THE VICTORIA HISTORY OF THE COUNTIES

OF ENGLAND

A HISTORY OF CHESHIRE

VOLUME V, PART 2

INSCRIBED TO THE MEMORY OF HER LATE MAJESTY

QUEEN VICTORIA

WHO GRACIOUSLY GAVE THE TITLE TO AND

ACCEPTED THE DEDICATION OF THIS HISTORY

THE VICTORIA HISTORY
OF THE COUNTIES OF
ENGLAND

THE UNIVERSITY OF LONDON

INSTITUTE OF HISTORICAL RESEARCH

Publication of this volume was aided by grants from the Scouloudi Foundation, in association with the Institute of Historical Research, by the Isobel Thornley Bequest Fund, and by the County History Trust.

A HISTORY OF
THE COUNTY OF
CHESTER

EDITED BY C. P. LEWIS AND A. T. THACKER

VOLUME V, PART 2

THE CITY OF CHESTER

CULTURE, BUILDINGS, INSTITUTIONS

PUBLISHED FOR THE

INSTITUTE OF HISTORICAL RESEARCH

BY BOYDELL & BREWER · 2005

First published 2005

A Victoria County History publication
in association with The Boydell Press
an imprint of Boydell & Brewer Ltd
PO Box 9 Woodbridge Suffolk IP12 3DF UK
and of Boydell & Brewer Inc.
PO Box 41026 Rochester NY 14604–4126 USA
website: www.boydell.co.uk
and with the
University of London Institute of Historical Research

ISBN 1 904356 03 6

A catalogue record for this book is available from the British Library

Typeset by Joshua Associates Ltd, Oxford
Printed in Great Britain by
St Edmundsbury Press Ltd, Bury St Edmunds, Suffolk

CONTENTS OF VOLUME FIVE, PART TWO

ILLUSTRATIONS

PREFACE

THIS BOOK, Part 2 of *The City of Chester*, is the fifth to appear in the Cheshire series. Once again, we would like to record our gratitude to all the many individuals, institutions, and trusts who have supported this project, through writing, research, and funding. We offer renewed thanks in particular to John and Valerie Hess and all the members of the Appeal Committee (Dr. A. J. P. Campbell, Mr. W. Leathwood, Mrs. D. McConnell, and Mr. T. J. Strickland) for their energy and enthusiasm in raising funds at a very difficult time. We also owe an especial debt of gratitude to the County History Trust, the Marc Fitch Fund, the Scouloudi Foundation, and the Isobel Thornley Bequest Fund, whose generosity enabled us to proceed with the compilation of the combined index of the two parts of the work. Grateful thanks are due too to Dr. Derek Nuttall for generously making available unpublished research on printing in Chester and to Noelle Thomas for her work on Curzon Park. David Burroughs (Chester Diocesan Adminstrator), Jill Collens (Historic Environment, Cheshire County Council), Ian Dunn (Cheshire County Librarian), Jonathan Pepler (Cheshire County Archivist), and Simon Ward (Chester Archaeology, Chester City Council) all gave valuable help at a late stage.

Taken together, the two parts of *The City of Chester* mark a first for the V.C.H. in several ways. Most importantly they comprise the first history of a town or city to appear in the series in two volumes. The two parts have been designed to be complementary and yet each to take its place as a free-standing book. Part 1 covered the general history and topographical development of the city in chronologically arranged chapters subdivided according to broad themes. Part 2 is devoted to major buildings, institutions, and cultural activities, each treated in detail in discrete encyclopaedic entries, themselves usually broadly chronological in arrangement. Grouped together for the first time in five overarching chapters, they complement the general history in Part 1. Detail, which would hold up the narrative in Part 1, informs analysis of the specific building, institution, or activity in Part 2. Great care has been taken to provide cross-references between the two parts and a general introduction to the history of the city appears in both.

The two books which form *The City of Chester* have also pioneered a new design for the V.C.H. series as a whole, and we are most grateful to our designer, Tony Kitzinger, for his work. A new typeface, Minion, has been employed, together with a new structure of headings, to make the text more spacious, inviting, and legible. We have complemented that redesigned text with considerably more illustrations than usual, and in this book, although not in Part 1, they have been integrated into the text.

After Part 1 of this volume went to press, in 2002, Dr. Lewis resigned as county editor, leaving the Cheshire V.C.H. without staff at the time of writing. In 2003 a V.C.H. website, www.cheshirepast.net, was established, publishing draft text and providing details of publications and events.

The following individuals and institutions are thanked for permission to reproduce illustrations which are their copyright: The British Library (Part 2, Figs. 72–3, 76, 81, 83, 85, 87, 90, 151, 153); Cheshire and Chester Archives and Local Studies (Part 1, frontispiece, Figs. 5, 7–9, 12, Plates 1, 7–8, 15–20, 22–5, 27, 30–9, 41–2, 44, 47–9, 51–2, 54, 58; Part 2, Figs. 26, 38, 44, 55–6, 64, 75, 123, 127, 137, 156, 181); Cheshire Museums Service (Part 1, Plates 28–9); Chester Archaeological Society (Part 1, Plates 9–14, 21; Part 2, Fig. 15); Chester Archaeology (Part 1, Plates 4–5); Chester City Council (Part 2, Fig. 171); Chester History and Heritage (Part 1, Figs. 26, 40, 43, 45–6, 50, 53, 55–7, 59–61; Part 2, Figs. 8, 52, 59, 66, 109); Chester Photographic Survey and individual photographers credited in the list of illustrations (Part 2, Figs. 2, 6, 10, 12, 18, 20, 23, 29, 33, 35–6, 43, 47, 57–8, 61, 65, 98, 101–3, 149, 158, 161, 163, 168, 170, 173, 178, 180, 184); Courtauld Institute of Art (Part 1, Plate 6); Richard Gem (Part 2, Fig. 105); Grosvenor Museum (Part 1, Plate 3); Roland Harris (Part 2, Fig. 139); A. F. Kersting (Part 2, Figs. 86, 92, 97, 116, 129, 131, 134, 145, 148, 160, 177); Lovelock, Mitchell, and Partners (Part 2, Fig. 179); T. J. Strickland (Part 1, Fig. 2); University College Chester (Part 2, Fig. 176); Simon Ward (Part 1, Fig. 6).

ABBREVIATIONS

A.-S.	Anglo-Saxon
Acct(s).	Account(s)
Acts of P.C.	*Acts of the Privy Council of England* (H.M.S.O.)
Add. Ch.	Additional Charter(s)
Add. MS.	Additional Manuscript(s)
Alum. Cantab. to 1751	*Alumni Cantabrigienses, Part 1, to 1751*, comp. J. Venn and J. A. Venn
Alum. Cantab. 1752–1900	*Alumni Cantabrigienses, Part 2, 1752–1900*, comp. J. Venn and J. A. Venn
Alum. Oxon. 1500–1714	*Alumni Oxonienses, 1500–1714*, ed. J. Foster
Ann. Cest.	*Annales Cestrienses*, ed. R. C. Christie (R.S.L.C. xiv)
Ann. Rep.	*Annual Report*
App.	Appendix
Arch.	*Archaeology, –ical*
Archit.	Architecture, –al
Archives and Records, ed. Kennett	*Archives and Records of the City of Chester*, ed. A. M. Kennett
B.L.	British Library
Bk(s).	Book(s)
Bldg(s).	Building(s)
Blk. Prince's Reg.	*Register of Edward the Black Prince preserved in the Public Record Office* (H.M.S.O.)
Bodl.	Bodleian Library, Oxford
Boro.	Borough
Brit.	Britain, British
Burne, *Chester Cath.*	R. V. H. Burne, *Chester Cathedral from its Founding by Henry VIII to the Accession of Queen Victoria*
Burne, *Monks*	R. V. H. Burne, *The Monks of Chester*
C.A.S.	Chester Archaeological Society
C.C.A.L.S.	Cheshire and Chester Archives and Local Studies (formerly Cheshire Record Office), Duke Street, Chester
C.H.H.	Chester History and Heritage (formerly part of Chester City Record Office), St. Michael's church, Bridge Street Row, Chester
C.J.	*Journals of the House of Commons*
Cal.	Calendar
Cal. Chart. R.	*Calendar of the Charter Rolls preserved in the Public Record Office* (H.M.S.O.)
Cal. Ches. Ct. R.	*Calendar of County Court, City Court, and Eyre Rolls of Chester, 1259–97, with an Inquest of Military Service, 1288*, ed. R. Stewart-Brown (Chetham Soc. N.S. lxxxiv)
Cal. Chester City Cl. Mins. 1603–42	*Calendar of Chester City Council Minutes, 1603–42*, ed. M. J. Groombridge (R.S.L.C. cvi)
Cal. Close	*Calendar of the Close Rolls preserved in the Public Record Office* (H.M.S.O.)
Cal. Cttee. for Compounding	*Calendar of the Proceedings of the Committee for Compounding, &c., 1643–1660, preserved in the State Paper Department of Her Majesty's Public Record Office* (H.M.S.O.)
Cal. Fine R.	*Calendar of the Fine Rolls preserved in the Public Record Office* (H.M.S.O.)
Cal. Inq. Misc.	*Calendar of Inquisitions Miscellaneous (Chancery) preserved in the Public Record Office* (H.M.S.O.)
Cal. Inq. p.m.	*Calendar of Inquisitions post mortem and other analagous documents preserved in the Public Record Office* (H.M.S.O.)
Cal. Lib.	*Calendar of the Liberate Rolls preserved in the Public Record Office* (H.M.S.O.)
Cal. Papal Pets.	*Calendar of Entries in the Papal Registers relating to Great Britain and Ireland: Petitions to the Pope* (H.M.S.O.)
Cal. Papal Reg.	*Calendar of Entries in the Papal Registers relating to Great Britain and Ireland: Papal Letters* (H.M.S.O. and Irish MSS. Com.)

Cal. Pat.	*Calendar of the Patent Rolls preserved in the Public Record Office* (H.M.S.O.)
Cal. S.P. Dom.	*Calendar of State Papers, Domestic Series, preserved in the Public Record Office* (H.M.S.O.)
Cal. Treas. Bks.	*Calendar of Treasury Books preserved in the Public Record Office* (H.M.S.O.)
Cal. Treas. Papers	*Calendar of Treasury Papers preserved in Her Majesty's Public Record Office*, ed. J. Redington
Cart. Chester Abbey	*The Chartulary or Register of St. Werburgh's Abbey, Chester*, ed. J. Tait (2 vols., Chetham Soc. N.s. lxxix, lxxxii)
cat.	catalogue
Cat. Anct. D.	*A Descriptive Catalogue of Ancient Deeds in the Public Record Office* (H.M.S.O.)
Cath.	Cathedral
Census	printed reports of the decennial Census of Population
Cent.	Century, Centuries
Ch.	Charter(s) *or* Church
Charters of A.-N. Earls	*The Charters of the Anglo-Norman Earls of Chester, c. 1071–1237*, ed. G. Barraclough (R.S.L.C. cxxvi)
Ches. Chamb. Accts.	*Accounts of the Chamberlains and other Officers of the County of Chester, 1301–60*, ed. R. Stewart-Brown (R.S.L.C. lix)
Ches. Hist.	*Cheshire History*
Ches. in Pipe R.	*Cheshire in the Pipe Rolls, 1158–1301*, ed. R. Stewart-Brown and M. H. Mills (R.S.L.C. xcii)
Chester Chron.	*Chester Chronicle* [newspaper]
Chester City Cl. Mins.	*Chester City Council Minutes* [printed and bound volumes from 1896]
Chester Customs Accts.	*Chester Customs Accounts, 1301–1566*, ed. K. P. Wilson (R.S.L.C. cxi)
Chrons.	*Chronicles*
Cl.	Council
Close R.	*Close Rolls of the Reign of Henry III preserved in the Public Record Office* (H.M.S.O.)
Colln.	Collection
Complete Peerage	G. E. C[okayne] and others, *The Complete Peerage* (2nd edn. 1910–98)
Ct. R.	*Court Roll*
Cttee.	Committee
D.K.R.	*Reports of the Deputy Keeper of the Public Records*
D.N.B.	*Dictionary of National Biography*
Diary of Henry Prescott	*The Diary of Henry Prescott, LL.B., Deputy Registrar of Chester Diocese*, ed. J. Addy and P. McNiven (3 vols., R.S.L.C. cxxvii, cxxxii, cxxxiii)
Dir.	Directory
Domesday Surv. Ches.	*Domesday Survey of Cheshire*, ed. J. Tait (Chetham Soc. N.s. lxxv)
E.E.T.S.	Early English Text Society
E.H.R.	*English Historical Review*
Eccl.	Ecclesiastical
Econ. H.R.	*Economic History Review*
Eg.	Egerton
Eng.	England, English
f./ff.	folio, –s
Fam.	Family
G.E.C. *Baronetage*	G. E. C[okayne], *Complete Baronetage*
Gastrell, *Not. Cest.*	*Notitia Cestriensis, or Historical Notices of the Diocese of Chester, by [Francis] Gastrell [Bishop of Chester]*, ed. F. R. Raines, i (Chetham Soc. [1st ser.], viii)
Gent. Mag.	*Gentleman's Magazine*
H.C.	House of Commons
H.L.	House of Lords
Harl.	Harleian
Harris, *Chester*	B. E. Harris, *Chester* (Bartholomew City Guides, 1979)
Hemingway, *Hist. Chester*	J. Hemingway, *History of the City of Chester* (2 vols., 1831)
Hewitt, *Med. Ches.*	H. J. Hewitt, *Medieval Cheshire: A Social and Economic History of Cheshire in the Reigns of the Three Edwards* (Chetham Soc. N.s. lxxxviii)
Hist.	History, Historical

Hist. Soc.	Historical Society
Hughes, *Stranger's Handbk.* (1856) [1882]	T. Hughes, *The Stranger's Handbook to Chester* ([1st edn.] 1856) [1882 edn.]
Ind.	Industry, –ies, –ial
Irel.	Ireland
J.C.A.S.	*Journal of the Chester Archaeological Society* (formerly called *Journal of the Chester and North Wales Architectural, Archaeological, and Historic Society*, and variants)
Jnl.	*Journal*
Johnson, 'Aspects'	A. M. Johnson, 'Some Aspects of the Political, Constitutional, Social, and Economic History of the City of Chester, 1550–1662' (Oxf. Univ. D.Phil. thesis, 1971)
Jones, *Ch. in Chester*	D. Jones, *The Church in Chester, 1300–1540* (Chetham Soc. 3rd ser. vii)
King's Vale Royal	*The Vale-Royall of England, Or, the County Palatine of Chester Illustrated* (publ. D. King, 1656; facsimile reprint 1972): [i] = [W. Smith], *The Vale-Royall of England*; [ii] = [W. Webb], *A Description of the City and County Palatine of Chester*; [iii] = [S. Lee], *Chronicon Cestrense*
King's Works	*The History of the King's Works*, ed. H. M. Colvin
L. & P. Hen. VIII	*Letters & Papers, Foreign and Domestic, of the Reign of Henry VIII, preserved in the Public Record Office, the British Museum, and elsewhere in England* (H.M.S.O.)
L.J.	*Journals of the House of Lords*
Lavaux, *Plan of Chester*	A. de Lavaux, *Plan of the City and Castle of Chester* [1745]
List of Clergy, 1541–2	*A List of Clergy for Eleven Deaneries of the Diocese of Chester, 1541–2*, ed. W. F. Irvine (R.S.L.C. xxxiii)
Lond.	London
Lond. Gaz.	*London Gazette*
Lucian, *De Laude Cestrie*	*Liber Luciani de Laude Cestrie*, ed. M. V. Taylor (R.S.L.C. lxiv)
Lysons, *Ches.*	D. and S. Lysons, *Magna Britannia: Cheshire*
m./mm.	membrane, –s
Mins.	Minutes
Morris, *Chester*	R. H. Morris, *Chester in the Plantagenet and Tudor Reigns*
Morris, *Siege of Chester*	R. H. Morris, *The Siege of Chester, 1643–6*, ed. P. H. Lawson [also published in *J.C.A.S.* xxv]
MS.	Manuscript
n.s.	new series
O.E.D.	*Oxford English Dictionary*
O.S.	Ordnance Survey
o.s.	old series
orig. ser.	original series
Ormerod, *Hist. Ches.*	G. Ormerod, *The History of the County Palatine and City of Chester*, revised and enlarged edn. by T. Helsby (1882)
Oxf.	Oxford
P. & G. Dir. Chester	Phillipson and Golder, *Directory for Chester and its Immediate Neighbourhood* [various edns.]
P.N. Ches.	*The Place-Names of Cheshire*, ed. J. McN. Dodgson (English Place-Name Society)
P.R.O.	Public Record Office, Kew
Par.	Parish
Parl.	Parliament, –ary
pers. comm.	personal comment
Pevsner, *Ches.*	N. Pevsner and E. Hubbard, *The Buildings of England: Cheshire*
Proc.	*Proceedings*
Q. Sess.	Quarter Sessions
R.O.	Record Office
R.S.L.C.	Record Society of Lancashire and Cheshire
Rec. Ser.	Record Series
Red Bk. Exch.	*The Red Book of the Exchequer*, ed. H. Hall
REED: Chester	*Records of Early English Drama: Chester*, ed. L. M. Clopper
Reg.	Register(s)
Rep.	Report

31st Rep. Com. Char.	*Thirty-first Report of the Commissioners Appointed to Enquire Concerning Charities*, H.C. 103 (1837–8), xxiv
Rep. Com. Mun. Corp.	*Reports from Commission on Municipal Corporations in England and Wales*, H.C. 116 (1835), xxvi
Rev.	Review
rot./rott.	rotulet, –s
s.n.	under the name
s.v./s.vv.	under the word/words
Sel. Cases in K.B.	*Select Cases in the Court of King's Bench*, ed. G. O. Sayles (7 vols., Selden Soc.)
Sel. R. Chester City Cts.	*Selected Rolls of the Chester City Courts, Late 13th and Early 14th Centuries*, ed. A. Hopkins (Chetham Soc. 3rd ser. ii)
ser.	series
Sheaf	*The Cheshire Sheaf* [preceded by series number, followed by volume number within the series]
Soc.	Society
sqq.	and following pages
T.H.S.L.C.	*Transactions of the Historic Society of Lancashire and Cheshire*
T.L.C.A.S.	*Transactions of the Lancashire and Cheshire Antiquarian Society*
TS.	Typescript
Univ.	University
V.C.H.	*Victoria County History*
Valor Eccl.	*Valor Ecclesiasticus, tempore Henr. VIII* (Record Commission)

CLASSES OF ORIGINAL RECORDS

EDT   Tithe
EDV   Visitation

Church Commissioners
EEB   Bishopric of Chester

Public Records
NVA   Inland Revenue District Valuer

Parish Records
P 1   Chester Holy Trinity
P 15   Chester St. Bridget
P 16   Chester St. Martin
P 17   Chester Christ Church
P 20   Chester St. Mary
P 29   Chester St. Oswald
P 32   Backford
P 51   Chester St. John
P 63   Chester St. Peter
P 64   Chester St. Olave
P 65   Chester St. Michael
P 98   Lache cum Saltney
P 161   Hoole
P 162   Chester St. Paul
P 176   Upton by Chester

Quarter Sessions
QAB   Buildings and Gaols
QAM   Committee Minutes
QJB   Sessions Books
QJF   Sessions Files

Subject Files
SF   Subject Files

Wills and Probate Records
WS   Supra Series

CHESTER CITY RECORDS

Assembly
ZAB   Assembly Books
ZAC   Assembly Committees
ZAF   Assembly Files

City Council
ZCA   Boundary Reports
ZCB   Council Minute Books
ZCCB   Committee Minute Books
ZCCF   Committee Files
ZCH   Charters
ZCHB   Cartularies
ZCHC   Charities
ZCHD   Corporation Deeds
ZCL   Corporation Lawsuits
ZCLA   Acts of Parliament
ZCX   Council Manuscripts

Private Records
ZCR 3   St. Michael's Parish: William Jones's Almshouses
ZCR 15   Chester Deeds
ZCR 16   Chester Waterworks Co.

ZCR 24   Lowe Family (silversmiths)
ZCR 36   Blue Coat School
ZCR 55   Chester Methodist Circuit
ZCR 56   Miscellaneous
ZCR 60   Thomas Hughes (antiquary)
ZCR 62   Dr. J. C. Bridge (papers about music festivals)
ZCR 63   J. P. Earwaker (antiquary)
ZCR 78   George Street Primitive Methodist Church
ZCR 94   Chester Primitive Methodist Circuits
ZCR 102   St. John's Parish (MS. map)
ZCR 111   George Street Primitive Methodist Church
ZCR 119   Frank Simpson (antiquary)
ZCR 131   Chester and District Skin Dispensary
ZCR 137   Chester United Gas Co.
ZCR 145   Chester Literary and Philosophical Society (ZCR 145/1–14) and Water Tower Museum (ZCR 145/15–43)
ZCR 151   Queen Street Congregational Church
ZCR 158   Great Boughton Congregational Church
ZCR 163   Chester Literary and Philosophical Society
ZCR 167   Blacon Congregational Church
ZCR 193   St. Michael's Parish: William Jones's Almshouses
ZCR 222   St. Andrew's United Reformed (formerly Presbyterian) Church
ZCR 225   Hoole Congregational Church
ZCR 234   Pipers Ash Methodist Church
ZCR 238   Hamilton Street Methodist Church
ZCR 241   Cheshire County Mental Hospital
ZCR 242   Chester Football Club Ltd.
ZCR 269   Chester Infirmary (printed correspondence of Dr. Cumming)
ZCR 270   Chester Methodist Circuit
ZCR 276   United Methodist Church (formerly Methodist New Connexion)
ZCR 286   Queen Street Welsh Methodist Church
ZCR 300   Chester Waterworks Co.
ZCR 366   J. H. Taylor and Sons (boat builders)
ZCR 372   Chester Race Course Committee (printed poster)
ZCR 419   Royal Chester Rowing Club
ZCR 466   Hurleston Family
ZCR 469   Aldersey Family
ZCR 498   Deeds (house in Stanley Place)
ZCR 517   Chester Ladies Hockey Club
ZCR 536   Chester Municipal Charities
ZCR 542   Chester Mechanics' Institution
ZCR 546   Jack Douglas (personal papers)
ZCR 572   Chester Evangelical Free Church Council
ZCR 575   Blacon Townswomen's Guild History Project
ZCR 599   Owen Jones Charity
ZCR 600   Chester Municipal Charities (printed report)
ZCR 662   Hoole Baptist Church

ZCR 712   Chester Municipal Charities
ZCR 745   William Vernon and Sons Ltd. (builders and contractors)
ZCR 750   Drawers of Dee (craft guild)
ZCR 758   R. L. Astrella (photographs, 1944)
ZCR 842   Chester Sports and Leisure Association
ZCR 856   Upton Mental Hospital

Accumulations of Deeds and Papers
ZD/BC   Snow Family
ZD/DNA   Chester District Nursing Association
ZD/HT   Henry Taylor (antiquary)
ZD/JWW   Jolliffe, Wickham, and Wood (solicitors)
ZG/HS   W. R. Hornby Steer (papers of Harrison family of Chester)
ZG/Mc   Various

Council Departments
ZDE   Education
ZDES   Education: School Records
ZDF   Fire Service
ZDH   Health
ZDPO   Police
ZDPU   Publicity
ZDS   Surveyor
ZDT   Town Clerk

Guilds
ZG   Guild Records

Hospitals
ZHC   Chester City Hospital
ZHI   Chester Royal Infirmary
ZHW   Countess of Chester Hospital and predecessors

Mayor
ZMB   Mayors' Books
ZMCP   Mayors' Company Papers
ZMF   Mayors' Files
ZMFR   Freemen's Rolls and Registers
ZMIP   Inner Pentice Files
ZML   Mayors' Letters
ZMMP   Mayors' Military Papers
ZMP   Proclamations
ZMPM   Portmote Court Minute Book
ZMR   Portmote Court Rolls
ZMSR   General Court Rolls (Portmote and Pentice)

Murengers
ZMUB   Account Books
ZMUR   Account Roll

Coroners
ZQCI   Inquests

Crownmote
ZQCR   Court Rolls

Quarter Sessions
ZQAG   Gaol and House of Correction
ZQAR   River Dee
ZQJC   Commissions of the Peace
ZQRL   Licensed Victuallers
ZQRP   Deposited Plans
ZQSE   Examinations and Depositions

Petty Sessions
ZQPA   Minute Books
ZQSF   Quarter Sessions Files

Sheriffs
ZSB   Sheriffs' Books
ZSBC   Sheriffs' Court Books (Pentice Court)
ZSBO   Sheriffs' Bonds: Officers
ZSBT   Toll Books
ZSFE   Execution Orders
ZSIG   Gaol Indentures
ZSPR   Passage Court Rolls
ZSR   Pentice Court Rolls

Treasurers
ZCAS   Assessments: Subsidies, Aids, and Taxes
ZTAB   Account Books
ZTAR   Account Rolls and Rentals
ZTAV   Vouchers

Town Clerk
ZTCC   Papers Relating to Corporation Business

Statutory and Local Authorities
ZTRB   Dee Bridge Commissioners
ZTRH   Hoole Urban District Council
ZTRI   Police (Improvement) Commissioners
ZTRU   Chester Poor Law Union

Other Records
Cowper   Collectanea Devana of Dr. William
 MSS.   Cowper

THE CITY OF CHESTER

THIS VOLUME, published in two parts, provides a full treatment of most aspects of Chester's history from Roman times to the year 2000.[1] The two parts are complementary. The chapters in Part 1 give a general account of the city, covering administrative, political, economic, social, and religious history, divided into six periods: Roman, Early Medieval (400–1230), Later Medieval (1230–1550), Early Modern (1550–1762), Late Georgian and Victorian (1762–1914), and Twentieth-Century (1914–2000). The topographies of Roman and 20th-century Chester form integral parts of the first and last chapters,[2] while a separate chapter deals with Topography 900–1914. Part 2 of the volume contains detailed accounts of particular topics, institutions, and buildings, grouped in five sections: Local Government and Public Services; Economic Infrastructure and Institutions; The Churches and Other Religious Bodies; Major Buildings; and Leisure and Culture. Part 2 has a full index to the whole volume, including subjects; Part 1 an index only of persons and places mentioned in that part.

DEFINING CHESTER

Until the 19th century what was meant by 'Chester' was unproblematic. The Roman fortress with its adjacent civilian settlement was succeeded in the early Middle Ages by a small fortified town on the same site. Probably in the 10th century two sides of the Roman walls were abandoned, and by the early 12th century the circuit of walls had reached its modern extent. Sizeable extramural suburbs grew up, including the separately named Handbridge south of the river, which has always been reckoned part of Chester. The suburbs were encircled by Chester's arable fields, meadows, and common pastures, with heaths to the north-east around Hoole, and a large area of marshland to the south-west at Saltney.

Beyond the immediate environs of walled town, suburbs, and farmland, an extensive territory depended upon Chester in the early Middle Ages, covering many townships with their own villages, hamlets, and farms. During the central Middle Ages many of the townships were incorporated into newly formed parishes, leaving a few outliers attached to the oldest Chester parishes of St. Oswald and St. John. They were never strictly speaking part of Chester, and their histories are not treated in this volume.

In the 10th and 11th centuries Chester hundred was one of twelve in Cheshire, but the creation of civic institutions in the 12th and 13th centuries led to the disappearance of the hundred and its replacement by the liberties of the city, the area within which the citizens enjoyed their various individual and corporate privileges. The liberties were first explicitly demarcated by a precise boundary in 1354 but must have existed long previously as a territory whose limits were generally known. They covered some 3,000 acres and included the abbot of Chester's manor north of the city, and an extensive area south of the Dee, focused on Handbridge. Both the manor of Handbridge and its open fields extended beyond the liberties into the township of Claverton to the south.[3]

On the north-east, north, and north-west the townships immediately beyond the liberties were Great Boughton, Hoole, Newton, Bache, and Blacon. The Hoole boundary was little more than ½ mile from the heart of Chester at the Cross (the central crossroads by St. Peter's church, also the site of the medieval High Cross). The approach to Great Boughton, 1½ miles distant from the Cross, lay through Chester's most important medieval and early modern suburb in Foregate Street and its continuation beyond the Bars, which was called Boughton. Right on the boundary from the early 12th century until the 1640s stood the leper hospital of St. Giles, occupying a tiny extra-parochial area called Spital Boughton. On the south-western side the boundary of the liberties coincided with the national boundary between England and Wales from 1536, when the Act of Union placed the lordship and parish of Hawarden in the newly created Welsh county of Denbighshire (it was transferred to Flintshire in 1541).[4]

From the 19th century Chester is less easy to define. The liberties circumscribed the formal extent of the city of Chester until minor adjustments were made in 1835, enlarging the municipal borough at the expense of Great Boughton, but already by then the town had spilled over the boundary through residential building in the adjoining parts of Great Boughton and Hoole. The arrival of the railway in the 1840s quickened the growth of Chester beyond the borough boundaries, creating new streets which were physically part of the city but administratively outside the remit of the borough council. North-east of the town, the main

1 Where not otherwise stated, what follows depends upon the findings presented more fully elsewhere in this volume.

2 A more detailed account of the topography of Roman Chester appeared in *V.C.H. Ches.* i. 117–85.

3 P. J. W. Higson, 'Pointers towards the Structure of Agriculture in Handbridge and Claverton prior to Parl. Enclosure', *T.H.S.L.C.* cxlii. 56–71.

4 R. R. Davies, *Lordship and Society in the March of Wales, 1282–1400*, 16, 48; *V.C.H. Ches.* ii. 7; G. Williams, *Recovery, Reorientation, and Reformation: Wales c. 1415–1642*, 268, 271.

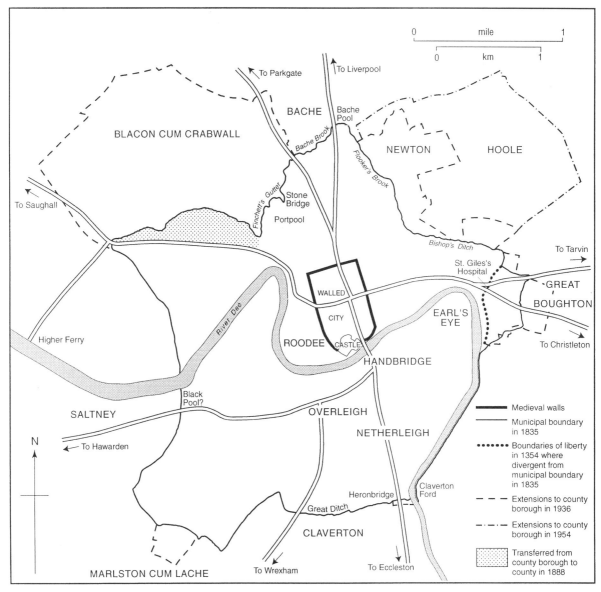

FIG. 1. *Chester: the city boundaries and neighbouring townships*

railway station was built on the boundary with Hoole, the nearer parts of which were rapidly built over. To the west, the railway brought industrial development and associated housing to a new suburb which straddled the boundary between Chester and the township of Saltney in Flintshire. For a variety of reasons there was no major extension of the city's boundaries until 1936, when the county borough incorporated parts of Great Boughton and Newton and most of Blacon, the last intended for a large new council-housing estate. Hoole remained a separate unit of local government (latterly an urban district) until it too was absorbed by Chester in 1954. Meanwhile the building of more new housing in the townships of Upton and Bache north of the city created a large built-up area which was not brought under Chester's control until 1974. Even after that date Saltney had to be excluded from Chester district because it was in

Wales and the national boundary was regarded by central government as inviolate.

The area described in both parts of this volume is essentially the medieval town and liberties, together with those parts brought within the borough boundary in 1835, 1936, and 1954, but only from the time of their incorporation into Chester. Saltney, Upton, Bache, and Great Boughton are discussed where appropriate, as in the accounts of 19th-century industry and 20th-century suburban housing. The earlier histories of all those townships are reserved for treatment elsewhere.

NAME AND SITUATION

The Roman name for the fortress built at the head of the Dee estuary was Deva, adopted directly from the British name of the river, and 'Deverdoeu' was still one of two alternative Welsh names for Chester in the late

12th century. Its other and more enduring Welsh name was Caerlleon, literally 'the fortress-city of the legions', a name identical with that of the great Roman fortress at the other end of the Marches at Caerleon (Mon.). The colloquial modern Welsh name is the shortened form, Caer. The early English-speaking settlers used a name which had the same meaning, 'Legacæstir', which was current until the 11th century, when – in a further parallel with Welsh usage – the first element fell out of use and the simplex name Chester emerged. From the 14th century to the 18th the city's prominent position in north-western England meant that it was commonly also known as Westchester.[1]

Chester's importance as a town has been shaped by its geographical position. The city centre and Handbridge occupy a ridge of sandstone interrupted by the river Dee. The western side of the ridge is a steep escarpment overlooking the Roodee, which until the 12th century was a tidal meadow at the head of a broad estuary extending some 20 miles to the open sea at Hilbre Island and Point of Ayr. The combination of factors made the site both the lowest point at which the river could be bridged (successively, and almost on the same spot, by the Romans and the Anglo-Saxons) and the limit of navigation in the estuary. Navigation and tides in the upper estuary were evidently restricted by a rocky natural feature underlying the man-made causeway or weir constructed just upstream from the Dee Bridge no later than the 1090s. Although little evidence of pre-Roman occupation of the site of Chester had come to light before 2000, local archaeologists then believed that there was likely to have been significant Iron Age activity in the vicinity.[2]

The geological strata underlying Chester comprise Pebble Beds to the east of Dee Bridge, the Roodee, and Bache, and Lower Mottled Sandstone to the west. Both are overlain by boulder clay except where the ridge protrudes in a line running from Heronbridge in the south through Handbridge and Queen's Park to the walled city. Further north there are pockets of glacial sands and gravels in Newton and Upton, while to the west the former bed of the upper estuary at Sealand, Lache, and the Roodee is composed of alluvium deposited as the river gradually assumed its modern course and width.[3] The Roman fortress did not occupy the highest point on the ridge, which lies at a little over 30 m. (100 ft.) just north of the city walls. To the north and east the land slopes gently down to about 23 m. (75 ft.) before rising again to a low ridge over 30 m. which runs south-east to north-west through Christleton, Hoole, Newton, and Upton. South and west of the Roman fortress there is a much steeper slope to below 5 m. (15 ft.) on the river bank and the Roodee. South of the river the land rises to about 24 m. (80 ft.) at the

southern boundary of the liberties. Within the city walls the natural ground levels have been much altered by almost two thousand years of building and demolition, with the effect of creating a much more level plateau.[4] The Dee describes a gently winding double bend through the city, flowing first north between Heronbridge and Handbridge on the left bank (within the liberties) and Great Boughton on the right (outside), turning sharply south-west around the meadows known historically as the Earl's Eye, passing in the relatively narrow gap between the walled city and Handbridge, and turning briefly north again around the Roodee. In ancient times the river flowed into the head of the open estuary at the Roodee but since the later Middle Ages it has been directed sharply south-west again for about a mile before finally turning north-west, after the 18th century into the straight canalized stretch which takes it through the reclaimed marshland of Sealand (Flints.) to the open part of the estuary below Flint.

CHESTER'S IMPORTANCE AND RANKING

Chester was for many centuries the most important place by far in north-western England. That was largely due to its location at the crossroads of the British Isles, where routes from southern Britain led into north Wales and the Irish Sea. On three occasions its role as the point of entry into the Irish Sea region for rulers based in the South made it prominent in national affairs. At the outset the Romans probably selected the site for their fortress because of its potential as a port for an assault on Ireland. In the 10th century the reoccupied fortress became the centre for attempts by English kings to dominate other rulers around the shores of the Irish Sea, notably in the carefully staged set-piece by which King Edgar demonstrated his overlordship by having them row him on the Dee in 973. Tribute in silver extracted from such rulers was turned into coin at Chester, whose mint was astonishingly prolific in the 10th century. Finally, the English conquest of north Wales in the 1270s and 1280s depended heavily on Chester as a base. The city's military and political importance to Edward I, which endured into the early 14th century, brought it great prosperity, notably through the victualling of armies and the supply of royal castles in north Wales.

Although never among the largest five or six English provincial towns, Chester was certainly in the second rank by the late Anglo-Saxon period and retained that status almost until 1700. Uncertainty about the numbers of inhabitants makes it impossible to assign a more precise ranking before 1801. In 1086 Chester was among a dozen towns with populations in the order of 2,000–2,500, behind seven with over 5,000 people

---

1 *P.N. Ches.* v (1:i), 2–7.
2 Inf. from Mr. Keith Matthews, Chester City Archaeology.
3 Geol. Surv. 1-inch map, sheets 108–9, solid and drift.

4 O.S. Map 1-inch, 7th ser., sheet 109 (1952 edn.); D. Mason, 'Chester: The Evolution and Adaptation of its Landscape', *J.C.A.S.* lix. 14–23.

each.[1] In the 1520s it was among sixteen towns with perhaps 3,500–5,000 inhabitants, when the six largest, other than London, had between 6,000 and 13,000 residents. By 1700 Chester's population was probably approaching 8,000, placing it in a second rank of some 25 towns with 5,000 or more people; the six largest towns after London then had between 10,000 and 30,000 people.[2] In the 18th century Chester continued to grow in absolute terms and it just about held its place, ranking 18th in England in 1801, the first year for which reliable population figures are available. It was then among the middling county towns, comparable with Shrewsbury, Worcester, Carlisle, Leicester, Derby, Oxford, Reading, Exeter, Cambridge, Colchester, and Ipswich but considerably smaller than such places as York, Norwich, Newcastle upon Tyne, and Bristol, let alone its near neighbours Liverpool and Manchester.[3] In the 19th century Chester slipped dramatically down the rankings as the new industrial towns of the North and Midlands swelled in size. By 1901 it was barely among the eighty most populous boroughs and cities, and even within Cheshire it had been overtaken by Stockport, Birkenhead, Crewe, and Wallasey.[4] In the 20th century Chester's prosperity and rising population allowed it to maintain that rank, overtaking many stagnant or declining northern towns (including Crewe and Wallasey) but eclipsed by a similar number of faster-growing towns, mostly in the South.[5]

At the time of the Norman Conquest Chester was in effect a provincial capital. With no larger place closer to it than York, Lincoln, and Oxford, it was the foremost town of western Mercia, covering the whole north-western and central Midlands, the Welsh borders, and the upper North-West beyond the Mersey. Later in the Middle Ages Chester's region contracted: Bristol overtook it as the most important west-coast port at an early date; Coventry rose to become an economic capital for the heart of the Midlands; and, nearer at hand, Shrewsbury was almost certainly as big as Chester by 1300 and deprived it of any significant economic role in the central Marches and mid-Wales.

Chester survived as a regional capital through the Middle Ages and into the 18th century, with no rival nearer than Shrewsbury, but it dominated a much smaller region than cities such as Bristol, Exeter, Norwich, and Newcastle upon Tyne, as well as being a smaller place in absolute terms. Its hinterland was poorer than most of theirs, and its overseas trade was much more limited. The hinterland in economic terms covered the western half of Cheshire and much of north-east Wales; it was the main market for the

agricultural produce of that area, to which it also supplied manufactured goods, both locally produced and imported, and a variety of services. It continued to perform that role well into the 19th century, though the region which it dominated gradually diminished in size as rival towns such as Wrexham and Birkenhead grew in size. As a resort of the propertied and leisured classes, however, Chester had a much larger reach for much longer: even in the early 19th century, for example, the races were frequented and the infirmary was patronized by well-to-do families from south Lancashire, north Shropshire, north Staffordshire, and north Wales as far as Anglesey.

CHESTER AND THE GROSVENORS

Chester had no patron from the later Middle Ages onwards to match the Roman army, the 10th-century West Saxon kings, or Edward I, all of whom had put the city at the centre of national affairs. From the 17th century it did, however, have the Grosvenors. Seated at Eaton from the earlier 15th century,[6] holder of a baronetcy from 1622 and a peerage from 1761, the head of the family was Earl Grosvenor from 1784, marquess of Westminster from 1831, and duke of Westminster from 1874. In 1677 the family acquired the Middlesex manor of Ebury, in Westminster, and from the later 18th century it rose very quickly to become one of Britain's wealthiest. The basis of their wealth was initially lead mining in Flintshire, but that was very soon overtaken by the vast urban rents accrued from the successive development of Mayfair (1720s–1770s), Belgravia (1820s–1850s), and Pimlico (1830s and later) on their London estate. From the 18th century the Grosvenors played a large part in the life of Chester as landlords and patrons. Eaton Hall was only three miles from the Cross, though outside the liberties. A fitting approach from Handbridge along tree-lined avenues to Eaton was created through a very carefully managed parliamentary inclosure in 1805.[7]

From the late 17th century to the late 1820s Grosvenor patronage in Chester had an overtly political purpose: to dominate the Assembly (the governing body of the city) and monopolize Chester's parliamentary representation. The family's social leadership was significant even when it was divorced from direct political interests after the 1820s. During the rest of the 19th century and the early 20th the marquess and dukes of Westminster paid for schools, curates, a new parish church, two public parks, and a nurses' home; they owned the advowsons of two of the city's parish churches, were patrons of Chester races, major benefactors of the infirmary and the new Grosvenor

1 H. C. Darby, *Domesday Eng.* 302–9, 364–8.
2 C. G. A. Clay, *Econ. Expansion and Social Change: Eng. 1500–1700*, i. 166–70.
3 *Census*, 1801.
4 *Survey Gazetteer of Brit. Isles*, ed. J. G. Bartholomew (1904 edn.), 896.

5 *Census*, 1991, *Key Statistics for Urban and Rural Areas: Great Britain*, pp. 20–35.
6 Ormerod, *Hist. Ches.* ii. 833.
7 P. J. W. Higson, 'Landlord Control and Motivation in the Parl. Enclosure of St. Mary's-on-the-Hill Parish, Chester', *T.H.S.L.C.* cxxxvii. 93–116.

Museum, supporters of innumerable philanthropic activities, and had the new Grosvenor Bridge named after them. In the later 20th century their property interests in Chester included the largest of the city's shopping centres (the Grosvenor Centre) and a huge business park on the southern outskirts.

CHESTER'S WIDER CULTURAL CONNEXIONS

Although Chester has had close links with Wales and Ireland at nearly every period, its wider cultural links have always been rather meagre. There seems not to have been a Jewish community in the Middle Ages. Manxmen settled in Chester from the later Middle Ages, and a few Spanish merchants visited in the 16th century. Negligible numbers of displaced persons and Commonwealth immigrants arrived in the years after the Second World War, and in 1991 the non-white element amounted to little more than 1,000 people in a population of almost 90,000.[1] At only two periods have the streets been full of foreign voices: in Roman times, the legionary garrison was made up of soldiers drawn from across the provinces of the Empire, and late 20th-century tourism filled the city centre with thousands of visitors from western Europe, north America, and further afield.

The city's location, however, long gave it a pivotal role in the affairs of the Irish Sea region. In the 1120s the historian Henry of Huntingdon regarded Chester's distinct attribute as being 'near to the Irish' (not the Welsh).[2] As long as the Dee remained navigable, Ireland was Chester's chief overseas trading partner, and as such the main source of Chester merchants' prosperity in the later Middle Ages and the 16th century. The city's political importance to the English Crown from the 1590s into the early 18th century arose because it was the main staging post on the route between the two capital cities: about 185 miles from London by road and 150 from Dublin by sea. Connexions with Ireland were again evident in the brief flourishing of linen imports in the later 18th century, in famine-induced Irish migration to the city in the earlier 19th century, and in the comically abortive Fenian plot against Chester castle in 1867. The Roman Catholic presence in the city from the mid 19th century was very largely of Irish origin. Irish migration to Chester peaked in the mid 19th century and then declined somewhat: in 1851, in the immediate wake of the Potato Famine, some 7 per cent of Cestrians were Irish-born, account-

ing for about 2,000 people, but by 1901 the level had fallen to 3 per cent (though of a considerably larger total population), and in 1991 stood at about 2 per cent.[3]

Welsh links have been more obviously to the fore in Chester's history, but they were mostly restricted to the north-eastern corner of the principality and the districts along the north coast, areas closely bound into Chester's economic hinterland. At all periods since the 11th century or earlier Welshmen have frequented Chester's markets, fairs, and shops; Chester was the market for Welsh grain, livestock, coal, lead, and slates; Welsh soldiers were shipped from Chester to fight in Ireland in the 1590s, and a Welsh pirate allegedly sold his booty in the city in the 1560s.[4] Chester loomed large in the consciousness of the north Welsh: the city gates were regarded as the limits of Welsh territory in the 12th century,[5] and the 'men of Chester' were vilified in anti-English poetry of the 15th century,[6] but there was probably always much migration from Wales to the city, larger by far than any town in north Wales itself until the mid 19th century, and even then still larger than Wrexham. Before the later 18th century it seems that most migrants were rapidly Anglicized and assimilated, contributing to a rich stratum of Chester surnames of Welsh origin. Possibly as many as a third of the 1,200 freemen who voted in the shrieval election of 1818, for example, had Welsh surnames, many doubtless of families long established in the city.[7] Welsh-language books were printed in Chester from the early 18th century,[8] and Welsh newspapers from the 1790s,[9] the period when separate Welsh-speaking congregations were first formed in the city. The existence of Welsh churches suggests that the numbers of settlers were large enough to sustain the language beyond first-generation migrants. By the 1860s, when there were five Welsh-speaking congregations in Chester, St. David's Day was a focus of collective expression which transcended denominational boundaries. There had been a Chester Cymmrodorion Society, Anglican and Tory in orientation, from 1822 but it evidently died out after local politics became less polarized in the 1830s. The revival of a Chester Welsh Society (Cymdeithas Cymry Caer) in 1892 was evidently non-aligned in politics and religion.[10] The Welsh-born population formed 11 per cent of the total in 1851 and almost as much in 1901 and 1951.[11] In 1991 over 6 per cent of the residents of

1 Census, 1991, Key Statistics for Urban and Rural Areas: North, p. 50.

2 Henry of Huntingdon, Historia Anglorum, ed. D. Greenway, 20–1.

3 Census, 1851, Birthplaces, p. 664; 1901, Ches. p. 90; 1951, Ches. p. 82; 1991, Ches. p. 88: 1,801 people born in both parts of Ireland living in Chester district as a whole.

4 G. Williams, Recovery, Reorientation, and Reformation: Wales c. 1415–1642, 368, 372, 379.

5 R. R. Davies, Conquest, Coexistence, and Change: Wales 1063–1415, 16.

6 G. Williams, Recovery, Reorientation, and Reformation: Wales c. 1415–1642, 9.

7 Based on analysis of Poll-Bk. for Sheriff, with Concise Hist. and Papers (1818, publ. M. Monk).

8 M. Parry, 'Chester Welsh Printing', J.C.A.S. xxi. 57–67; D. Nuttall, 'Hist. Printing in Chester', ibid. liv. 51–9.

9 Below, Newspapers.

10 T. Edwards, Chester Cambrian Societies, 1760–1906 (priv. print. 1906).

11 Census, 1851, Birthplaces, p. 664; 1901, Ches. p. 90; 1951, Ches. p. 82.

Chester district as a whole, wider than the city alone, had been born in Wales.[1]

THE CHARACTER OF CHESTER

Roman Chester is most plausibly represented and best understood as a military depot consisting of a walled fortress with a number of important extramural buildings, notably the amphitheatre, and an attendant civilian settlement. Archaeological investigations have revealed more about the fortress than about the town which served it.[2] There were long periods in which the Roman legion stationed at Chester was absent on duties elsewhere in Britain or further afield in the Empire, leaving only a skeleton garrison as depot caretakers. The ebb and flow of the military presence can hardly have failed to affect the civilian settlement, but it is difficult to say how far the latter may have had an independent existence. After the legion left for the last time, perhaps in 383, the character and extent of settlement at Chester is impossible to establish for a period of almost five centuries. It is clear that very substantial remains of the fortress walls and of stone buildings both inside and outside them survived for many centuries afterwards, and it seems probable that from the 7th century Chester was the centre of an extensive territory and had at least one major church.

Chester was re-established as a place of importance by the 10th century through the convergence of two circumstances. First, it was garrisoned again in the early 10th century during the course of Æthelflæd's military campaigns designed to secure the northern frontier of Mercia against the Vikings. In reoccupying Chester, Æthelflæd made it a centre of government, one of the fortified towns which later in the 10th century developed into the central places of the newly established Mercian shires. Cheshire was thus Chester's shire, and indeed was often known as Chestershire until the 15th century.[3] In addition, the city became a centre of trade for the Irish Sea region, with a small Hiberno-Norse quarter between the remains of the Roman fortress and the river Dee. Trade and government have been the mainstays of Chester's significance ever since.

Control of Chester in the early medieval period alternated between great regional magnates and the kings of England. Æthelflæd was ruler of a Mercia still partly independent of Wessex, but after her death Chester soon fell into the hands of the West Saxon kings, and on the eve of the Norman Conquest it was one of the series of sizeable Midland shire towns under royal lordship. After 1066 William I gave it to Earl Hugh, whose successors as earls of Chester ruled the city until 1237, when the earldom was annexed by the Crown. The fact that Chester belonged for over 150 years to Anglo-Norman earls rather than English kings, unlike most large towns, did not in practice make much difference to its development, though there may have been economic advantages from being the earls' headquarters. After 1237 the presence of senior palatine officials and a certain military presence at the castle affected the city's physical appearance and its prosperity. The palatine status of the county meant that Chester's administrative development was not straightforward. Cheshire had its law courts at Chester castle, in effect parallel to those at Westminster, and there were many conflicts of authority between the palatinate and the city's own courts. Chester did not return M.P.s to parliament until 1543. In many respects, however, the county palatine was assimilated to English administrative and judicial norms between the 1520s and the 1540s, though some of its distinctive institutions survived until the 1830s.[4]

In general the administrative development of Chester followed a course similar to that of other shire towns which were also regional capitals. Chester was already regarded as a city (*civitas*) in 1086. Institutions of self-government, notably the mayoralty, had developed by the 1230s, supplementing and eventually subordinating the sheriffs who had previously governed the city on behalf of the earls. Chester was created a county in its own right by the royal charter of 1506, and became successively a reformed municipal borough in 1835 and a county borough in 1889. Although the county borough was too small to resist absorption into a larger second-tier district council at local government reorganization in 1974, the style City of Chester was carried over as the name of the new district and the mayoralty was retained and indeed in 1992 elevated to a lord mayoralty.

Chester was also an ecclesiastical capital. For a few years after 1075 it served as the seat of the diocesan bishop earlier based at Lichfield and later at Coventry. The archdeaconry of Chester had a semi-independent status within the medieval diocese. The bishop's church in the city, St. John's, however, was always outranked by the great Benedictine abbey of St. Werburgh, founded by Earl Hugh in 1092. St. Werburgh's was rich and powerful, with a large monastic precinct within the city walls, a manor covering the northern part of the liberties, and control (initially) of the city's main annual fair. On the other hand, unlike abbeys in some smaller towns, St. Werburgh's was only one element in medieval Chester. The abbot and monks were frequently at loggerheads with the citizens, and as the civic authorities became more self-confident in the 14th and 15th centuries they gradually enlarged their rights at the expense of the abbey's, until the city's Great Charter of 1506 in effect confirmed Chester's independence from both St. Werburgh's and the county palatine.

Following the dissolution of the monastery in 1540

---

1 *Census*, 1991, *Ches.* p. 88.
2 D. J. P. Mason, *Roman Chester*, appeared after the chapter on 'Roman Chester' in Part 1 of this volume was completed.
3 *P.N. Ches.* i. 1.   4 *V.C.H. Ches.* ii. 33–7.

the abbey church became the seat of a new diocesan bishop in 1541, the monastic precinct and many of its buildings being retained by the new establishment. The precinct was a place somewhat apart from the city until the 1920s. That separation, and the commercial bustle outside the precinct walls, prevented Chester from ever becoming a Trollopean backwater in the manner of the smaller cathedral cities: although the cathedral dominated the town centre as a building it was only one among several influences as an institution.

Chester was also for most of its history a garrison town, a consequence of its situation in relation to Wales and Ireland. The Roman fortress, Æthelflæd's *burh*, the small earthwork and timber castle of the Normans, and the larger stone castle created by Earl Ranulph III and Henry III were successively superimposed upon one another. From the 11th century to the late 13th the city was the gathering place for armies setting out into north Wales, and from the late 12th century to the late 17th for expeditions to quell rebellions in Ireland. Chester's military importance was reflected in the long siege which it endured at the hands of parliamentarian forces during the English Civil War. After the Glorious Revolution, however, that significance fell quickly away, notwithstanding the Jacobite scares of 1715 and 1745. The castle was garrisoned in the 18th century by companies of invalid soldiers, giving the second-in-command in 1760, Lieut. Joseph Winder, the leisure to amuse himself by drawing a detailed panoramic view of the city.[1] Even so, Chester's military role had not been entirely eroded: with the invention of county-based regiments and regional commands in the later 19th century, it became an important Army recruiting centre and the headquarters of Western Command.

The economy of the medieval town was based on Chester's position as a port, a market with an extensive hinterland, a place of craft manufacture, and a centre for servicing the needs of the abbey, several other religious houses, and the palatine administration and garrison at the castle. The port of Chester included outlying anchorages in the Dee estuary which became of greater significance as the head of the estuary silted up in the later Middle Ages and restricted access to the city's own quays. From 1559, when it was brought into the national customs system, Chester was administratively the head port for the whole stretch of coastline from Anglesey to Lancaster.[2] It remained the largest port on those coasts until eclipsed by Liverpool. Liverpool did not begin its meteoric rise as a transatlantic and international port until the later 17th century, but it was already encroaching on Chester's Irish trade by

1500. In the 16th century Liverpool's location closer to the burgeoning textile industries of south Lancashire, and on an open estuary but with a good natural harbour, gave it distinct advantages over Chester.

Coasting trade and especially the trade with Ireland were always Chester's mainstays; overseas contacts were extremely limited in comparison with those of Bristol or the main ports of the east and south coasts. Moreover the progressive silting of the Dee meant that coasting and long-distance vessels increasingly had to unload into carts or shallow-draught boats at the minor ports further down the estuary. Although ships were built at the Roodee shipyard as late as 1869 and small seagoing vessels still occasionally visited Crane Wharf in the 1940s, Chester's maritime importance had ended centuries earlier.

By the later Middle Ages, when abundant documentation allows a full picture of the city's economy to be drawn, Chester craftsmen were making an enormous variety of goods. Given the pastoral bias of the city's immediate hinterland, the most important area of specialization was leather manufacture in almost every branch. Textiles were never of any great moment. Much corn was also grown in the neighbourhood until the concentration on dairying in the later 19th century, and the Dee corn mills, powered by penning up the river at the causeway above the bridge, were large and profitable. They acquired national renown through the opening words of Isaac Bickerstaffe's comic song, *The Miller of the Dee*, written for a traditional tune in 1762: 'There was a jolly miller once, lived on the river Dee'.[3]

The sale of agricultural produce, locally manufactured goods, and imports of all kinds in Chester's markets and fairs contributed greatly to the city's prosperity from an early period into modern times. Despite the huge changes in the nature of the national economy and in the means by which goods were distributed, retailing remained of prime importance to the city at the end of the 20th century. A very large proportion of late 20th-century visitors to Chester came 'for the shops', and the city had a retail sector far larger than its own population would have warranted.

The 'long 18th century' has been seen as the period when Chester was transformed from a town of craft manufactures and artisans into a 'leisure town',[4] a 'historic regional centre . . . on the way to the pleasant obscurity of county rather than national fame'.[5] Although the characterizations contain some truth, they are cruder than Chester's complexity deserves. Its 18th-century 'leisure industries' – theatre, the races,

1 *V.C.H. Ches.* v (1), frontispiece.
2 *Chester Customs Accts.* 3–7, 19, 73.
3 *Notes & Queries*, 3rd ser. iv. 49, 78, 277; R. Fiske, *Eng. Theatre Music in 18th Cent.* (2nd edn., 1986), 327–33, 343–4, 605; A. Nicholl, *Hist. of Eng. Drama, 1660–1900*, iii. 197–8, 237.
4 J. Stobart, 'Shopping Streets as Social Space: Leisure,

Consumerism and Improvement in an 18th-Cent. County Town', *Urban Hist.* xxv. 3–21; cf. P. Borsay, *The English Urban Renaissance: Culture and Society in the Provincial Town, 1660–1780*, 9, 20–1, 35–6.
5 E. A. Wrigley, 'Urban Growth and Agricultural Change', *The 18th-Cent. Town*, ed. P. Borsay, 48–9, 78–9.

and the comfortable lifestyles of coffee houses and conviviality described in the diaries of Henry Prescott, deputy registrar of the diocese between 1686 and 1719 – built on Chester's long-established position as a late-medieval and early-modern gentry capital. Craft manufacturing was certainly in slow decline throughout the later 18th century, but in a few trades did not die out until almost the end of the 19th. Moreover Chester did acquire some new heavy industries in association with the arrival of the canal (notably the canalside lead-works) and more particularly the railways, and has some claim to be regarded as a railway town, albeit one in which the railway diversified and strengthened a faltering local economy rather than creating a town from scratch, as at Crewe. A stress on Chester's standing as a Georgian resort also tends to underplay the significance of its leisure industries in the eras of the railway excursion and the mass ownership of motor cars. Already by 1896 the railways allowed noticeable numbers of American tourists and hordes of 'holiday-makers and pleasure-seekers' from Liverpool, Manchester, and the rest of Lancashire to make their way to Chester.[1] In the late 20th century the hordes became a torrent of millions of visitors each year and the fame of the most distinctive features of Chester's townscape – the city walls, the Rows, and the riverside – and of the most obvious aspects of its history and cultural heritage – notably the Romans and the mystery plays – spread world-wide, misunderstood and misrepresented though they frequently were.

1 G. L. Fenwick, *Hist. of Ancient City of Chester*, 253–4.

LOCAL GOVERNMENT AND PUBLIC SERVICES

LOCAL GOVERNMENT BOUNDARIES

THE MEDIEVAL LIBERTIES

The liberties of the city of Chester, first explicitly defined in 1354, derived from Chester hundred as it was constituted in 1086 (Fig. 1, p. 2). The hundred then comprised the city of Chester, the 'bishop's borough' and 'Redcliff' to its east, Newton to the north-east, and Handbridge and 'Lee' (later Netherleigh and Overleigh) south of the river Dee.[1] The term 'city' may have referred only to the walled town and its common fields to the north. Immediately east of the walls lay the bishop's borough, around St. John's church, and 'Redcliff', named from the red sandstone cliff between St. John's and the Dee. 'Redcliff' presumably covered all the extramural area later within St. John's parish, but the name was not in current use after the 11th century.[2] Newton was probably 'new' in relation to Chester itself. South of the river, Handbridge clearly extended beyond the hamlet of that name at the southern bridgehead and may also have included the detached part of St. Bridget's parish which comprised the meadows known later as the Earl's Eye. Netherleigh and Overleigh lay respectively further south and south-west. Chester hundred was bounded to the south by Marlston, Lache, and Claverton, east by Huntington and Great Boughton, and north by Blacon and Upton by Chester,[3] Upton being a large manor which certainly included Bache and probably Hoole.[4]

Chester hundred was not recorded again after 1086, and its rural parts north of the city (except Newton) and south of the river (with some additions) later fell within the liberties of the city. Newton was probably excluded from the liberties because it belonged to Chester abbey from the abbey's foundation c. 1092,[5] and there is no evidence that the city ever sought jurisdiction over it. The abbey's manor of St. Thomas, immediately outside the city's Northgate, however, was within the liberties, and an apparent attempt by Abbot Richard Oldham in the early 1480s to withdraw it met with failure.[6] In 1509, soon after

obtaining a royal charter conferring extensive privileges, the city followed up that victory over the abbey by confining the abbot's liberty to the precincts of the abbey.[7]

The liberties also excluded Chester castle, the seat in turn of comital, palatine, and county government,[8] together with a small area in front of the castle gate, called Gloverstone from the stone marking the limit of the city's jurisdiction. Gloverstone's own boundaries were obliterated by the early 19th-century alterations at the castle.[9] Later in the 19th century there was a separate civil parish of Chester Castle, coincident in area with the castle precincts and Gloverstone. It was not part of the municipal and county borough of Chester, lying within Chester rural district until local government reorganization in 1974.[10]

On the south the liberties as defined in 1354 extended beyond the former limits of Chester hundred, taking in part of Lache to the south-west,[11] and part of Claverton to the south-east.[12]

The boundary of the liberties was long left undefined. Earl Ranulph III c. 1200 confirmed the citizens' rights 'in the city of Chester' without saying where the city ended, and Earl John in the 1230s granted them liberties as citizens, without saying where they were exercised. The earliest reference to the liberties as a definite geographical area was in Edward I's charter of 1300, which was concerned, among other matters, with pleas 'within the city and its liberty' and the powers of bailiffs 'within the liberty of the city'.[13] Perhaps because of doubts about the limits, in 1351 the citizens offered to pay not only to have their charters ratified but also to have the boundary of their franchise fixed. The chamberlain and justice of Chester perambulated the boundary in 1353[14] and it was confirmed by the Black Prince's charter of 1354.[15]

The perambulation began in the south-east at Claverton ford on the Dee, and headed west by way of Heronbridge on the Chester–Eccleston road.[16] The whole of the southern boundary followed drainage

1 V.C.H. Ches. i. 325–6.   2 P.N. Ches. v (1:i), 80–1.
3 V.C.H. Ches. i. 340–1.   4 T.H.S.L.C. cxxxi. 159–60.
5 Ormerod, Hist. Ches. ii. 772–3.
6 Hemingway, Hist. Chester, i. 294.
7 Morris, Chester, 134–5.
8 Below, Castle: Administrative and Military Functions.
9 Morris, Chester, 107–11; C.C.A.L.S., QAB 2/6/54.

10 V.C.H. Ches. ii. 210–11; F. A. Youngs, Guide to Local Administrative Units of Eng. ii. 13.
11 Morris, Chester, 497–9.
12 e.g. Ormerod, Hist. Ches. ii. 821–2; 39 D.K.R. 220–1.
13 Morris, Chester, 482–3, 485–7, 490–3.
14 Blk. Prince's Reg. iii. 20–1, 104.
15 Morris, Chester, 495–9.   16 Para. based on ibid.

ditches, known at least in part as the Great (or Grey, or Green) ditch,[1] to the Chester–Wrexham road and then along field boundaries and another ditch to Lache Lane. It passed through Lache to the Black pool, a creek or inlet of the Dee, which it followed north to the river. It then crossed the river, in the 14th century a broad tidal estuary, to the mouth of a stream which at one time had been known throughout its course as Flooker's brook.[2] The northern boundary of the liberty then followed the brook past Pool Bridge, Stone Bridge, and Bache pool; further east the brook was called Bishop's ditch, which led east then south to the Roman road east of Chester. The boundary followed the road as far east as the eastern boundary ditch of St. Giles's hospital, which it followed south to the Chester–Tarporley road, next following the road a short way to Sandy Lane. Following the lane under the cliff on the right bank of the Dee, then the river bank itself, the boundary returned to the starting point at Claverton ford.

The boundary was identical to that defined in 1354 when it was viewed by the mayor in 1540, with changes only in some of the landmarks and minor place-names. For example a lane now ran along the boundary from Lache Lane to the Black pool, while a gallows stood by Black pool further towards the Dee, giving that part of the creek the name of Gallows pool. On the north bank of the Dee the 16th-century name for the lowest reach of Flooker's brook was Port pool, and east of Bache pool it was called Newton brook. East of St. Giles's the boundary was marked by a merestone.[3] By 1573 the point where the boundary crossed the Chester–Wrexham road was known as Hangman's hill, though the gallows which had once stood there had been removed.[4]

By 1573 parts of the boundary were in danger of being lost or forgotten through the neglect of ditches and the diversion of Flooker's brook.[5] Perhaps because of the risk of obliteration, the boundary was viewed more regularly from the later 16th century than seems previously to have been the case, in 1594, 1621, 1635, 1652, 1675, and 1686, when the Assembly ordered that perambulations were to take place every seven years.[6] From 1635, if not earlier, dated boundary stones were set up wherever needed during the perambulation. They survived into the later 20th century or were recorded earlier for 1635, 1652, 1686, 1702, 1708, 1715, 1736, 1750, 1785, 1807, 1812, and 1814.[7] Later perambulations of the boundary, by then extended, were made in 1841, 1857, 1866, 1873, 1913 (Fig. 2), and 1972, the last occasion ahead of the incorporation of Chester into a much larger local government district.[8]

FIG. 2. *Mayor Harry Dutton beating city bounds, 1913*

By the early 18th century the silting of the Dee estuary had made the course of the boundary across it uncertain. In 1713 Finchett's Gutter (the lower course of Flooker's brook below the Stone Bridge on Parkgate Road) was marked as the boundary between the liberties and Blacon, and in 1717 the Dee Navigation committee was ordered to make a new straight cut for part of it.[9] The later canalization of the river along the southern edge of the estuary and reclamation of land to its north led to the boundary's being pushed west to take in a triangular area formerly part of Blacon marsh. It was defined on the north by the old course of the river below Blacon Point and on the west by a line which ran straight north from the new cut at Saltney to Bumper's Lane, then waveringly north-west, all the while crossing fields laid out on reclaimed land. At its southern end the line was fixed in 1731, the date on a boundary stone set close to the Dee, but for the most part it ran through land permanently reclaimed only after a bank was raised in 1754, and was marked by stones set up by the parish of Hawarden (Flints.) in 1762 and the mayor of Chester in 1785.[10] It also formed the boundary between England and Wales.

1 *P.N. Ches.* v (1:i), 53.

2 Ibid. i. 24–5.

3 Morris, *Chester,* 210–12.

4 Ibid. 212–15.   5 Ibid.

6 Ibid. 215–18; *Cal. Chester City Cl. Mins. 1603–42,* 111–14, 181–4; C.C.A.L.S., ZAB 2, ff. 100–1, 181; ZAB 3, f. 5v.

7 *Rep. Com. Municipal Bndries.* H.C. 238, pp. 242–51 (1837),

xxvi; C.C.A.L.S., ZCA 1; ZAB 3, f. 103v.; 3 *Sheaf,* xii, p. 36.

8 3 *Sheaf,* x, pp. 41–3; Chester City Libr., file of press cuttings on beating the bounds (ref. supplied by Mr. G. Fisher); C.C.A.L.S., ZCA 12.

9 C.C.A.L.S., ZAB 3, ff. 207v.–208, 240v.–241.

10 *Rep. Com. Municipal Bndries.* pp. 247–9; T. Boydell, 'Plan of Lands of River Dee Co.' (1772).

By the 1830s the built-up area along Foregate Street and Boughton continued beyond the liberties into Great Boughton township, while along Hoole Road only a short gap separated the city from the hamlet of Flookersbrook, which straddled the boundary between Hoole and Newton townships. In 1835 the municipal boundary was enlarged to coincide with the parliamentary boundary extension of 1832, taking in the contiguously built-up part of Great Boughton as far as the Tarvin Road canal bridge, Filkins Lane, and Heath Lane, but leaving Flookersbrook outside.[1] In 1836 the added area was brought under the local improvement and police Act.[2]

The arrival of the railways at Flookersbrook in the 1840s obliterated a long stretch of the city boundary, which lay directly under the extensive area of sidings and railway company buildings around the station.[3] To the south-west of Chester, the railway was also responsible for the growth of the industrial suburb of Saltney, which straddled the city and national boundary.[4] Although the parliamentary constituency of Chester was enlarged in 1868 from Newton, Hoole, Saltney, and Great Boughton townships,[5] the municipal boundary did not follow suit, and the constituency in any case was extended again well beyond the town and its suburbs in 1918.[6] When Chester became a county borough in 1889 its boundaries were thus unaltered from those of 1835 and fell well short of the actual built-up area in several directions.[7]

Two boundary disputes with the county which had their origins in the 18th century were resolved in 1898. The Acts of 1788 and 1807 which authorized the rebuilding of the castle had provided that any land within the liberties bought by the rebuilding commissioners should be deemed part of the county.[8] The area opposite the castle entrance used for the militia barracks, and various pieces of land in Lower Bridge Street and Grosvenor Street had thus passed out of the city of Chester and into the county's jurisdiction. Although some of the property had been sold off by the county authorities, and all of it paid city rates, its status remained doubtful until the county agreed to restore it to the city, except for a triangle between the south-west corner of the castle and Grosvenor Road. In a separate case, *c.* 100 a. on the western side of Chester,

between the old bed of the Dee and Sealand Road, was claimed by both city and county. Although the boundary along the old bed had been perambulated as recently as 1873 and was marked by boundary stones,[9] the county and Blacon cum Crabwall civil parish had assessed the disputed area for rates, and it was agreed in 1897 to transfer it formally to Blacon. Both alterations came into effect in 1898,[10] reducing the area of the borough from 2,960 a. to 2,862 a.[11]

Suburban development immediately outside the borough boundary continued apace in the later 19th century and the early 20th, in Great Boughton, Newton, Upton, and especially Hoole,[12] where the boundary was difficult to trace through a maze of railway tracks and station buildings.[13]

In 1898 the city pressed unsuccessfully to incorporate the whole of Hoole urban district and parts of the civil parishes of Great Boughton, Newton, Saltney, and Sealand, the last two in Flintshire.[14] When the county borough boundary was eventually extended in 1936, Hoole remained independent and was indeed enlarged.[15] Newton civil parish was abolished and divided between Chester (153 a. on the west) and Hoole (288 a. on the east). Blacon cum Crabwall civil parish was also abolished and the greater part of it, 985 a., together with 8 a. in Little Saughall, was added to Chester in anticipation of a rapid growth of suburban housing there. Upton civil parish was unaffected. Elsewhere there were some additional but minor adjustments to the county borough. The boundary with Hoole was nudged north from the area of the station to a line which could be recognized on the ground, adding to Chester 47 a. which covered railway company property and the Chester Union workhouse. The city also gained 48 a. from Great Boughton which included a new housing estate south of Christleton Road, while the straight boundary of 1835 running from Sandy Lane to the Dee was kinked around the houses which had been built since then in Dee Banks. To the south the boundary was straightened at Heronbridge by taking 3 a. from Claverton, and extended to include 35 a. taken from Marlston cum Lache south of Lache Hall. As a result the area of the county borough was increased to 4,140 a. Hoole urban district, besides incorporating part of Newton, took 99 a. from the south end of Hoole Village civil parish, 11 a. from Guilden Sutton, and 5 a. from

1 *Rep. Com. Parl. Bndries.* H.C. 141, pp. 59–61 (1831–2), xxxviii; Act to Settle Parl. Divisions, 1832, 2 & 3 Wm. IV, c. 64, sched. O.5; *Rep. Com. Municipal Bndries.* 242–51; Municipal Corporations Act, 1835, 5 & 6 Wm. IV, c. 76, sched. A.

2 C.C.A.L.S., ZAB 6, pp. 203–4.

3 Ibid. p. 717; *Chester Chron.* 19 Sept. 1857; below, Railways.

4 *Census,* 1821–1901, for pop. of Flints. part.

5 *Rep. Bndry. Com. 1868* [3972], pp. 73–4, H.C. (1867–8), xx; Bndry. Act, 1868, 31 & 32 Vic. c. 46, s. 4, sched. 1.

6 *V.C.H. Ches.* ii. 140–1; Youngs, *Guide,* ii. 803.

7 *Rep. Com. Local Govt. Bndries. 1888,* H.C. 360 (1888), li; *V.C.H. Ches.* ii. 210–11.

8 Chester Castle Rebuilding Act, 1788, 28 Geo. III, c. 82; Chester Castle Gaol Act, 1807, 47 Geo. III, Sess. 2, c. 6 (Local and Personal).

9 3 *Sheaf,* x, pp. 41–3.

10 *Chester City Cl. Mins. 1896/7,* 354–8, 397, 441; C.C.A.L.S., ZCA 4; ibid. ZQRP 70; *Census,* 1901, *Ches.* 40.

11 C.C.A.L.S., ZCA 5, *Statement of Particulars,* p. 5.

12 *V.C.H. Ches.* ii. 207, 218, 224, 226, 229, 236.

13 O.S. Map 6-inch, Ches. XXXVIII (1882 edn.).

14 C.C.A.L.S., ZCA 5.

15 Rest of para. based on ibid. ZCA 7; *Census,* 1931, *Ches.* (Pt. 2), 7, 10–11.

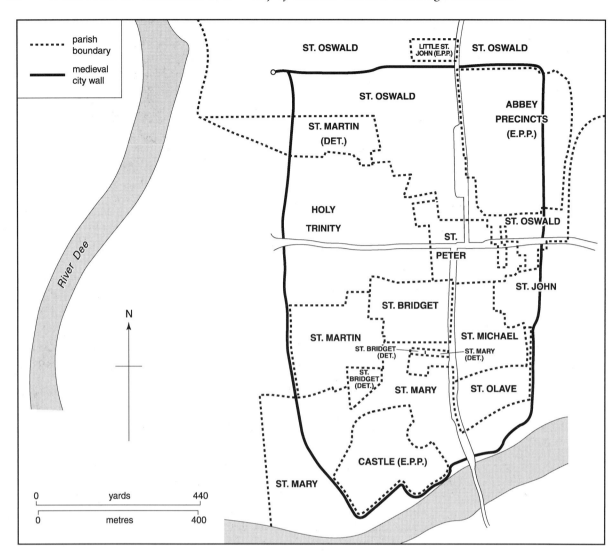

FIG. 3. *Parish boundaries: intramural area, c. 1875*

Great Boughton, so that its south-east boundary followed the Chester–Warrington railway line. Taking into account the loss to Chester, the urban district increased from 334 a. to 672 a.

In 1954 the Chester (Extension) Order dissolved Hoole urban district and incorporated most of it in Chester, omitting the rural 156 a. in the east, which were added to Hoole Village civil parish, and 18 a. at the hamlet of Piper's Ash, transferred to Guilden Sutton. Although the Order also added 22 a. from Upton to the county borough,[1] the greater part of Upton and Great Boughton were left out even though they had become increasingly suburban since the 1930s.[2] Likewise, East Saltney, a populous suburb of Chester across the Welsh border, remained outside the county borough.[3]

Under the 1972 Local Government Act Chester county borough and the rural districts of Chester and Tarvin were united in 1974 as Chester district,[4] stretching from the Mersey to the Shropshire border and including within one local government boundary, for the first time since the Middle Ages, the city, the castle, and all the continuously built-up area except for Saltney.

PARISH BOUNDARIES

Chester's nine medieval parishes were not mapped until 1833,[5] but there is no reason to suppose that the boundaries as then defined were substantially different from those of 1200, by which date all the churches were in existence. The parishes of St. Michael, St. Olave, and St. Peter lay within the medieval walls, and St. Martin's almost entirely so. St. Bridget's was partly extramural but confined to the liberties. Holy Trinity and St. John's extended beyond the liberties, and St. Mary's and St. Oswald's far beyond them. The

1 *Census*, 1961, *Ches.* 10.
2 *V.C.H. Ches.* ii. 207, 236.
3 *Census*, 1901–81.
4 Local Govt. Act, 1972, c. 70, sched. 3; Eng. Non-metro-

politan Districts (Definition) Order, 1972 (Statutory Instruments 1972, no. 2039); Eng. Non-metropolitan Districts (Names) Order, 1973 (Statutory Instruments 1973, no. 551).
5 J. Wood, *Map of Chester* (1833).

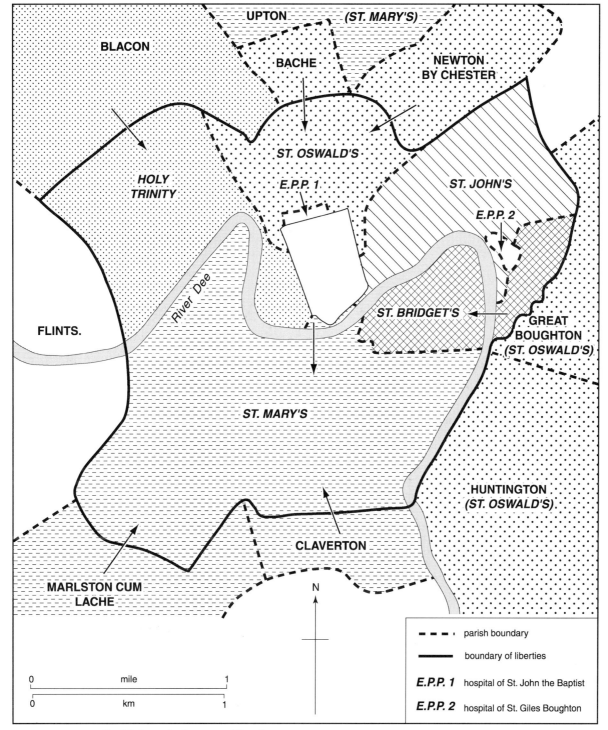

FIG. 4. *Parish boundaries: outer liberties*

partly extramural detached portion of St. Martin's parish in the Crofts may originally have been the parish of a tenth church, St. Chad's, which had disappeared before the Reformation.[1]

The evolution of the parishes and the final shape of their boundaries have been plausibly explained as the successive subdivision of territories attached to the two

oldest foundations, St. Oswald's and St. John's, as new churches were established from the 10th century onwards.[2]

St. Oswald's had the largest of the extramural parishes and perhaps also originally included all the area within the Roman walls except for the small part belonging to St. John's. In its final form, however, the

1 For fuller details: below, Medieval Parish Churches.
2 *J.C.A.S.* lxiv. 5–31, on which following acct. based; cf.

V.C.H. Ches. v (1), Early Medieval Chester: Chester in 1066, Church in Anglo-Norman Chester.

intramural part was confined to the north of the walled town. St. Oswald's was the church associated with the minster (later abbey) of St. Werburgh, and its parish also included much of the community's landed estate around the city, both within the liberties and without. Within the liberties the parish covered 468 a.; in all it extended to 7,736 a.[1]

St. John's parish, by contrast, was mainly extra-mural, coinciding with the probable extent of an early estate east of the Roman fortress belonging to the minster church, namely the bishop's borough and 'Redcliff' in the north-east part of the liberties and a small part (91 a.) of Hoole township.[2] The part within the liberties covered 257 a.

The third large parish, St. Mary's, lay on both sides of the river. To the north it included an area between the Roman walls and the Dee. South of the river it took in all the liberties except for Earl's Eye and extended beyond them to Claverton and Marlston cum Lache townships. The parish also had a large detached portion north of Chester, covering the townships of Upton by Chester and Little Mollington, to which Moston and part of Chorlton townships were added in 1599.[3] Within the liberties St. Mary's extended to 1,444 a.; in all it covered 4,307 a.

St. Peter's, probably the oldest of the smaller parishes, lay entirely within the Roman walls and covered only 7 a. Its irregular but rectilinear bound-aries seem to have followed property divisions, and included detached burgage plots on Eastgate Street. Its southern boundary followed lanes along the northern edge of a major Roman building.

St. Bridget's and St. Michael's parishes lay respect-ively west and east of Bridge Street in the southern part of the walled town, except that St. Michael's included some isolated burgage plots on the west side of the street. St. Michael's was entirely intramural and cov-ered only 8 a., whereas St. Bridget's also had as a detached part the meadows of Earl's Eye south of the river and covered 163 a.

St. Olave's (5 a.) and St. Martin's (16 a.) were small parishes with fairly regular boundaries, intramural except for part of the detached portion of St. Martin's.

Holy Trinity had the largest parish within the walls, and beyond them included most of the Roodee, Blacon marsh, and the manor of Blacon, the last being outside the liberties.[4] The part within the liberties covered 394 a.; including Blacon the parish covered 1,348 a.

There were four extra-parochial enclaves in the city: the precinct of St. Werburgh's, which included the

FIG. 5. *Parish boundary markers (St. Olave and St. Michael), Park Street*

Kaleyards outside the city wall (18 a.); the castle, with Gloverstone (9 a.); St. John's hospital outside the Northgate, also known as Little St. John's (1 a.); and Spital Boughton, the precinct of St. Giles's hospital at Boughton (3 a.).

The parish boundaries were much altered in the 19th and 20th centuries. The site of new St. Bridget's church in Grosvenor Street, formerly within St. Martin's and St. Mary's parishes, was transferred to St. Bridget's after the church was consecrated in 1829.[5] The parishes of St. Michael and St. Olave were united in 1839, and those of St. Bridget and St. Martin in 1842.[6] New ecclesiastical districts were formed in the suburbs from the mid 19th century: Christ Church, Newtown; All Saints, Hoole; St. Paul's, Boughton; and Lache cum Saltney.[7]

In the 1880s the intramural boundaries of the older parishes were rationalized. Within the walls St. Peter's was enlarged, while St. Oswald's and St. Mary's became wholly extramural when parochial functions were transferred to new churches built in the suburbs north of the city and in Handbridge.[8] Further changes were made in 1960 when St. Peter's parish was again enlarged and Holy Trinity became wholly extramural, the city-centre church being replaced by one in

---

1 Cf. 1620 perambulation: 3 *Sheaf*, iv, pp. 34, 37–9, 45, 47. The parish acreages in this section (rounded to the nearest acre) were supplied by Mr. P. Laxton, Department of Geography, University of Liverpool, from 1st edn. O.S. maps (surveyed 1869–77) and O.S. parish books of reference. Mr. Laxton is warmly thanked for allowing them to be used here.

2 Below, Collegiate Church of St. John.

3 Below, Medieval Parish Churches.

4 Ibid.

5 Ibid.; Dee Bridges Act, 1825, 6 Geo. IV, c. 124 (Local and Personal).

6 *Return of Pars. United and Disunited*, H.C. 227, p. 2 (1872), xlvi.

7 Below, Modern Parish Churches.

8 *Lond. Gaz.* 17 Feb. 1882, pp. 648–51; 27 Sept. 1887, pp. 5220–7; cf. below, Medieval Parish Churches.

Blacon.[1] In 1967 Little St. John's, which had acquired parochial functions, was united with St. Oswald's parish.[2] More significantly, under a Church Commissioners' Scheme of 1972 a united Chester parish for the central part of the city was created by merging the parishes of St. John, St. Oswald with Little St. John, Christ Church, St. Bridget with St. Martin, St. Peter, and St. Michael with St. Olave.[3] That scheme left the outer suburbs in the independent parishes of Holy Trinity without the Walls (Blacon), Lache cum Saltney, St. Mary without the Walls (Handbridge), St. Paul (Boughton), and Hoole, to which a new parish for Plas Newton was added (by dividing Hoole parish) in 1982.

WARD BOUNDARIES

Until the 1460s the administrative subdivisions of the city for civil purposes were four quarters based on the four main streets. Other divisions for the outlying areas beyond the walls were added later. From the 1480s the divisions were generally called wards; nine existed by 1507–8 and in 1533 there were fifteen.[4] Although nine of them (not the nine of 1507–8) were named from the parish churches, they were based upon logical divisions of the street plan rather than parish boundaries and had clearly evolved from the original four quarters.

To the north, St. Oswald's ward covered Northgate Street from the Cross to the Stoups in the corn market; Cornmarket ward ran from there to Parsons Lane (later Princess Street); and Northgate ward from Parsons Lane to the northern walls, including the Crofts. Beyond the northern walls St. Thomas's ward took in all the extramural area.

West of the Cross the north and south sides of Watergate Street were respectively covered by Trinity and St. Martin's wards.

In Bridge Street the west side from the Cross to Cuppin Lane formed St. Bridget's ward, the east side

from the Cross to Pepper Street St. Michael's ward. South of Cuppin Lane and Pepper Street, Beastmarket ward covered both sides of Bridge Street as far as Castle Lane and St. Olave's Lane. South from there, everything west of Bridge Street and Handbridge was in St. Mary's ward, and everything to the east in St. Olave's ward.

Heading east from the Cross, the first part of Eastgate Street as far as Fleshmongers Lane (later Newgate Street) and St. Werburgh's Lane formed St. Peter's ward. The lanes themselves and the rest of the street as far as the Eastgate comprised Eastgate ward. Outside the walls St. John's ward covered Foregate Street as far as Love Lane, and St. Giles's ward covered the Bars and Boughton.

By the 1600s the number of wards had been reduced to twelve by the absorption of Cornmarket ward into St. Oswald's, Beastmarket ward into St. Olave's, and St. Peter's ward into Eastgate. The twelve continued until 1835, being adopted, for example, as the divisions of the city for the purposes of the local improvement and police Acts of 1762 and 1784.[5]

After municipal reform in 1835 the city was divided into five electoral wards radiating from the city centre: St. Oswald's north-east, Boughton east, St. John's south-east, St. Mary's south-west, and Trinity north-west.[6] Their boundaries were altered and a sixth ward, Newton, was added when the county borough was enlarged in 1936. Hoole urban district, created in 1894 with two wards, East and West, also had a new ward called Newton added in 1936. When the urban district was incorporated into the city in 1954 its wards and the existing city ward of Newton were recast as Hoole and Newton wards, the other five city wards being unchanged.[7] After local government reorganization in 1974 the area of the former county borough and its suburbs was divided into six county-council wards and 15 (increased in 1999 to 16) city-council wards.[8]

MUNICIPAL BUILDINGS

COMMON HALL

The first common hall was probably built shortly before 1250, the last year in which the guild merchant met in the selds.[9] It certainly existed by 1337,[10] when it lay behind the selds, west of Bridge Street and just

south of Moothall or Commonhall Lane, itself in existence as a thoroughfare by the 1290s.[11] Later a second means of access from Bridge Street was provided a little further south by Pierpoint Lane, which may have become the main approach.[12]

Almost certainly the common hall was built as a

1 *Lond. Gaz.* 23 Dec. 1960, p. 8798; Order in Council, 21 Dec. 1960 (copy in Chester Dioc. Regy.).

2 Order in Council, 28 Nov. 1967 (copy in Dioc. Regy.).

3 *Lond. Gaz.* 30 June 1972, p. 7865.

4 *V.C.H. Ches.* v (1), Later Medieval Chester: City Government and Politics, 1350–1550 (City Government, 1430–1506; Charter of 1506); rest of para. based on C.C.A.L.S., ZAB 1, ff. 36–37v. (printed in 1 *Sheaf,* ii, pp. 146–7); the date 1533 is that of Henry Gee's first mayoralty, as given for the list of gable rents which follows in the manuscript: ibid. ff. 38–40.

5 3 *Sheaf,* iv, pp. 57–8, 60–1; C.C.A.L.S., ZCAS 1; ZCAS 2, esp. assessments of 1704, 1753, and 1799; *Rep. Com. Municipal*

Bndries. 235; J. Pigott, *Plan of Chester* (1823), shows ward bndries.

6 *Rep. Com. Municipal Bndries.* 234, 236–7.

7 *Census,* 1901–11; 1931, *Ches. (Pt. 1),* 3, 6; 1951, *Ches.* 3, 5; 1961, *Ches.* 2.

8 Ches. Co. Cl., *A to Z of County Councillors* [1993/4], 2; City of Chester (Electoral Changes) Order 1998 (Statutory Instruments 1998, no. 2866).

9 C.C.A.L.S., ZCR 469/542, f. 14v.

10 B.L. Add. Ch. 50142.

11 Ibid. Add. Ch. 50058.

12 Morris, *Chester,* 256; *J.C.A.S.* xxxii. 119.

meeting place for the guild merchant under the presidency of the mayor. Later, perhaps only after 1300 when the mayor became chief judicial officer, it seems also to have housed the principal civic court, the portmote, and to have become known as the moot hall.[1] In 1394 the assize of wine and in the mid 15th century full sessions of the portmote and mayoral inquests were held there. It also became the location of civic assemblies: in 1398, for example, the city treasurers presented their accounts there, and by 1506, and probably long before, it was where civic elections were held.[2] It was later remembered as the setting for 'the pleas of the city, and the courts thereof, and meetings of the mayor and his brethren'.[3] Described as the 'common hall of pleas' in the early 16th century,[4] it was then a modest two-storeyed building, of which the principal chamber on the upper floor was *c.* 24 ft. long and 18 ft. wide.[5]

A common hall continued in use on the site until *c.* 1510, when the building was converted into a chapel for the newly founded fraternity and hospital of St. Ursula.[6] In 1547, when the fraternity was dissolved, the chapel reverted to the corporation and was sold to the mayor-elect.[7] By 1592 it had become the meeting house of the Smiths and Cutlers' company, in whose possession it remained until 1778. It served as a nonconformist chapel from 1768, was converted into a dwelling house in 1806,[8] and was demolished in 1874.[9]

It is not certain where the mayoral courts were held in the earlier 16th century.[10] A building designated the common hall was in use for sessions of the portmote in 1540,[11] and the former chapel of St. Nicholas at the south-west corner of the abbey precinct was perhaps already being used for that purpose when the corporation leased it from the abbey in 1539.[12] At all events, in 1546 the Assembly determined to reconstruct the chapel as a new common hall. The profits of a recent common bargain of 52 tons of iron were devoted to the work, and the mayor, an ironmonger, also contributed towards the cost.[13] The chapel was converted by the

insertion of a floor, creating an upper chamber for use as a 'stately senate house' and a ground floor for the marketing and storage of wholesale goods.[14] In the upper chamber were held the meetings of quarter sessions, the fortnightly sessions of the portmote, and from 1551 many of the corporation's assemblies. In 1573 the thrice-weekly meetings of the sheriffs' court were transferred there from the Pentice.[15]

The new common hall was maintained by a keeper or clerk, generally a substantial citizen, who delegated the actual care of the building to an underkeeper.[16] It played a varied role in civic life. Foreign merchants were required to transact business there, and for a while it housed the King's school and the shambles for the country butchers.[17] In the early 17th century it also functioned as a playhouse.[18]

After an order of 1660 that the expenses for repair were to be borne by the keeper, the hall seems to have been neglected, and by 1686 its rebuilding was being considered.[19] In 1687, when it was allegedly 'ruinous and ready to fall down', the Assembly finally took action. A new lease was to be obtained from the dean and chapter, and money paid into the city treasury for the admission of freemen was to be appropriated to repair or rebuilding.[20] In 1692 it was decided to build a new common hall and a committee was appointed to prepare plans and estimates.[21] In 1694 the committee was authorized to sell the corporation's lease of the old building and in 1698 business was transferred to the new Exchange.[22] Though described as 'in great decay and unfit for use', the common hall survived and was thereafter put to various uses, including playhouse, music hall, cinema, and shop.[23]

EXCHANGE

The Exchange, also known at first as the new common hall, was erected between 1695 and 1698 at the corporation's expense but with contributions from William III, Peter Shakerley (former governor of the castle and a Tory M.P. for Chester from 1698), Francis Gell (projector of a plan to improve the Dee naviga-

1 B.L. Add. Ch. 50152.

2 C.C.A.L.S., ZCH 32; ZMB 1, ff. 16v., 41v.; ZMB 4, f. 7v.; ZMB 5, f. 174v.; ZMB 6, f. 35; ZSB 3, ff. 19, 60, 63, 67v., 91v., 97v.; ZSB 4, ff. 10, 30, 48, 51, 72v., 90, 95v., 97, 110, 118v. Thanks are offered to Dr. Jane Laughton for the references.

3 *King's Vale Royal*, [ii], 24.

4 *P.N. Ches.* v (1:i), 31.

5 *J.C.A.S.* xx. 34, 60; xxii. 118–20.

6 Ibid. xxii. 118–20; *V.C.H. Ches.* iii. 184; C.C.A.L.S., ZCHD 2/11.

7 *J.C.A.S.* xxxii. 123–4; C.C.A.L.S., ZCHD 2/11.

8 Lysons, *Ches.* 582; *J.C.A.S.* xx. 56–67; xxxii. 123–4; below, Protestant Nonconformity: Early Presbyterians and Independents.   9 *J.C.A.S.* xx. 67.

10 There is a hiatus in the portmote records, only three rolls surviving from 1507–50: C.C.A.L.S., ZMR 110–12.

11 C.C.A.L.S., ZAB 1, f. 48 and v.

12 3 *Sheaf*, xxx, p. 2; cf. below, Medieval Parish Churches: St. Oswald.

13 C.C.A.L.S., ZAB 1, f. 76v.; Morris, *Chester*, 398–9.

14 C.C.A.L.S., ZAB 1, ff. 77, 79; *Cal. Chester City Cl. Mins. 1603–42*, p. xxv.

15 *King's Vale Royal*, [ii], 39; Morris, *Chester*, 202–3; *Cal. Chester City Cl. Mins. 1603–42*, 79; C.C.A.L.S., ZAB 1, ff. 80 and v., 83, 85, 89v., 91v.

16 Morris, *Chester*, 203–4; C.C.A.L.S., ZAB 1, ff. 106v., 133, 184v.; *Cal. Chester City Cl. Mins. 1603–42*, 21, 42 n., 79, 137, 150.

17 C.C.A.L.S., ZAB 1, ff. 77, 79, 211, 219; *Cal. Chester City Cl. Mins. 1603–42*, 2, 79, 203; Morris, *Chester*, 203, 297; *V.C.H. Ches.* iii. 230.

18 C.C.A.L.S., ZAB 1, f. 331v.; ZQSF 51, nos. 55, 57–8.

19 Ibid. ZAB 2, f. 125v.; ZAB 3, f. 9.

20 Ibid. ZAB 3, f. 13.

21 Ibid. ff. 34v., 35v.

22 Ibid. ff. 46 and v., 67v.

23 Below, Places of Entertainment: Theatres and Music Halls, Cinemas.

FIG. 6. *The Exchange, south side, c. 1850*

tion), and the estate of Thomas Cowper of Overleigh Hall in the southern liberties. It stood on the site of the old shambles in the wide middle section of Northgate Street almost opposite Abbey Gate.[1] The architect is unknown.[2] The building, of brick with stone quoins and elevated on pillars, was adorned in 1712 with a life-sized statue of Queen Anne 'curiously gilt and painted' placed over the main entrance in the south front.[3] The lower storey formed an open piazza with a coffee house, initially in the south-west corner,[4] but later moved to the north-east corner.[5] The main apartments were in the upper storey, which comprised

'a fine magnificent room styled the common hall of pleas', with to the south the portmote court, 'extremely ornamental, wainscotted with oak and adorned with figures of carved work', and to the north the sheriffs' court.[6] Those apartments later functioned as an assembly or banqueting room, a court room, and a council chamber.[7]

In 1756 the Exchange, which had already been strengthened by the addition of 'several strong pillars', was showing signs of collapse. It was secured by enclosing the ground floor to house a row of shops, on which work continued until 1759,[8] and in 1801–2 was further adapted to plans by Thomas Harrison to provide for the court rooms and offices formerly in the Pentice.[9] In disrepair by 1839, it was destroyed by fire in 1862 (Fig. 7); most of the important contents including the city records and all except two large paintings were, however, saved.[10] The ruins of the Exchange were cleared after the fire and its site was taken into an enlarged Northgate Street. Until the new town hall opened on an adjoining site in 1869 the council met in the Chester Savings Bank in Grosvenor Street and its staff were housed in premises in Lower Bridge Street.[11]

PENTICE

By 1288 the sheriffs held their court in a building called the Pentice,[12] known from later evidence to have been a lean-to attached to the southern side of St. Peter's church.[13] In the late Middle Ages the court room was on the first floor at Row level, above shops which abutted the church on both south and east sides. By the 1430s there were at least seven shops,[14] and in the early 16th century at least nine, four facing the High Cross to the south and five at the southern end of Northgate Street to the east.[15] Probably the arrangement was ancient, since shops are known to have abutted St. Peter's church from the 1230s.[16]

By the mid 15th century, as later, the Pentice probably consisted of two parts, the main, southward-facing structure and a lesser northern section overlooking Northgate Street. In the 1460s there was a major reconstruction, probably of the larger southern range, which was levelled to the foundations and replaced with a new timber-framed building.[17] By

1 C.C.A.L.S., ZAB 3, ff. 13, 35v.–36, 46 and v., 48v.–49v., 54v.–59, 62–64v., 67v.–68, 74, 83–4, 85v.–86, 113; ZAF 47A/4; ZML 6/195; *Cal. S.P. Dom.* 1694–5, 461, 495; *Cal. Treas. Bks.* 1693–6, 1350; Lavaux, *Plan of Chester.*

2 Unlikely to have been Nicholas Hawksmoor, whose sketch for the embellishment of the 'townhouse' at Chester seems to date from after 1701: Wilton House, MS. F 6/27; cf. below, Cathedral and Close: Cathedral Church from 1541. Thanks are due to Mr. R. B. Hewlings for supplying a copy of the drawing and for comments on Hawksmoor's involvement.

3 C.C.A.L.S., DCC 16/120, pp. 46–7.

4 Ibid. ZAB 3, f. 94; cf. ZAB 4, ff. 48, 143, 175v.–176, 305, 311; *Diary of Henry Prescott*, i. 2, 16, 21, 30–4.

5 *J.C.A.S.* [1st ser.], ii. 102–3.

6 C.C.A.L.S., DCC 16/120, pp. 46–7.

7 Lysons, *Ches.* 382; Ormerod, *Hist. Ches.* i. 363; Hemingway, *Hist. Chester*, ii. 186; C.C.A.L.S., ZAB 3, f. 268; ZAB 5, pp. 120, 239.

8 C.C.A.L.S., DCC 16/120, pp. 46–7; ibid. ZAB 4, f. 168; ZTAV 2/42–3; Hemingway, *Hist. Chester*, ii. 185–6.

9 C.C.A.L.S., ZAB 5, pp. 148–9, 158, 160, 182.

10 Ibid. ZAB 6, p. 352; Ormerod, *Hist. Ches.* i. 363–4.

11 H. T. Dutton, *Chester Town Hall and its Treasures*, 6.

12 *Cal. Ches. Ct. R.* p. 154; cf. B.L. Harl. MS. 2162, f. 58; C.C.A.L.S., ZSR 5.

13 *King's Vale Royal*, [i], 39; B.L. Harl. MS. 2073, f. 88; Morris, *Chester*, 200.

14 B.L. Harl. MS. 2158, ff. 31v., 32v.–34v.

15 C.C.A.L.S., ZAB 1, f. 54; cf. B.L. Harl. MS. 2158, f. 40 and v.

16 B.L. Add. Ch. 49975; *J.C.A.S.* n.s. x. 17.

17 B.L. Harl. MS. 2158, ff. 49v.–50.

FIG. 7. *The Exchange on fire, 1862*

then besides being the place where the sheriffs transacted their business, the Pentice was also used by the mayor, in particular to settle disputes between citizens and foreign merchants.[1]

In 1497 the northern section was also reconstructed, and in 1573 there were further changes, comprising the heightening of the 'inner' and the reduction of the 'lesser' Pentice.[2] By then the structure had presumably assumed the form illustrated in the 17th century (Fig. 90, p. 156): a long timber-framed chamber, perhaps the inner Pentice, ran for much of the length of the south side of the church above a projecting undercroft, apparently built of stone. At the eastern end of the chamber was a higher building, of at least three storeys, perhaps the lesser or outer Pentice. At the western end was the timber-framed church house and rectory house of St. Peter's.[3] In the 17th century the Pentice was divided into three areas: an outer Pentice, 'open in day time ... for all persons to come into', a middle Pentice, 'where mayor and aldermen sit', and a further Pentice in two parts, one 'where the city officers are', the other, the inner Pentice, 'a place for private consultation'.[4]

The Pentice apparently continued to be the meeting place of the sheriffs' court until the mid 16th century.[5] After the abandonment of the old common hall *c.* 1510 it became a more important location for the administration of municipal business, and by the 1530s it was the main, perhaps only, meeting place of the Assembly.[6] With the adoption of St. Nicholas's chapel as a new common hall the importance of the Pentice

diminished. From 1550 the Assembly often met in the new building,[7] and in 1573 the shrieval court was also transferred there.[8] Increasingly the Pentice came under the control of the mayor. By the early 16th century he paid the salary and supplied the gown of the yeoman of the Pentice,[9] and in the late 16th century he was said to remain there most of the day transacting business. Besides the mayoral apartment it then included an adjoining room occupied by the mayor's clerks, in which judicial business was recorded and recognizances were taken. As later it probably housed the city records,[10] and by then too it had become the main venue for civic banquets.[11] In the late 16th and the 17th century it was the scene of other entertainments, including the 'shott', a drinking ceremony held each Sunday before the mayor and corporation processed to the civic service in St. Oswald's church and on other special occasions.[12] Gaming also took place there, and in the earlier 16th century the profits so made contributed significantly to the keeper's salary.[13]

In 1704 the south side of the Pentice was rebuilt, the late medieval timber-framing being replaced by a brick front with a stone balustrade and sash windows.[14] The new structure continued to incorporate shops at street level.[15] The northern section of the older building still survived and was used as a repository for the city's records, charters, and seal. Though no courts held formal sessions in the Pentice, it was the scene of a weekly public meeting of the mayor and J.P.s to hear complaints, make settlements, and redress grievances,

1 C.C.A.L.S., ZMB 6, f. 36 and v.

2 B.L. Harl. MS. 2125, f. 32; Morris, *Chester*, 200.

3 B.L. Harl. MS. 2073, f. 88; below, Medieval Parish Churches: St. Peter.

4 B.L. Harl. MS. 7568, f. 136v.

5 e.g. C.C.A.L.S., ZAB 1, f. 48 and v.

6 Ibid. ff. 48, 61, 62, 65v., 67 and v., 69v., 73v., 74v.

7 Ibid. ff. 76v.–77v., 78v., 82v., 86 and v.

8 Morris, *Chester*, 200, 203; B.L. Harl. MS. 2125, f. 32.

9 C.C.A.L.S., ZAB 1, f. 45v.   10 *King's Vale Royal*, [i], 39.

11 e.g. C.C.A.L.S., ZAB 1, ff. 253, 336; B.L. Harl. MS. 2125, f. 42; Harl. MS. 2133, f. 47v.; Harl. MS. 2150, f. 186 and v.; Add. MS. 11335, ff. 23v.–24; Add. MS. 29780, ff. 63–4, 161–2; *REED: Chester*, 139, 194, 259, 304–7.

12 *Tudor Chester*, ed. A. M. Kennett, 20; C.C.A.L.S., ZTAR 1/18.   13 C.C.A.L.S., ZAB 1, f. 91v.

14 Ibid. ZAB 3, ff. 126, 128.

15 Ibid. f. 200 and v.; ZAB 4, ff. 51, 58v., 68v., 86, 225v.

and was also used for meetings of, and public entertainments given by, the magistrates.[1] Guests included
the lord lieutenant of Ireland, who was feasted there on
several occasions in the earlier 18th century.[2] After the
rebuilding, however, no public balls were allowed
without a special order of the Assembly.[3]

In 1781 the Pentice was reduced in size and partly
reconstructed to designs by the local architect Joseph
Turner. The northern or back Pentice was taken down
to permit the widening of the southern end of Northgate Street, and the records kept there were transferred
to a new record room at the west end of the inner
Pentice adjoining the town clerk's office.[4] In 1800 the
record room was moved to the Exchange,[5] and in 1803
the rest of the Pentice and St. Peter's rectory house
were taken down to improve Eastgate Street.[6]

TOWN HALL

After the Exchange fire of 1862 a competition was
organized for a new town hall; entrants were to submit
designs which were 'substantial and economical' and in
accordance with 'the general features of this ancient
city', costing no more than £16,000. Some thirty
designs were submitted in 1864 and the competition
was won by the Belfast architect W. H. Lynn.[7]

The site chosen, occupied mainly by inns and alehouses, lay west of the Exchange, bounded by Princess
Street to the north, the Saracen's Head Inn to the
south, and the road to the new market hall to the rear.[8]
Work began in 1865 and lasted some four years,
prolonged by the increasingly strained relations
between corporation and architect. The principal difficulty was that Lynn's scheme cost more than £16,000,
and although the committee grudgingly accepted a
tender of £21,610, it continued to consider various
modifications. Nevertheless, in 1869 the new town hall
was completed. Built of red and grey sandstone in a
style best described as Venetian Gothic, its main façade
was symmetrical, of ten bays with a central tower. The
interior included a large assembly room, a court room
for the city quarter sessions, and on the first floor,
reached by a fine staircase rising in an apse, a council
chamber, mayoral suite, and committee room. The
basement was occupied by police offices, prison cells,
and kitchens. By 1881 the principal floor also included
a muniment room.[9]

Upon the completion of the town hall the corporation purchased the old butter market and, after some
argument, the then vacant and derelict Market and

FIG. 8. *Town Hall, c. 1880*

Saracen Inns to the south of the town hall. The butter
market was soon demolished to provide a dignified
open space in front of the new building, but the inns
did not finally disappear until 1882 when they were
replaced by an extension, adorned with a suitable
frontage by Lynn, linking market and town halls.[10]
The council chamber was rebuilt to designs by T. M.
Lockwood in 1897 after it had been seriously damaged
by fire.[11] In 1967, with the demolition of the market hall
and extension, there were considerable changes. The city
police removed to new buildings and part of their
premises was used to house the city's record office,
thereby moved into close proximity to the strongroom
constructed in the basement in 1935.[12] In 1973 most
council departments moved to new offices in the
Forum, recently built on the site of the market hall.[13]

In 1995 the furnishings included eight late 16th-
century painted boards depicting the Norman earls
and Edric Sylvestris (Eadric the wild), supposed
ancestor of the Sylvesters of Storeton in Wirral.
Formerly in the possession of the Stanleys of
Hooton, they were purchased by Sir Thomas Gibbons
Frost and presented by him to the city during his
mayoralty in 1883.[14] The civic paintings also included
a *Diana* by the 17th-century Dutch artist Jan van

1 Ibid. DCC 16/120, pp. 47–8.
2 Ibid. ZAB 3, ff. 152, 236, 264, 278v.; ZAB 4, ff. 2v., 82, 113.
3 Ibid. ZAB 3, f. 128.
4 Ibid. ZAB 4, ff. 339v., 340v.; Lysons, *Ches.* 582.
5 C.C.A.L.S., ZAB 5, f. 149.
6 Ibid. ff. 102v.–103; Lysons, *Ches.* 582 (gives date wrongly as
1805); Hemingway, *Hist. Chester*, i. 407–8; *J.C.A.S.* [1st ser.], iii.
375–6.
7 C.C.A.L.S., ZCCF 7; R. C. Gwilliam, 'Bldg. of Present
Town Hall, Chester', *J.C.A.S.* xlvii. 21–3; *Chester Town Hall*

(Chester, 1979).
8 Para. based on C.C.A.L.S., ZDS 5/3; ZDS 6/1–17; ZCCF 7;
J.C.A.S. [1st ser.], ii. 100–3; n.s. xlvii. 23–32.
9 *J.C.A.S.* lxii. 110–12.   10 C.C.A.L.S., ZDS 5/16–30.
11 Ibid. ZDS 6/18–35; *Chester City Cl. Mins. 1896/7*, 230–2;
1905/6, 848–9; *J.C.A.S.* lxii. 108.
12 C.C.A.L.S., ZDS 6/36; *J.C.A.S.* lxii. 110–12.
13 M. Lewis and S. Harrison, *From Moothall to Townhall*, 18;
Official Opening of the New Cl. Offices at the Forum (pamphlet at
C.H.H.).   14 Hemingway, *Hist. Chester*, ii. 186–7.

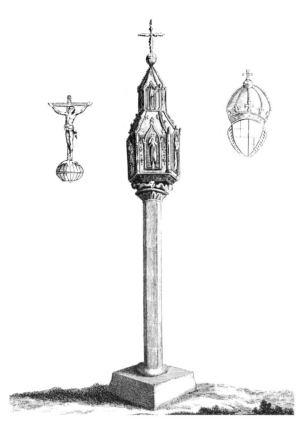

FIG. 9. *High Cross*

Oost, and portraits of George III, several members of the Grosvenor family (two by Benjamin West), and various recorders and mayors of the city. The mayoress's parlour contained nine portraits of the founders of local charities painted on wainscotting rescued from the council chamber of the Exchange.[1] The regalia included a civic sword dating from the 15th century, a mace given by Charles Stanley, earl of

Derby, during his mayoralty (1668–9), and a silver oar dating from 1719–20, symbolizing the mayor's authority as admiral of the Dee. The corporation began to accumulate silver plate in the early 16th century, its first acquisition being a goblet given by Hugh Aldersey, mayor 1528–9. In 1602, when a detailed inventory was drawn up, it possessed *c.* 28 items. By the outbreak of the Civil War there were considerably more. With the exception of the sword, however, all the ancient plate disappeared during the siege of Chester and the Interregnum. The corporation started to acquire plate again in the 1670s, and in 1995 possessed a fine collection dating from the late 17th century to the 20th.[2]

CROSSES

The High Cross, a focal point of the city markets and set up by the later 14th century, stood next to the entrance to St. Peter's church on a square pedestal with three or four steps. A new cross was made in 1476 and comprised an octagonal pillar surmounted by a head carved with images, 'tabernacle work', and a crucifix. Freshly gilded in 1603, it was pulled down after the fall of Chester in 1646.[3] After long remaining in private hands the surviving fragments from the head and base were erected with a new shaft in the Roman Garden near the Newgate in 1949 and restored to their original location at the Cross in 1975.[4]

Crosses were set up in other public spaces within the liberties. At Hough Green there was a hexagonal pillar surmounted by images of the Crucifixion and Virgin and Child, destroyed in 1646. A stone cross by a public way outside the Northgate was pulled down in 1584. Other crosses stood on the Roodee and by the road from the Bars to Spital Boughton, as well as in various ecclesiastical precincts.[5]

LAW COURTS

Besides its own courts, Chester was the location of courts held at the castle for the county at large. In the Middle Ages the county court, presided over by the justice of Chester, was the superior court for the whole county palatine, including the city. The other palatinate court, the Chester exchequer, operated under the authority of the chamberlain of Chester and heard cases concerned, among other matters, with debt.[6]

From 1543 the chief justice of Chester held criminal sessions on circuit for Cheshire, Flintshire, Denbighshire, and Montgomeryshire, the equivalent of the

assizes held for other circuits and known as the Court of Great Sessions. The sessions for Cheshire were held twice a year at the castle, usually in March or April, and September or October, and as elsewhere were accompanied by much ceremonial and became the focus of the county gentry's social season (Fig. 10).[7] The Chester exchequer, from the later 16th century overseen by the vice-chamberlain of Chester, became chiefly a court of equity jurisdiction until its business dried up at the end of the 18th century. In the later 16th century it vigorously attempted to enforce its

1 Hemingway, *Hist. Chester*, ii. 186–90. A tenth portrait described by Hemingway appears to have been lost.

2 C. N. Moore, *Silver of City of Chester*.

3 B.L. Harl. MS. 1944, f. 91; Harl. MS. 2073, f. 104; Harl. MS. 7568, f. 130; C.C.A.L.S., ZMB 6, f. 33v.

4 Hemingway, *Hist. Chester*, i. 404; Harris, *Chester*, 41.

5 B.L. Harl. MS. 2073, ff. 98–9; Harl. MS. 7568, f. 130; *Cal. Ches. Ct. R.* pp. 162–3; *P.N. Ches.* v (1:i), 33, 62–3, 67, 78; below, Collegiate Church of St. John; Sites and Remains of Medieval Religious Houses: Benedictine Nunnery.

6 *V.C.H. Ches.* ii. 2–3, 11–22.

7 Ibid. ii. 34–5, 37, 56–7.

FIG. 10. *High sheriff's coach at Cheshire assizes, early 20th century*

judgements in cases concerned with the city, which in the end had its autonomy confirmed.[1] The county J.P.s also usually held one quarter session a year in Chester, but their jurisdiction did not extend to the city, which from 1506 was a county in its own right.[2]

The Court of Great Sessions and the Chester exchequer were abolished in 1830, but Chester remained an assize town until both the assizes and quarter sessions were replaced nationally by Crown courts in 1971.[3] Among many trials at Chester assizes which attracted national attention perhaps the most notorious was that of the 'moors murderers' Ian Brady and Myra Hindley in 1966.[4]

MIDDLE AGES

Portmote

A borough court with 12 'lawmen' (*iudices*) existed in Anglo-Saxon times.[5] It is probably to be identified with the portmote, the principal medieval court of the city, first mentioned in the early 13th century, at which the city sheriff (then a single officer) presided and judgement was vested in a group of doomsmen (*judicatores*), a body perhaps descended from the lawmen and much the same in number.[6] The doomsmen determined custom, fixed the dates when the portmote met, postponed cases if they deemed the evidence insufficient, and acted as witnesses to property transactions recorded in court.[7]

As a court of record, where the principal citizens witnessed one another's land grants, the portmote's main business was probably pleas of real estate, initiated by plaint and writ.[8] By the mid 13th century, however, it was also concerned with minor criminal matters, though not with those serious crimes which constituted the Crown pleas.[9]

By the 1290s the court met every two or three weeks (occasionally consecutively) on Mondays, with long recesses at harvest, Christmas, Easter, and Midsummer,[10] the last coinciding with the fair and usually lasting three or four weeks.[11] Its procedures, which allowed for numerous postponements, were cumbrous and many cases did not come to judgement.[12] Those arrangements continued largely unchanged throughout the later Middle Ages, lengthy recesses at Christmas and Easter remaining normal but by no means obligatory;[13] until the 1480s the court also continued to be suspended for several weeks during the Midsummer fair.[14]

Throughout the 13th century the sheriffs (from perhaps the 1220s two in number) presided over the portmote and acted as its executive officers responsible for attachment of persons and distraint of goods, in which they were assisted by the city serjeants.[15] In 1300, however, Crown pleas were assigned to the mayor, who evidently heard them at sessions of the portmote, with the result that by 1305 he had come to preside over all sessions of the court. A separate court for Crown pleas emerged only in the later 14th century.[16]

1 Ibid. ii. 38–40; v (1), Early Modern Chester: City Government, 1550–1642 (Legal Administration).

2 Ibid. ii. 34, 45–7; v (1), Later Medieval Chester: City Government and Politics, 1350–1550 (Charter of 1506).

3 Ibid. ii. 59, 63.

4 e.g. [P. Holland], *Memories of Chester* (Halifax, 1997), [9].

5 *V.C.H. Ches.* i. 326, 343.

6 *J.C.A.S.* n.s. x. 19–20, 29.

7 *Sel. R. Chester City Cts.* pp. l–liv; *V.C.H. Ches.* v (1), Early Medieval Chester: City Sheriff and Portmote; Later Medieval Chester: City Government, 1230–1350 (Sheriffs and their Courts).

8 *Sel. R. Chester City Cts.* pp. xxiii–xlix.

9 e.g. *Cal. Ches. Ct. R.* pp. 4, 26.

10 *Sel. R. Chester City Cts.* p. xxi; C.C.A.L.S., ZMR 1–3, 5, 7–10.

11 Below, Fairs.

12 *Sel. R. Chester City Cts.* pp. xxiii–xlix.

13 C.C.A.L.S., ZMB 5, f. 51; ZMB 6, ff. 66v., 94v., 134v.

14 Ibid. ZMB 6, ff. 68v., 70v., 100, 101 and v.; B.L. Harl. MS. 1989, f. 454; Morris, *Chester*, 133–4.

15 *V.C.H. Ches.* v (1), Later Medieval Chester: City Government, 1230–1350 (Sheriffs and their Courts).

16 Ibid. (Charter of 1300 and City Government 1300–50); below, this section (Crownmote).

The mayor's association with the court was made explicit by his inclusion in the headings of the court rolls from the 1370s, and in the 15th century by the use of his name alone.[1] He routinely presided over judicial inquiries heard in sessions known as 'full' portmote, although the sheriffs were sometimes named and doubtless always present.[2] The common hall was the usual venue for such inquiries and probably also for regular sessions.[3]

The sheriffs continued to act as the court's executive officers in the later Middle Ages, responsible for the city gaol in the Northgate, executions, attachment, distraint, and the summoning of juries. In the more routine tasks they were assisted by four bailiffs, each responsible for one quarter of the city.[4] Judgement remained the preserve of the doomsmen, still provided on the basis of ownership of particular houses within the city. By then some of the most prominent owners, including the abbot of Chester and the heads of the Stanley and Egerton families, customarily appointed attorneys to serve on their behalf.[5] Such attorneys were generally drawn from the common pleaders of Chester's courts, although occasionally there were unusual appointments, such as a chaplain in 1404.[6] They also acted for townsmen involved in litigation, commonly serving for many years and accumulating an expertise which perhaps compensated for their lack of formal legal training.[7]

Throughout the later Middle Ages the portmote remained a court of record for property transactions enrolled before the mayor and sheriffs.[8] Wills and items of civic business were also enrolled from time to time.[9] It also remained the only court to hear pleas of real estate,[10] initiated by plaints which were probably written rather than verbal,[11] and often subject to lengthy delays.[12] The option of removing a case from the portmote to a higher court was apparently available to all litigants, but only by writ of error. Payment for

such a writ, 3*s.* 4*d.* in 1442–3 but later doubled, was relatively uncommon in the 15th century.[13]

In 1358 the citizens claimed that Crown pleas were heard before the mayor and sheriffs in the portmote and personal pleas before the sheriffs in the Pentice.[14] The mayor's civil jurisdiction was apparently largely confined to pleas of real estate, other types of plea being heard by the sheriffs, but in the later 14th century the portmote did hear some cases of debt, trespass, detinue (unlawful detention of personal property), and broken contract.[15] In the earlier 15th century such cases became fewer,[16] and the portmote seems increasingly to have confined its jurisdiction to pleas concerning land.[17] After 1430 and especially from the 1450s, however, that trend was reversed as growing numbers of personal actions were transferred from the Pentice.[18]

In the later 15th century judicial inquiries were heard in 'full' portmote in the common hall, at which jurors drawn from the four quarters of the city presented breaches of the peace and offences against the city's ordinances.[19] Similar inquiries held earlier had been conducted by the sheriffs or the mayor on various days of the week, but from the 1450s the mayor presided and the sessions always took place on Mondays,[20] often coinciding with a normal court hearing, and occasionally also with the crownmote.[21] There was a trend towards four 'full' portmotes a year, at intervals which suggest that they were quarter sessions in all but name.

A typical jury, which numbered from 12 to 24,[22] might include members of the Twenty-Four and Forty-Eight (forerunners of the aldermen and common councilmen of the city corporation), and constables from each quarter. Presentments were evidently made by ward.[23] Offences ranged from assault and prostitution to infringements of market regulations. Punishment was customarily by a monetary fine, the amount apparently depending upon ability to pay.[24]

1 e.g. C.C.A.L.S., ZMR 48, 50–1, 60, 62–4, 71, 78, 80, 90, 101, 104.

2 e.g. ibid. ZMB 4, ff. 7v., 34; ZMB 5, f. 174v.; ZMB 6, f. 35; ZSB 1, f. 133v.; ZSB 2, ff. 27v., 39v., 44v., 60; ZSB 3, ff. 3, 60v.; ZSB 4, ff. 10, 48, 123v.

3 e.g. ibid. ZSB 1, f. 133v.; ZSB 2, f. 85; ZSB 3, f. 19; ZSB 4, f. 30; ZMB 5, f. 200; ZMR 91, m. 1; B.L. Harl. MS. 2046, f. 33.

4 e.g. C.C.A.L.S., ZMB 1, f. 67; ZMB 2, f. 43v.; ZMB 3, ff. 71v., 81; ZMR 51, m. 1; ZMR 62, m. 1; ZMR 67, m. 1; ZMR 68, m. 1; ZSR 126, m. 2; ZSR 160, m. 1; ZSR 164, m. 1d.

5 e.g. ibid. ZMB 2, f. 95v.; ZMB 5, ff. 1, 41v., 69, 85; ZMB 7, ff. 80, 157; ZSB 1, f. 20v.; P.R.O., SC 6/800/1, m. 1d.; *Cat. Anct. D.* iii, C 3291.

6 C.C.A.L.S., ZMB 2, f. 29v.; ZMB 5, ff. 1, 41v.; ZMB 7, ff. 80, 118.

7 e.g. ibid. ZSR 289–308, 377–411; ZMB 3, f. 87v.; ZMB 4, f. 22v.; ZSB 2, f. 84; ZSB 3, ff. 1, 62; ZSB 4, f. 4.

8 e.g. ibid. ZMR 58, m. 1; ZMR 76, m. 1; ZMR 80, m. 1; ZMR 84, m. 1; ZMR 90, m. 1; ZMR 91, m. 1; ZMR 93, m. 1; ZMR 95, m. 1; ZMR 98, m. 1.

9 e.g. ibid. ZMR 75, m. 1 and d.; ZMR 77, m. 1; ZMR 85, m. 1.

10 Ibid. ZCHB 2, ff. 76–7; Morris, *Chester*, 553–4.

11 e.g. C.C.A.L.S., ZMR 51, m. 1; ZMR 59, m. 1; ZMR 60, m.

1d.; ZMR 62, m. 1.

12 Ibid. ZCHB 2, ff. 71–2; ZMR 51; ZMR 61; B.L. Harl. MS. 2057, f. 120 and v.; *Sel. R. Chester City Cts.* pp. xxx–xxxvii.

13 C.C.A.L.S., ZCHB 2, ff. 66v., 68 and v., 79, 82v.–84; ZMB 5, ff. 46v., 47v.; B.L. Harl. MS. 2158, ff. 196v., 205, 209v., 212; *Blk. Prince's Reg.* iii. 291–2.   14 *Blk. Prince's Reg.* iii. 291–2.

15 C.C.A.L.S., ZMR 82, 92, 99–100, 102, 109.

16 Ibid. ZMR 82.

17 *Sel. R. Chester City Cts.* pp. xix, xxiii.

18 C.C.A.L.S., ZSR 173, m. 1; ZSR 283, m. 1d.; ZSR 284, m. 1; ZSR 285, m. 1d.; ZSR 288, m. 1; ZSR 291, m. 1; ZSR 293, m. 1; ZSR 294, m. 1; ZSR 295, m. 1; ZSR 296, m. 1; ZSR 297, m. 1; ZSR 298, m. 1; ZSR 299, m. 1; B.L. Harl. MS. 2046, f. 33; below, this section (Pentice).

19 e.g. C.C.A.L.S., ZMB 4, f. 7v.

20 Inquiries held by sheriffs: ibid. ZMB 2, ff. 23, 106v.; ZMB 3, ff. 7v., 32, 44, 71; ZMB 4, ff. 6v., 72v.; by mayor: ZMB 4, ff. 34, 47, 53; ZMB 6, f. 35.

21 e.g. ibid. ZMB 5, ff. 11v., 15; ZMB 6, ff. 45, 58v.; ZSB 1, f. 134v.; ZSB 3, f. 63.

22 e.g. ibid. ZSB 2, ff. 39v., 45v., 59, 85; ZSB 3, ff. 60, 63, 91v.; ZSB 4, ff. 48, 51.   23 e.g. ibid. ZSB 3, ff. 37–40, 63–7.

24 e.g. ibid. ZSB 2, f. 25.

In the portmote the mayor also supervised the issuing of mainprizes, legal instruments which bound individuals or groups to keep the peace.[1] In the later 15th century few court sessions were without such business, especially at the final session of the mayoral year.[2] Subjects of mainprizes normally reappeared at a later session, when they either found further sureties or were dismissed by proclamation.[3] Evidently an effective device for controlling disruptive behaviour, the issuing of mainprizes apparently comprised much of the business transacted in the portmote court in the later 15th and early 16th century.[4]

Pentice

The sheriffs also operated in the Pentice court, where the procedure was more summary. The court, named from the structure in which it was held, a lean-to built against St. Peter's church,[5] was well established by 1288.[6] Its earliest surviving records date from 1297.[7] Although its wide range of business was at first apparently little different from that of the portmote, cases were determined personally by the sheriffs and there were no doomsmen. In 1290 the county court admitted the sheriffs' claim that cases of simple trespass should be heard before them and that they should take the fines.[8]

The rapid procedures of the Pentice made it especially suitable for dealing with offences such as forestalling and regrating, both of which had the effect of forcing up prices for buyers in the markets. It also had an important role in relation to the fairs: it was the only civic court to function during the Midsummer fair,[9] and from the late 13th century heard summary cases involving market traders (piepowder pleas) at Michaelmas.[10] The growth in the mayor's influence is evident in the fact that c. 1320–40 he presided over the Pentice court alongside the sheriffs.[11] When the court became once more exclusively shrieval much of its business had been eroded. By 1307 the mayor was already involved in piepowder cases,[12] and fair-time pleas disappeared from the Pentice entirely after the mid 14th century.[13] By then forestalling and regrating were also regulated in the portmote.[14] Such developments rendered business at the Pentice more and more routine.

In the 1390s it became customary for the Pentice to sit on Tuesdays, Thursdays, and Fridays, a pattern confirmed in 1506.[15] The sheriffs, who had resumed presidency of the court by 1358,[16] were as earlier assisted by four serjeants or bailiffs,[17] whose duties included summonsing, attachment, collecting fines, distraint, and assembling jurors.[18] The court dealt primarily with personal pleas which did not affect real property,[19] and fell into four main categories: debt, trespass, detinue, and broken contract. Pleas of debt were the most numerous, followed by pleas of trespass.[20] Suits were begun by plaint, sometimes in writing,[21] and all litigants were required to nominate pledges or hand over an item of property as a substitute.[22] Most causes did not proceed beyond the initial stage, either because the plaintiff failed to prosecute or the defendant to appear, or because agreement was reached out of court.[23] Those which did proceed to judgement were usually settled by the defendant's acknowledgment of a debt or admission of a charge.[24]

Throughout the period defendants could opt for a jury, a request with which plaintiffs invariably concurred.[25] In such cases, for which the shrieval court was apparently designated a 'passage' or 'panels' court, 12 jurors were assembled by the bailiffs with the assistance of four assessors (*triatores*), each representing a quarter of the city.[26] Although jurors gave decisions in cases at the Pentice throughout the later Middle Ages, the passage court was first expressly named in the 1460s.[27] Earlier, perhaps, jurors had been summoned on an *ad hoc* basis, the more formal procedures being established in response to an increasing demand for their presence in contested cases.[28] In the 15th century the passage court may have met only about eight times

1 e.g. ibid. ZMB 4, ff. 59–65v.; ZMB 5, ff. 74–80v.; ZMB 6, ff. 5v.–28v.; ZMB 7, ff. 83–94v., 162v.–189v.

2 Ibid. ZMB 6, ff. 26–28v., 137–40; ZMB 7, ff. 91–93v.

3 Ibid. ZSB 3, ff. 67, 69; ZMB 5, f. 79; ZMB 6, ff. 13v., 24, 44v.

4 D. J. Clayton, *Administration of County Palatine of Chester, 1442–85* (Chetham Soc. 3rd ser. xxxv), 240–77.

5 Above, Municipal Buildings: Pentice.

6 *Cal. Ches. Ct. R.* pp. 154, 156; *Sel. R. Chester City Cts.* pp. xv, xviii–xix.   7 C.C.A.L.S., ZSR 1.

8 *Cal. Ches. Ct. R.* pp. 154, 169–70, 177–8, 197.

9 C.C.A.L.S., ZSR 11, 25, 41, 44, 51, 59; below, Fairs.

10 B.L. Harl. MS. 2162, f. 58; below, this section (Court of Piepowder).

11 C.C.A.L.S., ZSR 33, m. 1d.; ZSR 39, m. 1; ZSR 42, m. 1; ZSR 48, m. 1; ZSR 50.

12 B.L. Harl. MS. 2162, f. 93.

13 Last recorded in C.C.A.L.S., ZSR 51, m. 2; ZSR 52, m. 1d.; ZSR 66, m. 1d.

14 e.g. ibid. ZQCR 2, 4–5.

15 Ibid. ZCH 32; Morris, *Chester*, 524–40.

16 *Blk. Prince's Reg.* iii. 291–2.

17 C.C.A.L.S., ZMB 3, f. 66v.

18 Ibid. ZMB 3, f. 20; ZSR 210, m. 1; ZSR 238, m. 1; ZSR 272, m. 1d.; ZSR 293, m. 1; ZSR 346, m. 2.

19 Ibid. ZCHB 2, f. 76; Morris, *Chester*, 553–4; *Blk. Prince's Reg.* iii. 291–2; *Sel. R. Chester City Cts.* pp. xvi–xxiii.

20 C.C.A.L.S., ZSR 183–93, 281–315, 330–68.

21 e.g. ibid. ZSR 126, m. 2; ZSR 132, m. 1d.; ZSR 157, m. 1.

22 e.g. ibid. ZSR 228, m. 1; ZSR 231, m. 1d.; ZSR 245, m. 1; ZSR 276, m. 1; ZSR 282, m. 1; ZSR 284, m. 1 and d.; ZSR 319, m. 1; ZSR 324, m. 1d.; ZSR 349, m. 3d.; ZSR 367, m. 1d.; ZSR 435, m. 1d.

23 e.g. ibid. ZSR 81, m. 1d.; ZSR 116, m. 1d.; ZSR 177, m. 1; ZSR 218, m. 1d.; ZSR 290, m. 1d.; ZSR 318, m. 1; ZSR 408, m. 1.

24 e.g. ibid. ZSR 170, m. 1; ZSR 182, m. 1d.; ZSR 205, m. 1d.; ZSR 266, m. 1 and d.

25 *Sel. R. Chester City Cts.* pp. xlv–xlvi.

26 e.g. C.C.A.L.S., ZSB 1, f. 50v.; ZSPR 1, mm. 8d., 16d.

27 Ibid. ZSPR 1; ZMB 5, f. 103v.

28 Johnson, 'Aspects', 147.

each year, a development which made justice in the Pentice less expeditious.[1]

The transfer of cases from the Pentice to the portmote, first recorded in 1430, became increasingly frequent in the 1450s, often at the request of leading citizens.[2] The reasons for removal remain obscure, but perhaps stemmed from dissatisfaction with the sheriffs' handling of the cases or from disquiet at the jurors' verdicts.[3] Occasionally a case in the Pentice was ended by a royal writ of *supersedeas*.[4]

Crownmote

The crownmote, which apparently emerged as a distinct court in the later 14th century,[5] was held in the common hall under the presidency of the mayor and in the presence of the sheriffs who, as the executive officers, assembled the jurors.[6] Sessions took place on Mondays, at approximately six-weekly intervals, sometimes coinciding with the portmote.[7] The court was normally in recess at Christmas and Easter,[8] but not apparently during the Midsummer fair.[9]

In 1399 the crownmote was declared the court in which defendants who failed to respond to the writ *capias* were to be outlawed.[10] Its other business included coroners' inquests into violent deaths,[11] indictments for trading offences and encroachments, and infringements of civic ordinances and of the Statute of Labourers,[12] matters which in the later 15th century were heard instead by the mayor in 'full' portmote and once at a 'great inquiry' in the common hall.[13] After *c.* 1450 mainprizes were occasionally issued by the court,[14] but only for more serious offences.[15]

Court of Piepowder

In the late 13th century rapid procedures for the convenience of non-Cestrian merchants were apparently administered in the Pentice. By the 1350s, however, piepowder law was pleaded before the mayor, probably in a separate court.[16] The court is known to have functioned during fair time only once, in 1486. The case, which involved two Spanish merchants and a spicer from Caernarfon, was doubtless heard by the mayor, whose portmote jurisdiction was at that period still restricted by the abbot's monopoly of jurisdiction during the fair. The mayor certainly presided over piepowder courts held before the door of St. Peter's church in 1470 and 1471, but neither was held during fair time. On each occasion the case had already been heard by the sheriffs in the Pentice, and the mayor secured a verdict from 12 jurors the following morning in order to give speedy justice to strangers.[17] The court apparently fell into disuse in the early 16th century.[18]

Court of Dee Mills

The ancient customs recorded in 1353–4 obliged the justice of Chester (an official of the palatinate) or his deputy to deal with trespasses committed at the Dee Mills and fishery, and excluded the city officials from all attachments and causes.[19] Profits from the court did not appear in later accounts, and in the late 14th century sessions were probably held only intermittently. A revival was attempted in 1402, perhaps because of the presence in Chester of Henry, prince of Wales, and his council; the mayor and sheriffs were ordered to proclaim a session to be held before the justice and chamberlain of the palatinate and to summon a jury drawn from the city and the mills.[20] It was perhaps intended to initiate regular sessions, and a judicial inquiry, nominally under the justice of Chester, was held at the mills in 1404.[21] Thereafter, however, inquiries in 1406, 1407, 1410, and 1411 were apparently conducted during sessions of the county court.[22] In 1415 indictments were again made separately at the mills,[23] and 11 similar sessions are known to have been held between then and 1448.[24] Their discontinuance later was probably related to the economic decline of the mills.[25]

Sessions of the court were timed to dovetail with the

1 Johnson, 'Aspects', 149–50, 153–9; C.C.A.L.S., ZSPR 6, m. 9; ZSPR 7, m. 1; ZSPR 10, m. 1.

2 C.C.A.L.S., ZSR 173, m. 1; ZSR 283, m. 1d.; ZSR 284, m. 1; ZSR 285, m. 1d.; ZSR 288, m. 1; ZSR 291, m. 1; ZSR 293, m. 1; ZSR 294, m. 1; ZSR 295, m. 1; ZSR 296, m. 1; ZSR 297, m. 1; ZSR 298, m. 1; ZSR 299, m. 1.

3 e.g. ibid. ZSR 309, m. 1 and d.; cf. ZSR 312, m. 1d.

4 e.g. ibid. ZSR 149, m. 1; ZSR 195, m. 1; ZSR 232, m. 1; ZSR 318, m. 1d.; ZSR 420, m. 1.

5 *Blk. Prince's Reg.* iii. 291–2; Morris, *Chester*, 554.

6 e.g. C.C.A.L.S., ZMB 1, f. 52; ZMB 2, f. 89v.; ZMB 6, f. 16v.; ZSB 3, f. 2.

7 e.g. ibid. ZSB 1, ff. 80–1; ZMB 5, ff. 48–60; ZMB 6, ff. 41–59; ZMB 9C, ff. 7–8v.

8 Ibid. ZMB 2, f. 33; ZMB 4, f. 69; ZMB 5, f. 101.

9 Ibid. ZMB 5, ff. 59, 101; ZMB 6, f. 164; ZMB 9C, f. 8v.

10 *36 D.K.R.* App. II, p. 99.

11 C.C.A.L.S., ZQCR 7.

12 Ibid. ZQCR 4, 8–11.   13 Ibid. ZMB 4, f. 34.

14 e.g. ibid. ZMB 4, f. 69 and v.; ZMB 5, ff. 15, 38v., 58v.–59,

81v., 212 and v.; ZMB 6, f. 29 and v.; ZMB 7, ff. 74–79v.; ZMB 9E, ff. 33–34v.

15 e.g. ibid. ZMB 5, ff. 125v., 152; ZMB 6, f. 29v.; ZMB 7, ff. 74, 152, 191; ZMB 9C, f. 8.

16 B.L. Harl. MS. 2162, ff. 58, 93; *Blk. Prince's Reg.* iii. 178; above, this section (Pentice).

17 B.L. Harl. MS. 2057, ff. 125–126v.

18 Johnson, 'Aspects', 143.

19 Eaton Hall, MS. 321; P.R.O., SC 6/784/5, m. 3; B.L. Harl. MS. 2081, f. 179; Morris, *Chester*, 105 n.

20 C.C.A.L.S., ZCHB 2, f. 71; B.L. Harl. MS. 2115, f. 69.

21 P.R.O., CHES 25/10, mm. 10, 14.

22 Ibid. mm. 22, 25d., 32–3; cf. CHES 25/11, mm. 1A–1B.

23 Ibid. CHES 25/11, m. 5.

24 Ibid. mm. 8, 19, 22; CHES 25/12, mm. 4, 18d., 20d., 26, 28d., 34d., 38d.; CHES 25/13, m. 1; CHES 25/14, m. 3d.

25 C.C.A.L.S., ZCH 28; P.R.O., SC 6/798/1, m. 1d.; J. Laughton, 'Aspects of Social and Economic Hist. of Late Medieval Chester, 1350–1500' (Camb. Univ. Ph.D. thesis, 1993), App. 3; below, Mills and Fisheries: Dee Corn Mills.

county court to facilitate the attendance of royal officers, clerical staff, and the county gentry, who served as jurors.[1] The court required two or three juries, one composed of townspeople to present offences committed by the millers, another of mill workers for offences committed against them, and a third of local gentry for offences committed beyond the liberties or by the mayor and sheriffs.[2]

Ecclesiastical Courts

Chester was the seat of the principal archdeaconry of the diocese of Coventry and Lichfield, and by the earlier 14th century its archdeacon possessed unusual powers,[3] eventually encompassing wills, instance and *ex officio* causes, and marriage and divorce. Those powers, which virtually excluded the bishops from first-instance jurisdiction in the city and shire,[4] were exercised in a court presumably held, as later, in St. John's church,[5] by locally based officials on behalf of the absentee archdeacons, an arrangement which on occasion led to extortion and abuse.[6] In the 15th century the archdeacon continued to exercise primary jurisdiction through his official in Chester,[7] at courts held, it seems, in the chapel of St. Nicholas as well as St. John's.[8] For the laity the main business remained testamentary and matrimonial.[9]

The bishop and abbot also held courts for their manors within the liberty.[10] The more significant was the abbot's, which originated with Earl Hugh I's grant of immune jurisdiction over the abbey tenants and those who offended at the Midsummer fair.[11] Held in the abbot's chapel of St. Thomas outside the North-gate, by the early 13th century it had doomsmen (*judices*), an indication that its procedures resembled those of the portmote.[12] Business included the register-ing of land grants.[13] Although in the earlier 13th century relations with the citizens were sufficiently amicable for civic officials to witness grants, by 1289 the existence of the court had become a source of conflict. The citizens alleged that it was a new court, injurious to the king's court in the city in that it withdrew the pleas initiated by the abbot's tenants

and any fines imposed upon them. The allegation was contested by St. Werburgh's.[14] The dispute was apparently never formally resolved, and in the mid 14th century the abbot still claimed exclusive jurisdic-tion during the Midsummer fair over all pleas except those of manslaughter.[15] In the 1350s the citizens again initiated pleas against the abbot in the borough courts, and his view of frankpledge was challenged.[16] In the early 15th century he was forced to defend his right to hold an annual court leet and to resist the attachment of his tenants in the Pentice court.[17] Each crisis resulted in a new definition of powers which left the abbey in a weaker position. In the early 1480s the sheriffs con-tinued to provoke conflict by distraining goods from the abbey's tenants,[18] and they enjoyed a significant victory in 1485, when in contravention of the abbot's rights they attached two women involved in a brawl during fair time and imprisoned them in the city gaol.[19] Nevertheless, the abbot's fair-time jurisdiction was not formally cancelled until the charter of 1506.[20]

In the later Middle Ages the prioress of St. Mary's also held a manorial court. Although her jurisdiction was extremely limited, it survived the citizens' attempt to extinguish it in 1391–2,[21] and in the 15th century the sheriffs were still unable to fine the nuns' tenants or make arrests on their land.[22]

EARLY MODERN, 1506–1660[23]

Effects of the Great Charter

The charter of 1506 amended the structure of the city's courts. While confirming that the portmote, Pentice, and crownmote were to be held as formerly, it added two others, the county court of the city and quarter sessions. The county court of the city, a necessary aspect of Chester's new status as a county in its own right, had little business. Quarter sessions on the other hand was responsible for trying all misdemeanours and most felonies in the city; in practice it took some business from the portmote but most from the crownmote, for which only the most serious felonies were reserved.[24] The changes and rationalization in the city courts' internal procedures coincided with a rise in the activity

---

1 e.g. P.R.O., CHES 25/10, mm. 10, 22, 33; CHES 25/12, m. 18d.

2 Ibid. CHES 25/10, mm. 10, 14, 22; CHES 25/11, mm. 8, 19; CHES 25/12, mm. 18d., 28d.

3 *V.C.H. Staffs.* iii. 31; P. Heath, 'Medieval Archdeaconry and Tudor Bishopric of Chester', *Jnl. Eccl. Hist.* xx. 244; *Great Reg. of Lich. Cath. known as Magnum Registrum Album*, ed. H. E. Savage (*Collns. Hist. Staffs.* 3rd ser. 1924), 237–8.

4 *V.C.H. Ches.* iii. 8–9; *Jnl. Eccl. Hist.* xx. 247–50.

5 *Jnl. Eccl. Hist.* xx. 246; below, Collegiate Church of St. John.

6 *Great Reg. of Lich. Cath.* 57; *V.C.H. Staffs.* iii. 142; *V.C.H. Ches.* iii. 8; *Cal. Papal Reg.* i. 529; *Jnl. Eccl. Hist.* xx. 244; *Cal. Ches. Ct. R.* pp. 188–9.

7 *Jnl. Eccl. Hist.* xx. 243–52.   8 3 *Sheaf,* v, p. 38.

9 e.g. ibid. xxxvi, p. 54; P.R.O., WALE 29/291; B.L. Harl. MS. 2020, f. 18; *Cal. Papal Reg.* viii. 331–2; Lich. Jt. R.O., B/A/1/12, ff. 133v.–135v.; *Jnl. Eccl. Hist.* xx. 246–7.

10 e.g. *Cal. Ches. Ct. R.* pp. 157, 165.

11 *Cart. Chester Abbey,* i, pp. 14, 21, 23.

12 Ibid. i, p. 49; *Sel. R. Chester City Cts.* p. li.

13 *Ancestor,* vi. 33.

14 *Cal. Ches. Ct. R.* p. 159; Burne, *Monks,* 42–3.

15 Ormerod, *Hist. Ches.* i. 287–8; below, Fairs.

16 *Blk. Prince's Reg.* iii. 178, 185, 190, 360–1.

17 C.C.A.L.S., ZCHB 2, f. 84 and v.; cf. ibid. ZCR 65/Bn.33.

18 e.g. P.R.O., CHES 29/187, mm. 5–6, 8 and d., 11.

19 C.C.A.L.S., ZMB 6, f. 101.

20 Ibid. ZCH 32; Morris, *Chester,* 524–40.

21 B.L. Harl. MS. 7568, f. 190v.; *V.C.H. Ches.* iii. 147.

22 e.g. C.C.A.L.S., ZSR 205, m. 1; ZSR 208, m. 1; ZSR 245, m. 1; P.R.O., CHES 25/16, m. 19d.

23 What follows draws heavily on Johnson, 'Aspects', 139–89.

24 Ibid. 180–1; Morris, *Chester,* 526, 528–30, 534, 536–9.

of the Cheshire courts based at the castle, which led to conflict between city and county jurisdictions.[1]

The main officials serving the city courts in 1506 were the clerk and the recorder. The clerk of the Pentice acted as clerk to all the city courts and soon became known as the town clerk. In the early 16th century the recorder came into conflict with the civic authorities by attempting to deliver judgement in the city courts; the matter was resolved in the corporation's favour in 1540, when a commission ruled that the recorder's role was simply to offer expert advice.[2]

Summonsing and attachment continued to be the business of the city's serjeants, who in the 16th century comprised four serjeants-at-mace elected by the Assembly, and four serjeants of the Pentice, the sheriffs' personal officers.[3] Serjeants-at-mace dealt with the summoning and attachment of freemen in both portmote and Pentice and of 'foreigners' (non-freemen) in the portmote,[4] while serjeants of the Pentice were empowered only to attach foreign defendants in the Pentice.[5] The arrangements led to repeated friction between the two sets of officials in the late 16th and 17th century.[6]

In 1657 the ancient tradition of serjeants-at-mace acting as attorneys was abolished; the Assembly decreed that instead the mayor, recorder, and sheriffs should nominate four other persons to serve in that capacity in the portmote and Pentice, expressly excluding any officer of the mayor or sheriffs.[7]

Portmote

In the early 16th century the portmote continued to meet regularly on alternate Mondays. Its status as the superior court of the city was confirmed by the regular attendance of the recorder from 1506.[8] Fees were higher than in the Pentice court, from which cases could be transferred either by writ of error or on petition. The portmote remained the principal court of record, the decisions of which could be questioned only by writ of error, and possessed exclusive jurisdiction over actions concerning landed property. The court also continued occasionally to enrol debts under Statute Merchant, but did not, in general, deal with cases in which the sum at issue was less than 40s., except in the case of disputed actions at the Pentice transferred by appeal.[9] Its business was limited in

comparison with the Pentice, and even as litigation increased in the later 16th and earlier 17th century it scarcely exceeded 150 cases a year.[10]

Pentice

Most cases involving small sums continued to be considered in the Pentice, the informal procedures of which were heard before the sheriffs and recorded by the clerk but not supervised by the recorder. Business comprised personal actions of debt (much the most numerous class), detinue of goods, assault, slander, and other invasions of the rights of one citizen by another.[11] Contested cases continued to be referred to a passage court, held irregularly but supposedly every few weeks,[12] a procedure which sometimes entailed delays of two or three months.[13] Litigants claimed that the officers of the passage court were corrupt and that the jurors were unfit to deal with complex business, and the more influential among them petitioned for their cases to be transferred to the portmote.[14]

By the earlier 16th century the volume of litigation, delaying tactics by defendants,[15] and the inefficiency of officials meant that the procedures of the Pentice court were scarcely expeditious. After 1506 the custom of awarding a case to the plaintiff if a defendant defaulted on three summonses had apparently been relaxed in favour of a fine for every day of failure to appear, though the large fines thus accrued by long-term defaulters were often commuted.[16] In 1545 the Assembly revived the custom of awarding such cases to the plaintiff,[17] and in a further attempt to discourage fraudulent delays ruled in 1575 that when a defendant denied a bond, bill, or similar instrument and the case was found against him, he could be imprisoned and fined.[18]

By the later 16th century the administration of the Pentice had many abuses. The courts were held irregularly at the pleasure of the sheriffs and not on the appointed three days a week;[19] despite admonition by the Assembly in 1570 and 1604,[20] of the prescribed 150 sessions only 37 were held in 1579–80, and in 1622–3 the number sank to 14, nearly all in October and November. The highest number recorded was 114 in 1592–3. Although the Assembly ordered monthly passages there were generally no more than four a year in the 1620s and 1630s, reaching up to 160 cases each session. Such a diminution was the more serious because of the increase in the court's business by some

1 *V.C.H. Ches.* v (1), Early Modern Chester: City Government, 1550–1642 (Legal Administration).

2 Johnson, 'Aspects', 161–2, quoting B.L. Harl. MS. 2057, ff. 122–3.

3 Johnson, 'Aspects', 146; Morris, *Chester*, 220, 534; *Cal. Chester City Cl. Mins. 1603–42*, pp. xii–xv.

4 Johnson, 'Aspects', 151, 163–4.

5 Ibid. 146, 163–5; C.C.A.L.S., ZAB 1, f. 108.

6 Johnson, 'Aspects', 164–7; C.C.A.L.S., ZAB 1, ff. 226, 251.

7 Johnson, 'Aspects', 166; C.C.A.L.S., ZAB 2, f. 115v.

8 Johnson, 'Aspects', 161.

9 Ibid. 144, 150–4.

10 Ibid. 160–1, quoting C.C.A.L.S., ZMB 33.

11 Johnson, 'Aspects', 145.

12 Ibid. 147.

13 Ibid. 153–4; B.L. Harl. MS. 2093, ff. 12, 29–32, 51.

14 Johnson, 'Aspects', 154, quoting C.C.A.L.S., ZMP 1, f. 5; ZMCP 1/11, 2/4, 2/17.

15 e.g. C.C.A.L.S., ZAB 1, ff. 75v.–76, 165v.

16 Johnson, 'Aspects', 149.

17 C.C.A.L.S., ZAB 1, ff. 75v.–76.

18 Ibid. f. 165v.

19 Ibid. f. 124; Johnson, 'Aspects', 154–5.

20 *Cal. Chester City Cl. Mins. 1603–42*, 16.

two thirds between the 1560s and the 1630s. The problem of insufficient sittings and delays continued to plague the court throughout the 17th century.[1]

Quarter Sessions and Crownmote

The establishment of quarter sessions enhanced the office of recorder; he, along with the mayor and those aldermen who had already served as mayor, constituted the city's justices of the peace.[2] Four J.P.s, including the mayor and recorder, formed a quorum. Other court officers included the serjeant of the peace (the mace-bearer), the four serjeants-at-mace, and the clerk of the peace, who was in practice always the clerk of the Pentice. As part of the rationalization of the courts in the early 16th century, minor offences and the binding over of citizens to keep the peace were transferred from the portmote. Quarter sessions also took over many of the criminal cases formerly heard in the crownmote, leaving the latter with only the most serious felonies and gaol deliveries. The crownmote's sittings, presided over by the same officers as quarter sessions, were reduced from *c.* 13 to three or four a year, at dates which were adjusted to dovetail with meetings of quarter sessions in order to facilitate the referral of serious cases to the senior court.[3]

A large part of the business of quarter sessions was to receive presentments made by the ward constables, usually for offences against the assize of ale and other minor misdemeanours. By the early 17th century it appears that very few of the fines levied were actually collected, a further example of the failure of the sheriffs to perform their duties. By then, too, the court played a significant part in administering the city's social legislation, a role closely monitored by the Assembly.[4]

County Court of the City

The main function of the court, which from 1508 met every month on Mondays under the presidency of the sheriffs, was to summon all those accused of felonies against the king for trial at the next crownmote. From 1543, when Chester was first represented in parliament, it was also responsible for declaring the election of the city's M.P.s.[5]

Ecclesiastical Courts

The special powers of the archdeacons and their courts were such that in 1535 Bishop Rowland Lee could claim that he had no authority in the archdeaconry.[6] The continued delegation of judicial powers to locally based officials engendered abuse and difficulties in enforcement, not remedied by the introduction in the 1520s of sessions outside Chester.[7] The archdeacon's court was held at St. John's church until 1541, when it was transformed into the consistory court of the new diocese and transferred to the cathedral.[8]

The charter of 1506 assigned all jurisdiction within the liberties to the mayor and citizens, and thereby brought to a head the long-standing conflict between the corporation and the abbey. When in 1507 Abbot Birkenshaw demanded recognizances to keep the peace after a brawl in Northgate Street, the disputed jurisdiction was referred to arbitration which in 1509 found in the city's favour; the abbot's authority was confined to the monastic precincts, his right to hold a fortnightly court in St. Thomas's outside the Northgate and to hear pleas during the Midsummer fair being abolished. Although Birkenshaw refused to accept the decision, St. Werburgh's never recovered its ancient rights.[9] After the Dissolution the dean's jurisdiction was confined to the manorial court of St. Thomas, held in Abbey Gate.[10]

DECLINE OF THE ANCIENT COURTS AFTER 1660

After 1660 the ancient city courts declined steadily in significance to become almost purely formal as the activities of quarter sessions expanded. The county court of the city was held for the purposes of conducting parliamentary elections until an Act of 1745 laid the responsibility on the sheriffs, after which it ceased to meet.[11] The crownmote remained the city's highest criminal court, presided over by the recorder, and in the early 1830s tried some 40 cases a year.[12] Quarter sessions met at first three times a year, reduced in the earlier 18th century to two principal sittings in spring and late summer, the January sessions being held merely as a formality and routinely adjourned. Criminal business mainly concerned assaults and petty theft.[13] In the later 18th century the quorum was the mayor and recorder alone (in breach of the charter of 1506), though often as many as eight or ten J.P.s attended.[14] Much routine judicial business was transacted on a relatively informal basis at weekly meetings of the mayor and at least one other J.P. in the inner

1 Johnson, 'Aspects', 156–60.

2 Morris, *Chester*, 525, 530, 532, 538.

3 Johnson, 'Aspects', 180–4; C.C.A.L.S., ZQCR 13; B.L. Harl. MS. 2057, ff. 97–9.

4 *Cal. Chester City Cl. Mins. 1603–42*, pp. xiv–xv, 187–8; Johnson, 'Aspects', 179–89; C.C.A.L.S., ZMB 28, *passim*; cal. of ZQSF 15–51.

5 Johnson, 'Aspects', 179; *V.C.H. Ches.* ii. 98; C.C.A.L.S., ZSB 5, f. 73; ZSB 9, f. 230.

6 C. Haigh, *Reformation and Resistance*, 1; *Jnl. Eccl. Hist.* xx. 247; *V.C.H. Ches.* iii. 9.

7 Haigh, *Reformation and Resistance*, 3–4, 14–19.

8 C.C.A.L.S., EDC 1/1–10, esp. EDC 1/10, ff. 146v., 155v., 158v.; *V.C.H. Ches.* iii. 13–14, 18–19, 38, 43.

9 *V.C.H. Ches.* iii. 142; Morris, *Chester*, 133–5.

10 Burne, *Chester Cath.* 249–52.

11 Parl. Elections Act, 1745, 19 Geo. II, c. 28; *The Trial at Large, in Several Informations in the Nature of a Quo Warranto, the King against Thomas Amery and John Monk* (Chester: J. Fletcher, 1786), 65.

12 *Rep. Com. Mun. Corp.* pp. 2623–4.

13 Ibid. p. 2624; C.C.A.L.S., ZQSF 79–131.

14 *Trial at Large of Quo Warranto, King vs. Amery and Monk*, 27, 29.

Pentice.[1] From such meetings emerged petty sessions, held twice weekly by 1835 and supplemented by daily sittings of the mayor and aldermen J.P.s to deal with minor offences and licensing.[2] About 1715 the portmote, apart from swearing in city officials and producers of bread and meat, handled only a few cases of debt and one or two property lawsuits, and by the 1750s had practically no business.[3] In the early 1830s it was still handling final concords and common recoveries, as well as 'frequent' cases concerning vessels in the Dee, under the mayor's admiralty jurisdiction.[4] Ordinary suits of debt and trespass continued to go before the Pentice court, but in numbers probably halved between the 1720s and the 1750s to fewer than 300. In the later 18th and early 19th century, although actions were still begun in the Pentice almost none came to trial because debtors normally paid what they owed on being served with the Pentice court's summons.[5]

In 1836 the city's quarter sessions were confirmed,

and thereafter commissions of the peace were issued by letters patent.[6] The meetings of petty sessions eventually evolved into the magistrates' court.[7] The portmote and Pentice also survived the reform of the corporation in 1835, meeting thereafter under the recorder four times a year. Their procedures were brought into line with those of the Westminster courts in 1870.[8] During the recordership of Horatio Lloyd from 1866 many Cestrians chose to bring their cases to be heard by him rather than in the county court, but when he was appointed a county court judge in 1874 the business followed him there and the portmote in effect ceased, though the town clerk continued to give notice each quarter that it and the Pentice would be held before the recorder.[9] The Pentice continued in being as the instrument for admitting the city's freemen, and after 1974 the district council was permitted to continue using the name of Pentice court for the equivalent ceremony.[10]

LAW AND ORDER

POLICING

From the late 16th century to the 18th the constables of each ward made monthly (occasionally fortnightly or weekly) reports to the Assembly on the numbers and lodging places of the unemployed poor and beggars,[11] often also reporting on fire hazards and nuisances.[12] From 1591 they were responsible for storing fire buckets, and from 1709 had oversight of fire-fighting.[13] References to constables are scarce after 1709.[14]

The earliest recorded watches, made up of unpaid citizens, were organized in 1625 and 1632 to exclude strangers from the city during the plague,[15] and an armed watch of 300 men was created to defend Chester in 1642.[16] There was a watch at the Pentice in 1659,[17] but the first clear reference to a permanent paid night watch was in 1703.[18] The Improvement Act of 1762 provided for the appointment of up to 60 able-bodied

watchmen, but the commissioners had only limited powers to raise revenue.[19]

Under the 1803 Improvement Act the commissioners acquired more effective financial powers and set up a force of 18 paid watchmen and an officer, who patrolled the city between 11 o'clock at night and an hour before dawn. Most of the watchmen were middle-aged or elderly labourers.[20] In 1811 the commissioners resolved to increase numbers to 24 and recruit younger men,[21] and from 1814 the Rows were patrolled also on winter evenings.[22]

Under the Municipal Reform Act of 1835 the council's watch committee took over responsibility for policing. The new force consisted of a superintendent, an inspector, two existing corporation constables, and 26 other constables, many of whom had been watchmen.[23] Eleven or twelve hours of duty a day were normal, mainly on the beat at night,[24] and from 1837 the police also acted as firemen;[25] the pay compared

1 C.C.A.L.S., ZMIP 1–198; *V.C.H. Ches.* v (1), Early Modern Chester: City Government and Politics, 1662–1762 (City Government).

2 *Rep. Com. Mun. Corp.* p. 2625.

3 C.C.A.L.S., ZMB 45; ZMB 50; ZMSR 140–86; *Archives and Records*, ed. Kennett, 23–4.

4 *Rep. Com. Mun. Corp.* p. 2624.

5 Ibid.; C.C.A.L.S., ZSBC 143; ZSBC 165; ZSPR 160, 163–4; ZAF 53, pt. 3, petition July 1744.

6 C.C.A.L.S., ZCH 43; ZQJC 1–4.

7 *Archives and Records*, ed. Kennett, 94–5.

8 *Pentice and Portmote Cts. of the City and Boro. of Chester: General Rules and Regulations* (Lond. 1870: copy in Liverpool Univ. Libr.).

9 H. T. Dutton, *Chester Town Hall and its Treasures*, 7; *Ches. Contemporary Biographies*, ed. W. T. Pike, 267.

10 *Archives and Records*, ed. Kennett, 23; C.C.A.L.S., ZMFR 16; ZMPM 1; ZMSR 187–237.

11 *Cal. Chester City Cl. Mins. 1603–42*, 134, 152–3, 196; C.C.A.L.S., ZAB 1, ff. 231v., 252v., 259v.; ZAB 2, f. 95v.

12 *Cal. Chester City Cl. Mins. 1603–42*, 99, 117, 141.

13 C.C.A.L.S., ZAB 1, f. 234; ZAB 3, ff. 47, 174; below, this chapter: Fire Service.

14 C.C.A.L.S., ZAB 4, f. 188v.

15 *Cal. Chester City Cl. Mins. 1603–42*, 135–6, 167; cf. C.C.A.L.S., ZAB 2, f. 98.

16 C.C.A.L.S., ZAB 2, f. 59 and v.   17 Ibid. f. 124v.

18 Ibid. ZAB 3, f. 115v.   19 2 Geo. III, c. 45.

20 Chester Improvement Act, 43 Geo. III, c. 47 (Local and Personal); C.C.A.L.S., ZTRI 2, ff. 10v.–11, 15v., 16v.–17.

21 C.C.A.L.S., ZTRI 2, ff. 175, 238v.–239; cf. ZTRI 3, f. 53.

22 Ibid. ZTRI 2, ff. 194v., 253, 291v.

23 Ibid. ZCCB 15, flyleaf, 9, 17, 19 Feb. 1836; cf. *Policing and Punishment in 19th-Cent. Britain*, ed. V. Bailey, 44.

24 C.C.A.L.S., ZCCB 15, 24 Oct. 1836.

25 Below, this chapter: Fire Service.

badly with that in nearby borough forces and did not attract good recruits. Dismissals, usually for drunkenness or sleeping on duty, greatly outnumbered resignations.[1] The basement of the Exchange was put into use as a permanent police station in 1839.[2]

The force was reduced in 1842 to a superintendent, two sergeants, and 16 men,[3] but was soon growing again, partly in response to public pressure.[4] Better pay for experienced officers was introduced in 1844 and extended in 1853.[5] Police work mostly consisted of patrols which reported the presence of prostitutes, drunks, and thieves in public houses. During race week additional constables were hired from outside the city, at the expense of the grandstand committee.[6] An old tradition was broken in 1837 when the police ceased to cry out the hour in order to increase their chances of capturing felons.[7] Their aim, like that of the watch, was crime prevention; there was little effort at investigation, and some financial pressure to refrain from prosecutions.[8]

The 1856 Police Act, establishing closer Home Office supervision and government grants, brought Chester into line with practice elsewhere, and the city soon had a police surgeon and its first detective.[9] The annual inspections exposed several weaknesses, notably the small size of the force and in 1864 the improperly close involvement in the management of the races of the chief constable since 1835, John Hill. He was compelled to resign.[10]

Hill's successor, George Fenwick, reduced the number of resignations due to low wages,[11] partly by introducing merit pay, a measure adopted by other forces in the mid 1860s.[12] A pay rise and new grading structure implemented in 1877 ensured much greater stability in the force.[13] Fenwick took an informed interest in the causes of criminality,[14] though his progressive ideas on dealing with juveniles were not

always backed by the council.[15] As in the period before 1856, police work was still largely confined to coping with drunkenness, petty theft, and vagrancy.[16] Large-scale public order offences were unusual, though there was an affray between the police and the militia in 1870[17] and race week and parliamentary elections continued to require extra police drafted from elsewhere.[18]

The abortive Fenian plot of 1867 to seize the castle helped to sour relations between the city force and the county constabulary.[19] Relations between the two forces had perhaps never been good and matters reached a head in 1870.[20] By then it was probably becoming clearer to the authorities in Chester that the Home Office favoured the larger county constabularies over small borough forces.[21]

The scope of police duties widened greatly between 1870 and 1900, largely through the need to enforce new legislation.[22] Policemen were permanently stationed in Saltney by 1880 and Boughton in 1882.[23] Pay and conditions were improved in the 1890s to bring Chester more closely into line with nearby forces,[24] though a weekly rest day was agreed only in 1909.[25] By 1920 the council was introducing nationally agreed pay scales and training.[26]

In the 20th century traffic control came to be a burdensome responsibility.[27] During the industrial unrest of 1909–11 the chief constable made arrangements with other police forces for mutual assistance and registered men willing to serve as special constables.[28] Local women's groups sought the appointment of women constables during the First World War,[29] but although a female probation officer to work with children was appointed in 1924,[30] no police-women joined the force until 1941.[31]

With a nominal strength of *c.* 70,[32] the Chester force was too small to meet the approval of the Home Office,

1 C.C.A.L.S., ZCCB 15, esp. 20 June 1836, 15 Oct. 1839, 15 Oct. 1853; *Public Administration*, xxxiv. 407.

2 C.C.A.L.S., ZCCB 15, 26 Oct. 1837, 16 July 1838, 1 Apr. 1839, 12 Sept. 1839, 7 Dec. 1843.

3 Ibid. 28 July 1842; cf. 6 Apr. 1843.

4 Ibid. 4 Dec. 1845, 28 Jan. 1847, 12 Mar., 9 Apr. 1850, 13 Apr. 1854.   5 Ibid. 6 Mar. 1844, 24 Oct. 1853.

6 Cf. ibid. 6 Jan. 1848, 18 Nov. 1850.

7 Ibid. 1 June 1837, 3 Dec. 1840.

8 Ibid. 5 May 1850; ZCCB 16, 23 July, 10 Aug. 1857.

9 Ibid. ZCCB 16, 11, 19, 22 Feb., 3 July 1856, 4 June 1857; cf. ibid. ZCCB 15, 2 Feb. 1854.

10 Ibid. ZCCB 16, 23 Oct. 1856, 5 Jan. 1857, 7 Jan., 21, 26, 28 Apr., 24 June, 18 Nov., 18 Dec. 1864, 19 Jan., 7 Feb., 2, 8, 21 Mar. 1865; cf. *Chester City Cl. Mins. 1897/8*, 529.

11 C.C.A.L.S., ZCCB 16, 4 Aug. 1864, 5 Jan. 1865.

12 Ibid. 19 Oct., 16 Nov. 1865; cf. C. Steedman, *Policing the Victorian Community*, 107.

13 C.C.A.L.S., ZCCB 17, pp. 356–7, 476; ZCCB 18, p. 182; cf. ibid. ZDPO 1/11, chief constable's reps. 1874–5, 1877–9.

14 Ibid. ZDPO 1/11, reps. 1869, 1872.

15 Ibid. ZCCB 16, 15 Nov., 12 Dec. 1866, 19 Jan., 13 Feb. 1867; ZCB 2, 13 Feb. 1867, 10 Feb., 9 June 1869; ZCB 3, ff. 19v., 22v.; ZDPO 1/11, chief constable's rep. 1883, pp. 5–6.

16 Ibid. ZDPO 1/11, rep. 1869, p. 3; rep. 1883, pp. 4–5; ZQPA 4.   17 Ibid. ZCCB 17, pp. 264–5, 269–72.

18 Cf. ibid. ZCCB 18, p. 396.

19 Ibid. ZCB 2, 13 Feb. 1867; ZCCB 16, 7 Mar., 3, 9 Oct. 1867; ZCCB 17, p. 2; P. Quinlivan and P. Rose, *Fenians in Eng. 1865–72*, 16–23.

20 C.C.A.L.S., ZCCB 16, 25 Feb., 4 Apr. 1861; ZCCB 17, pp. 192–5, 198, 206.

21 Ibid. ZCCB 17, p. 281; ZCCB 18, pp. 338, 343–4, 352.

22 Ibid. ZCCB 17, pp. 624–33, 646–7; ZCCB 18, pp. 78, 175, 343–4, 547; ZCCB 20, pp. 49–50, 61, 427, 430.

23 Ibid. ZCCB 18, pp. 413–14, 543, 575.

24 Ibid. pp. 111–12, 394.

25 *Chester City Cl. Mins. 1908/9*, 696.

26 Ibid. *1919/20*, 287; *1920/1*, 77–8; C.C.A.L.S., ZCCB 19, pp. 63–4; cf. *Chester City Cl. Mins. 1937/8*, 442; *1943/4*, 280–1; *1944/5*, 217; *1946/7*, 46.

27 e.g. *Chester City Cl. Mins. 1920/1*, 153–4.

28 Ibid. *1908/9*, 500; *1910/11*, 704; *1911/12*, 81–2.

29 Ibid. *1914/15*, 73; *1918/19*, 242; cf. R. R. Graves, *Goodbye to All That*.

30 *Chester City Cl. Mins. 1924/5*, 152, 241–2.

31 Ibid. *1940/1*, 974.

32 Ibid. *1938/9*, 760; *1945/6*, 120–1.

FIG. 11. *County constabulary headquarters*

nunnery, 'severely rectangular' and eight storeys high with an abstract design in cast concrete on the blank end wall facing the castle entrance (Fig. 11). It was the work of the county architect Edgar Taberner. The Foregate Street building was used as a headquarters for the county library service until it was demolished in 1969.[7] The county force also had a police station in Hoole by the early 1870s.[8]

FIRE SERVICE

The Assembly provided fire buckets in 1570, and a hook and a ladder for each ward in 1591, to be maintained by the constables.[9] From 1599 to 1633 or later strangers obtaining the freedom had to provide two buckets.[10] In 1671 thatching was banned as a fire precaution from the roofs of houses in the four main intramural streets and Foregate Street.[11]

The city's fire-fighting equipment was still limited to buckets, ladders, and hooks in 1695,[12] but the new waterworks inaugurated the previous year made more effective methods feasible. The city probably bought its first fire engine in 1705,[13] and in 1709 issued a comprehensive set of fire regulations. The constables were in charge of operations.[14] In 1709 the Assembly built a fire-engine house abutting the bishop's palace and not far from the waterworks company's cistern in Northgate Street. Ornamented with Corinthian pilasters and battlements, it was perhaps paid for by James Butler, 2nd duke of Ormonde.[15]

After 1803 the improvement commissioners bought new equipment and appointed seven part-time firemen, one of whom was to maintain the engines and drill his colleagues.[16] The water supply was controlled by an employee of the waterworks company.[17] Fire insurance companies were expected to contribute towards the cost of new engines,[18] though there was also at least one private engine in 1811,[19] and another from the castle was frequently used in the city.[20] In 1828 the commissioners had four engines, under the command of the leader of the city watch.[21] Between 1824 and 1831 the engines were moved to a new building behind the potato market towards the north end of Northgate Street,[22] perhaps in 1828 when the waterworks company moved its cistern to that site.[23]

Under the Municipal Corporations Act of 1835 the improvement commissioners at first retained control

which urged its amalgamation with the Cheshire Constabulary in 1932,[1] and again in 1946 after the Police Act of that year had abolished 45 non-county borough forces.[2] The Home Office hoped that Chester would agree to voluntary amalgamation but the watch committee first asked for permission to increase the establishment to 84 men,[3] and then demanded a public inquiry.[4] The inquiry was held in 1948, decided against the council, and the city police force was absorbed by the county in 1949.[5]

The ground floor of the new town hall, opened in 1869, was designed as the city's police station,[6] and remained in use after 1949. The county constabulary headquarters was located from 1884 in a building designed for the purpose by John Douglas in Foregate Street, of four storeys with a brick and terracotta façade and an elaborate Dutch gable. The county force moved in 1967 to a new building on the site of the medieval

1 *Chester City Cl. Mins. 1931/2*, 741.

2 Ibid. *1946/7*, 47–8; T. A. Critchley, *Hist. Police in Eng. and Wales, 900–1966* [1st edn.], 243.

3 *Chester City Cl. Mins. 1946/7*, 462.

4 Ibid. *1947/9*, pp. 341, 985.

5 Critchley, *Hist. Police*, 244.

6 Above, Municipal Buildings: Town Hall.

7 Harris, *Chester*, 114–15; *Chester Chron.* 6 Feb. 1970; *V.C.H. Ches.* ii. 92; C.P.S., Foregate St. (negs. N 4/27; POCK 10/21).

8 O.S. Map 1/2,500, Ches. XXXVIII.11 (1875 and later edns.).

9 C.C.A.L.S., ZAB 1, ff. 234, 258.

10 Ibid. f. 258; *Cal. Chester City Cl. Mins. 1603–42*, 21, 176.

11 C.C.A.L.S., ZAB 2, f. 170v.

12 Ibid. ZAB 3, f. 47.   13 Ibid. f. 139.

14 Ibid. f. 174; cf. *Diary of Henry Prescott*, i. 131, 219; ii. 348.

15 C.C.A.L.S., ZAB 3, ff. 175v., 186v., 194, 212v.; ibid. EDD 16/120, p. 48; Hemingway, *Hist. Chester*, ii. 15; G. and W. Batenham and J. Musgrove, *Ancient Chester*, print V.

16 C.C.A.L.S., ZTRI 2, ff. 48v.–49.

17 Ibid. f. 104.   18 Ibid. f. 174.

19 Ibid. f. 166v.   20 Ibid. f. 297.

21 Ibid. ff. 390v.–392v.

22 Hemingway, *Hist. Chester*, ii. 18–19.

23 Ibid. ii. 18, 329; cf. *Chester Chron.* 10 July 1846, p. 4; C.C.A.L.S., ZDF 2 (plan of proposed engine house, 1843).

FIG. 12. *Earl of Chester's Volunteer Fire Brigade, early 20th century*

of fire-fighting. They disbanded the fire brigade and transferred its duties to the city council's new police force.[1] Formal control of the fire service passed in 1838 to the city council's watch committee, which bought two new engines.[2] Because they were larger and required more water, the committee pressed the water-works company for additional fire hydrants and an improved supply,[3] but until the 1860s fire-fighting was hindered by the lack of hydrants, low pressure, and water shortages; if fire broke out at night the supply had to be turned on especially.[4] A continuous supply was gradually provided through dedicated fire mains.[5]

In 1843 the watch committee moved the engines to a rented building next to the Theatre Royal (the former St. Nicholas's chapel) and in 1854 from there to George Street. A new fire station in the potato market, planned since the 1840s, was opened only in 1856.[6]

Disputes between the watch committee and the waterworks company after a serious fire at the race-course grandstand in 1855 led to the collective resig-nation of the police force as firemen, though they were persuaded back with extra pay.[7] At the end of 1862 the destruction of the Exchange in a fire which, ironically, started in the police office chimney, exposed the inadequacy of the water supply and the ill-discipline and ineffectiveness of the brigade, especially in com-

parison with the soldiers who assisted at the blaze.[8] In the wake of the disaster the brigade was disbanded and replaced by a new force, the Earl of Chester's Volunteer Fire Brigade, with volunteer officers, paid men, and a paid, full-time superintendent responsible for drill and equipment but subordinate to the officers.[9] The arrangement sometimes caused friction.[10]

Equipment was still provided by the city, which bought its first fire engine with steam-powered pumps in 1874,[11] installed telegraph wires between the police office and the waterworks in 1876,[12] bells in the firemen's houses in 1877,[13] and telephones in the station and the captain's house in 1893.[14]

The council bought the land off the west side of Northgate Street on which the fire station stood in 1900,[15] and completed a new station, designed by James Strong as a half-timbered building with three arched entrances, in 1911.[16] Old cottages in Valentine's Court behind the station were replaced in the 1920s with six firemen's cottages and a superintendent's house fronting Northgate Street.[17]

Meanwhile in 1914 the city council's brigade was revived, consisting of a full-time superintendent and assistant, three sergeants and 18 firemen paid retaining fees, and an unpaid reserve, whereupon the Earl of Chester's Volunteers voluntarily disbanded.[18] More full-time firemen were appointed in the 1920s and

1 C.C.A.L.S., ZTRI 3, ff. 94v., 96v.; ZCCB 15, 6 July 1837.

2 Ibid. ZCCB 15, 14 May 1838, 3, 28 Dec. 1840.

3 Ibid. 8 Oct., 12 Nov., 17 Dec. 1840, 11 Feb. 1841, 21 Apr. 1842.

4 Ibid. 1 June 1843, 29 Aug. 1848, 22 Dec. 1852, 5 Jan. 1853, 27 Apr. 1854; ZCCB 16, 5, 12 Apr. 1855.

5 Ibid. ZCCB 16, Fire Mains.

6 Ibid. ZDF 2; ZCCB 15, 2 Nov. 1843, 4, 18 Apr. 1844; ZCCB 16, 3 Aug. 1854, 12 Apr. 1855, 7 July 1856.

7 Ibid. ZCCB 16, 5, 12, 26 Apr., 7, 18 May, 4 June, 7 July, 2 Aug. 1855.

8 Ibid. 8 Jan. 1863; ZCB 2, 14 Jan., 11 Feb. 1863.

9 Ibid. ZCCB 16, 17, 22 Oct. 1863, 7 Jan. 1864; cf. 7, 13 Apr. 1864, 8 June 1865.

10 Ibid. ZCCB 19, pp. 537–8, 542, 544–5, 552–3, 554; ZCCB 20, pp. 402–3.

11 Ibid. ZCCB 17, pp. 593, 693.

12 Ibid. ZCCB 18, pp. 41–2.

13 Ibid. pp. 174, 202–3, 263, 269–70, 316, 422, 485; ZCCB 19, pp. 423–5.   14 Ibid. ZCB 4, 8 Mar. 1893.

15 Ibid. ZCCB 20, p. 284; *Chester City Cl. Mins. 1899/1900*, 584; *1906/7*, 299, 665, 666–7; *1907/8*, 298.

16 *Chester City Cl. Mins. 1907/8*, 98; *1908/9*, 237; Harris, *Chester*, 87; C.C.A.L.S., ZDF 48, 50.

17 *Chester City Cl. Mins. 1914/15*, 78, 145; *1927/8*, 807–8; *1928/9*, 87; C.C.A.L.S., ZDS, uncatalogued Plans and Drawings, File 97/4, nos. 7, 14.

18 *Chester City Cl. Mins. 1906/7*, 300; *1913/14*, 524, 592–3.

1930s, starting with drivers,[1] and the unpaid reserve was dispensed with in 1937.[2]

The first motorized fire engine was bought in 1914.[3] The brigade began providing a service for rural areas outside the city boundary *c.* 1920,[4] and by 1937 covered Hoole urban district and Tarvin rural district, and was about to make similar arrangements with the rural district councils of Hawarden and Chester; in 1939 a substation was established at Ellesmere Port.[5]

As a preparation for war an auxiliary fire service was set up in 1938.[6] On the formation of the National Fire Service in 1941 Chester's brigade was taken over by a district which included Liverpool and Wirral,[7] and the city council regained control of the force only in 1947.[8]

It was apparent early in the 1950s that the Northgate Street fire station was too small and difficult of access,[9] but a new station was opened only in 1970, on the site of the Northgate railway station goods yard. Responsibility for fire services was transferred from the city to the county council in 1974 under the 1972 Local Government Act.[10]

MUNICIPAL PRISONS

Northgate Gaol

There was a town gaol at the Northgate in the custody of the serjeant of the gate by 1294.[11] In the mid 14th century that arrangement was believed to have existed time out of mind,[12] and although there was no formal grant of the right to keep a gaol, the citizens were empowered in 1300 to lodge there anyone arrested within the liberties, awaiting gaol delivery according to city custom, which amounted to the same thing.[13] The prison, and the gallows and pillory associated with it,[14] were often in the later Middle Ages managed by an underkeeper who paid the serjeant of the Northgate for his office. The serjeanty was hereditary from the 14th century. In 1498–9 the mayor and citizens laid claim to it; perhaps then and certainly by 1541 they established their right, and control of the prison passed to the city sheriffs.[15] They paid rent to the corporation and appointed a gaoler, styled keeper or underkeeper, and a hangman.[16] The Assembly removed appointments into its own hands in 1618,[17] but by the 1660s and

throughout the 18th century each October the incoming sheriffs reappointed the underkeeper or deputy keeper, who indemnified them against any escapes and undertook to find an executioner.[18] From 1767 the deputy keeper was paid an annual salary rather than left entirely dependent on fees and perquisites.[19]

Offenders were gaoled in the 16th and 17th centuries for gambling, adultery, insulting the mayor, debt, negligence on watch, and many other transgressions. Most seem to have been detained for only short periods,[20] except for debtors, some of whom in the 18th century remained in the Northgate for 10 years or more. Deserters from the army and convicts awaiting transportation were also held. Total numbers in the later 18th century seem rarely to have reached 20, and probably most of the time debtors were in the majority.[21] Charitable bequests and gifts made between 1594 and 1615 by Hugh and Robert Offley, Thomas Green, Valentine Broughton, and John Vernon provided small amounts of money for the prisoners to buy food and other necessities.[22]

The prison comprised a house built over the Northgate and dungeons below (Fig. 13).[23] By 1631 the gaoler had his own accommodation.[24] After St. John's hospital was rebuilt in 1717 the gaol had use of a garden and a room under the gallery in the chapel.[25] Debtors were lodged in the 'free house' over the gate, from where in 1540 they were at liberty to attend services in St. John's chapel, or to walk on the northern stretch of the walls or along Northgate Street as far as the Bull Inn.[26] About 1714 the recorder spent £140 on repairs.[27] An Assembly committee considered building a new gaol in 1773 but instead apparently repaired the existing buildings,[28] and in 1777 debtors were well housed in a series of rooms, gentlemen among them using the 'blue room' at a weekly rent of 5*s.* Felons had a spacious day room, but at night were confined in an underground cell merely 14 ft. by 8 ft., down a flight of 18 steps, without light, and ventilated only by two narrow pipes leading up to ground level. Women felons occupied a windowless upper dungeon. In the 1770s and 1780s there were rarely as many as eight debtors and ten felons imprisoned at any one time, and often far fewer. The

1 *Chester City Cl. Mins. 1923/4*, 160, 242; *1929/30*, 291; *1933/4*, 428–9.

2 Ibid. *1936/7*, 294–5, 511.

3 Ibid. *1913/14*, 525, 552; *1915/16*, 250.

4 Ibid. *1916/17*, 271, 299–300; *1919/20*, 436, 489, 557.

5 Ibid. *1937/8*, 44–6; *1938/9*, 874.

6 Ibid. *1938/9*, 50–3.   7 Ibid. *1940/1*, 846–8.

8 Ibid. *1947/9*, p. 58.

9 Ibid. *1952/3*, p. 246; *1957/8*, pp. 784–5.

10 Ibid. *1961/2*, pp. 231, 342; *1964/5*, p. 445; *1965/6*, p. 829; *1966/7*, pp. 91, 359; *1972/3*, p. 405; *1973/4*, p. 653; Harris, *Chester*, 87.   11 *Cal. Ches. Ct. R.* p. 188.

12 Below, City Walls and Gates: Gates, Posterns, and Towers (Northgate).

13 Morris, *Chester*, 493; *Brit. Boro. Chart. 1216–1307*, ed. A. Ballard and J. Tait, 170.

14 Morris, *Chester*, 556–7.

15 Ibid. 237; below, City Walls and Gates: Gates, Posterns, and Towers (Northgate).

16 *Cal. Chester City Cl. Mins. 1603–42*, pp. xiv–xv, 31, 39, 61.

17 Ibid. 90, 94, 166, 168, 180.

18 C.C.A.L.S., ZSBO 1–2.

19 Ibid. ZAB 4, ff. 248v.–249.

20 e.g. *Cal. Chester City Cl. Mins. 1603–42*, 5, 9, 16, 18, 40–1, 167, 189, 198; Morris, *Chester*, 185–6, 189–90, 234.

21 C.C.A.L.S., ZSIG 1–35.

22 *31st Rep. Com. Char.* 354–7, 373, 383, 385.

23 Morris, *Chester*, 529.

24 *Cal. Chester City Cl. Mins. 1603–42*, 168.

25 C.C.A.L.S., ZAB 3, f. 236.

26 Morris, *Chester*, 162–4.

27 C.C.A.L.S., ZTAB 2, f. 10; ZTAB 3, f. 58v.; ZTAB 5, f. 53; ZAB 3, ff. 122, 207v., 215v., 266v.–267.

28 Ibid. ZAB 4, ff. 296 and v., 301.

FIG. 13. *Old Northgate and gaol, before 1808*

authorities provided no food, and convicted felons and prisoners awaiting trial wore irons.[1] The cutting of the Chester canal in the 1770s separated the gaol from the chapel in the Blue Coat building, but in 1793 a foot-bridge was built to allow prisoners to attend chapel without going into the street.[2] In 1801 a new drop for executions was made,[3] but the prison was itself con-demned from 1803, when the Assembly decided to build a new gaol.[4] The old one was demolished with the Northgate in 1808.[5]

House of Correction (Bridewell)

In 1576 the Assembly implemented the Act of that year permitting J.P.s to set up a house of correction by buying part of the Quarrel, a deep quarry outside the walls east of the Northgate, and re-erecting there the timber-framed building which had formerly housed the corn market. It included workrooms on two storeys. In its courtyard a narrow space in the face of the quarry was used in the 17th century to confine refractory youths, and during the Interregnum Quakers, for a few hours in a tortured position where they could neither stand, sit, kneel, or lie. It was known, euphemistically, as Little Ease.[6] The bridewell was pulled down by the city's defenders during the Civil War siege, but was replaced in 1655–7 by a new house of correction on the same site. Initially intended to provide corrective employment for the able-bodied

destitute in tasks such as weaving cloth,[7] it came, like similar establishments elsewhere, to be used as a prison for minor offenders convicted by the magistrates. In the 1770s a workshop and two 'dungeons' were added. It was closed in 1808 and sold in 1817 to Joseph Fletcher, who converted the buildings into dwellings.[8]

New City Gaol

A new combined gaol and house of correction were built in 1807 and opened in 1808. The site, enclosed by a high wall, fronted the later City Walls Road between the Linenhall to the south and the infirmary to the north (Fig. 14, p. 34). The buildings, of brick, were designed by Thomas Harrison and had the gaol on the west and house of correction on the east, linked by a chapel serving both. The entrance from the walls had a neo-classical stone gateway, surmounted by the gal-lows.[9] The gallows was frequently used until 1867 because of the continuing custom that those convicted of capital offences anywhere in the county of Cheshire were to be hanged by the city sheriffs.[10]

The new gaol was built out of corporation funds, and the house of correction from the proceeds of a special city rate. They had a separate governor and keeper until the early 1830s, and were formally distinct, though in practice managed together, until the 1865 Prisons Act.[11] The gaol passed from the control of the sheriffs to that of the city's J.P.s in 1823. As originally

1 J. Howard, *State of Prisons* (1780 edn.), 405–6; J. Howard, *Acct. of Principal Lazarettos in Europe* (1791 edn.), 208.

2 Murray and Stuart, *Plan of Chester* (1791); C.C.A.L.S., ZAB 5, p. 72.   3 C.C.A.L.S., ZAB 5, f. 84.

4 Ibid. ff. 99v.–100; S. and B. Webb, *Eng. Prisons under Local Govt.* 63.

5 Below, City Walls and Gates: Gates, Posterns, and Towers (Northgate).

6 3 *Sheaf,* xxi, p. 33; below, Protestant Nonconformity: Quakers.

7 Johnson, 'Aspects', 196–202, 212–14; C.C.A.L.S., ZTCC 6; *V.C.H. Ches.* v (1), Early Modern Chester: Economy and Society, 1550–1642 (Social Conditions).

8 Webb, *Eng. Prisons,* 12–16; Murray and Stuart, *Plan of*

Chester (1791); Hemingway, *Hist. Chester,* i. 347–8; Howard, *State of Prisons,* 407; Howard, *Acct. of Lazarettos,* 208; C.C.A.L.S., ZAB 5, pp. 371–2, 379.

9 Hemingway, *Hist. Chester,* ii. 184; M. A. R. Ockrim, 'Life and Work of Thomas Harrison' (Lond. Univ. Ph.D. thesis, 1988), 426–7; H. Colvin, *Biographical Dict. of Brit. Architects* (1995), 468; engraving (wrongly dated to *c.* 1790) reproduced in E. M. Mumford, *Chester Royal Infirmary, 1756–1956,* 17; O.S. Map 1/500, Ches. XXXVIII.11.16–17 (1875 edn.); C.C.A.L.S., ZAB 5, ff. 123, 132.

10 *Rep. Com. Mun. Corp.* p. 2621; C.C.A.L.S., ZQAG; ZSFE 1–2; *V.C.H. Ches.* ii. 59–60.

11 Hemingway, *Hist. Chester,* ii. 184; *Rep. Com. Mun. Corp.* p. 2626; Webb, *Eng. Prisons,* 17.

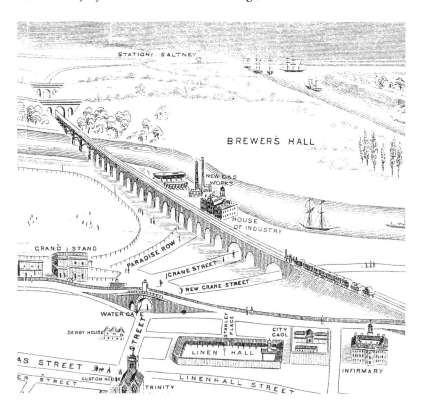

FIG. 14. *New city gaol
and nearby buildings, 1867*

built the two establishments could house 30 prisoners each, though not in separate cells. The Act of 1823, requiring prisoners to be classified,[1] necessitated alterations, completed by 1825. Twenty-seven separate cells, six workrooms, and two schoolrooms were made out of the existing accommodation, and at the same time a resident matron and turnkey were appointed.[2] Lodges on the east and west were demolished and the site was extended east so as to clear a space around the buildings and prevent escapes, which had previously been frequent.[3] Total expenditure down to 1831 was £7,400 on the gaol and £9,300 on the house of correction.[4]

The number of cells was sufficient in the 1820s, but less so in the 1830s, when during one race week they held as many as 85.[5] The gaol was commended in 1833 for its cleanliness, orderly management, and healthy situation,[6] but those advantages were soon lost through increasing pressure of numbers and an ineffective

governor: in the late 1830s defects were found in security, discipline, prisoners' employment, and staffing.[7]

Prison discipline was greatly improved under a new governor appointed in 1839,[8] but the shortage of cells and poor security were not remedied until 1847, when the day wards were converted into cells.[9] There were then 64 separate cells, again insufficient from the later 1860s. Overcrowding was especially acute in the women's quarters.[10] From the 1820s the prison regime included work, and after 1839 all prisoners were given regular employment. The staple tasks were mat-making and oakum-picking, with stone-breaking for men sentenced to hard labour, and laundry work and sewing for women.[11]

Most prisoners were locked up for breaches of the peace, vagrancy, or prostitution, and served short sentences.[12] In the year 1861–2, for example, only 9 of 413 prisoners were serving more than a year, and

1 4 Geo. IV, c. 64; Webb, *Eng. Prisons*, 73–5; *Acct. of Gaols, Houses of Correction, and Penitentiaries*, H.C. 135, pp. 6–7 (1819), xvii; *Rep. Com. Mun. Corp.* p. 2626.

2 *Reps. and Schedules pursuant to Gaol Acts*, H.C. 5, pp. 322–5 (1825), xxiii; H.C. 10, pp. 306–7 (1826), xxiv.

3 Hemingway, *Hist. Chester*, ii. 184–5.

4 C.C.A.L.S., ZTCC 187–8.

5 e.g. *Reps. and Schedules*, H.C. 46, p. 277 (1826–7), xix; H.C. 41, pp. 281–2 (1830–1), xii; H.C. 33, p. 280 (1835), xliv; *2nd Rep. Inspectors of Prisons: N. and E. Dist.* [89], p. 33, H.C. (1837), xxxii.   6 *Rep. Com. Mun. Corp.* p. 2626.

7 F. E. Jackson, 'Police and Prisons in Chester, 1830–50' (Manchester Univ. B.A. dissertation, 1966) (copy at C.H.H.), 49–50, citing city cl. mins.; *2nd Rep. Insp. of Prisons*, pp. 31–3; *4th Rep.: N. and E.* [199], pp. 26–9, H.C. (1839), xxii.

8 e.g. *6th Rep. Insp. of Prisons: N. and E.* [339], pp. 25–9, H.C.

(1841, Sess. 2), v; *8th Rep.: N. and E.* [517], pp. 106–10, H.C. (1843), xxv/xxvi.

9 *10th Rep.: N. and E.* [675], pp. 141–4, H.C. (1845), xxiv; *11th Rep.: N. and E.* [754], pp. 69–70, H.C. (1846), xxi; *13th Rep.: N.* [997], pp. 35–7, H.C. (1847–8), xxxvi; Jackson, 'Police and Prisons', 52–4.

10 e.g. *16th Rep. Insp. of Prisons: N. and E.* [1355], p. 39, H.C. (1851), xxvii; *23rd Rep.: Midland Dist.* [2504], p. 28, H.C. (1859, Sess. 1), xi; *27th Rep.: Mid.* [3038], p. 29, H.C. (1862), xxv; *29th Rep.: N.* [3326], pp. 8–9, H.C. (1864), xxvi; *30th Rep.: N.* [3520], p. 10, H.C. (1865), xxiii.

11 e.g. Jackson, 'Police and Prisons', 55; *Reps. and Schedules*, H.C. 2, p. 319 (1828), xx; *6th Rep. Insp. of Prisons*, p. 28; *13th Rep.* p. 36; *19th Rep.: N. and E.* [2102], p. 16, H.C. (1856), xxxiii; *30th Rep.* p. 10.

12 *13th Rep.* p. 36; *16th Rep.* p. 39.

most were on summary convictions of less than a month.[1] Every race week saw the gaol filled beyond its capacity.[2] Perhaps the most severe problem was the inability, through lack of space, to segregate prisoners of different categories. As standards rose elsewhere the gaol's defects became ever more apparent. The government inspectors pressed for improvements, though were aware that the constricted site made enlargement out of the question.[3] In 1871 they condemned the gaol, by then grossly overcrowded, as 'most unsatisfactory',[4] and it was closed by the Home Office in 1872 under the 1865 Prison Act, the inmates being removed to the county gaols.[5] The buildings were demolished soon afterwards,[6] and the Queen's school was later built on the site.[7]

PUBLIC UTILITIES

WATER SUPPLY

A piped water supply was designed as an integral feature of the Roman legionary fortress, though it was one of the last parts to be built, dated precisely to A.D. 79 by lead distribution pipes stamped with the consular date.[14] Since the large intramural bathhouse was also dedicated in that year, it would appear that the two were planned together. The aqueduct ran from springs at Boughton, east of Chester, where, in the 90s or later, the Twentieth Legion built a shrine with an altar dedicated to the nymphs and wells. Ceramic supply pipes have been found in and near Chester, three with a similar bore of over 160 mm. at the wide end.

In the Middle Ages most inhabitants were supplied from wells[15] or the river. The city's water carriers had formed themselves into a company, the Waterleaders, by *c.* 1500; they had links with the fishermen's company, the Drawers of Dee, and the two companies merged in 1603.[16] As elsewhere, aqueducts were built only by religious houses.[17] The Dominicans were licensed in 1276 to pipe water from Boughton through the city wall,[18] and two years later the abbey decided to

Police Lock-ups

By 1837 there were two overnight lock-ups for vagrants in the yard of the city gaol.[8] They were replaced in 1839 by two police cells next to the Exchange, which were far too small for the numbers confined there almost every Saturday and Sunday night.[9] The building was enlarged to six cells on two storeys in 1844 or 1845;[10] at least 1,000 people a year spent a night in them in the late 1840s.[11] They were destroyed in 1862 when the Exchange burned down, and two cells in the gaol were used as temporary lock-ups, causing much night-time disturbance,[12] until the new town hall, which incorporated a police station and cells in the basement, was opened in 1869.[13]

make an aqueduct from a well at Newton.[19] It presumably did not carry a large enough supply, for in 1282 Sir Philip and Isabel Burnel of Malpas gave the monks a spring at Christleton.[20] Earthenware pipes found in 1814 near Dee Hills House may have been part of the scheme.[21] The abbey encountered opposition from other landowners, who broke the pipe.[22]

In 1537 the last warden of the Franciscans, Dr. William Wall, began a conduit with lead pipes which ran from Boughton along the riverside to the Bridgegate.[23] A more northerly line would have been necessary to supply the friary, and Wall perhaps changed the line of the aqueduct when he knew that the friary was to be dissolved. It came to be used as a public supply,[24] but did not meet all the town's needs. A well sunk in Northgate Street in 1572 did not find water, and in 1573 the mayor, Richard Dutton, brought an unnamed workman from London to build a conduit from the Dee to the Cross.[25] By 1574 the plan had been altered: the corporation gave a contract to Peter Morris to excavate a spring at St. Giles's well in Spital Boughton and convey the water in lead pipes to the cross at St. Bridget's church. Morris was almost certainly Dutton's contractor of the previous year, for a Dutch hydraulic

1 *27th Rep.* p. 30.   2 e.g. *19th Rep.* p. 15.

3 e.g. *21st Rep.: N. and E.* [2250], p. 16, H.C. (1857, Sess. 2), xxiii.

4 *35th Rep.: N.* [C. 372], pp. 8–12, H.C. (1871), xxix.

5 *37th Rep.: N.* [C. 811], p. 9, H.C. (1873), xxxii; 28 & 29 Vic. c. 126, ss. 35–6.

6 O.S. Map 1/500, Ches. XXXVIII.11.16–17 (1875 edn.), surveyed 1872, shows vacant plot marked 'Disused'.

7 Below, Education: 1870–1920.

8 *2nd Rep. Insp. of Prisons*, p. 31.

9 *6th Rep.* p. 29; *8th Rep.* p. 110.   10 *10th Rep.* p. 144.

11 *16th Rep.* p. 40.   12 *29th Rep.* p. 9.

13 Above, Municipal Buildings: Exchange, Town Hall; this chapter: Policing.

14 Para. based on G. R. Stephens, 'Roman Aqueduct at Chester', *J.C.A.S.* lxviii. 59–61, 63; G. W. Shrubsole, 'Roman Earthenware Waterpipes in Grosvenor Mus.' *J.C.A.S.* n.s. v. 32.

Thanks are due to Mr. D. Hall and his colleagues at Chester Waterworks Co. for their assistance with this section.

15 Burne, *Monks*, 38 and frontispiece.

16 Below, Craft Guilds: List.

17 Cf. *V.C.H. Glos.* iv. 262; W. Urry, *Canterbury under Angevin Kings*, 205.

18 *V.C.H. Ches.* iii. 174; *Cal. Pat. 1272–81*, 165; J. H. E. Bennett, 'Black Friars of Chester', *J.C.A.S.* xxxix. 45.

19 Burne, *Monks*, 38; *Cal. Pat. 1272–81*, 279; *Cart. Chester Abbey*, ii, pp. 356–7; below, Cathedral and Close: Monastic Buildings to 1541.

20 Burne, *Monks*, 40–1.

21 Hemingway, *Hist. Chester*, i. 429.

22 Ormerod, *Hist. Ches.* ii. 176; B.L. Harl. MS. 2071, f. 75.

23 B.L. Harl. MS. 2125, f. 35; *V.C.H. Ches.* iii. 173.

24 Morris, *Chester*, 282; cf. C.C.A.L.S., ZAB 1, f. 78v.

25 Morris, *Chester*, 282–3; C.C.A.L.S., ZAB 1, f. 135v.

FIG. 15. *Old Bridgegate water tower, before 1782*

engineer of that name was active in London in the 1580s. Presumably it was intended that for much of the distance his conduit would follow the same route as Wall's. It is not certain that the plan was carried out.[1]

A more effective attempt to alter Wall's conduit was made in 1583, when the Assembly decided to have it realigned along Foregate Street and Eastgate Street to a cistern at the corner of the latter and Bridge Street. The site was chosen by four benefactors of the scheme, the three Offley brothers and John Rogers of London.[2] A stone cistern house was decorated with the arms of the city, the earls of Derby and Leicester, one of the Offleys, and Dr. Wall. The pipes were lead.[3] By 1586 the scheme was causing problems: the spring did not provide enough water and the mason had overspent. To produce a better supply other springs were diverted to the head of the conduit, work paid for by a voluntary subscription and mostly completed in 1586–7. It included a well house at Boughton, where the flow was turned on at five every morning and again between four and five in the afternoon to fill the cistern. Private citizens could have water laid on to their houses.[4]

The Dee provided a plentiful source of water throughout the year, but since it lay below most of

the town the only way to use it before the 16th century was to draw it out in buckets and fill barrels on water carts. In 1600 the corporation licensed John Tyrer to draw water from the river by a waterworks on the Bridgegate and lay pipes in the streets.[5] The works were completed and made over to the corporation in 1605. A hydraulic engine in the river fed two pipes leading to a tall turret above the Bridgegate, which acted as an air pipe to the long pipe running up Bridge Street to the cistern at the Cross.[6] Householders paid the city rent for domestic supplies.[7]

Tyrer's son, also John, was granted land at Boughton in 1621 to improve the supply to the cistern, and built a water tower outside the Bars.[8] In 1622 the corporation leased his father's waterworks back to him.[9] In 1632 Tyrer sold his interest to a consortium headed by Sir Randle Mainwaring,[10] but a dispute with Francis Gamull, who controlled the Dee Mills and causeway, led to Gamull's cutting off the supply.[11] The privy council decided that Gamull must allow the supply to continue, but soon afterwards it was interrupted when the causeway was damaged and the water tower destroyed during the siege of Chester.[12] Although the tower was rebuilt, it is not certain when the supply was resumed. The Assembly leased the works in 1673,[13] but

---

1 B.L. Harl. MS. 2093, ff. 209v.–210, 211v.–212; cf. N. Brett-James, *Growth of Stuart Lond.* 54.

2 C.C.A.L.S., ZAB 1, f. 190 (wrongly dated 1582 in B.L. Harl. MS. 2125, f. 42); cf. C.C.A.L.S., ZAB 1, f. 197v.

3 B.L. Harl. MS. 2093, ff. 205, 207, 214; Morris, *Chester*, 284, wrongly shows the long side of the conduit in Eastgate St.

4 Morris, *Chester*, 285–6; C.C.A.L.S., ZAB 1, ff. 200 and v., 204v., 245v.

5 C.C.A.L.S., ZAB 1, f. 262v.; ZCHB 3, f. 70; cf. B.L. Harl. MS. 2125, f. 46; Brett-James, *Growth of Stuart Lond.* 54.

6 C.C.A.L.S., ZCHB 3, f. 86 and v.; cf. B.L. Harl. MS. 2093, f. 208.

7 B.L. Harl. MS. 2083, f. 204; C.C.A.L.S., WS 1618, Edw. Button of Chester; WS 1621, Thos. Thropp of Chester; WS 1629, Godfrey Wynne of Chester; WS 1666, Chas. Farrington of Chester.

8 *Cal. Chester City Cl. Mins. 1603–42*, pp. xxxvi, 104, 109.

9 C.C.A.L.S., ZCR 300/1, no. 4.

10 Ibid. ZAF 17/30; cf. *Cal. Chester City Cl. Mins. 1603–42*, 172–3.

11 B.L. Harl. MS. 2083, ff. 206–209v.; below, Mills and Fisheries: Dee Corn Mills.

12 C.C.A.L.S., ZAB 2, f. 102v.

13 Ibid. f. 176v.; ZCHB 3, f. 200v.

they may not have been restored to full working order, for in 1681 a reservoir elsewhere was under consideration,[1] and in 1690–1 they were apparently not operational.[2] The conduit from Boughton to the Cross was also no longer working. The conduit house was turned into a shop as early as 1652, and the lead was ordered to be taken up in 1671,[3] though the building itself, or a successor built on its footings, remained standing on the corner of Bridge Street and Eastgate Street until the 1880s.[4]

In 1692 two water engineers, John Hadley of Worcester and John Hopkins of Birmingham, were given permission to repair the waterworks,[5] and immediately began buying up shares in the Bridgegate water tower,[6] from where they pumped water into a large cistern, built in 1694 on pillars above the shambles in Northgate Street.[7] By 1698 they were in debt and sold out to a consortium of eight shareholders later known as the Waterworks Company.[8] The new owners bought rights to some of the mill streams at the weir and the enterprise eventually became profitable, partly by leasing riverside premises for light industry and warehousing.[9] The water tower, a tourist landmark, was pulled down along with the Bridgegate in 1782.[10]

The pressure in the system was insufficient to supply Upper Northgate Street, where a well was opened in 1764.[11] The rest of the city had to manage with an intermittent supply at low pressure. The purity of the water does not seem to have occasioned complaint until the 1820s, in spite of the fact that it was drawn from the causeway, just below which the river was tidal. Spring tides, indeed, pushed salt water over the causeway. The state of the river in flood had concerned the Waterworks Company in 1710–11, when rubbish dumped at Dee Lane was carried downstream and damaged their machinery.[12] Purification was limited to placing a grating across the intake and raking it out. Little was spent on repairs or cleaning. An increase in expenditure in 1825 on repairs to pipes and new premises in Northgate Street[13] was evidently in reaction to demands voiced the previous year for a new supply, pumped by steam power so as to be under higher pressure. The promoters of the new supply favoured an intake more than a mile upstream from the causeway, at Barrel Well Hill in Boughton, where the water would also be freer of sewage because Boughton had few

FIG. 16. *Chester waterworks at Barrel Well, 1852*

houses.[14] A new waterworks company was to have seven directors and 160 shares at £50 each,[15] and a bill was presented to parliament to have the old company's monopoly revoked.[16] The old company at first fought back,[17] but when it became clear that the new company's bill was likely to be passed it agreed to rent out all its own pipes and cease operating.[18] The old works on the river continued only until the new one at Barrel Well was ready.[19]

The new company, named the City of Chester Waterworks Company, bought Barrel Well from the corporation in 1828. It took some time to become profitable,[20] so that investment in efficient pumping machinery and storage capacity was delayed. The first

1 Ibid. ZAB 2, ff. 194v.–195; cf. ZAB 3, f. 4v.
2 Ibid. ZCR 300/1, no. 19; D. Defoe, *Tour thro' Whole Island of Brit.* ed. G. H. Cole, ii. 470.
3 C.C.A.L.S., ZAB 2, ff. 99v., 172.
4 [P. Broster], *Chester Guide* [1st edn., 1781], 21.
5 C.C.A.L.S., ZAF 46B/5; ZAB 3, f. 34v.; ZCHB 3, ff. 235v.–236v.
6 Ibid. ZCR 300/1, nos. 21–4, 28–30.
7 Ibid. ZAB 3, f. 46.   8 Ibid. ZCR 300/1, nos. 39–43.
9 Ibid. nos. 47–8, 51, 51 bis, 62–3, 66.
10 Ibid. ZAB 4, ff. 342, 345.
11 Ibid. ff. 215, 224v., 233v., 235v., 250.

12 Ibid. ZAB 3, f. 181.   13 Ibid. ZCR 300/18.
14 *Chester Chron.* 23 Apr., 3 Sept. 1824.
15 Ibid. 17 Sept. 1824.
16 C.C.A.L.S., ZCR 300/3; Hemingway, *Hist. Chester*, ii. 339–40.
17 C.C.A.L.S., ZCR 300/18, accts. of 1825 and 1826.
18 Ibid. ZCR 300/2–3, 5; Chester Waterworks Act, 7 Geo. IV, c. 110 (Local and Personal).
19 C.C.A.L.S., ZCR 300/18; cf. *Chester Chron.* 10 July 1846, p. 4.
20 C.C.A.L.S., ZAB 6, p. 21; Hemingway, *Hist. Chester*, ii. 340.

priority was to lay mains, which were much extended between 1838 and 1840. A special council committee in 1841 recommended a new source of supply for the whole town from a spring recently tapped at Christleton, but the scheme was not implemented, probably because of the cost of buying out the company.[1]

The council took a sustained interest in the water supply after the cholera outbreak of 1849. The sanitary committee noted that there were not enough standpipes, that sewage from Boughton was seeping into the Dee just above the works, and that much of Handbridge was badly supplied. The Waterworks Company agreed to supply Handbridge by laying a pipe across the Dee Bridge.[2] It also decided to reconsider the intake, and in 1849 took on J. F. Bateman, one of the greatest Victorian hydraulic experts, as its consulting engineer.[3] Bateman wanted to build a tunnel under the river to catch springs in the rock, which he hoped would not need filtration;[4] the company spent over £1,000 on the scheme, but it was dropped in 1851.[5]

The city council appointed a new water supply committee in 1852, with a brief which included considering taking over the water supply. There were three main complaints: the water was not filtered,[6] despite the fact that untreated sewage was increasingly channelled into the river, some of it upstream from the weir;[7] the supply did not reach throughout the city; and it was intermittent,[8] partly because there was not enough storage capacity.[9] Demand for a constant supply was growing as more households installed water closets.[10]

Consultants hired in 1853 proposed an additional supply from springs outside the city at Ashton,[11] and the council's threat to obtain parliamentary powers forced the company to begin work on a constant supply of filtered water at high pressure.[12] Acting on

Bateman's plans it built filter beds, a reservoir, additional engines, and an elevated tank.[13] Work proceeded slowly and doubts continued to be expressed about the site of the intake, which was endangered by sewage from Boughton and Dee Lane.[14] Under pressure from the corporation, the company made some concessions and in 1857 obtained an Act which raised additional capital and reconstituted it as the Chester Waterworks Company.[15] Shortly afterwards the company agreed to move its intake to the south side of the river upstream from Huntington brook, from where water was piped to Barrel Well, though work began only in 1866.[16] The water tower at Barrel Well, which ensured adequate pressure and allowed storage, was opened in 1867.[17]

Filtration alone did not solve the problem of water pollution, and the company and the corporation were in dispute over the purity of the supply in 1871, when both sides produced expert analyses to back their case.[18] Concern after a serious pollution incident at Minera (Denb.) in 1879 led to co-operation between the city and local health boards upstream to check on industrial discharges and sewage outfalls.[19] In Chester itself, contamination by sewage continued from the suburbs south of the river and was eventually recognized as the cause of an alarmingly high level of typhoid. A report of 1890 pressed for restrictions on extracting water from the river during spring tides,[20] and in 1891 Bishop Jayne denounced the water supply as impure, to the irritation of the influential Charles Brown, who was both mayor and chairman of the Waterworks Company.[21] The company was, however, finally impelled to take action: it improved its filtration over the years 1895–9,[22] and its water analysis in 1897 and 1900,[23] but as late as 1910 water was not stored before filtration.[24]

A constant supply was provided in stages from 1868:

1 C.C.A.L.S., ZAB 6, pp. 302, 377, 387–8, 418–19, 435.
2 Ibid. ZCCB 34, pp. 307, 309, 316, 325, 329–33; ZCCB 35, pp. 1–2, 4.
3 G. M. Binnie, *Early Victorian Water Engineers*, 159–90.
4 Chester Waterworks Co., Directors' Min. Bk. I, 19 May 1854; cf. *Chester Chron.* 14 Dec. 1849 (garbled acct.).
5 C.C.A.L.S., ZCB 1, p. 154.
6 Ibid. p. 137; ZCCB 35, p. 221; cf. Binnie, *Water Engineers*, 71.
7 C.C.A.L.S., ZCB 1, p. 162.
8 Cf. G. F. Deacon, *On Systems of Constant and Intermittent Water Supply* (reprint. from *Mins. of Proc. of Inst. of Civil Engineers*, xlii), 9–10; Binnie, *Water Engineers*, 10; B. Luckin, 'Evaluating Sanitary Revolution: Typhus and Typhoid in Lond., 1851–1900', *Urban Diseases and Mortality in 19th Cent. Eng.* ed. R. Woods and J. Woodward, 111–12; C.C.A.L.S., ZCCB 36, p. 8.
9 C.C.A.L.S., ZCCB 35, p. 221; cf. ZCCB 36, p. 9.
10 Cf. M. J. Daunton, *House and Home in the Victorian City*, 249–56.
11 C.C.A.L.S., ZCB 1, 9 Sept. 1853; ZCCB 35, pp. 285–9; cf. ZCB 1, 22 Nov. 1853.
12 Ibid. ZCCB 35, pp. 291, 295–9; cf. ibid. ZCB 1, 10 Feb. 1854.
13 Ibid. ZCCB 36, pp. 311–13; Chester Waterworks Co., Min. Bk. I, 19 May, 28 June 1854.
14 *Chester Chron.* 9 Sept. 1854.

15 Ibid. 28 Oct. 1854; C.C.A.L.S., ZCCB 35, pp. 221–2; ZCCB 36, pp. 1–2, 7–9; Chester Waterworks Act, 7 Geo. IV, c. 110 (Local and Personal); Chester Waterworks Act, 20 & 21 Vic. c. 11 (Local and Personal).
16 C.C.A.L.S., ZCR 16.
17 Ibid. ZCCB 36, pp. 441, 456, 460–1; ZCCB 37, p. 47.
18 Ibid. ZCCB 37, pp. 38–47, 264–76; cf. *J.C.A.S.* N.S. v. 113–14; *Urban Diseases and Mortality*, ed. Woods and Woodward, 117–18; *Chester Chron.* 12, 19 Aug., 2, 9, 16, 23 Sept. 1871.
19 Below, this chapter: Sewerage; C.C.A.L.S., ZCCB 37, pp. 360–70; ZCCB 98, pp. 47–50, 52–7; *Annual Rep. of Medical Officer of Health* (1879), 12; cf. (1883), 6; (1897) (copies in C.C.A.L.S., ZDH 2/1–2).
20 *Annual Reps. of M.O.H.* esp. (1880), 4–5; C.C.A.L.S., ZCB 2, 13 Jan. 1869, 12 Jan. 1870, 11 Jan. 1871, 10 Jan. 1872; ZCB 3, ff. 40v., 99v.; ZCCB 39, pp. 69–72, 82–110, 112–14, 146; ZCCB 138, pp. 35–45; *Chester Chron.* 13 Sept. 1890.
21 *Browns and Chester: Portrait of a Shop, 1780–1946*, ed. H. D. Willcock, 160–2.
22 *Annual Rep. of M.O.H.* (1910), 92: copy in C.C.A.L.S., ZDH 2/4; ibid. ZCR 16, directors' reps., esp. 1895–9.
23 *Annual Rep. of M.O.H.* (1897), 7; (1898), 5; (1900), 5–6; (1901), 4: copies in C.C.A.L.S., ZDH 2/2.
24 *Annual Reps. of M.O.H.* (1907–10): copies in C.C.A.L.S., ZDH 2/4.

the whole town had water on Sunday mornings from 1871,[1] and capital raised under the 1874 Chester Waterworks Act[2] allowed the company to buy more efficient pumping engines from 1875[3] and meters to locate wastage in the mid 1880s.[4] From 1887 the supply throughout the system was continuous.[5] Public drinking fountains were provided in several of the main streets in the later 19th century, most prominently one donated in 1860 by the former mayor Meadows Frost at the junction of Bridge Street and Grosvenor Street.[6]

Further technical improvements in purification and filtration followed in 1911 (a reservoir allowing partial purification before filtration),[7] 1920 (rapid filters),[8] and the 1930s (chemical treatment).[9] The Waterworks Company built an octagonal concrete water tower south of Overleigh Road in 1935, and by 1957 was serving *c.* 90,000 consumers with an average daily consumption of 3.6 million gallons.[10] The supply of water from the Dee was guaranteed by the construction of reservoirs: the natural Bala Lake was deepened in the 1950s and Llyn Celyn was completed in 1965.[11] In 1974, without surrendering its independence, the company became a distributing agent of the publicly owned Welsh Water Authority, empowered to extract supplies from the Dee. The 1989 Water Privatization Act constituted it a water undertaker accountable to the Director General of Water Services; whereas previously, as a statutory company, it had limitations on capital borrowing and dividends, it was thereby allowed to become a public limited company and make profits, subject to the Director General's approval of price increases.[12]

SEWERAGE

Until the early 19th century public sewerage was limited to open gutters carrying away rainwater and street debris. Some householders disposed of their domestic waste by digging cesspits into the bedrock, which lay only 3–4 ft. below the surface; deep examples have been uncovered at the Linenhall and Northgate Brewery sites. The town ditch provided an easier, though illegal, alternative: seven citizens were indicted

for building cesspits there in 1293.[13] The street gutters, first mentioned in 1508, ran down both sides of the street until the late 16th century, when they were moved to the middle to make building encroachments easier.[14]

The improvement commissioners were empowered in 1803 to build sewers by raising loans not exceeding £1,000 in total.[15] They ordered tunnel drains, intended for rainwater, to be built in Watergate Street in 1807 and Lower Bridge Street in 1808.[16] Over the next twenty years most streets, especially within the walls, were provided with similar rainwater culverts, though when a drain was built in Foregate Street in 1826 householders were invited to pay for their private drains to be connected to it.[17] The most ambitious plan, in 1824, brought a drain down Cow Lane (later Frodsham Street) and St. John's Lane (later Street) and extended it to below the bridge in order to prevent the outfall from contaminating the waterworks intake at the weir.[18] By the 1840s, when the limit of the loans had long since been reached, the council found it difficult to undertake schemes of its own. The drainage of Northgate Street in 1844 was partly financed by private subscription.[19] The council encouraged private schemes, hoping in 1845 when the railway station was being built that nearby residents would construct their own drainage.[20]

The Chester Improvement Act of 1845 allowed the council to undertake large-scale sewerage projects, financed by borrowed money.[21] In 1846 it appointed an experienced sewerage engineer, B. Baylis, whose first tasks were to drain Newtown and the west of the town and lengthen the Northgate Street drain.[22] In 1847 he built 540 ft. of sewers in Boughton, 630 ft. in Northgate Street, and 771 ft. in Watergate Street, and was already connecting side streets to the sewers in Boughton and Foregate Street.[23]

Newtown, however, had to be drained from scratch. Baylis followed a practice common among Victorian engineers by combining his scheme for the area with the drains being laid by the railway companies.[24] In 1848 work continued in the area between the canal and Foregate Street, the middle stretch of Northgate Street,

1 C.C.A.L.S., ZCCB 36, p. 461; ZCCB 37, p. 47.

2 Chester Waterworks Act, 37 & 38 Vic. c. 65 (Local).

3 C.C.A.L.S., ZCR 16, directors' reps. from 1869, esp. 1881–3; ZCCB 97, pp. 809–12.

4 Ibid. ZCR 16, directors' reps. 1885–9; Deacon, *Systems of Water Supply*; cf. Chester Waterworks Co., Directors' Min. Bk. II, 26 Feb. 1885.

5 *Browns and Chester*, ed. Willcock, 160–2; C.C.A.L.S., ZCB 4, 12 Dec. 1888.

6 J. Williams, *Story of Chester*, 228–9.

7 Chester Waterworks Act, 1 & 2 Geo. V, c. 77 (Local).

8 C.C.A.L.S., ZCCF 9/25, p. 18; *Annual Rep. of M.O.H.* (1920): copy in C.C.A.L.S., ZDH 2/5.

9 Chester Waterworks Act, 20 Geo. V, c. 57 (Local).

10 *Chester Waterworks Co.* (priv. print. 1957), 7–9.

11 Welsh Water Authority, *Dee Regulation Scheme* (priv. print. [1979]).

12 Water Act, 1989, c. 15; cf. *Chester Chron.* 18 Aug. 1995, p. 4.

13 *J.C.A.S.* lvi. 8; P. J. Davey, *Chester Northgate Brewery Phase One, Interim Rep.* 22; P.R.O., CHES 25/1.

14 C.C.A.L.S., ZCHD 2/5, 7; ZAB 1, ff. 197v., 267; cf. Morris, *Chester*, 271.

15 C.C.A.L.S., ZAB 6, pp. 429, 510; Chester Improvement Act, 1803, 43 Geo. III, c. 47 (Local and Personal), s. 19.

16 C.C.A.L.S., ZTRI 2, ff. 39, 115v., 117, 122v.

17 Ibid. f. 364v.   18 Ibid. f. 341.

19 Ibid. ZTRI 3, f. 156 and v.

20 Ibid. ZAB 6, p. 613.

21 Ibid. ZCCB 47, 19 Dec. 1845, 16 Jan. 1846.

22 Ibid. ZAB 6, pp. 632, 664; ZCCB 47, 4 June, 2 July 1846, 6 Jan., 17 Feb. 1847; cf. *Chester Chron.* 27 Oct. 1869.

23 C.C.A.L.S., ZAB 6, pp. 718–19, 732.

24 Ibid. ZCCB 47, 6 Dec. 1847.

and Watergate Street,[1] and in 1849 a start was made in the quadrant between Watergate and Bridge Streets and in Handbridge.[2] As a main sewer was laid in each street, notices were served on owners and occupiers to connect their private drains to it.[3] Those further from the main sewers were required to install ashpits and privies.[4] Baylis laid short lengths of drain in different areas simultaneously, extending the existing sewers and adding new ones a little at a time. The method did not have happy results. To some extent it was forced on him by the council's parsimony and his reliance on outside small building firms. Judging from later criticisms, however, his work was also flawed by inattention to both detail and the whole. Baylis was careful to build the approved egg-shaped sewers and to trap drains,[5] but failed to deal successfully with ventilation and outfall. The main outfalls were the river at the bottom of Dee Lane for Foregate Street, Flooker's brook for Newtown, and the Dee at the bottom of Crane Street for the western part of the town; almost certainly Bridge Street and Northgate Street were drained into the river at the weir. Much of the city's sewage thus entered the river above the tidal reach. The outfall in Crane Street was so shallow that sewage backed up into houses at high tide, while those at Dee Lane and the weir stank during droughts.[6] Baylis probably ventilated the sewers by passing rainwater spouts into them, an inadequate method which later Victorians abandoned.[7] Water for flushing the drains was available only close to the canal, and malodorous and toxic fumes emanated from ventilators in the roadways.[8] The Waterworks Company, which had difficulties in maintaining an adequate supply, refused to allow the sewers to be flushed from its mains until 1880.[9]

The overcrowding, filth, and lack of drainage in the city's courts and yards were recognized as aiding the spread of the cholera outbreak of 1849, and a general plan to drain Handbridge, badly affected by the epidemic, was perceived to be an immediate necessity;[10] moves were also made on the slums around Princess Street and between George Street and St. Anne Street.[11]

In 1851 Baylis built an intercepting sewer to divert Newtown's waste away from Flooker's brook to the river at Dee Lane.[12] Its completion led to renewed concern about the effect of the outfall on drinking water,[13] and sewage from Northgate Street was diverted down Watergate Street.[14]

Most of the public streets were sewered by 1851, except the Nicholas Street area and Upper Northgate Street, which were completed in 1854.[15] Attention was then turned to private streets,[16] especially the courts, many of which had more than three houses for each privy.[17] Orders to drain many of the courts were issued in 1853,[18] the work being undertaken by the council and the cost borne by the owners. Private streets built after 1825 were sewered at the joint expense of owners and occupiers, who were expected to contract for the work themselves. Only if the city surveyor pronounced the sewerage and paving satisfactory would the council adopt the streets as public highways.[19] In 1854 a start was made on draining existing private streets.[20]

In 1855 irregularities were discovered in Baylis's accounts; he was dismissed and later convicted of embezzlement.[21] His successor, George Angelo Bell, remained in post barely a year, escaping to more lucrative private practice,[22] and the council economized on the salary of a qualified sanitary engineer by employing the deputy surveyor, on the grounds that most of the city had already been sewered.[23] Over the years 1857–9 he drained Hough Green and Curzon Park,[24] and extended the sewers in Princess Street, Liverpool Road, and Eaton Road.[25] The pace slowed after 1860, but quickened between 1867 and 1870 when several private streets were drained.[26] Meanwhile the council improved arrangements for the removal of night soil,[27] from 1872 taking over the work from private contractors.[28]

By the late 1860s the faults of Baylis's system were becoming apparent.[29] G. A. Bell had already advised ventilation in 1866,[30] and in 1869 after a damning report commissioned by the Local Government Board he was called in as a consultant and recommended

1 C.C.A.L.S., ZCCB 47, 15 May, 12 June, 10 July 1848; ZAB 6, p. 764.
2 Ibid. ZAB 6, pp. 831–42; cf. *Builder*, vii. 269.
3 C.C.A.L.S., ZAB 6, pp. 665, 670, 680.
4 Ibid. p. 831.
5 Ibid. p. 732; cf. G. M. Binnie, *Early Victorian Water Engineers*, 5–6; C.C.A.L.S., ZAB 6, p. 732; ZCCB 47, 24 July 1848, 2, 16 July 1849.
6 C.C.A.L.S., ZCB 1, 12 Sept., 10 Oct. 1856, 12 June 1857; ZCCB 51, pp. 131–2, 223–9; ZCCB 76, p. 295 .
7 Ibid. ZCCB 47, 9 Aug. 1847; *Builder*, vi. 35.
8 C.C.A.L.S., ZCCB 47, 15 May 1848.
9 *Annual Rep. of M.O.H.* (1880), 4: copy in C.C.A.L.S., ZDH 2/1; *Chester Chron.* 16 Sept. 1854.
10 C.C.A.L.S., ZAB 6, pp. 855–7.
11 Ibid. pp. 860–3, 867–71.
12 Ibid. ZCB 1, pp. 102, 119–23; *Builder*, ix. 448.
13 C.C.A.L.S., ZCB 1, pp. 156, 162; ZCCB 48, 9 Mar., 6 Apr. 1852.

14 Ibid. ZCCB 48, 27 Apr. 1852; ZCCB 51, pp. 131–2, 223–9.
15 Ibid. ZCB 1, 5 May, 14 July 1854; ZCCB 48, 29 Mar., 27 Apr., 17 May 1854.
16 Ibid. ZCCB 48, 10 Aug., 19, 26, 28 Oct., 16 Nov. 1852, 26 Apr. 1853.
17 Ibid. 14 Sept. 1852.   18 Ibid. ZCB 1, 9 Sept. 1853.
19 Ibid. ZAB 6, p. 757.
20 Ibid. ZCB 1, 13 Jan., 21 Apr. 1854.
21 Ibid. ZCCB 48, 11, 13, 16 July 1855; ZCB 1, 21 Sept. 1855, 11 Aug. 1856.
22 Ibid. ZCCB 48, 3, 19, 21 Sept. 1855; ZCB 1, 11 Aug. 1856.
23 Ibid. ZCB 1, 10 Oct. 1856.
24 Ibid. 9 Jan., 12 June 1857, 12 Feb., 13 Apr. 1858, 13 Apr. 1859.
25 Ibid. 9 Oct. 1857.
26 Ibid. ZCB 2, 13 Mar. 1867, 10 Feb., 9 Mar. 1869, 13 Apr., 14 Sept. 1870.   27 Ibid. 12 Feb. 1868.
28 Ibid. ZCB 3, f. 12.   29 Ibid. ZCB 2, 9 Dec. 1868.
30 Ibid. ZCCB 51, p. 101.

ventilation as an urgent necessity.[1] In 1872–5, alarmed by analysis of the drinking water, and with Bell as consultant, the council built intercepting sewers to collect the outfall from Baylis's drains, one running from the Bars to the Little Roodee and the other from Liverpool Road to a new treatment works by the Dee off Sealand Road, from where the treated effluent was discharged into the river.[2]

Once the northern intercepting sewer was under construction, it was possible to drain the growing north-western part of town, work completed by 1879.[3] Between 1881 and 1883 the council tackled Boughton.[4] Tarvin rural sanitary authority and Hoole local board connected their systems with Chester's intercepting sewers, the city contributing to the cost of the Hoole scheme in 1881.[5] In 1882 work began on an intercepting sewer from Queen's Park, which had been discharging its waste upstream from the weir, to below the weir, half the cost being paid by the residents.[6] Large houses and estates just outside Chester were connected one by one to the city's sewerage under private agreements.[7]

A report of 1890 on sanitation urged improvements to sewage disposal, and another intercepting sewer to carry sewage from the south side of the city under the river to the outfall works was built in 1897.[8] The works were enlarged between 1900 and 1905, after which they also treated sewage from Great Boughton, Christleton, Newton, Upton, and Bache,[9] and again in 1919.[10] An additional disposal works was constructed at Bumper's Lane in the early 1930s.[11] The area served by the council was extended along the Eaton and Wrexham roads in 1926, when the hydroelectric works on the Dee weir provided electrical pumping for a new intercepting sewer for Handbridge.[12] Blacon was connected to the system in 1936 and Saughall in 1951.[13] A duplicate northern intercepting sewer was planned in 1953 but incomplete in 1960.[14]

A major reconstruction of the Sealand works was begun in 1962.[15] In 1974 control of the treatment works was transferred from the city council to the Welsh Water Authority, which by 1987 was planning a large programme of improvements.[16]

GAS SUPPLY

The Chester Gas Light Company was formed after a public meeting in 1817; the local banker G. B. Granville was elected chairman (serving as such until 1845) and the share capital of £6,850 was quickly taken up.[17] The company hired the doyen of gas engineers, Samuel Clegg, to build the system, ensuring that its works in Cuppin Street, opened in 1819, was at the forefront of the emerging technology of gas supply.[18] The immediate intention was to replace the inadequate oil lamps which the improvement commissioners provided for street lighting.[19] The company won the contract to light the streets around its works in Cuppin Street in 1818,[20] and at least the main city streets were gas-lit by 1830.[21] The supply was inefficient and expensive, despite the relative cheapness of coal in Chester,[22] but the company forestalled complaints by paying retainers to the lamp rate collectors and by having on its committee many members of the improvement commission.[23] It also consciously subsidized the supply for street lighting in order to retain the commissioners' goodwill, but charged private customers enough to make large profits and pay handsome dividends in the period before 1838.[24]

In 1837 the city council took over responsibility for street lighting, and frequently complained about the quality and price of the supply. An attempt to threaten the company with a rival undertaking was beaten off in 1844, but continuous agitation forced the company to cut prices and modernize the system.[25] Private gasworks were built at the General railway station and by other businesses,[26] and eventually the council broke the

1 Ibid. ZCB 2, 8 Sept. 1870.

2 Ibid. 8 June 1870, 26 Mar. 1872; ZCB 3, ff. 6v., 14–15, 16v.–17, 41v., 57v., 66, 115v.–116v., 138v., 191, 209 and v.; O.S. Map 1/2,500, Ches. XXXVIII.10 (1898 edn.).

3 C.C.A.L.S., ZCB 3, ff. 129v.–130, 213, 243–245v., 355v., 447; O.S. Map 1/2,500, Ches. XXXVIII.11 (1875 edn.).

4 C.C.A.L.S., ZCB 3, f. 276 and v.

5 Ibid. ff. 476v.–477, 496, 511 and v.; ZCB 4, 14 Dec. 1881.

6 Ibid. ZCB 3, f. 534v.; ZCB 4, 12 July, 13 Sept. 1882.

7 Ibid. ZCB 4, 8 Mar. 1882, 12 May, 8 Dec. 1886.

8 Ibid. ZCB 5, 14 Oct. 1896.

9 Ibid. 16 June 1897; *Annual Rep. of M.O.H.* (1910), 92: copy in C.C.A.L.S., ZDH 2/4; *Chester City Cl. Mins. 1898/9,* 53–6, 274–9, 335, 471–7, 505; *1899/1900,* 447, 519–20; cf. *1904/5,* 397–8; *1906/7,* 374; *1907/8,* 241–3; *1911/12,* 37–8.

10 *Chester City Cl. Mins. 1916/17,* 13; *1918/19,* 59, 309–10; *1919/20,* 194.

11 Ibid. *1929/30,* 37, 816, 941; *1930/1,* 819–20; *1931/2,* 308, 310, 507, 621, 806.

12 Ibid. *1925/6,* 478; *1926/7,* 38–40.

13 Ibid. *1935/6,* 605–6, 794, 911–12; *1951/2,* p. 83.

14 Ibid. *1952/3,* pp. 772, 799; *1959/60,* pp. 549, 916.

15 Ibid. *1958/9,* p. 311; *1961/2,* p. 245; *1962/3,* p. 106; *1964/5,* p. 459.

16 Ibid. *1982/3,* pp. 403–4; *1984/5,* p. 290; *1985/6,* pp. 285–6; *1986/7,* p. 637; *1988/9,* p. 839.

17 J. F. Wilson, 'Competition in the Early Gas Industry: Chester Gaslight Co., 1817–56', *T.L.C.A.S.* lxxxvi. 89–90; *Browns and Chester,* ed. H. D. Willcock, 53; Chester Gas Act, 1858, 21 Vic. c. 6, preamble.   18 *T.L.C.A.S.* lxxxvi. 90–1.

19 Chester Improvement Act, 1762, 2 Geo. III, c. 45; C.C.A.L.S., ZTRI 2, ff. 2–7v., 18, 67 and v., 144v., 246.

20 C.C.A.L.S., ZTRI 2, f. 257 and v.

21 Ibid. ZCCB 15, 23 Jan. 1839; cf. Hemingway, *Hist. Chester,* ii. 338; *T.L.C.A.S.* lxxxvi. 92.

22 *Browns and Chester,* 55; C.C.A.L.S., ZTRI 3, f. 2v., Apr. 1834; cf. ibid. ZCCB 15, 5 Dec. 1842.

23 C.C.A.L.S., ZCB 1, pp. 34–5.

24 *T.L.C.A.S.* lxxxvi. 92–4.

25 Ibid. 95–100; cf. C.C.A.L.S., ZAB 6, pp. 526, 606; ZCCB 15, 5 Dec. 1842.

26 Hughes, *Stranger's Handbk.* (1856), 12–13; C.C.A.L.S., ZCCB 51, pp. 625, 630–1; O.S. Map 1/2,500, Ches. XXXVIII.11 (1875 and later edns.).

FIG. 17. *Gas lamps near St. Michael's, Bridge Street, 1849*

Gas Light Company's monopoly by sanctioning a rival undertaking proposed in 1851 by Samuel Highfield, the engineer to the company supplying Birkenhead. The council leased Highfield a site on the Roodee, where he completed a new gasworks in 1852, and awarded him the contract for street lighting in 1853. Highfield was probably backed financially by local business interests.[1] The council tried to prevent High-

field from amalgamating with the old Gas Light Company,[2] but he outwitted them by conveying his business in 1854 to a newly formed company, the Roodee Gas Company, whose main shareholder was the Radical politician E. G. Salisbury. Under Salisbury's wily management, the Roodee Company in effect bought out the Gas Light Company in 1856, forming the Chester United Gas Company (incorporated by Act of Parliament in 1858), with Salisbury as chairman and largest shareholder.[3] The council was forced to acquiesce in the new monopoly, gaining in return the closure of the Cuppin Street works, which caused serious pollution,[4] the power to appoint an inspector to test the pressure and illuminating power of the gas supplied,[5] and, from 1858, a seat on the board for the mayor.[6]

The new company enlarged its premises on the Roodee in 1865,[7] and raised additional capital under Acts of 1870 and 1880.[8] The quality of its supply was generally above the minimum required in the original Act,[9] and in the 1890s it supplied more powerful gas burners at a cut price in response to the threat of electricity.[10] Electric street lighting was installed from 1896,[11] and the last gas street lights were given up in 1905.[12]

Despite the loss of its largest customer, the gas company's financial position improved in the 1890s and 1900s as domestic demand for gas increased.[13] The Board of Trade allowed it to raise prices sharply in 1921,[14] and in 1933 it was authorized to supply a ring of villages around the city.[15]

The company was nationalized in 1948 and its responsibilities were taken over by the North Western Gas Board, which continued production at the Chester works in order to supply the city and Wirral.[16] The works closed in 1966 after pipelines had been laid to connect west Cheshire with Lancashire, north Wales, and the works at Ellesmere Port.[17] The gas holder on the Roodee was retained.[18] The supply to the city was converted to natural gas in 1970.[19]

ELECTRICITY SUPPLY[20]

The city council opposed private applications to supply electricity to Chester under the Electric Lighting Act of 1882,[21] and in 1889 decided to apply for powers

1 *T.L.C.A.S.* lxxxvi. 101–3; C.C.A.L.S., ZCB 1, pp. 101–2, 104, 146, 149, 211, 214, 217.
2 Cf. C.C.A.L.S., ZCB 1, 9 Sept. 1853, 21 Apr., 5 May 1854.
3 Ibid. 11 Aug. 1854, 14 Apr. 1858; *T.L.C.A.S.* lxxxvi. 103–4; Chester Gas Act, 1858, 21 Vic. c. 6, s. 71.
4 C.C.A.L.S., ZCB 1, 8 Feb., 11 Apr. 1856.
5 Ibid. 13 Mar., 6 Aug. 1857.   6 *T.L.C.A.S.* lxxxvi. 105.
7 C.C.A.L.S., ZCB 2, 14 Dec. 1864, 11 Jan. 1865.
8 Chester Gas Act, 1870, 33 Vic. c. 1; Chester Gas Act, 1880, 43 & 44 Vic. c. 9.
9 C.C.A.L.S., ZCB 2–3 *passim* (results of monthly gas tests).
10 Ibid. ZCB 4, 9 Mar. 1892.
11 Ibid. ZCB 5, 19 Sept. 1894, 14 Oct. 1896.
12 *Chester City Cl. Mins.* 1904/5, 436–7.

13 C.C.A.L.S., ZCR 137/9, directors' reps. to Dec. 1895, Dec. 1911.
14 *Chester City Cl. Mins.* 1920/1, 415–17, 542–3, 694.
15 Ibid. *1921/2*, 356, 358, 408; cf. C.C.A.L.S., ZCR 137/7.
16 North Western Gas Board, *Rep. and Accts. 1954–5*, App. 2 facing p. 60.
17 Ibid. *1965–6*, App. 2 facing p. 46.
18 *Chester City Cl. Mins.* 1967/8, p. 134; cf. ibid. *1974/5*, p. 429.   19 Ibid. *1970/1*, p. 511.
20 Section based, except where stated otherwise, on *Chester Electricity Undertaking: Jubilee, 1896–1946* (copy at C.H.H.).
21 45 & 46 Vic. c. 56; C.C.A.L.S., ZCCB 18, pp. 562, 581, 583, 586, 590; ZCCB 19, pp. 18–19, 21, 26, 69–71, 476, 482–6, 507, 512–13.

itself.[1] Having obtained authority by an Act of 1890[2] it then delayed even beginning to implement it until 1892 and hesitated over the choice of a system and a site for the generators until its hand was forced in 1895 by the threat of a rival scheme headed by the duke of Westminster.[3] In 1896 the council opened a coal-fired generating station in New Crane Street, mains were laid along the principal streets in the city centre, and electricity supply began. The number of customers rose from 211 in 1898 to 703 in 1903. In 1904 the city appointed Sydney Ernest Britton as its electrical engineer; he held the post until his death in 1946 and became a leading figure in his profession,[4] preparing many schemes for developing the local electricity supply, not all of which found favour with the council.

The New Crane Street works reached capacity in 1910 and work started the next year on a hydroelectric generating station on the site of the Dee Mills. The choice of Gothic detailing for the building, consciously in keeping with the architecture of the adjoining Dee Bridge, was influenced by the Chester Archaeological Society.[5] When it opened in 1913 it provided 40 per cent of Chester's electricity at a fifth of the price of coal-generated power. Rising demand from many more consumers meant that its output met only 2 per cent of requirements by 1946, and the hydroelectric plant was closed in 1951, the building being used thereafter as a water pumping station.[6] After the First World War Chester bought electricity from the government's munitions works at Queensferry (Flints.), and in 1923 acquired the power station itself. The overhead high-tension cables between Queensferry and Chester were among the first in the country. From 1932 the city was buying electricity from the Central Electricity Board's embryonic national grid in order to cope with demand which grew to over 23,000 consumers by 1946, most rapidly in the decade 1927–37.

Many of those customers were outside the city. Britton pioneered rural electrification in the 1920s, especially for dairy farmers, obtaining powers to supply Hoole and parts of Chester and Tarvin rural districts in 1923, with an extension in 1927 to cover 144 square miles. On the other hand, the council declined to implement his schemes for Chester to participate in a joint electricity authority for south Cheshire and north Wales (1920–3; it went ahead without the city) and to build a new power station at Queensferry (1937).

At nationalization in 1948 the corporation's system came under the Merseyside and North Wales Electricity Board (Manweb),[7] which in 1968–70 built its administrative headquarters in Sealand Road.[8] The buildings had as their centrepiece a seven-storeyed **Y**-plan office block which dominated the skyline looking west from the city centre until it was demolished in the 1990s.

LOCAL PUBLIC TRANSPORT

Public sedan chairs were in use in Chester by 1781, when regulations about conditions and fares were published in the earliest of the city's directories. The chairs, licensed by the improvement commissioners, were ordinarily available for hire between 9 o'clock in the morning and midnight. At assemblies, balls, plays, and other social events the chairmen had to form an orderly line, take up passengers in rotation, and not hold the chair for a particular person.[9] In 1796 there were probably 42 chairmen (that is, 21 sedan chairs), the number on the Grosvenors' payroll during an election campaign.[10] Twelve chairs were licensed in 1806.[11] It is not clear how long afterwards they survived.

Hackney cabs were started *c.* 1830,[12] and by mid century there were also waggonettes operating along Liverpool Road, private omnibuses run by the big hotels, and a public omnibus service between the main railway station and the town hall.[13] By 1902 there were well over a hundred licensed horse-drawn vehicles plying for hire in the city.[14] Despite lobbying by the cabmen the first motor taxis were licensed in 1908.[15]

The idea of a tram service from the station to the town centre was promoted in 1877 by T. Lloyd, manager of the Liverpool tramways.[16] A private limited company was formed under an Act of 1878[17] and laid standard-gauge tracks from the station to Saltney via City Road, Foregate Street, Eastgate Street, Bridge Street, Grosvenor Street, Grosvenor Road, and Hough Green, with a depot near the station. Lloyd

1 C.C.A.L.S., ZCCB 19, pp. 514–15, 526, 530.

2 Electric Lighting Orders Confirmation (No. 2) Act, 1890, 53 & 54 Vic. c. 187 (Local).

3 C.C.A.L.S., ZCCB 19, p. 602; ZCCB 20, pp. 35, 52–4, 73, 77, 91–2, 116–17, 121–2, 126–30, 135–6, 141, 144–5, 157, 209–10, 213–19; ZCCB 139, pp. 1–109.

4 Obituaries in *Chester Chron.* 29 June 1946; *Ches. Observer,* 29 June 1946.

5 G. Woodward, 'A Tale of Two Cities: Hydroelectricity at Chester and York', *Engineering Science and Education Jnl.* (Apr. 1997), 56.   6 Ibid. 60.

7 Electricity Act, 1947, 10 & 11 Geo. VI, c. 54, schedules.

8 Pevsner, *Ches.* 172.

9 [P. Broster], *Chester Guide* [1st edn., 1781], 70–3; *Jnl. of Transport Hist.* v. 210–11.

10 [F. O'Gorman], 'Decline of Unreformed Politics: Chester 1784–1826' (TS. at C.H.H., cited by kind permission of author), 11.

11 C.C.A.L.S., ZTRI 2, ff. 9, 80 and v.

12 Hemingway, *Hist. Chester,* i. 266 n.; ii. 434.

13 D. Gill and H. G. Dibdin, 'Chester Tramways, 1879–1930', *Tramway Rev.* vii (1952), 137.

14 *Chester City Cl. Mins. 1901/2,* 435–6.

15 Ibid. *1906/7,* 191–2, 303–5, 347–9; *1907/8,* 299, 389–90, 415–17, 479, 511–12, 843; *1908/9,* 156, 374, 408–9, 631.

16 This and next para. based, except where stated otherwise, on Gill and Dibdin, 'Chester Tramways', 137–47; W. D. Clark and H. G. Dibdin, *Trams and Buses of City of Chester* (Rochdale, 1979): copy at C.H.H.; and R. Phillips, *Chester City Transport, 1902–2002*: copy at C.H.H.

17 Chester Tramways Act, 1878, 41 & 42 Vic. c. 174 (Local).

FIG. 18. *Hackney cabs in Bridge Street, c. 1850*

FIG. 19. *General railway station omnibus in Eastgate Street, 1867*

was the first manager, and horse-drawn services started in 1879. The company also ran horse buses to Bache, Christleton, and Hoole. The Act permitted Chester corporation to buy the undertaking after 21 years, and the city made plans to do so after it opened an electricity generating plant in 1896.[1] Under an Act of 1901[2] the corporation bought the tramway company, electrified the system, and relaid the tracks at a gauge of 3 ft. 6 in. Horse buses were used while the work was under way but the corporation then disposed of them. Electric tram services from the Cross to Saltney in one direction and the station in the other began in 1903, and were extended eastwards in 1906 as far as the city boundary in Tarvin and Christleton roads. The old tramway company's manager appointed in 1885, John Gardner, served the corporation in the same capacity until 1915. By the early 1920s the tracks needed replacing and although the trams ran at a profit, carrying 2 million passengers a year at the start of the

decade and 4 million by the end, they were not recouping any of the capital outlay. The council replaced the tracks between the castle and Saltney in 1921 but accepted a report of 1928 that the cost of overhauling the whole system was too great and that it ought to abandon trams in favour of motor buses.[3] A ballot of ratepayers supported the change, and the last tram ran in 1930.[4]

The tramways committee had wanted to start a motor bus service to Bache, Handbridge, and Newton as early as 1905,[5] and periodically revived the idea of corporation motor buses or trolleybuses in the 1910s and 1920s,[6] but the council itself was reluctant, preferring to license other operators. They included H. H. Aldred along Liverpool Road and Garden Lane between 1907 and 1915,[7] Wrexham and District Transport to Saltney and Parkgate Road from 1914,[8] and the Chester-based Crosville Motor Company to Hoole, Newton, and Liverpool Road from 1919, Garden Lane from 1922, and Sealand Road from 1925.[9] The city council, meanwhile, declined in 1915 to co-operate with Hoole urban district council in subsidizing a service to Hoole and Newton.[10] Finally the deterioration of the tramway system forced its hand. It obtained powers to run municipal buses under the Chester Corporation Act of 1929[11] and began services in 1930 along the earlier tram routes,

1 Above, this chapter: Electricity.

2 Chester Corporation Act, 1901, 1 Edw. VII, c. 192 (Local), preamble and ss. 4, 27–8.

3 *Chester City Cl. Mins. 1927/8*, 284–92.

4 *Chester City Transport, 1983* (pamphlet at C.H.H.), 4–5.

5 *Chester City Cl. Mins. 1904/5*, 483–93, 599–601, 765–6; *1905/6*, 638–9, 801, 917, 1010–12; *1906/7*, 109, 464–5.

6 Ibid. *1911/12*, 689; *1912/13*, 35–6, 126; *1914/15*, 314–17; *1924/5*, 376, 744–5, 847; *1925/6*, 27, 121–3, 206, 284–5.

7 Ibid. *1906/7*, 309–11; *1907/8*, 186, 303–4; *1914/15*, 180.

8 Ibid. *1913/14*, 463, 590.

9 Ibid. *1918/19*, 145–6; *1921/2*, 279, 290; *1924/5*, 244–5.

10 Ibid. *1914/15*, 476–7.

11 19 & 20 Geo. V, c. 96 (Local), ss. 29–53.

FIG. 20. *Horse tram at City Road and Fore-gate Street junction, probably 1890s*

with extensions to Vicars Cross, Christleton village, and Saughall Road.[1] After the Road Traffic Act of 1930 the corporation negotiated with Crosville, by then a large business,[2] and agreed in 1932 to exchange routes so that corporation buses served most of the city except Hoole, Newton, and Upton (which were reserved for Crosville) but gave up their out-of-town destinations.[3] The municipal undertaking thereafter operated between a dozen and twenty routes, increasing its fleet from 20 buses in 1931 to *c.* 50 by 1955 and the number of passengers carried from 6.5 million in 1931 to a peak of over 15 million a year *c.* 1950, with a considerable reduction afterwards.[4]

After the government deregulated the bus industry in 1986, Chester City Transport (as it had been called since 1957) became a limited company owned by the city council; by 2001 it was one of fewer than 20 municipal passenger transport undertakings to survive. Deregulation also ended the route-sharing agreement with Crosville, and a period of fierce competition ensued; by the end of the 1990s 'bus wars' Chester City Transport had lost its service to Saltney but retained the others. The continuing fall in passenger numbers had already led to the development of other types of passenger service. Bus tours of the city, started in 1981, were from 1994 provided in conjunction with a private company, Guide Friday Ltd. A park and ride service was introduced from Boughton Heath to the city centre in 1983 and from Sealand Road in 1986, though the complementary services from Wrexham Road and Upton, started in

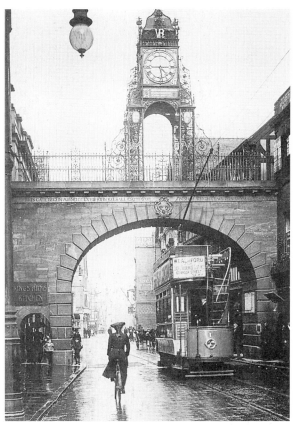

FIG. 21. *Electric tram at the Eastgate, c. 1910*

the 1990s, were put on by other bus operators licensed by the city council.[5]

The city's tram depot was adapted for buses in 1930 and extended several times afterwards, the original horse tram shed of 1878 remaining in use in 2000.[6] Most local services ran from Market Square until 1983, when a new bus exchange between Hunter Street and Princess Street was opened.[7]

POSTAL SERVICE

From the later 16th century, if not earlier, government mails between London and Dublin passed via Chester and Holyhead.[8] Government letters sent from Chester often reached London less than 30 hours later, and on average took 37½ hours.[9] In the 17th and 18th centuries the clerkship of the Chester road was the most important of the six divisions of the general post office in London.[10] Chester had a resident postmaster by 1561; in 1581 he and his colleagues at Conwy and Holyhead were the only three retained in government pay.[11] Early 17th-century postmasters also sent government mail to other places in the North as required.[12]

1 Rest of para. based, except where stated otherwise, on Clark and Dibdin, *Trams and Buses of Chester*, 37–48.

2 Below, Roads and Road Transport: Long-Distance Road Transport.

3 W. J. Crosland-Taylor, *Crosville: the Sowing and the Harvest* (1987), 59–61; *Chester City Transport, 1983*, 2.

4 Clark and Dibdin, *Trams and Buses of Chester*, 79.

5 Phillips, *Chester City Transport*, 2–3, 13, 35, 40, 46.

6 Ibid. 29; *Chester City Transport, 1983*, 4–5.

7 *Chester Observer*, 29 July 1983, p. 32.

8 *Inland Posts (1392–1672): Cal. of Hist. Docs.* ed. J. M. W. Stone, *passim*.

9 *Jnl. of Hist. Geography*, xxiv. 275–6.

10 H. Robinson, *Brit. Post Office: Hist.* (1970), 55, 110.

11 *Inland Posts*, ed. Stone, pp. 20, 213.

12 Ibid. p. 46.

Public letters were carried by the government's horse posts from 1635.[1] In May 1666 the London mail started from Chester at noon on Saturdays, Mondays, and Wednesdays, and could take as little as 40 hours. Packets were sent weekly from Chester to Dublin.[2] Stage coaches provided a slower service by 1675: they left London and Chester every Monday, Wednesday, and Friday and took between four and six days.[3] In 1700 a service was set up direct from Chester to Bristol and Exeter, one of the first two cross-country routes; at first it had a separate office in Chester,[4] which may have continued until the national bye-post was united with the general post office in 1799.[5] Other routes were soon added: in 1721 letters for Manchester, for example, were sent and received three days a week.[6] By the 1780s the post went daily to London and the North, five times a week to Dublin, and three times on the cross road to the South-West and into north Wales.[7]

The main Chester post office declined in relative importance from the late 18th century, especially after the Chester–Holyhead road was superseded in the 1820s by Telford's direct road through Shrewsbury, and later by railways.[8] In 1792 the Chester postmaster's salary was among the top six in England, commensurate with Birmingham, Liverpool, and Manchester,[9] but by 1840 it ranked only 22nd.[10] In 1833 the office's revenues came mainly from the provincial post (70 per cent) rather than the services to London (25 per cent), Dublin (3 per cent), or the local penny post (2 per cent).[11]

Until the mid 19th century almost all provincial post offices were run from the postmasters' own premises.[12] In 1787 and 1830 the Palin family kept the Chester office at a house in a yard off the north side of Foregate Street just outside the walls, later called Old Post Office Yard.[13] William Palin built a new office in 1842 on the east side of St. John Street behind the Blossoms Hotel, evidently to cope with the greatly increased business occasioned by the introduction of the national penny post in 1840.[14] The Post Office opened a new head office for the town in 1876 on the other side of St. John Street,[15] where it remained in 2000. By 1878 there were sub-offices in Boughton, Handbridge, and Hoole; others in the city centre and outlying areas followed later, especially as the suburbs grew. There were 9 in 1896, 12 in 1914, 17 in 1939, and 25 in 1974.[16] A sorting office facing Chester General station was opened in 1912,[17] and was replaced by a new building west of the Brook Street railway bridge in 1983.[18]

TELECOMMUNICATIONS

The telegraph arrived in Chester with the railway in the 1840s, and at first the only telegraph office was at the station.[19] The Post Office ran the service from 1870, when the telegraph companies were nationalized.[20] By 1896 there were telegraph offices in the main post office and the Boughton and Hoole sub-offices.[21]

There was a telephone exchange in 1882, probably opened that year, operated by the Liverpool and Manchester Exchange Telephonic Co. as a subsidiary of the United Telephone Co. and under Post Office licence.[22] The U.T.C. merged with its subsidiaries as the National Telephone Co. in 1891.[23] Its Chester exchange and regional head office were in Godstall Chambers, St. Werburgh Street. In 1898 there were 168 subscribers, mostly businesses.[24] The exchange was transferred to a new building next to the main post office in St. John Street in 1908[25] in anticipation of the Post Office's acquisition of the telephone system, which took effect in 1912.[26] It moved again in 1950 to a neo-Georgian building on the north side of Little St. John Street built for the purpose in 1939,[27] and in 1979 across the road to Dee House, the former Ursuline convent south of the Roman amphitheatre.[28]

BATHS AND WASH-HOUSES

Paying members of the public were allowed to use the warm slipper bath installed at the infirmary in 1773.[29] After the building was enlarged in the late 1820s there were two public baths (one for the wealthy on payment, the other for dispensary patients free) besides

1 *Cal. S.P. Dom.* 1635, 166, 299.

2 *Inland Posts*, ed. Stone, pp. 114, 151.

3 Robinson, *Brit. P.O.* 68.

4 Ibid. 81–2; H. Joyce, *Hist. Post Office to 1836*, 151.

5 *1st Rep. of Postmaster Gen.* [1913], p. 14, H.C. (1854–5), xx.

6 *4th Rep. of Postmaster Gen.* [2342], p. 67, H.C. (1857–8), xxv.

7 [P. Broster], *Chester Guide* [1st edn., 1781], 61–2.

8 Below, Roads and Road Transport: Roads (Holyhead Road and North Wales); Railways.

9 Joyce, *Hist. P.O.* 293.

10 *Return of Postmasters' Salaries*, H.C. (155), pp. 2–6 (1841 Sess. 1), xxvi.

11 C.C.A.L.S., ZCR 60/8/35.

12 *Return of Postmasters' Salaries*, p. 11.

13 *Broster's Dir. Chester* (1787), 100; Hemingway, *Hist. Chester*, i. 415; J. Hunter and S. Weston, *Plan of Chester* (1789).

14 Hughes, *Stranger's Handbk.* (1856), 16.

15 *22nd Rep. of Postmaster Gen.* [C. 1575], p. 5, H.C. (1876), xxi.

16 *Kelly's Dir. Ches.* (1878), 106; (1896), 193; (1914), 226–7; (1939), 79; *Kelly's Dir. Chester* (1974), 470.

17 C.C.A.L.S., ZCR 119/24, p. 189; *Chester City Cl. Mins.*

1906/7, 31.

18 Plaque on bldg.

19 J. Kieve, *Electric Telegraph: Social and Economic Hist.* 29–30, 38, 49, 53, 75.

20 Ibid. 152–77.

21 *Kelly's Dir. Ches.* (1896), 193.

22 C.C.A.L.S., ZCCB 55, pp. 181, 185, 191; J. C. Hemmeon, *Hist. Brit. Post Office*, 219–21.

23 Hemmeon, *Hist. Brit. P.O.* 222.

24 *Nat. Telephone Co. Dir.* (1896–7 and 1898–9): photocopies of pp. for Chester at C.H.H., pamphlets ('Colln. of extracts about telecommunications in Chester').

25 *Chester Exchange of Nat. Telephone Co.*: copy at C.H.H., C.A.S. libr., pamphlet box 22; *Chester City Cl. Mins. 1907/8*, 296, 386–7, 475; *J.C.A.S.* xiii. 136.

26 *60th Rep. of Postmaster Gen.* [Cd. 7573], pp. 68–9, H.C. (1914), xliv.

27 *Brief Hist. of Telecommunications in Chester*: photocopy at C.H.H., pamphlets ('Colln. of extracts about telecommunications in Chester').

28 *Ches. Observer*, 16 Feb. 1979.

29 C.C.A.L.S., ZHI 3, ff. 158v., 242, 258, 267, 270; ZHI 4, f. 48.

FIG. 22. *Water Tower baths, 1856*

FIG. 23. *Union Street baths, 1904*

four for in-patients. They could all be used for hot, cold, shower, or vapour baths.[1] The paying bath cost 1*s.* in 1811 and 2*s.* in 1852 and so was out of reach of all but the richest Cestrians.[2]

A subscription baths committee existed by 1847. In 1848 it secured from the city council a grant of £1,260 and the lease of a plot of land south-west of the Water Tower, where it opened a public baths and wash-house in 1849. Access was through a new opening in the city wall.[3] In 1850, with the baths losing money, the council adopted the Baths and Wash-houses Act of 1846, which permitted it to operate its own establishment.[4] It was only the eighth local authority to do so, far in advance of other towns of comparable size.[5] Those in favour of adoption were inspired by Liverpool's pioneering work in providing baths and wash-houses for the poor, but the motion was carried only on a casting vote.[6] The council took over the private committee's premises and debts.[7] The wash-house, a financial burden, was closed in 1851, reopened (for only two days a week) in 1852, and finally closed in 1855;[8] the equipment was sold in 1861.[9] The slipper and swim-

ming baths, however, were popular: 700 people a week swam or bathed in summer 1850 and 25 even in December.[10] Mindful of the need to subsidize baths for the poor, the council added a suite of private warm baths in 1853. They were divided into four classes, with prices ranging from 1*s.* to 2*d.*[11] The swimming pool was segregated socially by pricing its use at 1*d.* before 8 a.m. and after 5 p.m. and up to 6*d.* at more desirable times.[12] Water for the baths was drawn from the canal.[13] In 1852 the pool was heated to 70 degrees F. but in the 1860s had cold water all year round.[14] The baths were closed in 1878 and afterwards demolished.[15]

The Chester Floating Baths Co. opened a swimming bath in 1877, moored on the Dee at the Groves. Professor Mitchell and his daughter were hired as swimming teachers from the St. George's baths at Liverpool pierhead. The bath was open daily in summer, with prices ranging from 1*d.* upwards according to the time of day.[16] The council took it over in 1883[17] and considered replacing it in 1887–9 and again from 1894. A site in Union Street was found only in 1898 and new baths were opened there in 1901.[18] Meanwhile the floating bath was badly damaged when it drifted from its mooring on to the weir during a storm in 1899. It was temporarily repaired but in 1902 was sold and broken up.[19]

The Union Street baths were designed by John Douglas in his usual vernacular style.[20] The entrance block is of red brick with elaborate stone porches and a

1 Hemingway, *Hist. Chester,* ii. 199.

2 C.C.A.L.S., ZHI 11 (12 Mar. 1811); ZHI 13 (29 Oct. 1833); ZHI 14 (5 Nov. 1839); ZHI 15, ff. 15v., 27v.; ZCCB 77, newspaper cutting (10 June 1852) facing p. 1.

3 Ibid. ZCCB 30, 21 Apr., 8, 15 June, 13 July 1847, 18, 28 June, 6, 9 Aug., 9 Oct. 1849; *Chester Chron.* 16 June 1848.

4 9 & 10 Vic. c. 74 (Local and Personal); C.C.A.L.S., ZAB 6, pp. 882–3; *Chester Chron.* 21 Dec. 1849.

5 *Return of Places where Baths and Washhouses Acts have been Adopted,* H.C. 383, pp. 2–5 (1865), xlvii; cf., e.g., *V.C.H. Glos.* iv. 195, 202; *V.C.H. Oxon.* iv. 363; *V.C.H. Staffs.* xiv. 107–8.

6 C.C.A.L.S., ZCCB 77, newspaper cutting facing p. 1; *T.H.S.L.C.* cxxxvii. 117–36.   7 C.C.A.L.S., ZCCB 77, pp. 1–4.

8 Ibid. pp. 25, 28, 57–8, 80, 82 (no later ref. to washing); *White's Dir. Ches.* (1860), 100.

9 C.C.A.L.S., ZCCB 77, loose sheet advertising sale.

10 Ibid. pp. 6, 10.   11 Ibid. pp. 28–9, 38, 52–3, 62.

12 Ibid. loose sheet of prices.   13 e.g. ibid. p. 100.

14 Ibid. p. 23, 10 Jan. 1860, 12 Nov. 1866, 2 Oct. 1871.

15 Ibid. ZCCB 53, p. 867.

16 *Chester Chron.* 21 Apr. 1877, p. 6; 11 May 1878, p. 1; 10 May 1879, p. 1; 15 May 1880, p. 1.

17 Ibid. 9 June 1883, p. 8; C.C.A.L.S., ZCCB 54 (no refs. to baths sub-cttee. in 1881 or 1882); ZCCB 55, pp. 359–60, 364.

18 C.C.A.L.S., ZCCB 130, pp. 2, 7, 9, 11–12, 14, 26–9, 32–43, 45, 56–7, 115–16, 118–19, 123–4, 126, 143–4, 157–8, 184, 194, 203, 206, 208, 211, 213, 218–19, 231, 233, 236, 245; O.S. Map 1/2,500, Ches. XXXVIII.11 (1899 and 1911 edns.).

19 C.C.A.L.S., ZCCB 130, pp. 226–8, 230, 256, 261, 265–6.

20 Ibid. pp. 219, 221–2.

FIG. 24. *St. Oswald's parish graveyard, south-east of cathedral, 1830*

black-and-white timber-framed first floor. Behind it were two swimming pools, and slipper and vapour baths, with two classes of pricing. In the early years, females had the use of the better pool for a few hours three days a week[1] but most bathers were male: in the first full year of opening 4,000 tickets were sold to women but 57,000 to men.[2] The swimming pools remained in use by Chester Swimming Club in 2000.[3]

CEMETERIES

By 1830 seven of the nine parish churchyards in the city were regarded as overcrowded. New burial grounds had already been consecrated in 1810 for Holy Trinity, 1825 for St. Mary's, and 1829 at the new church of St. Bridget. St. John's was using the churchyard of the medieval hospital of St. Giles at Spital Boughton.[4]

A proposal in 1833 to use the Little Roodee as a municipal cemetery came to nothing.[5] In 1848 a group of subscribers obtained an Act of Parliament for incorporation as the Chester Cemetery Co. They included Richard Grosvenor, marquess of Westminster, and the dean and chancellor of Chester. The Act allowed the company, whose directors were to include the mayor and a representative of the marquess, to make a cemetery on land bought from the marquess and the corporation on the south bank of the Dee east of Grosvenor Bridge, and restricted burials in existing churchyards.[6] Most of the latter, together with the Roman Catholic and six nonconformist burial grounds, were closed in 1855, though St. John's churchyard was partly in use until 1875 and the new churchyard of St. Bridget's remained open until 1877.[7] Chester was thus one of the few places, including other cathedral and county towns and resorts, which obtained a general cemetery through a Local Act rather than under the Burials Act of 1853.[8]

The cemetery was laid out between 1848 and 1850 to a design prepared by Mr. Lister on the rocky site climbing south from the Dee to Overleigh Road, bounded west by Grosvenor Road and east by River Lane (Fig. 25). Lister made good use of a naturally picturesque spot, incorporating serpentine walks, a rustic bridge, a small lake, and much ornamental planting. The buildings – Anglican and nonconformist chapels, two lodges, and a chaplain's house – were designed by T. M. Penson. Graves were scattered in small groups.[9] The cemetery was much admired by contemporaries.[10] By 1894 there had been over 30,000 burials; in that year the company made a profit of £148 on its income of £945 and paid a dividend of 3 per cent to its 42 shareholders.[11] The chaplain's house was demolished between 1872 and 1898, the nonconformist chapel in 1907, and the lodges after 1967. Penson's Romanesque Anglican chapel, derelict by 1968, was pulled down in 1980,[12] and in the 1990s the cemetery was suffering from neglect and minor vandalism.

The cemetery company bought an additional 4 a. south of Overleigh Road under an Act of 1879.[13] The land, flat and treeless, was marked out on a rather

1 C.C.A.L.S., ZCCB 130, p. 245.

2 Ibid. p. 299.

3 Below, Sport after 1700: Other Sports (Swimming).

4 Hemingway, *Hist. Chester,* ii. 128–9, 144–5; below, Medieval Parish Churches.

5 *Chester Chron.* 5 Apr., 23 June, 8 Nov. 1833.

6 Chester Cemetery Act, 11 & 12 Vic. c. 100 (Local and Personal).

7 *Lond. Gaz.* 9 Feb. 1855, pp. 472–3; 2 Mar. 1855, pp. 899–900; 5 Feb. 1856, pp. 420–1; 29 Oct. 1875, pp. 5112–13; below, Medieval Parish Churches.

8 *Return of Parishes in which Cemeteries have been Constituted,* H.C. 102, pp. 1–3 (1863), xlvi.

9 Pevsner, *Ches.* 174, corrected by Chester Civic Trust,

Chester Cemetery, Overleigh (leaflet, 1994, at C.H.H.), citing *Chester Chron.*; O.S. Map 1/2,500, Ches. XXXVIII.15 (1874 edn.).

10 e.g. J. Romney, *Chester and its Environs Illustrated,* [40]; Hughes, *Stranger's Handbk.* (1856), 70–1; *Gresty and Burghall's Chester Guide* [1867], 35.

11 *Chester General Cem. Co.: Rep. of Directors, 1894:* copy at C.C.A.L.S., ZCLA 24.

12 O.S. Map 1/2,500, Ches. XXXVIII.15 (1874, 1899, and 1911 edns.); *Chester City Cl. Mins. 1906/7,* 734; *Ches. Observer,* 26 Apr. 1968; 'Victorian Society Cemetery Survey' (1981: copy at C.H.H.); C.P.S., Grosvenor Rd. (neg. G 22/11); Overleigh Rd. (negs. G 22/3–5).

13 Chester Cemetery (Extension) Act, 42 Vic. c. 14 (Local).

FIG. 25. *Overleigh cemetery, 1867*

regimented plan by 1894,[1] but was apparently not used until 1904.[2] In included a lodge and two chapels, built in brick with stone dressings: the Anglican one in vernacular style with a nave, north aisle, and low tower over the north-east porch; its nonconformist counterpart a plain box-like nave and aisle. Both survived in 2000, not in use as cemetery chapels,[3] though some burials were still then taking place on reserved plots.

The city council bought the cemetery in 1933 under enabling legislation of 1932.[4] It had to drop a planned extension because the adjoining land was unsuitable,[5] and instead prepared a new cemetery and crematorium on 30 a. on the eastern edge of the Blacon housing estate. Burials began there in 1942[6] and it remained in use as Chester's main cemetery in 2000. It included two areas maintained by the Commonwealth War Graves Commission, containing over 500 graves, mainly of men of the Canadian, Australian, and British air forces, and of Polish troops settled in the area in the 1940s.[7]

Burials also took place at the Chester Union workhouse from 1880 to 1900.[8]

MEDICAL SERVICES

The two medieval hospitals treating the sick and diseased, St. Giles's leper house at Spital Boughton and St. John's outside the Northgate, both survived the Dissolution but had ceased to provide medical care by 1537 and the early 17th century respectively.[9] In 1602–5 and 1647–8 the Assembly built plague cabins on the edge of the Roodee, between the Water Tower and the river.[10] A charity dispensing medicines to the poor was set up in 1721 with an endowment of £100 under the will of Peter Cotton. Its apothecary and surgeon were appointed by the city corporation,[11] and it still existed in 1757, when the governors of the newly established infirmary pressed the corporation to transfer the endowment to them.[12]

The general infirmary, opened in 1755, in time provided services more comprehensive than many voluntary hospitals, so that other medical institutions developed more slowly in Chester than in some similar towns.[13] The infirmary was especially distinguished by its pioneering fever wards (1784), which obviated the need for a separate fever hospital, and by a dispensing and out-patient service which ran on an unusually large scale. The only other voluntary dispensaries were therefore late, small, and specialized.[14] As befitted an important county town, Chester was exceptionally well served by medical men in the 18th century,[15] and dental practitioners were established from the 1790s.[16]

1 *Chester General Cem. Co.: Rep. of Directors, 1894.*

2 J. Williams, *Story of Chester*, 288.

3 Below, Other Churches: Greek Orthodox.

4 Chester Corporation Act, 22 & 23 Geo. V, c. 84 (Local), s. 4; *Chester City Cl. Mins. 1931/2*, 29–30, 881, 926; *1932/3*, 68, 293, 812, 1023.

5 *Chester City Cl. Mins. 1936/7*, 276, 416.

6 Ibid. *1937/8*, 68, 170, 461–2; *1939/40*, 61, 424, 820; *1941/2*, 644.

7 *War Dead of Commonwealth: Cems. and Chyds. in Ches.* i (Commonwealth War Graves Com. 1961), 39–40: copy in crematorium office.   8 C.C.A.L.S., ZHC 14.

9 *V.C.H. Ches.* iii. 178–83. Thanks are offered to Mr. Kevin Brown (archivist, St. Mary's Hosp., Paddington) and Mr. Jonathan Pepler (C.C.A.L.S.) for comments and advice on this

section. Research on the infirmary was largely the work of Dr. J. S. Barrow.   10 Hemingway, *Hist. Chester*, i. 144–5.

11 C.C.A.L.S., ZAB 3, f. 264v.

12 Ibid. ZAB 4, f. 173v.; ZHI 1, f. 108v.

13 e.g. Oxford and Gloucester: *V.C.H. Oxon.* iv. 360–3; *V.C.H. Glos.* iv. 269–75.

14 Below, this chapter: Chester Royal Infirmary, Other Dispensaries.

15 P. J. and R. V. Wallis, *18th-Cent. Medics* (2nd edn. 1988), comparing Chester entries in index of places with those for other towns.

16 C. Hillam, *Brass Plate and Brazen Impudence: Dental Practice in the Provinces, 1755–1855*, 17, 54 n. 15, 72, 78, 81, 92 n. 11, 128, 198–9, 204, 236, 240; J. R. Davey, 'Dentistry in Chester, 1790–1800', *Dental Historian*, xxviii. 20–30.

FIG. 26. *Chester infirmary, before 1830*

CHESTER ROYAL INFIRMARY

Chester infirmary was founded after William Stratford, physician, left £300 in 1753 to endow a county infirmary. He had the recent local examples of infirmaries in Liverpool (1744), Shrewsbury (1745), and Manchester (1752). A committee appointed at the Chester assizes drew up proposals and gathered subscriptions; the subscribers then elected a management committee, which formulated statutes, appointed the first staff, fitted up a temporary hospital in the Blue Coat school, and sought advice in Liverpool and Manchester.[1] Out-patients were treated from 1755; the first in-patient was admitted in 1756.[2] It was among the first dozen provincial infirmaries.[3] Renamed Chester Royal Infirmary in 1914,[4] it never received a royal charter and became a limited company in 1937.[5]

The infirmary was intended for those too poor to pay for medical care at home. Under the earliest statutes, it did not admit pregnant women, children under seven years, infectious diseases, or inoperable and incurable cases. Patients were admitted by subscriber's ticket on Tuesdays; emergencies at any time at the discretion of the medical staff. Only the apothecary and the matron were salaried; the honorary physicians and surgeons attended patients without payment on a rota.[6]

In 1758 the governors bought a site for a new hospital in the Crofts facing City Walls Road. The building, designed by William Yoxall and completed in 1761, was built of brick and formed a quadrangle round a courtyard; it was of two principal storeys with basements and attics. Offices occupied the raised ground floor and included a board room, library,

waiting and receiving rooms for the in-patients, and bedrooms and sitting rooms for the staff; long wards, each with 24 beds, were in the north and south ranges of the first and attic floors, men in the south range and women in the north; nurses' rooms, staircases, and the chapel were placed in the east and west ranges, one of the staircases in a projecting bay on the east, the other rising from the entrance hall on the west; the basements were too poorly lit, drained, and ventilated to be used. There was no provision to segregate patients with different types of illness, and no day rooms for those convalescing.[7] Despite the governors' complacent view in 1807 that the building was 'spacious and convenient',[8] there was growing dissatisfaction with it, led by Dr. George Cumming, honorary physician 1804–6 and thereafter a governor.[9] A report in 1824 concluded that the infirmary was 'essentially defective' in comparison with more recent hospital buildings.[10] After much controversy,[11] alterations were completed in 1830 by the county architect William Cole junior. He divided the long wards into smaller rooms, lowered the ground level on all sides except the south in order to allow the basements to be used, and inserted two new blocks within the central courtyard, narrowing it on the north and south. The courtyard blocks contained nurses' rooms, bathrooms, and W.C.s, and incorporated a corridor running round the inner side of the original building, permitting better use of the east and west ranges. Both original staircases were removed and a single staircase in the east range was substituted; Cole added a canted bay to the projecting eastern bay and moved the chapel into it on the first floor. It was now possible to make small day rooms as well as separate wards for different categories of patient, including surgical, medical, convalescent, accident, and ophthal-

1 C.C.A.L.S., ZHI 1, ff. 1–21; H. E. Boulton, 'Chester Infirmary', *J.C.A.S.* xlvii. 9; E. M. Mumford, *Chester Royal Infirmary, 1756–1956*, [3]; dates from P. Langford, *Polite and Commercial People: Eng. 1727–83*, 137.

2 C.C.A.L.S., ZHI 1, ff. 23, 29.

3 Langford, *Polite and Commercial People*, 136–7.

4 C.C.A.L.S., ZHI 22, p. 71.

5 Mumford, *Infirmary*, 16.

6 *Statutes of General Infirmary at Chester* (1763); *Statutes of*

General Infirmary at Chester (1799); *Laws, Orders, and Regulations of Chester Infirmary* (1816); *Rules for Government of Infirmary at Chester* (1854): copies in C.C.A.L.S., ZHI 316, 320.

7 Mumford, *Infirmary*, 7; Hemingway, *Hist. Chester*, ii. 196–9 and plan facing 204; C.C.A.L.S., ZHI 317, p. 10 and plan; for the architect: *Ches. Hist.* xxxiv. 25–8.

8 C.C.A.L.S., ZHI 10 (24 Mar. 1807).

9 Ibid. ZHI 9, f. 249v.; ZHI 10 (22 July 1806); ZHI 319.

10 Ibid. ZHI 317, p. 6.   11 Ibid. ZHI 319, pp. 1, 6.

mic cases. The same number of beds was provided as before, but the total space per bed was increased by over half. At the same time the rooms on the ground floor were rearranged to accommodate a separate suite for the dispensing department.[1]

The governors of the infirmary initially comprised the numerous individuals who subscribed 2 guineas a year or more, together with the honorary physicians and surgeons. General meetings of the governors appointed the staff and controlled policy; day-to-day management was carried out by a weekly board open to any governor.[2] The open weekly board was replaced from 1827 to *c.* 1833[3] and permanently in 1865 with a board of management comprising the honorary medical officers and representatives elected by the governors.[4] In the 20th century the board included elected governors, members of the medical staff, and representatives of Chester city and Cheshire, Denbighshire, and Flintshire county councils, local churches, and other bodies.[5]

In the early years the subscribers were mostly from Chester: 70 per cent in 1778/9 as against 18 per cent from the rest of the county and 12 per cent from north Wales. The proportion of non-Cestrians grew as the subscription list lengthened: by 1839/40 the figures were 41 per cent Chester, 38 per cent Cheshire, and 20 per cent north Wales.[6] In 1806 the board discouraged parishes from subscribing on the reasoning that subscriptions from individuals were easier to collect.[7] The railway companies operating from Chester subscribed from 1838 at the infirmary's request because of the frequency of accidents to their employees.[8] Subscribers and benefactors were entitled to nominate patients by ticket according to the value of their donations. The entitlement for subscribers of 2 guineas (much the commonest sum) was set at one in-patient or two out-patients in 1763 but was frequently changed: one of each from 1799; two in-patients and any number of out-patients from 1816; two and ten from 1831; and two and six from 1854.[9]

The cost of running the infirmary stood a little under £2,000 a year *c.* 1800 and rarely exceeded £3,000 before 1870.[10] As in most voluntary hospitals, subscriptions alone were never sufficient to meet

1 Ibid. ZHI 13 (16 Nov. 1830); ZHI 317; Hemingway, *Hist. Chester*, ii. 198–9 and plans facing 204.

2 *Statutes* (1763); *Statutes* (1799); *Laws* (1816); *Rules* (1854).

3 Hemingway, *Hist. Chester*, ii. 200, 206–7; C.C.A.L.S., ZCR 269/1.

4 C.C.A.L.S., ZHI 16 (23 Jan. 1865).

5 *Ann. Rep. of Chester General Infirmary* (1920, 1947): copies in C.C.A.L.S., ZHI 44, 48.

6 Boulton, 'Infirmary', 15; C.C.A.L.S., ZHI 92.

7 C.C.A.L.S., ZHI 24, p. 14.

8 Ibid. ZHI 14 (9 Oct., 11 Dec. 1838, 28 May 1839).

9 Ibid. ZHI 13 (25 Jan. 1831); *Statutes* (1763), 14–15; *Statutes* (1799), 10; *Laws* (1816), 5; *Rules* (1854), 5.

10 Para. based on *Ann. Rep.* (1840, 1856, and later edns.): copies in C.C.A.L.S., ZCR 24/42 and ZHI 31–48; ibid. ZHI 91–2.

(A)

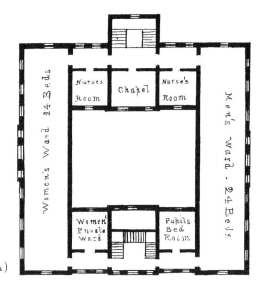

(B)

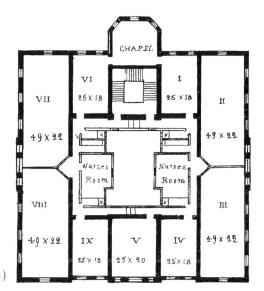

(C)

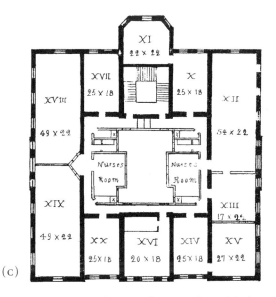

FIG. 27. *Chester infirmary, plans: (a) first floor, 1761; (b) first floor, 1830; (c) second floor, 1830*

running costs, even with a peak of *c.* 500 subscribers in the first two decades of the 19th century, let alone when their number dropped to 400 or fewer by mid century. Average annual subscriptions fell from £1,113 in the years 1806–20 to £959 in 1831–42 but recovered slowly to over £1,000 in the 1860s. There were periodic efforts to gain new subscribers, as in 1779, 1807, and 1831.[1] The financial gap was met partly by legacies and gifts, which amounted to almost half the subscription income in 1806–20 and over two thirds in 1831–42. Surpluses were invested, so that the income from dividends rose from £319 in 1806/7 to £651 in 1841/2. Fund-raising events in the earlier 19th century included church collections, subscription assemblies during Chester races, and a bazaar sale which brought in £1,500 in 1832. There was also regular income from the fees paid by medical apprentices (£210 for a five-year apprenticeship) and for treating patients belonging to other institutions in the city: the workhouse from 1784, the county gaol at Chester castle from 1785, and the city council's watch committee (for police constables and prisoners in police cells) from 1857.[2] The infirmary was nevertheless sometimes in severe financial difficulties: economy measures limited the number of in-patients to 60 in 1786, and to between 30 and 50 from 1799 to 1807.[3]

The number of in-patients admitted each year rose from under 300 in the 1760s and 1770s to average over 500 between 1787 and 1817 (even allowing for lower numbers in the 1800s) and over 600 in the 1820s.[4] In 1775 half the in-patients were from city parishes, a fifth from elsewhere in Cheshire, and a quarter from north Wales.[5] Unlike most other voluntary hospitals before the mid 19th century,[6] the Chester infirmary also treated many out-patients, who were of course mainly from the city. Out-patients outnumbered in-patients from the first.[7] Out-patient services were extended in 1764, when a dispensing service was set up to sell medicines at cost price to the poor,[8] though until *c.* 1783 only a few hundred people made use of it each year.[9] By the late 1780s (presumably because the

medicines were then given free) the numbers had grown to over 3,000 a year, and from 1791 the dispensary was open every day.[10] Under pressure from Dr. Cumming, the infirmary organized a separate dispensary branch with its own rooms and staff in 1829 to treat out-patients and home patients.[11] It was so successful that numbers had to be limited by a change in the rules a decade later.[12] The infirmary coped adequately with a disaster in 1772, when 23 were killed and 53 injured in a gunpowder explosion at a puppet show in Watergate Street.[13]

The infirmary at first had only one paid medical officer, the apothecary, who doubled as administrator.[14] The medical duties were separated from financial matters in 1794 and from the secretaryship possibly in 1815, when the post was renamed house surgeon.[15] By 1825 the house surgeon was spending most of his time visiting patients at home and in the workhouse and gaol.[16] An assistant was appointed in 1829 to take charge of home visiting, and a dispensing surgeon in 1831 for the out-patients.[17] The home visiting service was at its most extensive and burdensome *c.* 1900[18] and continued until 1921, by when the government's national insurance scheme had made it unnecessary.[19]

Until the 1850s the normal complement of honorary officers was three physicians and three surgeons.[20] Under John Haygarth, physician 1767–98, the infirmary became in 1784 the first in Britain to admit smallpox patients, who were isolated under rules which he had developed during the epidemic of 1777–8.[21] Haygarth's methods were widely admired and copied.[22] The infirmary treated smallpox and fever patients in rooms within the original building until 1851, but then excluded them in line with practice elsewhere.[23] Fever patients were required to pay for their maintenance, 4*s.* a week from 1784, 7*s.* from 1831; the money came either from their parish overseers or from the governors on whose tickets they had been admitted.[24]

The scale and nature of the infirmary's care changed with national trends from the 1860s. The number of

1 C.C.A.L.S., ZHI 4, ff. 89v.–91; ZHI 10 (24 Mar. 1807); ZHI 13 (25 Jan. 1831).

2 Ibid. ZHI 6, ff. 107, 125v.; ZHI 14 (9 Jan. 1844); ZHI 16 (9 June 1857).

3 Ibid. ZHI 6, f. 184v.; ZHI 9, ff. 127v., 141v., 153v.–154, 189v.; ZHI 10 (24 June 1806, 24 Mar. 1807); ZHI 24, pp. 7–16; *Statutes* (1799), 21–3.

4 C.C.A.L.S., ZHI 51–2; Hemingway, *Hist. Chester,* ii. 210.

5 Calculated from C.C.A.L.S., ZHI 52.

6 Figs. for 1787–1817 collected by infirmary in ibid. ZHI 24, pp. 1–6, 19–21; for 1863 by F. Buckle, *Vital and Economical Statistics of Hosps. for 1863.*

7 C.C.A.L.S., ZHI 51.

8 Ibid. ZHI 2, f. 23v.

9 Ibid. ZHI 6, f. 37v.

10 Ibid. ZHI 7 (15 Feb. 1791); ZHI 24, pp. 1–6, 19–21.

11 Ibid. ZHI 13 (17 Nov. 1829); ZHI 318, p. 7; ZHI 319, pp. 1–4, 8–9; Hemingway, *Hist. Chester,* ii. 199.

12 *Ann. Rep.* (1840).

13 Hemingway, *Hist. Chester,* ii. 6–7.

14 *Statutes* (1763), 20–3.

15 *Laws* (1816), 19–21; C.C.A.L.S., ZHI 7 (10 Jan. 1794); ZHI 12 (4 July 1815); cf. ZHI 9, ff. 87, 95v.

16 C.C.A.L.S., ZHI 318, p. 7.

17 Ibid. ZHI 13 (17 Nov. 1829); ZHI 319, p. 2.

18 e.g. *Ann. Rep.* (1897, 1898).

19 Mumford, *Infirmary,* 14.

20 *Rules* (1854), 16.

21 C.C.A.L.S., ZHI 6, f. 79v.; *D.N.B.*; J. Haygarth, *Inquiry How to Prevent Smallpox* (1784), esp. 8–9, 93, 118–20, 147–208.

22 e.g. J. Howard, *Acct. of Principal Lazarettos in Europe* (1791), 208–9; Hemingway, *Hist. Chester,* ii. 361; *Dr. Haygarth's Rules to Prevent Infectious Fevers* (1800): copy in B.L., printed bks., 1830.c.1, no. 146.

23 e.g. C.C.A.L.S., ZHI 10 (19 Mar. 1805); ZHI 14 (26 Feb. 1839); ZHI 15 (20, 27 May, 3 June 1851). The evidence contradicts Mumford, *Infirmary,* 32.

24 C.C.A.L.S., ZHI 6, f. 106v.; ZHI 13 (25 Jan. 1831).

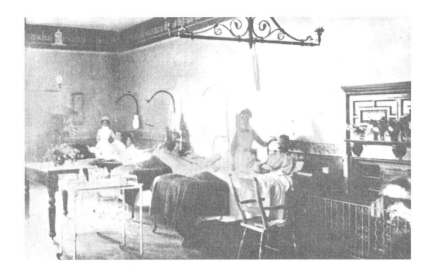

FIG. 28. *Infirmary ward, c. 1906*

in-patients grew inexorably from (in round figures) 700 admitted in 1867 to 1,550 in 1917 and 4,400 in 1937; out-patients from 5,000 to 6,000 and 14,000 in the same years; the average daily bed occupancy from 92 in 1900 to 182 in 1937.[1] The infirmary continued to serve a wide area: in 1873 half the in-patients were from Chester and about a quarter each from other places in Cheshire and north Wales.[2] In the 20th century there were proportionately fewer from Chester: in 1927 the city and county each accounted for about 30 per cent and the principality 40 per cent.[3]

The medical staff grew too. A dental surgeon was appointed in 1853, and an ophthalmic surgeon in 1885, both as honorary positions.[4] Including retired honorary officers kept on as 'consulting' surgeons and physicians,[5] by 1900 there were 11 honorary medical officers, increasing to 22 in 1920 and 28 in 1947. The salaried medical staff numbered 3, 6, and 11 in the same years.[6]

Modern nursing was introduced gradually in the 1860s and 1870s, though never through a Nightingale-trained matron. Efforts were made between 1865 and 1867 to replace the existing infirmary servants,[7] and from 1869 a deaconess appointed by the diocese of Chester assisted with training;[8] one of the first of the middle-class trainees was Rose, daughter of Canon Charles Kingsley.[9] The number of nurses, including probationers, grew from 13 in 1880 to 24 in 1890 and

52 in 1911. In 1947 the nursing and technical staff numbered 130.[10] In the late 19th and earlier 20th century the infirmary ran a district nursing service in poor areas and hired out private nurses to wealthier households.[11]

Separate wards for smallpox patients were opened in the grounds east of the old building in 1868.[12] They were in use until the city's isolation hospital was opened in 1899,[13] when they were converted into nurses' rooms.[14] The range of medical and surgical care available was continuously expanded in the later 19th and earlier 20th century in line with medical advances. For example, X-ray equipment was acquired in 1902 and a pathological laboratory in 1907 – both gifts of G. W. Hayes – and departments for gynaecology, psychiatry, and orthopaedics were established between 1924 and 1937.[15]

The increase in patients and staff necessitated new building on the 5-a. Infirmary field north of the original block, which had been bought in 1859 to prevent any building close to the hospital and as a recreational area.[16] The Humberston wing, extending south-east of the 1761 building and designed by T. M. Lockwood to provide rooms for nurses and servants, was opened in 1892.[17] The main impulse, however, came from a highly critical report on the existing buildings in 1909 by the hospital pundit Sir Henry Burdett,[18] which found that the wards were among the most cramped in the country.[19] The infirmary raised

1 *Ann. Rep.* (1867–1937, sampled at 10-year intervals).

2 Ibid. (1873).   3 Ibid. (1927).

4 C.C.A.L.S., ZHI 15 (25 May 1853); ZHI 18, p. 796.

5 *Rules* (1854), 18.

6 *Ann. Rep.* (1900, 1920, 1947).

7 C.C.A.L.S., ZHI 16 (28 Feb., 13 June, 31 Oct., 20 Nov. 1865, 30 Jan., 20 Feb., 9, 16 Oct., 24 Dec. 1866, 1, 29 Jan. 1867).

8 Ibid. ZHI 17, pp. 166, 179.

9 Ibid. pp. 253, 318.

10 Ibid. ZHI 18, p. 246; ZHI 19, p. 488; ZHI 21, p. 399; *Ann. Rep.* (1947).

11 e.g. *Ann. Rep.* (1877, 1878); C.C.A.L.S., ZHI 17, p. 694; ZHI 18, pp. 88–9; ZHI 19, p. 664.

12 C.C.A.L.S., ZHI 16 (28 Nov. 1865, 30 Jan. 1866, 29 Jan., 2 Apr., 4 June, 6 Aug. 1867); ZHI 17, pp. 4, 24, 47; Mumford, *Infirmary*, 11–12.

13 Below, this chapter: Isolation Hospitals.

14 C.C.A.L.S., ZHI 20, pp. 387, 391–6, 401, 441.

15 Mumford, *Infirmary*, 33; *Ann. Rep.* (1902).

16 C.C.A.L.S., ZHI 16 (29 Nov., 19 Dec. 1859); Mumford, *Infirmary*, 11.

17 Mumford, *Infirmary*, 12; *Ann. Rep.* (1892).

18 Mumford, *Infirmary*, 13; C.C.A.L.S., ZHI 21, pp. 307, 341–2, 356, 362–4.

19 H. C. Burdett, *Hosps. and Asylums of World*, iv. 197, 212; cf. ibid. 108, 115, 136, 144, 166, 168, 173, 179, 181, 183, 185, 194.

FIG. 29. *Chester Royal Infirmary, 1964: wards of 1913 and* (right) *1761 building*

over £30,000, and a new wing, designed by W. T. Lockwood in consultation with Paul Waterhouse, was opened by George V in 1914. It was named after the principal benefactor, Albert Wood. Refurbishment of the older buildings continued until 1917.[1] The Humberston wing was enlarged in 1923 and another new block was opened in 1931.[2] By 1939 there were 225 beds.[3]

Running costs became a major problem after *c.* 1870, growing slowly from under £3,000 a year to £7,000 by 1914, then accelerating to over £20,000 by 1920, £40,000 by 1940, and £90,000 in 1947. Subscriptions (which were more or less static after 1880), investment income, and payments for services were not meeting expenditure even in the 1870s, and the infirmary increasingly depended on private gifts and charitable fund-raising. From 1883 the 1st and 2nd dukes of Westminster gave usually £500 a year from visitors' entrance fees at Eaton Hall; annual church collections, disappointing *c.* 1860, revived from 1871 with the national Hospital Sunday campaign and raised *c.* £400 a year; and the Chester and District Working Men's Hospital Saturday Association (part of another national organization) was formed in 1886 to collect weekly payments from working men.[4] After 1918, as throughout the voluntary hospital sector, new methods of financing were adopted: the 'Oxford scheme' of weekly insurance payments was introduced in 1922,[5] and means-tested fees for non-members of the scheme followed in 1931, when the ticket system was finally abandoned. The financial saviour of the infirmary,

however, was the Deeside Voluntary Hospital Committee, set up in 1929 to collect employees' weekly contributions, which were deducted from pay and augmented by their employers. By 1938 the Deeside scheme had 55,000 members and an annual income of £23,500. Even so, when the infirmary was brought into the new National Health Service in 1948 it was running an annual deficit of £20,000 and selling its investments.[6] The infirmary continued as part of the N.H.S. until it was closed in 1994.[7]

CITY HOSPITAL (FORMER WORKHOUSE)

Patients from the workhouse on the Roodee were treated by the infirmary's physicians and surgeons from 1759,[8] and from 1784 the guardians of the poor were regular subscribers to the infirmary.[9] By 1830 they were paying £40 a year, a sum which Dr. Cumming of the infirmary thought should be increased to £150 to cover 1,500 cases a year.[10] By the 1850s others were being treated by the poor-law union's own medical officer.[11] From 1864 or 1865 all sick paupers were attended by him, and the guardians stopped using the infirmary's out-patient service.[12] Hospital wards with 247 beds were provided at the new workhouse built in Hoole Lane in the late 1870s.[13] The Local Government Act of 1929 transferred the workhouse to city council control, under which the hospital was at first named St. James's and later the City Hospital. In 1947 all the workhouse buildings were made over to the hospital.[14] They were demolished after the N.H.S. closed the hospital in 1991.[15]

---

1 Mumford, *Infirmary*, 13; C.C.A.L.S., ZHI 21, pp. 391, 398, 446, 456, 498; ZHI 22, pp. 49, 60–1, 131–2.

2 Mumford, *Infirmary*, 14; C.C.A.L.S., ZHI 23, p. 326.

3 *Hosps. Year-Bk.* (1940), 206.

4 *Ann. Rep.* (1856–1947).

5 Cf. *V.C.H. Oxon.* iv. 361.

6 C.C.A.L.S., ZHI 22, p. 502; ZHI 23, p. 234, loose sheet at pp. 343–4; ZHI 30 (23 Apr. 1948); *Hosps. Year-Bk.* (1940), 291.

7 Below, this chapter: National Health Service.

8 C.C.A.L.S., ZHI 51, f. 1; ZCR 60/2/43, f. 11.

9 Above, this chapter: Chester Royal Infirmary.

10 C.C.A.L.S., ZHI 319, p. 4.

11 *Return of Medical Provision in Poor-Law Workhouses*, H.C. 230, pp. 124–5 (1857–8), xlix (1).

12 *Ann. Rep. of General Infirmary* (1864/5).

13 C.C.A.L.S., ZTRU 36; *Return of Workhouse Hosps.* H.C. 0.120, p. 13 (1890–1), lxviii.

14 K. C. White, 'Chester City Hosp.' (TS. [1983] at C.H.H.), 2.

15 C.P.S., City Hospital; below, this chapter: National Health Service.

MATERNITY CARE

The main gap in the infirmary's medical provision was maternity care, deliberately so, because of the fear of cross-infection. In 1798 Dr. Griffith Rowland founded the Benevolent Institution as a subscription charity to provide midwives for poor women in Chester. Rowland acted alone as its surgeon until 1812; thereafter a panel of five or more gave their services free. The Institution was managed by a ladies' committee and employed a matron and four midwives. The income from annual subscriptions was £48 in 1799 and £140 c. 1820.[1] At first the midwives worked from their own homes, but in 1899 the duke of Westminster adapted a house in Grosvenor Street as a nurses' home. Then or a little later it also had two maternity beds. In 1904 the Institution was approved for training.[2] In 1897 the midwives attended 402 confinements.[3] After the National Insurance Act of 1911 gave maternity benefit to all insured women, the Institution was soon treating more patients privately than on subscribers' tickets. The ticket system had been dropped by 1920.[4]

The growing demand after the First World War for in-patient maternity care led the Institution to convert premises at no. 16 Whitefriars into an eight-bed maternity hospital, which opened in 1925; at the same time the Institution merged with the Chester District Nursing Association.[5] In 1937 a more extensive midwifery service was begun by a joint committee of the D.N.A. and the city council. The maternity hospital closed in 1938 after maternity wards were opened at the City Hospital,[6] and the home nursing service was taken over by the city council in 1948.[7]

OTHER NURSING

District nursing in the late 19th century was provided both by the infirmary and by the Chester Diocesan Deaconess Institution, established in 1869. The latter changed its name in 1900 to the Chester District Nursing Association.[8] In the early 20th century a lady superintendent and five district nurses, working from no. 10 Water Tower Street and supported by subscriptions and donations from individuals, churches, and charities, treated c. 1,000 cases and made over 20,000 visits a year. The D.N.A. united with the Benevolent Institution in 1925,[9] and continued in existence there-

after as a charitable organization, renamed the Chester Sick Poor Fund in 1953.[10]

ISOLATION HOSPITALS

Although the infirmary treated smallpox and other infectious diseases, it refused in 1832 and 1849 to take in cholera patients.[11] Temporary cholera hospitals were built on the land which became Grosvenor Park during the outbreak of 1866, and at Infirmary field in 1892.[12]

The city council opened its own isolation hospital on the south side of Sealand Road almost at the city boundary in 1899 to meet its statutory obligation to provide treatment for patients with certain notifiable infectious diseases, among which scarlet fever, diphtheria, and typhoid were the most common. The hospital was designed by Harry Beswick with an administration block and four separate pavilion wards, accommodating 46 patients in all. It cost £21,300. In 1900 the corrugated-iron buildings at Infirmary field were moved to an even more remote site off Bumper's Lane, south of the isolation hospital, and arranged as two wards for up to 12 smallpox patients.[13] Besides cases from the city, the hospital took in patients paid for by neighbouring local authorities as well as some private referrals from further afield, though it was reluctant to make permanent arrangements which reserved a fixed number of beds for the use of other authorities except after 1905 for the Tarvin, Malpas, and Tarporley joint hospital board.[14] The hospital usually had between 10 and 20 patients at any one time, and coped with more serious outbreaks by putting up temporary accommodation. When smallpox infected 67 people in 1903, for example, the council's public health committee put up tents near the smallpox wards. Its other measures including opening vaccination points in Lower Bridge Street and Saltney, closing schools in Handbridge, and cancelling or postponing some of the regular summer entertainments, and fatalities were restricted to just six. In 1909 tents were again used for an outbreak of scarlet fever.[15] The hospital took tuberculosis patients from 1914 under an arrangement with the county council, but stopped doing so in 1938 when the Cheshire Joint Sanatorium was enlarged.[16] The smallpox wards, virtually disused after 1903, housed German prisoners of war in 1918–19.[17] As part of the changes leading up to the creation of the National Health Service, the isola-

1 Hemingway, *Hist. Chester*, ii. 211, 364–6; C.C.A.L.S., ZD/DNA 1; ZD/DNA 2/1.

2 C.C.A.L.S., ZD/DNA 3; *Chester Courant*, 15 Mar. 1899.

3 C.C.A.L.S., ZD/DNA 5.

4 Ibid. ZD/DNA 11, 15.

5 Ibid. ZD/DNA 4/3; ZD/DNA 18–19, 51.

6 Ibid. ZD/DNA 63, pp. 4–5; ZD/DNA 64, p. 4.

7 Ibid. ZD/DNA 73, pp. 2–3.

8 *Burdett's Hosps. and Charities* (1900), 668; C.C.A.L.S., ZD/DNA 73, p. 2.   9 C.C.A.L.S., ZD/DNA 28, 50.

10 Char. Com. file 214343.

11 C.C.A.L.S., ZHI 13 (3 July 1832); ZHI 15 (21 Aug. 1849).

12 *Ann. Rep. of Chester Infirmary* (1866, 1894).

13 *Annual Rep. of Medical Officer of Health* (1897), 6; (1898), 4; (1900), 4–5: copies in C.C.A.L.S., ZDH 2/2; *Chester City Cl. Mins.* 1898/9, 539–40, 595; 1899/1900, 51, 140, 264–5, 317, 321–2, 486; 1900/1, 178, 231.

14 *Chester City Cl. Mins.* 1898/9, 531; 1899/1900, 45–6, 96, 139, 143, 321; 1901/2, 471–3; 1903/4, 316–18; 1904/5, 985, 992–3; 1931/2, 698; 1934/5, 87; 1937/8, 687.

15 Ibid. 1902/3, 625–6, 628–30, 636, 639, 743, 842–3, 1054; 1908/9, 678; *passim* via indexed refs. to isolation hospital.

16 Ibid. 1914/15, 327–8; 1937/8, 686, 1009.

17 Ibid. 1917/18, 433, 465; 1918/19, 315.

tion hospital was closed in 1947 and patients were treated at Clatterbridge Hospital on Wirral until isolation wards were opened at the City Hospital. The buildings at Sealand Road were made over to the city council's public assistance committee and reopened in 1948 as an old people's home, Sealand House.[1]

PSYCHIATRIC CARE

There were two private madhouses in Foregate Street in 1787 but none was licensed thereafter.[2] A county lunatic asylum was opened in 1829 under the legislation of 1828.[3] The magistrates bought a 10-a. site, later enlarged to 55 a., on elevated ground west of Liverpool Road on the boundary of the city and Bache. The asylum was designed by William Cole junior and built in red brick with simple stone dressings to a conventional neo-classical design. It was mainly of two storeys with full-height basements and had a long range of 21 bays facing Liverpool Road and shorter return wings to the rear at each end. The main range consisted of a pedimented central block of five bays and an extra storey, flanking wings of five bays, and three-bay end pavilions, projecting by one bay and with canted full-height bays on their side elevations. The basements of the main range were occupied by the kitchen, stores, laundry, brewhouse, and bakehouse. In the central block there were offices for the medical superintendent, matron, and other staff on the ground floor; the committee room, doubling as the chapel, and bedrooms for the senior staff on the first floor; and servants' bedrooms on the second floor. The rest of the building accommodated 20 private patients and 70 paupers, and allowed for segregation by class and sex. Women occupied the wings on the north, men those on the south. On each side the private patients had bedrooms in the ground floor of the main range, with a gallery to the rear commanding views over the countryside to the west. The most disturbed patients were in the basements of the return ranges, and other paupers on the first floor above them. Each category of inmates had a separate 'airing ground' complete with a covered walk for use in poor weather. The corner pavilions were taken up by day rooms with bay windows, bathrooms, and warders' offices, the last having internal windows into the day rooms as well as external ones looking over the airing grounds.[4] In 1853, following an

unfavourable report by the Lunacy Commissioners, the first resident medical superintendent was appointed; in 1854 he abolished mechanical restraint and allowed most patients to work, play games, and go for walks.[5] The number of patients grew almost continuously until the 1960s, passing 500 in the 1860s, 1,000 c. 1910, 1,500 in the 1920s, and reaching almost 2,000 in the 1930s. The staff similarly increased from 37 in 1848 to 255 (including 15 medical staff) in 1938.[6]

Building kept pace with the growth in numbers.[7] North and south wings accommodating 80 patients were added to the original block in 1849, and two east wings containing day rooms in the 1870s. All were of two storeys. Two detached ward blocks, designed by T. M. Penson with Gothic detailing, were built between 1857 and 1862 to the west. The chapel was moved before 1849 to the upper floor of a short wing added on the west. A free-standing chapel, in Early English style, was completed west of the original block in 1856 and survived in 2000. It has a short chancel, a nave of six bays, and north and south porches, and is in brick with stone dressings and slate roofs.

A complete new hospital with five ward blocks accommodating 404 men was built between 1895 and 1898 north of the original asylum to designs by Grayson and Ould, and on its completion the earlier wards were given over to women patients. The county architect, Harry Beswick, designed a block for epileptic patients (completed 1912), a 440-bed infirmary annexe at the north end of the site (1915), and a new isolation hospital at the south end (1916, later demolished). A nurses' home was built in 1938.

The name of the asylum was changed to the County Mental Hospital in 1921, Upton Mental Hospital when it joined the N.H.S. in 1948, and Deva Hospital in 1950.[8] In 1960 it acquired a former military hospital a mile up the road at Moston as a 370-bed annexe.[9] The capacity of the hospital was reduced drastically from 1964 as successive concepts of 'care in the community' were substituted for hospitalization, and by 1991 it had only 473 beds.[10]

OTHER DISPENSARIES

A dispensary for skin complaints was established in 1889 at rented premises in City Walls Road near the infirmary. It was funded mainly by subscribers and

1 *Chester City Cl. Mins.* 1945/6, 78, 522; 1946/7, 264; 1947/9, 299.

2 *Broster's Dir. Chester* (1787), 89, 94; *Return of Houses Licensed for Lunatics*, H.C. 267, p. 1 (1819), xvii.

3 *V.C.H. Ches.* ii. 72.

4 Hemingway, *Hist. Chester*, ii. 226–9 (the plan which should face p. 229 is in some copies misplaced facing p. 205); *Return of Lunatic Asylums and Licensed Houses*, H.C. 299, pp. 2–3 (1857–8), xlix (1).

5 *Rep. of Ches. Lunatic Asylum* (1855), pp. 9–10: copy in C.C.A.L.S., ZHW 53; ibid. ZCR 241/1.

6 *Rep. of Ches. Lunatic Asylum* (1848, 1858, 1868, 1878): C.C.A.L.S., ZHW 49, 56, 63, 68; *Burdett's Hosp. Annual* (1890),

313; *Burdett's Hosps. and Charities* (1900), 583; (1910), 547; (1920), 614; (1930), 522; *Hosps. Year-Bk.* (1940), 174.

7 O.S. Map 1/2,500, Ches. XXXVIII.7 (1880, 1899, 1911, and 1938 edns.); archit. description based on I. H. Goodall, 'Historic Bldgs. Rep.: Countess of Chester Hosp.' for R.C.H.M.E. (TS. 1993 in possn. of V.C.H.); thanks are offered to Dr. Goodall for a copy of the rep.

8 Inf. from Deva Hosp. Hist. Group (Ms. Jan Hore).

9 B. A. Wall, *A World of its Own: A Personal Acct. of Chester's Psychiatric Hosps., 1829–1976*, 56, 60–9.

10 *Hosps. Year Bk.* (1960), 304; (1970), 294; *Hosps. and Health Services Year Bk.* (1984), 346–7; later edns. to (1991); *Chester Observer*, suppl. Sept. 1979 (C.C.A.L.S., ZCR 639/1).

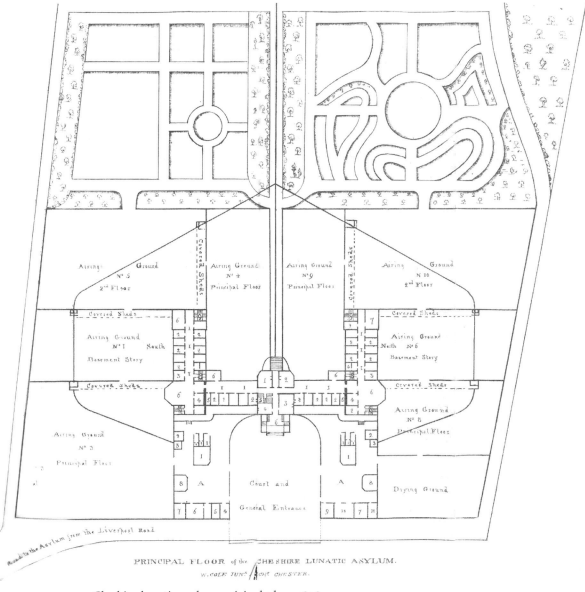

FIG. 30. *Cheshire lunatic asylum, original plan, 1828*

survived until national health insurance was introduced in 1912; it provided free treatment to an average
of over 800 patients a year on an income rarely more
than £100.[1] There was a Homoeopathic Institution in
Lower Bridge Street in 1855,[2] and a free homoeopathic
dispensary was founded by Edward Thomas (d. 1906)
in Pepper Street in 1878. He and his son Dr. Edward
Haynes-Thomas ran it until *c.* 1912. It was supported
by subscribers and in 1889 treated 248 patients on an
income of £50.[3]

NATIONAL HEALTH SERVICE

Plans to co-ordinate the work of the Royal Infirmary
and the City Hospital were being made from 1929,[4]

and by 1945 they were working closely together under
the auspices of the wartime Emergency Medical
Service.[5] On the formation of the National Health
Service in 1948, they were grouped with smaller
hospitals at Boughton Heath (the former Tarvin
poor-law union workhouse), Ellesmere Port, and
Runcorn under the Chester and District hospital
management committee (H.M.C.). The mental hospital had its own H.M.C. Both came under Liverpool
regional board and were united as West Cheshire
H.M.C. in 1965. They were reorganized in 1974
within Cheshire area health authority and in 1982
came under Chester health authority, in Mersey
region, which ran all the health services within the

1 *Burdett's Hosps. and Charities* (1900), 514; (1910), 486;
(1920), 504; C.C.A.L.S., ZCR 131/1 (includes *Ann. Rep.* for
1892–1911).

2 *Slater's Dir. Ches.* (1855), 41.

3 *11th Ann. Rep. of Chester Free Homoeopathic Dispensary.*
copy in possn. of Miss M. G. Haynes-Thomas, Chester, who is

warmly thanked for making it available; *Chester Chron.* 29 Dec.
1906, 6 Jan. 1930; inf. from Miss Haynes-Thomas.

4 Mumford, *Infirmary*, 14; C.C.A.L.S., ZD/DNA 55, p. 6;
ZD/DNA 56, p. 4.

5 Ministry of Health Hosp. Surv., *Hosp. Services of North-
Western Area* (H.M.S.O. 1945), 81–2, 168–9.

local authority districts of Chester and most of Ellesmere Port.[1]

After 1948 the Royal Infirmary specialized in surgery and out-patients, and the City Hospital in chronic illness, and chest, maternity, paediatric, and general medical cases, a division foreshadowed by their strengths before nationalization.[2] Pre-war plans for the expansion of the infirmary were eventually revived and a large out-patient and casualty department was opened on Infirmary field in 1963.[3] After the creation of the West Cheshire H.M.C., it was decided in 1968 to concentrate all the district's hospital services at the Liverpool Road site (hitherto the county mental hospital), which in anticipation was renamed West Cheshire Hospital.[4] The maternity unit

was transferred from the City Hospital to a new building at the south end of the site in 1971.[5] A new general wing was opened in 1983, when several departments moved from the infirmary, and the City Hospital was left as a 120-bed geriatric unit.[6] The City Hospital closed entirely in 1991 when geriatric care was moved, and the rest of the departments still at the infirmary moved to Liverpool Road in 1994. West Cheshire Hospital was renamed the Countess of Chester Hospital in 1984.[7]

PRIVATE HOSPITAL

A private hospital, the Grosvenor Nuffield, was opened in Wrexham Road with 30 beds in 1975 and was enlarged in 1984 to accommodate 40 beds.[8]

CHARITIES FOR THE POOR

Endowed charities for the poor in Chester, as in other large corporate towns, fell into two main groups: those controlled by the corporation and those in the hands of the individual parishes. The municipal charities were much more valuable but were largely restricted to the families of freemen of the city; the parochial charities were more widely available but tended to provide more limited benefits.

MUNICIPAL CHARITIES

From the later 16th century the Assembly controlled a growing number of charities, many founded to benefit freemen or their families, and some of which also provided for payments to the mayor, aldermen, or officers, or endowed a civic feast. At the outbreak of the Civil War the city spent over £2,000 of the capital sums belonging to one particular type, the loan charities, on defensive works and munitions. A new wave of benefactions began in the late 1650s and continued into the early 18th century, a period in which the Assembly also took over the endowment of St. Giles's hospital (1660) and gained full control of St. John's hospital (1702). Its management of the charities in the 18th century was at best lax and in some respects clearly corrupt. The corporation kept no separate accounts for the municipal charities, but merged their income in its general funds, from which it diverted a great deal to non-charitable purposes. St. John's hospital, by far the richest charity, was the

most severely plundered. In addition the corporation sold what were supposed to be permanent rent-charges in order to pay its debts, let charity property to aldermen and councilmen on long leases at low rents, and from the 1740s connived at the craft guilds' misapplication of the Owen Jones charity. By the late 1820s the city was receiving over £1,400 a year from charity endowments, and held a further £1,100 capital for the loan charities, but was spending little over £600 a year on charitable purposes.[9]

With the support of several of the parish vestries, interested in keeping poor rates down, a local solicitor, John Faulkner the younger, began a suit against the Assembly in 1829.[10] It was overtaken by the Municipal Corporations Act, 1835, which ended corporation control of the charities,[11] and by a Chancery order of 1837, which created the independent Chester Municipal Charities Trustees and assigned them a mortgage on corporation property which was sufficient to cover the outgoings of the charities reliant upon capital sums held by the corporation. In 1874 one of the trustees, the younger William Brown, nephew and namesake of the first chairman, argued that the original terms of many charities were unsuited to contemporary needs, and instead favoured pensions 'of respectable amount, subject to annual reappointment, conditional upon good behaviour', provisions which were adopted for several of them.[12] The gownsmen charities and three others were united and their purposes altered in 1892;

1 *Hosps. Year Bk.* (1950/1, 1960, 1970); *Hosps. and Health Services Year Bk.* (1984).

2 *Hosp. Services of NW.* 81–2, 168–9; *Hosps. Year Bk.* (1950/1), 715; Mumford, *Infirmary*, 26, 36.

3 *Hosp. Services of NW.* 81; Mumford, *Infirmary*, 35; inscr. on bldg.

4 C.H.H., newspaper cuttings, iii. 61 (5 Jan. 1968).

5 *Ches. Observer*, 22 Oct. 1971.

6 White, 'Chester City Hosp.' 4; M. Brown, 'Reorganisation of Chester Health District' (TS. 1981 at C.H.H.), 3–4, 8, 10.

7 C.C.A.L.S., TS. list of hospital recs.; C.H.H., newspaper

cuttings, xxxii. 170, 172 (28 Nov. 1991).

8 *Hosps. and Health Services Year Bk.* (1984), 530; (1986), 457; inf. from hospital.

9 *31st Rep. Com. Char.* 343–87; details of individual chars. below, this chapter.   10 C.C.A.L.S., P 51/13/5.

11 5 & 6 Wm. IV, c. 76, s. 71.

12 *Hist. Municipal Chars. of Chester, 1837–75* (printed for trustees, 1875), pp. iii, 5, 7, 9, 34–8 (copy at C.H.H.); C.C.A.L.S., ZD/CT 1, *passim*; ZCR 712/4/1–2; *Browns and Chester: Portrait of a Shop, 1780–1946*, ed. H. D. Willcock, 127–8.

FIG. 31. *St. John's hospital seal, 1730*

the maximum pension payable was raised in 1901 to 12*s.* a week; and in 1929 the range of benefits available was widened, particularly to cover medical assistance.[1]

Under a Scheme of 1976 the Municipal Charities, united with those of Maria Grey Egerton, George Cotgreave, and Elizabeth Wilding, were divided into an almshouse charity (St. John's hospital, Green and Wardell's, and Wilding's) and a relief in need charity (all the rest except Owen Jones's). Five eighths of the income of Owen Jones's was added to the relief in need charity, the rest going to educational purposes. In 1994 the income of the almshouse charity was *c.* £60,000, and of the relief in need charity *c.* £50,000, intended first for resident or formerly resident freemen or their widows, and secondly for other residents.[2]

Almshouses

St. Giles's Hospital St. Giles's leper hospital, established at Spital Boughton east of the city in the 12th

century, was demolished by Chester's royalist garrison in 1643, and the site and endowments were granted to the corporation in 1660. Its history is treated elsewhere.[3] The hospital was not rebuilt and its revenues were united with those of St. John's hospital.[4]

St. John's Hospital St. John's hospital outside the Northgate was founded in the 1190s for 13 poor men.[5] It, too, was destroyed during the Civil War siege, but was rebuilt after the Restoration. The city charter of 1685 gave the reversion of the hospital wardenship to the corporation, which came into possession in 1703 and applied the surplus revenues to maintain Sir Thomas Smith's almshouses, the house of correction, and Northgate gaol. The corporation rebuilt the hospital complex in 1715–17 with a rear courtyard which included six one-storeyed almshouses for women.[6] The almswomen shared £30 a year under the will of Alderman Joseph Crewe, proved 1801.[7] Mismanagement greatly reduced the value of the hospital's rents; by 1836 they were worth £600 a year, of which only £85 was spent on the almspeople, the rest being carried to the corporation's general account as it had been since *c.* 1762.[8] An action at law to establish what estates belonged to the hospital and to vest them in the Municipal Charities Trustees was begun in 1838 but not completed until a Chancery Scheme, evidently of 1852, ordered the almshouses to be rebuilt to house 13 paupers who received 10*s.* a week each.[9] As rebuilt in 1854 the almshouses each included a sitting room, bedroom, and scullery (Fig. 32, p. 60).[10] A Charity Commission Scheme of 1892 assigned the substantial surplus to pay pensions to other townspeople.[11] Under a Scheme of 1976 the hospital, still supporting 13 almshouses, was absorbed by the Chester Municipal Almshouse Charity,[12] and the almshouses, around a courtyard behind the Blue Coat school, remained in use in 2000.

Sir Thomas Smith's Almshouses Almshouses were established under the will of Roger Smith, proved 1508, who left a house in Commonhall Lane (later Street) primarily for the use of aldermen or common councilmen or their widows.[13] In 1509 his brother Sir Thomas Smith and the other executors agreed instead to build six almshouses on land in the same lane given by the corporation. Failing nomination by the mayor, the almspeople were to be appointed by the prioress of St. Mary's nunnery. The endowment

1 C.C.A.L.S., ZDT 3/3, 5, 8; below, this section: Gownsmen.

2 Char. Com. file 218916.

3 *V.C.H. Ches.* iii. 178–80; below, Sites and Remains of Medieval Religious Houses: Hospital of St. Giles.

4 *31st Rep. Com. Char.* 345–6.

5 Its history is treated in *V.C.H. Ches.* iii. 180–3.

6 *31st Rep. Com. Char.* 345–6; below, Sites and Remains of Medieval Religious Houses: Hospital of St. John the Baptist.

7 *31st Rep. Com. Char.* 366; *Char. Digest Ches. 1862–3*, 2–3.

8 *31st Rep. Com. Char.* 347–54.

9 C.C.A.L.S., ZCR 36/33, 130; ZD/CT 1 (22 July 1846, 5 Apr., 20 July 1847, 22 Mar. 1848, 26 Jan. 1852); *Hist. Mun. Chars.* 13–15; *P. & G. Dir. Chester* (1871), 13.

10 *White's Dir. Ches.* (1860), 96; *Kelly's Dir. Ches.* (1906), 215.

11 C.C.A.L.S., ZDT 3/3.

12 Above, this chapter: Municipal Charities (intro.).

13 *V.C.H. Ches.* iii. 183–4; P.R.O., PROB 11/16, f. 68.

FIG. 32. *St. John's hospital almshouses*

provided £8 a year as stipends. In 1510 the executors were licensed to convert the almshouses into a chantry and hospital dedicated to St. Ursula. The hospital survived the dissolution of the chantries in 1547 as almshouses. In 1836 the charity housed six freemen's widows, who each received 6s. 8d. a quarter.[1] There were no funds for repairs to the buildings, which eventually became unfit for use, and vacancies among the six places had to be left unfilled. A plan to rebuild them was abandoned, and under a Charity Commission Scheme of 1871 the Municipal Charities Trustees sold the building (which was later demolished), invested the proceeds in consols, and applied the income along with the other municipal charities.[2]

Harvie's Almshouses   Harvie's almshouses originated in Robert Harvie's gift to Chester corporation in 1662 of a house in Claverton Lane (later Duke Street) for six almspeople chosen by lot, with a preference for freemen. He also left a share in the Dee Bridge waterworks to provide income for repairs and to pay stipends of 40s. a year, with a gown and badge every third year. Any residue after other payments to members of the corporation went to the poor of St. Olave's parish. The corporation exchanged the waterworks share in 1692 for an annuity of £6 payable to the almsmen by the (Old) Chester Waterworks Company, which thereafter ran the charity. From 1692 there was thus no revenue specifically assigned to maintain the almshouses, which were described as 'ruinous' in 1836 and as 'much dilapidated' in 1850;[3] they were none the less evidently kept in some sort of repair (Fig. 33). They were transferred to the Municipal Charities Trustees in 1888.[4] Under a

Scheme of 1892 vacancies were left unfilled, the building was sold and later demolished, and the income was diverted to a pension.[5]

Grosvenor Almshouses   The Grosvenor almshouses in New Crane Street originated in 1820 when Robert, Earl Grosvenor, bought 12 cottages for the use of aged freemen and provided pensions of 2s. 6d. a week each. Non-freemen were admitted from 1892. About 1907 the cottages were replaced by six new houses in Hugh Street, Handbridge, and the weekly pension (5s. since 1874) was raised to 10s.[6]

Green and Wardell's Almshouses   Green and Wardell's charity as restructured after 1858 also provided almshouses.[7]

Loan Charities

Sir Thomas White's   In 1566 Sir Thomas White left property to Bristol corporation, among other purposes to pay £104 by annual turns to Chester and 23 other towns. In each town the money was to be loaned interest-free to four young freemen, preferably clothiers, at £25 apiece. The loans were to be repaid after 10 years, when the capital would be available for new loans.[8] The beneficiaries were not allowed to retail ale or beer, and in 1661 transgressors in Chester were ordered to repay their loans.[9] Eleven payments of £104 were received by Chester corporation between 1566 and 1836, theoretically providing 44 recirculatable loans of £25, but in fact the corporation put much of the capital to other uses. By the 18th century loans were rare; there were only three after 1748, the last in 1760.[10] In 1838 the Municipal Charities Trustees sued the corporation for 11 payments of £100.[11] Under a

1 *31st Rep. Com. Char.* 381–2; C.C.A.L.S., ZCHC 12.
2 *Hist. Mun. Chars.* 11–12, 56–7; *Gresty and Burghall's Chester Guide* [1867], 76; below, this section: Gownsmen.
3 *31st Rep. Com. Char.* 362–4; *Bagshaw's Dir. Ches.* (1850), 69, 83–4; C.C.A.L.S., ZCR 300/1, no. 33; ZCHC 5.
4 C.C.A.L.S., ZDT 3/62.
5 Ibid. ZDT 3/3.

6 3 *Sheaf*, xviii, p. 79; *Kelly's Dir. Ches.* (1906), 216, 234.
7 Below, this section: Other Municipal Charities.
8 *31st Rep. Com. Char.* 371–2.
9 C.C.A.L.S., ZAB 2, f. 131.
10 Ibid. ZCHC 14; *31st Rep. Com. Char.* 372–3.
11 *Report of Finance Cttee. as to Chars. laid before [Chester] Town Cl.* (1839), 9–11 (copy in C.C.A.L.S., ZCR 600/1).

FIG. 33. *Harvie's almshouses, awaiting demolition, 1903*

Chancery Scheme of *c.* 1841 loans of £25, £50, £75, and £100 on similar terms to those originally specified were made available to freemen under the age of 35. Almost £550 was out on such loans in 1862.[1]

The Offley Brothers' Three loan charities were established by the Offley brothers, wealthy Londoners from a family originating in Chester. Hugh Offley by will proved 1594 left £200 to be lent to four young men (two merchants and two retailers) for three years in sums of £50, each paying 30*s.* annual interest which was to be spent on the poor and other objects. Robert Offley by will proved 1596 gave £600 to be lent in sums of £25 to 24 young men over the age of 24, half of them former apprentices in the city and all chosen by lot, to enable them to set up in business. Their interest payments of 10*s.* a year were distributed partly in sums of 10*s.* to 20 poor freemen. William Offley by will proved 1600 left £300 to be lent to 12 young freemen, former apprentices, in sums of £25 each, repayable after five years with 14*s.* annual interest, which was mainly distributed in weekly doles of 2*d.* cash and 1*d.* in bread to 12 poor householders nominated by each of the nine city parishes in rotation.[2] All three Offley loan charities were applied irregularly after 1621 and ceased altogether when the capital out on loan was called in by the Assembly in 1642–3 and spent defending the city.[3]

Other Loan Charities Alderman Fulk Aldersey by will effective 1611 left £200 for loans of £25 each to eight former Chester apprentices, to be repaid after seven years, paying 25*s.* a year interest, mainly for distribution at the rate of 13*s.* 4*d.* to each of the nine city parishes. Regular payments were made between 1613 and 1643, when the capital was spent on defence.[4]

Dame Elizabeth Booth, a widow of Bath, gave £400 in 1619 for loans of £20 each to 20 freemen for four years. The interest payments at 5 per cent were divided among the poor of several parishes in Cheshire and Lancashire, 5*s.* going to St. John's hospital almshouses. Although the capital was called in and spent on defence during the siege of Chester, the corporation continued to dispense £17 15*s.* a year towards the objects of the charity, including 5*s.* for St. John's hospital.[5]

Bequests to the corporation to lend to manufacturers willing to give work to the poor included 200 marks by Ralph Worsley (effective 1575), £3 6*s.* 8*d.* annual interest by Hugh Atwyll (date unknown), and £200 by John Vernon (will proved 1617). Half of Worsley's bequest was lost by 1608, Worsley's and Vernon's were last used for loans in 1623,[6] and all three sums were spent on defence in 1642–3 and not replaced.[7]

Gownsmen

Besides £200 for his loan charity John Vernon by will proved 1617 left £800 to buy land worth £50 a year to

1 *Char. Digest Ches. 1862–3*, 2–3; *Hist. Mun. Chars.* 12, 58–62; C.C.A.L.S., ZCR 712/2/1.
2 *31st Rep. Com. Char.* 383–6; P.R.O., PROB 11/84, ff. 294v.–300v. at 297v.; PROB 11/87, ff. 230–7 at 231–2; PROB 11/96, ff. 300v.–303v. at 301–2; 3 *Sheaf,* xv, pp. 28–9.
3 *31st Rep. Com. Char.* 387.

4 Ibid. 367–8.
5 Ibid. 362; *Char. Digest Ches. 1862–3*, 2–3; C.C.A.L.S., ZDT 3/3.
6 C.C.A.L.S., ZAF 11/106–10; ZCHC 15; 3 *Sheaf,* xiv, pp. 58–9.
7 *31st Rep. Com. Char.* 386–7.

FIG. 34. *John Vernon's charity badge*

benefit the poor. The Assembly spent the £1,000 on an estate at Guilden Sutton. After endowing a sermon and other purposes, £40 of the annual income was given in quarterly payments of 20s. each to 10 poor church-going guildsmen aged over 60 and chosen by lot. Every three years they received a gown embroidered on the sleeve with Vernon's name, giving rise to the name gownsmen.[1]

The terms of Vernon's will were adopted by others, and the corporation managed the gown charities together, keeping a common list of applicants by 1709.[2] Gownsmen were elected for life but could be removed for misconduct. Eventually the number of company or lot gownsmen, named after their principal qualification or the manner of their election, reached 29. There were also nine gift gownsmen, freemen not chosen by lot or required to be members of a guild. All received a gown bearing the donor's badge. By 1836 the gowns were worn only on special occasions, and by 1875 the surviving badges had been retrieved by the Municipal Charities Trustees.[3]

Two gift gowns were endowed from an £8 rent-charge left by Richard King (will proved 1667); six lot

gowns from £650 left by Richard Bird (d. 1681); and four lot gowns from the Star Inn and other property left by Richard Harrison (will proved 1686). Thomas Williams (will proved 1736), Richard Sneyd (will proved 1774), Charles Boswell (1784), Richard Ledsham (will proved 1784), John Scasebrick (1785), Henry Hesketh (1787), and Joseph Crewe (will proved 1801) gave sums between £100 and £120 to provide for one lot gown each.[4] Two more lot gowns were created under the wills of Thomas Rathbone (dated 1815) and Thomas Bradford (proved 1821), each with an endowment of £120.[5] By will proved 1810 Robert Jones, a shoemaker, left £100 for a gift gownsman from his own trade.[6] Other bequests of £100 or £120 increased the stipends of the 14 senior lot gownsmen by 20s. each: Thomas Cotgreave (will proved 1791) for the five oldest; James Broadhurst (will proved 1798) for the next four; and John Jones (will dated 1822) for the next five.[7] Under a Scheme of 1892 the gownsmen charities and those of Richard Bavand, William Lewis, and Sir Thomas Smith were to be spent instead at the trustees' discretion on medical aid, provident clubs, apprenticeships, emigration, reading rooms, museums, or grants in money or kind.[8]

Owen Jones's Charity

Owen Jones, a wealthy Chester butcher originally from Soughton (Flints.), by will proved 1659 left £200 and land in Denbighshire and Cheshire to benefit the poor members of every one of Chester's craft guilds in rotation.[9] The initial income was £27 a year, of which £20 was available for distribution. Part of the endowment was invested in buying the Bridgegate tolls in 1667 as a source of future revenue, but after 1744 the charity derived far greater wealth from royalties on the lead mines newly opened on its 83 a. at Minera (Denb.). Between 1761 and 1779 the mines produced almost £13,000 in royalties, but difficulties in draining the mines hindered their exploitation after the 1780s and they were finally abandoned in 1824. The royalties were invested, principally by advancing a capital sum of £10,640 to the corporation on a 4 per cent mortgage, thus providing an annual income for the charity of £425 12s. The mayor and sheriffs as trustees delegated their powers to the aldermen and stewards of the guilds, who by the 1780s were dividing the proceeds indiscriminately among their members, whether poor or rich, as each guild came round in rotation. Admission to the guilds was closely regulated, some

1 *31st Rep. Com. Char.* 373–5; P.R.O., PROB 11/129, ff. 68–80AV. at 76v.–78v.
2 C.C.A.L.S., ZAB 3, f. 175 and v.; ZAF 48A/3; ZAF 48C/54; ZAF 48D/18; ZAF 49A/24; ZAF 49C/9.
3 *31st Rep. Com. Char.* 375, 377; *Hist. Mun. Chars.* pp. 11, xli–lv; C.C.A.L.S., ZD/CT 1 (14 June, 16 Aug., 29 Nov. 1837).
4 *31st Rep. Com. Char.* 366, 377–80.
5 Ibid. 379; C.C.A.L.S., WS 1821, Thos. Bradford of Chester.
6 *31st Rep. Com. Char.* 377.

7 Ibid. 380–1; C.C.A.L.S., WS 1815, Jas. Broadhurst of Chester.
8 C.C.A.L.S., ZDT 3/3; above, this section: Almshouses (Sir Thos. Smith); below, this section: Other Municipal Charities (Bavand, Lewis).
9 Para. based on *31st Rep. Com. Char.* 368–71; *Rep. Com. Mun. Corp.* p. 2628; P.R.O., PROB 11/293, ff. 225–8; C.C.A.L.S., ZCR 599/1; ZCR 712/1/1; ZCHC 6; ZD/CT 1 (31 July 1839); *Industrial Minera: Lead Mines and Quarries of Minera*, ed. J. Bennett, 40–2, 44.

choosing to admit new members at inflated premiums, others to exclude new guildsmen as their own turn for the bonanza approached. In 1785 the mayor and sheriffs resumed control and began to require from beneficiaries both a sworn statement of their poverty and a receipt. In 1803, when no poor members of the Grocers' company could be found, the guild sued the mayor for the money anyway. In 1808 Chancery ordered that only poor guildsmen were to benefit, and capped the pay-out to each man at £40 (reduced to £10 in 1839). To that end the annual rotation guild by guild was abandoned in favour of distribution in the order of companies originally prescribed, but without restricting payments in any one year to just one guild. From that date also the availability of the charity was advertised each year and the town clerk kept accounts. In 1836 the annual income stood at £465 12s., which the Municipal Charities Trustees increased to £867 9s. 8d. in 1873 by selling some of the charity's land as building plots. Under a Scheme of 1871 an educational charity was endowed with £2,000, the amount distributed among the guilds each year was limited to £400, and the remainder was paid out in pensions of up to £20 a year to needy guildsmen.[1]

Other Municipal Charities

The following are arranged in order of their foundation.

Simon Harding by will proved 1582 left £1 3s. 4d. a year from a rent-charge in London to be distributed among 20 poor people. The bequest was lost by 1643.[2]

Besides his loan charity Hugh Offley by will proved 1594 left a rent-charge of £5 to be applied as specified by him in writing; it was later represented by £5 a year which the corporation paid in respect of Offley's charity and that of Matthew Anderton, who by will proved 1693 had left money to extend Offley's bequest. On the first Sunday of each month the churchwardens of eight city parishes in rotation (all bar St. Olave's) sent 18 of their poor to St. Peter's church to receive a penny loaf and 3d. in cash each.[3]

Thomas Green by deed of 1602 gave property partly to benefit 20 poor householders, being freemen or their widows, who were each to receive 6s. 8d. a year. The income came from a house in Eastgate Street, which was let to an alderman on a 99-year lease in 1759 at only £11 a year, albeit in a ruinous condition. By 1836 its real rental value was almost £150.[4] When the lease

fell in, the Municipal Charities Trustees spent £1,200 given by their chairman, William Wardell, in building a hotel on the site; he also built six almshouses on the west side of Crook Street in 1859 (Fig. 35, p. 64). The charity was renamed Green and Wardell's charity, and the increased income, £145 in 1862, provided 6s. a week each for the almsmen.[5] After 1892 the surplus was carried to the general municipal charities account.[6] The Crook Street almshouses were demolished in 1973 during the redevelopment of the city centre.[7]

Alderman Richard Bavand by will proved 1603 left a rent-charge of 20s. to be distributed each year in cash to 20 poor people.[8] In 1892 it was united with the former gownsmen charities.[9]

Alderman Valentine Broughton by will proved 1603 left the corporation land at Holt (Denb.) and Iscoyd (Flints.) to benefit 48 poor freemen or their families and for other purposes, and the residue from another estate in Wrexham to be used for the marriage of poor freemen's daughters. The freemen were supposed to receive 6s. 8d. each but by 1700 the sum made available by the corporation had been halved and was distributed as 13s. 4d. for the poor of each of the twelve wards. Similarly in 1615 the corporation limited the sum available for marriages to £5 a year, and by 1836 was paying it to freemen's daughters without reference to marriage at all. Thus by 1836 most of the income of £131 2s. was absorbed by the corporation, leaving only £37 10s. for distribution.[10] A Chancery Scheme of 1855 was ineffective because the endowments were insufficient, and the original estate was not transferred to the Municipal Charities Trustees until 1860.[11] Under a Scheme of 1892 £16 a year was assigned to poor freemen, £53 14s. to the other purposes originally specified, and the residue to young women.[12]

Alderman Philip Phillips by will proved 1611 left a shop in Eastgate Street to endow a distribution of bread six times a year to the poor of St. Michael's or any other parish chosen by the mayor. The amount was fixed as a rent-charge of £2, though the shop remained in corporation hands and was actually rented for £73 in 1833.[13]

Robert Singleton by will proved 1612 left a half share of a house in Foregate Street to benefit the poor; 25s. was distributed in 1618 and £4 in 1626, after the corporation had bought the other half from Singleton's devisee. The corporation sold the property in 1630 for an annual fee-farm of £12, but the house was destroyed during the Civil War and the income fell to £2. The

1 *Hist. Mun. Chars.* 19–29; C.C.A.L.S., ZDT 3/3; *Browns and Chester*, ed. Willcock, 129.

2 *31st Rep. Com. Char.* 383; P.R.O., PROB 11/64, ff. 8v.–10.

3 *31st Rep. Com. Char.* 376, 388, 390, 394, 398, 400–1, 410.

4 Ibid. 354–5.

5 *Char. Digest Ches. 1862–3*, 2–3; *Hist. Mun. Chars.* 15–17; *P. & G. Dir. Chester* (1871), 13; *Kelly's Dir. Ches.* (1906), 215, 227.

6 C.C.A.L.S., ZDT 3/3.

7 C.P.S., Crook St. (negs. POCK 43/2–4).

8 *31st Rep. Com. Char.* 355–6.

9 C.C.A.L.S., ZDT 3/3; above, this section: Gownsmen.

10 *31st Rep. Com. Char.* 356–61; C.C.A.L.S., ZCHC 3; 3 *Sheaf*, viii, pp. 63–6, 68–9, 71, 74–5, 77–80, 83–4, 87, 90, 92, 94–6, 99.

11 *Hist. Mun. Chars.* 17–18, 70–1.

12 C.C.A.L.S., ZDT 3/3.

13 Ibid. WS 1611, Phil. Phillips of Chester; *31st Rep. Com. Char.* 361.

FIG. 35. *Green and Wardell's almshouses, Crook Street, 1965*

corporation sold the fee-farm in 1828 and made no further payments.[1]

Alderman John Brereton by will proved 1631 left a rent-charge of £3 10s. for the poor of seven city parishes. St. John's parish received 20s. for 20 poor people; Holy Trinity, St. Mary's, St. Oswald's, and St. Peter's 10s. each for 10; and St. Bridget's and St. Michael's 5s. each for five. All payments were made at St. Peter's church on the Friday after St. George's Day, and the charity became known as St. George's money.[2]

Robert Whitby left £100 by will proved 1656, primarily to support godly ministers but for the poor if not needed for that purpose; its fate after 1660 is not known and any payments were long discontinued by 1836.[3]

John Lancaster by will proved 1676 but taking effect 14 years after his death left an estate in Shordley and Hope Owen (both Flints.) to pay £36 a year to six aged freemen. Probably from the inception of the charity in 1690 the estate was leased indiscriminately with the lands of St. John's hospital, and the corporation paid £24 a year to six almsmen chosen by the mayor and sheriffs.[4] The recipients were issued with a badge similar to those worn by the gownsmen. By 1862 a Chancery Scheme had re-established the separate endowment of 95 a., later sold, which produced £96 a year.[5]

William Crompton by will dated 1695 left the reversion of 13 a. in Higher Kinnerton (Flints.) to the corporation and the rector and churchwardens of Dodleston (in which parish Higher Kinnerton lay) to distribute the income among aged poor parishioners attending church at St. Peter's and Dodleston, half for each parish. In 1836 the rental income was £18, which the corporation divided between the parishes. In St. Peter's it was spent on clothing and fuel.[6]

William Lewis gave £200 stock in 1808 to maintain a freeman's widow with young children who had never received parish relief, or a freeman's widow aged over 66; the charity produced £6 a year.[7] In 1892 it was united with the former gownsmen charities.[8]

Judith Ball by will proved 1866 left £2,200 to the Municipal Charities Trustees for St. Oswald's parish. It was paid out in quarterly pensions of £2 10s. to six people.[9]

PAROCHIAL CHARITIES

Changes in the boundaries of the ancient city-centre parishes in the 20th century made the administration of parochial charities difficult, and under a Scheme of 1988 the eleemosynary charities of St. Bridget's, St. John's, St. Martin's, St. Michael's (except William Jones's almshouses and the Robert Oldfield foundation), St. Oswald's, and St. Peter's were united as the Chester Parochial Relief in Need Charity, for the benefit of those living within the area served by the united benefice of Chester. The charities in St. Olave's were added in 1990, and in 1994 the trustees distributed *c.* £30,000 in grants to individuals and institutions, about half coming from the real estate held by the St. Michael's consolidated charities.[10] The parishes of St. Mary and Holy Trinity retained control of their own charities in 1996.

1 *31st Rep. Com. Char.* 366–7; P.R.O., PROB 11/120, ff. 142–3.
2 *31st Rep. Com. Char.* 375–6.
3 Ibid. 366; P.R.O., PROB 11/254, ff. 241v.–246 at 245.
4 *31st Rep. Com. Char.* 364–5.
5 *Char. Digest Ches.* 1862–3, 2–3; *Hist. Mun. Chars.* 18, 72–3.
6 *31st Rep. Com. Char.* 365.
7 Ibid. 377.
8 C.C.A.L.S., ZDT 3/3; above, this section: Gownsmen.
9 *Hist. Mun. Chars.* 30; C.C.A.L.S., ZDT 3/3.
10 Char. Com. file 1001314.

Holy Trinity[1]

Peter Ince by will dated 1644 left a rent-charge of £2 12s. to buy bread for 12 poor parishioners, with a preference for members of the company of Painters, Glaziers, Embroiderers, and Stationers.

Robert Fletcher of Cork (Irel.) by deed of 1674 gave four cottages at Lady Barrow's Hay in the Crofts to be used as almshouses for four aged widows, together with a rent-charge of £4 4s. to pay each of them 20s. a year and for repairs.[2] By 1850 the repair fund was no longer being kept up,[3] and under a Scheme of 1874 the churchwardens were permitted to sell the almshouses and apply the income instead to benefit four poor widows.

Henry Bennett at an unknown date left £25, the interest to be distributed among 12 poor widows. It was invested in a rent-charge of £1 12s.[4]

John Grosvenor by will proved 1702 left £3 a year to be divided among 10 householders. By 1836 it had been replaced by an annual distribution of 1s. 6d. to each of 40 paupers.

Thomas Kenyon by will proved 1711 left houses in Lower Lane (later Linenhall Street) to provide annuities for 12 poor widows. About 1730 the parish spent other legacies amounting to £221 on building additional houses, and the income rose steadily from £8 15s. in 1750 to £59 by 1820, distributed weekly in bread and quarterly in cash to widows. In 1994 the sum available each year was only £112.[5]

Mary Morris by will proved 1848 left £200 stock, the proceeds to be divided each year among poor widows. James Dixon by will dated 1865 left £100 for the poor at the rector's discretion. General Thomas Gerrard Ball left £1,000 in 1881, the interest to be divided among three men and three women aged over 60.[6] Jane Churton by will proved 1908 left £1,000 for the poor in cash or kind.

The parish also benefited from four municipal charities.[7] The charities remained under parochial control and in 1994 produced £250, distributed to the needy in small sums.

Several other charities were lost by 1836.

St. Bridget[8]

Ralph Proby by will proved 1606 left £10 for a weekly distribution of bread, supplemented by his executor

Peter Proby to a total value of £18.[9] In 1836 the dole amounted to 14 loaves given to 14 people selected by the incumbent. The charity had evidently ceased by 1862,[10] but was probably being applied instead in St. Michael's parish.[11]

Thomas Wilcock by will proved 1638 left a rent-charge on land in the Wirral township of Willaston for weekly bread for 12 poor householders. The income had risen by 1834 to £8 5s., distributed in bread at Christmas to poor parishioners.[12]

Richard Harrison by will proved 1686 left money to buy land, the rent from which was to benefit up to 10 of the poorest parishioners, excluding residents of Sir Thomas Smith's almshouses. Land was purchased at Wimbolds Trafford and the trustees paid £3 a year to each of 10 paupers who remained beneficiaries for life or until they entered the workhouse or an almshouse.

Alderman Townsend (presumably Robert, recorder of Chester 1754–87) gave a rent-charge of £2 for bread.

Hannah Griffiths at an unknown date left £50 for bread; the charity was applied for some years after 1798, but the parish spent most of the capital in obtaining probate of her will in 1813 and what remained was carried to the church rate account.

Four cash bequests amounting to £60 were invested in land which in 1836 produced £5 5s. a year, divided among 14 parishioners chosen for life by the minister and churchwardens. From five other bequests totalling £27 the churchwardens were then also paying 15s. twice yearly to 15 paupers, but those payments had ceased by 1862.[13]

The parish also benefited from four municipal charities.[14] The parochial charities were consolidated with those of St. Martin's (the parishes having been united in 1842) under a Scheme of 1889, though each group was still applied within its own ancient parish.[15]

St. John the Baptist

One of Henry Smith's extensive charities, established in the 1620s, benefited St. John's and 20 other parishes scattered across England from an estate at Stoughton (in Thurnby, Leics.). In the early 19th century St. John's share amounted to up to £15 a year, which the churchwardens distributed in clothing, food, and

1 Acct. based, except where stated otherwise, on *31st Rep. Com. Char.* 390–2; Char. Com. file 216444; cf. C.C.A.L.S., P 1/19–21.

2 C.C.A.L.S., P 1/399–400; for the location cf. *P. & G. Dir. Chester* (1871), 13.

3 *Bagshaw's Dir. Ches.* (1850), 69, 91.

4 Cf. below, this section: St. Peter.

5 Cf. C.C.A.L.S., P 1/390, 393–5, 397.

6 Ibid. P 1/402.

7 Above, this chapter: Municipal Charities (Loan Charities: Wm. Offley, Fulk Aldersey; Other Municipal Charities: Hugh Offley and Mat. Anderton, Jn. Brereton).

8 Acct. based, except where stated otherwise, on *31st Rep. Com. Char.* 392–4; C.C.A.L.S., P 15/15/1.

9 P.R.O., PROB 11/108, ff. 143–4; 3 *Sheaf*, vii, pp. 14–15, 32–3, 72, 93–4.   10 *Char. Digest Ches. 1862–3*, 4–5.

11 Below, this section: St. Michael.

12 C.C.A.L.S., WS 1638, Thos. Wilcock of Chester; cf. below, this section: St. John the Baptist.

13 *Char. Digest Ches. 1862–3*, 4–5.

14 Above, this chapter: Municipal Charities (Loan Charities: Wm. Offley, Fulk Aldersey; Other Municipal Charities: Hugh Offley and Mat. Anderton, Jn. Brereton).

15 C.C.A.L.S., ZDT 3/56–7.

fuel.[1] Under a Scheme of 1884 the benefits were extended to include medical assistance.[2]

Alderman Edward Batho by will proved 1629 left various rent-charges from which 20*s.* was intended for 40 poor spinners and working people at 6*d.* a head; 10*s.* for nine paupers and the parish clerk at 1*s.* apiece; and 10*s.* in bread for 10 poor people on the first Sunday of each month.[3]

Thomas Wilcock by will proved 1638 left £20 a year, being the rent from 77 a. at Willaston (in Wirral), most of which was to be distributed by the churchwardens of St. John's: 2*s.* in bread among 24 householders every Sunday and 40*s.* in cash every quarter among 40 poor householders. The rest was for the parson and parish officers of St. John's and the poor of St. Bridget's and Neston (in which parish the estate at Willaston lay). In 1709 the estate was conveyed by Wilcock's great-grandson George Wilcock to trustees for the three parishes involved. The proportion which each received remained fixed as the rent increased, an arrangement confirmed by a Scheme of 1890. From 1796 St. John's used the surplus from its share beyond the original purposes of the charity to pay 1*s.* a week to each of the eight occupants of the parish almshouses.[4] The parish's share for bread and cash payments in 1862–3 was £42 13*s.* 4*d.* out of £64.[5] Under a Scheme of 1882 any residue above £5 4*s.* earmarked for bread was applied for the general benefit of the poor.[6]

John Stockton by will dated 1698 left 6*s.* a year to the parish poor, and his widow Eleanor Stockton in 1710 added 5*s.* a year, both charged on a garden in the Groves. The intention was to give 6*d.* to each of 22 paupers, but by 1835 the churchwardens were instead giving 1*s.* a year to half that number,[7] and in 1862 were distributing it in bread.[8]

Peter Leadbeater at an unknown date left £26 to endow a weekly distribution of bread to six poor people. By 1836 the churchwardens were instead providing for the distribution of £1 6*s.* a year from the church rates.[9]

The parish almshouses in Little St. John Street were probably established after the Dissolution in succession to the fraternity of St. Anne. Their foundation deed was allegedly still in existence in 1630, when the eight resident almswomen petitioned the bishop to order repairs at the expense of the then owners of lands which had once belonged to the fraternity.[10] In 1738 Mrs. Deighton Salmon rebuilt the almshouses as a row of four single-storeyed houses each of four rooms, in return for the right to nominate the almspeople during her lifetime. In 1796 they housed eight women, in 1836 sixteen, and in 1871 eight again.[11] The almshouses were not endowed, but they were maintained from church rates, and the occupants paid no rent and received money from Wilcock's charity and coal from Henry Smith's.[12] Bequests for the almswomen were made by Mary Garratt (will proved 1841, for coal: £111 in consols in 1890), Frances and Elizabeth Orange (wills proved 1851 and 1855: £109 in consols in 1890), Sarah Sinclair (will proved 1856: £196 in consols in 1890), and the duke of Westminster (date unknown: rent-charge of £1). Under a Scheme of 1890 the trustees were permitted to sell the almshouses and apply the income to pensions.[13] The city council bought the dwellings in 1899 with the intention of refurbishing them, but then changed its mind and demolished them in 1901.[14]

The parish used cash benefactions for the poor amounting to £199 to establish a poorhouse, and the proceeds from selling the poorhouse after 1762 to build a gallery in the church. It made charitable distributions from the church rates and after 1803 instead from pew-rents from the gallery, by order of the bishop, usually in bread and bacon. By 1835 the income had fallen to £6 8*s.* 6*d.*,[15] and when the gallery was removed, probably in the restoration of 1859, the charity ceased altogether.[16]

Harvey's charity, evidently a cash bequest, was put towards buying the grazing of the churchyard for the parish in 1794; in its place 15*s.* a year was allotted from the church rates and distributed at the churchwardens' discretion.[17]

By will proved 1881 Jane Kearsley left *c.* £100, later invested in consols, for the parish poor.[18]

The parish also benefited from four municipal charities.[19] The surviving parochial charities were consolidated by a Scheme of 1890.[20]

1 *31st Rep. Com. Char.* 397; *4th Rep. Com. Char.* H.C. 312, pp. 448–50 (1820), v; *11th Rep. Com. Char.* H.C. 433, pp. 796–7 (1824), xiv; C.C.A.L.S., P 51/18/1–2.

2 C.C.A.L.S., ZDT 3/52; ibid. P 51/18/7–17.

3 Ibid. WS 1629, Edw. Batho of Chester; ibid. P 51/18/129–30; *31st Rep. Com. Char.* 397.

4 *31st Rep. Com. Char.* 395–6; C.C.A.L.S., WS 1638, Thos. Wilcock of Chester; ibid. P 51/18/18–128; ibid. ZDT 3/54.

5 *Char. Digest Ches. 1862–3,* 4–5.

6 C.C.A.L.S., ZDT 3/51.

7 Ibid. P 51/18/131; *31st Rep. Com. Char.* 399.

8 *Char. Digest Ches. 1862–3,* 4–5.

9 *31st Rep. Com. Char.* 398.

10 B.L. Harl. MS. 2150, no. 23.

11 C.C.A.L.S., P 51/12/2, p. [48] from end; *P. & G. Dir. Chester* (1871), 13.

12 *31st Rep. Com. Char.* 396–7.

13 C.C.A.L.S., ZDT 3/53.

14 *Chester City Cl. Mins. 1899/1900,* 41, 43–4, 93, 124, 126; *1900/1,* 223, 292.

15 *31st Rep. Com. Char.* 398–9.

16 *Char. Digest Ches. 1862–3,* 4–5; below, Medieval Parish Churches: St. John.   17 *31st Rep. Com. Char.* 398.

18 C.C.A.L.S., ZDT 3/53.

19 Above, this chapter: Municipal Charities (Loan Charities: Wm. Offley, Fulk Aldersey; Other Municipal Charities: Hugh Offley and Mat. Anderton, Jn. Brereton).

20 C.C.A.L.S., ZDT 3/53.

St. Martin[1]

Robert Shone by will proved 1678 and William Terry by will proved 1728 each left £1 a year, spent on bread.[2] The two charities were administered with those of St. Bridget's parish under a Scheme of 1889.[3]

Other sums amounting to over £60 left for the poor were spent on the church fabric between 1720 and 1723.

The parish also benefited from three municipal charities.[4]

John Langdale's bequest (date unknown) of £10 for the poor disappeared when it was loaned to a bankrupt, probably in 1782.

St. Mary on the Hill[5]

One of Henry Smith's many charities, set up in the 1620s, provided a variable income for the parish and 13 others elsewhere in the country from an estate at Tolleshunt D'Arcy (Essex), amounting to £5 in 1641 and £10 15s. in 1835, spent on bread. It was given as clothing in 1862.[6]

The parish invested many small bequests totalling £263 at an unknown date in the 10-a. Llay farm at Gresford (Denb.), the income from which rose gradually by 1836 to £22, given in bread.

Other accumulated sums were used to build a north gallery in the church in 1756, the pew-rents being spent also on bread. After 1816 income from the pews was replaced by £4 a year from church rates. Together with cash raised from the sale of timber at Llay farm *c.* 1815, the parish had £7 18s. available for distribution in bread and money each Easter.

An unidentified Mr. Harrison at an unknown date left £20, the interest to be distributed in bread; in 1836 it was given to 20 poor widows.

Charlotte Dicas at an unknown date gave a rent-charge of 12s., which was put with the 10s. received by the parish from John Brereton's municipal charity and distributed as 1s. to each of 22 poor widows.

The parish also benefited from three other municipal charities.[7]

The above charities were united under a Scheme of 1889 and spent on subscriptions to benevolent institutions or relief in cash or kind at the discretion of the trustees; in 1993–4 they distributed £3,605, mainly to charitable organizations in the city generally.[8]

Frances Elizabeth Matilda Mawdesley by will proved

1891 left £800 for coal at Christmas; the income was spent as directed until 1995, when a small accumulated balance was transferred to the parochial charity trustees.[9]

John Ramsden by will proved 1905 left £120 stock for the poor in cash or kind. In the early 1990s it was distributed in the form of electricity stamps; it, too, was united with the parochial charities in 1995.[10]

St. Michael

William Jones's Almshouses By deed of 1658 William Jones of the Middle Temple gave to local trustees a newly built brick almshouse adjoining St. Michael's church in Pepper Street. It was to house six single women and four men, all aged over 55 and regular churchgoers, and was supported by an estate in Chester and Holt (Denb.). Jones framed rules for the conduct of the almspeople, who received 1s. a week each.[11] The income in 1862–3 was £171.[12] The cottages in Pepper Street were sold in 1948 and later demolished for the development of the Grosvenor shopping precinct. Under a Scheme of 1960 four bungalows in Upton were bought as replacements; a further Scheme of 1969 allowed the trustees to sell them and buy instead the recently restored Nine Houses (actually six in number) in Park Street.[13]

Apprenticeship Charities By will dated 1695 Robert Oldfield left the reversion of his estate at Dunham on the Hill to provide £20 a year for the minister of St. Michael's and apprenticeships and university scholarships for poor freemen's sons. His widow died in 1715 and the charity was regulated by a Chancery Scheme of 1722. The trustees added to the estate by investing surpluses, so that it comprised 196 a. by 1830 (reduced to 110 a. by 1862), when the income had risen steadily to £432 a year (£694 in 1862). Expenditure averaged barely £150 because few were eligible to benefit, despite the efforts of the trustees to enlarge its terms. Only two applications for university grants were ever received, and both were refused on the grounds that the applicants did not need charity. Most of the money was spent on apprenticeship fees of £10 or £15 for poor boys born in the parish. From 1819 those who served their time faithfully were given £5, raised to £10 in 1837. Between 1759 and 1835 Oldfield's charity provided 296 apprenticeships.[14] Under a Scheme of 1895 the charity was turned into an educational foundation,

1 Acct. based, except where stated otherwise, on *31st Rep. Com. Char.* 400.

2 C.C.A.L.S., WS 1686, Rob. Shone of Chester; WS 1728, Wm. Terry of Chester.

3 Above, this section: St. Bridget.

4 Above, this chapter: Municipal Charities (Loan Charities: Wm. Offley, Fulk Aldersey; Other Municipal Charities: Hugh Offley and Mat. Anderton).

5 Acct. based, except where stated otherwise, on *31st Rep. Com. Char.* 401–2.

6 *32nd Rep. Com. Char. Pt. 1*, H.C. 108, pp. 776–8 (1837–8),

xxv; *Char. Digest Ches. 1862–3*, 6–7; C.C.A.L.S., P 20/17/1.

7 Above, this chapter: Municipal Charities (Loan Charities: Wm. Offley, Fulk Aldersey; Other Municipal Charities: Hugh Offley and Mat. Anderton).

8 Char. Com. file 215406.

9 Ibid. file 256212; C.C.A.L.S., P 20/17/8–21.

10 Char. Com. file 254852.

11 *31st Rep. Com. Char.* 405–9; C.C.A.L.S., ZCR 3/51–7; ZCR 56/4–8; ZCR 193.　　12 *Char. Digest Ches. 1862–3*, 6–7.

13 Char. Com. file 213838.

14 *31st Rep. Com. Char.* 402–5; C.C.A.L.S., P 65/12/28.

with a continuing provision for apprenticeships, formalized as the Robert Oldfield Apprenticing Foundation under a Scheme of 1962. It was not always possible to find beneficiaries for the apprenticeships, and in such years the income was transferred to the educational foundation. The three other apprenticing charities in the parish were united with it in 1989.[1]

By will proved 1681 Jonathan Goldson gave an annual rent-charge of £5 to apprentice a poor freeman's son of the parish every third year, to which Joseph Basnett by will proved 1696 added £2 every third year.[2] John Matthews (d. *c.* 1800) left £350 in stock to apprentice another poor child each year; it produced £10 10*s.* a year and was reserved for girls.[3]

Other Charities   The Consolidated Charities were created from the bequests of the Revd. Thomas Leftwich, who by will dated 1746 left £10 to buy devotional books for the poor; Hannah Leftwich, who by will proved 1750 left £40, the interest to be given annually to old maids; and Elizabeth Potter, who by will proved 1782 left £40 to benefit those living in William Jones's almshouses. The three sums were used to buy a shop in Bridge Street, the rent from which produced £4 for the poor in the 1830s.[4] By 1862 the income was £53, eight ninths of which was still given to the poor.[5]

A general bread fund was established from separate bequests made between 1622 and 1731 totalling £112 10*s.* Five per cent a year (£5 12*s.* 6*d.*) from the church rates was given out in bread at Christmas but ceased many years before 1862.[6] Proby's gift, perhaps transferred after 1836 from St. Bridget's parish,[7] was a rent-charge of 12*s.* for bread, in existence by 1862.[8] Henry Smith's charity, paid from the same estate in Leicestershire which benefited St. John's parish, yielded usually £10–£12 a year for bread in the 19th century,[9] declining by the 1930s to £5, spent on groceries.[10]

The parish also benefited from five municipal charities.[11] Under a Scheme of 1940 all the parish charities except William Jones's almshouses and Robert Oldfield's foundation were managed together and much of the income was accumulated; in 1975–6, for instance, out of £829 income, £324 from the

consolidated charities was transferred to Jones's almshouses and £90 was spent on Christmas food parcels for the elderly.[12]

St. Olave

The Revd. Benjamin Culme of Freshwater (Hants) by will proved 1768 left £100 to apprentice poor children at £5 a time. By 1836 a balance of £37 had been accumulated through the lack of qualified applicants.[13] Catherine Aubrey by will dated 1790 gave £20 to the minister to benefit the poor at his discretion. It was invested with Culme's legacy and £1 in bread was distributed annually.[14] The parish also benefited from the municipal charity of William Offley and Fulk Aldersey.[15]

St. Oswald[16]

Alderman Edward Batho by will proved 1629 left rent-charges of 30*s.* a year for bread;[17] by 1862 10*s.* had been lost and the remaining £1 was given in cash.[18]

Edward Russell in 1666 left a rent-charge of £2 10*s.* to provide bread to 12 poor parishioners on Sundays; no record of payments was found in 1836 but the charity was later revived.[19]

By 1717 £1 a year from Thomas Green's municipal charity was being paid to the churchwardens of St. Oswald's; in 1836 it was distributed among 30 poor widows.[20]

Legacies or gifts to the poor of £10 from each of John Mather (d. 1700 or 1701), Peter Cotton (will proved 1716), and the Revd. Thomas Aubrey (will proved 1759) were used to repair the church, but the churchwardens instead distributed bread worth 30*s.* each year.[21]

Separate legacies amounting to at least £454 and possibly £478 were used to buy and fit out a parish workhouse in 1729. It was later leased and the income was diverted to the church rate.

The parish also benefited from five municipal charities.[22] The charities of Batho, Russell, and St. Oswald's portions of two of the municipal charities were united under a Scheme of 1889.[23]

Elizabeth Burkinshaw by will proved 1913 left

1 Char. Com. file 525892.
2 *31st Rep. Com. Char.* 409; C.C.A.L.S., WS 1680, Jona. Goldson of Chester; WS 1696, Jos. Basnett of Chester.
3 *31st Rep. Com. Char.* 410; cf. C.C.A.L.S., P 65/12/22.
4 *31st Rep. Com. Char.* 409–10; C.C.A.L.S., P 65/12/9–15; WS 1750, Hannah Leftwich of Boughton.
5 *Char. Digest Ches.* 1862–3, 6–7.
6 Ibid.; *31st Rep. Com. Char.* 410.
7 Above, this section: St. Bridget.
8 *Char. Digest Ches.* 1862–3, 6–7.
9 *31st Rep. Com. Char.* 410; *Char. Digest Ches.* 1862–3, 6–7; cf. above, this section: St. John the Baptist.
10 C.C.A.L.S., ZCR 536/73/1–13.
11 Above, this chapter: Municipal Charities (Loan Charities: Wm. Offley, Fulk Aldersey; Other Municipal Charities: Hugh Offley and Mat. Anderton, Philip Phillips, Jn. Brereton).
12 Char. Com. files 216443, 525904; C.C.A.L.S., P 65/12/54.

13 *31st Rep. Com. Char.* 388; P.R.O., PROB 11/940, ff. 302–6; C.C.A.L.S., P 64/6.   14 *31st Rep. Com. Char.* 388.
15 Above, this chapter: Municipal Charities (Loan Charities).
16 Acct. based, except where stated otherwise, on *31st Rep. Com. Char.* 388–9.
17 C.C.A.L.S., WS 1629, Edw. Batho of Chester; cf. above, this section: St. John the Baptist.
18 *Char. Digest Ches.* 1862–3, 6–7.
19 C.C.A.L.S., ZDT 3/50.
20 Cf. above, this chapter: Municipal Charities (Other Municipal Charities).
21 3 *Sheaf,* xx, p. 11; C.C.A.L.S., WS 1759, Thos. Aubrey of Eccleston (naming St. Olave's not St. Oswald's).
22 Above, this chapter: Municipal Charities (Loan Charities: Wm. Offley, Fulk Aldersey; Other Municipal Charities: Hugh Offley and Mat. Anderton, Jn. Brereton, Judith Ball).
23 C.C.A.L.S., ZDT 3/50.

money to benefit the most deserving poor parishioners. It produced *c.* £3 a year.[1]

St. Peter[2]

Thomas Cowper by will proved 1697 left a rent-charge of £2 13s. 4d. for a weekly distribution of bread to 12 people.

Alderman Henry Bennett by will dated 1708 left £25, the interest to be paid to 12 widows at Christmas. The capital was never handed over, but instead the parish received £1 12s. a year from land in the Cheshire township of Whitby.

John Witter by will dated 1734 left a rent-charge of £1 a year for bread.

The parish also benefited from five municipal charities, including that of William Crompton.[3] Under a Scheme of 1927 the Chester branch of Crompton's was separately managed by the rector and churchwardens of St. Peter's.[4]

William Pritchard by will proved 1905 left an endowment for the parish poor. All the parochial charities were consolidated with the Chester Parochial Relief in Need Charity under a Scheme of 1988.[5]

Individual benefactions lost before 1836 amounted to £290.

PRESBYTERIAN (LATER UNITARIAN) CHARITIES

William Trafford by will proved 1640 left £100 for unspecified charitable purposes in Chester. It was invested with another bequest for the benefit of Frodsham in 18 a. at Huntington, which in 1686 produced £6 a year, of which £1 went to Frodsham and £5 to the poor of Chester. By 1828 the income was £40 a year, which, apart from the fixed payment to Frodsham, was mainly spent on the Unitarian minister and school. The poor, who had received small sums every year between 1719 and 1828, were thereafter excluded.[6]

Timothy Dean by will proved 1729 left land in Handbridge, after the death of his wife, to benefit Presbyterian ministers and their widows. He also left cottages at Quarry Head in Handbridge (located at the corner of the later Queen's Park Road) to be turned into almshouses for two men and two women. The income in 1832 was £75, mostly spent on ministers and ministers' widows; the four almspeople received 10s. a month each. Timothy's widow Jane Dean by will proved 1730 left a further £350 to build and endow a

separate almshouse for four Presbyterian women. It was put up on land near the chapel in Trinity Lane (later Street) and was rebuilt in 1862; land in Tarvin was bought as an investment. In 1836 the residents each received £6 a year.[7] Under a Scheme of 1889 the two were united as the Almshouse Charities of Timothy Dean and Jane Dean to support four almswomen and two male pensioners, and the site of Timothy's almshouse, demolished after 1850,[8] was sold. Jane's almshouses were taken down in the mid 1930s, and the charity was converted wholly to a pension charity under a Scheme of 1937. £1,000 was paid out in pensions in 1987.[9]

Samuel Hignett of Holt (Denb.) by will proved 1707 left £100 to the minister of the Presbyterian chapel in Chester to benefit its poorer members. Half was invested and the income from it was distributed. In 1836 it produced £4 a year.[10]

Priscilla Leconby by will proved 1802 left shares in the River Dee Company partly to benefit poor members of the congregation. The annual dividend was £16 4s. 4d. by 1836, when the poor's share was added to Hignett's charity and largely given to the chapel Sunday school on the grounds that poor members of the congregation were already provided for.[11]

OTHER CHARITIES

Mary Tilley (d. 1793) by will proved 1815 left £1,000 to the senior physician of Chester infirmary, who after the death of her sisters was to invest £400 to maintain four maiden women over the age of 50, born and living in Chester, and nominated by the superintendents of the Blue Girls' school.[12] The charity became known as the Blue Girls Charity and was supplemented under the wills of Elizabeth Garratt (proved 1840, £496 in stock), Mary Garratt (proved 1841, £1,739 in stock), and Frances Elizabeth Matilda Mawdesley (proved 1891, £1,000). The first three were transferred to the control of the school's committee of ladies under a Scheme of 1899, and the last was added under another of 1976. They were united as the Mary Garratt Charity under a Scheme of 1994, when £130 was distributed in annuities.[13]

Charlotte Susanna Beard by will proved 1803 established a charity for the general benefit of the poor, which under a Scheme of 1949 was transferred to the management of trustees appointed by the city council and distributed in clothing, bedding, and fuel.

1　Ibid. ZCR 536/77/1–11.

2　Acct. based, except where stated otherwise, on *31st Rep. Com. Char.* 389–90.

3　Above, this chapter: Municipal Charities (Loan Charities: Wm. Offley, Fulk Aldersey; Other Municipal Charities: Hugh Offley and Mat. Anderton, Jn. Brereton, Wm. Crompton).

4　C.C.A.L.S., P 63/10/2; Char. Com. file 220399.

5　Char. Com. file 1001314 (the Scheme wrongly lists all but Pritchard's as belonging to St. Oswald's parish).

6　*31st Rep. Com. Char.* 411–13.

7　Ibid. 413–15; C.C.A.L.S., WS 1729, Tim. Dean of Chester;

WS 1730, Jane Dean of Chester; *P. & G. Dir. Chester* (1878/9), 13.

8　*Bagshaw's Dir. Ches.* (1850), 70.

9　*P. & G. Dir. Chester* (1919/20), 28; Char. Com. files 243388, 243388 A/1.

10　*31st Rep. Com. Char.* 415.

11　Ibid. 416; C.C.A.L.S., WS 1802, Priscilla Leconby of Chester.

12　*31st Rep. Com. Char.* 411; C.C.A.L.S., WS 1815, Mary Tilley of Chester.

13　Char. Com. file 215690.

The accumulated capital of *c.* £1,900 was transferred to the Chester Municipal Relief in Need Charity in 1990.[1]

Helen Catherine Tidswell by will proved 1919 left *c.* £2,400 to create the Richard Tidswell Trust, which paid pensions of 10*s.* a week to five married couples, one of them in Chester.[2]

Margaret Collins by will proved 1925 left £3,000 to be administered by trustees chosen jointly by the city's Council of Social Welfare (later called the Council for Voluntary Service) and the priest of St. Werburgh's Roman Catholic church; invested in stock, it produced £93 a year, distributed among a handful of old people or families.[3]

1 Char. Com. file 240349; not recorded in *31st Rep. Com. Char.*
2 C.C.A.L.S., ZDT 3/70.
3 Char. Com. file 228216.

ECONOMIC

INFRASTRUCTURE AND

INSTITUTIONS

POPULATION

Estimating the size of Chester's population at the time of the Norman Conquest is no easier than for other large towns. In 1066 there were reportedly 487 houses there, of which 431 paid tax and 56 belonged to the bishop of Lichfield. In 1086 there were said to be 205 fewer, a total of 282. The 21 belonging to St. John's and St. Werburgh's minsters[1] were probably included in those totals.[2] An average household size of five would give a population in 1066 of 2,435 and in 1086 of 1,410. Those totals seem too low.[3] There were almost certainly other houses exempt from tax, especially in 1086, when the reduction by 205 since the pre-Conquest number probably represented a tax concession rather than an actual count of occupied dwellings. A more realistic estimate of the population would be up to 3,000 in 1066 and still 2,000 or more in 1086.

The six small rural manors south of the river at Handbridge, Overleigh, and Netherleigh had 13 tenants in 1086, perhaps *c.* 65 people in all, and there were two oxmen in 'Redcliff' besides the bishop's tenants enumerated with the urban population.[4]

The county's palatine status, exclusion from parliamentary representation, and consequent exemption from national taxes make it particularly difficult to estimate Chester's population later in the Middle Ages.[5] If the city was about the same size as Shrewsbury (as it was in both 1086 and the early modern period), its population may have been 4,000 or fewer in 1377, after the ravages of the Black Death,[6] though

a different means of calculation has placed it as high as 4,600 or more.[7]

The only medieval date for which a more informed estimate can be made is 1463, when a total of 480 'inhabitants' (meaning male householders) paid a tax levied by the mayor. The figure included residents of Handbridge and Foregate Street as well as people living within the walls, but excluded several other categories.[8] Of those excluded, the abbot's tenants outside the Northgate can be estimated at 35 (as in the 1390s),[9] the nuns' tenants at 75 (as, plausibly, in 1526),[10] the householders of Gloverstone at 20,[11] the secular clergy at 70,[12] and the staff of the castle garrison at 10.[13] Poor households, exempt from the tax, may have constituted a fifth of the total.[14] There were thus in the order of 740 households in all, amounting to perhaps 3,000 people if the average household size was four, or 3,700 if it was five. In addition there were some 70 monks, nuns, and friars,[15] perhaps with servants not already reckoned.

Epidemics swept Chester regularly in the 16th century and probably ensured that the population fluctuated markedly over time. The more serious episodes were those of 1506–7 (when 'sweating sickness' killed 91 householders in three days), 1517–18 (described as 'plague'), 1528 (when 41 died in one day and night of the 'sweat'), 1537, 1550, and 1556 (all 'plague'), 1558 ('Stubb's bile'), 1563 (plague again), and 1574.[16]

Chester's population in the 1520s may have been,

1 *V.C.H. Ches.* i. 342–4 (nos. 1a, 1e, 12, 14).

2 Contrary to what is said ibid. i. 325.

3 Cf. H. C. Darby, *Domesday Eng.* 307; J. C. Russell, *Brit. Medieval Population,* 50.

4 *V.C.H. Ches.* i. 356, 358 (nos. 182–3, 210–12, 218).

5 Ibid. ii. 23–4, 35; M. Jurkowski, C. L. Smith, and D. Crook, *Lay Taxes in Eng. and Wales, 1188–1688,* p. xxx; R. W. Hoyle, *Tudor Taxation Recs.: Guide for Users,* 10, 56–7.

6 Shrewsbury estimated as 3,671: A. Dyer, *Decline and Growth in Eng. Towns, 1400–1640,* 64, 72–3; cf. *Towns and Townspeople in 15th Cent.* ed. J. A. F. Thomson, 9; Russell, *Brit. Medieval Population,* 145.

7 M. J. Bennett, *Community, Class, and Careerism: Lancs. and Ches. in Age of Sir Gawain and the Green Knight,* 60–1.

8 B.L. Harl. MS. 2158, ff. 45v.–47v.

9 Ibid. Add. MS. 36764.

10 *J.C.A.S.* xiii. 105–9, where the number of tenants of houses, as against other forms of property, seems to lie between 61 and 88; cf. 114 tenants in 1588: *V.C.H. Ches.* v (1), Early Modern Chester: Demography.

11 A guess based on the fact that there were 30 houses in 1801: Morris, *Chester,* 111.

12 From the figures given in Jones, *Ch. in Chester,* 10–11.

13 Cf. 12 in 1313: *Ches. Chamb. Accts.* 81.

14 Cf. apparently 17 per cent in 1631 and 26 per cent in 1664: *V.C.H. Ches.* v (1), Early Modern Chester: Demography (Population Statistics).

15 Jones, *Ch. in Chester,* 11–12.

16 B.L. Harl. MS. 2125, ff. 36v., 60v.; *L. & P. Hen. VIII,* xii (2), p. 288; Ormerod, *Hist. Ches.* i. 234–6.

like Shrewsbury's, around 3,500.[1] From the 1560s much more reliable data are available.[2] By 1563 the number of people had risen to at least 4,700, continuing to grow quickly and peaking at over 6,000 in 1586 before falling almost as sharply to *c.* 5,200 in 1603. The double epidemic of 1603–5 killed almost 2,000 people but the population had recovered by 1610 to its level of before the plague, and grew vigorously to reach 6,500 before 1630 and over 7,500 in 1644. At the end of the siege in 1646 there were still 6,000 civilians in Chester. Recovery from the plague of 1647–8, which killed over 2,000, was slow to start but the population reached *c.* 6,750 in 1660, over 7,000 in 1664, and over 8,000 in 1725.

Probably the population was growing steadily throughout the 18th century, and certainly by 1800 it had embarked upon a period of sustained growth. In 1774 Dr. John Haygarth counted 14,713 people in 3,428 families in the nine city parishes and the cathedral precinct, but it is not clear whether his figures covered only the town, or also included some or all of the rural townships which belonged to some of the Chester parishes.[3] The count of 15,174 for the 1801 census was for the town alone, but had evident (if minor) defects in the omission of the cathedral precincts and in a figure for St. Mary's parish which had to be adjusted later. Its figure of 3,377 for St. Oswald's parish seems too low in comparison with Haygarth's of 4,027.[4] Smaller falls in the numbers of residents in St. Olave's, St. Mary's, and St. Peter's parishes between the two dates can be explained by wealthier families' abandoning the city centre, especially Lower Bridge Street, in the later 18th century,[5] but the discrepancy for St. Oswald's cannot be easily explained unless Haygarth had included the inhabitants of its rural townships.

The number of people living within the liberties of Chester rose to 16,140 in 1811,[6] sharply to 19,949 in 1821, and more steadily to 21,344 in 1831 and 23,115 in 1841, part of the last increase being due to the boundary extension into Great Boughton effected in 1835.[7] The growth in population over the next thirty years was strikingly more rapid, to 27,766 in 1851, 31,110 in 1861, and 35,257 in 1871, representing more than a doubling of the number of people in the sixty years since 1811. It then almost levelled off, adding less than 20 per cent more in the next sixty years: 37,208 in

1881, 37,354 in 1891, 38,539 in 1901, 39,252 in 1911, 40,965 in 1921, and 41,668 in 1931.[8]

At the same time, however, the suburban areas outside the city boundary were growing more rapidly than the municipal borough (from 1889 county borough) itself, even though only relatively small numbers were involved. Hoole township contained only 177 people in 1801 but there were *c.* 5,900 in the smaller Hoole urban district during the period 1911–31; Upton had 173 in 1801 and 2,667 in 1931; Newton 141 and 2,581 at the same dates; Great Boughton 544 and 2,690;[9] the whole of Saltney (Flints.) 156 in 1821 and the built-up civil parish of East Saltney 2,642 in 1931.[10] Even Blacon, not seriously affected by new building before the Second World War, had a population of 788 in 1931.[11] Not all the inhabitants of those townships lived in suburban Chester, but the total urban population clearly exceeded 55,000 by 1931, and another estimate for the same date, covering a wider urban fringe, put it at 61,500,[12] compared with fewer than 42,000 within the county borough alone.

Between 15,000 and 20,000 people continued to live in suburban Chester but outside the town's local government boundary until the county borough was abolished in 1974. The absorption of Blacon, part of Newton, and other areas into the city in 1936 transferred a population of well over 4,000 to Chester, helping to take its figure to 48,360 in 1951, when Hoole U.D. (including the rest of Newton) contained 9,058, Upton 6,343, Great Boughton 3,165, and East Saltney 4,144.[13] Most of Hoole was added to Chester in 1954, taking the county borough to 60,006 in 1961 and 62,919 in 1971. East Saltney was static in that period at *c.* 4,100 but Upton continued to grow to 7,708 in 1961 and 10,441 in 1971, when it was exceptionally populous for a mere civil parish, while Great Boughton had 4,673 people in 1961 and 7,832 in 1971. The county borough and those three satellite civil parishes together with the small civil parish of Bache included 71,138 people in 1951, 76,431 in 1961, and 85,447 in 1971. A wider definition of the urban area made in the 1960s put Chester's population at 78,000 in 1951 and 84,300 in 1961.[14]

From 1971 Chester's population, however defined, was falling. The 15 urban wards of the new Chester district created in 1974 had housed 82,678 people in 1971 (of whom 19,759 were outside the county

1 Dyer, *Decline and Growth*, 66, 72–3; *Towns and Townspeople*, ed. Thomson, 9.

2 Rest of para. based on details in *V.C.H. Ches.* v (1), Early Modern Chester: Demography.

3 *Philosophical Trans. of Royal Soc.* lxviii. 151.

4 *Census*, 1801.

5 *V.C.H. Ches.* v (1), Topography, 900–1914: Early Modern and Georgian (Residential Development, 1760–1840).

6 Para. based on ibid. ii. 210–11.

7 Above, Local Government Boundaries: Modern Boundary Extensions.

8 From 1881 the figs. include those returned separately for

Chester Castle civil parish.

9 *V.C.H. Ches.* ii. 207, 218, 224, 226, 229, 236.

10 *Census*, 1821–1931 (not separately enumerated in 1801 or 1811).   11 *V.C.H. Ches.* ii. 206, 218.

12 T. W. Freeman, H. B. Rodgers, and R. H. Kinvig, *Lancs., Ches., and Isle of Man*, 180.

13 Rest of para. based on *V.C.H. Ches.* ii. 204, 207, 210–11, 218, 236; *Census*, 1951, *Flints.*; above, Local Government Boundaries: Modern Boundary Extensions. The figs. for Chester include Chester Castle civil parish.

14 Freeman, Rodgers, and Kinvig, *Lancs., Ches., and Isle of Man*, 180.

borough boundary), falling to 77,384 in 1981, and 75,984 in 1991. The last two figures were for those people in Chester on census night; the population normally resident was only 75,422 in 1981 and 75,458 in 1991.[1] All those figures excluded East Saltney, which contained 4,455 people in 1981 and 4,530

in 1991.[2] The continuously built-up 'Chester urban area' (as defined for Census purposes), which extended further into Wales to include West Saltney and Broughton as well as the Cheshire villages of Moston, Rowton, Christleton, and Waverton, had 89,848 inhabitants in 1981 and 89,628 in 1991.[3]

ROADS AND ROAD TRANSPORT

ROADS

Chester has always lain at the convergence of many roadways, both national and local, which have both reflected and reinforced its standing as a regional capital. It was the focal point of Roman military roads in northwest Britain,[4] several stretches of which remained in use in later centuries, often together with river crossings, notably the Dee Bridge in Chester itself.[5] East of the city Roman roads crossed the river Gowy at Stamford and Trafford, later the site of fords and eventually, by the 13th century, of bridges.[6] In the Middle Ages political considerations made Chester an important staging post for north Wales and Ireland.[7] The Gough map of *c.* 1360 depicted the London–Chester–Caernarfon and the Bristol–Chester roads, the latter one of the few non-London roads shown.[8] The most important local roads were the saltways connecting Chester with Northwich, Middlewich, and Nantwich.[9] The main roads were improved and in some cases realigned under turnpike Acts passed between 1743 and 1787. They generally became the trunk and major roads of the 20th century, the busier ones being replaced by motorways or dual carriageways from the 1970s.[10]

The London Road

The Roman road to London left Chester by the south gate of the fortress, bridged the Dee, and recrossed the river at Aldford. A direct line took it to Wroxeter (Salop.) on Watling Street and thus to London. In

Cheshire the few lengths followed by modern roads include that between Handbridge and Eaton park.[11] The Roman road was disused by the 14th century, when the London road went instead over Stamford Bridge to Nantwich, Woore (Salop.), and Stone (Staffs.), where it converged with the road from Carlisle and the North to become one of the main national thoroughfares.[12] In 1676 and 1780 carts set out via Stamford Bridge but riders used an alternative 'horse road' through Christleton, crossing the Gowy further south at the bridge called Hockenhull Platts before rejoining the main road at Duddon heath.[13]

The London road was turnpiked from Staffordshire southwards by the 1720s, and from Chester to the Staffordshire border in 1743.[14] The Cheshire portion came under a separate turnpike trust in 1755.[15] The Acts of 1743 and 1755 prevented the trustees from building a tollgate anywhere between Nantwich and Chester, severely restricting the trust's income. As a result the condition of the road, which was heavily used, remained poor until an Act of 1769 empowered the trust to make further improvements.[16] The road was disturnpiked in 1883.[17] Designated the A51 in the 20th century, it remained the main London road until the M6 and M1 were fully opened in 1972. Access to the southbound M6 from Chester was improved when a new link road to the motorway east of Nantwich was built in the mid 1980s. Thereafter the shortest route to London followed the old road via Tarvin, Tarporley, and Nantwich, all three of which were bypassed in the 1980s.[18]

1 *Census*, 1981, *Ward and Civil Parish Monitor: Ches.* p. 4; ibid. 1991, p. 10; for definition of urban wards: Chester City Cl., Economic and Tourism Development Unit, *Analysis of 1991 Census Data* (copy at C.H.H.).

2 *Census*, 1981; inf. from Flints. County Cl., Planning Dept.

3 *Census*, 1981, *Key Statistics for Urban Areas: North*, p. 23; for definition of built-up area: ibid. pp. 5–6, 8–9; ibid. 1991, *Key Statistics for Urban and Rural Areas: North*, p. 22.

4 *V.C.H. Ches.* i. 116, 118, 216.

5 Below, this chapter: Bridges and Other River Crossings (Dee Bridge).

6 *P.N. Ches.* iii. 261; iv. 108–9, 133–5.

7 *V.C.H. Ches.* v (1), Early Medieval Chester: Chester and the Ealdormen and Earls of Mercia; Chester and the Anglo-Norman Earls; Later Medieval Chester: City and Crown, 1237–1350; City and Crown, 1350–1550.

8 *Map of G.B. c. 1360 known as the Gough Map* (Bodl. facsimile, 1958).

9 *T.L.C.A.S.* liv. 94–5 and map facing 92; B. P. Hindle, *Medieval Rds.* 49.

10 For details: below, this section.

11 *V.C.H. Ches.* i. 216–18; I. D. Margary, *Rom. Rds. in Brit.* (1967), 170–5, 183–7, 289–94, 296–9, 318–23.

12 *Gough Map*; F. M. Stenton, 'Rd. System of Medieval Eng.' *Econ. H.R.* [1st ser.], vii. 8–10; W. Harrison, *Description of Eng. [1577]* (1877 edn.), iii. 111; W. Smith, *Particular Description of Eng. 1588*, ed. H. B. Wheatley and E. W. Ashbee, 71; G. Scott Thompson, 'Rds. in Eng. and Wales, 1603', *E.H.R.* xxxiii. 239; *Diary of Henry Prescott*, i. 120; ii. 328, 400–1, 548, 599.

13 J. Ogilby, *Britannia* (facsimile edn. 1939), plates 21–4; *T.L.C.A.S.* ix. 114–15; K. W. L. Starkie, 'The Lond.–Chester Rd., via Hockenhull Platts', *Ches. Hist.* xxxviii. 40–9.

14 W. Albert, *Turnpike Rd. System in Eng. 1663–1840*, 227; 17 Geo. II, c. 24.

15 Litchfield and Chester Rds. Act, 1755, 28 Geo. II, c. 52.

16 9 Geo. III, c. 94.

17 Annual Turnpike Acts Continuance Act, 1876, 39 & 40 Vic. c. 39, no. 76.

18 Edns. from 1963 of rd. atlases publ. by Bartholomew and Automobile Association.

The Holyhead Road and North Wales

The Roman roads into north Wales left the London road some way south of the fortress at Chester in order to avoid the marshes around Saltney.[1] The more southerly of the two routes, to Caer Gai (Merion.), is largely marked by modern roads. The more northerly ran parallel to the north Wales coast from Balderton to Holywell (Flints.), then turned west across the mountains to Caernarfon.[2]

By the 14th century the route instead followed the coast to Flint, Rhuddlan (Flints.), Conwy (Caern.), and Bangor (Caern.).[3] In the later 16th century it took a long inland detour from Flint to Denbigh and back to the coast at Conwy.[4] By the 1670s the road left Chester by the Dee Bridge and Hough Green, crossed Saltney heath to Bretton (Flints.) and proceeded thence through Hawarden across Halkyn mountain to Denbigh. From there it followed what in the 20th century were minor and mostly unclassified roads, heading north-west to Bettws-yn-Rhos (Denb.), and then west to the Conwy ferry and eventually Holyhead (Ang.).[5]

In the turnpike era the mountainous stretches beyond Denbigh were abandoned by most traffic in favour of a more northerly route to Conwy through St. Asaph and Abergele (Denb.).[6] The stretch from Chester via Northop to Holywell and beyond was turnpiked in 1756, and the Chester–Northop road came under a separate district in 1828.[7] As a whole the Chester–Holyhead road was described in 1822 as 'very imperfect': poorly surfaced, hilly, and under the divided management of seven turnpike trusts.[8] Responsibility for its maintenance remained divided, and the Chester district was disturnpiked in 1883.[9] The road to Bangor, later designated a trunk road, the A55, was improved in stages from the late 1960s.[10]

Even before Thomas Telford's improvement of the Holyhead road through mid Wales there was an alternative to the London–Chester–Holyhead road via Shrewsbury, Llangollen, Llanrwst (both Denb.), and

Bangor, described in 1778 as 'a hard, smooth, level road . . . 27 miles nearer than by Chester',[11] and by 1789 passable in all weather.[12] Further improvement by the Holyhead Road Commissioners and Telford had by 1822 made the London–Chester–Holyhead route superfluous, though local traffic from Chester still used it.[13] Chester's significance as a centre for road traffic was thereby very much reduced.

The Dee fords at Blacon Point and Shotwick provided another route into north-east Wales.[14] After the canalization of the river in the 1730s and the reclamation of Sealand, new roads were laid out by the Dee Company under the River Dee Act of 1743 to serve the ferries which replaced the fords.[15] The main road ran the length of Sealand from the end of New Crane Street in Chester to the Lower King's Ferry (later Queensferry), and other roads branched from it to the Higher Ferry, Great Saughall, and Shotwick. They were transferred from the management of the Dee Company to the local authorities in 1894.[16] Roads leading to the Lower Ferry were effectively turnpiked between 1826 and 1838; under the last Act a new through road was made from the Mersey ferries to Queensferry, taking away from Chester all the direct traffic between Liverpool and north Wales.[17] The Lower King's Ferry Turnpike Trust expired in 1882.[18]

After a bridge was opened at Queensferry in 1897[19] Sealand Road became a busy route between Chester and the industrial districts of Deeside. Use of the Queensferry bridge as a western Chester bypass for traffic to and from north Wales increased when a new road leading to it (the A5117) was built in the early 1930s from Helsby on the Chester–Warrington road.[20]

The Welsh Borders

In the Middle Ages the important road south from Chester through the Welsh Marches steered east of the Roman road from Wroxeter to Caerleon (Mon.) to take in Shrewsbury, Worcester, Gloucester, and Bristol. Between Chester and Shrewsbury the route *c.* 1360 was through Overton (Flints.) and Ellesmere (Salop.), but

1 *V.C.H. Ches.* i. 219.

2 Margary, *Rom. Rds. in Brit.* 346–51.

3 *Gough Map*; *Econ. H.R.* [1st ser.], vii. 10.

4 Harrison, *Description [1577]*, iii. 111; Smith, *Particular Description*, 1588, 71; *E.H.R.* xxxiii. 239.

5 Ogilby, *Britannia*, plates 21–4; *Diary of Henry Prescott*, i. 20, 245; ii. 463, 508, 540.

6 Paterson, *Rds.* (1778), cols. 77–80; (1789), cols. 95–8; (1807), i, cols. 179–86; (1822), 188–93.

7 Shrewsbury and Wrexham Rd. Act, 1756, 29 Geo. II, c. 93; 9 Geo. IV, c. 74 (Local and Personal).

8 *3rd Rep. Sel. Cttee. State of Rds. from Lond. to Chester and Holyhead*, H.C. 275, pp. 35–51 (1822), vi.

9 Annual Turnpike Acts Continuance Act, 1876, 39 & 40 Vic. c. 39, no. 73.

10 Edns. from 1963 of rd. atlases publ. by Bartholomew and Automobile Association.

11 Paterson, *Rds.* (1778), cols. 81–2.

12 Ibid. (1789), cols. 100–1.

13 Ibid. (1822), 179–88.

14 Below, this chapter: Bridges and Other River Crossings (Medieval Fords and Ferries).

15 17 Geo. II, c. 28, s. 24; below, Water Transport: River; cf. H. W. Owen, *Place-Names of E. Flints.* 130.

16 Queen's Ferry Bridge Act, 1894, 57 & 58 Vic. c. 180 (Local), s. 60.

17 Saltney and Flint Turnpike Acts, 1788, 28 Geo. III, c. 101; 1809, 49 Geo. III, c. 11 (Local and Personal); Lower King's Ferry Turnpike Acts, 1826, 7 Geo. IV, c. 86 (Local and Personal); 1829, 10 Geo. IV, c. 86 (Local and Personal); 1835, 5 & 6 Wm. IV, c. 88 (Local and Personal); 1838, 1 & 2 Vic. c. 19 (Local and Personal).

18 Annual Turnpike Acts Continuance Act, 1882, 45 & 46 Vic. c. 52, no. 2.

19 Below, this chapter: Bridges and Other River Crossings (Later Ferries and Bridges).

20 *Newnes' Motorists' Touring Maps and Gazetteer* (1931, 1936 edns.).

c. 1480 went instead further east through Malpas and Whitchurch.[1]

The Whitchurch road was diverted by stages over most of its length away from the Roman line. The ancient ford at Aldford, still used *c.* 1070,[2] had been abandoned by *c.* 1200, when the way from Chester to Aldford went instead by the Eastgate and the right bank of the Dee.[3] In later centuries it served only as a minor road connecting Chester with the villages in the Dee valley and the bridge over the Dee at Farndon. It was a turnpike as far as Worthenbury (Flints.) between 1854 and 1877.[4]

By 1315 the main Whitchurch road bypassed Aldford altogether, following a line through Boughton and Christleton and then east of the modern main road to No Man's Heath.[5] That remained the route in later centuries,[6] heavily used by traffic for Shrewsbury and London. A few miles in Cheshire were a turnpike 1705–26,[7] and the entire road from Chester to Whitchurch and Birmingham was turnpiked in 1759.[8] The trust was wound up in 1877.[9] In the 20th century the road was designated a trunk road as the A41 and remained the main road between Chester and Shrewsbury. It was also the way to Bristol[10] until the M6 and M5 were opened between the mid 1960s and 1971.[11]

The other principal way to Shrewsbury and the Marches was via Wrexham. That road left the city by the Dee Bridge and Handbridge and branched west from the Roman road to Aldford along what was called Bromfield or Wrexham Lane.[12] In the 17th century the road led on beyond Wrexham to mid Wales, Brecon, and Cardiff,[13] but the Chester–Wrexham part was turnpiked in 1756 as an extension of the Shrewsbury and Wrexham turnpike, whose trust supervised other roads which gave access from Chester to Flint, Holywell, and Mold.[14] Beyond Handbridge a new stretch was built west of the original line. The Chester–Wrexham road was under a separate trust from

1828[15] and was disturnpiked in 1877.[16] In the 20th century it was numbered the A483, which continued to Oswestry, Newtown (Mont.), and Brecon. By the early 1990s the whole route from Chester to Oswestry and beyond had been replaced by a fast new road, mostly dual carriageway.[17]

East and North-East

The Roman transpennine road from Chester left the fortress at the east gate, crossed the river Gowy at Stamford Bridge and headed in an almost straight line to cross the Weaver at Northwich before turning north for Manchester.[18] Most of that road remained in use as a primary route in 2000. In the Middle Ages the Northwich–Chester section, diverted through Kelsall and Tarvin, was a saltway also known as 'Lynstrete', 'the road to the Lyme'.[19] In the late 16th century it was regarded as the way not only to Manchester but to cross the Pennines.[20] Its condition may have been poor, since by the late 17th century the preferred route to Manchester went instead through Frodsham, Warrington, and Salford (Lancs.).[21] The road via Northwich and Altrincham was turnpiked in stages between 1753 and 1769 and thereafter the two routes were probably regarded as alternatives.[22]

The route to Manchester through Frodsham and Warrington followed what was probably a Roman road[23] to cross the Mersey by Warrington bridge.[24] In the 1370s the road left Chester by the Northgate and turned right along Bag Lane (later George Street),[25] but later the route went from the Eastgate along Cow Lane, a road which in the 19th century was successively renamed Warrington Street and Frodsham Street.[26] Beyond Flookersbrook bridge the original course was along the line later taken by Kilmorey Park, Newton Hollows, Mannings Lane, and the Street as far as Trafford Bridge.[27] The road was realigned through the villages of Hoole and Mickle Trafford when it

1 *Gough Map*; *Econ. H.R.* [1st ser.], vii. 5, 8; Wm. Worcester, *Itin.* ed. J. H. Harvey, 331.

2 Ormerod, *Hist. Ches.* ii. 754.

3 Lucian, *De Laude Cestrie*, 63–4.

4 17 & 18 Vic. c. 86 (Local and Personal); Annual Turnpike Acts Continuance Act, 1876, 39 & 40 Vic. c. 39, no. 97.

5 *P.N. Ches.* i. 42; iv. 91.

6 e.g. Ogilby, *Britannia*, plates 56–7; *Diary of Henry Prescott*, i. 90, 234.

7 4 & 5 Anne, c. 9; Albert, *Turnpike Rd. System*, 202.

8 33 Geo. II, c. 51.

9 Annual Turnpike Acts Continuance Act, 1876, 39 & 40 Vic. c. 39, no. 59.

10 Smith, *Particular Description, 1588*, 70; Ogilby, *Britannia*, plates 56–7; Paterson, *Rds.* (1778), cols. 170–1.

11 Edns. from 1963 of rd. atlases publ. by Bartholomew and Automobile Association.

12 *P.N. Ches.* i. 39; v (1:i), 58.

13 Ogilby, *Britannia*, plates 63–4; cf. Paterson, *Rds.* (1778), cols. 180–1.

14 Shrewsbury and Wrexham Turnpike Act, 1751, 25 Geo. II, c. 22; Shrewsbury, Wrexham, and Chester Turnpike Act, 1756,

29 Geo. II, c. 93.

15 9 Geo. IV, c. 77 (Local and Personal).

16 Annual Turnpike Acts Continuance Act, 1872, 35 & 36 Vic. c. 85, no. 109.

17 Edns. from 1963 of rd. atlases publ. by Bartholomew and Automobile Association.

18 *V.C.H. Ches.* i. 218–19; Margary, *Rom. Rds. in Brit.* 300–2.

19 *P.N. Ches.* i. 40–1.

20 Smith, *Particular Description, 1588*, 71.

21 Ogilby, *Britannia*, plates 89–90.

22 Cranage Green and Altrincham Turnpike Act, 1753, 26 Geo. II, c. 62; Altrincham and Manchester Turnpike Act, 1765, 5 Geo. II, c. 98; Chester and Woore Turnpike Act, 1769, 9 Geo. III, c. 94; Paterson, *Rds.* (1778), col. 181; (1789), col. 218; (1807), ii, cols. 436–40; (1822), 441–5.

23 Margary, *Rom. Rds. in Brit.* 304–5; *V.C.H. Ches.* i. 221.

24 e.g. Hewitt, *Med. Ches.* 1–2.

25 P.R.O., CHES 19/1, m. 27 (Mr. P. H. W. Booth is thanked for the ref.); *V.C.H. Ches.* v (1), Topography, 900–1914: Later Medieval (Extramural and Suburban Development).

26 *P.N. Ches.* v (1:i), 65–6.

27 Ibid. i. 40; iv. 146.

was turnpiked as far as the existing turnpike at Warrington in 1786.[1] It was disturnpiked in two parts in 1870 and 1883.[2]

The turnpiking of the Warrington–Stockport road in 1820[3] added another possible route between Chester and Manchester, and it was that, via Frodsham and Altrincham, which was designated the A56 in the 20th century. The road was improved in the 1960s and superseded in the 1970s by the M56 motorway, which also provided the main access from Chester to the M6 northbound and the M62 into Yorkshire.[4]

In the Middle Ages the saltway from Middlewich to Chester went via Winsford bridge to join the North-wich–Chester road just east of Kelsall.[5] It remained in use in the 20th century.

Wirral

Stretches of a Roman road from the Northgate along Wirral have been discovered, presumably leading to the anchorage at Meols.[6] After the medieval decline of the harbour there the roads into Wirral were of no more than local importance. Their main function as roads to Chester market is implied by the name Portway, which in the 13th and 14th centuries was applied to at least three of them, from West Kirby, Whitby, and Ince.[7] Perhaps more important was 'Blakestrete', which in 1357 led from Chester to the Mersey ferry at Birkenhead.[8] The Dee fords at Blacon Point and Shotwick and the Wirral outports were reached by the sands at low tide or by rough tracks along the coast.[9]

In the early 18th century it took a day to travel to Liverpool and back, via Eastham,[10] but the rise of Liverpool and the emergence of Parkgate as a resort and harbour for Ireland demanded better roads into and across Wirral. Existing roads to Parkgate and the Mersey ferries were turnpiked in 1787, the latter being regarded as a main route from Liverpool to the south.[11] The Wirral roads were disturnpiked in 1883.[12]

In the 20th century, the road from Chester to Birkenhead increased in importance, taking traffic generated by the growth of Ellesmere Port, the sub-

urbanization of mid Wirral, and the opening of the first Mersey road tunnel between Birkenhead and Liverpool in 1934.[13] As the route between Liverpool and Chester it was, however, entirely superseded when the M53 Wirral motorway, connected to the second Mersey road tunnel at Wallasey, was opened in 1971 north of Childer Thornton and extended by 1984 to the outskirts of Chester.[14]

Bypasses

In the 20th century Chester was besieged by through traffic (Fig. 36) and a ring-road outside the city boundary was agreed upon as a necessity as early as 1922.[15] Planning began in 1924 and a short section in Lache was opened in 1928 and named Circular Drive. A longer stretch between Moston and Long Lane east of the city was open by 1950.[16] The completion of the road was impeded by protracted negotiations with neighbouring authorities, cuts in local government expenditure in 1931, the reduction of the central government grant for road-building in 1934, the out-break of the Second World War, post-war lack of funds, and the failure of the Ministry of Transport to make it a priority in the 1960s.[17] In the end the idea of a complete ring-road was given up in favour of a dual-carriageway southerly bypass, opened in 1977, which linked the eastern bypass with the improved A55 and other roads into north Wales. The eastern bypass was itself bypassed when the M53 was linked to the south-ern bypass in the early 1990s. At about the same time a partial western bypass was constructed linking Liverpool Road, Parkgate Road, and Sealand Road.[18]

BRIDGES AND OTHER RIVER CROSSINGS
Dee Bridge

Chester was the lowest bridging point on the Dee from earliest times. Almost certainly the Romans built a bridge on or near the site of the later structure; its remains were identified on the river bed in 1984 and a massive stone wall in Lower Bridge Street has been interpreted as part of a causeway leading to it.[19] Its fate after the Roman army left Chester is uncertain.

1 26 Geo. III, c. 139; Salford, Warrington, and Bolton Turn-pike Act, 1753, 26 Geo. II, c. 63.

2 Annual Turnpike Acts Continuance Acts, 1869, 32 & 33 Vic. c. 90, no. 30; 1876, 39 & 40 Vic. c. 39, no. 72.

3 1 Geo. IV, c. 28 (Local and Personal).

4 Edns. from 1963 of rd. atlases publ. by Bartholomew and Automobile Association.

5 *P.N. Ches.* i. 47–8; iii. 173.

6 *V.C.H. Ches.* i. 219; Margary, *Rom. Rds. in Brit.* 299–300.

7 *P.N. Ches.* i. 39, 49; iv. 141.   8 Ibid. i. 39–40; iv. 232.

9 C. Armour, 'Trade of Chester and Dee Navigation' (Lond. Univ. Ph.D. thesis, 1952), 152; below, this chapter: Bridges and Other River Crossings (Medieval Fords and Ferries).

10 *Diary of Henry Prescott*, i. 14, 103; ii. 481.

11 27 Geo. III, c. 93; Paterson, *Rds.* (1778), col. 91; (1789), col. 113.

12 Annual Turnpike Acts Continuance Act, 1876, 39 & 40 Vic. c. 39, no. 90.

13 *Mersey Tunnel* (Liverpool, [1951]), 84.

14 Edns. from 1963 of rd. atlases publ. by Bartholomew and Automobile Association.

15 P. Abercrombie, S. Kelly, and T. Fyfe, *Deeside Regional Planning Scheme*, pp. xi, 35, 48–51, map 1.

16 *Newnes' Motorists' Touring Maps and Gazetteer* (1936, 1950 edns.).

17 *Chester City Cl. Mins.* 1922/3, 713–14; 1923/4, 58, 148–9, 231, 341, 431, 549, 620; 1924/5, 112, 144, 202, 478, 683; 1925/6, 319, 381, 556; 1926/7, 615; 1927/8, 305, 397, 442, 469; 1928/9, 67, 71, 250, 821; 1929/30, 661, 847–8, 974–5, 977; 1930/1, 27, 84–8, 183, 348–9, 536, 743–4, 1128; 1931/2, 71–2; 1933/4, 314, 602, 649, 991; 1934/5, 66, 233–4, 340–1, 525–6, 916; 1935/6, 55–6; 1936/7, 62; 1937/8, 76, 755–6; 1944/5, 222; 1945/6, 136, 580–1; 1958/9, pp. 493–4; 1962/3, pp. 210, 225, 840; 1964/5, pp. 568, 1037; 1965/6, p. 379; 1966/7, p. 105; 1971/2, pp. 42, 680.

18 Edns. from 1963 of rd. atlases publ. by Bartholomew and Automobile Association.   19 *V.C.H. Ches.* i. 174.

FIG. 36. *Heavy traffic in Bridge Street, 1930s*

By 1066 there was again a bridge, the burden for the repair of which fell upon the men of Cheshire as a whole.[1] In 1182–3, when the earldom was in royal wardship, work was done on that bridge or its successor, but by 1227 it was claimed that it had collapsed.[2] Money was again spent on repairs in 1241–2 and between 1250 and 1254.[3] Further work, including the erection of a brattice in the middle of the bridge, was carried out in the 1270s,[4] but in 1279 or 1280 the entire structure was allegedly carried away by a sea flood.[5]

Until 1280 the responsibility for repairing the bridge rested firmly with the comital administration and was paid for out of the revenues from the county as a whole.[6] By 1285, however, the men of Cheshire were claiming that the city of Chester ought also to contribute to the costs,[7] and in 1288 it was agreed that the landholders and inhabitants of the liberty would sustain the southern part of the bridge provided the county continued to take care of the rest. The terms of the agreement make it clear that by 1288 the bridge comprised stone piers and a timber superstructure together with a causeway of compressed earth and stone at the southern end.[8]

The destruction of the bridge in 1279 or 1280 led to proposals that Chester abbey should also contribute towards its maintenance. Although in 1284 the abbot obtained a royal order in support of any exemption proved by his charters, the matter was raised again after

a fresh collapse in 1316, when Abbot Thomas Birchills complained that the sheriff of Cheshire had improperly distrained oxen at his grange of Little Sutton to enforce a contribution to the repairs. Examination of the county records showed that the abbey had never so contributed and judgement was given in favour of the abbot.[9]

By 1346 the bridge once more required attention. Responsibility for its repair was again disputed and a claim against the abbot of St. Werburgh's was revived.[10] In 1347 the Black Prince's mason and surveyor, Henry of Snelson, was charged with oversight of the work, and in 1348 payment was made to the justice of Chester, Sir Thomas Ferrers, for repair to the piers and arches of the bridge, and to the tower which by then stood at the southern end.[11] Nevertheless, in 1351 it was still 'in such plight that no one [could] pass over it'.[12] In that year it was agreed that the abbot and the shire should contribute for a final time to the repair and thenceforward be discharged of the responsibility for ever.[13] A quarry was purchased to obtain the stone necessary to complete the work, and by 1354 the bridge was once more open.[14] During its closure a ford and a ferry were maintained by the keeper of the passage of Dee.[15] Evidently, however, work still remained to be done, for in 1357 and 1358 it was found necessary to order the mayor and citizens to make all speed with that part of the bridge which was their responsibility, and to complete the work in stone to match the rest.[16]

1 Ibid. i. 250–1, 343; *Domesday Surv. Ches.* 85.
2 *Ches. in Pipe R.* 8; *Ann. Cest.* 55.
3 *Ches. in Pipe R.* 71; *Cal. Lib.* 1240–5, 53, 59.
4 *Ches. in Pipe R.* 109, 120.
5 *Ann. Cest.* 107; *Cal. Fine R.* 1272–1307, 119.
6 *Ches. in Pipe R.* 100–1, 109; *Cal. Lib.* 1251–60, 282.
7 *Sel. Cases in K.B.* i (Selden Soc. lv), 157–8.
8 28 D.K.R. 7; 3 *Sheaf*, xxi, pp. 32–3.
9 *J.C.A.S.* xxx. 70–2, quoting B.L. Harl. MS. 2071, f. 89;

P.R.O., CHES 29/30, m. 1d.
10 *Blk. Prince's Reg.* i. 37. Cf. ibid. iii. 87–8.
11 Ibid. i. 83; *Ches. Chamb. Accts.* 126.
12 *Blk. Prince's Reg.* iii. 9.   13 Ibid. iii. 15, 19, 22, 88.
14 *Ches. Chamb. Accts.* 169, 221.
15 Ibid. 119, 141, 179–80, 221; P.R.O., SC 6/783/15, m. 1; SC 6/784/2, m. 1; SC 6/784/3, m. 1; SC 6/784/5, m. 1; below, this section (Medieval Fords and Ferries).
16 *Blk. Prince's Reg.* iii. 275, 298.

FIG. 37. *Dee Bridge from east, 1810s*

In 1387, when the bridge was once more 'destroyed and broken', the entire responsibility for its repair was apparently placed upon the citizens of Chester; to assist in the work they were granted a murage (a special tax usually assigned to the repair of the city walls), together with 'all the profits of the passage of the said water at Dee'.[1] The new work was protected by an order, promulgated in 1394 and still in force in 1533, forbidding the passage of carts with iron-bound wheels.[2] It included a tower at the southern end, to finish which it was decided in 1407 to devote half the income from the ensuing five years' murage.[3] That end of the bridge was again repaired or renewed at the end of the 15th century.[4]

Almost certainly the bridge which still spanned the river in 2000 was substantially that reconstructed after 1387. Built of the local red sandstone, it originally consisted of eight arches, later reduced to seven (four segmental and three pointed), surmounted by a carriageway with a stone parapet;[5] the southern gatehouse, which survived until the 1780s, stood between the sixth and seventh arches from the Chester side.[6]

By the later 16th century the bridge was described as ruinous,[7] and from the 1570s to the 1590s leases of the gatehouse at the southern end obliged the tenant to carry out repairs, apparently to the bridge itself as well as to the buildings upon it; in 1594, for example, the lessee Thomas Lyniall undertook to repair the structure and to build 'fair and beautiful houses' on the tower and south side.[8] Nevertheless, its condition remained a matter of civic concern and the Assembly appointed surveyors for its repair in 1623.[9]

During the siege of Chester the bridge seems to have sustained no permanent damage. Charles I crossed it twice in 1645, protected from the besiegers' view on his return journey by specially erected blinds; and the parliamentarians, unable to shake the citizens' hold over it, bypassed it by building a bridge of boats a short distance upstream.[10] Maintenance remained a civic concern and further repairs were carried out in 1660 and 1704.[11]

Towards the end of the 18th century anxiety was expressed about the narrowness and inconvenience of the bridge and its approaches. The steep descent in Lower Bridge Street was eased, the Bridgegate rebuilt, and the gatehouse at the Handbridge end demolished.[12] Nevertheless, the structure itself remained 'very narrow and dangerous'.[13] The canalization of the Dee had, no doubt, exacerbated the inconvenience to travellers, since the heavily used fords lower down the river had been replaced by less convenient ferries. Fresh complaints were voiced at a public meeting in 1818, and for some years it was debated whether the better solution would be to widen the existing bridge or to build another.[14] Both policies were eventually adopted. In 1824 the corporation decided that care of the old bridge should be vested in the trustees of the planned new bridge, and improvements were carried out in 1826. The bridge was widened by 7 ft. on the upstream side by adding an iron-plate footpath and railings, and the road surface was macadamized.[15] Tolls taken at the bridge tollhouse were let for over £3,000 in 1826 and 1827, but in 1829 the city judged it more profitable to retain direct control and a paid collector was appointed.[16] Tolls continued to be levied until 1885.[17]

1 C.C.A.L.S., ZCH 20; Morris, *Chester*, 503.
2 Morris, *Chester*, 261 n.; C.C.A.L.S., ZSB 7, f. 16.
3 C.C.A.L.S., ZCH 25; Morris, *Chester*, 509.
4 *King's Vale Royal*, [i], 78; [ii], 190.   5 Ibid. [i], 37.
6 R. Stewart-Brown, 'Old Dee Bridge at Chester', *J.C.A.S.* xxx. 63–78; C.C.A.L.S., ZAB 4, ff. 352, 356.
7 C.C.A.L.S., ZAB 1, f. 148.
8 Ibid. ff. 169, 206v.; ZCHB 3, f. 62v.; Morris, *Chester*, 232 n.
9 *Cal. Chester City Cl. Mins. 1603–42*, 122.
10 Morris, *Siege of Chester*, 110, 121, 131.

11 C.C.A.L.S., ZAB 2, f. 126; ZAB 3, f. 122.
12 Ibid. ZAB 4, ff. 336, 343, 345, 352, 356; below, City Walls and Gates: Gates, Posterns, and Towers (Bridgegate).
13 T. Pennant, *Tours in Wales*, i. 139.
14 C.C.A.L.S., ZTRB 1; below, this section (Grosvenor Bridge).
15 C.C.A.L.S., ZAB 5, pp. 480–1; ZTRB 1, ff. 46, 52v.–53; *J.C.A.S.* xxx. 77; *Gresty and Burghall's Chester Guide* [1867], 43.
16 C.C.A.L.S., ZTRB 1, ff. 15 and v., 53v., 62v., 75.
17 *J.C.A.S.* lxi. 65.

FIG. 38. *Grosvenor Bridge from west, soon after opening*

The opening of the Grosvenor Bridge in 1832 created a new and much more convenient route out of the city towards north Wales, leaving the old Dee Bridge mainly to local traffic. It was adequate for such use,[1] but improvements carried out at Handbridge in the 1920s gave it a new lease of life as a thoroughfare, and in 1933 the city council's improvement committee began to consider a further widening.[2] By 1935, however, it had been agreed that it would be preferable to install traffic lights to restrict traffic using the bridge to one direction at a time.[3] Lights remained there in 2000.

Grosvenor Bridge

In 1818 a committee was elected at a public meeting at the Exchange to promote a Bill for an additional bridge over the Dee at Chester and to commission an architect for it. The bridge was to be situated on a new road to run from the Wrexham road, south of the river, to the Two Churches in Bridge Street, a scheme which involved the destruction of St. Bridget's church. Thomas Harrison was chosen as architect and Thomas Telford and Marc Isambard Brunel were also consulted.[4] An Act of 1825 established commissioners to implement the scheme.[5] The elderly Harrison resigned as architect in 1826, to be succeeded by one of his pupils, William Cole junior. Harrison's final scheme for a bridge with a single stone span of 200 ft. was apparently adopted with

only one significant amendment: plain abutments with niches and pediments were substituted for the paired columns in the original plans.[6] The bridge was opened by Princess Victoria in October 1832. Built largely of Peckforton and Chester sandstone, with granite voussoirs, it was believed to be the largest single-span stone bridge then in existence and impressed contemporaries by its elegance and as a feat of civil engineering.[7] The work also involved the construction of tollhouses and gates and substantial embankments along the approaches. Grosvenor Bridge remained under the control of the Dee Bridge Commissioners until 1885, when they were bought out by the city corporation and the tolls were abolished.[8]

Suspension Bridge

Another ornament to the city was the pedestrian suspension bridge built by James Dredge in 1852 to link the Groves with the new residential suburb of Queen's Park.[9] Having become unsafe, it was taken over by the corporation, which replaced it with a new structure in 1923 (Fig. 39, p. 80).[10] It survived in 2000.

Medieval Fords and Ferries

Besides the Dee Bridge, there were other crossing points within or near the city liberties in the Middle Ages. By the later 13th century a ford downstream from Chester and just outside the liberties at Blacon

1 Below, this section (Grosvenor Bridge).

2 *Chester City Cl. Mins. 1932/3*, 215, 989, 1021, 1028; *1933/4*, 78, 1010.

3 Ibid. *1934/5*, 54, 224, 501.

4 J. W. Clarke, 'Bldg. of Grosvenor Bridge', *J.C.A.S.* xlv. 43, 51–2. In 1826 Brunel produced a drawing for a single-span bridge: C.C.A.L.S., ZG/HS [Acc. 871].

5 *J.C.A.S.* xlv. 43–5, based on C.C.A.L.S., ZTRB.

6 *J.C.A.S.* xlv. 51–4; C.C.A.L.S., ZTRB 1, ff. 24–25v., 31v.–32v., 39–40v.; ZTRB 164–5.   7 *J.C.A.S.* xlv. 51, 54.

8 Ibid. 55 (where the date is wrongly given as 1865); ibid. lxi. 65; C.C.A.L.S., ZTRB 57.

9 Hughes, *Stranger's Handbk.* (1856), 39–40; J. Romney, *Chester and its Environs Illustrated*, [53].

10 *Chester City Cl. Mins. 1920/1*, 142, 270, 302, 473, 537–8, 621–2, 660; Pevsner, *Ches.* 160.

FIG. 39. *Suspension bridge of 1923, from the Groves*

FIG. 40. *Queen's Ferry, mid 19th century*

Point was in the custody of the Mainwaring family in time of war.[1] Perhaps, too, the ford known later to have been located upstream at Boughton was already used.[2]

By the mid 14th century a ferry in Chester itself functioned under the control of a comital keeper at periods when the Dee Bridge was not passable.[3]

Below the Dee Bridge and Blacon ford was Shotwick ford, of strategic importance in the early 14th century when it carried a road used by the king's army called 'Saltesway', which began on Hoole heath and bypassed Chester to the north.[4] Because the route from Chester by the Dee Bridge into north Wales involved a long detour through Lower Kinnerton to avoid the Saltney marshes, travellers preferred the fords down river, especially since they thereby escaped the tolls charged at the bridge. Nevertheless, a journey across the estuary's shifting sands was hazardous, and many were drowned making the crossing.[5]

Later Ferries and Bridges

The Dee fords downstream from Chester were destroyed by the cutting of a new river channel in the 1730s, and were replaced by two ferries. Under an Act of 1744 the River Dee Company was to supply the boats and maintain the roads leading to them. The Higher Ferry was at Saltney; the lower ferry was originally called King's Ferry, but was renamed Queen's Ferry (later giving rise to the place name Queensferry) after Victoria's accession.[6]

Both ferries were eventually superseded. The Victoria Jubilee toll bridge opened in 1897 to replace the lower ferry. In 1926 it was rebuilt and made free of toll and in 1962 it was supplemented by the Queensferry bypass bridge a little to the east.[7] The higher ferry, at Saltney, was replaced by a footbridge in 1968.[8]

Other Bridges within the Liberties

The northern boundary of the liberties, formed by the stream known variously as Flooker's brook, Newton brook, and Finchett's Gutter, was crossed from an early period by stone bridges at Portpool, where it drained into the Dee, and on the Mollington road. One of the 13th-century names for the former was Wyardesbridge, possibly from a pre-Conquest personal name. To the south of the Dee, a bridge carried the road to Eccleston across the watercourse which formed the limit of the city liberties.[9] At Saltney, too, the boundary between the city and Flintshire was marked by a stone bridge in the late Middle Ages.[10] A little to the east at Hough Green a further bridge was built by the city corporation in 1598–9 to ease the passage of loaded horses, carts, and waggons through the Hollow Way.[11]

1 *Cart. Chester Abbey*, ii, pp. 462–3; 3 *Sheaf*, lix, pp. 12–13.

2 Eaton Hall MSS., Box Pp. 2, quoted in 4 *Sheaf*, v, p. 6.

3 *Ches. Chamb. Accts.* 119, 141, 179–80; P.R.O., SC 6/783/15, m. 1; SC 6/784/5, m. 1; SC 6/785/3, m. 1; SC 6/785/8, m. 1; C.C.A.L.S., ZCH 20.

4 *P.N. Ches.* iv. 130; *Great Diurnal of Nic. Blundell*, i (R.S.L.C. cx), 143; iii (R.S.L.C. cxiv), 49–50.

5 e.g. C.C.A.L.S., ZQCI 11/27; ZQCI 12/25; ZQCI 12/43; ZQCI 13/19; ZQCI 14/3; ZQCI 14/22; ZQCI 14/26; ZQCI 15/7;

ZQCI 15/35; ZQCI 16/12; ZQCI 16/25; ZQCI 16/43; ZQCI 17/1–2; ZQCI 18/22; 3 *Sheaf*, x, p. 55.

6 3 *Sheaf*, xi, p. 7; lix, pp. 12–15; 4 *Sheaf*, v, p. 44; E. Davies, *Flints. Place-Names*, 142; Dee Navigation Amendment Act, 17 Geo. II, c. 28.

7 3 *Sheaf*, lix, pp. 14–15.   8 4 *Sheaf*, v, p. 44.

9 *P.N. Ches.* v (1:i), 55–6, 70–2.

10 B.L. Harl. MS. 7568, f. 168v.

11 C.C.A.L.S., ZAB 1, ff. 255, 258.

FIG. 41. *Carriers' waggons at Falcon Inn, Lower Bridge Street, c. 1830*

In 2000 no trace remained of any of those bridges. They appear to have survived until the 17th century or later, and indeed in 1691 the bridge at Hough Green was repaired. The stone bridge at Portpool probably disappeared with the canalization of the Dee, while the others were presumably made redundant when the streams which they crossed were covered over.[1]

LONG-DISTANCE ROAD TRANSPORT

By the 1580s regular carriers by waggon and packhorse plied between Chester and London, then an eight-day journey.[2] In the 1710s mail carriers ran from Chester to Liverpool, Manchester, Kendal (Westmld.), St. Asaph (Flints.), Oswestry (Salop.), and Oxford, among other places.[3] By the 1790s there were three main depots for long-distance waggons, the Wool Hall in Northgate Street and two inns in Foregate Street, the Blossoms and the Hop Pole. Between them they sent goods daily to London, Birmingham, and Liverpool; thrice weekly to Wrexham, Whitchurch (Salop.), Warrington, Manchester, and Middlewich; and weekly to Oswestry and Shrewsbury. There was also a dense network of carrying services throughout north Wales, running weekly or less frequently to market towns as far distant as Beaumaris (Ang.), Caernarfon, Pwllheli (Caern.), Bala (Merion.), and Welshpool (Mont.). They used a different set of inns, especially the King's Head in Whitefriars and the White Bear and the Falcon in Lower Bridge Street.[4] Such services

survived until the railways were built in the early 1840s.[5]

Nearby market towns without a direct railway link had road carriers to Chester for much longer. In 1855 services were advertised to Hawarden (Flints.), Mold (Flints.), Denbigh, Ruthin (Denb.), Cerrig-y-Drudion (Denb.), Farndon, Malpas, Whitchurch, Tarporley, Northwich, Runcorn, Warrington, Neston, and Parkgate.[6] As the railway lines became denser, many of those were also discontinued, but carriers still ran to Hawarden, Malpas, and Neston in the 1890s and to Farndon and Tarporley as late as 1923.[7]

For passengers, a stage-coach service between Chester and London was first projected in 1653 by the operators of the London–York coaches.[8] A service had certainly been started by three London partners before 1657. It ran thrice a week in summer, travelling via Stone (Staffs.) and taking four days, but only once a week in winter. Alternative routes were evidently used in the early, experimental years of the service, one via Stone, Lichfield, and Coventry, and another via Newport (Salop.), Wolverhampton, and Birmingham.[9] In the 1660s it settled into a pattern which remained stable into the mid 18th century. The journey took four days in summer and six in winter and mostly stopped at the same inns for dinner and lodgings. As with other early stage-coach services, the different partners in the business were each responsible for one stretch of the road. In the 1680s, for example, the Londoner John

1 B.L. Harl. MS. 7568, f. 167v.; *P.N. Ches.* v (1:i), 55–6, 62, 70–2.

2 T. S. Willan, *Inland Trade*, 13; E. Kerridge, *Trade and Banking in Early Modern Eng.* 9–13; C. Armour, 'Trade of Chester and State of Dee Navigation' (Lond. Univ. Ph.D. thesis, 1956), 2–3, 116, 152–3.

3 *Diary of Henry Prescott*, i. 278; ii. 305, 307, 312, 314, 330, 471, 474, 477, 548, 556, 561, 587, 590; above, Public Utilities: Postal Service.

4 [P. Broster], *Chester Guide* [1st edn., 1781], 62–4; *Poole's Dir. Chester* [1791/2], 37.

5 e.g. *Pigot's Commercial Dir.* (1818/20), 107; *Parry's Dir. Chester* (1840), [97]; below, Railways.

6 *Slater's Dir. Ches.* (1855), 41.

7 *P. & G. Dir. Chester* (1871), 15; *Kelly's Dir. Ches.* (1892), 193–4; (1923), 243.

8 *Perfect Diurnall*, 4 Apr. 1653. The references for this para. were kindly supplied by Mr. D. J. Gerhold (Putney) from a draft of his *Stage-Coaches and Carriers in the 17th Cent.* (in preparation).

9 *Mercurius Politicus*, 2 Apr., 22 Oct. 1657; 1 Apr., 6 May 1658; 17 Mar. 1659.

and by 1818 there were as many as eight a day. Manchester could be reached directly by road or by a connecting packet boat on the canal at Preston Brook. At the high point of the coaching era in the 1830s there were also direct coaches at least daily to Shrewsbury, Birmingham, Welshpool, Wrexham, and Oswestry. The main coaching inns were the White Lion and the Pied Bull in Northgate Street and the Yacht in Watergate Street.[4]

Long-distance coaching was destroyed by the railways, but horse-drawn omnibuses continued to ply local routes not served by rail. In 1855 there were daily services for passengers to Mold, Ruthin, Flint, and Holywell (Flints.); Tarvin, Northwich, Knutsford, and Manchester; and Malpas and Whitchurch, all setting out from the Eastgate Inn.[5] Tarporley, Tarvin, and Kelsall still had horse omnibuses from Chester twice a week in 1880.[6]

The first motor bus service from Chester began in 1911 to Ellesmere Port, which was not served directly by rail.[7] The service was operated by Crosville Motor Co., which had been founded in 1906 by George Crosland-Taylor to build motor cars but quickly abandoned that enterprise. Passenger transport became the sole business, other routes were soon added, and the company expanded first by putting on workmen's services to munitions factories on Deeside during the First World War, and then hugely after 1918 by aggressive business tactics against its rivals in a largely unregulated market. The company was bought by the London, Midland, and Scottish Railway in 1929 and passed to Tilling-B.A.T., the national bus company, a year later. By 1935 Crosville was one of the biggest bus operators in the country, with 47 depots and 1,000 vehicles carrying 100 million passengers on routes concentrated in north and mid Wales, Cheshire, and south-west Lancashire. The company had offices and engineering works at Crane Wharf and a depot at Liverpool Road.

By 1927 Crosville ran 48 routes from Chester, reaching throughout west Cheshire and north-east Wales.[8] At first there were numerous other small bus operators from the city, mostly based in the villages around Chester, but Crosville gradually bought them up or forced them out of business, so that its only long-term local rival was the Wrexham & District Transport Co., which ran a few services into Wales. The city council normally refused to license rival operators on routes which already had a good bus service, reinforcing Crosville's near-monopoly, though

FIG. 42. *Coach at Albion Hotel, Lower Bridge Street, 1852*

Holloway operated the Chester end from premises at Whitchurch (Salop.), where he had two coaches and three teams of four horses. He clearly ran the same sort of service as that taken between Chester and London by Nicholas Blundell of Little Crosby (Lancs.) in the summers of 1717 and 1723: dinner on the first day at Whitchurch, the first night's lodging at Newport, and dinner on the second day at the Welsh Harp at Stonnall (in Shenstone, Staffs.), where the next partner's part of the service began. Blundell's stops further south were at Coventry (lodgings), Northampton (dinner), Woburn (Beds.) (lodgings), and St. Albans (Herts.) (dinner).[1]

From the 1770s services to London (now taking only two days on improved roads) and other major towns proliferated, reaching a peak in the 1830s.[2] In the later 1770s competition on the London service brought prices down and offered alternative routes, thus making a direct connexion between Chester and a much larger range of provincial towns. The first regular coaches to Liverpool, via Eastham ferry, ran in 1784,[3]

1 Liverpool R.O., 920 MD 173–5 (diary of Sir Willoughby Aston); *Great Diurnal of Nic. Blundell*, ii (R.S.L.C. cxii), 208–9; iii (R.S.L.C. cxiv), 105, 116; T. Pennant, *Journey from Chester to Lond.* (1782 edn.), 137; Corporation of Lond. R.O., Orphans Inventories 2170; ibid. Repertories 64, f. 51.

2 *Adams's Weekly Courant*, 31 Mar. 1761, p. 3; rest of para. based on *Cowdroy's Dir. Chester* (1789), 67–8; *Poole's Dir. Chester* [1791/2], 36–7; *Pigot's Commercial Dir.* (1818/20), 108; Hemingway, *Hist. Chester*, ii. 334; H. Hughes, *Chronicle of Chester*, 121–2, 125–6, 130–4.

3 Hemingway, *Hist. Chester*, ii. 335.

4 E. M. Willshaw, 'Inns of Chester, 1775–1832' (Leic. Univ. M.A. thesis, 1979: copy at C.H.H.), 56–81.

5 *Slater's Dir. Ches.* (1855), 41.

6 Ibid. (1880), 23.

7 Para. based, except where stated otherwise, on W. J. Crosland-Taylor, *Crosville: the Sowing and the Harvest* (1987); R. Phillips, *Chester City Transport, 1902–2002*, 13–14; B. Bracegirdle, *Engineering in Chester: 200 Yrs. of Progress*, 33–5.

8 *Chester City Cl. Mins.* 1926/7, 739–49.

FIG. 43. *Delamere Street bus station*

the policy also protected small operators where they survived.[1] Crosville started coach services to London in 1928,[2] and in the 1930s began running many excursions and tours.[3]

When bus services were deregulated in 1986 Crosville was split up, but both the Welsh and the Merseyside companies which were formed passed into the successive ownership of British Bus plc and the Cowie Group, emerging after 1997 respectively as Arriva Cymru and Arriva North West, which between them provided services from Chester to nearby towns in Cheshire, north-east Wales, and Merseyside.[4] The Liverpool Road bus depot, however, belonged in 2000 to a rival bus company, FirstGroup.

WATER TRANSPORT

RIVER NAVIGATION

The site of Chester marked the division between the navigable waters of the upper Dee and those of the estuary; vessels might come to it from both upstream and downstream, but at Chester itself from the 11th century or earlier the river was blocked by a weir or causeway, passable only at the highest tides and probably built at a natural interruption in the watercourse.[5]

Although barges sailed on the river between Bangor bridge and Chester until the 19th century and pleasure craft plied upstream from the city thereafter, the estuary was always the more important waterway.[6] It gave access to the Irish Sea and made Chester for much of its history a main point of arrival and departure for travellers from and to Ireland. In Roman times there may have been a quay west of the legionary fortress,[7] but by the 12th century the main anchorage seems to have been to the south, marked presumably by the Romanesque arch of the Shipgate.[8] The course of the river downstream from Chester was always uncertain, and its shifting sandbanks were remarked upon as early as the 12th century.[9] In the endless movement of those 'skittering sands' lay a perennial problem for the city: the maintenance of suitable anchorages to accommodate sizeable ships. By the 13th century the earliest and nearest, Portpool, had been created at the western edge of the city liberties.[10] Thereafter anchorages were established further down the Dee, at Shotwick, Burton, Denhall (in Ness), Neston, Gayton, Heswall, 'Redbank' (later Dawpool) in Thurstaston, and Point of Ayr (in Llanasa, Flints.).[11] In the 14th and 15th centuries 'Redbank' was much the most important, but Burton and Denhall rose to significance in the early 16th century. Those closest to the city, Portpool and Shotwick, were affected by silting; they were disused from the later Middle Ages, and a quay established at Shotwick in 1449 proved of little value. The fluctuations in the fortunes of the others reflected a succession of shifts in the river's course rather than progressive silting downstream.[12]

1 Ibid. *1912/13* and later years, indexed refs. s.vv. Bus, Motor Bus, esp. *1921/2*, 163, 196, 223–4, 255–6.

2 Ibid. *1927/8*, 803.

3 Bracegirdle, *Engineering in Chester*, 34.

4 Inf. from company website: www.arriva.co.uk.

5 *V.C.H. Ches.* v (1), Topography: Later Medieval (Street Plan within the Walls).

6 Hemingway, *Hist. Chester*, ii. 300.

7 *V.C.H. Ches.* i. 179.

8 Lucian, *De Laude Cestrie*, 23, 45–6; below, City Walls and Gates: Gates, Posterns, and Towers (Shipgate).

9 Lucian, *De Laude Cestrie*, 46.

10 Ormerod, *Hist. Ches.* i. 198; *King's Vale Royal*, [ii], 50; *P.N. Ches.* v (1:i), 70.

11 *Chester Customs Accts.* 20–62; *Ches. Chamb. Accts.* 26, 93, 123, 129, 214, 229, 235, 238, 240, 249, 255–6, 271, 275; G. W. Place, *Rise and Fall of Parkgate* (Chetham Soc. 3rd ser. xxxix), 12, 33–4, 53–7.

12 Place, *Rise and Fall*, 33–4; C. Armour, 'Trade of Chester and Dee Navigation' (Lond. Univ. Ph.D. thesis, 1952), 57.

The right to establish anchorages far beyond the limits of the city liberties was an aspect of Chester's control of the whole of the Dee estuary. The citizens' rights were first specified in the charter of 1354, which allowed them to levy tolls and other customs and to make attachments for offences committed in the water of Dee between the city and Arnold's Eye, at Hilbre Point, the extremity of the estuary.[1] The grant, which is generally taken to be the origin of the mayor's powers as 'admiral' of the Dee, claimed to continue ancient custom.[2] The citizens' privileges were clarified in 1506: they were to have the 'searching' of the Dee from Heronbridge to Arnold's Eye, oversight of nets, weirs, and fishing, and the collection of fines from all transgressions.[3] Heronbridge was on the boundary of the liberties upstream from the city. By the 17th century the citizens' rights were usually exercised by a water bailiff, appointed by the Assembly and often a serjeant-at-mace.[4] As a symbol of his authority the city in 1719 commissioned a silver oar, still in 2000 among the civic plate.[5]

The citizens' privileges appear to have overlapped with those of the serjeant of Dee. Robert of Eaton first laid claim to that office in the earlier 14th century, regarding himself as keeper of the river banks from Eaton weir to Arnold's Eye, with rights over fishing, wrecks, and ferries, and an entitlement to toll from every vessel.[6] The main obligation of the office, to keep the river clear of obstructions, was evidently a pressing matter when it was first recorded; in 1358, for example, the justice and chamberlain of Chester were ordered to seize nets and other fishing devices which impeded the progress of boats upstream to the Dee Bridge.[7]

The office of serjeant was retained by Robert's descendants, the Grosvenors, until the 18th century, with the assistance from the mid 17th century of the Chester fishermen's guild, the Drawers of Dee.[8] By then, however, the corporation appears to have been uncertain about the relationship of the Grosvenors' office to its own admiralty powers. In 1705, for example, the mayor claimed that the office of serjeant of Dee belonged to the city. The alderman of the Drawers of Dee, who was deputizing for Sir Richard Grosvenor, 4th Bt., responded by sailing alone from Eaton to Chester, and thence to Hilbre and back in the

company of the Drawers, in the course of which he seized illegal fishing stakes. He conducted a similar progress in 1710.[9] The dispute was evidently over by 1722, when Sir Richard Grosvenor appointed as his deputy the mayor who had challenged him in 1705. By the early 19th century the Grosvenors had apparently given up their claims.[10]

In 1541 the corporation adopted a plan to build a new harbour some 10 miles down the Dee estuary at Lightfoot's Pool in Little Neston, and the king ordered 200 trees to be delivered to the mayor for that purpose.[11] In 1548, in response to a petition from the city for aid with the work, the orders were repeated and augmented by a grant of £40 for seven years.[12] Despite a further appeal for a royal grant in 1551,[13] the city was forced to raise funds locally; between 1555 and 1560 voluntary rates and special assessments were imposed on the guilds, parishes, and citizens, and special payments were exacted from members of the corporation.[14] Work was evidently well under way by 1565, when a salaried overseer was appointed.[15] In 1566, however, the 'great pier of stone' which formed the main feature of the haven was largely overthrown in a gale.[16] To repair the damage a further special assessment was made in 1568 on the citizens and the guilds, and councilmen were ordered to oversee the work at their own cost.[17] By 1570 much of the new quay had been finished.[18]

The New Haven, otherwise known as Neston Quay or New Quay, eventually comprised an anchorage protected by a stone pier.[19] The project, which was probably never completed, remained a constant burden on the city's finances throughout the later 16th century, despite appeals to the Crown for grants out of customs revenue in 1576 and 1589.[20] Its repair was aided by the Ironmongers' company in 1571,[21] and was the subject of further orders by the Assembly in 1576, 1587, and 1598.[22] The city's last recorded expenditure upon it was in 1604.[23] Although it remained in use until the 1690s or later, the New Haven's position as head of navigation for larger vessels was gradually undermined by the anchorage newly developed near by at Parkgate.[24] In 1763 the corporation granted the petition of one of its aldermen to use some of the stones of the pier, by then known as the Old Quay, to

1 *P.N. Ches.* iv. 300.

2 C.C.A.L.S., ZCH 8; Morris, *Chester*, 498–9.

3 C.C.A.L.S., ZCH 32; Morris, *Chester*, 529–30.

4 e.g. C.C.A.L.S., ZAB 1, f. 276; ZAB 3, ff. 238, 246v.; ZAB 4, ff. 86v., 310, 329v.; ZAB 5, p. 323; *Cal. Chester City Cl. Mins. 1603–42*, 75, 92 n.

5 C.C.A.L.S., ZAB 3, f. 246v.; C. N. Moore, *Silver of City of Chester*, 7 and plate 11.

6 Morris, *Chester*, 500–1; 4 *Sheaf*, v, pp. 1–2.

7 *Blk. Prince's Reg.* iii. 304.

8 e.g. 4 *Sheaf*, v, pp. 2–4, 6–8.

9 Ibid. pp. 7–8; Hemingway, *Hist. Chester*, ii. 321–2.

10 Hemingway, *Hist. Chester*, ii. 321–2.

11 Morris, *Chester*, 459, citing the 'Great Letter Bk.'

12 Morris, *Chester*, 459–60; *Acts of P.C. 1547–50*, 546.

13 Morris, *Chester*, 460; B.L. Harl. MS. 2082, f. 14.

14 *T.H.S.L.C.* lxxix. 144–7, 160–74; Morris, *Chester*, 460; C.C.A.L.S., ZAB 1, ff. 91, 94, 96v.

15 *T.H.S.L.C.* lxxx. 87; Morris, *Chester*, 461; C.C.A.L.S., ZAB 1, f. 108v.   16 *T.H.S.L.C.* lxxx. 88.

17 Ibid. 89–91; C.C.A.L.S., ZAB 1, ff. 117–18.

18 *King's Vale Royal*, [ii], 119.

19 *T.H.S.L.C.* lxxix. 142–3, 150, 152–9; Place, *Rise and Fall*, 16.

20 Morris, *Chester*, 461; C.C.A.L.S., ZAB 1, ff. 167, 219.

21 *T.H.S.L.C.* lxxix. 149.

22 Ibid. 149–50; C.C.A.L.S., ZAB 1, ff. 167, 211v., 253v.–254.

23 *Cal. Chester City Cl. Mins. 1603–42*, 14; Place, *Rise and Fall*, 17.

24 Place, *Rise and Fall*, 15–17.

develop a colliery, and in 1790 it ordered that the remaining ashlar and other stone be valued and sold. It was finally disposed of in 1799.[1]

By the early 17th century, schemes were afoot to improve the Dee navigation. Commissioners of Sewers, appointed in 1607 to survey the river and remove obstructions, decreed that a breach of 10 yd. be made in the causeway at Chester.[2] Although favoured by the J.P.s of Flintshire and Cheshire, the order was vigorously opposed by the city corporation, two city companies, and the proprietor of the Dee Mills, on the grounds that the removal of the causeway would ruin the mills and damage the new system of water supply.[3] In 1609 the privy council quashed the commissioners' order.

In 1646 the citizens of Chester themselves successfully petitioned parliament to be allowed to demolish the causeway and the mills,[4] but the only effect of the several breaches made was to make the river more shallow and sandy. Despite the appointment of labourers to carry out the work in 1648, the mills and causeway survived.[5]

In 1666 the citizens alleged that the river had become so shallow that vessels as small as 20 tons could no longer reach Chester, and in 1670 they were granted leave to bring a Bill before parliament to improve the navigation.[6] The engineer Andrew Yarranton, who surveyed the estuary in 1674, was the first to suggest the solution ultimately adopted, namely the construction of a new channel along the Welsh side of the estuary, reclaiming 3,000 a. of potentially rich arable.[7]

In the late 1680s and early 1690s fresh proposals were put to the corporation for making the Dee navigable and reclaiming land.[8] Although the schemes aroused the opposition of those claiming rights on the sands and marshes of the estuary, in 1698 the corporation agreed with Francis Gell, a London merchant, that in return for a grant of tolls and reclaimed land he

should make the Dee navigable for vessels of 100 tons at all tides.[9] An Act of 1700 authorized the corporation to collect special dues on coal, lime, and limestone to finance a new channel, and to appoint seven commissioners to oversee the work; it also provided for ferries to replace the old fords.[10] After a break of six years the work begun by Gell restarted in 1708 with a new undertaker, Nicholas Jennings, who promised to complete it in three years. Little was achieved, however, and work probably largely ceased in 1712,[11] though maintenance continued in the late 1710s,[12] when the city's agents were still collecting the duties intended to pay for the works.[13] The work made the city's wharves and warehouses near the Watergate obsolete by 1707, but the replacement wharf constructed near the Roodee was destroyed by flooding in 1720,[14] and by 1730 almost no ships came up to the city.[15] Instead most goods were transferred to lighters or carts at Parkgate.[16] About 1730 navigation to Chester ceased altogether after breaches in the dykes destroyed the channel.[17]

In 1732 the project was revived by Nathaniel Kinderley, who sought funding to make the river navigable for ships of 200 tons. He followed Yarranton in proposing a new cut across Saltney marshes and estimated that *c.* 6,000 a. would be reclaimed to set against the cost. Despite considerable opposition from interests in Liverpool and Parkgate, in 1733 an Act authorized Kinderley to cut a new channel from Chester towards Flint to a depth of 16 ft. at a moderate spring tide. Once the new channel was open, the 40 undertakers of the project, of whom fewer than a third were Chester men, were authorized to collect dues from ships using it. They were also granted the profits from any land reclaimed.[18]

Cutting began in 1734, and the river was diverted into its new channel in 1737. In 1741, by a further Act, the undertakers, who needed to raise additional capital, became the River Dee Company.[19] The cost

1 *T.H.S.L.C.* lxxix. 152; Place, *Rise and Fall*, 242, 252.

2 For what follows see T. S. Willan, *River Navigation in Eng. 1600–1750* (1964 edn.), 18–20; R. Bennett and J. Elton, *Hist. of Corn Milling*, iv. 98–105; Hist. MSS. Com. 7, *8th Rep. I, Corp. of Chester*, p. 382; Armour, 'Dee Navigation', 61–2; *Cal. Chester City Cl. Mins. 1603–42*, 33–4; C.C.A.L.S., ZAF 7/35–41; B.L. Harl. MS. 2003, ff. 144–227, 230–59; Harl. MS. 2082, ff. 17–39; Harl. MS. 2084, *passim*.

3 B.L. Harl. MS. 2003, f. 164.

4 Armour, 'Dee Navigation', 63–4; Hist. MSS. Com. 5, *6th Rep., House of Lords*, p. 172; *Cal. S.P. Dom. 1645–7*, 475; C.C.A.L.S., ZAB 2, f. 87v.

5 Armour, 'Dee Navigation', 64; T. S. Willan, 'Chester and Navigation of Dee, 1600–1750', *J.C.A.S.* xxxii. 64; Bennett and Elton, *Hist. Corn Milling*, iv. 120–3; C.C.A.L.S., ZAB 2, f. 88v.

6 *Cal. S.P. Dom. 1665–6*, 436; 1670, 87; cf. Place, *Rise and Fall*, 7, 34; R. Craig, 'Some Aspects of Trade and Shipping of River Dee in 18th Cent.' *T.H.S.L.C.* cxiv. 100; Armour, 'Dee Navigation', 65, 187; C.C.A.L.S., ZAB 2, f. 153v.; ZML 3, nos. 442–3.

7 *D.N.B.*; A. Yarranton, *Eng.'s Improvement by Sea and Land* (2 pts., 1677–81), i. 191–2; Place, *Rise and Fall*, 32, 35, 39–40; *J.C.A.S.* xxxii. 65.

8 Armour, 'Dee Navigation', 67–72; Place, *Rise and Fall*, 22,

25–6; *J.C.A.S.* xxxii. 65; C.C.A.L.S., ZAB 3, ff. 12v., 41.

9 Place, *Rise and Fall*, 40; *J.C.A.S.* xxxii. 65–6; Armour, 'Dee Navigation', 72–8; C.C.A.L.S., ZAB 3, ff. 65v.–66v., 68, 74, 77v.–80, 82; ZML 4, nos. 534–7, 544–5, 553, 558.

10 Dee Navigation Act, 11 & 12 Wm. III, c. 24.

11 Armour, 'Dee Navigation', 72–81; C.C.A.L.S., ZAB 3, ff. 153, 156, 166–8, 169v., 173 and v., 197v., 240 and v.; ZML 4, nos. 601, 632.

12 C.C.A.L.S., ZAB 3, ff. 240 and v., 245v.

13 Ibid. ff. 106, 125 and v., 142, 163v., 183v., 189v., 203v., 216, 236, 251.

14 D. Defoe, *Tour through Eng. and Wales* (Everyman edn.), ii. 70; C.C.A.L.S., Cowper MSS., pp. 267–8; cf. ibid. ZAB 3, ff. 148v., 265 and v.

15 *Contemporary Descriptions*, ed. D. M. Palliser, 21.

16 *C.J.* xxi. 812–13; xxii. 44; cf. *T.H.S.L.C.* cxiv. 101 n.; Armour, 'Dee Navigation', 88–9.

17 C.C.A.L.S., ZAB 4, f. 35.

18 Armour, 'Dee Navigation', 81–92; Dee Navigation Act, 6 Geo. II, c. 30; *J.C.A.S.* xxxii. 66; *V.C.H. Ches.* ii. 132–3; cf. C.C.A.L.S., ZAB 4, ff. 35–6, 37v.–38, 40, 45, 47–8.

19 Armour, 'Dee Navigation', 96; River Dee Co. Act, 14 Geo. II, c. 8; B.L. Add. MS. 11394, ff. 29–31.

FIG. 44. *New Crane Wharf, mid 19th century*

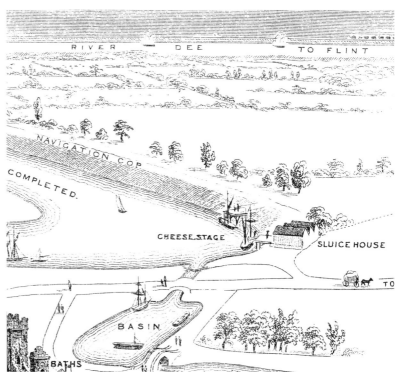

FIG. 45. *Cheese Wharf, 1867 (looking west)*

had proved much greater and the income from the new dues much less than expected. An Act of 1744 reduced the levies in an attempt to encourage trade, and they remained insufficient to meet outgoings, enlarged by the requirement to maintain two ferries and the roads which led to them.[1] Reclamation involved the company in expensive work to restore boundaries and roads disrupted by the new channel, which as a result was not properly maintained. In 1752 the company claimed to have lost £60,000. It eventually agreed to pay Sir John Glynne of Hawarden a yearly sum to compensate for his loss of

common rights and to maintain a new south bank. Since that sum exceeded the receipts from the tolls, the company remained in difficulties and apparently paid no dividend until 1775.[2]

The new cut nevertheless made the city accessible during spring tides to ships drawing up to 15 ft. in the 1770s.[3] By the mid 1740s a wharf had been re-established west of the Roodee and there were large timber yards near by. About 1760 the city built a new warehouse for cheese, with its own quay, just to the north, and was planning a further dock, warehouses, and a new road from the Watergate, later called New

1 Armour, 'Dee Navigation', 97; Dee Navigation Amendment Act, 17 Geo. II, c. 28.
2 Armour, 'Dee Navigation', 101–3; *J.C.A.S.* xxxii. 67.

3 *Contemporary Descriptions*, ed. Palliser, 25; *T.H.S.L.C.* cxiv. 102–3; cf. Armour, 'Dee Navigation', 105–8; C.C.A.L.S., ZAB 4, f. 182v.

Crane Street.[1] By 1781 New Crane Wharf was lined with the warehouses of the city's merchants and capable of taking vessels up to 350 tons.[2]

The Act of 1744 empowered the corporation to appoint one of two supervisors who were to take soundings in the river and report to the city or county justices if at three successive tides the depth of the channel fell below 15 ft.[3] The city, however, took little interest in the river or the company in the century after the Act. By the early 19th century, the old watercourse had largely silted up and the company's maintenance of the new channel was under attack. Although Thomas Telford, who worked for the company between 1817 and 1828, expressed himself satisfied with the state of the river, by 1850 it was regarded as hazardous.[4]

In 1835 the city's admiralty powers were abolished and in 1841 its supervisory role over the river was vested in a council committee.[5] The corporation remained concerned about the company's neglect of the navigation, and there were several schemes for its improvement in the 1830s and 1840s.[6] In 1846 the Tidal Harbours Commission criticized the company for its interest in land reclamation at the expense of the new cut, and in 1850 an Admiralty inquiry into the Dee conservancy condemned the ruinous state of the navigation, attributing it to the negligence of the company and to the long-standing apathy of the city council.[7] Continuing dissatisfaction with the state of the navigation led in 1889 to the transfer of the company's powers to the Dee Conservancy Board, which also became the pilotage authority for the river until 1938, when that power was vested in Trinity House. In 1965 the board was replaced by the Dee and Clwyd River Authority, after 1974 a division of the Welsh Water Authority.[8]

CANALS

Improvements to the river Weaver after 1730 served to channel trade from central Cheshire away from Chester to the Mersey,[9] and the Trent and Mersey Canal Act of 1766 threatened to strengthen still further the dominance of Liverpool over the Dee.[10] Despite that threat, no apparent opposition to the Trent and Mersey Bill

TABLE 1: *Subscribers to the Chester Canal Navigation, July 1772*

Area	No.	£	Percentage of Capital
Chester	65	18,700	48.57
Cheshire gentry	11	8,200	21.30
Nantwich	38	4,300	11.17
London	7	2,900	7.53
North-east Wales	4	2,100	5.45
Middlewich	1	1,000	2.60
Warrington	2	1,000	2.60
Liverpool	2	300	0.78
Total	130	38,500	100.00

Source: C.C.A.L.S., ZQRP 1/1 (printed *List of Subscribers, 1772*)

was voiced in Chester, but within two years of its passage there was a proposal for a canal to link Chester to the new canal at Middlewich and surveys were commissioned from the canal engineer James Brindley.[11] Jealous of their own traffic, the Trent and Mersey company and the duke of Bridgewater, Francis Egerton, owner of the Bridgewater Canal which connected with it, opposed any link with the proposed Chester Canal.[12] The latter was nevertheless authorized in 1772,[13] permitting the building of a canal 14 ft. wide from Chester to Nantwich and Middlewich.[14] Most of the capital was raised in Chester or from the Cheshire gentry.[15] The project was undermined, however, by a requirement that the new canal should keep at least 100 yd. away from the older undertaking at Middlewich. As a result, the Middlewich branch was not begun. There were also arguments with the River Dee Company over access to the river at Chester, and many engineering problems. Although the canal between Chester and Nantwich opened in 1779, it was a dead end and attracted little traffic. The project was a financial disaster and during its first 10 years was threatened with closure.[16] No dividends were paid during the company's independent existence between 1772 and 1813.[17]

Within the city the new canal changed the townscape

1 Lavaux, *Plan of Chester*; Armour, 'Dee Navigation', 44–5, 126; C.C.A.L.S., ZAB 4, ff. 98 and v., 101, 141v., 145, 150v., 157v., 184v., 195v.

2 [P. Broster], *Chester Guide* [1st edn., 1781], 29.

3 17 Geo. II, c. 28.

4 Armour, 'Dee Navigation', 104–9; *Chester and River Dee*, ed. A. Kennett, 10; C.C.A.L.S., ZCCF 6/18.

5 Municipal Corporations Act, 5 & 6 Wm. IV, c. 76, s. 108; C.C.A.L.S., ZCCB 34, pp. 16–17; ZCCF 6; ZQAR.

6 C.C.A.L.S., ZCCF 6/1–5, 12.

7 Armour, 'Dee Navigation', 109; *Chester and Dee*, ed. Kennett, 10–11; C.C.A.L.S., ZCCF 6/17–18.

8 *Chester and Dee*, ed. Kennett, 11; C.C.A.L.S., ZQAR; Dee Conservancy Act, 52 & 53 Vic. c. 156 (Local); Clwyd R.O., *River Dee* (Source Guide, 1987).

9 C. Hadfield, *Canals of W. Midlands* (1985), 19.

10 Ibid. 42; E. A. Shearing, 'Chester Canal Projects: Part I', *Jnl. Rly. & Canal Hist. Soc.* xxviii. 98; 6 Geo. III, c. 96.

11 Shearing, 'Canal Projects', 98; Hadfield, *Canals of W. Mids.* 42; C.C.A.L.S., ZTAV 2/55, vouchers for Chester Canal; ibid. ZAB 4, f. 264.

12 Hadfield, *Canals of W. Mids.* 42–3.

13 12 Geo. III, c. 75.

14 E. A. Shearing, 'Chester Canal Projects: Part II', *Jnl. Rly. & Canal Hist. Soc.* xxviii. 152.

15 Above, Table 1.

16 Hadfield, *Canals of W. Mids.* 43–5; C.C.A.L.S., ZAB 4, f. 313 and v.

17 Hemingway, *Hist. Chester*, ii. 324; J. R. Ward, *Finance of Canal Bldg. in 18th-Cent. Eng.* 175–6.

substantially. From a tidal basin linked to the Dee north of Crane Wharf the canal climbed a staircase of five wide locks, the largest in Britain when built, with chambers cut from the solid sandstone. It then entered

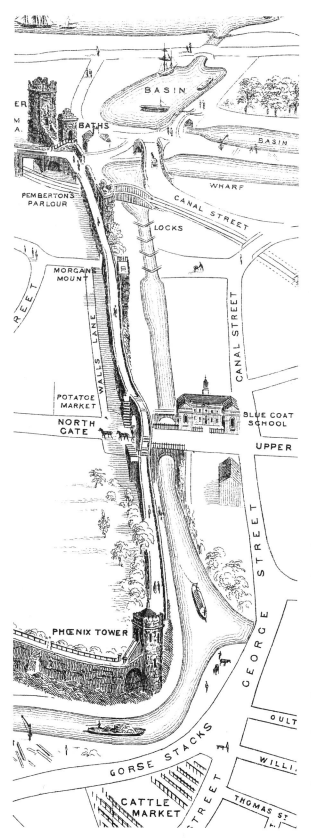

FIG. 46. *Canal and north city wall, 1867*

a deep cleft below the northern city walls, a section expected to need a tunnel but which proved to be along the rubbish-filled Roman defensive ditch.[1] The cutting was spanned by Northgate Street bridge and from 1793 by a narrow stone footbridge, designed by Joseph Turner, architect of the new Northgate, linking Northgate gaol and Little St. John's chapel in the Blue Coat school building.[2] From the main city wharf, later called Victoria Wharf, east of Cow Lane bridge the canal took a straight course eastwards across the fields and gardens north of Foregate Street and Boughton, beginning a steady climb to Nantwich at Hoole Lane lock.[3]

Chester's canal was saved from ignominious closure by the 'Canal Mania' of the 1790s. The Ellesmere Canal Act was passed in 1793,[4] and although the scheme took 12 years to complete[5] it ultimately connected the city to a much wider hinterland. The first section, opened in 1795, linked Chester to the Mersey at Netherpool (later Ellesmere Port). Connexion to the Chester Canal and the Dee involved substantial works, finished in 1797,[6] which resulted in the unusual layout still in use in 2000. The Northgate staircase was severed below the third lock, the lower two locks were filled in, and the Chester Canal swung sharply north to an end-on junction with the Ellesmere at Tower Wharf. The bend proved awkward for horse-drawn boats and was made worse when the railway cut across the cramped site below the locks, reducing the available space still further.[7] The link with the river for both canals diverged from the Wirral line at Whipcord Lane and fell parallel to the main route through two locks to reach the tidal Dee Basin.[8] The tidal basin itself had proved difficult of access and prone to silting, and a new entrance with a tidal lock was opened in 1801 south of the original line, no trace of which survived in 2000.[9] A dry dock for repairing canal boats was built at the junction between the two branches in 1798 and a large boat-building yard developed on the west bank, while the North Basin and warehouses were built on the east bank by Tower Wharf in 1802.[10] That basin was filled in and the warehouses were demolished during the 20th century but the dry dock survived in 2000 and plans were in hand to restore the basin as additional mooring space for pleasure craft.

1 R. J. Dean, 'Ellesmere Canal Packet' (TS. 1967 at C.H.H.), 3–5.

2 Harris, *Chester*, 84; P. M. Owens, *Canals: Booklist to Mark Bicentenary of Chester Canal*, 2: copy at C.H.H.; C.C.A.L.S., ZAB 5, p. 72; cf. ibid. p. 458.

3 Owens, *Booklist*, 2; Murray and Stuart, *Plan of Chester* (1791); *Nicholson/Ordnance Surv. Guide to Waterways, 2: Central*, ed. D. Perrott (1987), 115.

4 33 Geo. III, c. 91.

5 Hadfield, *Canals of W. Mids.* 166–96; Ward, *Finance of Canal Bldg.* 51–3, 90.

6 Hadfield, *Canals of W. Mids.* 169.

7 Below, Railways.

8 Dean, 'Ellesmere Canal Packet', 3–4 and maps.

9 Ibid. 4; Hadfield, *Canals of W. Mids.* 170, states 1802.

10 Dean, 'Ellesmere Canal Packet', 4.

FIG. 47. *Canal, west of waterworks, 1957: Steam Mill* (left), *leadworks* (right)

The Wirral line of the Ellesmere Canal proved a great success. It was navigable by flats, the standard craft of the Mersey and Weaver,[1] and goods could be brought directly to Chester by water from Liverpool and other points on the Mersey. Lancashire coal, for example, became cheap enough to compete with that from north Wales.[2] A service of passenger packet boats was provided from the opening of the canal, the journey to Liverpool optimistically timed at three hours, and 15,000 passengers a year were using it by 1801.[3] The service continued until the opening of the Chester and Birkenhead Railway in 1840.[4] The new link to the Mersey attracted a leadworks and corn mills to the canal side.[5] Successful as it was, the new canal served ultimately to demonstrate that Chester's waterborne traffic could be carried more effectively through Liverpool and the Mersey than through its own port. Although the increase in imported grain after 1860 initially made the canal more important, eventually it became more economic to open new mills on the Mersey and the canal-borne trade to Chester ceased, probably around the time of the First World War.[6] The trade in timber brought from the

Mersey to the yards at Cow Lane bridge also ceased soon after 1918.[7]

The opening of the Wirral line of the Ellesmere Canal revived the debt-ridden Chester Canal,[8] and its prospects improved further with the expansion of the Ellesmere company's system. In 1806 Chester was linked by a circuitous new canal (later called the Llangollen Canal) to the Denbighshire coalfield near Ruabon, as well as to Whitchurch (Salop.) and Montgomeryshire. It joined the Chester Canal at Hurleston near Nantwich. Plans for a direct link between Chester and Wrexham foundered because of cost and engineering difficulties.[9] The interdependence of the Chester and Ellesmere companies led to their merger in 1813.[10] In 1826 the passing of the Birmingham and Liverpool Junction Canal Act engendered a scheme linking the end of the Chester Canal at Nantwich with the main canal system at Autherley Junction near Wolverhampton.[11] The name of the new canal (Birmingham and Liverpool), opened in 1835, was indicative of its primary objective, and Chester was merely an intermediate point on its route. Faced with a new short route from the Midlands to the North-West, the Trent and Mersey

1 E. Paget-Tomlinson, *Mersey & Weaver Flats* (1974), 10.

2 Hemingway, *Hist. Chester*, ii. 326.

3 Dean, 'Ellesmere Canal Packet', 6; 3 *Sheaf*, ii, p. 119; viii, p. 26.

4 e.g. J. Broster, *A Walk Round the Walls and City of Chester* (1821 edn.), 28.

5 *V.C.H. Ches.* v (1), Late Georgian and Victorian Chester: Economy and Society (The Economy, 1762–1840: Industry and Transport).

6 Ibid. (The Economy, 1871–1914: Industry); C.H.H., Y 1/1/396.

7 R. E. Tovey and D. A. Williams, 'Chester Canal Trail' (TS. 1975 at C.H.H.).   8 Hadfield, *Canals of W. Mids.* 179.

9 C. Armour, 'Trade of Chester and Dee Navigation' (Lond. Univ. Ph.D. thesis, 1952), 151.

10 Hadfield, *Canals of W. Mids.* 179.

11 7 Geo. IV, c. 95 (Local and Personal); rest of para. based on Hadfield, *Canals of W. Mids.* 181–2, 185, 204.

FIG. 48. *Salt warehouse and timber yard, Cow Lane bridge, 1903*

Canal agreed to the completion of the Chester Canal's Middlewich branch and the disputed junction, though stiff tolls for traffic passing that way were exacted. The link opened in 1833, but the original aim of diverting Trent and Mersey traffic to Chester and the Dee had vanished. The main impact on the city's canal trade was to bring salt in bulk from the Middlewich area for local distribution from a wharf west of Cow Lane bridge, a traffic which ceased soon after 1918.[1]

To counter the threat from railways, the Chester and Ellesmere and the Birmingham and Liverpool Junction canals united in 1845, becoming the Shropshire Union Railways and Canal Company in 1846. The new concern was immediately leased in perpetuity to the London and North Western Railway, but the Shropshire Union continued to have considerable autonomy and was operated vigorously because much of its network lay in the territory of the Great Western

Railway.[2] A direct benefit to Chester was the location of the administrative headquarters of the whole Shropshire Union system at Tower Wharf. The company developed its own carrying business, and by 1870 had almost a monopoly of traffic on both the wide canal to Nantwich and the narrow canal beyond and to Middlewich. The boats were controlled from Chester[3] and many were built at the company's boatyard in the city.[4] From 1878 the city council was responsible for registering and inspecting the company's craft under the provisions of the Canal Boats Act, 1877.[5] Two hundred and fifty-two boats were working in 1878, and the number had risen to *c.* 400 by 1895.[6] Wide boats and flats traded between the Mersey Docks, Ellesmere Port, and Chester, the main traffic to Chester being in grain, fertilizer,[7] timber, and pig lead.[8] For narrow boats, engaged almost entirely in through traffic between Ellesmere Port and the Midlands or the Welsh Borders, Chester was merely a port of call and registration.

Chester's significance for the Shropshire Union system was primarily administrative, a function which proved vulnerable. The boatyard was sold in 1917,[9] and in 1921, faced with rapidly rising losses, the company hastily abandoned its carrying operation.[10] Although some of the fleet carried on under other owners,[11] trade on the canal to and through Chester had been dealt a mortal blow. Between 1922 and 1931 only 13 boats were added to the Chester register, while in 1925 alone 86 were scrapped.[12] The Shropshire Union company was taken over by the L.N.W.R. in 1922, and although part of the Shropshire Union system continued to be managed from Tower Wharf, Chester ceased to be the canal's head office.[13] After nationalization in 1948 most administrative functions were concentrated in Northwich.[14] Trade through the Dee branch ended in 1939 when Courtaulds' steam flats stopped running between the Mersey and Flint, and the last regular commercial traffic on the main line disappeared in 1957,[15] although carriage by narrow boat continued spasmodically until the early 1970s.[16] The demise of goods traffic was offset by the growth of pleasure boating, a development pioneered in 1935 by Inland Hire Cruisers of Christleton.[17] The canal's environmental and tourist value was recognized in the 1960s, and it was still much used and well maintained in 2000 (Fig. 49).[18]

1 Tovey and Williams, 'Canal Trail'.
2 Hadfield, *Canals of W. Mids.* 231–51; Owens, *Booklist*, 3.
3 C.C.A.L.S., ZDH 1/11.
4 e.g. *Chester Chron.* 25 Apr. 1874, 14 July 1894.
5 C.C.A.L.S., ZDH 1/1–6.   6 Ibid. ZDH 1/1–3.
7 Paget-Tomlinson, *Mersey Flats*, 22.
8 C.C.A.L.S., ZDH 1/11.   9 Ibid. ZCR 366.
10 Hadfield, *Canals of W. Mids.* 248.
11 Ibid. 248–9; P. J. Aspinall and D. M. Hudson, *Ellesmere Port*, 126.
12 C.C.A.L.S., ZDH 1/6; ZDH 1/11, list of cancelled registrations.

13 Hadfield, *Canals of W. Mids.* 249–51.
14 *Nicholson/Ordnance Surv. Guide*, 173.
15 *Chester Canal Boat Rally, 1972*, 20: copy at C.H.H.; Hadfield, *Canals of W. Mids.* 25.
16 Inland Waterways Association, *Bulletin*, xciii (May 1970), 20–1; xcix (Nov. 1971), 36; Harris, *Chester*, 37; R. Wilson, *Too Many Boats: Brit. Waterways' Narrow Boat Carrying Fleets*, 34–5; *Chester Canal Boat Rally, 1972*, 20.
17 Local inf.
18 e.g. Inland Waterways Association, *Bulletin*, lxxxv (Nov. 1968), 14; *Chester Chron.* 6 Sept. 1968, 12 Dec. 1975, 18 Aug. 1995 supplement.

FIG. 49. *Visitors' canal boats at Tower Wharf*

RAILWAYS

There were abortive railway schemes in the mid 1820s to link Birmingham and Birkenhead via Chester, and by 1835 for a branch from the city to the Grand Junction's Birmingham–Warrington line at Crewe.[1]

The Chester and Crewe and the Chester and Birkenhead Railways were incorporated separately in 1837,[2] and both lines were opened in 1840, by when the former was owned by the Grand Junction.[3] The line from Crewe entered the city alongside the canal in Boughton; that from Birkenhead came in through Upton and Newton, east of Liverpool Road.[4] They met on the city boundary north-east of Chester at the hamlet of Flookersbrook, a low-lying area which the railway companies drained. Their stations, near one another and reached along Brook Street, were wooden shacks and converted houses, including Brook Lodge,

which survived in a derelict condition into the 1940s or later.[5] Although the two lines connected, there were no through trains.[6]

After the Chester–Crewe line was authorized those already interested in a rail connexion between Holyhead (Ang.) and the Midlands proposed a line from Holyhead to Chester. The Chester and Holyhead Railway Company was incorporated in 1844 to build on a route much of which had already been surveyed by George Stephenson.[7] To carry the line out of Chester, Stephenson proposed a route leading west from Brook Street, with a tunnel under Upper Northgate Street, the line then emerging to bridge the canal, cut through the north-west corner of the city walls, and cross the Roodee on a viaduct leading to a bridge over the Dee.[8] The first two miles to Saltney were

FIG. 50. *Train for north Wales passing under city walls, 1867*

1 W. H. Chaloner, *Social and Economic Development of Crewe, 1780–1923*, 15–16, 21, 23; *Chester Chron.* 18 Feb. 1825, 20 Nov. 1835.　　2 P. E. Baughan, *Chester and Holyhead Rly.* i. 29.

3 *Chester Chron.* 18, 25 Sept., 2 Oct. 1840.

4 O.S. Map 6-inch, Ches. XXXVIII (1882 edn.).

5 H. J. Hewitt, *Bldg. of Rlys. in Ches. to 1860*, 30; above,

Public Utilities: Sewerage; C.P.S., London, Midland, and Scottish Railway Station.

6 *Correspondence between Post Office and Grand Junction Rly.* H.C. 164, pp. 702–3, 714 (1842), xxxix.

7 Baughan, *Chester and Holyhead Rly.* i. 30–2, 35–40.

8 C.C.A.L.S., ZAB 6, pp. 535, 542.

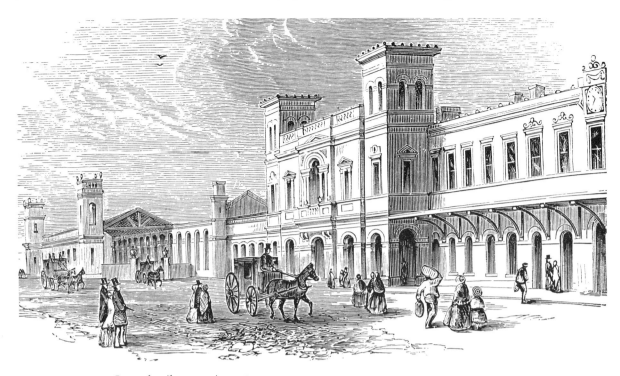

FIG. 51. *General railway station, 1890s*

shared by the Shrewsbury and Chester Railway, a company formed by merger in 1846.[1] The lines diverged at Saltney Junction, near Hough Green, the Holyhead line heading due west into Wales, the Shrewsbury line curving south to cross the main road (later Chester Street) by a bridge and leave the city parallel with the national boundary. A station and later extensive sidings were built at Saltney. The G.W.R. closed the station to passengers in 1917 but reopened it in 1932. At Saltney Wharf on the Dee were more sidings and a goods station which closed in 1937.[2]

The Shrewsbury and Chester opened its line as far as Ruabon (Denb.) in 1846 and to Oswestry and Shrewsbury in 1848.[3] A serious accident took place in 1847, when one of the cast-iron girders of the Dee bridge broke, plunging a train into the river and killing five people.[4] The bridge was repaired and in 1870–1 was rebuilt in brick and wrought iron.[5]

The Chester and Holyhead Railway was opened to Bangor (Caern.) in 1848 and to Holyhead in 1850.[6] A line to Mold (Denb.), branching from the Holyhead line just outside the city, was opened in 1849 by the same company.[7] It was extended to Denbigh in 1869,

thus providing access along lines already open to Ruthin (Denb.) and Corwen (Merion.).[8]

The Chester and Birkenhead had meanwhile been absorbed in 1847 into the Birkenhead, Lancashire, and Cheshire Junction Railway. In the same year the new company opened a branch from its main line at Helsby to a junction just east of Brook Street station in Chester.[9]

By the late 1840s Chester was thus already a busy rail junction whose stations were quite inadequate. A general station, to be run jointly by the companies concerned, was first mooted in 1845 and approved in 1847.[10] Completed in 1848, it was designed by Francis Thompson on the lines of his earlier station at Derby, as a long two-storeyed Italianate building in dark red brick with facings of Storeton stone.[11] There was only one through platform, over 1,000 ft. long, and a scissors junction allowed up trains to use one end and down trains the other. Offices for the railway companies were housed on the first floor, with booking hall, refreshment rooms, and other passenger accommodation beneath.[12]

As generally in the early 1840s,[13] passenger traffic was far more lucrative than goods: in 1846 the Chester

1 *Chester Chron.* 11 Sept. 1846.
2 O.S. Map 6-inch, Ches. XXXVIII (1882 edn.); C. R. Clinker and J. M. Firth, *Clinker's Reg. of Closed Stations* (1971 edn.), 29 and n.
3 *Chester Chron.* 30 Oct., 6 Nov. 1846; L. James, *Chronology of Construction of Britain's Rlys. 1778–1855*, pp. 44, 55.
4 *Chester Chron.* 18 June 1847; cf. ibid. 28 May, 4 June 1847.
5 Baughan, *Chester and Holyhead Rly.* i. 109–10.
6 Ibid. i. 82, 132.   7 James, *Chronology of Rlys.* p. 56.

8 W. L. Steel, *Hist. of L.N.W.R.* 314; *Bradshaw's Rly. Manual* (1869), p. 74.
9 James, *Chronology of Rlys.* pp. 30, 60; C.C.A.L.S., ZAB 6, p. 634; *Chester Chron.* 31 July 1846, 5 Mar. 1847.
10 Baughan, *Chester and Holyhead Rly.* i. 86–8.
11 Pevsner, *Ches.* 159; Hughes, *Stranger's Handbk.* (1856), 11.
12 V. R. Anderson and G. K. Fox, *Historical Surv. of Chester to Holyhead Rly. Track Layouts and Illustrations* (Poole, 1984), fig. 1.
13 T. R. Gourvish, *Rlys. and the Brit. Economy, 1830–1914*, 27.

and Birkenhead carried over 173,000 passengers who brought in over £15,600, while goods and mails accounted for under £2,500. The line to Ruabon carried over 60,000 passengers in its first six months.[1] Chester was nevertheless an obvious site for a large goods depot. In 1841 the newly appointed secretary of the Grand Junction, Mark Huish, began a goods agency at Chester,[2] and by 1849 the goods yard employed a staff of 67, handling 180,000 tons a year,[3] rising by 1855 to up to 80 trains a day carrying 684,000 tons a year.[4] Although the gap between freight and passenger income narrowed, the number of passengers also rose steadily to almost 1,500,000 in 1858, of whom nearly 300,000 were through passengers and over 350,000 were excursionists visiting Chester. There were nearly 100 passenger trains a day in 1855.[5]

In and after the 1850s there was great rivalry between the two main companies operating trains from Chester: the London and North Western (L.N.W.R.), into which the Grand Junction had been merged in 1846, and the Great Western (G.W.R.), which took over the Shrewsbury and Chester in 1854. The L.N.W.R., which had operated the trains on the Holyhead and Mold lines from their opening, took over the Chester and Holyhead company in 1858 and later acquired others, so that it could run trains from Chester throughout north Wales. A branch line from Tattenhall Junction on the Chester–Crewe line to Whitchurch (Salop.), opened in 1872, enabled the L.N.W.R. to run trains from Chester into G.W.R. territory at Shrewsbury. One area of contention between the two companies was resolved by compromise: in 1860 the Birkenhead, Lancashire, and Cheshire Junction was vested in them jointly, to be run as a separate concern, the Birkenhead Railway.[6]

By the mid 1860s Chester General station had passed from the General Station Committee to a joint committee of the L.N.W.R. and G.W.R. There were refreshment rooms from the start and a bookstall by 1860.[7] The Queen Hotel opposite the station was opened in 1860.[8] City Road, suggested in 1846 to link the station more directly with the town,[9] was built in the early 1860s jointly by the station committee and the city council.[10]

A large area of land was eventually taken over for railway purposes around General station. To its north, a triangle of tracks allowing interchange between the lines to Saltney and Birkenhead was surrounded

FIG. 52. *Northgate station, 1960s*

by sidings. The goods depot lay north-east of the passenger station.[11]

Further expansion of the local rail network was proposed in the early 1860s,[12] but the Act of 1867 for a line from Mouldsworth to a new station in Windmill Lane (later Victoria Road) was not implemented for some years. It was opened by the Cheshire Lines Committee (C.L.C.) in 1875, primarily for a passenger service to Manchester.[13] The line entered the city through Newton, crossed over the Birkenhead line at Brook Lane and curved sharply south to Northgate station, built virtually over the Upper Northgate Street tunnel. There was no connexion between the new line and the existing ones.[14] In 1876 Northgate station had *c.* 20 staff and its goods yard east of the passenger station was handling *c.* 1,000 tons a month.[15] A new line from Northgate station to Birkenhead, Connah's Quay (Flints.), and Wrexham was authorized in 1888 for the Manchester, Sheffield, and Lincolnshire Railway (renamed the Great Central in 1897), one of the proprietors of the C.L.C. The line, opened in 1890, passed under Liverpool Road, over Parkgate Road,

1 *Chester Chron.* 7 Aug. 1846, 30 Apr. 1847.

2 T. R. Gourvish, *Mark Huish and the L.N.W.R.* 51.

3 P.R.O., RAIL 114/11.

4 Hughes, *Stranger's Handbk.* (1856), 12.

5 Ibid.; P.R.O., RAIL 114/20.

6 Steel, *Hist. L.N.W.R.* esp. 256, 299, 339, 374; James, *Chronology of Rlys.* pp. 24, 30, 41, 44, 50; Gourvish, *Mark Huish*, 127, 210; C.C.A.L.S., ZCB 1, 5 May 1854, 13 Feb. 1860.

7 P.R.O., RAIL 114/18, 16 Nov. 1860; Hughes, *Stranger's Handbk.* (1856), 12; cf. *Chester Chron.* 8 May 1875; P.R.O., RAIL 404/118, 1 Jan. 1876; RAIL 404/123.

8 G. A. Audsley, *Handbk. to Chester* (1891), 27.

9 *Chester Chron.* 25 Dec. 1846.

10 C.C.A.L.S., ZCB 1, 13 Aug., 10 Sept. 1862.

11 O.S. Map 6-inch, Ches. XXXVIII (1882 edn.).

12 C.C.A.L.S., ZCB 1, 8 Jan. 1862; ZCB 2, 13 Dec. 1865; P.R.O., RAIL 404/1, p. 65 (7 Dec. 1864); cf. C.C.A.L.S., ZAB 6, pp. 634–5; *Chester Chron.* 2 June 1866.

13 *Chester Chron.* 8 May 1875; P.R.O., RAIL 110/7, p. 18; RAIL 110/131.

14 O.S. Map 6-inch, Ches. XXXVIII (1882 edn.).

15 P.R.O., RAIL 110/100, nos. 2488, 2492.

across an embankment, and out through Sealand (Flints.), with stations at Liverpool Road and Blacon.[1]

Chester General greatly enlarged its passenger accommodation in 1890, building two new through platforms with their own suite of refreshment and waiting rooms.[2] The main line to Saltney was given extra tracks between 1900 and 1904, necessitating major engineering works to widen the tunnels, the Roodee viaduct, and the bridge over the Dee.[3]

In 1887 over 100 passenger trains left Chester each weekday, a number which rose to *c.* 200 in 1910 and 1938.[4] In the 1890s Chester was regarded as 'a great railway centre . . . one of the most important in England'.[5] The L.N.W.R. and G.W.R. both ran services to London, the former via Crewe, the latter via Shrewsbury and Birmingham. The L.N.W.R.'s other main line from Chester was to Holyhead and Llandudno (Caern.), with many connecting services in north Wales. It also ran direct trains from Chester on the line to Mold, Denbigh, and Corwen, to Shrewsbury via Whitchurch, and to Liverpool via Runcorn. The Birkenhead Railway's trains ran to Liverpool via Birkenhead, and to Manchester Exchange via Warrington. All those services were from General station. From Northgate station the C.L.C. ran a service to Manchester Central via Northwich, and the Great Central one to Connah's Quay. When the railway companies were grouped in 1923 the L.N.W.R. became part of the London, Midland, and Scottish Railway (L.M.S.R.) and the Great Central part of the London and North Eastern Railway (L.N.E.R.). The Birkenhead Railway was jointly managed by the L.M.S.R. and the G.W.R. In the 1920s and 1930s the enlarged companies ran direct trains to places as far away as Aberdeen, Dover, Bournemouth, and Pwllheli (Caern.).

From the 1950s British Railways began to withdraw services and close stations and lines. Liverpool Road station was closed to passengers in 1951 and Saltney finally in 1960;[6] services to Whitchurch ceased in 1957 when the branch from Tattenhall Junction was closed,[7] and those to Connah's Quay and New Brighton in 1968 when the same fate met the lines west from Northgate station. Blacon station also closed then. Northgate station itself closed in 1969 once services to Manchester Oxford Road were able to operate from Chester General.[8] The station was afterwards demolished and its site and that of sidings to the north were redeveloped with housing estates.

Chester nevertheless retained frequent trains to many destinations, and in 1995 there were *c.* 150 every weekday, serving the lines to Crewe and London, Liverpool, Manchester via both Warrington and Northwich, north Wales, and Wolverhampton via Wrexham and Shrewsbury.[9]

MARKETS

GENERAL PRODUCE MARKETS

There was a market beside St. Peter's church in the later 11th century.[10] In the later Middle Ages held on Wednesdays and Saturdays,[11] it was the principal regional market, and in 1357 was expressly protected by an order against buying and selling within four leagues of the city except in other established market towns.[12] In fact Chester had no serious rivals as the neighbouring markets were minor and held on days which avoided Chester's own.[13]

By the late 12th century the main focus of the market lay south and east of St. Peter's in the broad space forming the northern end of Bridge Street and the westernmost part of Eastgate Street.[14] The area was called a *forum* in the early 12th century, when it seems to have been fronted by shops and important houses.[15] Later it contained the pillory and the High Cross.[16] The original market place evidently incorporated the north-western corner of Eastgate Street opposite St. Peter's, in the 11th century apparently an open space surfaced with extremely worn Roman tiles.[17] By the 13th century that site was occupied by the Buttershops, a permanent structure which perhaps superseded temporary stalls. Dairy stuffs were sold there in the early 14th century,[18] and by the later 15th it was associated

1 R. Christiansen, *Regional Hist. of Rlys. of G.B.: W. Midlands*, 181; *Chester Chron.* 5 Apr. 1890; C.C.A.L.S., ZCB 4, 11 Apr. 1888, 9 Jan. 1889; O.S. Map 6-inch, Ches. XXXVIII. NW., SW., SE. (1900 edn.).   2 *Chester Chron.* 3 May 1890.
3 Christiansen, *Regional Hist.: W. Midlands*, 168–86; R. O. Holt, *Regional Hist. of Rlys. of G.B.: NW.* 44–50, 84–5.
4 Para. based on *Bradshaw's Rly. Guide* (Aug. 1887), 22–3, 187, 204–5, 212–17, 301; (Apr. 1910), 80–5, 456–7, 472–5, 478, 480, 482, 493, 670–1; (July 1938), 112–14, 498–500, 503–4, 506–7, 514, 923, 1075.
5 *Chester in 1892, Illustrated* (publ. Robinson, Son, and Pike), 14.
6 Clinker and Firth, *Clinker's Reg.* 29.
7 C. R. Clinker, *L.N.W.R.: Chronology 1900–60*, 13, 17.
8 Clinker and Firth, *Clinker's Reg.* 29; *Chester Chron.* 14 Mar.,

10 Oct. 1969.
9 Ches. Co. Cl., *Ches. Rail Services* (1994–5).
10 Orderic Vitalis, *Historia Ecclesiastica*, ed. M. Chibnall, iv. 136; cf. *Charters of A.-N. Earls*, pp. 1–2, 20–1 (nos. 1, 11).
11 Morris, *Chester*, 553.
12 *Blk. Prince's Reg.* iii. 261.
13 P.R.O., C 53/85, m. 2; C 53/162, m. 26; C 66/66, m. 3; D. Sylvester, *Historical Atlas of Ches.* 26–7; *Burton in Wirral: A Hist.* ed. P. H. W. Booth, 264; Ormerod, *Hist. Ches.* i. 288.
14 Lucian, *De Laude Cestrie*, 47.
15 *Charters of A.-N. Earls*, pp. 15, 24, 44 (nos. 8, 13, 28).
16 C.C.A.L.S., ZCHD 2/1; *P.N. Ches.* v (1:i), 12.
17 K. Matthews, *Excavations at Chester: Evolution of Heart of City, Investigations at 3–15 Eastgate St.*, 1990–1, 15–16.
18 C.C.A.L.S., ZQCR 2, m. 1d.

FIG. 53. *Watergate tollhouse, 1818*

with the milk stoups, iron vessels from which milk was sold.[1] Marketing also seems to have extended west from St. Peter's along Watergate Street, where by the mid 14th century the fish market, also called the Fishboards, was located at the eastern end on the south side,[2] while on the north side next to the church lay the butchers' shambles.[3]

In the time of Earl Ranulph II (1129–53) a second market was established on the fairground outside the abbey gatehouse in Northgate Street, a location referred to as a *forum* by the early 14th century and perhaps by the 1220s.[4] By the later 16th century the main site of the markets had shifted there from St. Peter's, although much selling of perishables still took place at *tabulae*, either stalls in the main streets or stallboards in the Rows.[5]

Tolls were charged at the main gates on goods entering and leaving the city, but there were apparently no levies until the 1540s at the markets themselves, the dispersed nature of which would have made collection difficult.[6] The markets were regulated in the Pentice court (which literally overlooked the original market place in front of St. Peter's) in the late 13th and early 14th century, and thereafter in the portmote or crownmote.[7] In 1506 the mayor was made clerk of the market.[8] From the late 15th century the markets were increasingly tightly controlled.[9] Already in the

1470s there had been complaints that 'foreign' fishmongers (i.e. non-citizens) were trading at places away from the Fishboards,[10] and from 1506 all fish and flesh was required to be sold in the customary place.[11] In 1532 the Assembly ordered that all fresh fish be taken to the Fishboards, where the city fishmongers had the privilege of buying and selling during the first permitted hour of trading.[12]

The establishment of a new common hall in St. Nicholas's chapel adjoining the Northgate Street market place in 1545 marked a further stage in the tightening of corporation control,[13] and from 1547 all merchandise was required to be sold in bulk there. The wholesale market thus inaugurated was administered by a new official, the keeper of the common hall, who took fees on sales to pay for the upkeep of the building.[14] In 1549 non-free traders were still conducting clandestine transactions among themselves, and the Assembly forbade foreigners to purchase goods in the common hall, and freemen to buy on their behalf.[15] Similar orders were repeated at intervals throughout the 16th century but proved difficult to enforce.[16]

From the later 16th century better arrangements were made for sales at market by suppliers from outside the city. In the late 1570s the Assembly provided a separate shambles for country butchers, and after a brief spell in the Northgate gaol members

1 *P.N. Ches.* v (1:i), 23; Morris, *Chester*, 69, 257, 295–6; *King's Vale Royal*, [ii], 21.

2 C.C.A.L.S., ZCHD 2/1; Morris, *Chester*, 295; *J.C.A.S.* xlv, map facing p. 1.

3 J. Laughton, 'Chester Butchers' (unpublished TS. kindly loaned by author); Morris, *Chester*, 297.

4 *Cart. Chester Abbey*, i, pp. 52–3, 251; *Charters of A.-N. Earls*, pp. 33–4, 232–3 (nos. 23, 231).

5 Morris, *Chester*, 295; C.C.A.L.S., ZCHD 2/1; ZQCR 5, 11; below, The Rows: Physical Form ('Porches' and Stallboards).

6 *V.C.H. Ches.* v (1), Later Medieval Chester: Economy and Society, 1230–1350 (Tolls, Customs, and Prises); Economy and Society, 1350–1550 (Corporation and Regulation of Trade).

7 *Sel. R. Chester City Cts.* p. xviii; B.L. Harl. MS. 2162, f. 6;

C.C.A.L.S., ZAF 1, ff. 3–4; ZMB 1, ff. 2, 5, 6v.–7, 16v., 36, 37v., 52v., 69; ZMB 4, ff. 34, 53; ZQCR 2, 4–5, 10–11; ZSB 5, f. 35 and v.; ZSR 1, m. 1d.; ZSR 14, m. 2; Morris, *Chester*, 401–2.

8 C.C.A.L.S., ZCH 32.

9 Johnson, 'Aspects', 229, 244–5; Morris, *Chester*, 522; *V.C.H. Ches.* v (1), Later Medieval Chester: Economy and Society, 1350–1550 (Corporation and Regulation of Trade).

10 Morris, *Chester*, 402.

11 Ibid. 530, 538.

12 C.C.A.L.S., ZAB 1, ff. 64v.–65.

13 Above, Municipal Buildings: Common Hall.

14 C.C.A.L.S., ZAB 1, f. 77 and v.; Morris, *Chester*, 398–400.

15 C.C.A.L.S., ZAB 1, f. 79; cf. ibid. ZMB 1, f. 106v.

16 e.g. ibid. ZAB 1, ff. 77v., 91v., 106–7, 112, 116v., 121, 131–2, 191v., 199v.; Morris, *Chester*, 400.

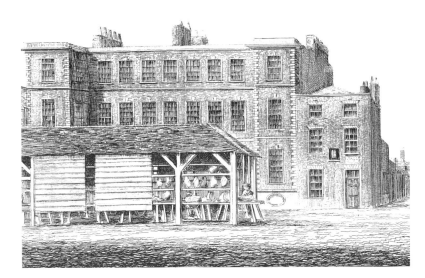

FIG. 54. *Butchers' shambles west of the Exchange, before 1812*

of the Butchers' company were forced to acquiesce.[1] In 1586 country bakers were also allowed to sell within the city on market days.[2] Attempts were made by the Bakers' company in 1623 to suppress a bread market outside the liberties at Gloverstone and allegedly backed by 'great persons'.[3]

FIG. 55. *Market traders in Eastgate Street, 1829*

Gradually the more important produce markets were resited in Northgate Street. The Assembly established a new shambles underneath the common hall in 1578,[4] and in 1582 had the former shire hall at the castle dismantled and re-erected in Northgate Street for the country butchers.[5] The shambles thereafter remained in Northgate Street, rehoused in 1695 in a new building, which by 1728 accommodated both city and country butchers, large numbers of the latter attending on Wednesdays and Fridays.[6] In 1734 it was joined by the fish market, moved from the site of the medieval Fishboards in Watergate Street.[7]

In the late 16th and 17th century dairy and garden produce was still mainly sold near the Cross,[8] but the fruit and vegetable market moved to Northgate Street by 1690, and in 1705 the Assembly acted to prevent the sale of fruit, herbs, and roots at stalls in front of the Pentice.[9] Butter, poultry, and cheese, however, continued to be sold in Bridge Street in 1741.[10] Cheese was an increasingly important commodity, sold in both Bridge Street and Northgate Street by the later 18th century.[11]

In 1758 there was an unsuccessful attempt to establish a toll-free market in Gloverstone, where a few country butchers and bakers had been selling inferior meat and bread since the early 18th century.[12] Perishable goods such as fruit, vegetables, and fish were still sold primarily in open market, and the corporation tried to ensure that townspeople could buy for themselves before retailers and country carriers.[13]

In the early 19th century the state of the markets was thought highly discreditable to the city. The flesh and fish shambles clustering around the Exchange

1 C.C.A.L.S., ZAB 1, ff. 174–5; Morris, *Chester*, 297, 438–42.

2 C.C.A.L.S., ZAB 1, f. 207; Morris, *Chester*, 420–1.

3 *Cal. Chester City Cl. Mins. 1603–42*, 124 n.

4 C.C.A.L.S., ZAB 1, f. 219; Morris, *Chester*, 297.

5 B.L. Add. MS. 39925, f. 21.

6 C.C.A.L.S., ZAB 3, ff. 46, 47v.; ibid. EDD 16/120, p. 52.

7 Ibid. ZAB 1, f. 217v.; ZAB 4, ff. 68, 107v.; Morris, *Chester*, 295–6.

8 *King's Vale Royal*, [i], 36; *Cal. Chester City Cl. Mins. 1603–*

42, 125; S. I. Mitchell, 'Urban Markets and Retail Distribution, 1730–1815, with Particular Reference to Macclesfield, Stockport, and Chester' (Oxf. Univ. D.Phil. thesis, 1974), 158.

9 C.C.A.L.S., ZAB 3, ff. 29, 136.

10 Ibid. ZAB 4, f. 98.

11 *T.H.S.L.C.* cxliv. 1–46; *Broster's Dir. Chester* (1781), 21–2.

12 Mitchell, 'Urban Markets', 173; 3 *Sheaf*, xx, p. 90.

13 Mitchell, 'Urban Markets', 170–7; C.C.A.L.S., ZAB 3, ff. 90 and v., 110; ZAB 4, f. 5.

FIG. 56. *Vegetable and fish markets south of the Exchange, c. 1830*

FIG. 57. *Market hall, 1965*

were described as nuisances, 'a collection of covered wooden stalls . . . in a very filthy condition', while fruit and vegetables were sold in various places, and poultry and butter in the open in Eastgate Street or Bridge Street.[1] The growing desire to resite the more offensive markets led to the virtual removal of the shambles from Northgate Street in 1812.[2] In 1827, however, on the initiative of the mayor, Henry Bowers, provision for the markets was concentrated in Northgate Street and greatly improved. A new shambles with an adjoining market house for butter was erected north of the Exchange, and a new fish and vegetable market to the south (Fig. 56). The poultry market was relocated on the east side of the street, adjoining the bishop's palace, and the potato market was moved from the east side of the Exchange

to the west side of Northgate Street near the North-gate.[3]

The city's growing population meant that the new shambles and butter market were too cramped as early as 1837, and in 1844 the council resolved to remove them from Northgate Street.[4] The Improvement Act of 1845 empowered it to buy land, replace the existing buildings, and change the times of the markets.[5] By then, Saturday had become the principal market day.[6] Eventually, in 1863, the corporation established a general public market, open daily with especially long hours on the former market days.[7] It was housed in a new building on the west side of Northgate Street (Fig. 57), designed by W. H. and J. M. Hay of Liverpool, consisting of a hall divided into three aisles by cast-iron columns, roofed with cast-iron girders and glass, and

1 Hemingway, *Hist. Chester*, ii. 15.

2 C.C.A.L.S., ZAB 5, p. 127; ZAC 1, f. 28 and v.

3 Hemingway, *Hist. Chester*, ii. 14–16; *Rep. Com. Mun. Corp.* p. 2627.   4 C.C.A.L.S., ZAB 6, pp. 191, 556.

5 Chester Improvement Act, 1845, 8 & 9 Vic. c. 15 (Local and Personal), ss. 185–7, 189, 216–17.

6 *Bagshaw's Dir. Ches.* (1850), 76.

7 C.C.A.L.S., ZCCB 31; ZCCF 3.

FIG. 58. *Market hall interior, 1962*

with a baroque façade of cream sandstone.[1] The original arrangement had butchers and provision dealers in stalls around the sides, farm and market garden produce and fruit sold from stalls in the centre, fishmongers in a bay to the right of the entrance, and crockery dealers at the rear of the building.[2]

The market was enlarged in the 1880s. The extensions were designed by J. Matthews Jones (the city surveyor) and W. H. Lynn to harmonize with Lynn's town hall.[3] The side facing Northgate Street (or, as it was now called, Market Square) was completed in 1882 with a Venetian Gothic front linking it with the town hall. On its opening the old shambles was converted into a wholesale meat and vegetable market.[4] A second extension at the rear of the market hall was completed in 1886 as a wholesale market for vegetables and cheese.[5] In 1898 the former Wesleyan chapel at the south-west corner of the market hall was converted into a fish market.[6] The potato market was evidently moved to the former poultry market next to the bishop's palace in 1863, but seems to have disappeared by the 1880s.[7]

The Victorian market hall was demolished in 1967, except for a fragment of the façade spanning the entrance to Hamilton Place, and replaced by a new building behind the town hall, linked to the Forum shopping precinct which went up on the site of the old market hall. It was still in use in 2000.[8]

LIVESTOCK MARKETS

Before 1529 the livestock market was apparently held in Bridge Street and Lower Bridge Street, but in that year it was confined to the latter, presumably because of the nuisance caused by the animals.[9] Evidently they remained a problem, because in 1596 a proposal was put to the Assembly to take a toll of ½d. for every calf brought to market in return for cleansing the site.[10] A horse market was held on the Gorse Stacks in the late 16th century,[11] and a swine market in Eastgate Street until 1640.[12] The horse market formerly held in Northgate Street was relocated near the Bars in Foregate Street in 1677.[13] By the 18th century the cattle market was established in Upper Northgate Street, where by 1820 it was obstructing the road.[14] The 1845 Improvement Act provided for the purchase of land, and in 1850 a new site, the Paddock, was found in George Street, adjoining the Gorse Stacks. The weekly market continued to be held there on Saturdays, and the site was also used for monthly cattle fairs.[15] The market was roofed over with corrugated iron in 1950 and remained in use until 1970, when a new cattle market was opened by the city council in Sealand Road, adjacent to the corporation abattoir built in 1964 to replace one opened in Queen Street in 1925.[16]

1 C.C.A.L.S., ZDS 5/1–12; *Builder*, 7 Feb. 1863; *Morris's Dir. Ches.* (1864), 6.

2 *Gresty and Burghall's Chester Guide* [1867], 66.

3 C.C.A.L.S., ZCCB 54, pp. 482–3, 504, 508, 515–16, 542, 551–3, 586; ZCCB 55, pp. 179, 184, 186; ZDS 5/13–19.

4 Ibid. ZDS 5/16–32; ZCCB 54, pp. 484–5; ZCCB 55, p. 195.

5 Ibid. ZCCB 56, pp. 235–6, 245, 270, 285–6, 293, 396.

6 Ibid. ZCR 119/24; ZDS 5/45.

7 Ibid. ZCCB 55, pp. 375, 397; O.S. Map 1/2,500, Ches. XXXVIII.11 (1875, 1899 edns.).

8 *Chester Chron.* 29 July 1967; *Ches. Observer*, 23 June 1967.

9 C.C.A.L.S., ZAF 1, f. 9v.   10 Ibid. f. 245v.

11 Wm. Smith's map of Chester: Morris, *Chester*, facing p. 256.

12 *Cal. Chester City Cl. Mins.* 1603–42, 207.

13 C.C.A.L.S., ZAB 2, ff. 108, 185; cf. ibid. f. 119v.

14 Ibid. ZAB 3, f. 131; cf. ZAB 5, f. 207.

15 Ibid. ZAB 5, p. 413; ZAB 6, pp. 26, 536, 553, 556; ZCCB 30.

16 A. D. Statham, *City of Chester Livestock Market* (copy at C.H.H.), 2–3; *Chester City Cl. Mins.* 1923/4, 614, 686–8; 1924/5, indexed refs. s.vv. Slaughter-Houses: Queen St.; 1925/6, 134; 1953/4, p. 443; 1956/7, p. 291; 1959/60, pp. 282, 406; 1961/2, pp. 69, 659; 1964/5, pp. 208, 327; 1969/70, p. 892.

CORN MARKET

A corn market existed by 1275, when it was attached to the residence of the wealthy Robert le Barn.[1] In the 1290s it also contained a malt kiln. Presumably then as later it lay in Eastgate Street, which from an early date also contained Bakers' Row and St. Giles's bakehouse.[2] By the mid 14th century the market was on the south side of the street and included a Row.[3]

At some time between 1439 and the 1530s the corn market moved to Northgate Street.[4] Like the general markets it was tightly controlled by the Assembly after 1506. From 1533 corn could be sold only in the market and after an appointed hour: purchase before 1 p.m. was restricted to citizens buying for their own households, after which the city bakers were allowed to buy for commercial purposes, and only at 2 p.m. was the market thrown open to the 'common people'.[5] Housed in a new building on the west side of Northgate Street in 1556, it was moved to the east side by the bishop's palace in 1574 but after protests from the chapter the building was dismantled in 1576 and reused elsewhere as a house of correction. A new corn market was erected on the site,[6] but by 1651 had moved further north near Little Abbey Gate.[7] In the earlier 17th century the city remained strongly protectionist towards the corn trade, prohibiting private sales from inns or cellars in 1615, and granting the serjeants-at-mace control of measuring grain sold in open market in the 1620s.[8]

After the Exchange was built in the 1690s the corn market was resited on its northern side, north of the butchers' shambles,[9] but by then the open market in grain was in severe decline.[10] In 1859 a corn exchange was built by George Chivas on the site of Manchester Hall off Eastgate Street.[11] Built of red sandstone and Gothic in style, the building included a large top-lit hall entered through a long passage from Eastgate Street, and a range of offices facing the cathedral graveyard, with access from the city walls.[12] It was managed by a committee of ten subscribers and two representatives of the city council and had space for 40 stands; the weekly Saturday corn market lasted until the early 20th

century.[13] The building itself, which from the beginning was also used for public meetings, lectures, and exhibitions, survived until the 1920s and by 1928 had been replaced by a branch of Woolworth's.[14]

WOOL, FLAX, AND LINEN MARKETS

The site of the medieval wool and cloth market is unknown, but the trade was probably centred in the selds in Bridge Street and regulated from the old common hall near by in Commonhall Lane.[15] In 1549 the wool market was established in Northgate Street, presumably in order to be near the new common hall,[16] and from the 1580s on market days cloth sellers rented the first floor of the common hall itself, which thus became known as the wool hall.[17]

The flax and linen market had no fixed location. In Eastgate Street in 1657, later in the century it apparently alternated between Watergate Street and Bridge Street, being held sometimes at street level but more often in the Row.[18] A cloth market was established in Bridge Street in 1705,[19] but from the mid 18th century the cloth trade was concentrated at the fairs.[20]

COAL AND LIME MARKETS

In 1677 the coal market was being held in Bridge Street.[21] It moved shortly afterwards to a site near the Newgate,[22] but had returned to Bridge Street by 1700. In 1711 sales of coal and lime were removed from the main streets to specialized market places established in Handbridge and between the New Tower and Watergate Street, both of which lay close to the river and so were more convenient for such bulky commodities.[23] The arrival of the canal in Chester later in the century led to the abandonment of dedicated market places for coal, and in 1840 three of the coal merchants operating in the city had riverside premises, five were by the canal, and one had already moved to Brook Street to be near the newly built railway. Ten years later all but two of Chester's eleven coal merchants and colliery agents were in Brook Street. New premises, the Coal Exchange, were built for them on Black Diamond Street, just off Brook Street, in the 1850s. The Exchange

---

1 P.R.O., E 315/47/139.

2 Ibid. CHES 25/1; WALE 29/272; *J.C.A.S.* n.s. ii. 166–8; *V.C.H. Ches.* v (1), Topography, 900–1914: Later Medieval (Street Plan within the Walls).

3 C.C.A.L.S., DVE 1/CI/32.

4 Ibid. ZD/HT 26; *J.C.A.S.* n.s. ii. 182–3; Morris, *Chester*, 257.

5 Morris, *Chester*, 396–8; C.C.A.L.S., ZAB 1, ff. 87–8.

6 *King's Vale Royal*, [i], 88; Morris, *Chester*, 227, 256, 298–9, 528; C.C.A.L.S., ZAB 1, ff. 111v., 169v., 261; above, Law and Order: Municipal Prisons (House of Correction).

7 J. Speed, *Map of Ches.* (1616); Morris, *Chester*, 227; C.C.A.L.S., ZAB 2, ff. 108, 197.

8 *Cal. Chester City Cl. Mins. 1603–42*, 79, 141, 186.

9 C.C.A.L.S., ZAB 3, ff. 49, 63v.; Lavaux, *Plan of Chester*; above, Municipal Buildings: Exchange.

10 Mitchell, 'Urban Markets', 162–3.

11 Ormerod, *Hist. Ches.* i. 364; *White's Dir. Ches.* (1860), 106;

O.S. Map, 1/500, Ches. XXXVIII.11.18 (1875 edn.).

12 *Gresty and Burghall's Chester Guide* [1867], 54.

13 *White's Dir. Ches.* (1860), 106; *P. & G. Dir. Chester* (1871), 17; *Kelly's Dir. Ches.* (1878), 104.

14 *Kelly's Dir. Ches.* (1923), 249; (1928), 88.

15 *V.C.H. Ches.* v (1), Later Medieval Chester: Economy and Society, 1230–1350 (Trades and Industries).

16 C.C.A.L.S., ZAB 1, f. 77v.

17 Ibid. ZAB 1, f. 219; Morris, *Chester*, 297, 398; Lavaux, *Plan of Chester*.

18 e.g. C.C.A.L.S., ZAB 2, ff. 112, 116v., 145, 151v., 156v., 162, 185 and v.

19 Ibid. ZAB 3, f. 131.

20 Below, Fairs.

21 This para. was contributed by C. P. Lewis.

22 C.C.A.L.S., ZAB 2, ff. 185v., 189.

23 Ibid. ZAB 3, ff. 78v., 183v.; ZAF 47c/57; ZAF 49c/22.

FIG. 59. *Coal Exchange,*
1960s

was a plain brick building, domestic in appearance, three-storeyed in the centre and two-storeyed to either side, which contained offices for the different firms. To its rear, approached through two arches in the central block, were extensive coal yards and railway sidings. Further offices were built in the yards in later years.

Between 15 and 20 coal merchants, some also dealing in bricks, lime, gravel, and other building materials, were based there until the 1950s. With the fall in the domestic use of coal thereafter their number had fallen to five when the Exchange was demolished in 1970 as part of the inner ring-road scheme.[1]

FAIRS

Earl Hugh I granted Chester abbey, probably in 1092, all the tolls, rents, and issues of a fair lasting three days about the feast of St. Werburg 'in the summer' (20–22 June), and assigned jurisdiction over it to the abbot's court and the proceeds to the monks.[2] There is no reason to suppose that the fair was new then, and indeed its existence may explain the creation of the feast of St. Werburg in the summer, a largely local affair not celebrated very widely.[3]

In the 1120s Earl Ranulph I confirmed the grant, specifying that all pleas and forfeitures during fair time should be dealt with in the abbot's court by the abbot's officials or the sheriff of the city. He also compensated the sheriff for losses sustained by the grant of the fines to the monks, an indication that such revenues had accrued to the sheriff's predecessors, the pre-Conquest reeves of Chester, and hence further evidence that the fair pre-dated Earl Hugh's grant.[4] Earl Ranulph II (1129–53) added stalls before the abbey gate, restricted trading elsewhere in the city while the fair lasted,[5] and later extended responsibility for policing the fair to the

barons of Cheshire, arrangements which suggest that it was already too big an event to be left to the city sheriff alone. It is significant that routes to Chester from north Wales and north of the Mersey had to be protected for the duration of the fair.[6]

By the early 13th century fairs were held in the city on the feasts of the nativity of St. John the Baptist (24 June) and Michaelmas (29 September), and outsiders were restricted to trading at those times.[7] The June fair, which was the abbey's, evidently extended beyond its original three days, and was the subject of an agreement in 1209 whereby Stanlow abbey provided St. Werburgh's with 24 cartloads of thatching each 16 June, presumably as roofing materials for booths.[8]

In the late 13th century the abbey's rights were disputed. The abbot claimed that during fair time all sales should take place either at the community's own stalls (*seldae*) on the fairground in front of the abbey gate or in the adjoining street; the mayor and citizens asserted that they could buy and sell elsewhere within the city. In 1284 it was agreed that the citizens could

---

1 *Parry's Dir. Chester* (1840), 56; *Bagshaw's Dir. Ches.* (1850), 111; *White's Dir. Ches.* (1860), 144–5; *Kelly's Dir. Ches.* (1878), 111, and later edns.; *Kelly's Dir. Chester* (1970), 152; C.P.S., Black Diamond Street.

2 *Cart. Chester Abbey*, i, pp. xiii, 21, 39–46; *Charters of A.-N. Earls*, pp. 6, 9, 14–16, 21–2, 32–3 (nos. 4, 8, 12, 22).

3 *V.C.H. Ches.* v (1), Early Medieval Chester: Church in Anglo-Norman Chester.

4 *Cart. Chester Abbey*, i, pp. 47–8; *Charters of A.-N. Earls*, pp. 22–5 (no. 13).

5 *Charters of A.-N. Earls*, pp. 32–4 (nos. 22–3); *Cart. Chester Abbey*, i, pp. 52–3, 68–9.

6 *Charters of A.-N. Earls*, pp. 34–5, 79–80 (nos. 24, 67); *Cart. Chester Abbey*, i, p. 69.

7 C.C.A.L.S., ZCH 7; cf. ZCH 8.

8 *Cart. Chester Abbey*, i, p. 201.

erect and trade at 'stalls and stands' (*seldae et ementoria*) by the graveyard gate and alongside the graveyard wall but not between the graveyard and abbey gates. The community was not to let its houses there to city merchants while the citizens' stalls remained unlet, but might let them to 'foreign' merchants (meaning non-locals) or even local men if the citizens' stalls proved insufficient. The monks also conceded that at fair time the citizens could buy and sell anywhere within the city, saving the abbey's privileges during the two and a half days around the feast of the Translation of St. Werburg (21 June). In return they received an annual payment of £2 6s. 8d.,[1] still exacted in 1360 although by then the citizens were in arrears.[2]

The dispute evidently resulted from an attempt by the abbot to enlarge his trading monopoly over a fair which by then lasted well beyond the three days granted by Earl Hugh I. By the 1290s the fair extended a fortnight either side of Midsummer Day, and was presumably more important than the autumn fair which lasted for only a week either side of Michaelmas.[3] Merchandise included cloth.[4] The fairs' significance in the 13th and early 14th century is indicated by special arrangements made by some citizens to obtain extra trading space while they were on, and by the continuing contribution of Cheshire landholders to policing the fairs and the routes which led to them.[5]

In the mid 14th century the abbot retained extensive rights over the Midsummer fair, including all tolls and fines levied during the three days around the Translation of St. Werburg. All pleas arising then, except those relating to manslaughter, were held in his court, and he was entitled to the chattels of those convicted and hanged. In addition, he could restrain ships in port from trading and had power to discipline all sellers of victuals. Tolls were taken on horses, oxen, sheep, pigs, wool, skins, and copper or bronze pots and bowls. In the case of livestock, an especially important commodity, the levy fell equally upon buyer and seller.[6] Tolls at the four main gates were doubled in fair time.[7]

In the late 14th and early 15th century the fairs still lasted a month at Midsummer and a fortnight at Michaelmas, with shorter core periods when most activity took place.[8] More and more, however, they were subjected to civic control in the mayor's piepow-

der court, and in 1484 after a scuffle in Northgate Street during the Midsummer fair the mayor ordered the city sheriffs to arrest the participants and imprison them in the Northgate, an action recorded by the town clerk as 'on behalf of our liberty against the abbot at fair time'.[9] The charter of 1506 assigned all jurisdiction in the city to the mayor and sheriffs, and its implicit abolition of the abbot's privileges at the Midsummer fair was confirmed in 1509.[10]

By the mid 16th century the city also managed the horse fairs, then held at both Midsummer and Michaelmas on the Gorse Stacks and of regional importance.[11] Its control was evident in the division of the fair tolls among the sheriffs' officers in the early 17th century, a custom which gave rise to dissension and eventually caused the Assembly to require the sheriffs to present the fair accounts to the city auditors.[12] By then the corporation also decided upon the duration of free trading permitted at the fair to merchants who were not citizens of Chester.[13] Fear of the plague brought further civic intervention, including regulation of the admission of strangers and goods to the city at Michaelmas in 1625, and the cancellation of the fairs in 1631, 1636, and 1650.[14]

By the later 17th century, when the Midsummer show was transferred to Whitsun week and then in 1678 abandoned,[15] the fairs seem to have been in decline. In 1685, however, Charles II granted the city a third fair, for horses and horned cattle, held on the last Thursday in February, and in 1705 that fair was moved to a new site in Foregate Street.[16] It was probably an occasion for the sale of other commodities, for the traditional sign giving notice of a fair, a hand or glove mounted on a pole, was suspended from the Pentice for its duration.[17]

By *c.* 1700 the fairs were beginning to revive. In 1704 the corporation defined anew the limits of free trading for non-citizen mercers as extending from six days before to six days after the two ancient fair feast days.[18] They also regulated the hop fair held under the common hall.[19] By 1718 ironmongery made at Coalbrookdale (Salop.), especially pots and kettles, and later also china, were sold regularly at Chester fairs.[20] In the 1720s and 1730s disputes over trading space in the Rows and at the Cross suggest that traders from

1 *Cal. Ches. Ct. R.* pp. 122–3; P.R.O., CHES 29/5, m. 2.

2 *Blk. Prince's Reg.* iii. 399–400.

3 *Cal. Ches. Ct. R.* p. 182; P.R.O., CHES 29/59, m. 23.

4 C.C.A.L.S., ZMR 3, mm. 2d., 5.

5 *V.C.H. Ches.* v (1), Later Medieval Chester: Economy and Society, 1230–1350 (City and its Hinterland); Ormerod, *Hist. Ches.* i. 288.

6 Ormerod, *Hist. Ches.* i. 287–8; *Blk. Prince's Reg.* i. 18.

7 P.R.O., CHES 29/59, m. 23; cf. Morris, *Chester*, 555.

8 Morris, *Chester*, 553; *V.C.H. Ches.* v (1), Later Medieval Chester: Economy and Society, 1350–1550 (Chester and its Region).

9 *Blk. Prince's Reg.* iii. 178; B.L. Harl. MS. 2057, ff. 133–4; C.C.A.L.S., ZMB 6, f. 101; Burne, *Monks*, 131–2.

10 Morris, *Chester*, 133–5, 524–40; C.C.A.L.S., ZCH 32; B.L.

Harl. MS. 1989, f. 87v.; *V.C.H. Ches.* iii. 142.

11 *King's Vale Royal*, [ii], 23; Hemingway, *Hist. Chester*, i. 418; C.C.A.L.S., ZSBT 1–2.

12 *Cal. Chester City Cl. Mins. 1603–42*, 145 n., 152 n., 170, 177, 181, 222.

13 e.g. C.C.A.L.S., ZAB 1, f. 238v.; Johnson, 'Aspects', 275.

14 *Cal. Chester City Cl. Mins. 1603–42*, 136–7, 168, 189; C.C.A.L.S., ZAB 2, f. 94v.

15 Below, Plays, Sports, and Customs before 1700: City Watches and Midsummer Show (Midsummer Watch or Show).

16 C.C.A.L.S., ZCH 39, m. 5; ZAB 3, f. 131.

17 Ibid. ZAB 3, f. 5.

18 Ibid. f. 117.

19 Ibid. f. 136.

20 Mitchell, 'Urban Markets', 41–2, 50.

London and all over the North of England were accustomed to occupy premises in the city at fair time.[1]

The revival saw the growth of both wholesaling and retailing. Hops were a feature of the autumn fair, concentrated in warehouses behind the Blossoms and Hop Pole inns in Foregate Street. Trade in livestock, focused on the February fair, seems to have served the city's immediate hinterland but not beyond.[2] The chief activity of the 18th-century fairs was, however, the trade in cloth. By the earlier 18th century Manchester merchants were attending in order to trade in cotton goods, and in the 1740s their presence was so marked that Eastgate Row North was known as Manchester Row. In 1751 a new warehouse, Manchester Hall, was opened between Eastgate Street and St. Werburgh Street; in the early 19th century it contained 44 shops along two ranges.[3]

Even more important was the development of the Irish linen trade, already in being by 1700 but much increased from the 1740s. Its rapid growth led to the construction east of Northgate Street of a linen hall, a private speculation by William Smith, an innholder and former alderman of Chester.[4] In 1743–4 Smith built 29 small shops, furnished with counters and a gallery, which were let during the fairs to linen drapers, all of whom came from Dublin except for one from Liverpool. By 1746 Smith had built a further 14 shops at the southern end of the original structure, also let mostly to Dublin drapers. By 1749 the hall had been enlarged again with the addition of another 22 shops on the northern side, all of which were let to traders from Dublin and Liverpool by 1752. Drapers from elsewhere, including Wolverhampton, Shrewsbury, Drogheda, and Chester itself, took up shops in 1754 and 1755,[5] and a second linen hall was built close to Smith's by Charles Boswell between 1755 and 1762.[6] By 1755 the linen fair had also spread to the Exchange.[7] The growth in activity engendered disputes in the 1770s about the double tolls traditionally exacted at fair time, and eventually they were enforced by constables stationed at each of the four main gates into the city.[8]

The linen trade reached its peak in the 1770s and 1780s.[9] The focus remained the fairs, opening on 5 July and 10 October after the change of calendar in 1752, and each lasting for a fortnight.[10] In the mid 1770s a group of 37 English and Irish merchants each subscribed £100 towards new premises. The New Linen-

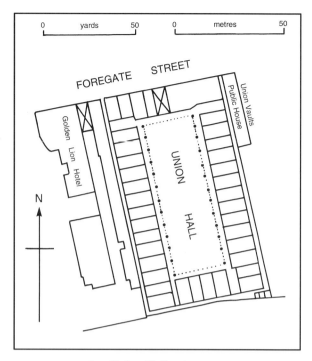

FIG. 60. *Union Hall, 1872*

hall, built on land purchased from the Stanley family, was opened in 1778 between Watergate Street and Breward Street, soon known as Linenhall Street.[11] It comprised a rectangular courtyard around which were arranged 36 double shops to east and west and 23 single shops to north and south, all built in brick.[12] All 95 shops were let in 1778, mostly to Irish traders, but thereafter numbers rapidly declined. In 1805 only c. 60 were let, and in 1815 c. 45. In 1823, when lettings had fallen to 29, including four used for cotton goods, the proprietors were recommended to surrender their rooms in order to escape liability for rent.[13] By 1831 the Irish linen trade through Chester was dead.[14]

Even so, the fairs retained their wholesaling functions much longer than others in the area.[15] Their vitality was reflected in the wide range of goods sold and in the building of new premises. In 1809 the Old Linenhall, by then dilapidated, was supplemented by the Union Hall, erected south of Foregate Street by tradesmen from Manchester and elsewhere attending the fairs. A rectangular brick building of three storeys, it contained 60 single and 10 double lock-up shops, arranged on two floors around the sides of a galleried courtyard with cast-iron pillars, and a top floor con-

1 Mitchell, 'Urban Markets', 41–2, 50; C.C.A.L.S., ZAB 4, ff. 17v.–18, 87.

2 Mitchell, 'Urban Markets', 40–1; Hemingway, *Hist. Chester*, i. 417; ii. 335; P.R.O., CHES 16/132.

3 Mitchell, 'Urban Markets', 41–9; C.C.A.L.S., ZAB 4, f. 141; J. Wood, *Map of Chester* (1833); Hemingway, *Hist. Chester*, i. 412.

4 Mitchell, 'Urban Markets', 43; C. Armour, 'Trade of Chester and State of Dee Navigation' (Lond. Univ. Ph.D. thesis, 1956), 275–6.   5 C.C.A.L.S., DLB 1548/Chester.

6 Ibid. EDD 3913/3/5, pp. 44–5, 87–8; B.L. Add. MS. 5836,

f. 226.

7 C.C.A.L.S., ZHI 1, f. 4v.

8 Ibid. ZAB 4, ff. 287–288v., 328v.

9 Mitchell, 'Urban Markets', 43–7.

10 Hemingway, *Hist. Chester*, ii. 335; Ormerod, *Hist. Ches.* i. 370–1.

11 *P.N. Ches.* v (1:i), 9, 15; C.C.A.L.S., ZCR 498/2.

12 C.C.A.L.S., ZG/Mc 11, 15; Hemingway, *Hist. Chester*, ii. 12.

13 C.C.A.L.S., ZG/Mc 15; cf. ibid. ZTCC 139.

14 Hemingway, *Hist. Chester*, ii. 12.

15 Mitchell, 'Urban Markets', 40.

sisting of long halls where clothiers from Yorkshire set up their stalls.[1]

In 1815 the Commercial Hall was opened north of Foregate Street. A private speculation, it was also a rectangular brick building and had 56 single and 20 double shops arranged on two floors around a galleried iron-pillared court, approached from Foregate Street and Frodsham Street.[2] The hall was occupied during fair time by traders from London, Glasgow, Manchester, Derby, Nottingham, Birmingham, and Sheffield, selling goods of every description, but with an emphasis on hardware and cutlery.[3]

In 1830 the fairs were still 'great marts for the sale of various sorts of goods'. They were inaugurated by a horse and cattle fair, at which great quantities of leather were also sold. Thereafter fustians, printed cottons, and muslins from Lancashire, hardware from Sheffield and Birmingham, flannels from Wales, and woollens from Yorkshire were marketed in the halls. By then the emphasis had shifted away from wholesaling to shopkeepers from Cheshire and north Wales in the opening days of the fair, and towards more general retailing in the last week.[4] By the early 1850s wholesaling fairs in the purpose-built halls were largely extinct, since railways now allowed retailers from Chester and elsewhere to travel to the manufacturing districts and deal with their suppliers at source.[5]

In place of the general fairs there was a multiplication of more specialized events. From the 1820s there were six livestock fairs; in addition to that held on the last Thursday in February, they were held on the first Wednesday in April, May, September, and November, and the second Wednesday in December.[6] In 1830 they were augmented by fairs for cheese, butter, bacon, and other agricultural produce, held on the same days in the New Linenhall and Commercial Hall.[7] The cheese fairs became important local events held in the New Linenhall the day before the livestock fairs.[8] In 1850 the corporation began monthly cattle fairs, including one on 10 October, the date of the 'old Cheshire fair'.[9] By 1864, however, the ancient

fairs had lost their pre-eminence: 5 July and 10 October were merely two among eleven dates in the year.[10] In 1871 an additional wool fair was held in the Linenhall in June, and there were seven cheese fairs.[11] The number of livestock fairs had risen to 13 by 1892, and cheese fairs were then held in the market hall on the third Wednesday of every month. By then the ancient fair days were entirely disregarded.[12] In the 1880s there was a separate monthly horse fair, held on Thursdays near the entrance to the Union Hall in Foregate Street until 1884, when it was removed to the cattle market in George Street.[13] By 1905 there were monthly horse fairs and monthly or twice-monthly cheese fairs.[14] That pattern remained largely unchanged until the 1930s.[15]

Of the buildings associated with the fairs, the Old Linenhall was dilapidated in 1831 but still used as shops and warehouses.[16] It had disappeared by 1872 and was presumably destroyed when St. Werburgh Street was extended.[17] The New Linenhall survived as the cheese market until its closure in 1876, and was eventually replaced by stabling for Chester races.[18] The Union Hall remained in use as shops and warehousing for Yorkshire clothiers until after 1850.[19] It was still intact in 1911, but shortly thereafter the street frontage and part of the south range were demolished. The western wing had been destroyed by 1966 (Fig. 61, p. 104), and in 1992 the remaining buildings were pulled down.[20] The Commercial Hall also remained in retail use until after 1850.[21] Still intact and used as warehousing in 1910, it continued to house workshops and stores until c. 1950, but had gone by 1966.[22] Manchester Hall, described in 1831 as a 'poor irregular building', was replaced by a corn exchange in 1859.[23]

A custom associated with the fairs was the practice of suspending a wooden hand or glove from a long pole attached to the Pentice, from shortly before the fairs started until their close. The earliest known reference to the usage was in 1687, when the citizens sought to extend it to the new livestock fair.[24] The origins of the custom are unknown, though it was clearly ancient.

1 Hemingway, *Hist. Chester*, i. 419; J. Williams, *Story of Chester*, 244; *Chester Arch. Service Newsletter*, 1992 (4), p. 1.

2 Hemingway, *Hist. Chester*, i. 418–19; O.S. Map 1/500, Ches. XXXVIII.11.18 (1875 edn.).

3 Hemingway, *Hist. Chester*, i. 419; *Ches. Dir.* (1840), 80.

4 Hemingway, *Hist. Chester*, ii. 335–6; 3 *Sheaf*, ii, pp. 119, 121.

5 J. Romney, *Chester and its Environs Illustrated*, [35].

6 Hemingway, *Hist. Chester*, ii. 336; Ormerod, *Hist. Ches.* i. 370.

7 Hemingway, *Hist. Chester*, ii. 336; *Ches. Dir.* (1840), 80.

8 C.C.A.L.S., ZCCB 30, 11 Apr. 1850; Romney, *Chester Illustrated*, [4].   9 *Bagshaw's Dir. Ches.* (1850), 76, 78.

10 *Morris's Dir. Ches.* (1864), 6.

11 *P. & G. Dir. Chester* (1871), 17.

12 *Kelly's Dir. Ches.* (1892), 186.

13 Ibid.; 3 *Sheaf*, xxxvi, p. 20; J. Williams, *Story of Chester*, 244.

14 *P. & G. Dir. Chester* (1905/6), 30.

15 Ibid. (1919/20), 37; (1935/6), 45; *Kelly's Dir. Ches.* (1910), 219; (1923), 235; (1934), 76.

16 Hemingway, *Hist. Chester*, i. 419.

17 O.S. Map 1/500, Ches. XXXVIII.11.18 (1875 edn.); *V.C.H. Ches.* v (1), Topography, 900–1914: Victorian and Edwardian (City Centre).

18 *P. & G. Dir. Chester* (1871), 17; below, Chester Races; Harris, *Chester*, 100.

19 *Ches. Dir.* (1840), 80; *Bagshaw's Dir. Ches.* (1850), 78; W. Willis, *Pictorial Plan of Chester* (1860).

20 O.S. Map 1/2,500, XXXVIII.11 (1911 edn.); 1/1,250, SJ 4066 (1966 edn.); J. M'Gahey, *Bird's Eye View of Chester* (1855); C.C.A.L.S., NVA 1/2, nos. 3668–3713; *Chester Arch. Service Newsletter*, 1992 (4), p. 1.

21 *Bagshaw's Dir. Ches.* (1850), 78; Willis, *Pictorial Plan* (1860).

22 4 *Sheaf*, iv, p. 2; *P. & G. Dir. Chester* (1935/6), map; O.S. Map 1/1,250, SJ 4066 (1966 edn.); C.C.A.L.S., NVA 1/1, nos. 1284–1302.

23 Ormerod, *Hist. Ches.* i. 364; O.S. Map 1/500, Ches. XXXVIII.11.18 (1875 edn.).   24 C.C.A.L.S., ZAB 3, f. 5.

FIG. 61. *Union Hall, 1989*

The glove surviving in 2000, which appears to have been repainted often, was inscribed with the names of Earl Hugh II of Chester and the guild merchant, and the date 1159, in a form dating probably from the 17th century. It is likely that the custom developed, perhaps at a very early date, as a symbol of the exceptional privileges and protection which the authorities in Chester accorded to traders from outside the city at fair time.[1] After the demolition of the Pentice in 1803 the glove was instead displayed from the south-east corner of St. Peter's church. By then it was customarily hung out 14 days before the fairs and continued on display until their close.[2] In 1836 the custom was discontinued and the glove then in use passed into private hands. It was later purchased by Joseph Mayer, and in 2000 was in Liverpool Museum.[3]

MILLS AND FISHERIES

DEE CORN MILLS

The survival of millstones of appropriate size suggests that there may have been Roman power mills at Chester.[4] Otherwise there is no evidence for milling until the late 11th century, but probably, given its position at the centre of a relatively extensive arable area and the presence of water power on the Dee, the city had its own corn mills from an early date.

The corn mills were located at the Chester end of the weir or causeway just west of the Dee Bridge, a site which in 2000 was occupied by a former hydroelectric generating station.[5] Although almost certainly they were always controlled by the secular authorities, Earls Hugh I and Richard apparently intended that they should include a mill for Chester abbey.[6] Possibly they were augmented in Earl John's time;[7] by 1237 there were six mills on the site.[8]

From earliest times the mills were exceptionally valuable. In 1237 they were leased for the enormous sum of £100, half the earl's revenue from the entire city and over twenty times that for most other mills of the period.[9] That the figure nevertheless reflected genuine income is suggested by the large sums which the king received when the mills were administered directly in 1237.[10] The ultimate source of that income was the earl's monopoly over corn milling within the city and its liberties: all corn and malt, except the abbot's, was ground at the Dee Mills and was subject to the payment of toll in kind (also called multure), probably then as later levied as a sixteenth of the grain brought for grinding.[11] The custom was established before *c.* 1200, when Earl Ranulph III exempted the nuns of Chester and his chancellor-clerk Peter from the tolls.[12]

The earl's rights probably bore heavily on the inhabitants, for at Earl John's death in 1237 the mills were destroyed by the citizens, despite the fact that they were themselves lessees of one mill for an annual rent of two tuns of wine. The mills were eventually restored at the king's expense.[13] It is unlikely that such large

1 R. Stewart-Brown, 'Notes on Chester Hand or Glove', *J.C.A.S.* xx. 144–7.

2 Hemingway, *Hist. Chester*, ii. 335–6; Ormerod, *Hist. Ches.* i. 370.   3 *J.C.A.S.* xx. 123, 132–9.

4 O. Bott, 'Cornmill Sites in Ches. i', *Ches. Hist.* x. 59.

5 Above, Public Utilities: Electricity.

6 *Charters of A.-N. Earls*, pp. 4, 15–16 (nos. 3, 8); below, this chapter: Abbot's Mills.

7 Cf. ref. to his new mills in Ches.: *Charters of A.-N. Earls*, p. 451 (no. 450); *Cart. Chester Abbey*, i, pp. 96–7.

8 *Ches. in Pipe R.* 34.

9 Ibid.; pers. comm. Dr. R. Holt, Birmingham Univ.

10 e.g. *Ches. in Pipe R.* 55, 64.

11 C.C.A.L.S., ZCHB 1, f. 15v.; below, this section.

12 *Charters of A.-N. Earls*, pp. 225, 280 (nos. 224, 281).

13 *Ches. in Pipe R.* 27, 39; *Close R.* 1234–7, 538.

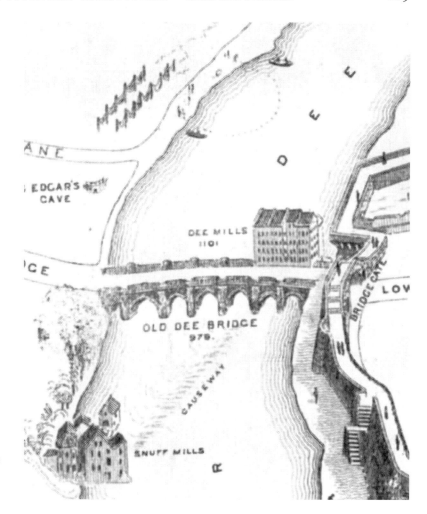

FIG. 62. *Dee Mills and fisheries, 1867; the salmon cage is the small building next to the snuff mills*

sums derived entirely from corn ground for local use, especially since there is no evidence that the monopoly extended outside the liberties. Indeed by the 13th century there were numerous other mills near by.[1] More probably Chester had by the late 12th century become an entrepôt for corn, serving Ireland, Wales, and north-west England, and inflating the profits of the Dee Mills by tolls levied in kind on corn brought into Chester for grinding before being shipped out again as flour.[2]

Although the king rented out the mills in the first year after the annexation of the earldom, thereafter they returned to royal hands, perhaps because the damage sustained in 1237 had reduced their profitability. Certainly the revenues in 1238–9 were well below the earlier annual rental value.[3] In 1241, however, the mills were repaired out of the revenues of the

county,[4] and thereafter profits probably increased.[5] By 1245 they were again leased, to Roger of Mold, steward of Chester.[6]

In the early 1270s the mills were leased to Richard the engineer.[7] When he renewed the lease for five years in 1275 Richard was charged £140 a year, and in addition was to maintain the mills and causeway at his own cost.[8] By 1279 he was evidently in arrears, and the king considered granting the mills to his new monastic foundation of Vale Royal.[9] In 1281, however, Richard received a fresh three-year grant of the mills together with the Dee fishery for the very large annual sum of £200.[10] The grant was renewed in 1284 for twelve years,[11] and by 1300 Richard had been made lessee of the Dee Mills, fishery, and bridge for life.[12]

Initially, Richard undoubtedly encountered some difficulty in meeting the rent due for the mills and

1 *Ches. Hist.* xi. 53–4.

2 *V.C.H. Ches.* v (1), Early Medieval Chester: Trade and Economic Life, 1070–1230; Later Medieval Chester: Economy and Society, 1230–1350 (City and its Hinterland); *Ct. R. of Ldship. of Ruthin and Dyffryn-Clwyd*, ed. R. A. Roberts, 41, 45 (thanks are due to Dr. Jane Laughton for those references); for the corn market: *V.C.H. Ches.* v (1), Topography, 900–1914: Later Medieval (Street Plan within the Walls).

3 *Ct. R. Ruthin*, 42, 50.   4 Ibid. 71; *Cal. Lib.* 1240–5, 53.

5 *Ches. in Pipe R.* 64.

6 Ibid. 86, 89, 92; *Cal. Lib.* 1245–51, 91.

7 *Ches. in Pipe R.* 108.

8 *Cal. Pat.* 1272–81, 105; *Cal. Fine R.* 1272–1307, 52.

9 B.L. Harl. MS. 2064, f. 19; R. Bennett and J. Elton, *Hist. of Corn Milling*, iv. 61.

10 *Cal. Fine R.* 1272–1307, 153.

11 Ibid. 206–7; *Cal. Pat.* 1282–92, 135.

12 *Ches. Chamb. Accts.* 1.

fishery, and by 1286 he was apparently £100 in arrears.[1] A partnership with a second lessee, Hugh of Brickhill, failed in 1287.[2] Richard's difficulties were caused by flood damage to the mills, causeway, and fishery in the mid 1280s,[3] and by local resistance to his attempts to exploit his rights. In 1289, for example, certain tenants of lands associated with the castle were exempted from paying multure because their holdings had been granted in exchange for land surrendered to Vale Royal.[4] Richard attempted to enforce the monopoly by seizing corn and malt which was sent for grinding outside Chester, and even by confiscating bread baked elsewhere.[5]

In 1290 the king remitted £100 of the annual rent to enable Richard to erect two additional mills on the site, and for the remainder of the lease fixed the sum at £200.[6] By 1298 substantial works were begun upon all five mills next to the Dee Bridge. Then housed under two roofs in groups of two and three, they were moved to an adjacent site and completely rebuilt, perhaps because of alterations to the causeway.[7] The mills' importance in the late 13th century is illustrated by the scale of that reconstruction and by the quantities of wheat (1,752 qr.) ground for the king's use over seven months in 1282 and 1283.[8]

Richard the engineer was lessee of the mills and fishery until his death in 1315.[9] Thereafter the lease passed to Robert of Glasham,[10] and later still to the abbot of Chester, who in 1335 claimed that he had been forced to rent the mills against his will. The ensuing inquiry established that the arrangements disclaimed by Abbot William Bebington had begun under his predecessor Thomas Birchills (d. 1323). The abbot was discharged from his responsiblity for the mills, which were leased instead to two leading citizens, Richard of Capenhurst and Thomas of Strangeways.[11] By 1339, however, they were in the keepership of the chamberlain of Chester,[12] a leading official of the palatine earldom, and they remained directly managed until 1341 when they were once more leased.[13]

The earl's difficulties in leasing the mills may indicate that he was demanding too much in rent. Nevertheless in 1346 they and the fishery were leased for three years to Bartholomew of Northenden for over £240 a year.[14] To make them more attractive, in 1347–8 the earl repaired the bridge and built structures at both ends to protect the mills and causeway.[15]

The Black Death sharply reduced the mills' prosperity, and when Northenden renewed the lease in 1349 the rent had been reduced to *c.* £166.[16] After his murder,[17] the mills were held until 1353 at the reduced sum by his associate Robert of Bredon, rector of St. Peter's in Chester,[18] but even so, they probably remained unprofitable, for in 1351 the citizens complained of new levies by the millers. In response, the justice and chamberlain of Chester were ordered to check and authenticate all the corn measures in use at the mills.[19]

The Black Prince resumed direct control in 1353.[20] In the ensuing year the recorded revenues amounted to only £94, but in 1354–5 they improved to £170.[21] Besides the keeper, the staff then consisted of a master, three yeomen (*valetti*), three boys (*garciones*), and six apprentices (*pagetti*), two in the corn and four in the malt mills. Both the staff and the rental were still below the levels recorded in the 1340s.[22]

The customs which had obtained in the mills 'since beyond the memory of man' were carefully recorded in 1353–4, perhaps because of the complaints of 1351. All the inhabitants of the city had to grind their corn in the mills and surrender a sixteenth of the grain as toll. The abbot and monks of Chester, the abbot of Dieulacres (Staffs.), Sir Peter Thornton as heir of Peter the clerk, and two other named individuals were exempt from paying toll. The master of the mill and his staff were entitled to a share of the multure levied, in the form of unmilled grain, flour, and malt. Severe penalties were decreed against those infringing the regulations, and the lessee or keeper of the mills was to hold a court to deal with them.[23] The court, which seems to have been held only intermittently, was presided over by the justice of Chester (the chief judicial officer of the palatinate) or his representative, and the fines exacted were reckoned as part of the revenues of the mills. In 1355 they were the third most valuable item on the account.[24]

The mills' principal profits in the 1350s, however, came from selling the grain received as tolls paid in kind. The main types were wheat, wheat flour, and unmilled oat malt, the last being by far the largest item.

1 *Cal. Ches. Ct. R.* p. 56.   2 Ibid. pp. 123–5.

3 Ibid. p. 151; *Cal. Close, 1288–96,* 182–3; *Ches. in Pipe R.* 156. Cf. B.L. Harl. MS. 2083, ff. 125–6.

4 *Cal. Inq. Misc.* i, p. 428; Bennett and Elton, *Hist. Corn Milling,* iv. 62–3; B.L. Harl. MS. 2083, f. 126; *Cal. Close, 1288–96,* 106, 182. Cf. *Cal. Chart. R. 1257–1300,* 282.

5 *Cal. Ches. Ct. R.* pp. 153, 164, 166–7.

6 *Cal. Close, 1288–96,* 77, 182.

7 P.R.O., E 101/486/10, 12; *Cal. Close, 1296–1302,* 145, 183.

8 *Cal. Close, 1279–88,* 202–3.

9 *Ches. Chamb. Accts.* 78, 83.   10 Ibid. 89.

11 *Cal. Close, 1333–7,* 407–8; *36 D.K.R.* App. II, p. 127.

12 *36 D.K.R.* App. II, p. 173.

13 Ibid. pp. 82, 114, 125, 144, 221, 226, 255, 414, 429, 438.

14 Ibid. p. 363; *Ches. Chamb. Accts.* 119.

15 *Ches. Chamb. Accts.* 126–7.

16 Ibid. 140; P.R.O., SC 6/783/15.

17 P.R.O., SC 6/783/15; *V.C.H. Ches.* v (1), Later Medieval Chester: City Government and Politics, 1350–1550 (Decay of the Guild Merchant).

18 *Ches. Chamb. Accts.* 160; P.R.O., SC 6/784/2.

19 *Blk. Prince's Reg.* iii. 70.   20 Ibid.

21 *Ches. Chamb. Accts.* 221.

22 Eaton Hall, Ch. 321; Hewitt, *Med. Ches.* 35–41, 191–3; Morris, *Chester,* 101–2; P.R.O., SC 6/784/5, m. 3; SC 6/784/11, m. 2d.

23 Morris, *Chester,* 101–2.

24 P.R.O., SC 6/784/5, m. 3.

Other products included wheat malt, milled oat and barley malt, 'milldust', and maslin. In the mid 1350s the keeper accounted for up to 100 qr. wheat, 24 qr. wheat flour, 28 qr. wheat malt, 239 qr. unmilled oat malt, and 40 qr. milled oat malt a year,[1] quantities which presumably represented the earl's sixteenth of what had been processed at the mills.[2]

In 1355 the causeway was raised to provide extra power, and the corn mills, together with the new fulling mills and fishery, were leased to Robert of Bredon and three associates.[3] Robert retained the lease with one or more of those associates until 1369 and then alone until his death in 1377. The period was one of relatively prosperous stability, with the annual rent remaining constant at *c.* £200 until the mid 1360s, and thereafter increasing to £240.[4]

The considerable quantities of millstones acquired, often from Anglesey, in the later 1350s and 1360s imply either that the causeway then powered many corn mills, or that heavy use required frequent replacements.[5] A reserve of suitable stones was kept on hand, and in 1361–2 the lessees accounted for 30 millstones.[6] Throughout the period there were also constant repairs to the mills themselves and to the causeway.[7]

After 1377 the mills were no longer leased. With one brief and unsuccessful exception, they were directly managed until *c.* 1500 by 'keepers and approvers' who were paid a wage.[8] The reasons for the change are unclear, but presumably relate to fluctuations in the price of corn in the 1370s and 1380s and to the continuing decline in prices, especially of oats in the late 14th and 15th century.[9] In his first year, Thomas of Moston, Robert of Bredon's executor and keeper 1378–90,[10] accounted for annual revenues of only just over £230, less than the previous rent.[11] By 1380–1 the sum had risen to over £333,[12] but in 1386–7 it dropped again to just under £200.[13] In fact, throughout his keepership Moston was substantially in arrears in handing over the revenues from the mills, perhaps because the charges for which he had to

account were not wholly realistic.[14] Moston's difficulties may have engendered long-standing irregularities and extortions. In the late 1380s he and his millers were accused by the citizens of Chester of taking additional tolls, falsifying the traditional measures (the 'schole' and the 'tolhop'), and imposing cash charges. In addition, Moston was alleged to have maintained a staff of only three 'masters', instead of the traditional six and a 'superior master', and to have appropriated the dues of the unfilled posts.[15]

Sales of wheat and oat malt remained the principal source of profit. In 1380–1, a good year, the keeper accounted for the sale of some 171 qr. wheat, 39 qr. wheat malt, 298 qr. oat malt, 40 qr. milled oat malt, and 77 qr. maslin,[16] a pattern which remained fairly constant throughout the 1380s and 1390s.[17] Revenues declined in the 1390s, when lower prices outweighed increased multure,[18] and the keepers, increasingly designated 'clerks',[19] remained mostly in arrears.[20]

In 1391, despite the increasing difficulties, the mills and fishery were once again leased, to John Walsh at £240 a year,[21] an arrangement opposed by the citizens of Chester, who sought the lease themselves.[22] In fact the mills were taken back into the king's hands after only a year, and although in 1393 they were leased once more to Walsh,[23] in 1394 they were permanently resumed by the king.[24] They remained in the hands of royal keepers, who usually exercised their office through deputies, for the rest of the Middle Ages.[25]

In 1394 two malt mills were destroyed by fire.[26] In 1398, after the mayor and citizens had again complained of the millers' extortions, the king conceded that for the next four years all those who lived within the liberties should grind their grain and malt free of any additional tolls charged above the customary sixteenth. In the ensuing accounts, the keeper did not answer for the sale of any milled oat malt, 'feemalt', flour, or the dust produced by milling. Wheat, maslin, unmilled oat malt, and wheat malt were, however, unaffected and the charge on the keeper was not

1 Hewitt, *Med. Ches.* 191–2; P.R.O., SC 6/784/5, m. 3.
2 *Blk. Prince's Reg.* iii. 317.
3 Ibid. iii. 209–10, 310, 423; B.L. Harl. MS. 2081, ff. 179–87; Morris, *Chester*, 105; P.R.O., SC 6/784/6, m. 1; SC 6/784/7, m. 1.
4 P.R.O., SC 6/784/11, m. 2; SC 6/785/3, m. 1; SC 6/785/5, m. 1d.; SC 6/785/8, m. 1d.; SC 6/785/10, m. 1; SC 6/786/2, m. 3d.; SC 6/786/10, m. 1; SC 6/787/5, m. 1; SC 6/787/7, m. 1; SC 6/787/8, m. 1.
5 e.g. *Acct. of John de Burnham, Chamberlain of Chester*, ed. P. H. W. Booth and A. D. Carr (R.S.L.C. cxxv), 205; *Ches. Chamb. Accts.* 241.
6 P.R.O., SC 6/785/10, m. 1.
7 e.g. ibid.; *Acct. of John de Burnham*, 90–1; *Blk. Prince's Reg.* iii. 273; *Ches. Chamb. Accts.* 251, 271.
8 P.R.O., SC 6/787/9, m. 3.
9 *T.H.S.L.C.* cxxviii. 42–4; *Agrarian Hist. of Eng. and Wales, iii, 1348–1500*, ed. E. Miller, 443–55.
10 P.R.O., SC 6/787/8, m. 1; *36 D.K.R.* App. II, p. 354.
11 P.R.O., SC 6/787/9, m. 3.
12 Ibid. SC 6/788/2, m. 3; cf. SC 6/788/3, m. 4.
13 Ibid. SC 6/789/5, m. 3.

14 e.g. ibid. SC 6/788/2, m. 3; SC 6/789/5, m. 3; *36 D.K.R.* App. II, p. 354.
15 C.C.A.L.S., ZCHB 1, ff. 15–16v.; Morris, *Chester*, 112–14.
16 P.R.O., SC 6/788/2, m. 3.
17 e.g. ibid. SC 6/790/5, m. 4; SC 6/790/7, m. 3; SC 6/790/8, m. 4; SC 6/790/9, m. 3; SC 6/790/10, m. 4; SC 6/790/11, m. 6; SC 6/791/3, m. 5; SC 6/791/5, m. 4.
18 Ibid. SC 6/788/2, m. 3; SC 6/790/5, m. 1.
19 e.g. *36 D.K.R.* App. II, pp. 326, 354. The earliest record of the title occurs in 1384, when the office was distinct from that of keeper: ibid. 227. In the early 15th cent. the clerk was the keeper's deputy: P.R.O., SC 6/791/6, m. 7; SC 6/791/7, m. 6; SC 6/792/1, m. 7; SC 6/792/10, m. 5.
20 e.g. P.R.O., SC 6/790/5, m. 4d.; SC 6/790/10, m. 4.
21 *Cal. Fine R. 1391–9*, 35.
22 *36 D.K.R.* App. II, p. 96.
23 P.R.O., SC 6/790/3, m. 3.
24 Ibid. SC 6/790/5, m. 4.
25 e.g. ibid. SC 6/790/8, m. 4; SC 6/790/10, m. 4; SC 6/791/1, m. 6; SC 6/791/5, m. 1.
26 Ibid. SC 6/790/5, m. 4d.

significantly reduced, presumably because the mills' principal business was not the grinding of corn for the citizens but the collection of toll on grain passing through Chester.[1]

In 1399 the keeper, Thomas Marshall, a serjeant of the duke of Norfolk, was replaced by Henry Strangeways, almost certainly a member of a prominent Chester family.[2] Strangeways was made keeper for life,[3] but by 1401 had been succeeded by Robert Castell, an esquire of the young Prince Henry who throughout his long period of office (1401–36) was an absentee.[4] By then the income from the mills was undoubtedly falling. The concession of 1398 to the citizens of Chester was revoked in 1400, on the grounds that the revenues were smaller than formerly; at the same time the millers were permitted to increase their fees and take additional wages.[5] Moreover the court held in the mills was revived, primarily, it seems, to pursue those accused of grinding their corn elsewhere.[6] Such actions were perhaps stimulated by the fact that 1400–1 was an exceptionally poor year: receipts amounted to only *c.* £170.[7] By 1413 they had dropped to an even lower level, and arrears remained a problem.[8]

For much of the 15th century the keepership of the corn mills and fishery was granted to royal yeomen, such as Thomas Pulford (1436–61),[9] and William and David Malpas (1464–75),[10] or local gentlemen, such as Robert Hanbury (1485–1503).[11] Daily administration was left to deputies under whom profits declined, complaints about extortion by the mills' officials were frequent, and the mills' jurisdiction eventually lapsed.[12]

The main cause of the decline in profits was the low price of grain and malt, coupled with some reduction in the quantities collected as multure. The reduction became more pronounced in the mid 15th century. By 1444–5 the annual revenue had fallen to *c.* £96 and Pulford accounted for the sale of only some 93 qr. wheat, 188 qr. unmilled oat malt, 14 qr. milled oat malt, and 25 qr. wheat flour.[13] By 1463–4 his successor Ranulph Bold, a protonotary of the justice of Chester, was charged for only 23 qr. wheat, 69 qr. unmilled oat malt, and 9 qr. milled oat malt.[14] Even at that reduced

level of operations the keepers continued to experience difficulties, and in 1470 their arrears were cancelled.[15]

In 1503 the corn mills were again leased, at an annual rent of £50.[16] Although the lessee, Hugh Hurleton the younger, who already held the fishery, died shortly afterwards, they were retained by his widow, and by 1514 the family also held the fulling mills.[17] In 1532 the corn mills were leased to Robert Brooke, but he assigned his interest to Ralph and Thomas Goodman, who increased profits by energetically enforcing their monopoly.[18] When the king granted the corn mills and fishery to Sir Richard Cotton in 1553, their annual value had risen by nearly £40.[19] In 1567 the Goodmans, who continued to operate the corn mills, began proceedings against the lessee of the former abbey mills at Bache and the proprietors of other watermills and windmills in the environs of the city for infringing their monopoly. Most allowed the case to go by default, but Margaret Bavand, lessee of Bache watermill, continued to defy the prohibition until 1571, when she was fined and imprisoned.[20]

Ralph Goodman died in 1570 and his interest passed to William Goodman, while serving as mayor, who died in 1579 having renewed the lease of the mills and fishery in 1575 from Cotton's widow at the large rent of £140.[21] In 1583 Goodman's widow married Alderman Edmund Gamull, later mayor, who in 1588 paid £600 in advance to renew the lease at the reduced rent of £100.[22] When Gamull became proprietor, the Dee millers were again accused of extortion. Alderman John Hankey, himself a former miller, challenged the monopoly and established a horse mill which ground for the citizens at the ancient rate of a sixteenth. Although in 1585 Gamull obtained a ruling from the palatinate exchequer court in support of his monopoly, he was ordered to take only the customary toll, and either to accept rent for Hankey's new mill or to purchase it from him.[23] Evidently satisfied with that judgement, and perhaps prompted by the extra custom generated by the needs of troops employed in the Irish wars of the 1580s and 1590s, in 1600 Edmund Gamull's son Thomas (d. 1613) bought the mills and fishery from

1 P.R.O., SC 6/790/7, m. 3; SC 6/790/8, m. 4; SC 6/790/9, m. 3; SC 6/790/10, m. 4; *36 D.K.R.* App. II, p. 98; B.L. Harl. MS. 2003, ff. 228–9.

2 *36 D.K.R.* App. II, p. 454.   3 *Cal. Pat.* 1399–1401, 11.

4 Ibid. 1422–9, 49; P.R.O., SC 6/791/5, m. 1; SC 6/791/6, m. 7; SC 6/791/7, m. 6; SC 6/792/10, m. 5; SC 6/794/10, m. 7.

5 *36 D.K.R.* App. II, p. 454; P.R.O., SC 6/791/1, m. 6.

6 C.C.A.L.S., ZCHB 2, f. 71; Bennett and Elton, *Hist. Corn Milling,* iv. 66.

7 P.R.O., SC 6/791/3, m. 5.

8 Ibid. SC 6/791/5, m. 1; SC 6/791/6, m. 7; SC 6/791/7, m. 6; SC 6/792/1, m. 5; SC 6/792/10, m. 5; *36 D.K.R.* App. II, p. 87.

9 P.R.O., SC 6/798/7, m. 6; *Cal. Pat.* 1424–6, 419; 1429–36, 144, 513; *37 D.K.R.* App. II, pp. 197–8, 603, 675.

10 *37 D.K.R.* App. II, p. 506; P.R.O., SC 6/798/10, m. 6.

11 P.R.O., SC 6/Hen. VII/1500–1, 1518–19.

12 Above, Law Courts: Middle Ages (Court of Dee Mills).

13 P.R.O., SC 6/796/10, m. 7.

14 Ibid. SC 6/798/10, m. 6; *37 D.K.R.* App. II, p. 56; cf. P.R.O., SC 6/799/10, m. 4d.; SC 6/800/10, m. 4 and d.

15 P.R.O., SC 6/799/7, m. 4d.; *37 D.K.R.* App. II, pp. 159, 422, 506.

16 *37 D.K.R.* App. II, pp. 198, 395–6; cf. B.L. Harl. MS. 2083, f. 123.

17 *L. & P. Hen. VIII,* i (2), p. 1309; *39 D.K.R.* 158.

18 Bennett and Elton, *Hist. Corn Milling,* iv. 84–5; B.L. Harl. MS. 2081, f. 167v.; Harl. MS. 2083, ff. 132–3.

19 Morris, *Chester,* 105; C.C.A.L.S., ZCHD 12/1/1; B.L. Harl. MS. 2081, ff. 167v., 190–8.

20 Bennett and Elton, *Hist. Corn Milling,* iv. 86–91; B.L. Harl. MS. 2081, ff. 109v.–110, 253–70; Harl. MS. 2083, ff. 94–114.

21 C.C.A.L.S., ZCHD 12/2–3.

22 Ibid. ZCHD 12/4.

23 Bennett and Elton, *Hist. Corn Milling,* iv. 92–4; B.L. Harl. MS. 2081, ff. 199–200; Harl. MS. 2083, f. 602; C.C.A.L.S., ZAB 1, f. 189.

Cotton's heirs. Shortly afterwards Gamull built a new corn mill, bringing the number up to five and a malt mill, all housed under two roofs. By then he had few rivals in the locality: most of the citizens, the Bakers' company, and many who dwelt within a 10-mile radius of Chester brought their corn and malt to be ground at the Dee Mills.[1]

In 1601 Gamull undertook to supply water and power to John Tyrer's new waterworks, in return for an agreement to deny water to any who infringed his milling monopoly. Shortly afterwards his mills were seriously damaged.[2] In 1607 some of the citizens, abetted by neighbouring gentry, proposed to demolish the weir, thereby ruining the corn and fulling mills and the waterworks. Gamull was among those instrumental in ensuring that the privy council quashed the orders that a breach be made in the causeway.[3]

Edmund Gamull died in 1616 and since his heir, Thomas's son Francis, was a minor, the highly profitable estate was managed by Francis's stepfather Edward Whitby, recorder of Chester. By the 1620s one at least of the mills was leased to John Brerewood, who had married into the Gamull family.[4] Increasingly, legal action was required in the face of ever more open infringements of the monopoly. The city's small tradesmen patronized cheaper mills, and despite it being customary for the 'poorer sort' to grind their corn without payment of toll, Whitby still sought to enforce his ward's rights. In 1622 the tradesmen appealed to the Assembly, apparently unsuccessfully, to intervene with Whitby on their behalf.[5] In 1623 a recently erected horse mill in Boughton was suppressed.[6]

After Tyrer's death in 1634, the waterworks was purchased by a group of citizens, led by a former alderman, Sir Randle Mainwaring, who immediately dissolved the link with the mills. Francis Gamull, by then of age, initiated legal proceedings, but apparently failed to secure the restoration of the old arrangements.[7] In 1635 there were further attacks on the monopoly. A new horse mill was built within the liberties, and its proprietor and other citizens also made use of a watermill outside the city. Gamull

again instituted legal proceedings and the defendants were ordered to suppress their mills. In response, a group of city maltsters combined to buy ready-ground malt openly from sources outside the city, and in 1637 professed themselves prepared to face imprisonment rather than submit.[8]

After the fall of Chester, parliament deprived Gamull, an ardent royalist, of his income from the mills and ordered that they be demolished at the city's expense.[9] In 1647 the aldermen, merchants, and citizens petitioned afresh for an order to take down the causeway and mills,[10] and in 1648 the Assembly appointed overseers and labourers to carry out the work.[11] Defenders of the mills, however, alleged that their loss would disadvantage both the city and the government, and greatly reduce the production of biscuit required for troops bound for Scotland and Ireland.[12] Their arguments carried weight because of the large income which the state derived from leasing the mills. The mills therefore survived.[13]

By the 1650s the millers' monopoly had been broken and their income was correspondingly reduced; in 1654, although the leaseholders paid £179 in rent, the profits were allegedly only £44. By then Gamull was dead and the mills were vested in his five coheiresses. The husband of one having purchased two other shares, the resulting three fifths, after passing to the Westons and the Shaws, were sold in 1743 to Edward Wrench, who acquired a fourth share in 1753 and bought out the reserved rent due to the Cottons in 1776.[14] The mills burned down in 1789, but were rebuilt and extended soon afterwards by E. O. Wrench. They were advertised for sale in 1807,[15] but evidently remained unsold, for in 1808 Wrench purchased the fifth and final share.[16] The property was again advertised for sale in 1811, when it comprised '18 pair of stones, suitable warehouses, drying kilns, [and] complete machinery'. It was burned down in 1819[17] and rebuilt, and in 1830 contained 22 pairs of stones, let to several tenants by E. O. Wrench the younger.[18]

After further destruction by fire in 1847, the corn mills were worked by Alderman William Johnson, who

1 Bennett and Elton, *Hist. Corn Milling*, iv. 94–5, 100–1; B.L. Harl. MS. 2081, ff. 167v., 217v.–218, 221v.; Harl. MS. 2082, f. 25; C.C.A.L.S., ZCHD 12/5–9; ZCHD 12/13/1–2.

2 Bennett and Elton, *Hist. Corn Milling*, iv. 95–6; B.L. Harl. MS. 2081, ff. 40–92; above, Public Utilities: Water.

3 Bennett and Elton, *Hist. Corn Milling*, iv. 96–105; B.L. Harl. MS. 2083, f. 208; C.C.A.L.S., ZAF 7/35–41; ZCHD 12/10; above, Water Transport: River.

4 Bennett and Elton, *Hist. Corn Milling*, iv. 106–9; B.L. Harl. MS. 2081, ff. 167v., 222; Harl. MS. 2082, f. 6v.; Harl. MS. 2091, f. 307v.; C.C.A.L.S., ZCHD 12/13/1–2.

5 Bennett and Elton, *Hist. Corn Milling*, iv. 107–8; B.L. Harl. MS. 2081, ff. 169–71, 217v.

6 Bennett and Elton, *Hist. Corn Milling*, iv. 109–11; B.L. Harl. MS. 2081, ff. 121–53.

7 Bennett and Elton, *Hist. Corn Milling*, iv. 111–13; B.L. Harl. MS. 2081, ff. 38–92.

8 Bennett and Elton, *Hist. Corn Milling*, iv. 113–19; B.L. Harl.

MS. 2081, ff. 2–37v., 111v.–120; Harl. MS. 2083, ff. 2–91, 173–203.

9 Morris, *Siege of Chester*, 208; Bennett and Elton, *Hist. Corn Milling*, iv. 122; B.L. Harl. MS. 2057, f. 56; *Cal. S.P. Dom. 1645–7*, 474–5; C.C.A.L.S., ZAB 2, ff. 76–78v.

10 Hist. MSS. Com. 5, *6th Rep., House of Lords*, 172.

11 Bennett and Elton, *Hist. Corn Milling*, iv. 122; C.C.A.L.S., ZAB 2, ff. 87–88v.

12 C. Armour, 'Trade of Chester and Dee Navigation' (Lond. Univ. Ph.D. thesis, 1952), 64; above, Water Transport: River.

13 *Cal. Cttee. for Compounding*, iii, p. 1875; *J.C.A.S.* xxxii. 64.

14 Armour, 'Dee Navigation', 64; Bennett and Elton, *Hist. Corn Milling*, iv. 122–3; Hemingway, *Hist. Chester*, i. 375; C.C.A.L.S., ZCHD 12/17–23, 25, 59, 68, 71, 90–3.

15 Bennett and Elton, *Hist. Corn Milling*, iv. 123; C.C.A.L.S., ZAB 5, p. 45; ZCHD 12/107.

16 Hemingway, *Hist. Chester*, i. 375.

17 Ibid. i. 374; Bennett and Elton, *Hist. Corn Milling*, iv. 123; 3 *Sheaf*, xlvii, p. 61.   18 Hemingway, *Hist. Chester*, i. 373.

FIG. 63. *Dee Mills, mid 19th century*

installed rolling machinery.[1] In 1885 Johnson acquired a share in the mills from the Wrench family, and, after yet another fire in 1895, the whole property was purchased by the corporation. The buildings were used for storage until they were demolished in 1910.[2]

DEE FULLING MILLS

The fulling mills were located in Handbridge at the eastern end of the causeway. There appear to have been mills on the site by the mid 12th century, since the tithes of a mill 'beyond the bridge' were bestowed on Chester abbey in a grant attributed to Earl Richard I (1101–20) but more probably issuing from Ranulph II (1129–53).[3] In 1298–9 two mills 'across the bridge' received new *claves*[4] and mill houses.[5]

In 1355 new mills were built on the site and thereafter their business was definitely the fulling of cloth.[6] Leased from 1355 to 1376 to Robert of Bredon,[7] thereafter the fulling mills were managed directly by the Crown, and their revenues, generally under £10 a year, were recorded in the accounts presented by the keeper of the mills.[8] With the building of a new mill in 1392, they were leased separately for £3 a year.[9]

Difficulties between the lessees and their men were resolved in 1395 when both sides were bound to keep the peace towards each other.[10]

In the 15th century the fulling mills continued to be leased separately, usually to citizens and clothworkers of Chester for *c.* £10 a year.[11] The lease was held in the 1480s by a consortium which included Hamlet Goodman, member of a family destined to have a long association with the mills.[12]

By 1514 the three fulling mills were leased to Nicholas Hurleton, whose family already held the corn mills and fishery.[13] After Nicholas's death, they apparently passed together with the other properties to Robert Brooke, and were assigned by him to Ralph Goodman.[14] They were not sold with the corn mills in 1553, and remained with the Goodmans until 1577.[15] Brooke evidently retained an interest for in 1557 he sought to renew the lease for a further term, beginning in 1574.[16] In 1577, however, they passed to John Bingley and others, presumably members of the Fullers and Clothworkers' company, which was said in 1607 to have long rented the mills and to hold them by a lease recently renewed.[17]

1 Bennett and Elton, *Hist. Corn Milling*, iv. 123; 1 *Sheaf,* ii, p. 242; *White's Dir. Ches.* (1860), 145; J. H. Norris, 'The Water-Powered Corn Mills of Ches.' *T.L.C.A.S.* lxxv/lxxvi. 63.

2 Bennett and Elton, *Hist. Corn Milling*, iv. 123; C.C.A.L.S., ZCHD 12/125.

3 *Charters of A.-N. Earls*, pp. 15–16, 36–8 (nos. 8, 26); *Cart. Chester Abbey*, i, pp. 43, 76.

4 The meaning of *clavis* is unclear. The Dee *claves* were made by carpenters and situated 'at the head' (*in capite*) of the mills.

5 P.R.O., E 101/486/10, 12; above, this chapter: Dee Corn Mills.

6 *Ches. Chamb. Accts.* 230; P.R.O., SC 6/784/6, m. 1.

7 e.g. P.R.O., SC 6/784/6, m. 1d.; SC 6/784/11, m. 2d.; SC 6/785/3, m. 1d.; SC 6/787/7, m. 1; SC 6/787/8, m. 1.

8 e.g. ibid. SC 6/787/9, m. 3; SC 6/788/2, m. 3; SC 6/788/3, m. 4; SC 6/789/5, m. 3.

9 *36 D.K.R.* App. II, pp. 88, 141; cf. P.R.O., SC 6/790/1, m. 3.

10 *36 D.K.R.* App. II, p. 543; P.R.O., SC 6/790/6, m. 3d.; SC 6/790/10, m. 4.

11 e.g. P.R.O., SC 6/790/10, m. 4; SC 6/791/6, m. 7; SC 6/794/10, m. 7; SC 6/796/10, m. 7; SC 6/797/10, m. 7; SC 6/798/10, m. 6; SC 6/799/10, m. 4d.; *36 D.K.R.* App. II, p. 544; *37 D.K.R.* App. II, pp. 341, 547.

12 P.R.O., SC 6/Hen. VII/1501; cf. SC 6/Hen. VII/1518–20, 1522; SC 6/Hen. VIII/275; *37 D.K.R.* App. II, p. 315.

13 *L. & P. Hen. VIII*, i (2), p. 1309; P.R.O., SC 6/Hen. VIII/287; SC 6/Hen. VIII/294; *37 D.K.R.* App. II, p. 158.

14 P.R.O., SC 6/Edw. VI/63.

15 e.g. ibid. SC 6/Eliz. I/293, 301, 303.

16 *39 D.K.R.* 36.

17 e.g. P.R.O., SC 6/Eliz. I/303–4, 317, 322; SC 6/Jas. I/139; B.L. Harl. MS. 2081, f. 216; Harl. MS. 2082, f. 25; Harl. MS. 2084, ff. 106v.–107.

Burned down in the siege of Chester, the mills were restored at the instance of the Clothworkers, whose trade depended upon them.[1] They continued in the company's possession until 1725, when two were sold to George Scott, a paper maker. Scott, who had been based at the site since c. 1705, was also lessee of the third mill, which had been sold to the waterworks company. By 1745 he was operating two paper mills and a mill for grinding logwood (a dye), tobacco, and snuff.[2] By 1757 one of the mills had been acquired by Edward Wrench to grind snuff, while the two in Scott's ownership ground snuff and logwood.[3]

The Scott family's interest was acquired c. 1805 by Robert Topham, a skinner, and Joseph Evans, a needle-maker,[4] and in 1828 Topham also bought the Wrenches' mill, together with the Dee fishery.[5] By then Topham's property comprised snuff and tobacco mills, leased to a tobacco manufacturer, skinners' workshops, and some dwellings.[6] Evans's share of a mill, used to make needles until his bankruptcy in 1833, was sold in 1845 to Thomas Nicholls, a tobacco maker.[7] The Nichollses continued to operate on the site throughout the later 19th century, and in 1895 bought the rest of the property from the Tophams.[8] By 1911 the mills, which had passed to the duke of Westminster, were acquired by H. E. E. Peel and Sir Henry Robertson, owners of important fisheries on the Dee.[9] The tobacco factory remained in operation until 1954, when it closed and the site was acquired by the city. The buildings were demolished in the mid 1960s and replaced by housing,[10] but the mill leat survived and a waterwheel was restored by Chester Civic Trust in 1988–9.[11]

DEE FISHERIES

The earl of Chester inherited from his Anglo-Saxon predecessor important fishing rights which included a fishery recorded in 1086 under the manor of Eaton; it then had six fishermen rendering annually 1,000 salmon.[12] The earliest unquestioned record of the fishery at Chester itself is the grant by Earl Ranulph II (1129–53) of a tithe of the profits from the fish taken at the Dee Bridge.[13] Thereafter the earl granted favoured religious houses such as Calke (Derb.),

Garendon (Leics.), and Chester nunnery rights to fish in the Dee above or below the bridge.[14] The monks of Wenlock (Salop.), in particular, were allowed to fish wherever they wished downstream of the bridge or upstream to Eaton, using seine nets, stall nets, and float nets, and were given a house in which to maintain a fisherman to man their boat.[15]

Such grants were continued by Earl Hugh II (1153–81), to the communities of Bordesley (Worcs.) and Trentham (Staffs.).[16] Under Hugh and Ranulph III (1181–1232) fishing rights were also extended to laymen, including officers of the earldom such as Roger the constable and Peter the clerk, tenants such as Robert Lancelyn, and citizens of Chester such as Nicholas son of Robert and Andrew son of Mabel.[17] The right to maintain a boat on the Dee was hereditary; that granted to Peter the clerk, for example, had descended by the 14th century to his great-grandson Peter Thornton.[18] It was also alienable, for c. 1270 such a right was granted by Stephen, son of Richard the fisherman, to his sister Ellen.[19] By the 14th century named fisheries were established in the river, such as 'Mabbes stalls' at Portpool, to which four nets were attached.[20]

By the late Middle Ages the fisheries were policed by the serjeants of the Dee and by the mayor and corporation, whose role as conservators, confirmed by the 1506 charter, eventually made the serjeants redundant.[21] Fish continued to abound in the river until the early 19th century. By 1830, however, when the fisheries were worked by c. 32 rowing boats, numbers were down and prices had risen, allegedly because of the netting of young fry with small-meshed nets and the netting of the millrace at the weir.[22] In 1866 the River Dee Fishing Board was established with powers to protect the salmon fisheries through licensing and the establishment of a hatchery. A fish pass at the weir, first proposed in 1869, was built in 1913 or 1914 by agreement between Chester corporation, the River Dee Fishing Board, and the owners of the weir. It comprised a 'ladder' of four broad pools, constructed parallel with the weir at the Handbridge end. The fortunes of the fisheries varied in later years. The 1920s were generally good, the 1950s relatively poor.

1 B.L. Harl. MS. 2081, ff. 216–217v.; Harl. MS. 2082, f. 25; Harl. MS. 2084, ff. 106v.–107; C.C.A.L.S., ZAF 28/16–17.

2 C.C.A.L.S., ZCHD 13/16.   3 Ibid. ZCHD 12/107.

4 Ibid. ZCHD 13/1–9.   5 Ibid. ZCHD 12/107.

6 Hemingway, *Hist. Chester*, i. 378–9.

7 C.C.A.L.S., ZCHD 13/10–14.

8 Ibid. ZCHD 13/17–20; *Bagshaw's Dir. Ches.* (1850), 104; *P. & G. Dir. Chester* (1871), 97.

9 R. Wilding, *Miller of Dee*, 120.

10 *P. & G. Dir. Chester* (1919/20), 111; *Kelly's Dir. Chester* (1938), 72; (1952), 80; (1954), 80; *Chester Chron.* 30 July, 26 Dec. 1955; *Ches. Observer*, 10 May 1968; Wilding, *Miller of Dee*, 17.

11 Inscription at site.

12 *V.C.H. Ches.* i. 249 (nos. 16–17).

13 *Charters of A.-N. Earls*, pp. 36–8 (no. 26). For evidence that Earl Richard's grant of a tithe of salmon taken at the Dee is a later interpolation see ibid. pp. 14–16, 37; *Cart. Chester Abbey*, i, p. 43.

14 *Charters of A.-N. Earls*, pp. 56–7, 59–61, 112–13 (nos. 41, 45, 99).

15 Ibid. pp. 122–3 (no. 109).

16 Ibid. pp. 156–60 (nos. 149, 151–2); cf. pp. 209–11, 246–7, 313–14 (nos. 207, 209, 247, 314).

17 e.g. ibid. pp. 190–1, 243–5, 249–50, 266–7, 279, 312–13 (nos. 185, 244, 250, 268, 280, 313).

18 Morris, *Chester*, 558.   19 B.L. Add. Ch. 75142.

20 Ibid. Add. Ch. 72271; *P.N. Ches.* v (1:i), 74.

21 Above, Water Transport: River.

22 Hemingway, *Hist. Chester*, ii. 322–3.

FIG. 64. *Fishing with bag nets in King's Pool, 1760*

From the 1970s there was a decline in the numbers of fish caught, though there were signs of improvement in the 1990s.[1]

By far the most important fishery was the King's Pool, situated by the Dee Bridge.[2] In the Middle Ages hurdles were attached to the bridge, presumably as a frame for the nets,[3] but by the later 16th century they had been superseded by a device known as the salmon cage, fixed within the tailrace of the fulling mills on the Handbridge side.[4] The King's Pool, which belonged to the earl, passed to the Crown in 1237 and was leased by the 1270s; in 1278 it was granted to the citizens of Chester for three years at an annual rent of £50, with a proviso to protect the poor.[5] In fact the citizens seem to have held the fishery for only two years, for in 1280 it passed to Richard the engineer and from 1281 was linked with the mills, again at an annual rent of £50.[6] Richard is the first person known to have leased the mills and the fishery together, but thenceforth they were generally inseparable, except for a brief period in the mid 1350s, when the keeper of the fishery accounted separately for *c.* £10.[7]

In 1347–8 the earl spent considerable sums repairing the arches and parapet of the Dee Bridge for the benefit of the fishery.[8] Rented with the mills during the tenure of Robert of Bredon, thereafter the fishery appears in the keeper's accounts. By then the profits were mainly from the sale of salmon, but other fish included lampreys, eels, whiting, and sparling. The annual income was *c.* £40.[9]

The fishery was again briefly leased with the mills in the 1390s,[10] but throughout the earlier 15th century the revenues, which rarely rose above £25, were generally accounted for by the keeper.[11] By 1463 the fishery was leased for *c.* £16.[12] It was still leased in 1475, when it was held by the widow of Hugh Hurleton, janitor of the castle, and an associate at an annual rent of £24.[13] It remained in the hands of the Hurleton family until 1532, when it passed to Robert Brooke.[14] In 1553 it was sold with the corn mills to Sir Richard Cotton, and thereafter generally descended with them.[15] In 1661 it was held by Francis Gamull's widow Elizabeth, but thereafter, like the mills, it was divided among Gamull's coheiresses.[16] In 1746 the then owners, Edward Wrench and John Brerewood, were in dispute with George Scott, whose regulation of the channels and gates near his paper mills had allegedly impaired the fishery. By 1800, when the annual rental from the fishery was £120, its income derived largely from salmon, although as earlier eels and lampreys were also taken.[17]

In 1828 the fishery was purchased by Robert Topham from E. O. Wrench; by then, however, it was in decline, and in 1831 the annual rent was only

---

1 P. M. Cohen, 'Hist. of Water Management on River Dee' (Manchester Univ. Ph.D. thesis, 1986), 30–1; Wilding, *Miller of Dee,* 120–4.

2 *Cal. Fine R.* 1272–1307, 153.

3 *Cal. Close,* 1288–96, 182–3; *Ches. in Pipe R.* 156.

4 B.L. Harl. MS. 2081, ff. 99v., 217v.; Harl. MS. 2084, f. 106; Cohen, 'Water Management', 31.

5 *Cal. Fine R.* 1272–1307, 92.

6 Ibid. 119, 153, 206; *Cal. Close,* 1279–80, 70.

7 *Ches. Chamb. Accts.* 221.   8 Ibid. 126.

9 P.R.O., SC 6/787/9, m. 3.

10 Ibid. SC 6/790/3, m. 3.

11 Ibid. SC 6/790/10, m. 4; SC 6/791/6, m. 7; SC 6/794/10, m. 7; SC 6/796/10, m. 7.

12 Ibid. SC 6/798/10, m. 6; cf. SC 6/799/10, m. 4d.

13 *37 D.K.R.* App. II, p. 198.

14 P.R.O., SC 6/800/10, m. 4 and d.; SC 6/Hen. VII/1500–1, 1518–20, 1522; SC 6/Hen. VIII/275, 287, 294; SC 6/Edw. VI/63; B.L. Harl. MS. 2081, ff. 190–8.

15 C.C.A.L.S., ZCHD 12/1/1; B.L. Harl. MS. 2081, ff. 190–8; Harl. MS. 2084, f. 106v.; Hemingway, *Hist. Chester,* i. 378–9.

16 C.C.A.L.S., ZCHD 12/17–22; ZCHD 13/16.

17 Ibid. ZCHD 13/16; 3 *Sheaf,* xviii, p. 69; Hemingway, *Hist. Chester,* i. 379; ii. 322.

FIG. 65. *Fishing with draft net below Dee Bridge, c. 1890*

£60.[1] Still in the hands of the Tophams in the 1870s, the fishery was increasingly controlled by the Salmon Fishery Acts. In 1869 an inquiry was held to investigate the removal or alteration of the fishing equipment installed at the mills. By then the salmon cage served merely as a fish pass. The cage, which had come with the weir to the duke of Westminster, was sold in 1911 to the fishery owners Peel and Robertson, who directed that on their deaths it and the weir should be offered for sale to the conservators of the River Dee Fisheries.[2]

ABBOT'S MILLS

The abbot of Chester's mills, the only watermills within the liberties except for the Dee Mills, lay north of Chester on Bache brook.[3] The site of the mill pool, near Bache railway station, was still identifiable in 1995. In the abbey's so-called foundation charter, dated 1092 or 1093, Earl Hugh I is said to have granted the community a site for a mill at the Dee Bridge.[4] The only other reference to the abbot's mill by the Dee is highly dubious: Earl Richard (1101–20), in confirming his father Earl Hugh's gifts to the monks, also granted them the site of a mill 'at the nearer end of the bridge' together with a mill at Bache.[5] That the grant of the riverside site was a later interpolation into the text of the charter is suggested by the fact that in the mid 12th century it was ignored by the compiler of Earl Ranulph II's 'great charter', which confirmed in detail the grants of his predecessors, including Earl Richard's grant of the mill at Bache.[6] Most probably, the abbot's mills were always at Bache, and the record of both Hugh I's

and Richard's grants by the Dee Bridge reflects monastic tradition relating to an unrealized claim to a riverside site.

By the late 13th century the abbot's millers were, like those of the earl, important local figures.[7] Especially prominent was David the miller, sheriff of Chester at least twice in the 1280s and 1290s.[8] That David was the abbot's miller is suggested by the fact that he was the tenant of all the abbot's holdings in Bridge Street[9] and in the 1290s also acquired extensive holdings in Bache.[10]

The abbot's mills passed with the rest of the abbey's property to the new cathedral in 1541.[11] They were among the property reserved by the Crown in 1553 to be regranted to the dean and chapter.[12] In the later 16th century they were held by Alderman Thomas Bavand and his widow Margaret, under whom there was a dispute with the Gamull family over the milling monopoly.[13] Although by *c.* 1607 Bache mill was allegedly often inoperative from lack of water,[14] in 1613 the then lessee, Alderman Edward Dutton, perhaps spurred on by the Gamulls' example at the Dee Mills, took steps to preserve his own rights over certain tenants of the abbey's former possessions who had set up a handmill of their own to grind malt. His efforts were evidently resisted, for in 1616 their leader was fined for failing to resume grinding at Bache.[15]

The mill remained in the hands of the dean and chapter until 1816. By then used for preparing skins, it was sold to a Mr. Brodhurst.[16] It had disappeared by 1872.[17]

1 C.C.A.L.S., ZCHD 12/107; Hemingway, *Hist. Chester*, i. 379; ii. 322.

2 *Chester Chron.* 11 Dec. 1869, 22 Mar. 1873; C.C.A.L.S., ZCHD 13/21; Cohen, 'Water Management', 31; Wilding, *Miller of Dee*, 120.   3 B.L. Harl. MS. 2081, f. 218.

4 *Charters of A.-N. Earls*, pp. 2–11 (no. 3); *Cart. Chester Abbey*, i, pp. 13–37.

5 *Charters of A.-N. Earls*, pp. 15–16 (no. 8); *Cart. Chester Abbey*, i, pp. 55, 57.

6 *Charters of A.-N. Earls*, p. 42 (no. 28).

7 *Cal. Ches. Ct. R.* p. 180.

8 e.g. B.L. Add. Ch. 72249, 72256; C.C.A.L.S., ZMR 2, m. 1d.

9 *Cart. Chester Abbey*, ii, p. 341.

10 P.R.O., WALE 29/249; 36 D.K.R. App. II, p. 35.

11 *L. & P. Hen. VIII*, xvi, pp. 5–6; Ormerod, *Hist. Ches.* i. 274.

12 Ormerod, *Hist. Ches.* ii. 776; *Cal. Pat.* 1553 and App. 1547–53, 100.

13 Above, this chapter: Dee Corn Mills; B.L. Harl. MS. 2081, ff. 253–70.   14 B.L. Harl. MS. 2081, f. 218.

15 Ibid. Harl. MS. 2083, ff. 160–166v.

16 Ormerod, *Hist. Ches.* ii. 776; C.C.A.L.S., EDD 10/2/1.

17 O.S. Map 6-inch, Ches. XXXVIII (1882 edn.).

The abbot also had a windmill outside the Northgate by the late 14th century.[1] Having passed with the water-mill to the dean and chapter and been leased to the Bavands,[2] the 'great windmill' was taken down in 1643 to prevent its use by parliamentary forces during the siege.[3]

OTHER MILLS[4]

By *c.* 1600, despite the Dee millers' vigorous attempts to defend their monopoly, horse mills and windmills were from time to time established within the liberties, but probably none was operative for long.[5] A list compiled in the earlier 17th century mentioned two decayed windmills and four horse mills still in use.[6] A windmill was certainly standing on Hough Green between 1652 and 1708 and perhaps survived in 1721 when the name Windmill Hill remained known. In 1739 two of the city's bakers had a grant of two plots of waste land on the green, one near the gate leading to Brewer's Hall and the other at Red Hill, with permission to dig clay for bricks to build two windmills. No further reference to the windmills is known and it not certain that they were erected.[7]

CRAFT GUILDS

Like other corporate towns, Chester had a system of craft guilds or companies through which urban manu-facturing and retailing were regulated in the later Middle Ages and the early modern period. Their names and the composition of each by different occupations underwent many changes. The companies were closely connected with the corporation, not least because the freedom of the city and membership of a guild went hand in hand. The guilds staged Chester's civic pageants, both the medieval 'mystery plays' and the secularized processions and events which succeeded them after the Reformation. In most other towns craft guilds atrophied and disappeared in the earlier 18th century with the ending of civic involvement in eco-nomic regulation. At Chester, however, the guilds survived, turning themselves into a type of social club and focusing on the convivial side of their activities which had been present from the start.

ORIGINS

Associations of craftsmen existed in Chester by the early 14th century, a time when the unitary guild merchant, in theory representing all the city's trades, still flourished.[8] The Shoemakers' company later claimed to have been established as the guild of St. Martin before 1285–6 (though later still it alleged a 12th-century origin),[9] while in the 1410s the Tailors asserted a less precise claim to have existed since ancient times,[10] and certainly had some form of collective identity soon after 1300, when they made a small annual payment to the earl of Chester to ensure that no-one 'communed' with them on 3 September (the feast of the Translation of St. Gregory the Great).[11] Both companies may have emerged from what were originally religious guilds formed by groups of craftsmen following the same trade, since they alone of all the companies were called guilds before 1500, when the preferred terms were art (*ars*), craft (*artificium*), or simply the occupational name.[12]

From the 1360s the Tanners and the Shoemakers enjoyed exclusive and collective privileges in the leather-dressing trade,[13] and during the earlier 15th century many other craft fellowships emerged as corporate bodies which participated in the Corpus Christi festival and could be represented in the city courts by their stewards. Probably most were in being by the 1420s, perhaps crystallized by what was appar-ently a reorganization and elaboration of the Corpus Christi play shortly before 1422.[14] The earliest docu-mented references to individual guilds stretched over a long period. The Bakers, Glovers, Weavers, Fletchers, Coopers, Barbers, Goldsmiths, Ironmongers, Carpen-ters (or Wrights), and Smiths certainly existed by the 1420s;[15] the Fishmongers, Drapers, Masons, Mercers, and Drawers of Dee (fishermen) were first noticed by

1 *P.N. Ches.* v (1:i), 67, 74; Ormerod, *Hist. Ches.* i. 274.

2 B.L. Harl. MS. 2081, f. 253.

3 Bennett and Elton, *Hist. Corn Milling,* iv. 59.

4 For steam mills: *V.C.H. Ches.* v (1), Late Georgian and Victorian Chester: Economy and Society.

5 O. Bott, 'Cornmill Sites in Ches. iv', *Ches. Hist.* xiv. 32.

6 B.L. Harl. MS. 2081, f. 173.

7 C.C.A.L.S., ZAB 2, ff. 98v., 184; ZAB 3, ff. 160v., 258; ZAB 4, ff. 25v., 26v., 28 and v.; ZCHD 5/21–4; cf. *P.N. Ches.* v (1:i), 61.

8 *V.C.H. Ches.* v (1), Later Medieval Chester: City Govern-ment and Politics, 1350–1550 (Decay of the Guild Merchant). This chapter is based in part on research and earlier drafts by J. Laughton (1350–1500), J. I. Kermode (1500–50), G. C. F. Forster (1550–1702), and A. P. M. Wright (1702–62).

9 P.R.O., CHES 38/26, m. 9 (printed in 3 *Sheaf,* xxx, p. 26); B.L. Harl. MS. 2054, f. 64.

10 B.L. Harl. MS. 2115, f. 163; C. Gross, *Gild Merchant,* i. 115 n.

11 *Ches. Chamb. Accts.* 37, 74; P.R.O., SC 6/771/3, m. 8; SC 6/771/5, m. 14; cf. C.C.A.L.S., ZMR 7, m. 4.

12 C.C.A.L.S., ZSR 110, m. 1d.; ZSR 156, m. 1; ZSR 235, m. 1d.; ZSR 453, m. 1d.; ZMB 3, f. 60; P.R.O., CHES 38/26, m. 9 (printed in 3 *Sheaf,* xxx, p. 26); cf. C.C.A.L.S., ZSR 147, m. 1; ZSR 153, m. 1 and d.; ZSR 160, m. 1d.; ZSR 203, m. 1; ZSR 272, m. 1d.; ZSR 310, m. 1; ZSR 350, m. 1; ZSR 362, m. 1.

13 *Blk. Prince's Reg.* iii. 428, 486; 36 *D.K.R.* App. II, pp. 23, 224; P.R.O., SC 6/785/9, m. 1, and later accts. to SC 6/786/10, m. 1; SC 6/787/2, m. 1, and later accts.

14 Below, Plays, Sports, and Customs before 1700: Chester Plays (Corpus Christi Procession and Play).

15 C.C.A.L.S., ZSR 145, m. 1; ZSR 146, m. 1; ZSR 147, m. 1; ZSR 151, m. 1d.; ZSR 153, m. 1; ZSR 156, m. 1 and d.; ZSR 165, m. 1d.; ZSR 166, m. 1d.; ibid. ZG 7/23 (printed in R. M. Lumiansky and D. Mills, *Chester Mystery Cycle: Essays and Documents,* 204–5).

name in the 1430s;[1] the Saddlers and Skinners in the 1440s; the Butchers in the 1450s; the Cooks in the 1460s;[2] the Dyers in the 1470s;[3] the Painters in the 1480s;[4] and the Vintners and the Tapsters and Hostellers *c.* 1500.[5] Some of the larger trades also had separate organizations of journeymen: bakers, shoemakers, and tailors by the 1420s,[6] weavers by the 1440s,[7] and glovers by the 1490s.[8]

Nineteen guilds agreed their entry fees in 1475–6 under the supervision of the mayor,[9] but six others not party to the agreement clearly existed by then. By *c.* 1500 the 24 parts of the Corpus Christi play were staged by probably 26 craft guilds and the Worshipful Wives, evidently a religious guild. Of the companies known to have existed before *c.* 1500, only the Painters did not participate.[10]

ORGANIZATION BEFORE 1700

Most guilds initially covered a single craft or a number of closely allied trades. The Smiths' company, for example, included locksmiths, farriers, and cutlers,[11] while the Weavers, Walkers (fullers of cloth), and Chaloners (blanket weavers) evidently formed a single entity.[12] In 1488 the Cooks' company also included innkeepers.[13] Already by the 1420s some trades were collaborating with others in order to stage a Corpus Christi pageant: the Fletchers, Bowyers, and Stringers with the Coopers and Turners, for instance, and the Weavers, Walkers, and Chaloners with the Shearmen.[14] Sharing of costs continued later: in 1521 the Smiths agreed with the Founders and Pewterers to continue their joint contributions.[15] Some of the pageant groupings resulted in the formation of guilds which combined men following disparate trades, but others were simply *ad hoc*, if long-lasting, arrangements between what always remained separate companies. The Masons and Goldsmiths, for example, put on a pageant together by the 1430s but were distinct guilds,[16] as were the Cappers and Mercers *c.* 1520.[17] Some crafts which were either wholly new or newly prominent after the mid 15th century never formed a guild of their own: makers of felt caps were

part of the Skinners' company by 1489,[18] and glaziers belonged to the Painters' company by 1482.[19]

Changes in the arrangements of the pageants between *c.* 1500 and the Reformation precipitated a restructuring of certain guilds. Three guilds (the Tanners; the Cappers and Pinners; and the Painters, Glaziers, Embroiderers, and Stationers) put on their own pageants for the first time. Conversely the Cooks' guild merged with that of the Tapsters and Hostellers to put on a single play, and the Ironmongers similarly collaborated with the Fletchers and Coopers. The last arrangement, however, did not lead to permanent union in a single guild, perhaps because at the Reformation they separated again in order to replace the pageant previously put on by the Worshipful Wives.[20]

Only two companies were chartered by the city before 1500: the Bakers in 1463 and the Fletchers and Bowyers in 1468. Both charters simply reaffirmed the guild's own regulations. The Fletchers' rules probably represented common practice, for example in regulating entry fees and the length of apprenticeships, forbidding master craftsmen from taking work from their fellows, setting a limit to the length of the working day, and punishing infringements by a monetary fine.[21] Standardized regulations made it easier for the guilds to control their members, but the courts of the city and even the palatinate were a further resort.[22] In 1475–6 twelve companies fixed their entry fees at 6*s.* 8*d.* for apprentices and 13*s.* 4*d.* for strangers, three at 6*s.* 8*d.* and 10*s.*, and one at 3*s.* 4*d.* and 6*s.* 8*d.*, while three others left the matter to be determined by the mayor and his brethren.[23] From the 15th century guild members were also required to pay annual dues.[24]

The size of individual guilds before 1500 is difficult to determine. Nineteen men witnessed the Fletchers and Bowyers' charter in 1468,[25] and in the 1490s both the Bakers and the Butchers had a membership of *c.* 18.[26] About 1576 the Cappers and Dyers had 6 members each, the Saddlers, Fishmongers, and Goldsmiths 9, the Skinners 10, the Barbers and Mercers 15 each, the Fletchers and Weavers 19 each, the Joiners 21, the Butchers 23, the Drapers 26, and the Smiths 33.[27]

---

1 C.C.A.L.S., ZSR 203, m. 1; ZSR 230, m. 1d.; ZSR 232, m. 1d.; ZSR 236, m. 1; B.L. Harl. MS. 2158, ff. 193 and v., 194v.–195; *REED: Chester*, 8–9.

2 C.C.A.L.S., ZSR 261, m. 1d.; ZSR 272, m. 1d.; ZSR 310, m. 1; ZSR 314, m. 1d.

3 Morris, *Chester*, 443.   4 C.C.A.L.S., ZSR 342, m. 1.

5 *REED: Chester*, 22.

6 C.C.A.L.S., ZSR 145, m. 1; ZSR 151, m. 1d.; ZSR 156, m. 1.

7 Ibid. ZSR 251, m. 1.   8 Ibid. ZSR 389, m. 1.

9 Ibid. ZMB 6, f. 30 and v. (printed with many errors of transcription in Morris, *Chester*, 443).

10 B.L. Harl. MS. 2104, f. 4 (printed in *REED: Chester*, 22–3).

11 B.L. Harl. MS. 2054, f. 23.

12 C.C.A.L.S., ZMR 85, m. 1 (printed in Lumiansky and Mills, *Essays*, 205–6); cf. C.C.A.L.S., ZSR 239, m. 1d.; ZSR 273, m. 1d.; ZSR 289, m. 1.

13 C.C.A.L.S., ZSR 356, m. 1.

14 Ibid. ZG 7/23; ZMR 85, m. 1.

15 Ibid. ZMB 12, f. 24v.

16 Ibid. ZSR 213, m. 1; ZSR 358, m. 1 and d.; B.L. Harl. MS. 2150, f. 85v. (printed in Lumiansky and Mills, *Essays*, 259–60); cf. C.C.A.L.S., ZSR 156, m. 1d.; ZSR 236, m. 1.

17 B.L. Harl. MS. 1996, f. 120.

18 C.C.A.L.S., ZSR 366, m. 1d.; cf. ZSR 382, m. 1; ZSR 387, m. 1d.

19 Ibid. ZSR 342, m. 1, naming as company stewards men surnamed Stainer and Glazier; ZSR 467, m. 1.

20 *REED: Chester*, 22–3, 25–6, 29–38, 245, 250–1.

21 C.C.A.L.S., ZG 7/19; B.L. Harl. MS. 2054, f. 36v.

22 e.g. C.C.A.L.S., ZSB 1, f. 51; ZSR 272, m. 1d.; P.R.O., CHES 25/11, m. 3.

23 C.C.A.L.S., ZMB 6, f. 30 and v.

24 e.g. ibid. ZSR 150, m. 1; ZSR 293, m. 1; ZSR 351, m. 4d.

25 Ibid. ZG 7/19.

26 Ibid. ZMB 7, f. 120; ZMB 8, ff. 60v., 128.

27 B.L. Harl. MS. 1996, ff. 7–20v.

Women were not eligible for permanent membership, but by *c.* 1490 some widows were allowed to join certain guilds, notably the Butchers' and Bakers' companies, after their husbands' deaths; their membership seems to have been permitted only until such time as a male relative replaced them at the head of the family business.[1] About 1575 there were five widows in the Smiths' guild and one in each of the Fishmongers' and Butchers'.[2]

From the 1530s more guilds sought to strengthen their powers by obtaining charters. Only the Barbers' charters of 1540 and 1550 (from the Assembly),[3] and the Bakers' of 1552 (a royal inspeximus of the monopoly conferred by Arthur, prince of Wales, as earl of Chester in 1495)[4] were not explicitly charters of incorporation. Existing companies which were newly incorporated included the Weavers in 1583,[5] the Wrights, Carpenters, Slaters, and Sawyers in 1584,[6] and the Brewers in 1607,[7] all by the mayor, and the Merchant Drapers and Hosiers in 1577, by the Crown.[8]

The Assembly also created new guilds, in part by formally incorporating groups of trades which had long co-operated in the Whitsun and Midsummer pageants, like the Painters, Glaziers, Embroiderers, and Stationers in 1534,[9] the Innholders, Victuallers, and Cooks in 1583,[10] and the Mercers and Ironmongers in 1605.[11] The Drawers of Dee and Waterleaders petitioned the Assembly for a similar charter in 1578, apparently in vain, and in 1603 united without one.[12] The Assembly also created wholly new guilds for the Linendrapers in 1552[13] and the Joiners, Carvers, and Turners in 1566,[14] and incorporated the city's curriers into the Saddlers' company in 1639.[15] In 1725 it refused to incorporate a group of 10 apothecaries as a separate company, insisting that they remain part of the Mercers and Ironmongers' guild with which they had long been associated.[16] The charters placed the guilds on a firmer legal footing and emphasized their dependence on the city authorities. The Assembly was wary of royal charters, which usually granted wider privileges, for example to the Merchant Drapers in

1577 and the Brewers in 1634. Other guilds revised their constitutions and ordinances to strengthen control over members.[17] Record keeping also became more systematic, at least 15 company books apparently starting between 1580 and 1660.[18]

In the early 1420s the title of master was sometimes given to officers representing a guild or the light which it maintained for devotional purposes,[19] but in non-religious contexts guild officers were invariably called aldermen and stewards.[20] The working officials were the stewards, two in number, whose election possibly always took place on the feast day of the company's patron saint.[21] Most companies also had two aldermen, though there were some variations. In 1472 the Saddlers had four,[22] and a few companies managed with only one at various times, including the Bakers in the late 15th century and the earlier 16th,[23] the Linendrapers under their charter of 1552,[24] and the Drawers of Dee in 1572.[25] The Merchant Drapers switched to a master and two wardens under their charter of 1577,[26] followed in 1607 by the Brewers, under an Assembly charter (master and two stewards) varied by a royal charter of 1634 (master and two wardens),[27] and in 1679 by the Bricklayers when they became a separate company; the last, however, went back to an alderman and two stewards *c.* 1826 and two aldermen and two stewards in 1832.[28]

Stewards or wardens usually served for two years each, the aldermen or masters for longer. In combined guilds there were rules to ensure that no single occupation monopolized the offices. The aldermen and masters conducted the meetings held quarterly or more frequently; the stewards and wardens kept records, enforced attendance, and supervised finances. Income was derived from admission fees, fines for the breach of ordinances, and quarterly dues, called quarterage and usually between 3*d.* and 6*d.* a head. Admission fees in the 16th and 17th centuries varied from under £1 to £12 or even more, with a dinner in addition or an extra fee in lieu. Regular expenditure included the amounts spent on feasting and drinking

1 C.C.A.L.S., ZMB 6, ff. 121v.–122; ZMB 7, ff. 120, 156.

2 B.L. Harl. MS. 1996, ff. 10, 20; Harl. MS. 2054, f. 22; cf. ibid. ff. 44 and v., 53.

3 *J.C.A.S.* xviii. 105–10.

4 B.L. Harl. MS. 2054, ff. 37–38v.; *Hist. MSS. Com. 7, 8th Rep. I, Chester,* p. 402; *Cal. Pat.* 1553 and App. 1547–53, 134–5.

5 B.L. Harl. MS. 2054, f. 36; *Hist. MSS. Com. 7, 8th Rep. I, Chester,* p. 402.

6 B.L. Harl. MS. 2054, ff. 42–3; *Rep. Com. Mun. Corp.* p. 2634.

7 B.L. Harl. MS. 2054, f. 55 and v.

8 *Cal. Pat.* 1575–8, no. 3572.

9 B.L. Harl. MS. 2054, ff. 88–91.

10 *Hist. MSS. Com. 7, 8th Rep. I, Chester,* pp. 402–3.

11 B.L. Harl. MS. 2054, ff. 55v.–56.

12 *Ibid.* f. 54; C.C.A.L.S., ZCR 750/1, p. 16.

13 B.L. Harl. MS. 1996, ff. 95–6.

14 *Ibid.* Harl. MS. 2054, ff. 3–8v.

15 *Ibid.* ff. 56v.–57.

16 C.C.A.L.S., ZAB 4, ff. 2–3.

17 M. J. Groombridge, 'City Guilds of Chester', *J.C.A.S.* xxxix. 93–108; Morris, *Chester,* 386–8; Johnson, 'Aspects', 244–7; 3 *Sheaf,* i, pp. 23–4.

18 C.C.A.L.S., TS. lists of guild records.

19 e.g. *ibid.* ZSR 145, m. 1; ZSR 146, m. 1; ZSR 147, m. 1; ZSR 150, m. 1.

20 e.g. *ibid.* ZSR 403, m. 1d.; ZSR 453, m. 1d.; P.R.O., CHES 2/144, m. 7 (printed in Lumiansky and Mills, *Essays,* 207–9); CHES 38/26, m. 9.

21 e.g. C.C.A.L.S., ZSR 150, m. 1; *REED: Chester,* 518.

22 Lumiansky and Mills, *Essays,* 207–9.

23 B.L. Harl. MS. 2054, ff. 36v.–38v.; *Cal. Pat.* 1553 and App. 1547–53, 134–5.

24 B.L. Harl. MS. 1996, ff. 95–6.

25 *Hist. MSS. Com. 7, 8th Rep. I, Chester,* pp. 365–6; cf. C.C.A.L.S., ZCR 750/1, p. 3.

26 *Cal. Pat.* 1575–8, no. 3572.

27 B.L. Harl. MS. 2054, f. 55 and v.; *J.C.A.S.* n.s. v. 18–19.

28 *J.C.A.S.* xxii. 69, 86.

at meetings or special occasions; the expenses of litigation or any other unforeseen demands had to be met by special levies.[1]

ECONOMIC REGULATION

Eventually each company had a set of ordinances, similar for all guilds and subject to Assembly approval.[2] They included rules about secrecy, the wearing of livery, and attendance at brother guildsmen's funerals, but more significantly covered working, trading, and employment practices. An apprenticeship of seven years was normally required,[3] but certain guilds demanded more: the Barbers twelve years, the Drapers nine, and the Shoemakers eight. At different dates the Butchers, the Joiners, Turners, and Carvers, and the Tanners all obliged newly qualified apprentices to serve as journeymen before they could join the company. From the later 16th century some guilds restricted entry by imposing a high fee or insisting on a qualifying period before a new member could take apprentices. Guilds also controlled the numbers of journeymen employed and limited the scope of their work. In 1599 the Assembly prohibited associations of journeymen, a ban ignored apparently with impunity by journeymen shoemakers who retained their own fraternity until the 1630s or later.[4]

The guilds were also concerned from the 15th century to preserve their monopoly against outsiders and against residents within the liberties who worked without belonging to the relevant company.[5] Those dwelling on the castle demesne or within the abbey precinct were immune, and in the late 14th and early 15th century non-freemen could work elsewhere in the city on payment of a small annual fine, though the practice died out between the late 1420s and c. 1450 as the guilds grew stronger.[6] In the earlier 16th century, with the support of the Assembly, some guilds became more active in enforcing their monopolies. The Tailors, for example, seem to have brought at least two or three cases every year between 1500 and 1550, and the Carpenters, Dyers, Skinners,

Tanners, and Smiths were also assiduous in hounding 'foreign' traders, 'foreign' clearly meaning anyone not a freeman of Chester.[7] Even at the height of the guild system in the later 16th and earlier 17th century, however, the guilds did not find it easy to enforce their rights against unqualified competitors in Gloverstone and the cathedral precincts, or from the countryside. By the 1630s Gloverstone in particular was crowded with non-guild traders and craftsmen who claimed the right to sell their wares in the city's markets without hindrance.[8]

During the first third of the 18th century at least some guilds were still active in economic regulation, passing and sometimes enforcing rules about the number of apprentices who might be taken on and the length of apprenticeships,[9] and restraining members who tried to entice journeymen away from other masters by offering higher wages.[10] Some still tried to control access to their raw materials,[11] notably the Tanners in the 1710s.[12] Most effort, however, was directed towards preventing non-members from trading in the city. The Feltcappers frequently took action, though it took two costly lawsuits over 10 years before they finally put a non-member working from Boughton out of business in 1740.[13] The Shoemakers were vigorous in making prosecutions in the 1720s and 1730s,[14] and the Bricklayers in 1737 fined members who sold bricks to unfree journeymen working on their own account.[15] Such efforts gradually petered out after the 1730s,[16] and by 1750 they had all but stopped. The Brewers frequently asserted their monopoly before 1761, but not at all afterwards, and they last regulated the price of ale in 1762.[17]

By then the support of the city authorities had ebbed away. Already by the 1720s they were normally willing to grant the freedom to men who had not served a full apprenticeship locally.[18] Complaints about non-freemen making and retailing goods continued in the 1730s and 1740s, and the Assembly still occasionally ordered fines, which had to be sued for in the portmote court, and even closed a few

1 Ibid. xxxix. 95–8; D. Woodward, *Men at Work: Labourers and Bldg. Craftsmen in Towns of N. Eng. 1450–1750*, 33, 73; Johnson, 'Aspects', 247–51; extensive extracts from guild records in *J.C.A.S.* xviii. 98–203; xx. 51–121; xxi. 77–149; xxii. 55–90.

2 Para. based on *J.C.A.S.* xxxix. 98–9; *T.H.S.L.C.* cxix. 93, 98–100; Woodward, *Men at Work*, 30–5; Johnson, 'Aspects', 230, 251–60; C.C.A.L.S., ZAB 1, ff. 116v., 259v.

3 C.C.A.L.S., ZG 7/19; ZSR 121, m. 1; ZSR 269, m. 1d.; ZSR 338, m. 1; ZSR 425, m. 1; ZSR 439, m. 1; ZSR 454, m. 1d.; ZSR 468, m. 1d.; ZSR 471, m. 1d.; B.L. Harl. MS. 2046, f. 41v.

4 C.C.A.L.S., ZAB 1, f. 277; *Cal. Chester City Cl. Mins. 1603–42*, 1–2, 140; *J.C.A.S.* xx. 15–17; xxxix. 99; Woodward, *Men at Work*, 78–9; Johnson, 'Aspects', 263–70.

5 e.g. C.C.A.L.S., ZSR 222, m. 1d.; ZSR 235, m. 1 and d.; ZSR 247, m. 1; ZSR 339, m. 1d.; ZSR 351, m. 2; ZSR 396, m. 1d.; ZSR 433, m. 1d.

6 Ibid. ZMB 1, f. 33; ZMB 2, ff. 26–7, 58v.–59; ZMB 3, ff. 45 and v., 100–101v.; ZSB 1, ff. 39v., 65, 66v., 118, 139; ZSB 2, f. 41.

7 Ibid. ZSR 445, m. 1; ZSR 504, m. 9; ZSR 506, mm. 51d.,

56d., 60d.; ZSR 522, m. 33; ZSR 535, mm. 23, 32.

8 Ibid. ZAB 2, f. 21v.; *Cal. Chester City Cl. Mins. 1603–42*, 132; Johnson, 'Aspects', 292–6; P.R.O., PC 2/38/230, 501; PC 2/39/385; PC 2/41/373; PC 2/42/478; PC 2/44/292; *Cal. S.P. Dom. 1628–9*, 340, 545.

9 e.g. C.C.A.L.S., ZG 5/1, f. 200; ZG 19/1, f. 48; *J.C.A.S.* xviii. 103–4; xxi. 109–11; xxii. 75–7; cf. C.C.A.L.S., ZAB 3, f. 98v.; ZAB 4, f. 42.

10 e.g. C.C.A.L.S., ZG 8/6, s.a. 1728, 1730, 1734, 1739.

11 e.g. *J.C.A.S.* xviii. 127.

12 Ibid. xliv. 41–9; C.C.A.L.S., ZG 21/4, petition at front.

13 *J.C.A.S.* xxi. 100–5; C.C.A.L.S., ZG 19/1, f. 57.

14 e.g. C.C.A.L.S., ZG 8/6, s.a. 1722–3, 1725, 1735; ZG 19/1, f. 63.

15 *J.C.A.S.* xxii. 71–2.   16 e.g. ibid. xviii. 151; xx. 24.

17 *Rep. Com. Mun. Corp.* p. 2633; cf. pp. 2634, 2636.

18 e.g. C.C.A.L.S., ZAB 3, ff. 100v., 119, 125, 126v.–127, 132 and v., 144v., 160, 161v., 175, 272, 277v.; ZAB 4, ff. 11, 30v., 33v., 44, 68, 70v., 74.

FIG. 66. *Assay Office, Goss Street*

illegal shops.[1] Its increasingly half-hearted policy was finally undermined after it sued a grocer trading in Gloverstone in 1758. After prolonged legal man-oeuvres a ruling was given in 1766 that the city was not entitled to sue unfree traders in its own court, since the freemen jurors there had a vested interest in the case.[2]

The one exception to the collapse of the guilds' regulatory powers was the Goldsmiths' company, which, paradoxically, had not enjoyed any such role in the 16th century, when local goldsmiths had been subject to the London livery company.[3] In the earlier 17th century London craftsmen dominated the provincial market to such an extent that the trade almost ceased in Chester, its guild kept alive during the Civil War and Interregnum by a single member. In the 1660s new demand for church plate led to a revival, especially after the guild decided *c.* 1663 to admit watchmakers.[4] By 1687 there were eight members, sufficiently self-confident to set up an assay office which kept a register of makers' marks and certified the fineness of all silver and gold offered for sale in Chester.[5] The office was closed under an Act of 1697 but reopened under the

Plate Assay Act of 1700, which made Chester an official assay town, incorporated the goldsmiths and silver-smiths under two wardens, and re-established the office of assay master, to be elected by the company.[6] The Chester assay office continued until 1962, when the premises in Goss Street, dating from 1749, were closed and its responsibilities were transferred to Birmingham.[7]

RELIGIOUS AND CEREMONIAL ROLE BEFORE 1700

The guilds were social and until the Reformation religious organizations as much as economic ones, with concerns which focused on burial of the dead and camaraderie with the living. Members of the Smiths' company, for example, were fined in 1501 for failing to attend a brother's funeral.[8] Their religious concerns probably pre-dated their role as craft regulators, and were still well to the fore in the early 15th century, when craft organizations were commonly termed fraternities.[9] At least some maintained a light on an altar in one of the city's churches, among them the Carpenters in the Carmelite church, and the

---

1 C.C.A.L.S., ZAB 4, ff. 71v.–72, 81v., 84, 117 and v.; ZAF 52, pt. 2, petition 1736; cf. ibid. ZG 6/4, July 1744.

2 Ibid. ZAB 4, f. 177; ibid. ZCL 119A–v.

3 M. H. Ridgway, 'Chester Goldsmiths from Early Times to 1726', *J.C.A.S.* liii. 1–189 at 15–16.

4 Ibid. 22, 84–6.   5 Ibid. 91–4.

6 Ibid. 96–7, 107–10; Plate Assay Act, 1700, 12 & 13 Wm. III,

c. 4.

7 M. H. Ridgway, *Chester Silver, 1727–1837*; idem, *Chester Silver, 1837–1962*, esp. 32, 45; *Goldsmiths Rev.* (1992/3), 28–33; dated rainwater head appears on C.P.S., Goss St. (neg. W 15/22).

8 B.L. Harl. MS. 2054, f. 23.

9 e.g. C.C.A.L.S., ZSR 145, m. 1; ZSR 146, m. 1; ZSR 147, m. 1; ZSR 150, m. 1; ZSR 151, m. 1d.; ZSR 166, m. 1d.

Tanners on the altar of St. Mary Calvercroft at St. John's.[1] Several bore the name of the patron saint on whose festival the officers were elected, including the Shoemakers that of St. Martin, the Smiths St. Eligius (Loy), and the Weavers the Blessed Virgin.[2]

Above all the guilds played a crucial role in the civic ceremonial of Chester,[3] taking part in the Corpus Christi procession and play, in the Whitsun pageants which succeeded them *c.* 1500 and were staged until the 1570s, and in the Midsummer show from its beginnings perhaps in the late 1490s until its demise in 1678. In each the companies processed or performed in a set order probably first assigned by the mayor. The order did not reflect their relative social or economic standing, and there were only a few obvious connexions between the subject of a pageant and the business of the guild which performed it, with the Drawers of Dee putting on Noah's Flood, the Carpenters the Nativity, the Bakers the Last Supper, and the Iron-mongers the Crucifixion, while the Mercers, richest of all the guilds, staged the Gifts of the Magi. A few companies had other, particular roles in the annual round of customs: the Butchers' and Bakers' guilds provided the bull which was baited when a new mayor took office, and the Drapers, Saddlers, and Shoemakers participated in the Shrove Tuesday festival. The Corpus Christi play in particular made large demands upon the guilds and their members: in 1437, for example, the Masons paid 3*s.* a head.[4] The high cost of putting together an elaborate spectacle was a factor in the stability of the guilds after the 1420s, and certainly affected the combination of separate trades into united guilds.[5]

Such ceremonial activities encouraged other forms of solidarity among guild members. Fellow guildsmen regularly supported each other in court, loaned one another money, witnessed the admission of craft associates to the franchise, and acted as executors to each other's wills.[6]

ACTIVITIES AND ORGANIZATION AFTER 1700

In the later 18th century the Assembly sometimes still had occasion to deal with the guilds over matters concerned with their corporate economic activities. For instance in the 1760s and 1770s it prevented the Bakers' company from storing firing for its members'

ovens on the Gorse Stacks, and dealt with both the Glovers and the Skinners over the tenancy of the Little Roodee, which had been used since the 1710s for drying skins (Fig. 67, p. 120).[7] Membership of the guilds, however, was falling sharply in the mid 18th century: the Cordwainers dropped from *c.* 45 in the early 1730s to *c.* 25 by the 1750s,[8] the Skinners from *c.* 25 in the late 1720s to 10 in 1760,[9] and the Tailors from *c.* 40 in the 1730s to fewer than 10 in the early 1750s.[10] One of the 26 companies went out of existence altogether: the Drawers of Dee wound up in or soon after 1746, in part apparently because they had been unable to prevent non-members from fishing in the Dee.[11] The others survived principally because they were beneficiaries of the Owen Jones charity, a modest affair used to benefit poor guildsmen until the 1750s, when it began to generate large sums of money from the royalties on lead worked under its land at Minera in Denbighshire.[12] The annual income, which until 1808 was divided strictly among the guilds in annual rotation, in the order in which they had processed at the Whitsun and Midsummer shows, exceeded £300 in the 1770s and £400 in the 1790s. Although after 1785 the Assembly required recipients to swear to their poverty before receiving a share, that did not stop all 26 members of the Barbers' company receiving £15 1*s.* apiece in 1792, or all 19 members of the Smiths', including the mayor and his son, £19 10*s.* each in 1797.[13] The abuse of the charity was ended only after 1808. Its existence preserved the guilds. The only new guild created, the Bricklayers (incorporated in 1683), took its place in the order of precedence after the company from which it separated, the Cappers, and the two divided one full share of the charity between them.[14]

With the decline of economic regulation in the earlier 18th century the guilds were already turning themselves into private dining clubs. The dinner traditionally held after the annual meeting became more important than the meeting itself, and typically sociable rules such as fining members for swearing were kept up or introduced.[15] Until the late 18th or early 19th century the guilds also joined in the civic celebrations held on Oak Apple Day (marking the restoration of Charles II, 29 May), 5 November, coronation days, when war was declared,[16] and when the bounds of the liberties were beaten.[17] Throughout

1 Ibid. ZSR 330, m. 1; 3 *Sheaf*, xxxvi, p. 54; cf. C.C.A.L.S., ZSR 302, m. 1.

2 C.C.A.L.S., ZMB 3, f. 60; ZSR 150, m. 1; ZSR 166, m. 1d.; ZSR 302, m. 1.

3 Para. based on details given below, Plays, Sports, and Customs before 1700.

4 C.C.A.L.S., ZSR 236, m. 1.

5 Above, this chapter: Organization before 1700.

6 e.g. C.C.A.L.S., ZSR 86, m. 1; ZSR 118, m. 1; ZSR 133, m. 1d.; ZSR 217, m. 1; ZSR 288, m. 1d.; ZSR 361, m. 1; ZSR 362, m. 1d.; ZSR 417, m. 1; ZSR 446, m. 1; ZMB 3, ff. 56, 105v.; ZMB 4, f. 46; ZMB 5, ff. 131, 155 and v., 184; ZMB 6, f. 38.

7 Ibid. ZAB 3, ff. 177v., 269; ZAB 4, ff. 223 and v., 233v., 293v.

8 Ibid. ZG 8/6, s.a. 1731, 1733, 1740, 1750, 1754.

9 Ibid. ZG 19/2, s.a. 1728, 1730, 1740, 1750, 1760.

10 Ibid. ZG 22/1, s.a. 1735, 1745, 1752–5, 1760.

11 Ibid. ZCR 750/1, pp. 18, 54, 62, loose note after p. 62.

12 Rest of para. based, except where stated otherwise, on above, Charities for the Poor: Municipal Charities (Owen Jones's Charity).

13 *J.C.A.S.* xviii. 145; xx. 93–5; cf. xxi. 131–2.

14 Ibid. xxii. 80.   15 e.g. ibid. xx. 13, 28.

16 e.g. ibid. xx. 35; xxi. 140–1; xxii. 85–6.

17 e.g. ibid. xx. 97.

FIG. 67. *Skinners' Houses on Little Roodee, before 1782*

the 18th century they contributed towards a prize for the St. George's Day horse race.[1]

From the mid 18th century admission fees fluctuated wildly, and in particular were raised to as much as £20 in some companies as their turn for the Owen Jones charity approached. Such large sums, and indeed ordinary revenues, were spent on a dinner, the residue being divided up equally among the members each year. From *c.* 1830, however, entry fees were forced down to 3*s.* 4*d.* by a legal ruling. While some companies took care to keep numbers low, a handful in the late 18th and early 19th century were still forcing men to join,[2] though any residual claim to stop non-freemen from trading was destroyed when a prosecution failed in 1825.[3]

The stimulus given to the guilds by the Owen Jones charity clearly began to fail after 1808, and two companies, the Fishmongers and the Dyers, became extinct apparently between 1794 and 1815.[4] The 23 which survived in 1835 had an average of 17 members, but numbers varied widely from the Innkeepers' 64 and the Bakers' 42 to those of four guilds which had only two or three.[5] Several guilds almost disappeared later in the 19th century or early in the 20th: the Skinners, for example, never had more than five members between 1812 and 1914,[6] the Barbers fell to only one or two between 1901 and 1911,[7] and the Butchers were believed in 1918 to have failed altogether.[8] Even by 1835 many guilds had lost their

seals and charters, though all but two kept a banner for display at their annual dinner.[9]

The guilds revived from the late 19th century. Some local historians were showing an interest in them in the 1890s,[10] and by the 1900s Frank Simpson had begun to study their records.[11] In 1890, in response to a further reorganization of the Owen Jones charity, the guilds united in order to lobby for the right to appoint representatives as trustees of the charity.[12] A new body, the Freemen and Guilds of the City of Chester, had its own officers, but each guild continued to exist under a single steward.[13] Gradually the guilds became more active socially and charitably. A thrift club to support sick members was formed *c.* 1903,[14] and in 1910 Simpson tracked down enough members to stage a version of the Midsummer Show as part of the Chester Historical Pageant, wearing gowns designed by himself.[15]

The guilds then continued as a series of male social clubs, some more active than others, with a further revival of interest from the 1950s which gathered pace after the Freemen and Guilds acquired the redundant Holy Trinity church, in use as a guildhall from 1967.[16] Most of the guilds had their own annual round of social activities, especially dinners and dances; they had a say in distributing small annual sums from the charities of Owen Jones, John Lancaster, and Sir Thomas White;[17] and from 1968 a number gave annual prizes for day-release students in appropriate

---

1 *J.C.A.S.* xviii. 156–8; xx. 84–5; C.C.A.L.S., ZAB 3, ff. 140v., 212; below, Chester Races.
2 *Rep. Com. Mun. Corp.* pp. 2633–7.
3 G. L. Fenwick, *Hist. of Ancient City of Chester,* 247.
4 *J.C.A.S.* xviii. 157–8; C.C.A.L.S., ZTCC 132.
5 *Rep. Com. Mun. Corp.* pp. 2633–7.
6 *J.C.A.S.* xxi. 46–8, 93.   7 Ibid. xviii. 179–80.
8 3 *Sheaf,* xv, p. 27.
9 *Rep. Com. Mun. Corp.* pp. 2633–7.
10 *J.C.A.S.* n.s. v. 1–27.

11 Ibid. xviii. 98–203; xx. 5–121; xxi. 77–149; xxii. 55–90.
12 *Deva Pentice,* ix. 13.
13 Ibid. v. 19.
14 *Ches. Observer,* 4 Feb. 1928 (copy in C.C.A.L.S., ZCR 546/40).
15 *Chester Historical Pageant Press Notes* (1910), p. 16: copy at C.H.H., Y 7/46; *J.C.A.S.* xviii. 117; cf. ibid. xxi. 148.
16 *Deva Pentice,* i–xxviii, *passim,* esp. i. 24 and (for guildhall) i. 23; iii. 5; vi. 4; xii. 2–8; xiv. 4.
17 e.g. ibid. iii. 15–16.

subjects.[1] By the 1970s there were *c.* 500 freemen of the city, all eligible to apply for admission to a guild. After women were allowed to become freemen in 1992[2] (over 200, mostly daughters of existing freemen, were admitted in the first two years),[3] the council left it to individual guilds to decide whether to admit women to membership; at least some did so immediately.[4]

MEETING PLACES

Although there were no guildhalls by that name in Chester, permanent meeting places for the guilds emerged by the late 16th century, such as the house belonging to the Tailors' company near the Newgate which was demolished in 1596.[5] The other meeting places mostly belonged to the city. Several companies met in the Phoenix Tower, which the corporation was leasing before 1600 jointly to the Painters and the Barbers, who used the upper room themselves and sublet the lower room to other guilds. The two principal companies surrendered their lease in 1773.[6] The other towers in use were the Water Tower, which the Bakers may have rented in the 1630s[7] and the Grocers were certainly using in 1772,[8] and the Saddlers' Tower, in use by the company of that name by the mid 16th century and until 1774.[9] The old common hall in Commonhall Street was leased by 1592 to the Smiths' company, which bought the building in 1700 and sublet to several other guilds, but the building was disused by 1768.[10] The Skinners' hall stood by the city walls at the end of Duke Street in the 1740s,[11] and was possibly distinct from the Glovers' meeting place, also in Duke Street, which they rebuilt in 1713, sublet to other guilds, and sold *c.* 1797.[12] Both the Weavers and the Shoemakers occupied houses in St. John's churchyard in the 18th century, the Weavers apparently ceasing to use theirs between 1755 and 1775.[13] By 1835 all but two guilds were meeting at inns,[14] the exceptions being the Skinners, who used the new common hall (St. Nicholas's chapel), and the Innholders, who met at the Exchange.[15]

LIST OF CRAFT GUILDS[16]

The variant forms of guild names given here are not comprehensive, but an attempt has been made to include every separate craft which was ever acknowledged as being part of a guild. The 23 guilds surviving in 2000 are named in bold.

Apothecaries. See Mercers (before 1605); Mercers, Grocers, Ironmongers, and Apothecaries (after 1605).

Bagmakers. See Wet and Dry Glovers.

Bakers. Earliest record *c.* 1422.[17] Called Bakers and Millers 1550s and later 16th cent. Pageant: Last Supper.

Barbers, Surgeons, Wax and Tallow Chandlers. Earliest record of Barbers *c.* 1423.[18] Called Barbers and Chandlers (sometimes specifying Wax, or Tallow, or both) or Barbers, Chandlers, and Leeches mid and later 16th cent.; Barber-Surgeons and Tallow Chandlers earlier 17th cent.; Barbers and Chandlers (or Tallow Chandlers) 18th cent.; Barbers, Surgeons, Wax and Tallow Chandlers 19th cent. Pageant: Abraham and Isaac.

Barkers. See Tanners.

Beerbrewers. See Brewers.

Bellfounders. See Dyers.

Bowyers. See Fletchers, Bowyers, and Stringers (before later 15th cent.); Fletchers, Bowyers, Coopers, and Stringers (after later 15th cent.).

Brewers. Incorporated by Assembly as Beerbrewers 1607 and by Crown as Brewers 1634.[19] Collaborated with Drawers of Dee and Waterleaders for pageant in earlier 17th cent.[20] and later replaced Drawers of Dee in order of guilds.

Bricklayers. Collaborated with Cappers, Pinners, Wiredrawers, and Linendrapers for pageant before 1603. Separated by Assembly from that guild 1619.[21] Incorporated as separate guild by Assembly 1683.[22]

Butchers. Earliest record 1457.[23] Apparently incorporated by Assembly 1665.[24] Pageant: Temptation of Christ.

1 C.C.A.L.S., ZCR 546/37.
2 *Deva Pentice*, x. 7; xv. 25–6; xxiv. 3; xxv. 7.
3 Ibid. xxvi. 2; xxvii. 2.
4 Ibid. xxv. 9–10; xxviii.
5 *J.C.A.S.* xxxix. 96.
6 Ibid. xviii. 129–41; below, City Walls and Gates: Gates, Posterns, and Towers (Phoenix Tower).
7 *Cal. Chester City Cl. Mins. 1603–42*, 166; *J.C.A.S.* xxxix. 96.
8 *Rep. Com. Mun. Corp.* p. 2636.
9 Ibid. pp. 2636–7; below, City Walls and Gates: Gates, Posterns, and Towers (Saddlers' Tower); Morris, *Chester*, 245.
10 Above, Municipal Buildings: Common Hall; *J.C.A.S.* xx. 56–67.
11 *J.C.A.S.* xxi. 89 and plate facing.
12 Ibid. xxxix. 96; 3 *Sheaf*, xx, p. 59; *Rep. Com. Mun. Corp.* p. 2635.
13 *Rep. Com. Mun. Corp.* pp. 2635, 2637.
14 e.g. *J.C.A.S.* xviii. 142; xx. 36.

15 *Rep. Com. Mun. Corp.* pp. 2633–7.
16 List based, except where stated otherwise, on lists in Morris, *Chester*, 443 (1475–6); *REED: Chester*, 22–3 (*c.* 1500), 31–8 (early banns for play), 242–6 (later banns), 249–52 (1574), 474–6 (proclamation for Midsummer Show); *T.H.S.L.C.* lxxix. 161–74 (1550s); *J.C.A.S.* xx. 9 (1757); xviii. 157–8 (1794); C.C.A.L.S., ZTCC 132 (1815); *Rep. Com. Mun. Corp.* pp. 2632–7 (1835); Harris, *Chester*, 188–9 (1979); *Deva Pentice*, xxviii, back cover (1995).
17 C.C.A.L.S., ZSR 145, m. 1.
18 Ibid. ZSR 153, m. 1.
19 B.L. Harl. MS. 2054, f. 55 and v.; *Rep. Com. Mun. Corp.* p. 2633; Hist. MSS. Com. 7, *8th Rep. I, Chester*, p. 403.
20 Cf. B.L. Harl. MS. 2054, f. 53.
21 *REED: Chester*, 317, 485–6.
22 C.C.A.L.S., ZAB 2, ff. 192, 197.
23 Ibid. ZSR 310, m. 1.
24 *Rep. Com. Mun. Corp.* p. 2635.

Cappers, Pinners, Wiredrawers, and Linendrapers.
Cappers' guild emerged after *c.* 1500.[1] Called Cappers
and Pinners early 16th cent.; Cappers, Wiredrawers,
and Pinners 1550s and later 16th cent. Linendrapers,
then Bricklayers joined to assist with pageant before
1603.[2] Called Cappers, Pinners, Wiredrawers, Bricklayers, and Linendrapers early 17th cent. Bricklayers
separated 1619.[3] Afterwards called Cappers, Pinners,
Wiredrawers, and Linendrapers. Pageant: Balaam and
Balaak.

Cardmakers. See Skinners and Feltmakers (later 16th
cent.); Smiths, Cutlers, and Plumbers (*c.* 1576
onwards).

Carpenters. See Wrights and Slaters.

Carvers. See Wrights and Slaters (*c.* 1576 only);
Joiners, Carvers, and Turners (1566 onwards).

Chaloners. See Weavers.

Chandlers. See Barbers, Surgeons, Wax and Tallow
Chandlers.

Clockmakers. See Goldsmiths.

Clothworkers. See Shearmen (early 17th cent.);
Masons (from 18th cent.).

Cooks. Earliest record 1460.[4] Still a separate guild
c. 1500, afterwards merged with Tapsters and Hostellers to form Cooks, Tapsters, and Hostellers.

Cooks, Tapsters, and Hostellers. Evidently an amal-
gamation in early 16th cent. of two guilds: Cooks, and
Tapsters and Hostellers. Called Cooks, or Cooks and
Hostellers earlier 16th cent.; Cooks and Tapsters 1550s;
Cooks, Tapsters, and Hostellers, or Cooks, Tapsters,
Hostellers, and Innkeepers later 16th cent. Part of
amalgamated guild from 1583 (see Innholders,
Cooks, and Victuallers). Pageant: Harrowing of Hell.

Coopers and Turners. Earliest record 1422, when
already collaborating for pageant with Fletchers, Bowyers, and Stringers.[5] Called Coopers 1475–6.[6] Later
merged in Fletchers, Bowyers, Coopers, and Stringers.

Cordwainers and Shoemakers. Earliest record 1364.
Called Tawyers (*alutarii*) and Shoemakers (*sutores*)
1360s;[7] Corvisers 15th and earlier 16th cent. and
1550s; Corvisers or Shoemakers later 16th cent.; Cordwainers (or Shoemakers) earlier 17th cent.;[8] Cordwainers 18th, 19th, and sometimes 20th cent. Pageant:
Entry into Jerusalem.

Corvisers. See Cordwainers and Shoemakers.

Curriers. See Saddlers and Curriers.

Cutlers. See Smiths, Cutlers, and Plumbers.

Daubers. See Wrights and Slaters.

Drapers. See Merchant Drapers and Hosiers.

Drawers of Dee. Earliest record 1438, as Fishermen
(*piscatores*). Called Drawers of Dee (occasionally
Drawers in Dee) 15th and 16th cent.; Owners and
Drawers of Dee Water later 16th cent.[9] Collaborated
for pageant with Waterleaders from 16th cent. or
earlier; amalgamated with them 1603. Disbanded in
or soon after 1746, certainly before 1757.[10] Pageant:
Noah's Flood. Brewers were associated with them for
pageant in earlier 17th cent. and later replaced them in
order of guilds.

Dyers. Earliest record 1475–6, as Hewsters.[11] Called
Hewsters or Dyers 16th cent.;[12] Dyers and Hewsters
earlier 17th cent.; Dyers 18th cent. Bellfounders collaborated for pageant later 16th cent. but probably not
part of guild. Disappeared probably between 1794 and
1815. Pageant: Antichrist.

Embroiderers. See Painters, Glaziers, Embroiderers,
and Stationers.

Feltcappers or Feltmakers. See Skinners and Feltmakers.

Fishermen. See Drawers of Dee.

Fishmongers. Earliest record 1434.[13] Disappeared
apparently between 1794 and 1815. Pageant: Pentecost.

Fletchers, Bowyers, and Stringers. Earliest record
1422, when already collaborating for pageant with
Coopers and Turners.[14] Chartered as Fletchers and
Bowyers 1468.[15] Called Bowyers and Fletchers 1475–
6.[16] Later merged in Fletchers, Bowyers, Coopers, and
Stringers.

Fletchers, Bowyers, Coopers, and Stringers. Prob-
ably an amalgamation in later 15th cent. of two guilds:
Fletchers, Bowyers, and Stringers; and Coopers and
Turners. Called Fletchers and Coopers *c.* 1500; Fletch-
ers, Bowyers, and Coopers (or Fletchers, Bowyers,
Coopers, and Stringers) earlier 16th cent.; Fletchers,
Bowyers, Stringers, Coopers, and Turners (order of
crafts varies) later 16th cent. Turners removed to
Joiners, Carvers, and Turners' guild 1566. Afterwards
called Fletchers, Bowyers, Coopers, and Stringers.
Sometimes called Coopers in later 20th cent. Pageant:
Flagellation, closely connected with Ironmongers'
pageant (Crucifixion).

Founders and Pewterers. Earliest record 1521.
Already collaborating for pageant with Smiths,[17] and
soon merged with them.

Fullers. See Weavers.

Furbers or Furbishers. See Smiths, Cutlers, and
Plumbers.

Fusters. See Saddlers and Curriers.

1 Cf. *REED: Chester*, 25–6.   2 Ibid. 485–6.
3 Ibid. 317.   4 C.C.A.L.S., ZSR 314, m. 1d.
5 Ibid. ZG 7/23; *REED: Chester*, 6–7.
6 C.C.A.L.S., ZMB 6, f. 30.
7 *Blk. Prince's Reg.* iii. 472; *Rep. Com. Mun. Corp.* p. 2635;
Hist. MSS. Com. 7, *8th Rep. I, Chester*, p. 402; P.R.O., SC
6/787/2, m. 1.
8 Cf. B.L. Harl. MS. 2054, f. 82.
9 C.C.A.L.S., ZG 10/1.

10 Ibid. ZCR 750/1, f. [1], pp. 3, 16, loose note at end.
11 Ibid. ZMB 6, f. 30.
12 Cf. *REED: Chester*, 26–7, 111–12; B.L. Harl. MS. 1996,
f. 19.
13 C.C.A.L.S., ZSR 203, m. 1.
14 Ibid. ZG 7/23; *REED: Chester*, 6–7.
15 C.C.A.L.S., ZG 7/19 (part printed in *REED: Chester*, 12).
16 C.C.A.L.S., ZMB 6, f. 30.
17 *REED: Chester*, 24–5; *J.C.A.S.* xx. 11.

Girdlers. See Skinners and Feltmakers (later 16th cent.); Smiths, Cutlers, and Plumbers (*c.* 1576 and earlier 17th cent.).

Glaziers. See Painters, Glaziers, Embroiderers, and Stationers.

Glovers. See Wet and Dry Glovers.

Goldsmiths. Earliest record 1422.[1] Incorporated by Act of Parliament 1700.[2] Called Goldsmiths and Clockmakers 18th and early 19th cent. Pageant: Massacre of the Innocents, jointly with Masons.

Grocers. See Ironmongers (earlier 17th cent.); Mercers, Grocers, Ironmongers, and Apothecaries (after 1605).

Haberdashers. See Skinners and Feltmakers.

Hatmakers or Hatters. See Skinners and Feltmakers.

Headmakers. See Smiths, Cutlers, and Plumbers.

Hewsters. See Dyers.

Hosiers. See Merchant Drapers and Hosiers.

Hostellers. See Tapsters and Hostellers (*c.* 1500); Cooks, Tapsters, and Hostellers (16th cent.).

Innholders, Cooks, and Victuallers. Incorporated by Assembly as Innholders, Victuallers, and Cooks 1583[3] (previously two guilds: see Cooks, Tapsters, and Hostellers; Vintners). Called Cooks, Innholders, and Victuallers earlier 17th cent.; Vintners, Innholders, Cooks, and Victuallers late 18th cent.

Innkeepers. See Cooks, Tapsters, and Hostellers.

Ironmongers. Earliest record 1422.[4] Called Ironmongers and Ropers 1550s and later 16th cent.; Ironmongers and Grocers earlier 17th cent. Part of amalgamated guild from 1605 (see Mercers, Grocers, Ironmongers, and Apothecaries). Pageant: Crucifixion, closely connected with Fletchers' pageant (Flagellation). Separate Midsummer pageant even after amalgamation.

Joiners, Carvers, and Turners. Incorporated by Assembly 1566.[5] Turners had previously been associated with Fletchers, Bowyers, Coopers, and Stringers; Joiners and Carvers with Wrights and Slaters.

Leeches. See Barbers, Surgeons, Wax and Tallow Chandlers.

Linendrapers. Incorporated by Assembly 1552.[6] Merged with Cappers, Pinners, and Wiredrawers later 16th cent., definitive from 1603.

Masons. Earliest record 1436.[7] Incorporated by Assembly with Plasterers 1705.[8] Called Clothworkers, Walkers, and Masons (or Clothworkers and Masons) 18th and early 19th cent.; Masons 20th cent. Pageant: Massacre of the Innocents, jointly with Goldsmiths.

Mercers. Earliest record 1437–8.[9] Called Mercers and Spicers 1550s and later 16th cent.; Mercers and Apothecaries earlier 17th cent. Part of amalgamated guild from 1605 (see Mercers, Grocers, Ironmongers, and Apothecaries). Pageant: Gifts of the Magi. Separate pageant even after amalgamation.

Mercers, Grocers, Ironmongers, and Apothecaries. Incorporated by Assembly as Mercers and Ironmongers 1605[10] (previously two guilds: see Ironmongers; Mercers). Called Mercers, Grocers, Ironmongers, and Apothecaries (occasionally Grocers, Ironmongers, Mercers, and Apothecaries) by 1757.

Merchant Drapers and Hosiers. Earliest record of Drapers 1437.[11] Incorporated by Crown as Merchant Drapers and Hosiers 1577.[12] Pageant: Adam and Eve.

Merchant Taylors. Earliest record of Tailors 1302.[13] Called Tailors until early 19th cent.; Merchant Tailors 1835; Merchant Taylors late 20th cent. Pageant: Ascension.

Millers. See Bakers.

Owners and Drawers of Dee Water. See Drawers of Dee.

Painters, Glaziers, Embroiderers, and Stationers. Earliest record of Painters and Glaziers 1482–3.[14] Embroiderers and Stationers collaborated for pageant earlier 16th cent. Incorporated by Assembly as Painters, Glaziers, Embroiderers, and Stationers 1534.[15] Pageant: Shepherds.

Parchment Makers. See Wet and Dry Glovers.

Pewterers. See Founders and Pewterers (1521); Smiths, Cutlers, and Plumbers (1550s onwards).

Pinners. See Cappers, Pinners, Wiredrawers, and Linendrapers.

Plasterers. See Masons.

Plumbers. See Smiths, Cutlers, and Plumbers.

Pointers. See Wet and Dry Glovers (mid 16th cent.); Skinners and Feltmakers (later 16th cent.).

Pursers. See Wet and Dry Glovers.

Ropers. See Ironmongers.

Saddlers and Curriers. Earliest record of Saddlers 1448.[16] Called Saddlers and Fusters 16th cent. Incorporated by Assembly as Saddlers and Curriers 1639.[17] Pageant: Supper at Emmaus.

Sawyers. See Wrights and Slaters.

Shearmen. Earliest record 1429, when perhaps part of Weavers' guild.[18] Separate guild by 1467.[19] Called Shearmen 16th cent.;[20] Shearmen and Walkers 1550s; Clothworkers and Walkers, or Walkers and Shearmen early 17th cent.[21] Not recorded as a guild later, but see

1 C.C.A.L.S., ZG 7/23; *REED: Chester*, 6–7.
2 Plate Assay Act, 12 & 13 Wm. III, c. 4.
3 Hist. MSS. Com. 7, *8th Rep. I, Chester*, pp. 402–3.
4 C.C.A.L.S., ZG 7/23; *REED: Chester*, 6–7.
5 B.L. Harl. MS. 2054, ff. 3–8v.
6 Ibid. Harl. MS. 1996, ff. 95–6.
7 C.C.A.L.S., ZSR 213, m. 1.
8 Ibid. ZAB 3, f. 136; ZAF 48B/94.
9 *REED: Chester*, 8–10.
10 B.L. Harl. MS. 2054, ff. 55v.–56.

11 C.C.A.L.S., ZSR 232, m. 1d.
12 *Cal. Pat.* 1575–8, no. 3572.
13 *Ches. Chamb. Accts.* 37, 74; P.R.O., SC 6/771/3, m. 8; SC 6/771/5, m. 14.   14 C.C.A.L.S., ZSR 342, m. 1.
15 B.L. Harl. MS. 2054, ff. 88–91.
16 C.C.A.L.S., ZSR 261, m. 1d.
17 B.L. Harl. MS. 2054, ff. 56v.–57.
18 C.C.A.L.S., ZMR 85, m. 1; *REED: Chester*, 7–8.
19 *REED: Chester*, 11.
20 Cf. ibid. 29.   21 Cf. B.L. Harl. MS. 2054, f. 65.

Masons (whose guild included Clothworkers). Pageant: Prophets of Antichrist and Doomsday.

Shoemakers. See Cordwainers and Shoemakers.

Silkweavers. See Weavers.

Skinners and Feltmakers. Earliest record of Skinners 1449.[1] Called Skinners 15th cent.; Skinners and Feltcappers later 15th cent.;[2] Skinners and Hatmakers, or Skinners, Cardmakers, and Hatters 1550s; Skinners, Cardmakers, Hatters, Pointers, and Girdlers (or omitting Hatters) or Skinners and Haberdashers[3] later 16th cent.; Feltmakers,[4] or Skinners and Feltmakers early 17th cent.; Feltmakers and Skinners 18th and early 19th cent. Pageant: Resurrection.

Slaters. See Wrights and Slaters.

Smiths, Cutlers, and Plumbers. Earliest record of Smiths 1427.[5] Merged with Founders and Pewterers after 1521.[6] Called Smiths earlier 16th cent.; Smiths, Furbers (or Furbishers, or Cutlers), and Pewterers 1550s and later 16th cent.; Smiths, Pewterers, Girdlers, Plumbers, Cardmakers, and Furbers c. 1576;[7] Smiths, Cutlers, Pewterers, Cardmakers, and Plumbers earlier 17th, 18th, and early 19th cent. (sometimes adding Spurriers, Girdlers, and Headmakers earlier 17th cent.); Smiths, Cutlers, Cardmakers, and Plumbers 1835. Pageant: (pre-Reformation) Purification; (post-Reformation) Christ in the Temple.

Spicers. See Mercers.

Spurriers. See Smiths, Cutlers, and Plumbers.

Stationers. See Painters, Glaziers, Embroiderers, and Stationers.

Stringers. See Fletchers, Bowyers, and Stringers (before later 15th cent.); Fletchers, Bowyers, Coopers, and Stringers (after later 15th cent.).

Surgeons. See Barbers, Surgeons, Wax and Tallow Chandlers.

Tailors. See Merchant Taylors.

Tallow Chandlers. See Barbers, Surgeons, Wax and Tallow Chandlers.

Tanners. Earliest record 1361.[8] Called Barkers later 15th cent.; Barkers and Tanners later 16th cent.; Tanners 1550s and from early 17th cent. Pageant: Creation and Fall of Lucifer.

Tapsters and Hostellers. Earliest record c. 1500,[9] afterwards merged with Cooks to form Cooks, Tapsters, and Hostellers.

Tawyers. See Cordwainers and Shoemakers.

Thatchers. See Wrights and Slaters.

Tilers. See Wrights and Slaters.

Turners. See Coopers and Turners (earlier 15th cent.); Fletchers, Bowyers, Coopers, and Stringers (later 15th cent. to 1566); Joiners, Carvers, and Turners (after 1566).

Victuallers. See Innholders, Cooks, and Victuallers.

Vintners. Earliest record c. 1500.[10] Connected with Merchants (not a craft guild) 1550s and collaborated with them for pageant later 16th cent. Part of amalgamated guild from 1583 (see Innholders, Cooks, and Victuallers). Pageant: Three Kings.

Walkers. See Weavers (15th and 16th cent.); Shearmen (16th and early 17th cent.); Masons (18th and early 19th cent.).

Water Carriers. See Waterleaders.

Waterleaders. Earliest record after c. 1500, when collaborating for pageant with Drawers of Dee. Also called Water Carriers earlier 17th cent.[11] Merged with Drawers of Dee 1603.[12]

Wax Chandlers. See Barbers, Surgeons, Wax and Tallow Chandlers.

Weavers. Earliest record 1422.[13] Called Weavers, Walkers, and Chaloners (or Weavers and Walkers (or Fullers) or Weavers and Chaloners) 15th cent.[14] Evidently included Shearmen 1429 but not 1467.[15] Called Weavers and Walkers 16th cent.; Weavers 1550s. Incorporated by Assembly as Weavers 1583.[16] Called themselves Weavers and Silkweavers 1633 or 1634;[17] Weavers 18th cent. and later. Pageant: Judgement Day.

Wet and Dry Glovers. Earliest record of Glovers 1422.[18] Called themselves Glovers, Pursers, Bagmakers, and Pointers 1556.[19] Also called Glovers and Parchment Makers 1550s and later 16th cent. Called Wet and Dry Glovers occasionally earlier 17th cent., regularly 19th and 20th cent. Pageant: Raising of Lazarus.

Wiredrawers. See Cappers, Pinners, Wiredrawers, and Linendrapers.

Wrights and Slaters. Earliest record of Wrights (alias Carpenters) 1422.[20] Called Wrights and Slaters earlier 16th cent.; Wrights, or Wrights, Slaters, and Tilers 1550s; Wrights, Slaters, Tilers, Daubers, and Thatchers later 16th cent.; Joiners, Wrights, Carvers, and Slaters c. 1576.[21] Incorporated by Assembly as Wrights, Carpenters, Slaters, and Sawyers 1584.[22] Pageant: Nativity.

1 C.C.A.L.S., ZSR 272, m. 1d.

2 Ibid. ZSR 366, m. 1d.; ZSR 382, m. 1; ZSR 387, m. 1d.

3 B.L. Harl. MS. 1996, f. 17.

4 Ibid. Harl. MS. 2104, f. 129v.

5 C.C.A.L.S., ZSR 165, m. 1d.

6 *REED: Chester*, 24–5; cf. *J.C.A.S.* xx. 11.

7 B.L. Harl. MS. 1996, f. 14.

8 *Blk. Prince's Reg.* iii. 428.

9 *REED: Chester*, 22.

10 Ibid.

11 B.L. Harl. MS. 2054, f. 53.

12 C.C.A.L.S., ZCR 750/1, p. 16.

13 Ibid. ZSR 146, m. 1.

14 Cf. ibid. ZSR 239, m. 1d.; ZSR 273, m. 1d.; ZSR 289, m. 1.

15 Ibid. ZMR 85, m. 1; *REED: Chester*, 11.

16 B.L. Harl. MS. 2054, f. 36; Hist. MSS. Com. 7, *8th Rep. I, Chester*, p. 402.

17 B.L. Harl. MS. 2054, ff. 70v.–71.

18 C.C.A.L.S., ZSR 146, m. 1.

19 3 *Sheaf*, i, pp. 23–4.

20 *REED: Chester*, 6–7.

21 B.L. Harl. MS. 1996, f. 16.

22 Ibid. Harl. MS. 2054, ff. 42–3; *Rep. Com. Mun. Corp.* p. 2634.

THE CHURCHES AND OTHER RELIGIOUS BODIES

COLLEGIATE CHURCH OF ST. JOHN

A late tradition, unverifiable but not implausible, ascribes the foundation of St. John's to Æthelred, king of Mercia (674–704), in 689.[1] Other information on the pre-Conquest church is scarce. King Edgar is said to have prayed in the minster (*monasterium*) of St. John in 973, and in the reign of Edward the Confessor it was enriched with 'precious ornaments' by Earl Leofric (d. 1057).[2] To those details may be added the survival of some scraps of physical evidence: some 40 coins from the reign of Edward the Elder (899–924), found just west of the present church,[3] and fragments of several crosses, probably memorials dating from the 10th century, recovered from St. John's churchyard and among the rubble of the collapsed tower in the late 19th century (Fig. 68, p. 126).[4] The crosses, and others from Wirral and north Wales, were probably made at a workshop based on St. John's, using stone from the nearby quarry.[5] Such evidence suggests that St. John's was an important church in later Anglo-Saxon Chester. Certainly by 1086 it was a collegiate foundation served by a dean (*matricularius*) and seven canons, who held eight houses in the city exempt from customary dues.[6] It was sited in the episcopal manor of 'Redcliff', and as the bishop's principal church in a city where he had considerable rights and possessions before 1066 it may already have housed an episcopal stool.[7]

A further indication of the early importance of St. John's is its possession of burial rights within the city and its environs.[8] In the late 12th century agreements were made with the monks of St. Werburgh's to preserve their common privileges. The two communities allowed St. John's hospital outside the Northgate to have a graveyard but restricted burial there to the brethren and poor of that house. The nuns of Chester were permitted to bury within their precinct on condition that the two communities provided the ministers and took two thirds of the offerings, and that the nuns did not invite Chester residents to be buried among them. Similar agreements were made with the friars as the occasion arose.

Those burial rights presumably dated from before 1100, and together with the fact that the church was collegiate by 1086 imply that St. John's was a church of high status, founded at an early period, and probably royal, with income from and pastoral duties initially over a large territory.[9] The extent of that early 'parish' is uncertain, but almost certainly it was mainly extra-mural. When first recorded, St. John's parochial responsibilities within the walls were restricted to a small area around the Newgate, presumably the location of the eight houses mentioned in 1086; outside the walls, however, they included much of the eastern part of the liberties around Boughton, besides a few fields in Hoole township outside the city boundary.[10]

After the Conquest St. John's became briefly the principal church of Lichfield diocese. In 1075 Bishop Peter formally moved his see to Chester, but by 1102, and probably as early as 1087, his successor Robert de Limesey had removed to Coventry.[11] Nevertheless, the bishop and archdeacon retained residences within the

1 B.L. Harl. MS. 2071, p. 3; R. Higden, *Holy Life and Hist. of St. Werburg* (Chetham Soc. [o.s.], xv), 86; *Ann. Cest.* 10. All cite a lost work of Gerald of Wales. Thanks are offered to the rector of Chester and the Revd. D. Gale for making the church available for inspection, to Mr. E. Rimington, conservation assistant, Chester district cl., for describing recent work on the ruins, and to Mr. F. I. Dunn and Mr. J. P. Greene for discussion of the church's architectural history.

2 John of Worcester, *Chronicle*, ed. R. R. Darlington and P. McGurk, ii. 424–5, 582–3; *Ann. Cest.* 14.

3 T. Hughes, 'On Some Coins Discovered in Foundations of St. John's Church, Chester', *J.C.A.S.* [o.s.], vii. 289–308; R. P. Mack, 'St. John's Church, Chester, Hoard of 1862', *Brit. Numismatic Jnl.* xxxvi. 36–9.

4 S. C. Scott, *Hist. of St. John the Baptist Church and Parish*, 241, 269.

5 J. D. Bu'lock, *Pre-Conquest Ches.* 77, 81–3; *T.L.C.A.S.* lxviii. 1–9; R. Bailey, *Viking Age Sculpture*, 177–82.

6 *V.C.H. Ches.* i. 344; Jones, *Ch. in Chester*, 10; *Valor Eccl.* v. 203.   7 *V.C.H. Ches.* i. 342–4.

8 Graveyard first mentioned c. 1300: B.L. Harl. MS. 2162, f. 420; rest of para. based on *Cart. Chester Abbey*, ii, pp. 299–302.

9 Cf. J. Campbell, 'Church in A.-S. Towns', *Studies in Church Hist.* xvi. 123–6.

10 C.C.A.L.S., EDV 7/1/2; EDV 7/2/2; *V.C.H. Ches.* i. 344; cf. C.C.A.L.S., ZCR 102; above, Local Government Boundaries: Parish Boundaries.

11 F. Barlow, *Eng. Church 1066–1154*, 48.

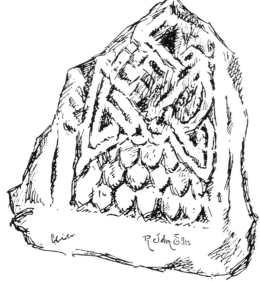

FIG. 68. *Anglo-Saxon crosses at St. John's church*

precincts of St. John's;[1] presumably it was not immediately clear that Limesey's move had definitively ended the bishop's close association with the church, though by the time of Bishop Stavensby (1224–38) the chapter of St. John's had abandoned any rights in episcopal elections.[2] St. John's remained the headquarters of the local ecclesiastical administration: ordinations were usually held there, and one of the canons

was often archdeacon. In the 16th century wills were usually proved at the church before the archdeacon's official, and in 1386 it was the location of a sitting of the Earl Marshal's court hearing the heraldic dispute between Sir Richard Scrope and Sir Robert Grosvenor.[3]

By the 12th century the precinct included other churches and chapels as well as the bishop's residence. A 'basilica' dedicated to St. Mary, outside the walls and near St. John's, to which in the late 12th century there was a choral procession from St. John's on Sundays and holy days, was presumably the minster (*monasterium*) of St. Mary which in 1086 lay in the same area.[4] Another apparently subordinate institution was the chapel of St. James, which by the late 12th century was associated with an anchorite and believed locally to be the last refuge of King Harold after his defeat at Hastings.[5] Its status is uncertain. Described as a chapel and held by the dean in 1341,[6] in 1589 it was termed the 'old parish church or chapel'.[7] Anchorites were supplied to a hermitage 'by the church' or 'below the graveyard' between 1342 and 1363 by the Cheshire monasteries of Vale Royal, Norton, and Birkenhead.[8] The anchorite's chapel was held in 1549 by Robert Bowyer, the first vicar of St. John's after the Dissolution. It was probably the earlier 14th-century oratory on a rock beside the quarry south of St. John's (Fig. 69), which was reputed an anchorite's cell in the later 16th century, by which time the Chester Shoemakers' guild met in it.[9]

The early endowments of St. John's are difficult to determine. In 1086 it apparently had only the small manor of 'Redcliff', but that may simply reflect the integration of the church's holdings with the bishop's.[10] Fresh grants are recorded in the 13th century.[11] By the later Middle Ages the church had intramural property near Bridgegate and in the Crofts, as well as around Newgate,[12] but the bulk of its possessions lay around the precinct in St. John's Lane and Foregate Street,[13] or scattered through the town fields.[14] The church's annual income in the early 13th century was probably over £250, and it benefited also from local patronage.[15] Philip of Orby, justice of Chester *c.* 1208–29, founded a chantry with two chaplains.[16] Later tradition ascribed to his foundation the grant of the churches of Overchurch, Guilden Sutton, and two in Chester, St. Martin's and St. Bridget's, though at least some of them may already

1 Lucian, *De Laude Cestrie*, 11–12, 41; Hemingway, *Hist. Chester*, ii. 75; B.L. Harl. MS. 2073, f. 98; 3 *Sheaf*, xxxvii, pp. 17–18.

2 Ormerod, *Hist. Ches.* i. 93; Jones, *Ch. in Chester*, 5.

3 Morris, *Chester*, 146, 171; Jones, *Ch. in Chester*, 113.

4 *V.C.H. Ches.* i. 344.

5 Gerald of Wales, *Opera* (Rolls Ser.), vi. 140; R. Higden, *Polychronicon* (Rolls Ser.), vii. 244; Lucian, *De Laude Cestrie*, 56; A. T. Thacker, 'King Harold at Chester', *Middle Ages in NW.* ed. T. Scott and P. Starkey, 155–76.

6 Morris, *Chester*, 168–9.

7 Jones, *Ch. in Chester*, 45.

8 Lich. Jt. R.O., B/A/1/2, f. 115v.; B/A/1/3, f. 138v.; *V.C.H. Ches.* iii. 127; 3 *Sheaf*, lv, pp. 48–9, 68; Ormerod, *Hist. Ches.* i. 353–4.

9 P.R.O., SC 12/6/24A; B.L. Harl. MS. 2073, ff. 97v.–99.

10 *V.C.H. Ches.* i. 269–70, 344; *Domesday Surv. Ches.* 28.

11 e.g. 3 *Sheaf*, xxxvi, p. 20.

12 1 *Sheaf*, i, p. 187; B.L. Add. Ch. 72211.

13 e.g. B.L. Add. Ch. 50102, 50105; *36 D.K.R.* App. II, p. 91.

14 Jones, *Ch. in Chester*, 51–2, 63–4; *P.N. Ches.* v (1:i), 84; P.R.O., E 315/419, ff. 20–1; SC 12/6/24A, ff. 5–9.

15 Jones, *Ch. in Chester*, 78, 81.

16 Ibid. 103; *V.C.H. Ches.* ii. 3; cf. 3 *Sheaf*, xx, p. 60.

FIG. 69. *Anchorite's chapel*

have been connected with St. John's.[1] Orby's family was long associated with the church. In 1258 or 1259 his son Philip gave three salt-houses in Northwich, and the family continued to appoint chantry priests until the death of Sir John Orby before 1354 left his daughter and heir Joan as a ward of the Black Prince.[2]

Although in the 12th century canons of St. John's subscribed local charters, by the 14th they had become largely absentee and appeared at visitations only by proxy. Their choir duties were performed by eight vicars.[3] By the 13th century there was also a sacristan appointed by the dean and responsible for the discipline of the vicars.[4] The senior of the two cantarists of the Orby chantry, the petty canon as he became known, came to be regarded as the leading figure among the lesser clergy. He enjoyed a large income and was often of the same social standing as the canons.[5]

From the 13th century St. John's reputation was enhanced by the possession of an important relic, the so-called Rood of Chester. It existed by 1256 or 1257, when Fulk of Orby provided a mark of silver annually for lights before it,[6] and appears to have been enshrined in a golden cross-shaped reliquary adorned with an image.[7] It was so greatly venerated both in the locality and much further afield that in the late 13th and early 14th century St. John's was known as the church of the Holy Cross.[8]

In 1291 St. John's derived its income almost wholly from spiritualities.[9] By 1318 it held the appropriated benefices of Farndon, Holt (Denb.), Shocklach, Guilden Sutton, and Overchurch, and of St. Martin's, St. Bridget's, and St. Chad's in Chester.[10] Three or four of those had been acquired in the 13th century with the establishment of the Orby chantry, and others probably much earlier; in 1352, for example, the dean alleged that Farndon and the chapelries of Holt and Shocklach had been annexed to his deanery 'time out of mind'.[11] All except Holt and St. Chad's remained attached to St. John's until the Dissolution.[12] In addition the college acquired the Cheshire benefices of Stoke, appropriated in 1349,[13] and Plemstall, transferred by Shrewsbury abbey in 1382 and appropriated in 1393. All the livings were served by stipendiary curates drawn from the lesser clergy, except Plemstall, where the bishop ordained a vicarage a decade after the appropriation.[14]

Other sources of income included the parish tithes, glebe,[15] and offerings to the Rood, which in the 14th century amounted to perhaps £70 a year and constituted the biggest single item.[16] From the late 13th century there were also occasional profits from ecclesiastical justice, some of which involved payments to maintain the fabric.[17]

The canons were paid from a common fund, and there were increasing difficulties about their entitlements. In 1318 income was divided into three main groups: the great tithes, annexed to the deanery, and the profits from the glebe, divided equally between the dean and the canons of the fifth and sixth stalls; offerings to the Rood and the altarage of St. John's, devoted primarily to the vicars' stipends and the resident canons' commons, with the remainder distributed weekly among the chapter; and revenues from

1 Jones, *Ch. in Chester*, 101–2; *Blk. Prince's Reg.* iii. 152; 3 *Sheaf*, xviii, pp. 27–8. Overchurch: 3 *Sheaf*, xx, p. 60; Guilden Sutton: *Domesday Surv. Ches.* 88.

2 His rights eventually descended to the Breretons of Brereton: Ormerod, *Hist. Ches.* iii. 548.

3 Jones, *Ch. in Chester*, 10, 32–3, 50; *Cart. Chester Abbey*, i, p. 94; ii, p. 336.

4 *J.C.A.S.* N.S. x. 25; Jones, *Ch. in Chester*, 10, 48, 50.

5 Jones, *Ch. in Chester*, 10, 14, 25, 50, 101–2; *Valor Eccl.* v. 202.

6 *Cal. of Deeds and Papers of Moore Fam.* (R.S.L.C. lxvii), p. 146; for date: 3 *Sheaf*, xxxiv, p. 31; W. Beamont, *Cal. of Ancient Charters preserved at Eaton Hall, Ches.* MS. 43; below, Lists of Mayors and Sheriffs.

7 3 *Sheaf*, xxii, p. 39.

8 e.g. ibid. pp. 37–40; *Tax. Eccl.* 258; Jones, *Ch. in Chester*, 51; C.C.A.L.S., Cowper MSS., i, f. 12v.; *V.C.H. Ches.* v (1), Later Medieval Chester: Religion (Religious Cults).

9 *Tax. Eccl.* 248.

10 Jones, *Ch. in Chester*, 70; Lamb. Pal., Reg. Arundel, i, f. 379.

11 *Blk. Prince's Reg.* iii. 74.

12 Holt was lost *c.* 1360: *Cal. Inq. Misc.* iv, p. 46.

13 Lich. Jt. R.O., B/A/1/2, f. 126.

14 Jones, *Ch. in Chester*, 70.

15 B.L. Harl. MS. 2162, ff. 423v.–424.

16 Jones, *Ch. in Chester*, 78–9.

17 *Cart. Chester Abbey*, ii, p. 460; B.L. Harl. MS. 2162, f. 421.

the appropriated churches, divided among members of the chapter resident in the previous year.[1] Provision for the lesser clergy was inadequate, and in the 14th century the bishop increasingly intervened on their behalf. After his visitation of 1331, Bishop Northburgh enjoined that the vicars should be removed only with his consent, that their salaries be paid at the customary times, and that they be provided with a common dwelling and meanwhile have the right to lodge in the canons' houses. He also ordered that part of the offerings to the Rood be set aside to buy new vestments and ornaments.[2] In 1346 he further directed that the vicars' stipends be increased and that four choristers be appointed to assist them in singing the offices.[3] Those injunctions were disregarded, and by 1348 the canons' determination to maintain their incomes had brought the fabric to near ruin and reduced the vicars' stipends to such an extent that services were endangered.[4] In his visitation of that year Bishop Northburgh found the church in disrepair, the books, vestments, and ornaments consumed with age, and his regulations about the vicars ignored. He restricted the incomes of the dean and canons for the following 10 years, and ordered that each newly installed member of the chapter should contribute to the cost of new vestments and ornaments. He also attempted to reform the college's finances, and annulled the long leases by which the chapter had farmed out not only the appropriated rectories but also their shares of the common fund.[5]

In 1349, perhaps in response to the bishop's strictures, Sir Peter Rutter, lord of the manor of Thornton le Moors, granted the dean and chapter the church of Stoke in return for the establishment of a perpetual chantry. Its two chaplains, to be chosen by the dean, were also to join the vicars in celebrating the offices.[6] After complaints by some of the vicars, the bishop made further injunctions in 1353 to ensure that their incomes were paid regularly and improved,[7] but the matter was clearly not entirely settled and was the subject of additional regulation at the metropolitan visitation of 1400.[8]

Such pressure from the bishop provoked dissension within the chapter. In 1347 the dean ordered, with the bishop's approval, that the offerings and small tithes of Farndon, Shocklach, Holt, St. Bridget's, and St. Martin's were to be devoted to augmenting the vicars' stipends.[9] His action changed the arrangements of 1318 and brought to a head the question of the

dean's rights over the appropriated churches. The two or three canons apparently resident at the time claimed that the revenues from those churches should be collected by one of their number and divided among them. The dean disagreed, and both sides appealed to the Black Prince. The disputed revenues were seized into the prince's hand, and the collegiate clergy, left without income, threatened to leave St. John's.[10]

Conspicuous in the lawsuit was the assumption, also made in 1318, that Overchurch, Guilden Sutton, and the Chester churches were to provide for the college as a whole and not simply for the Orby chantry; but in 1352 the cantarist sued at Canterbury for his full rights as a canon of St. John's and the court gave sentence in his favour.[11] In 1354 the Black Prince intervened as guardian of the Orby heiress to protect the chantry's interests, ordering that the salary of one of its chaplains be paid, but conceding that the churches associated with Orby's grant were never exclusively appropriated to the chantry.[12] The dean eventually won a partial victory. In 1397 he still retained Farndon, Shocklach, Overchurch, and Plemstall, leaving the canons only Guilden Sutton and the Chester churches.[13] Thereafter, however, his position was eroded, and by the 1530s only Plemstall remained appropriated to the deanery.[14]

In 1353 and 1354, in the midst of those disputes, two successive deans exchanged the deanery for other benefices. The beneficiary of the later transaction was challenged in 1357 by Alexander Dalby, a royal clerk who based his claims on a papal provision and was confirmed in the deanery in 1359.[15] Dalby came to a church facing increasing financial difficulties. Income fell to c. £220 by 1393 and to little more than £100 in the early 15th century.[16] The chapter's continued leasing of the tithes of the appropriated churches probably contributed to that decline, for it seems rarely to have received a fair rent.[17] Another factor was the reduction in offerings to the Rood, which had fallen to c. £50 by the early 16th century.[18] In the circumstances it is not surprising that some of the institutions for which the dean and chapter had earlier been responsible apparently lapsed. One such was the grammar school, in existence by 1353 when the master and boys attended services in a chapel dedicated to the Virgin situated in St. John's churchyard and popularly known as the White chapel.[19] Nothing further is recorded of the school, which had disappeared by the 16th century.[20]

Despite such difficulties, St. John's retained its role

1 *Valor Eccl.* v. 202; Jones, *Ch. in Chester*, 51–8.
2 Lich. Jt. R.O., B/A/1/3, f. 41.
3 Ibid. f. 118v.   4 Ibid. f. 112 and v.
5 Ibid.; *Reg. of Roger de Norbury, Bp. of Lich.: Abstract* (Collns. Hist. Staffs. [1st ser.], i), 274; Jones, *Ch. in Chester*, 88.
6 Lich. Jt. R.O., B/A/1/2, f. 126; B/A/1/3, f. 128.
7 Ibid. B/A/1/3, ff. 129v., 132v., 133v.
8 Lamb. Pal., Reg. Arundel, i, f. 484.
9 Lich. Jt. R.O., B/A/1/3, f. 132.

10 *Blk. Prince's Reg.* iii. 74–5.   11 Ibid. 64.
12 Ibid. 152.
13 *Cal. Pat.* 1396–9, 248.
14 *Valor Eccl.* v. 202–3.
15 *Blk. Prince's Reg.* iii. 277, 288, 326.
16 Jones, *Ch. in Chester*, 78–9.
17 Ibid. 88.   18 Ibid. 78–9.
19 Lich. Jt. R.O., B/A/1/3, f. 133v.
20 Not mentioned in *Valor Eccl.* or Dissolution records.

in civic life. Apparently from the 13th century it was the scene of ceremonies connected with the licensing of minstrels, and in the 15th century the guild procession for the feast of Corpus Christi finished at the church.[1] The Rood was still venerated in the 15th century, and the cult had even spread to Bordeaux.[2] At home, gifts continued to be made to it throughout the later Middle Ages: a ring in 1467, £20 from the son of a former mayor in 1489, and five large candles from an alderman in 1505, for example.[3] Its advocacy was still valued in the early 16th century, when a man from Winwick (Lancs.) left 6s. 8d. to anyone willing to undertake a pilgrimage to the Rood on his behalf, and the courtier William Smith caused three gold marks to be offered for the soul of his late master, Henry VII.[4] As late as 1518 Nicholas Deykin made provision for a priest to celebrate at the altar of the Holy Rood for eight years after his death.[5] The relic remained sufficiently important for three or four of the canons' stalls to be known as prebends of the Holy Cross.[6]

St. John's also continued to attract chantry endowments, presumably because the vicars could readily be employed for services commemorating the dead.[7] By the 16th century the vicars had accumulated considerable holdings given to finance such services and known as the obit lands,[8] though many bequests were for temporary commemorations. In 1398, for example, John Hatton gave £20 for a chaplain to say mass for four years, and in 1518 Nicholas Deykin left £45 for a priest to celebrate at St. Catherine's altar. Both probably expected collegiate vicars to be employed as cantarists.[9]

The guild or fraternity of St. Anne, which had close links with the vicars, was apparently founded in 1361 and refounded in 1393.[10] The wardens or masters seem often to have been drawn from the clergy of St. John's: between 1396 and 1420, for example, they included Ranulph Scolehall, chaplain of the Orby chantry.[11] The fraternity's own chantry seems originally to have been within the collegiate church, but presumably after the refoundation a separate building was established in the precinct east of St. John's.[12]

In the 1530s the college's income was somewhat over £150, still principally from the appropriated churches

and the Rood, the latter contributing a third of the total. The value of the canons' prebends had fallen, and the position of the vicars was relatively improved; by then they drew more than the canons from the common fund. The petty canon, with almost £16 a year, enjoyed an income second only to the dean's. The canons thus had little incentive to reside.[13] In the mid 1530s the college sustained a major financial loss with the removal of the Rood.[14] In response Bishop Rowland Lee, at the instance of Thomas Cromwell, in 1539 reduced the lesser clergy to two conducts, four vicars choral, and four chantry priests.[15] The changes improved the lot of the remaining vicars,[16] but also occasioned resentment. Two of them 'withdrew certain plate' and obtained a letter from Cromwell supporting their claim to have been wronged by the dean and chapter. The petty canon's chantry suffered especially; in 1539 Peter Brereton, the petty canon, complained that revenue was wrongfully withheld and that one of the chantry priests had been unjustly expelled. He petitioned the king, and c. 1542 the dean, Richard Walker, replied alleging that he had suspended the disputed payments since the removal of the Rood and the loss of the oblations.[17] The petty canon's chantry seems to have been suppressed in 1543, when its endowments were leased to the founder's heir, Richard Brereton, in whose hands they remained in 1557.[18]

Standards of behaviour among the lesser clergy were not exemplary in the period before the Dissolution. In 1536 four of the vicars were found to be unchaste,[19] and probably in the 1540s the two chantry priests of St. Anne's, William Horseman and Thomas Pyncheware,[20] allegedly broke into and damaged houses adjoining the fraternity's building.[21]

The creation of the bishopric of Chester in 1541 provided a fresh threat to St. John's. The archdeacon's court, hitherto held in the collegiate church, was removed in that year to the cathedral.[22] Although the dean's claim to be exempt from the authority of the new bishop was recognized in 1542, the privilege was soon lost.[23] Thereafter, the college seems to have feared the worst, and disposed of property in a series of very long leases.[24] Finally in 1547 or 1548 the college, with its

1 *REED: Chester*, pp. li, liii–liv, 15–16, 38–9, 461–6, 486–9; below, Plays, Sports, and Customs before 1700: Chester Plays (Corpus Christi Procession and Play), Music and Minstrelsy (Minstrels' Court).

2 *V.C.H. Ches.* v (1), Later Medieval Chester: Religion (Religious Cults).

3 Jones, *Ch. in Chester*, 51; 3 *Sheaf*, xix, p. 4; xxiii, pp. 37–8; E. Baines, *Hist. of County Palatine and Duchy of Lancaster* (1888–93 edn. by J. Croston), v. 73; B.L. Harl. MS. 2176, f. 276.

4 S. C. Scott, *Hist. of St. John the Baptist Church and Parish*, 33; pers. comm. Dr. Steven Gunn, Merton Coll., Oxf., citing P.R.O., E 36/214, f. 161v.   5 3 *Sheaf*, xiv, pp. 8–9.

6 Ormerod, *Hist. Ches.* i. 313; *Valor Eccl.* v. 203.

7 Cf. Lich. Jt. R.O., B/A/1/3, f. 133v.

8 Jones, *Ch. in Chester*, 56; P.R.O., SC 12/6/24A.

9 3 *Sheaf*, xiii, p. 49; xxxvi, p. 9; Jones, *Ch. in Chester*, 106.

10 *V.C.H. Ches.* v (1), Later Medieval Chester: Religion

(Guilds, Confraternities, and Chantries).

11 3 *Sheaf*, xxxvi, *passim*; lv, p. 86; *V.C.H. Ches.* ii. 25–6.

12 *Blk. Prince's Reg.* iii. 409; Jones, *Ch. in Chester*, 64–5.

13 *Valor Eccl.* v. 202–4; Jones, *Ch. in Chester*, 12–13.

14 3 *Sheaf*, xviii, pp. 27–8; Jones, *Ch. in Chester*, 102–3.

15 *L. & P. Hen. VIII*, xiv (1), p. 96.

16 Jones, *Ch. in Chester*, 57.

17 Ibid. 130; *L. & P. Hen. VIII*, xiv (1), p. 96; 3 *Sheaf*, xviii, pp. 27–8.   18 Jones, *Ch. in Chester*, 102–3.

19 *L. & P. Hen. VIII*, x, p. 142.

20 *List of Clergy, 1541–2*, 3; P.R.O., E 301/8/1; SC 6/Edw. VI/65–7; SC 12/6/24A.   21 3 *Sheaf*, xviii, p. 49.

22 C.C.A.L.S., EDC 1/10, ff. 117, 125v., 130.

23 *V.C.H. Ches.* ii. 15; *L. & P. Hen. VIII*, xvi, p. 654; xvii, p. 258; cf. C.C.A.L.S., EDA 3/1, ff. 51–2.

24 *L. & P. Hen. VIII*, xix (1), pp. 290–1; B.L. Harl. MS. 1994, f. 571; Harl. MS. 2046, f. 20.

FIG. 70. *St. John's church, nave looking east, 1858*

staff of dean, seven canons (five with livings elsewhere), and four vicars, was dissolved. The appropriated churches, the prebendal lands and other property in Chester, the obit lands, the chantry rents, and the possessions of the fraternity of St. Anne were all taken into the king's hands. The whole east limb of the church and four bells also fell to the king.[1]

The design of the Romanesque east end, probably of four bays with eastern towers terminating in three apses, suggests that it was begun *c.* 1100 under Bishop Limesey; it is related to other west Midland churches of that date, such as Shrewsbury, Hereford, and Much Wenlock. Work was then interrupted, to resume between *c.* 1125 and *c.* 1150, perhaps with a reduced scheme incorporating a central tower, transepts, a nave of six bays, and a west bay with north and south towers. By 1200 construction appears to have reached roof level as far as the east end of the nave, but further west only the arcades and perhaps the lower parts of the aisle walls had been built. The nave triforia appear to date from *c.* 1200, and the clerestories, surviving aisle windows, north doorway, and porch from the early 13th century.[2]

In the late 13th century a square building of two storeys was built in the angle between the chancel aisle and the south transept; perhaps a chapter house, in the 16th century it was described as the house of the 'church priests'.[3] After its completion, however, the fabric of the church seems to have been neglected, and in 1349 repairs were deemed necessary.[4] It was perhaps about then that the east end was remodelled, probably to accommodate the increasing number of chantries. The work comprised a polygonal Lady chapel flanked by square-ended chapels to north and south; stone-vaulted and richly carved, it was closely related to contemporary work in the south transept of the abbey and to parts of the chancel and north transept at Nantwich.[5]

St. John's seems generally to have remained in poor condition, and in 1415 the dean and chapter were granted a royal licence to collect alms for the rebuilding of the church and college, then described as ruinous.[6] Building and repair continued almost to the Dissolution: in 1463 and 1471 the church roof was referred to as newly covered,[7] and between 1518 and 1523 the north-west tower was rebuilt.[8] The

1 P.R.O., E 301/8/1; SC 6/Edw. VI/65–7; SC 12/6/24A.

2 R. Gem, 'Romanesque Archit. in Chester *c.* 1075–1117', *Medieval Arch., Art, and Archit. at Chester*, ed. A. Thacker, 38–41; S. Ward, 'Recent Work at St. John's and St. Werburgh's', ibid. 45–7; *Arch. Jnl.* xciv. 307–8.   3 B.L. Harl. MS. 2073, f. 99.

4 Lich. Jt. R.O., B/A/1/2, f. 126.

5 J. M. Maddison, 'Decorated Archit. in NW. Midlands' (Manchester Univ. Ph.D., 1978), 265–6; B.L. Harl. MS. 2073, ff. 95, 97v., 99.   6 *Cal. Pat.* 1413–15, 285.

7 3 *Sheaf,* xxix, pp. 29, 40.

8 R. V. H. Burne, 'The Falling Towers of St. John's Church', *J.C.A.S.* xxxvi. 15–16; B.L. Harl. MS. 2073, f. 93.

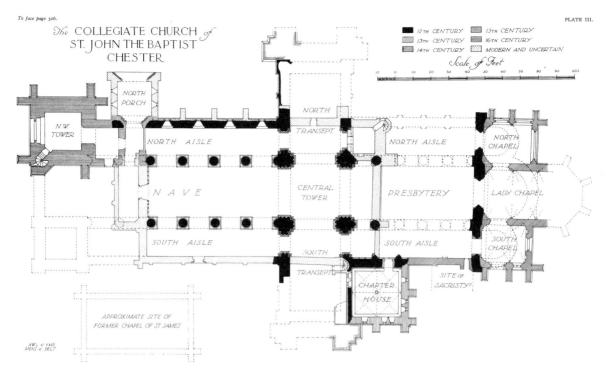

FIG. 71. *St. John's, plan* (Arch. Jnl. *xciv, facing p. 306*)

church, however, probably remained incomplete. There seems never to have been a central tower, and it is unlikely that the west front was finished to the original designs, which would not have accommodated the spiral staircase inserted south of the north-west tower. Nevertheless, the nave was certainly longer than at present by at least one bay, for the west wall cuts through the arches of the triforium and arcade.[1]

At its dissolution the church stood in a sizeable precinct (Fig. 72, p. 132), which included to the east the irregular and perhaps courtyarded building of the St. Anne's fraternity, and to the south the large chapel of St. James and a small anchorite's cell. A further chapel, the Calvercroft chapel, was also probably a separate structure.[2] All around were the clergy houses, including those of the bishop, dean, canons, vicars, and cantarists; other houses for the vicars lay just outside the precinct on Vicars Lane. Most of those buildings survived the dissolution. The chapels of the anchorite, Calvercroft, and St. James, the last put to use as a store, were held by the first parochial vicar; the fraternity house passed to Sir Hugh Cholmondeley, one of the royal commissioners; the dean's house was taken by Hugh Glazier, mayor of Chester 1602–3; and another clergy house was occupied by Alexander

Cotes, an early lay rector. All later disappeared, probably destroyed in the Civil War siege of Chester. St. John's itself survived as a parish church after the Dissolution.[3]

DEANS[4]

R. de Verdun, occurs *c.* 1187[5]
Bertram, occurs *temp.* Richard I and John[6]
Simon, fl. *c.* 1226–41[7]
Richard Aldcroft, ?[8]
William Brickhill (or Birchills), by 1287–1308/9[9]
Randle Torald, 1309–10
William Wish or Wych, 1311[10]
Adam Ayremynne, 1321–?
Stephen Kynardesley, 1323–?
Thomas Clopton, 1325–8
Nicholas Northburgh, 1329
Peter Russell, 1329–34
William Appletree, 1334–9
John Marsh, 1339–53
Richard Birmingham, 1353–4
Hugh Threekingham, 1354–5
Alexander Dalby, 1355–66/7
disputed succession, *c.* 1357
Richard Birmingham (reappointed?), 1357

1 *J.C.A.S.* xxxvi. 1–20.
2 3 *Sheaf*, xiii, p. 52; below, Medieval Parish Churches: St. John.
3 B.L. Harl. MS. 2073, ff. 95, 97v.–99v.; P.R.O., SC 12/6/24A; *Cal. Pat.* 1553 and App. 1547–53, 221; Scott, *Hist. St. John's Church*, 55–60; below, Medieval Parish Churches: St. John.
4 Unless otherwise stated list based on Jones, *Ch. in Chester*,

123–30.
5 Ormerod, *Hist. Ches.* i. 307; ii. 276.
6 Ibid. i. 307.   7 Ibid.
8 Ibid.
9 For 'Brickhill': e.g. C.C.A.L.S., DVE 1/CI/14.
10 Thus Ormerod, *Hist. Ches.* i. 307, but probably dean of Christianity for Chester.

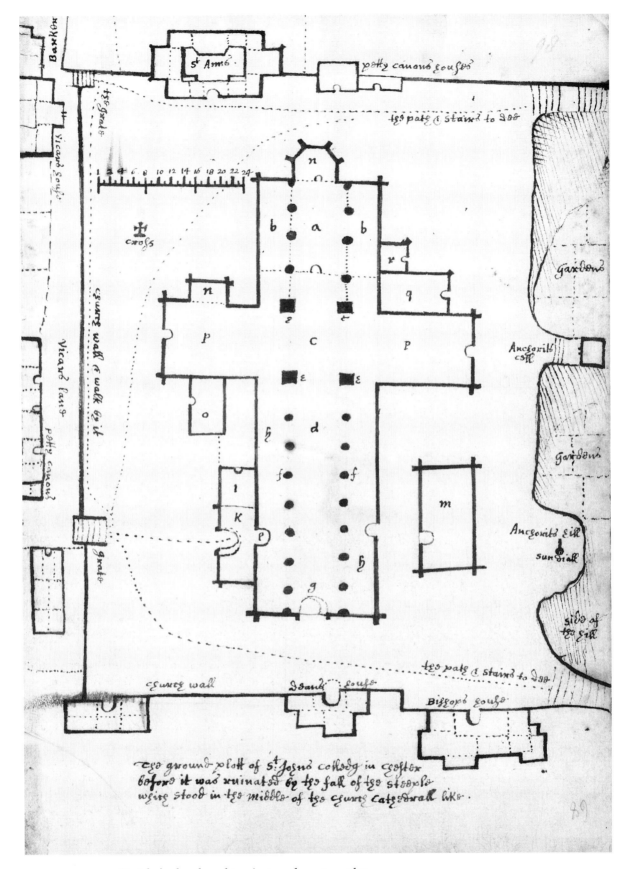

FIG. 72. *St. John's church and precinct, 17th-century plan*

KEY: The key to the plan is lost, but other plans by the same hand record the less obvious features:

k: north porch

l: small house adjoining north porch

m: St. James's chapel

n (at east end): the Lady chapel ('a fine little chapel or the *sancta sanctorum*, part ruinated')

n (east of north transept): 'a little low chapel'.

o: a house added to the north transept, reputedly the meeting house of the 'woollen and linen websters'

q, r: a house or some chambers belonging to the college priests.

John Woodhouse, by 1370–1395
John Leyot, 1395–1422/3
Roger Leyot, 1423–31
Walter Shirington, 1431–8
Humphrey Rodeley, 1438
Thomas Heywood, 1438–44
Roger Asser, 1444–71
Thomas Milly, 1471–88

Christopher Talbot, 1489–92/3
Hugh Oldham, 1493–4
Thomas Mawdesley, 1494–?
Robert Lawrence, occurs 1500[1]
Ralph Cantrell, 1505–?1531
Geoffrey Blythe, 1531–40/1
Richard Street, 1541
Richard Walker, 1542–8

MEDIEVAL PARISH CHURCHES

HOLY TRINITY

The church existed by the late 1180s and its dedication suggests an origin in the late 12th century.[2] Soon afterwards its priest was mentioned in terms which

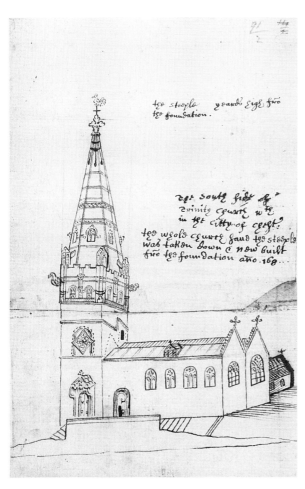

FIG. 73. *Holy Trinity in late 17th century*

suggest that it was associated with St. Peter's.[3] Probably it was founded by the Montalt family, barons of Mold (Flints.), with whom early rectors seem to have been connected.[4]

The parish lay in the west of the city, extending from the walls of the legionary fortress to the Dee, and thus reaching beyond the medieval city walls to cover the Roodee. It also included the manor of Blacon, beyond the liberties.[5] In 1882 and 1960 the intramural portions and the Roodee were assigned to St. Peter's, leaving Holy Trinity as the parish church for Blacon alone.[6] The city-centre church was closed in 1961 and replaced as the parish church by a new building in Blacon.[7]

Advowson, Income, and Property

The living is a rectory and has never been appropriated. Until the early 14th century the advowson belonged to the barons of Mold, whose heir in 1335 transferred it for life to Isabella, widow of Edward II. With her death in 1358 it passed to the Black Prince, who in 1361 gave it to William Montagu, earl of Salisbury. After forfeiture to the Crown it was granted in 1401 to Sir John Stanley of Lathom (Lancs.), with whose descendants, the earls of Derby, it remained until *c.* 1989, when they transferred it to the bishop of Chester.[8]

The income was always modest. In 1291 the church was valued at £6 13s. 4d.,[9] and throughout the 15th century at less than half that sum.[10] In 1535 it was worth £8 15s. 6d.[11] Income was derived mainly from the tithes of Blacon and from lands in Crabwall and the city;[12] from 1401 the Roodee was tithe free.[13] In the Interregnum the income, still only £10, was augmented by £100 a year.[14] At the Restoration that additional sum was lost, and the parishioners agreed to increase the income by *c.* £18 a year from voluntary contributions.[15] In the early 18th century the city corporation made certain allowances in lieu of grazing on the

---

1 Ormerod, *Hist. Ches.* i. 308.
2 F. Bond, *Dedications of Eng. Churches*, 4; Ormerod, *Hist. Ches.* i. 327, 429; C.C.A.L.S., DVE 1/RI/2.
   3 Lucian, *De Laude Cestrie*, 25–6, 51–2; *J.C.A.S.* lxiv. 28–9.
   4 C.C.A.L.S., DVE 1/RI/2; *J.C.A.S.* n.s. ii. 154.
   5 *J.C.A.S.* lxiv. 28–9.
   6 *Lond. Gaz.* 17 Feb. 1882, pp. 648–51; 23 Dec. 1960, p. 8798.
   7 Below (Church Life).
   8 Jones, *Ch. in Chester*, 22; Ormerod, *Hist. Ches.* i. 327, 330–2; *Cal. Inq. p.m.* ii, p. 83; *Cal. Pat.* 1334–8, 129; *Blk. Prince's Reg.*

iii. 390, 419; *Chester Dioc. Handbk.* 1988/9, p. 39; 1989/90, p. 40.
   9 *Tax. Eccl.* 245, 248.   10 Jones, *Ch. in Chester*, 14.
   11 *Valor Eccl.* v. 208.
   12 C.C.A.L.S., EDV 8/24/2.
   13 Ibid. ZCHB 2, f. 47v.; *King's Vale Royal*, [ii], 180.
   14 *Mins. of Cttee. for Relief of Plundered Ministers, and of Trustees for Maintenance of Ministers, 1643–54* (R.S.L.C. xxviii), 208, 216; *1650–60* (R.S.L.C. xxxiv), 3–4, 7, 13, 24, 43, 70, 81–2, 139, 161, 245–6; C.C.A.L.S., ZAB 2, f. 28.
   15 C.C.A.L.S., P 1/11.

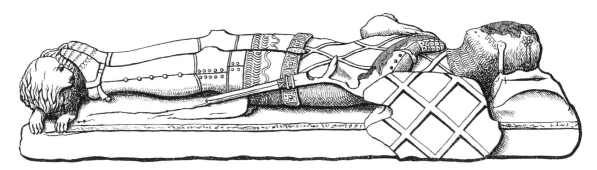

INSCRIPTION ROUND THE MARGIN, PART OF WHICH IS STILL LEGIBLE.

[HIC · IACET · IOHAN]NES · [DE] · W[HITM]ORE · OBIIT · III · [KA]L · OCTOB · M · DO · MCCCLXX[I]III

FIG. 74. *Effigy of John Whitmore (d. 1374), Holy Trinity*

Roodee, and in the 1720s the living was worth £33 11s.[1] The income from tithes more than doubled between 1696 and 1754.[2] In 1834 the benefice was worth £290, a figure at which it remained until the later 19th century.[3]

Although land belonged to it in the 13th century and to the rector in the late 14th, thereafter the church had no glebe.[4] In 1532 it was given a house in Watergate Street, and in 1537 it had a garden.[5] The parsonage house in existence in 1696 was unoccupied after 1735 and had fallen into ruin and been taken into the churchyard by 1778.[6]

The first known burial in the church was in 1374 (Fig. 74).[7] A churchyard existed by 1554,[8] and an additional burial ground in Bedward Row on land bought from the corporation was consecrated, complete with chapel, in 1810.[9] Both were closed in 1855, and the Bedward Row cemetery was sold to the city corporation in 1886 and afterwards built over.[10]

Church Life

Medieval rectors included some who were relatively well connected, and others who were clearly rich.[11] How far they were resident is uncertain, but by the mid 1540s both the rector and the parish maintained stipendiary chaplains.[12] By the later Middle Ages Holy Trinity was a fashionable church, and many leading citizens were buried there.[13] In the 16th century the city

corporation worshipped there often enough to require a case for the civic sword.[14]

Holy Trinity was also the parish church of the sailors' quarter.[15] By the 17th century there was a Manx community in the parish, and the north aisle was dedicated to St. Patrick, the patron of Man, by 1539.[16]

The church had vestments, books, and ornaments valued in 1553 at £6 11s., second only in the city to St. Mary's.[17] They were still in use in 1547,[18] but by 1549 the altars and the tabernacle had been removed. As early as 1551 objects connected with the old religion were being sold, and in 1553 the church retained little besides a chalice, altar cloths, surplices, and bells.[19] In Mary's reign many items were replaced or bought back from those to whom they had been sold in 1551, only to be dispersed again from 1560. Although the parishioners temporarily retained mass vestments and a censer, by 1566 they had taken down the rood loft, and in 1574 paid to have images in the windows defaced.[20]

In the 1590s the rector gave sermons only every quarter and was negligent in other duties.[21] Though Edmund Hopwood (rector 1615–32) was more assiduous and was paid extra by his parishioners for reading morning prayers, in the 1630s his successor, Richard Wilson (1632–69), was also accused of neglecting his liturgical duties.[22] In 1637–8, in accordance with

1 C.C.A.L.S., ZAB 3, ff. 184, 185v., 193; ZAB 4, f. 19 and v.; Gastrell, *Not. Cest.* i. 121.

2 3 *Sheaf*, lix, p. 35; C.C.A.L.S., EDV 8/24/2.

3 Gastrell, *Not. Cest.* i. 121 n.; Ormerod, *Hist. Ches.* i. 327; *White's Dir. Ches.* (1864), 4–5.

4 *Cart. Chester Abbey*, ii, p. 342; *Cal. of Deeds and Papers of Moore Fam.* (R.S.L.C. lxvii), 149.

5 3 *Sheaf*, xliv, p. 39; *J.C.A.S.* xxxviii. 107; C.C.A.L.S., ZSB 7, ff. 80v.–81.

6 3 *Sheaf*, xlvi, pp. 45–6; lix, p. 35; C.C.A.L.S., EDV 7/1/11; cf. EDV 7/2/9; EDV 7/4/231; EDP 70/1/3.

7 *J.C.A.S.* n.s. vi. 42–8; Morris, *Chester*, 350; Pevsner, *Ches.* 153.   8 3 *Sheaf*, i, p. 2.

9 C.C.A.L.S., EDA 2/10, pp. 519–28, 530; P 1/17; ibid. ZAB 5, pp. 262–3.

10 Ibid. EDA 2/28, p. 307; EDP 70/2; P 1/17.

11 Jones, *Ch. in Chester*, 169–72.

12 *List of Clergy, 1541–2*, 2; P.R.O., E 301/8/1.

13 Jones, *Ch. in Chester*, 113; Morris, *Chester*, 350–1; 3 *Sheaf*, xviii, pp. 99, 101.   14 *J.C.A.S.* xxi. 156.

15 Ibid. 158–9; Jones, *Ch. in Chester*, 113.

16 3 *Sheaf*, xviii, p. 99; xliv, p. 59; *J.C.A.S.* lv. 33–4; Gastrell, *Not. Cest.* i. 122.

17 *J.C.A.S.* xxxviii. 96–8; B.L. Harl. MS. 2177, f. 19 and v.; Morris, *Chester*, 151.

18 3 *Sheaf*, xviii, pp. 53–4.

19 Morris, *Chester*, 153; *J.C.A.S.* xxxviii. 87–8, 113.

20 *J.C.A.S.* xxxviii. 98–100, 120–1, 123–5, 128.

21 Ibid. n.s. v. 412; 3 *Sheaf*, i, p. 68.

22 *J.C.A.S.* xxxviii. 169; York, Borthwick Inst., V.1633/CB.2.

Archbishop Neile's instructions, the church was refurbished and its seats made uniform. The ensuing removal of two chancel pews set aside for the mayor and some of the aldermen provoked a dispute with the Assembly, and in 1640 fresh accommodation was provided for them.[1]

Wilson probably left Holy Trinity in the early 1640s, but in 1646 there must have been a minister, since baptisms were held there for other parishes.[2] By 1648 Thomas Upton, a Presbyterian, had been intruded into the living.[3] Upton left and Wilson was restored in 1660, but the changes did not pass without opposition: in 1663 the newly erected royal arms were destroyed by two parishioners and the church still lacked a surplice.[4] Later in the century relations with nonconformists appear to have been cordial, and several close relatives of the leading Chester Presbyterian Matthew Henry were buried in the church.[5] When Henry himself died in 1714 his funeral at Holy Trinity was attended by eight Anglican and nonconformist ministers.[6]

For much of the 18th and early 19th century incumbents were also cathedral dignitaries. William Smith (1735–80) became dean of Chester in 1758,[7] and Thomas Maddock (1786–1825) was a prebendary at his appointment.[8] Since both also held other livings most of the duties at Holy Trinity fell to curates. Communicants in their time averaged *c.* 80 at the monthly communions and up to 180 on the greater festivals.[9]

In the 1860s under Edward Marston (rector 1862–95) the church was rebuilt under the influence of the Oxford Movement, and there was a weekly communion and a surpliced choir.[10] Those traditions were retained by his successor L. M. Farrall (rector 1895–1927), and in 1926 the south aisle was made into a Lady chapel.[11] By the 1930s Sunday services included choral eucharist twice a month.[12] After 1951 more definitely Anglo-Catholic services were introduced; at Blacon from 1960 there were regular sung masses and occasional requiem masses. In the early 1960s ecumenical services were held at Blacon both with the Roman Catholics and with the Congregationalists.[13]

In 1929 a mission church dedicated to St. Chad was opened near the railway station in Blacon to replace an earlier mission room which had come into use by 1921.[14] In 1961 St. Chad's and the parish church were closed and replaced by a new building also in Blacon.[15] A church centre, including a chapel dedicated to the Holy Family, was opened *c.* 1987 in Melbourne Road, Blacon, and in 2000 the parish church and the chapel were served by an incumbent and a curate.[16]

Buildings

The redundant church of Holy Trinity in Watergate Street is built of red sandstone and comprises a chancel of two bays, an aisled and clerestoried nave of six, and a south-west tower and spire, all built in the later 1860s (Fig. 75, p. 136). There is no structural division between nave and chancel. An earlier church on the site, built on or near the west gate of the legionary fortress, was a two-aisled structure,[17] repaired in 1593 and extensively restored in 1637.[18] In 1678 the south side was taken down and rebuilt, and in 1728 the tower and north side were similarly treated.[19] The spire was removed in 1811.[20] Galleries were added in 1750 and 1761, and the north aisle was enlarged in 1774.[21] A new south gallery with two tiers of free seats was erected in 1826.[22]

In 1864 the old church was demolished; its replacement, consecrated in 1869, was designed by James Harrison in the Decorated style.[23] A screen designed by Douglas and Minshull was added in 1898.[24] Further alterations took place in 1926 when the aisles were converted into side-chapels.[25] In 1963 the redundant church became a guildhall and most of the fittings, except the screen, were removed.[26] Surviving mayoral monuments included the armoured effigy of John Whitmore (d. 1374), and a brass reused for Henry Gee (d. 1545).[27]

The mission church of St. Chad built in Blacon in 1929 had a chancel with north vestry and south organ chamber, and a nave with a south porch and west bell

1 C.C.A.L.S., EDC 5/1639/20; P 1/11.

2 B.L. Harl. MS. 2177, f. 67v.

3 *Calamy Revised*, ed. A. G. Matthews, 500; W. Urwick, *Hist. Sketches of Nonconformity in Ches.* 13.

4 C.C.A.L.S., P 1/11; York, Borthwick Inst., V.1662–3/CB.2, f. 4v.

5 L. M. Farrall, *Holy Trinity Parish Reg.* 448, 452–3, 456.

6 Ibid. 468; *D.N.B.*

7 C.C.A.L.S., EDP 70/1/2; Burne, *Chester Cath.* 216–17.

8 C.C.A.L.S., EDP 70/1/2.

9 Ibid.; EDV 2/35–6; EDV 7/1/11; EDV 7/3/112; EDV 7/4/231.

10 Ibid. P 1/291; *P. & G. Dir. Chester* (1878/9), 22.

11 *Kelly's Dir. Ches.* (1896), 197; *P. & G. Dir. Chester* (1921/2), 47–8; C.C.A.L.S., EDP 70/2.

12 *P. & G. Dir. Chester* (1935/6), 50.

13 C.C.A.L.S., P 1/3063/16/5; *Holy Trinity Parish News* (1945–50).

14 *Chester Dioc. Cal.* (1921), 76; (1930), 162; C.C.A.L.S.,

P 1/3063/16/1.

15 C.C.A.L.S., EDV 8/24/3–4.

16 *Chester Dioc. Handbk. 1987/8*, p. 33; *Chester Dioc. Year Bk. 1999/2000*, p. 44.

17 Ormerod, *Hist. Ches.* i. 327; *J.C.A.S.* lvi. 6; lxiv. 28.

18 C.C.A.L.S., P 1/11; EDC 5/1639/20.

19 Ibid. P 1/11; P 1/13; EDD 16/120, p. 29; 3 *Sheaf*, xxxi, p. 77; xlviii, p. 27; Gastrell, *Not. Cest.* i. 122; B.L. Harl. MS. 2073, f. 91, no. 2.

20 C.C.A.L.S., P 1/14; 3 *Sheaf*, xiv, p. 24; xliv, p. 60; Hemingway, *Hist. Chester*, ii. 93.

21 C.C.A.L.S., EDA 2/6, pp. 96, 398; EDA 2/7, ff. 165–167v.; P 1/147–54.

22 Ibid. P 1/157.

23 Ibid. P 1/158–265; Ormerod, *Hist. Ches.* i. 327.

24 C.C.A.L.S., EDA 2/29, p. 79; P 1/290.

25 Ibid. EDP 70/2; P 1/3063/4/6.

26 Ibid. EDP 78/3.

27 *J.C.A.S.* n.s. vi. 41–8; xxi. 152–7; Pevsner, *Ches.* 153.

FIG. 75. *Holy Trinity as rebuilt in 1869*

FIG. 76. *St. Bridget's before 1690*

turret; the chancel and nave were under one roof, with weatherboarded walls.[1]

The church of Holy Trinity without the Walls at Blacon was built in 1960 to designs by A. C. Bennett, a local architect; constructed of a steel frame with brick cladding, it comprises chancel, nave, and south tower.[2]

ST. BRIDGET

The church existed in the time of Earl Ranulph II (1128/9–1153),[3] and may well have originated much earlier; the dedication and the site in the south of the city suggest an Irish-Norse foundation in the 10th or 11th century.[4] The medieval church was replaced on a different site in 1829 and when the new church was closed in 1891 the congregation moved to the redundant church of St. Mary on the Hill, remaining there until the parish was merged into the united benefice of Chester in 1972.[5] The original parish included a detached portion south of the river, the Earl's Eye, which was transferred to St. Mary's in 1887.[6]

Advowson, Income, and Property

In the 12th century the advowson belonged to the lords of Aldford, but after a dispute it was quitclaimed to Earl Ranulph II.[7] Later it seems to have been granted to the Orby family, for in the earlier 13th century it formed part of Philip of Orby's endowment of his chantry in St. John's church.[8] By 1318 and perhaps by 1298–9, when St. Bridget's was served by a chaplain, St. John's had appropriated it.[9] A lengthy dispute between the deans and canons over the profits was resolved in 1397 in favour of the canons.[10] At the Dissolution the church seems to have passed to the Crown and incumbents continued to be known as curates, but by the early 17th century it was a rectory in the gift of the bishop of Chester.[11] In 1842 the living was united with that of St. Martin's,[12] and in 1972 the parish became part of the united Chester benefice. The parish church then in use, St. Mary on the Hill, was thereupon closed.[13]

The church was always poor and in 1535 St. John's received only £1 a year from the appropriated tithes.[14] By the 1720s the total value of the living was £33 18s., of which £16 came from voluntary contributions and £11 15s. from tithes of land south of the Dee.[15] Augmentations in 1755 and 1814, together with an

---

1 C.C.A.L.S., P 1/3063/17/1–2.

2 Ibid. EDV 8/24/3–4; [R. W. Harper], *Church of Holy Trinity Without-the-Walls* [Chester, 1993], 10–11.

3 G. Ormerod, *Introductory Memoir on Ches. Domesday Roll* (1851), 7–9; P.R.O., KB 26/152, m. 10; B.L. Harl. MS. 1967, f. 158; *E.H.R.* xxxviii. 497.   4 *J.C.A.S.* lxiv. 17–23.

5 Below (Buildings); below, this chapter: St. Mary on the Hill (Church Life).

6 C.C.A.L.S., EDA 2/28, pp. 426–52; *Lond. Gaz.* 27 Sept. 1887, pp. 5220–7.

7 Ormerod, *Hist. Ches.* i. 340; iii. 96.

8 3 *Sheaf*, xviii, pp. 27–8; *Blk. Prince's Reg.* iii. 152.

9 Jones, *Ch. in Chester*, 7; *Blk. Prince's Reg.* iii. 74; 3 *Sheaf*, xix, p. 92.   10 Above, Collegiate Church of St. John.

11 C.C.A.L.S., EDV 1/1; EDV 1/3, ff. 21, 48; EDV 2/4; Ormerod, *Hist. Ches.* i. 340, 342; Gastrell, *Not. Cest.* i. 98–9.

12 C.C.A.L.S., P 16/6/2.

13 *Lond. Gaz.* 30 June 1972, p. 7865.

14 *Valor Eccl.* v. 203.

15 Gastrell, *Not. Cest.* i. 98; C.C.A.L.S., EDV 7/1/1.

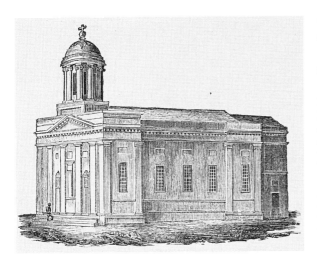

FIG. 77. *St. Bridget's, new church*

increase in the value of the tithes, brought the income to £68 3*s.* 2*d.* in 1809 and £150 in 1834, the last figure including St. Martin's.[1] The tithes were commuted in 1845 when they were worth £39 a year.[2] In 1874 the annual value of the united benefice of St. Bridget and St. Martin was £200.[3]

A parsonage house adjoining the church was taken down in the late 17th century, and thereafter there was none until 1857 when the parish was given, by the architect Thomas Harrison's daughter, the house of *c.* 1820 which Harrison had built for himself off Castle Esplanade. It was occupied until 1914 when the rector moved to the former parsonage house of St. Mary's.[4]

Burials were taking place in the church by the early 16th century.[5] A graveyard to the north-east was replaced in 1785 by one to the south of the church, enlarged in 1790.[6] It was closed in 1829 and replaced by a new graveyard beside the new church. That in turn was closed in 1877.[7]

Church Life

A chantry was established in St. Bridget's in the 1270s by John Arneway, mayor of Chester, with a priest maintained by the abbot of St. Werburgh's.[8] It was still maintained in the 1540s when the chaplain received £4 a year.[9] In 1528 a parishioner made pro-

vision for a priest to say mass in the church for as long as the money would serve.[10]

St. Bridget's was never well provided with vestments and ornaments, which in 1553 were valued at only 13*s.* 3*d.*[11] In 1578 it had no Bible. Absenteeism went unpunished,[12] perhaps because the church had puritan leanings: the puritan divine Christopher Goodman, who returned to his native Chester *c.* 1570, seems to have been associated with St. Bridget's and was buried there in 1603.[13]

There was a rapid turnover of incumbents in the early 17th century, suggesting an especially undesirable living.[14] Matters improved with the appointment of the composer Francis Pilkington (rector 1616–38), who although also precentor of the cathedral and minister at St. Martin's continued to treat St. Bridget's as his principal cure, securing benefactions from the mayor, Sir Thomas Smith.[15] The association with St. Martin's was revived under later incumbents,[16] but the two livings were separated in 1725.[17]

Curates were employed in the late 17th century and throughout the 18th, when the rectors included pluralists and the unsatisfactory Thomas Parry (1720–54), who in 1730 was suspended for neglect.[18] In 1778 the sacrament was administered monthly to *c.* 40 communicants and to almost double that number on the great feasts.[19] Under Richard Massie (rector 1810–32), who until the 1820s did the duty himself, numbers rose to *c.* 140 at the great feasts.[20]

Curates continued to be employed, especially from 1875 to 1914, when St. Bridget's was held by two successive archdeacons of Chester.[21] An organ and singers were introduced in 1836, and by 1900 the principal Sunday morning service alternated between matins and sung eucharist. Communicants numbered up to 30 on Sundays and up to 200 at Easter.[22] Those traditions of worship were maintained but numbers thereafter gradually declined until the closure of the church in 1972.[23]

Buildings

The first church of St. Bridget was built on or near the western abutment of the south gate of the legionary fortress on the western side of Bridge Street almost

1 C.C.A.L.S., EDV 7/1/1; Hemingway, *Hist. Chester*, ii. 114; C. Hodgson, *Queen Anne's Bounty* (2nd edn. 1845), p. ccxlix; Gastrell, *Not. Cest.* i. 98 n.

2 C.C.A.L.S., EDT 94/1.

3 *Morris's Dir. Ches.* (1874), 8.

4 Gastrell, *Not. Cest.* i. 98; 3 *Sheaf*, xliii, pp. 37–8; *J.C.A.S.* N.S. xi. 16–17; C.C.A.L.S., EDV 8/22/2; H. Colvin, *Biographical Dictionary of Brit. Architects* (1995), 469.

5 *Lancs. and Ches. Wills and Inventories*, i (Chetham Soc. [o.s.], xxxiii), 35–6.

6 3 *Sheaf*, xxxi, p. 33; C.C.A.L.S., P 15/13/1; EDA 2/8, p. 554.

7 *J.C.A.S.* N.S. xi. 15–16; 3 *Sheaf*, lix, p. 48.

8 *Cart. Chester Abbey*, ii, p. 469; Jones, *Ch. in Chester*, 109; 37 *D.K.R.* App. II, p. 779; B.L. Harl. MS. 2147, f. 31.

9 *List of Clergy, 1541–2*, 2; P.R.O., E 301/8/1.

10 *Lancs. and Ches. Wills*, i. 36.   11 Morris, *Chester*, 151.

12 3 *Sheaf*, lvii, pp. 76–7.   13 Ibid. xxx, p. 54; *D.N.B.*

14 Ormerod, *Hist. Ches.* i. 342.

15 *D.N.B.*; *New Grove Dictionary of Music and Musicians*, ed. S. Sadie, s.n. Pilkington; Gastrell, *Not. Cest.* i. 98.

16 York, Borthwick Inst., V.1662–3/CB.2, f. 29v.; C.C.A.L.S., EDA 1/4; EDV 2/8, 14–18; Ormerod, *Hist. Ches.* i. 332, 342; Gastrell, *Not. Cest.* i. 99.

17 C.C.A.L.S., EDP 72/1/1; EDV 2/19–21.

18 Ibid. EDP 72/1/1; EDV 2/11–14, 19–21.

19 Ibid. EDV 7/1/1; cf. EDV 7/2/1; EDV 7/3/103.

20 Ibid. EDP 72/1/1; EDV 7/4/52; EDV 7/7/121.

21 Ibid. EDP 72/1/1–2; *Chester Dioc. Cal.*

22 *J.C.A.S.* N.S. xi. 18; C.C.A.L.S., P 15/7/1–2.

23 C.C.A.L.S., P 15/7/3–8.

opposite St. Michael's. A single-celled, probably late-medieval building survived until *c.* 1690, when it was totally reconstructed in local stone with funds raised largely by briefs granted in 1684–5 and 1694.[1] The new church was repaired in 1727 and again in 1785, when it was refaced in stone under the direction of 'Mr.', probably Joseph, Turner.[2] By 1825, however, the whole structure was unsafe.[3] Proposals for a new church were under consideration from 1818, and in 1829 St. Bridget's was taken down to make way for Grosvenor Street.[4]

A new church was erected opposite the castle entrance to a neo-classical design by William Cole junior which owed much to designs by his master, Thomas Harrison (Fig. 77).[5] Opened in 1829, it was restored in 1861 under the direction of James Harrison.[6] It was demolished in 1892.[7]

ST. JOHN

In 1547 or 1548 the collegiate church of St. John was dissolved.[8] The royal commissioners reserved for the parishioners the nave, one bell, and £21 6*s.* 8*d.* a year to support a vicar and curate, who were appointed from the former collegiate vicars.[9] For their accommodation they were assigned one of the college's houses, and the new vicar also held other collegiate property.[10]

Advowson, Income, and Property

The advowson passed to the Crown and was granted in 1585 to Sir Christopher Hatton, who promptly sold it to Alexander King. In 1587 King in turn sold it to Alexander Cotes, in the possession of whose descendants it remained until sold to Earl Grosvenor, later 1st marquess of Westminster, in 1810. The Grosvenors retained the advowson until 1972 when St. John's became part of the newly established Chester parish, served by a team ministry. The patronage board then set up included the duke of Westminster.[11]

The value of the living remained unchanged until 1646, when parliament granted an augmentation of £100 from the confiscated revenues of the cathedral.[12] In the 1650s the minister was still in difficulties,[13] and in 1660 the augmentation ceased. In the 1720s the assured value of the benefice was only just over £30, but voluntary contributions brought in a further £30

FIG. 78. *St. John's from south-east, c. 1816*

or more,[14] and by 1757 the income was further increased by pew rents from the new south gallery built within the church in 1741.[15] Even so, in 1789 the incumbent regarded his income as 'very inconsiderable'.[16] In 1803 more pew rents were assigned to the vicar,[17] and in 1804 a grant from Queen Anne's Bounty was used to buy land which brought in £7 10*s.* a year,[18] increasing the vicar's assured income to a modest £47.[19] Further augmentations were made by parliamentary grant in 1811, 1812, and 1817.[20]

In 1860 the income stood at a respectable £237, but thereafter it was diminished by the closure of the churchyard, increasing resistance to pew rents, and the creation of separate parishes in Boughton and Hoole in 1879.[21] Eventually the Ecclesiastical Commissioners made a further augmentation of £60 a year in 1876.[22]

Church Life

After the Dissolution the parish was left with copes, vestments, and other items worth only 11*s.* 2*d.* in 1553.[23] The parishioners' difficulty in maintaining the building culminated in disputes with the patron which were resolved in 1596 by an agreement that he should keep up the chancel and its aisles and they the rest of the church. To assist them in particular in rebuilding

---

1 Ormerod, *Hist. Ches.* i. 340; C.C.A.L.S., ZAB 3, f. 12v.; 2 *Sheaf,* i, p. 88; 3 *Sheaf,* xxiv, pp. 14–15, 27; xxxi, p. 33.

2 C.C.A.L.S., P 15/13/1; 3 *Sheaf,* xxxi, p. 33.

3 C.C.A.L.S., EDV 7/7/121; *J.C.A.S.* n.s. xi. 7–8.

4 C.C.A.L.S., ZTRB 1, 18, 57; *J.C.A.S.* n.s. xi. 13–14.

5 H. Colvin, *Biographical Dictionary of Brit. Architects* (1995), s.n. Cole.

6 C.C.A.L.S., P 15/8/3; EDP 72/3.   7 Ibid. P 15/8/10.

8 Above, Collegiate Church of St. John, where its parochial functions in the Middle Ages are discussed.

9 P.R.O., E 301/8/1.

10 Ibid. SC 12/6/24A; *Cal. Pat.* 1553 and App. 1547–53, 221.

11 C.C.A.L.S., P 51/10/2; *Lond. Gaz.* 30 June 1972, p. 7865.

12 *Mins. of Cttee. for Relief of Plundered Ministers, and of Trustees for Maintenance of Ministers, 1643–54* (R.S.L.C.

xxviii), 208.

13 *Cal. S.P. Dom.* 1653–4, 122.

14 Gastrell, *Not. Cest.* i. 99.

15 S. C. Scott, *Hist. of St. John the Baptist Church and Parish,* 137–8, 159.

16 C.C.A.L.S., EDV 7/2/2.

17 Ibid. P 51/7/4–5; Scott, *Hist. St. John's Church,* 186.

18 C.C.A.L.S., EDV 7/4/132.

19 Hemingway, *Hist. Chester,* ii. 74.

20 C. Hodgson, *Queen Anne's Bounty* (2nd edn. 1845), p. ccl; Scott, *Hist. St. John's Church,* 187.

21 *White's Dir. Ches.* (1860), 86; C.C.A.L.S., P 51/7/43–58; P 51/10/22; P 51/11/18.

22 C.C.A.L.S., P 51/10/22; P/51/10/32.

23 Morris, *Chester,* 151.

the tower, they were given the remaining building materials on the site.[1]

By the 1630s the vestry had been augmented by a group of commissioners concerned with the disposing of seats and apparently appointed by the bishop.[2] In 1637 it was determined to make the seats uniform and adorn the church, which soon acquired a new pulpit and cover, altar rails, the royal arms, and new seats.[3] In 1641, however, the altar rails were removed,[4] and in 1643 the minister was ejected by the city authorities as a parliamentarian.[5]

During the siege of Chester, parish life apparently functioned normally until 1645, when Foregate Street was overrun by the parliamentary forces. By then the interior of the church had been wrecked, and between 1645 and 1647 communion was apparently suspended. In 1646 the minister was deprived and replaced by a parliamentarian pastor, Peter Leigh, who in 1648 signed the Cheshire attestation of Presbyterian ministers. Under his regime much effort was expended in making the interior fit for the new forms of worship, and the church acquired seats from the cathedral and a basin to replace the discarded font.[6]

Leigh was ejected in 1662 and replaced by Alexander Featherstone, a pluralist soon accused of scandalous life.[7] In the same year the old font was restored to use, although the church continued to lack other accompaniments of Anglican worship until 1663. By 1665 there was little amiss.[8] Improvements thereafter included the acquisition of plate in 1667 and 1674,[9] the construction of a gallery with free sittings between 1677 and 1679,[10] and the insertion of new altar rails and a reredos in 1692.[11]

By 1708 the pew commissioners were almost extinct and the bishop intervened with nine new appointments.[12] North and south galleries were added in 1727 and 1741 at private expense.[13] The parish declined in social standing in the 18th century, and included numerous nonconformists and Roman Catholics; in 1778, although the vicar was resident, held two Sunday services, and read prayers on Wednesdays, Fridays, and saints' days, communicants numbered fewer than 100 at the monthly celebrations and 300 at the great festivals.[14] By 1825, although congregations were large and increasing, the number of communicants seems to have fallen, to 50 and 150 respectively.[15] By then the vicar had a curate, and in 1830

FIG. 79. *St. John's, 1855, looking from north aisle into nave*

another was appointed for the new chapel of ease at Boughton. The creation in the 1840s of ecclesiastical districts for Boughton and Newtown reduced the area of St. John's pastoral responsibilities,[16] but even so congregations remained large, and in 1851 were estimated at *c.* 500 at morning prayer and 360 at evensong.[17]

The organ used in Westminster Abbey at the coronation of Queen Victoria was brought to the church in 1838. A fund was started to pay for the organist, choral services were celebrated twice every Sunday, and in 1845 the vestry started paying the organist's salary out of the church rate.[18]

Although the parish declined further in numbers

1 C.C.A.L.S., P 51/10/1.

2 Ibid. P 51/7/1; P 51/10/1; P 51/12/1.

3 Ibid. P 51/12/1; *V.C.H. Ches.* iii. 33–5; York, Borthwick Inst., V.1633/CB.2, ff. 434v.–435.

4 C.C.A.L.S., P 51/12/1.

5 *Ches. Q. Sess. Rec. 1559–60* (R.S.L.C. xciv), 140.

6 Scott, *Hist. St. John's Church*, 80, 82–4; C.C.A.L.S., P 51/12/1.

7 *Calamy Revised*, ed. A. G. Matthews, 320–1; *Alum. Oxon. 1500–1714*, s.n. Featherstone; C.C.A.L.S., EDV 1/34, f. 22v.

8 C.C.A.L.S., P 51/12/1; EDV 1/34, ff. 1–2; York, Borthwick Inst., V.1662–3/CB.2, f. 1v.

9 Scott, *Hist. St. John's Church*, 107–9.

10 Hemingway, *Hist. Chester*, ii. 81.

11 C.C.A.L.S., P 51/12/1–2.   12 Ibid. P 51/7/1.

13 Ibid. EDA 2/5, pp. 124–6; 3 *Sheaf*, xxiv, pp. 18–19; Scott, *Hist. St. John's Church*, 133–4, 137–8, 159.

14 C.C.A.L.S., EDV 7/1/2; EDV 7/2/2.

15 Ibid. EDV 7/7/122.

16 Ibid. P 51/26/1; below, Modern Parish Churches: Christ Church, Newtown; St. Paul, Boughton.

17 P.R.O., HO 129/459.

18 Scott, *Hist. St. John's Church*, 206–11, 213–14; 1 *Sheaf*, i, p. 29.

and wealth in the later 19th century, the incumbency of S. C. Scott (1875–1915) was marked by signs of vitality.[1] In 1876 the mission church of St. Barnabas was established in Sibell Street to serve a working-class district, and in the 1880s the Ecclesiastical Commissioners and the 3rd marquess (later 1st duke) of Westminster made grants to pay an additional curate to work there.[2] At St. John's, improvements were in accordance with prevailing liturgical standards. The 18th-century galleries and box pews had been swept away in the 1860s, and in 1870 new stone altar rails were installed. In 1875 Scott consulted his cousin Sir George Gilbert Scott and Morris and Co. about the provision of a new reredos, and their recommendations influenced the final design by John Douglas. A new lectern was purchased in 1887, and a south-east chapel was established in 1894.[3]

Under Scott services continued to focus chiefly on matins and evensong, but his successor, J. D. Polehampton, introduced High Church practices with a daily eucharist and a sung celebration every Sunday.[4] Eucharistic vestments had been introduced by the 1920s, and in 1926 the rural dean declared that St. John's was 'the best equipped church in these things' in his deanery.[5] By then the south-east chapel had been refurbished by Sir Charles Nicholson as a Lady chapel, with a new screen and a reredos reconstructed from that of 1692.[6] The catholic tradition was retained; in 1936 Bishop Fisher authorized the reservation of the sacrament in the south-east chapel,[7] and in 1981 there was still a weekly sung eucharist with a vested celebrant.

In 1972 St. John's became the principal church of the newly established parish of Chester, which also included St. Thomas of Canterbury in Parkgate Road, Christ Church in Newtown, and St. Peter's. The parish was served in 2000 by a rector, two team vicars, and a non-stipendiary curate.[8] St. Barnabas's mission church closed *c.* 1988.[9]

Building

The church of St. John the Baptist is built of red sandstone, and comprises a galleried choir of one bay, a crossing, an aisled nave of four bays with triforium and clerestory, and a north porch, all of which represents the surviving central portion of a building once much larger. The medieval church

FIG. 80. *St. John's from west, 1855*

suffered from neglect after the dissolution of the college,[10] and in the early 1570s the north-west tower fell down, ruining the west end of the church.[11] The collapse of the chancel followed in 1581. Although in that year the Crown granted the parishioners the entire church, they repaired only the central portion, rebuilding the tower, making a new west front, and cutting off all the eastern chapels.[12]

The church was kept in good condition in the earlier 17th century, but suffered severe damage, especially internally, after its capture by the parliamentarians and use as a gun battery in 1645.[13] Despite restoration in 1646 and further work on the tower in 1660, the chancel was out of repair in 1665.[14] By 1719 the minister and churchwardens had to seek assistance for major repairs, including reroofing and rebuilding the aisle walls and steeple.[15] A brief was issued, which by 1720 had raised over £1,200, and in 1728 the church was said to be in good condition.[16] The chancel, however, was out of repair throughout the later 18th century, and was restored only in the early 19th, when

1 C.C.A.L.S., P 51/11/18; S. Harrison, 'Revd. Samuel Cooper Scott and his Diary', *J.C.A.S.* lxi. 61–78.

2 C.C.A.L.S., P 51/10/33–5; P 51/11/18.

3 Ibid. P 51/7/68, 185–6, 191–4; P 51/27/1; Scott, *Hist. St. John's Church*, 238, 248–9, 275, 288.

4 *P. & G. Dir. Chester* (1878/9), 23; (1921/2), 48–9; *Kelly's Dir. Ches.* (1910), 225; (1914), 232.

5 C.C.A.L.S., P 51/11/16.

6 Ibid. EDP 73/2; inscription on screen.

7 C.C.A.L.S., P 51/7/247.

8 *Lond. Gaz.* 30 June 1972, p. 7865; *Chester Dioc. Year Bk. 1999/2000*, p. 44.

9 *Chester Dioc. Handbk.* (1987/8), p. 33; no entry in (1988/9).

10 P.R.O., SP 12/10, f. 318.

11 3 *Sheaf*, xxx, pp. 23–4; R. V. H. Burne, 'The Falling Towers of St. John's Church', *J.C.A.S.* xxxvi. 1–20.

12 *Cal. S.P. Dom.* 1581–90, 25; 3 *Sheaf*, xlvii, pp. 42–3; C.C.A.L.S., ZMMP 3/55; B.L. Harl. MS. 2073, ff. 97v.–99.

13 Scott, *Hist. St. John's Church*, 74–5, 77.

14 Ibid. 50, 80, 82–4; C.C.A.L.S., P 51/12/1; ibid. EDV 1/34, ff. 1–2.

15 3 *Sheaf*, xlviii, p. 26; C.C.A.L.S., ZQSF 92, nos. 186–7.

16 2 *Sheaf*, i, p. 58; 3 *Sheaf*, xlviii, p. 26; Scott, *Hist. St. John's Church*, 129–30, 292.

the transepts were also restored and given new windows.[1]

The whole church was restored in the 1860s by R. C. Hussey, who rebuilt the south wall, provided new roofs, fittings, and round-headed windows in the clerestories, and inserted a new west window designed by T. M. Penson in the Norman style. The whole cost £9,000, towards which the marquess of Westminster gave £4,000.[2] In the 1870s further work was done in the churchyard, which was partly closed for burials in 1855 and completely in 1875.[3] The project resulted in the excavation of the ruins and the removal of the houses built among them in the 18th century to disclose the vaulted undercroft east of the south transept. It also brought to light many architectural fragments.[4]

In 1881 the tower, which had clearly been unsafe for some time, fell down, also ruining the north porch. On the advice of J. L. Pearson the tower ruins were reduced and tidied, leaving only the stump still standing in 2000; the north porch was rebuilt to its original design by John Douglas, who added a small belfry and clock tower on the north-east.[5] The ruins of the east end, which passed into the guardianship of Chester corporation in 1955,[6] were consolidated and repaired between 1976 and 1980.[7]

The monuments include three mutilated 14th-century effigies, that of Agnes of Ridley (d. 1347) being half-length with the lower part of the body enclosed in a coffin carved with vine leaves. Notable tombs in the south-east chapel are those of Lady (Diana) Warburton (d. 1693) and Cecil Warburton (d. 1729). At the west end armorial fragments survive from the tomb of Alexander Cotes, erected in 1602 and destroyed in the Interregnum. There are also several monuments on panels, painted by the Randle Holmes between 1628 and 1682.

ST. MARTIN

The church existed by the late 12th century, when St. Martin was described by the monk Lucian as one of the 'guardians' of Chester.[8] The parish was originally restricted to the south-west of the city between the Roman and medieval walls, but later included a detached area in the Crofts perhaps once associated

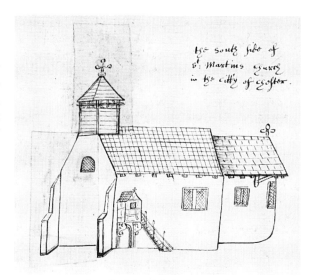

FIG. 81. *St. Martin's in late 17th century*

with the vanished church or chapel of St. Chad.[9] That portion was transferred to Holy Trinity in 1887 and to St. Peter's in 1960.[10]

Advowson, Income, and Property

The advowson probably belonged to the Orby family in the early 13th century, since it was among those granted to the collegiate church of St. John by Philip of Orby, justice of Chester, to endow a chantry.[11] St. John's had appropriated the living by 1318.[12] After the dissolution of the college St. Martin's seems to have remained a curacy until 1637, when it became a rectory in the gift of the bishop of Chester.[13] The bishop presented in 1664, but thereafter until the early 18th century the church was supplied with curates by the dean and chapter or after election by the parishioners.[14] From 1725 the bishop again presented rectors until the benefice was united with St. Bridget's in 1842.[15]

The living was always poor, and no medieval valuations exist. In 1541–2 the incumbent was described as living, in an obscure phrase, 'from the fruits of the parish' (*ex fructibus parochiae*).[16] In 1720 the annual income was only £1 16s., but after augmentations in 1725, 1782, 1787, and 1802 it rose to £76 18s.[17] In 1834, after another augmentation, it and St. Bridget's were together worth £150.[18]

1 Scott, *Hist. St. John's Church*, 149, 160–1, 190; C.C.A.L.S., EDV 7/3/104; EDV 7/4/132; EDV 7/7/122.

2 C.C.A.L.S., EDA 2/22, ff. 148–52; Scott, *Hist. St. John's Church*, 222–33.

3 Scott, *Hist. St. John's Church*, 201, 203, 217–18, 221, 245–8; C.C.A.L.S., P 51/8/1–55.

4 Scott, *Hist. St. John's Church*, 241–3; C.C.A.L.S., P 51/7/188.

5 C.C.A.L.S., P 51/7/121–4, 126–47; Scott, *Hist. St. John's Church*, 255–8, 265–70.   6 C.C.A.L.S., P 51/8/40–55.

7 Inf. from Mr. E. Rimington, conservation assistant, Chester district cl.

8 Lucian, *De Laude Cestrie*, 56.   9 *J.C.A.S.* lxiv. 26–9.

10 *Lond. Gaz.* 27 Sept. 1887, pp. 5220–7; 23 Dec. 1960,

p. 8798.

11 *Blk. Prince's Reg.* iii. 152; 3 *Sheaf*, xviii, pp. 27–8.

12 Jones, *Ch. in Chester*, 7.

13 C.C.A.L.S., EDV 1/1; EDV 1/3, ff. 21, 48; EDV 2/4; York, Borthwick Inst., V.1633/CB.2, ff. 437v.–438; Gastrell, *Not. Cest.* i. 104.

14 C.C.A.L.S., EDP 72/1/1; EDV 2/6, 8, 11; Gastrell, *Not. Cest.* i. 104.

15 C.C.A.L.S., EDV 2/12–21; P 16/6/2; Ormerod, *Hist. Ches.* i. 333.   16 *List of Clergy, 1541–2,* 2.

17 Gastrell, *Not. Cest.* i. 103; C. Hodgson, *Queen Anne's Bounty* (2nd edn. 1845), p. ccl; Hemingway, *Hist. Chester*, ii. 99–100.

18 Gastrell, *Not. Cest.* i. 103 n.

In the early 17th century there was a structure over the porch similar to the rectory houses of other Chester churches,[1] but by 1778 the living had no residence.[2] A churchyard existed by 1662 and a monument formerly in the church recorded a burial there in 1644.[3] The churchyard was closed in 1855.[4]

Church Life

St. Martin's had no stipendiary chaplains in 1541–2, and the vestments and ornaments surrendered in 1553 were of so little value that they were given away to the poor.[5] The church generally had its own incumbent in the later 16th century, though in 1565 it was held together with St. Olave's.[6] In the earlier 17th century it seems often to have been held with St. Bridget's, and there is some evidence of neglect; in 1633 and 1634 the curate was presented for not reading prayers on the prescribed days.[7]

Despite the presentation of a rector in 1664, the church thereafter seems to have been served by minor canons of the cathedral.[8] In 1699, however, the parishioners chose as their minister the curate and later rector of St. Bridget's, thus resuming an association between the two parishes which lasted until the 1720s.[9] He and later incumbents seem usually to have performed the duty themselves unless old or incapacitated.[10] In 1778 the rector preached two Sunday sermons in summer and one in winter, and administered holy communion every six weeks and on the great festivals to an average of *c.* 30 people.[11] By the early 19th century numbers had increased to *c.* 50 at the monthly communions and up to 120 at the great feasts.[12]

In 1823, under a non-resident rector, the parishioners met to consider union with St. Bridget's. They rejected the proposal on the grounds that they had recently improved the church, and the union was delayed until 1842.[13] After the union, services were discontinued at St. Martin's except in 1849–50, when St. Michael's congregation met there.[14] By 1867, however, St. Martin's had reopened as the parish church for the Welsh in Chester.[15] Links with the

Welsh dated from 1826, when a Sunday evening lecture in Welsh had been established, and they continued until 1964.[16]

Building

The church of St. Martin, which was situated near the south-west corner of the legionary fortress, was by the 17th century a small, two-celled building with a bellcote.[17] It had fallen into ruin by *c.* 1720, and in 1721 was replaced with a small, aisleless building of brick with stone dressings, with a tower but no chancel.[18] Repaired *c.* 1820 and again in 1869, it was enlarged in 1882 and demolished to make way for the inner ring-road after its sale to the city council in 1964.[19] Its pre-Reformation font was transferred to St. Bridget's in 1861 and to St. Mary's on the Hill in 1892.[20]

ST. MARY ON THE HILL

The church was granted by Earl Ranulph II to Chester abbey in the mid 12th century, when it was described as 'of' or 'by' the castle,[21] with which it remained closely associated. The part of the parish inside the walls was very small, but outside there were extensive detached parts, comprising in the south Handbridge and the townships of Claverton[22] and Marlston cum Lache, and in the north Upton by Chester and Little Mollington.[23] The southern portion was virtually coextensive with the castle demesne, while that to the north was originally held by the earl and his tenants; the link seems to have been the honor of Chester, and the parish was probably formed in the earlier 12th century.[24] In 1599 the parishioners successfully claimed that Moston township and half of Chorlton were in their parish and not Backford.[25] Marlston cum Lache was included within the new parish of Lache cum Saltney in 1855, and Upton became a separate parish in 1882.[26] In 1887 St. Mary's acquired Earl's Eye and lost the intramural areas north of the river, which were assigned to St. Michael's with St. Olave's, and St. Bridget's with St. Martin's.[27] Little Mollington and Moston were transferred to other parishes in the early 20th century.[28]

1 Ormerod, *Hist. Ches.* i. 332; cf. above, this chapter: St. Bridget; below, this chapter: St. Michael, St. Peter.

2 C.C.A.L.S., EDV 7/1/5.

3 Ibid. DBE 37/3; York, Borthwick Inst., V.1662–3/CB.2, f. 6.

4 C.C.A.L.S., P 16/5/1.

5 *List of Clergy*, 1541–2, 2; Morris, *Chester*, 151.

6 C.C.A.L.S., EDV 1/1; EDV 1/3, ff. 21, 48; EDV 2/4.

7 Ibid. EDV 1/32, f. 31; York, Borthwick Inst., V.1633/CB.2, ff. 437v.–438; above, this chapter: St. Bridget.

8 Gastrell, *Not. Cest.* i. 104; Burne, *Chester Cath.* 130, 146–8.

9 C.C.A.L.S., EDP 72/1/1; EDV 2/12–21.

10 Ibid. EDP 72/1/1.   11 Ibid. EDV 7/1/5.

12 Ibid. EDV 7/3/106; EDV 7/4/157; EDV 7/7/114.

13 Ibid. P 16/6/2.

14 *White's Dir. Ches.* (1860), 86; *J.C.A.S.* [o.s.], ii. 393–4.

15 *Chester Guide* (1867), 99; *Morris's Dir. Ches.* (1874), 8; *J.C.A.S.* n.s. xii. 22.

16 *Kelly's Dir. Chester* (1962), p. A8; (1964).

17 Ormerod, *Hist. Ches.* i. 332.

18 Gastrell, *Not. Cest.* i. 103 n.; 3 *Sheaf*, xlviii, p. 30; C.C.A.L.S., P 16/6/1.

19 C.C.A.L.S., P 16/6/2; *J.C.A.S.* n.s. xii. 22; *Kelly's Dir. Ches.* (1892), 184; *Chester City Cl. Mins.* 1963/4, p. 958.

20 *J.C.A.S.* [o.s.], ii. 393–4.

21 *Cart. Chester Abbey*, i, pp. 59, 253; ii, p. 286.

22 Extra-parochial by late 19th cent.: *Census*.

23 Ormerod, *Hist. Ches.* i. 333.

24 *J.C.A.S.* lxiv. 5–31.

25 Ormerod, *Hist. Ches.* ii. 362; C.C.A.L.S., P 32/1/1, f. 46; cf. *Cal. S.P. Dom.* 1655–6, 331.

26 Below, Modern Parish Churches: Holy Ascension, Upton; St. Mark, Saltney.

27 *Lond. Gaz.* 27 Sept. 1887, pp. 5220–7.

28 *Kelly's Dir. Ches.* (1910), 56; (1923), 494; (1928), 286.

Advowson, Income, and Property

Chester abbey retained the advowson throughout the Middle Ages. In 1354 it was licensed to appropriate the living, but the move seems to have been opposed by the bishop, and incumbents continued to be styled rector.[1] In 1396 the licence of 1354 was renewed and briefly implemented, the rectory of St. Mary's being united with that of St. Olave's and served by a vicar and perpetual chaplain. The appropriation was quashed in 1402.[2]

At the dissolution of the abbey the advowson passed to the dean and chapter of the new cathedral, who in 1546 granted it to Sir Thomas Garden.[3] In 1553 it was alienated to Sir Richard Cotton, and by 1554 had passed to the Brereton family, in whose possession it remained until sold to the Wilbrahams of Dorfold (in Acton) after 1623. They first presented *c.* 1642, and retained the living until it passed by marriage to the Hill family in 1772. In 1819 it was sold to Earl Grosvenor, later 1st marquess of Westminster, in the possession of whose descendants it remained in 2000.[4]

From the later 12th century the rector paid an annual pension of 4 marks to St. Werburgh's.[5] Presumably because of its association with the earls, the benefice was one of the richest in Chester, valued in 1291 at £10 13s. 4d.,[6] in 1379 at 80 marks, and in 1535 at £52.[7] The living remained valuable after the Reformation, worth £60 in 1559,[8] £140 in the 1720s, £322 in 1834,[9] and over £400 later in the 19th century.[10] Revenues were derived mainly from tithes, only the township of Marlston cum Lache, known as the nuns' lands, being virtually exempt.[11] The tithes were commuted in the 1840s.[12]

The rector's property, first mentioned in the early 14th century, presumably included a parsonage house. In the 1550s it stood near the church.[13] By 1328 St. Mary's also possessed a graveyard, perhaps originally for the burial of prisoners from the castle.[14]

Church Life

St. Mary's retained links with the palatine administration throughout the Middle Ages. In the late 12th century the earl and his court worshipped there;[15] in the 13th some incumbents were associated with palatine officials, and by the 14th the church was regarded as a suitable reward for such men. Many rectors were members of local landed families, and were often absentee pluralists. Alan Retford (rector 1327–35), for example, was a royal clerk and prebendary of Chichester, and John Brereton (1534–42) a canon of St. Paul's in London.[16]

Stipendiaries were employed as curates at St. Mary's before the Reformation, and there was at least one chantry chaplain, endowed by William Troutbeck in 1444. The church seems to have become a favoured burial place for the well-to-do; Randle Brereton, for example, in 1537 left £5 a year for two years for a priest to sing masses at his grave in St. Catherine's chapel, located in the north aisle. In 1549 a chantry priest was supported from the rents of property in the city.[17]

Before the Reformation St. Mary's possessed notable images of St. Stephen and the Virgin, and an abundance of vestments, ornaments, and sacred vessels.[18] It was also the starting point for the most important event in the annual round of civic ceremonial, the Corpus Christi procession.[19] The old services continued unimpaired until 1547, but thereafter change was rapid: in 1547 the rood was taken down and the church whitelimed, presumably to obliterate wall-paintings; in 1549 a prayer book, two psalters, and the *Paraphrases* were bought; in 1550 the holy water stoup was removed, the altars were taken down, and the parson married; finally, in 1553 the royal commissioners confiscated church goods which were sold for £10 13s. 6d., more than any other church in Chester. The parishioners' attempts to retain the choicest vestments were largely unsuccessful.[20]

After Queen Mary's accession the married incumbent was deprived in 1554, and money was spent on new altars, a new rood, and gilding a new image of the Virgin,[21] but under Elizabeth the rood was once again removed in 1559, and in 1562 the altars and rood loft were taken down, the church was painted, and the ten commandments were set up. The organ, probably taken down in 1553, was not disposed of until 1574, and the holy water bucket and censer were sold only in

---

1 Jones, *Ch. in Chester*, 173–4; *Blk. Prince's Reg.* iii. 161, 203.

2 Jones, *Ch. in Chester*, 67, 173–4; *Cal. Pat.* 1394–6, 11; 1396–9, 8–9, 42, 136.

3 Ormerod, *Hist. Ches.* i. 333.

4 Ibid. i. 340; *Cal. Pat.* 1553 and App. 1547–53, 100; J. P. Earwaker, *Hist. of St. Mary-on-the-Hill*, 2, 81–99; *Chester Dioc. Year Bk.* 1999/2000, p. 44.

5 *Cart. Chester Abbey*, i, pp. 252–3.

6 *Tax. Eccl.* 248.　　　　　7 *Valor Eccl.* v. 208.

8 P.R.O., SP 12/10, p. 320.

9 Gastrell, *Not. Cest.* i. 105.

10 *Bagshaw's Dir. Ches.* (1850), 62; *Morris's Dir. Ches.* (1874), 8; *Slater's Dir. Ches.* (1890), 136.

11 C.C.A.L.S., EDV 8/26/1–2; 3 *Sheaf*, xix, p. 7.

12 C.C.A.L.S., EDT 96/1; P 20/18/1, 15, 17.

13 Ibid. ZTAR 1/9, m. 3; ZTAR 1/20, m. 3.

14 Ibid. ZMR 31, m. 2; J. P. Earwaker, 'Ancient Parish Bks. of St. Mary's on the Hill', *J.C.A.S.* n.s. ii. 136–7; *Cal. of Norris Deeds* (R.S.L.C. xciii), 112.

15 Lucian, *De Laude Cestrie*, 61.

16 *Cal. Pat.* 1399–1400, 300; 3 *Sheaf*, xxxiii, p. 71; Jones, *Ch. in Chester*, 20, 173–6.

17 *List of Clergy*, 1541–2, 1; 3 *Sheaf*, xvii, p. 30; *Cal. Pat.* 1548–9, 313; P.R.O., E 301/8/1; SC 12/6/24A; SC 12/6/64.

18 3 *Sheaf*, xix, p. 4; Earwaker, *Hist. St. Mary's*, 3–5.

19 Below, Plays, Sports, and Customs before 1700: Chester Plays (Corpus Christi Procession and Play).

20 Earwaker, *Hist. St. Mary's*, 4–6, 81, 230–40; C.C.A.L.S., P 20/13/1, lists on flyleaf and under 1553.

21 C.C.A.L.S., P 20/13/1; Earwaker, *Hist. St. Mary's*, 5–6.

FIG. 82. *St. Mary's,
medieval wall paintings as
in 1843*

1573. By the 1630s the church was well provided with the necessities of Anglican worship.[1]

Throughout the later 16th and earlier 17th century, when rectors were absentees, St. Mary's appears to have been served by curates, sometimes with unsatisfactory results.[2] Francis Edwards (1623–42), although absentee, appears to have tried to force his evidently Caroline sympathies on the parish, unsuccessfully attempting to prevent the parishioners from exercising their customary right to sit in the chancel stalls, and employing as curate a royalist protégé of Bishop Bridgeman.[3] His successor, Richard Hunt, was ejected *c.* 1646, and replaced by William Peartree, who signed the Cheshire ministers' attestation in 1648. Reinstated after Peartree's death in 1655, Hunt appears to have conformed; the font was discarded in 1657 and the chancel was so neglected that in 1659 it was unusable.[4]

Hunt died in 1662. His successor, Nicholas Stevenson, a former Presbyterian,[5] found the church seriously out of repair, though not wanting in the essentials of Anglican worship.[6] Stevenson was probably resident, but his successor, Richard Wright (1674–1711), a prebendary of Chester cathedral, was not and in the 1690s his curate, Hugh Burches, was so established a figure at the church that he was styled rector in the registers.[7] Absenteeism and the employment of curates continued throughout the 18th century, under a succession of well-born rectors, including members of the Wilbraham and Brooke families, who whether resident or not usually maintained curates.[8]

By 1800 communion was administered monthly and at the great festivals to between 60 and 100 people.[9] A Sunday evening lectureship, managed by a committee of subscribers, lasted from 1822 until 1857, and one lecturer, Charles Tayler (incumbent of St. Peter's 1836–46), preached to congregations numbering 1,200.[10] Under William Massie (rector 1847–56) attendances at matins reached 500.[11] Curates were maintained throughout the 19th century, originally at the incumbents' expense and later through a voluntary fund established by the 1880s.[12]

In 1887 a new church in Handbridge replaced St. Mary's on the Hill, which, however, reopened in 1891 as the parish church of St. Bridget's.[13] By the early 20th century, under Henry Grantham (rector 1882–1922), St. Mary's in Handbridge offered a moderate Anglicanism, with a weekly early communion and matins the principal morning service.[14] A more catholic tradition had been established by the 1930s, when there was a weekly sung eucharist and the English Hymnal was in use.[15]

Buildings

The redundant church of St. Mary on the Hill is built of red sandstone and comprises a chancel with side chapels, an aisled and clerestoried nave with north and

1 Earwaker, *Hist. St. Mary's*, 6–7.

2 P.R.O., SP 12/10, p. 320; 3 *Sheaf,* i, p. 34; York, Borthwick Inst., V.1633/CB.2, f. 437.

3 *V.C.H. Ches.* iii. 34; C.C.A.L.S., P 20/13/1.

4 Earwaker, *Hist. St. Mary's,* 7–8; C.C.A.L.S., P 20/13/1.

5 Earwaker, *Hist. St. Mary's,* 85–6, 89–90.

6 York, Borthwick Inst., V.1662–3/CB.2, f. 4.

7 Earwaker, *Hist. St. Mary's,* 89–91; C.C.A.L.S., P 20/1/1.

8 Earwaker, *Hist. St. Mary's,* 91–9; 3 *Sheaf,* xl, p. 31; C.C.A.L.S., EDP 74/1/3; EDV 7/1/4; EDV 7/2/3.

9 C.C.A.L.S., EDV 7/1/4; EDV 7/2/3; EDV 7/3/107; EDV 7/4/159; EDV 7/7/115.

10 Ibid. EDP 74/1; Earwaker, *Hist. St. Mary's,* 200–1; *D.N.B.*

11 *J.C.A.S.* [o.s.], iv. 403; P.R.O., HO 129/459/63.

12 C.C.A.L.S., P 20/13/3; P 20/15/1; EDP 74/1/3–4.

13 Ibid. P 15/8/10; P 20/8/45; EDA 2/29, p. 1.

14 Ibid. P 20/15/1; *Kelly's Dir. Ches.* (1892), 192; (1902), 211; (1906), 221; (1910), 225; (1914), 232; *P. & G. Dir. Chester* (1921/2), 49.

15 C.C.A.L.S., P 20/15/2; *P. & G. Dir. Chester* (1933/4), 45; (1935/6), 51.

south porches, and a west tower. Nothing remains of the Norman church. The earliest parts of the surviving building seem to be the chancel arch and a reused base in the north arcade, both probably early 14th-century. Building activity was under way in 1358,[1] and in the late 14th century the existing tower was built. Between 1433 and 1444 William Troutbeck added the south chapel,[2] which until 1661 housed the monuments of his family.[3] At about the same time the south aisle was probably remodelled. There was further building in the 1490s, when bequests were made for the tower and for repairs,[4] and by the early 16th century the church had been largely reconstructed. The arcades appear then to have been remodelled, and a clerestory and a new oak-panelled camber-beamed roof were put into the nave;[5] the north aisle and north chapel are of a similar date, and the older north doorway was probably then reset. Additional repairs in the 1530s included retiling the floor and refurnishing the chancel with the choir stalls of Basingwerk abbey (Flints.).[6] North and south porches were built in 1542, the former with stones from St. Mary's nunnery; a chamber over one of them accommodated one of the church's priests.[7] Frequent internal redecoration in the later 16th century and the earlier 17th included the painting of the commandments and other scriptural texts on the walls, and the royal arms by Randle Holme (I) in 1622.[8]

The church suffered badly in the Civil War and Interregnum. The tower was damaged in the siege of Chester and in 1646 the church lost its stained glass. Although repaired in 1657, the tower was deprived of its upper stages in 1659 on the orders of the governor of Chester castle.[9] By then the chancel was ruinous, and in 1661 the Troutbeck chapel fell down, destroying the monuments.[10] Piecemeal repairs were made between 1676 and 1680 to St. Catherine's chapel in the north aisle and to a porch; in 1693, after it had been granted to the parishioners by Charles Talbot, earl of Shrewsbury, the Troutbeck chapel was reconstructed; in 1715 the upper stages of the tower were renewed;[11] and galleries were erected in 1703, 1728, 1756, and 1793.[12]

In 1861–2 the church underwent a major restoration by James Harrison. The tower was raised, the church repewed, plaster stripped from walls and pillars, and a plaster ceiling removed from the south aisle.[13] In 1891–2 under J. P. Seddon work undertaken for St. Bridget's congregation included the removal of the galleries and the insertion of new windows in the north aisle; the tower arch was also opened out, the nave roof repaired,

FIG. 83. *St. Mary's, tower and porch in 1641*

and the south clerestory and north porch rebuilt.[14] In the 1930s the remaining plaster ceilings in the Troutbeck chapel, aisles, and chancel were replaced by oak roofs, and a three-light window was inserted above the west arch of the chapel.[15]

The fittings, including a font and pulpit from St. Bridget's and reused early 17th-century altar rails, were removed after the church's closure in 1972. The church contains monuments to Philip Oldfield (d. 1616), a reclining effigy enclosed by a railing; Thomas Gamull (d. 1613) and his wife, a tomb-chest with effigies; and the Randle Holme family, wall monuments in the north aisle. Traces of elaborate late medieval wall paintings, uncovered in 1843, survive at the east end of the south aisle (Fig. 82).

After its closure for worship in 1972 the church passed into the hands of the county council, which used it, under the name of St. Mary's Centre, for conferences and other meetings.

The large church of St. Mary without the Walls, which is built of red sandstone, consists of a chancel, transepts (the north a vestry), an aisled nave of eight bays with porches, and a west tower and spire. It was

---

1 *Blk. Prince's Reg.* iii. 318.

2 Earwaker, *Hist. St. Mary's*, 31–2; *Talbot Deeds, 1200–1682* (R.S.L.C. ciii), 48.

3 2 *Sheaf*, i, p. 80; Hemingway, *Hist. Chester*, ii. 104–5.

4 3 *Sheaf*, xvii, p. 69; xviii, p. 92; xxii, p. 77.

5 *T.L.C.A.S.* lii. 107–8; E. Barber, 'Nave Roof of St. Mary's Church', *J.C.A.S.* n.s. viii. 67–80.

6 Earwaker, *Hist. St. Mary's*, 211; C.C.A.L.S., P 20/13/1.

7 Earwaker, *Hist. St. Mary's*, 4; C.C.A.L.S., P 20/13/1.

8 C.C.A.L.S., P 20/13/1.

9 Ibid.; Earwaker, *Hist. St. Mary's*, 7–8.

10 C.C.A.L.S., P 20/13/1.

11 Ibid. P 15/8/9; P 20/13/1; Earwaker, *Hist. St. Mary's*, 8; *T.L.C.A.S.* lvii. 111.

12 C.C.A.L.S., EDA 2/3, f. 267 and v.; EDA 2/5, pp. 147–50; EDA 2/6, pp. 284–5; EDA 2/9, pp. 170–2.

13 Ibid. P 20/8/38–43.

14 Earwaker, *Hist. St. Mary's*, 19–20; *Chester Dioc. Gaz.* (1891), pp. 2–3, 42, 91.

15 C.C.A.L.S., P 15/8/20–2; EDP 74/2; *T.L.C.A.S.* lii. 107–8.

FIG. 84. *St. Mary without the Walls, Handbridge*

erected in 1887 in the Early Pointed style at the expense of the 1st duke of Westminster. The architect was F. B. Wade of London.[1] The south transept was converted into a chapel in 1909 by Philip Lockwood, and a porch was added at the south-west entrance in 1914.[2] The fittings include a reredos with mosaics by Clement

Heaton to designs by Frederick Shields, erected between 1889 and 1896.[3]

ST. MICHAEL

In the mid 12th century a 'monastery' of St. Michael in Chester was supposedly among the gifts of William fitz Niel to Norton priory.[4] It was presumably the 'mighty minster' of St. Michael later said to have been burned in the great fire of 1180.[5] A parish church with the same dedication, apparently on the existing site, was first mentioned in 1178.[6] The parish was entirely intramural and its boundaries suggest that it was formed at the same time as its neighbour St. Bridget's.[7] It was united with St. Olave's in 1839,[8] and was incorporated in the new parish of Chester in 1972, when the church closed for worship.[9]

Advowson, Income, and Property

St. Michael's was probably in the charge of a parochial chaplain in the Middle Ages, but the identity of the patron or appropriator is unknown. If the church was indeed William fitz Niel's then the advowson was presumably held by the canons of Norton, at least until the earlier 14th century, though it was not among their possessions at the Dissolution.[10] After the Reformation the benefice was a perpetual curacy in the gift of the bishop of Chester.[11]

The living was always poor. In 1541–2 the incumbent was said to live 'from the fruits of the church' (*ex fructibus ecclesiae*), and in 1547–8 his successor had a clear income of only *c.* £4.[12] By the 1570s assessments were made on the parishioners to pay the minister's stipend.[13] Even in the 1720s, after a number of legacies, the incumbent seems to have remained largely dependent on voluntary contributions amounting to *c.* £20 a year.[14] Augmentations in 1772, 1791, 1810, and 1814 took the value of the living to £44 10*s.* in 1809, and £84 in 1834.[15] By 1864 it had reached £173.[16]

A chamber over the west porch may have served as a parsonage house in the late 16th century,[17] and in the early 17th the minister was given a house in Bridge Street Row.[18] No. 43 Bridge Street, a mid 17th-century timber-framed building which survived in 2000, was left as a rectory house by Lettice Whitley in 1659 and was used as such, perhaps intermittently, until 1907.[19] The small churchyard, first mentioned in the 1480s, was closed in 1854.[20]

---

1 C.C.A.L.S., P 20/8/52.
2 Ibid. P 20/8/100, 113, 121–51; EDP 74/2.
3 Ibid. P 20/8/60–98, 165; EDA 2/29, p. 437; EDP 74/2; Earwaker, *Hist. St. Mary's*, 18.
4 *Cal. Chart. R.* 1327–41, 124.
5 H. Bradshaw, *Life of St. Werburge of Chester* (E.E.T.S. orig. ser. lxxxviii), p. 187.
6 Ormerod, *Hist. Ches.* i. 694; Lucian, *De Laude Cestrie*, 47, 49, 60–1.
7 *J.C.A.S.* lxiv. 17–24.
8 Ormerod, *Hist. Ches.* i. 345.

9 *Lond. Gaz.* 30 June 1972, p. 7865.
10 Jones, *Ch. in Chester*, 103; *Cal. Chart. R.* 1327–41, 124.
11 Gastrell, *Not. Cest.* i. 108.
12 *List of Clergy*, 1541–2, 2; P.R.O., E 301/8/1.
13 C.C.A.L.S., P 65/8/1.   14 Gastrell, *Not. Cest.* i. 108.
15 Ibid.; C. Hodgson, *Queen Anne's Bounty* (2nd edn. 1845), p. ccl; Hemingway, *Hist. Chester*, ii. 122.
16 *Morris's Dir. Ches.* (1864), 4.
17 Below (Building).   18 C.C.A.L.S., P 65/8/1.
19 *Rows of Chester*, ed. A. Brown, 158–9.
20 C.C.A.L.S., P 65/12/34; ibid. ZCHD 2/5.

FIG. 85. *St. Michael's in late 17th century*

Church Life

Provision for chantry priests, perhaps temporary, was made in 1384, 1439, and 1505;[1] by the mid 16th century there was perhaps one chantry chaplain in addition to the incumbent.[2]

The church contained an image of St. Michael by 1401.[3] It possessed relatively few vestments and ornaments, and those sold by the royal commissioners in 1553 realized only 5s. 9d.[4] The vestments and other appurtenances of catholic worship, including an altar stone, dismantled and in a coffer, survived until 1565, after which they were sold and the remaining Marian fittings were taken down. The rood loft and the vaults over the two altars survived until 1568.[5]

The poverty of the living caused it to be held in plurality with St. Olave's in the mid 16th century and the 1630s.[6] Nevertheless in the early 17th century the church was apparently used for civic services, for in 1606 and 1609 Randle Holme (I) was paid for painting the rest for the city sword.[7] By 1633 St. Michael's was much neglected, the chancel full of pews, and the incumbent accused of failing to catechize and to church women correctly.[8] Further disorder culminated in the parishioners' destruction of the chancel screen,

and in 1637 they were ordered to erect a new one, make the seats in the chancel uniform and facing the holy table, and receive the sacrament not in their pews but at the altar rail.[9] The instructions were observed only until 1641–2, when the screen and altar rails were removed.[10]

By 1650 the parish had a strongly Presbyterian minister in William Cook.[11] Arrested for aiding Sir George Booth's rebellion and taken to London in 1659, he had returned by 1660, when he gave £10 towards restoring the seats in St. Michael's, but he was ejected in 1662 for refusing to conform.[12] Thereafter the church seems to have had no minister until John Hancock was presented in 1685.[13] The congregation, however, retained its nonconformist sympathies, and in the 1680s Hancock's Wednesday and Friday lectures were attended by the Presbyterian Matthew Henry.[14]

Throughout the 18th century the living was held by prebendaries or, more usually, minor canons of Chester cathedral.[15] In 1778 holy communion was celebrated monthly and on the great festivals, and communicants numbered between 70 and 120. Thereafter attendances declined to 50 or fewer in 1825.[16] From 1826 the incumbent, Joseph Eaton the younger (1796–1850), who was clerk to the cathedral chapter, employed a curate, and assistant clergy continued to be needed under his successor James Haworth (1850–93), who became insane.[17] St. Michael's retained a tradition of moderate Anglicanism, with in the 1870s holy communion generally restricted to a weekly early celebration, an arrangement which persisted largely unchanged in the 1930s.[18]

Building

The redundant church of St. Michael is a mostly 19th-century rebuilding of a much repaired medieval church. It is of buff-coloured sandstone and comprises a chancel with a north chapel, and a nave with a north aisle. Since it is built over the remains of the eastern abutment of the south gate of the legionary fortress, its entrance is well above street level.[19] Fragments of 12th-century masonry were discovered during restoration c. 1850.[20] The earliest part of the present structure, the north arcade with its octagonal piers, probably dates from the 15th century; money was left for building work in 1413 and 1439.[21] In the 1490s the chancel was

1 3 *Sheaf*, xvii, p. 105; xviii, pp. 93–4; xxxvi, pp. 59–60.
2 Gastrell, *Not. Cest.* i. 109 n.
3 *Cat. Anct. D.* vi, C 5282.
4 Morris, *Chester*, 151, 153.   5 C.C.A.L.S., P 65/8/1.
6 Ibid. EDV 1/1; EDV 1/3; EDV 2/4; P.R.O., SP 12/10, p. 320; 3 *Sheaf*, i, p. 34; York, Borthwick Inst., V.1633/CB.2, f. 436.
7 C.C.A.L.S., P 65/8/1.
8 York, Borthwick Inst., V.1633/CB.2, ff. 435v.–436.
9 C.C.A.L.S., EDC 5/1640/60.
10 Ibid. P 65/8/1; EDC 5/1639/9.
11 *Calamy Revised*, ed. A. G. Matthews, 132–3.
12 W. Urwick, *Hist. Sketches of Nonconformity in Ches.*

pp. xxxvi, 21–3; C.C.A.L.S., P 65/8/1; ibid. ZML 3, no. 390.
13 e.g. C.C.A.L.S., EDV 2/6.
14 3 *Sheaf*, lvii, p. 28.
15 Burne, *Chester Cath.* 197; Gastrell, *Not. Cest.* i. 108; C.C.A.L.S., EDV 2/12–27; EDV 7/2/4.
16 C.C.A.L.S., EDV 7/1/6; EDV 7/2/4; EDV 7/3/108; EDV 7/7/116.
17 Ibid. EDP 75/1; Burne, *Chester Cath.* 253.
18 *P. & G. Dir. Chester* (1878/9), 23; (1935/6), 51.
19 F. H. Thompson, *Deva*, 21.
20 *J.C.A.S.* [o.s.], i. 199.
21 C.C.A.L.S., ZMR 75; 3 *Sheaf*, xvii, p. 105.

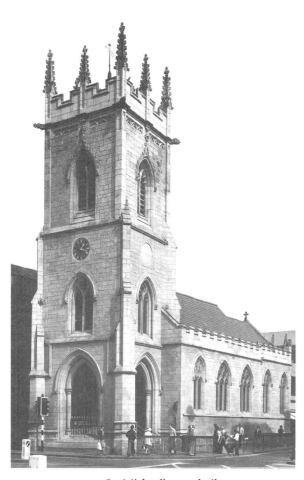

FIG. 86. *St. Michael's as rebuilt 1849–51*

rebuilt, and it was probably then that the arch-braced roof with decorated panels was installed.[1]

In 1582 the church was almost entirely rebuilt with a slate roof, a wooden steeple, and a porch chamber presumably like the rectory house at St. Peter's.[2] In 1610–11 further work was done, including a carved ceiling and, probably, the nave roof, which has tie-beams and crown posts.[3]

The church suffered in the Civil War, and *c.* 1678 the chancel had again to be rebuilt, the medieval roof being adapted to fit the new structure, which was perhaps extended northwards.[4] In 1708–10 the steeple was replaced with a square stone tower,[5] eventually capped by a cupola.[6]

By the 1840s the whole church was unsafe. Between 1849 and 1851 it was virtually rebuilt in a late Decorated style by James Harrison, only the north arcade, part of the north wall, and the roofs (but not the ceilings) being retained.[7] After the closure of the church in 1972 it was reopened by the city council as a heritage centre in 1975.[8]

ST. OLAVE

The church was given in 1119 by Richard the butler to Chester abbey.[9] Its dedication, to the Norwegian King Olaf killed in 1030, may be as early as the mid 11th century.[10] The very small parish, which lay within the medieval walls but outside the Roman ones, may have been carved out of a larger parish focused on St. Bridget's, which also had Scandinavian associations.[11]

Advowson, Income, and Property

The living was a rectory in the gift of Chester abbey in the Middle Ages.[12] It was united with St. Mary's in 1394, separated in 1406, and thereafter independent until 1460 or later.[13] At the dissolution of the abbey the advowson seems to have passed into private hands, and in the earlier 17th century belonged to the Vawdrey family. After a prolonged dispute it was sold in 1661 to Hugh Harvey, in whose possession it remained in 1685. Before 1722, perhaps in the 1690s, the living passed to the bishop of Chester, and afterwards was regarded as a perpetual curacy until its union with St. Michael's in 1839.[14]

The value of the benefice was always negligible and in 1394 the bishop considered it insufficient to support a rector.[15] In 1414 and 1459 papal dispensations made allowances for the poor endowments.[16] In 1541–2 the incumbent was said to live 'from the fruits of the church' (*ex fructibus ecclesiae*),[17] but that seems to have been exceptional, and in 1699 there was no income except for surplice fees.[18] The living was augmented in 1723 and 1771, and perhaps in 1726 and 1744, but by 1778 some of the augmentations had been withdrawn.[19] A legacy of 1732 added £10 a year.[20] In 1809 the living was valued at £42 1*s.*, and after further augmentations in 1810 and 1823, it had increased to £89 by 1834.[21]

---

1 3 *Sheaf*, viii, p. 84; xxix, p. 74; *King's Vale Royal*, [i], 77; [ii], 190; *T.L.C.A.S.* lii. 131–2.

2 C.C.A.L.S., P 65/8/1; Ormerod, *Hist. Ches.* i. 343.

3 C.C.A.L.S., P 65/8/1; Hemingway, *Hist. Chester*, ii. 121; *T.L.C.A.S.* lii. 123–4.

4 C.C.A.L.S., P 65/8/2–3.

5 Ibid. P 65/8/2–3; ibid. ZAB 3, f. 163v.

6 Ibid. P 65/8/3; 3 *Sheaf*, xlviii, p. 27.

7 *Chester Guide* [*c.* 1854], 107–8.

8 Below, Museums: Other Museums.

9 *Cart. Chester Abbey*, i, pp. 41, 57.

10 B. Dickens, 'Cult of St. Olaf', *Saga Bk. of Viking Soc.* xii. 53–80.

11 *J.C.A.S.* lv. 50–4; lxiv. 19–21.

12 Ormerod, *Hist. Ches.* i. 344–5.

13 Jones, *Ch. in Chester*, 67–8, 177.

14 C.C.A.L.S., EDC 5/1685/6; EDP 75/5; Gastrell, *Not. Cest.* i. 110; Ormerod, *Hist. Ches.* i. 344.

15 Jones, *Ch. in Chester*, 67–8, 177.

16 *J.C.A.S.* lv. 53.

17 *List of Clergy, 1541–2*, 2.

18 C.C.A.L.S., EDP 75/6; cf. Gastrell, *Not. Cest.* i. 109.

19 C. Hodgson, *Queen Anne's Bounty* (2nd edn. 1845), p. ccl; C.C.A.L.S., EDV 7/1/7; EDV 7/2/5; Ormerod, *Hist. Ches.* i. 345; Hemingway, *Hist. Chester*, ii. 125.

20 C.C.A.L.S., EDV 7/3/109.

21 Hodgson, *Queen Anne's Bounty*, p. ccl; Gastrell, *Not. Cest.* i. 109 n.

There was no parsonage house.[1] The churchyard, which existed by the 17th century, was closed for burials in 1851.[2]

Church Life

Several rectors in the 14th and early 15th century, especially after 1406, appear to have been pluralists.[3] No incumbents are known between 1460 and 1540, though services were evidently still held in the church and modest bequests were occasionally made to it.[4] In 1541–2 it had a stipendiary curate as well as an incumbent.[5] Nevertheless, in 1553 the royal commissioners found so little of value in the items surrendered that they distributed them to the poor.[6]

In the later 16th century and the early 17th St. Olave's seems to have been held in plurality with St. Michael's.[7] Their incumbent in the 1620s and 1630s, Roger Gorst, apparently officiated irregularly at St. Olave's until his death in 1660, but in 1666 it was said that public prayers, preaching, and the administration of the sacraments had been largely discontinued for many years. Christenings and burials were still occasionally held, and there were interments in the chancel in the 1680s.[8]

In 1693 a curate was licensed to St. Olave's, and in 1694 he also became minister of St. Michael's.[9] The two livings were held together until 1724, when St. Olave's was given its own incumbent.[10] It retained its independence until 1839.[11] By 1778 there were two Sunday services, with communion monthly and on the three great festivals, and between the 1780s and 1825 the number of communicants varied between 10 and 40, though congregations were considerably larger.[12] The numbers were insufficient to maintain the church. In 1839 it closed and services were transferred to St. Michael's,[13] although weekday services were held in it in the 1870s.[14]

Building

The redundant church of St. Olave is a small, aisleless, single-celled building of red sandstone. The present structure, which is entered from a small west terrace several feet above street level, is of uncertain date, although earlier than the mid 17th century. The east end is clearly a later addition.[15] Although money was

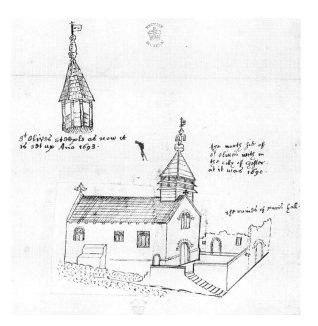

FIG. 87. *St. Olave's in 1690*

left for the repair of the church in 1548,[16] in 1633 the interior was unpaved and strewn with rushes.[17] In 1662 the churchwardens were presented for not repairing the church, and though some attempt at remedy was apparently made in the later 1660s the building soon fell into severe decay. In 1699 the chancel was ruinous, and the bishop appealed for funds.[18] The reconstruction of the east end presumably dates from the ensuing restoration in the early 18th century.[19] Further work included the replacement of the bell-cote in 1802, and the installation of new seating in 1819.[20] After its closure the church was kept in repair, and in 1858–9 it was thoroughly restored by James Harrison for use as a school.[21] In 1995 the building was in the care of the city council.

ST. OSWALD

Ancient Parish

The parish of St. Oswald, king and martyr, originated in association with the minster church which eventually became the Benedictine abbey of St. Werburgh. A late tradition that the cult of St. Oswald was

1 C.C.A.L.S., EDV 7/7/117.
2 Ibid. EDA 2/20, p. 362; EDC 5/1661/8; P 64/1/1.
3 Jones, *Ch. in Chester*, 177.
4 3 *Sheaf*, xxiii, pp. 2–3; *Lancs. and Ches. Wills and Inventories*, ii (Chetham Soc. [o.s.], li), 8.
5 *List of Clergy*, 1541–2, 2.
6 Morris, *Chester*, 151.
7 Above, this chapter: St. Michael.
8 York, Borthwick Inst., V.1633/CB.2, f. 441; C.C.A.L.S., EDC 5/1666/8; EDC 5/1673/27; EDC 5/1685/6.
9 Gastrell, *Not. Cest.* i. 110; C.C.A.L.S., EDV 2/11.
10 C.C.A.L.S., EDV 2/18–19.
11 Ibid. EDV 2/20–75.
12 Ibid. EDV 7/1/7; EDV 7/2/6; EDV 7/3/109; EDV 7/4/179;

EDV 7/7/117.
13 Ibid. P 64/1/1; P 64/2; P 64/3/4; P 64/4. From 1850 directories and handbks. gave the date of closure as 1841: *Bagshaw's Dir. Ches.* (1850), 63; *White's Dir. Ches.* (1860), 87; Hughes, *Stranger's Handbk.* (1856), 74.
14 *P. & G. Dir. Chester* (1878/9), 33.
15 Ormerod, *Hist. Ches.* i. 344.
16 3 *Sheaf*, xviii, p. 88; C.C.A.L.S., ZMB 28, ff. 67v., 70.
17 York, Borthwick Inst., V.1633/CB.2, f. 441.
18 Ibid. V.1662–3/CB.2, f. 7 and v.
19 Gastrell, *Not. Cest.* i. 109.
20 Hemingway, *Hist. Chester*, ii. 125–9; C.C.A.L.S., P 64/5.
21 *White's Dir. Ches.* (1860), 87; Ormerod, *Hist. Ches.* i. 345; *Chester Record*, 21 May 1859.

introduced when the minster was refounded by Æthel-flæd of Mercia gains plausibility from the fact that she translated the same saint's remains to Gloucester in 909.[1] The parish was termed indifferently St. Oswald's and St. Werburgh's in the 13th century, when the parishioners used the altar of St. Oswald in the abbey nave as their chief place of worship.[2]

The parish possessed burial rights in the city and its environs, originally shared only with St. John's, the other early minster church in the city. Besides the churchyard south of the abbey nave, it had by the later 12th century a cemetery outside the Northgate, associated with the chapel of St. Thomas of Canterbury and served by the monks of St. Werburgh's. Its burial rights were guaranteed by agreements with St. John's and by a papal bull in the late 12th and 13th century.[3] The parish probably originally comprised much of the city together with a sizeable extramural territory. After other parishes were carved out of it, it covered a large discontinuous area embracing the north-east part of the walled city, the abbot's manor of St. Thomas outside the Northgate, and, beyond the liberties, to the north Bache, Newton, Croughton, Wervin, and Crabwall (in Blacon township), and to the east and south-east Great Boughton, Churton Heath, Huntington, Lea Newbold, and Saighton; further afield lay Iddinshall and Hilbre Island. The parish in that form perhaps represented the remains of a once much greater Anglo-Saxon unit, together with some outliers added to it only after they became part of St. Werburgh's estates.[4] In the 19th century the parish was much reduced. Newton was lost in two stages in 1843 and 1867, and Great Boughton in 1846.[5] Bruera chapelry (Huntington, Lea Newbold, Saighton, and Churton Heath) became an independent parish in 1868. In 1882, a year after the new chapel of St. Thomas of Canterbury in Parkgate Road replaced St. Oswald's as the parish church, the intramural portions were transferred to St. Peter's. After 1889 the hamlet of Crabwall was lost to Holy Trinity, and in the 1930s Wervin and Croughton were also detached from the parish. By 1951 the parish comprised only the area

outside the Northgate and Bache. Anomalously it still also included the small civil parish of Iddinshall, almost 10 miles east of the city, which, however, had a population in that year of just six people.[6] United with Little St. John's in 1967, St. Oswald's was incorporated in the new parish of Chester in 1972, St. Thomas of Canterbury remaining in use as one of four churches serving the parish.[7]

In the 13th century St. Oswald's had dependent chapelries at Bruera, Wervin, and Great Boughton, served by chaplains maintained by the vicar.[8] By the 17th century, though Bruera survived, Wervin was in ruins and Great Boughton had disappeared.[9] In the later 16th century parishioners from Newton and Great Boughton were allotted seats in St. Oswald's, and most, if not all, of the townships paid assessments to provide new fittings.[10] In the early 17th century many country people attended sermons in the church.[11]

Advowson, Income, and Property

The benefice remained a rectory in the patronage of St. Werburgh's until its appropriation in the early 13th century, after which vicars were appointed and paid by the abbey.[12] In 1397 St. Werburgh's was licensed to suppress the vicarage, but it seems to have survived, though perhaps with smaller endowments.[13] After the dissolution of the abbey the dean and chapter of the cathedral became the impropriators.[14]

The living was outstandingly rich before its appropriation.[15] Thereafter the vicar received 40s. a year and a place at the abbot's table, a provision increased in the later 13th century by the grant of land in Bruera.[16] In 1291 the church was valued at £6 13s. 4d.[17] By the 1360s the vicar had some property in Chester, and in the 1390s there was a vicarage house, apparently near the churchyard.[18] In 1535 the vicar possessed only a small glebe and a very modest share of the parochial tithes and offerings, in all amounting annually to only 33s. 4d. The rest went to the abbey, whose share was worth over £70.[19]

In 1646 parliament granted the minister £120 a

1 H. Bradshaw, *Life of St. Werburge of Chester* (E.E.T.S. orig. ser. lxxxviii), 150–3; *A.-S. Chronicle*, ed. D. Whitelock, 61; F. Wainwright, *Scandinavian Eng.* 84–5; H. P. R. Finberg, *Glos. Studies*, 34, 60.

2 *Cart. Chester Abbey*, i, pp. 113–14, 118–19, 131–3; *Cal. Ches. Ct. R.* p. 206.

3 3 *Sheaf*, xlv, pp. 43–7; *Cart. Chester Abbey*, i, pp. 113–14; ii, pp. 300–1; above, Collegiate Church of St. John.

4 Ormerod, *Hist. Ches.* i. 304–5; C.C.A.L.S., P 29/7/2, p. 316; *Cart. Chester Abbey*, i, pp. 118–19; 3 *Sheaf*, iv, pp. 16–17.

5 Cf. below, Modern Parish Churches: All Saints, Hoole; St. Paul, Boughton.

6 *Lond. Gaz.* 17 Feb. 1882, pp. 648–51; Ormerod, *Hist. Ches.* i. 355; ii. 575, 762; C.C.A.L.S., EDT 51/1; P 29/7/7; *Kelly's Dir. Ches.* (1928), 152, 443; (1934), 137, 447; (1939), 141, 452; P. Sulley, *Hundred of Wirral*, 109; *Census*, 1951, *Eccl. Areas* (Eng.), 148; *V.C.H. Ches.* ii. 218.

7 Order in Council, 28 Nov. 1967 (copy in Chester Dioc.

Regy.); *Lond. Gaz.* 30 June 1972, p. 7865.

8 *Cart. Chester Abbey*, i, pp. 119, 131.

9 Ibid. i, p. 119; C.C.A.L.S., EDC 5/1664/67; *Mins. of Cttee. for Relief of Plundered Ministers, and of Trustees for Maintenance of Ministers, 1643–54* (R.S.L.C. xxviii), 112–13; Gastrell, *Not. Cest.* i. 118.   10 C.C.A.L.S., P 29/7/1–2.

11 G. T. O. Bridgeman, *Hist. of Church and Manor of Wigan*, ii (Chetham Soc. N.S. xvi), 298–9.

12 *Cart. Chester Abbey*, i, pp. 118–19; Jones, *Ch. in Chester*, 178–9.

13 *Cal. Pat.* 1396–9, 136; Jones, *Ch. in Chester*, 68.

14 Gastrell, *Not. Cest.* i. 111–12; 3 *Sheaf*, i, p. 32.

15 Jones, *Ch. in Chester*, 66–7.

16 *Cart. Chester Abbey*, i, p. 119.

17 *Tax. Eccl.* 248.

18 3 *Sheaf*, xxxvi, p. 32; xliv, pp. 49, 51.

19 Jones, *Ch. in Chester*, 68–9, 89–90; *Valor Eccl.* v. 205–6; B.L. Harl. MS. 2071, f. 47.

FIG. 88. *St. Nicholas's chapel, 1854*

year,[1] and by 1649 there was a vicarage house in the cathedral precinct valued at £4 a year.[2] At the Restoration the augmentation was lost, and the living was further impoverished by the failure of several of the outlying townships to render any dues.[3] In the 1720s the benefice was worth only £27 a year, of which the house represented £9. The income came mostly from Easter dues and surplice fees, though small sums were also derived from the lesser tithes and a pension paid by the dean and chapter.[4] No augmentation was made in the 18th century, and in 1804 the living remained small.[5] In the 1830s the vestry engaged in unsuccessful litigation to recover dues from the outlying townships.[6] Thereafter, however, the value rose to £250 in 1850 and £300 in the 1870s.[7] The Ecclesiastical Commissioners made grants towards a new parsonage house in 1868 and 1880, and a further small augmentation in 1907.[8]

Church Life

In the 13th century the parishioners were responsible for repairing the south nave aisle of the abbey, which served as the parish church.[9] By then a chaplain assisted the vicar at St. Oswald's altar four days a week.[10] Shortly after 1348 the monks removed the congregation to the chapel of St. Nicholas in the south-west corner of the abbey precinct, where the parish continued to worship until 1539, when it moved back to the abbey and the chapel was leased to the city.[11]

While occupying St. Nicholas's chapel, the church contained an altar to St. Leonard in 1397,[12] and attracted chantry endowments in 1408 and 1528.[13] In 1541, shortly after the parishioners returned to St. Werburgh's, there were five stipendiary priests, including one maintained by a warden of the fraternity of St. Anne,[14] but the church's possessions were valued at only £4 3s. 2d. in 1553. The parishioners' part of the cathedral was in disrepair in 1557, and by 1559 the parish was encumbered with a non-resident vicar and a negligent curate.[15] Conditions seem to have improved little by 1578,[16] and the problem of the churchyard, long a subject of complaint, was resolved only when it was paved in 1593 and enclosed and levelled in 1619.[17]

Despite its poverty and neglect St. Oswald's was the most 'eminent and spacious' church in Chester, because from 1539 it was sited in the south transept of the cathedral. The mayor and corporation regularly attended services, notably on Sunday afternoons, when they heard a sermon by one of the city preachers.[18] The church contained a joint seat for the mayor and bishop and there was much competition for the other pews, especially in the early 17th century. In 1624 the vestry appointed seating commissioners, mainly to secure better seats for the richer parishioners.[19] The ensuing rearrangement resulted in a bitter dispute between Bishop Bridgeman and the corporation. When the bishop returned to Chester in 1626 after two years' absence he found that the parishioners had allotted

1 *Mins. of Cttee. for Relief of Plundered Ministers, and of Trustees for Maintenance of Ministers, 1643–54* (R.S.L.C. xxviii), 208–9.

2 Gastrell, *Not. Cest.* i. 112 n.

3 C.C.A.L.S., EDV 7/1/8.

4 Gastrell, *Not. Cest.* i. 111.

5 C.C.A.L.S., DBE 30, f. 84.

6 Ibid. P 29/7/5; Hemingway, *Hist. Chester*, ii. 67.

7 *Bagshaw's Dir. Ches.* (1850), 64; *White's Dir. Ches.* (1864), 7.

8 C.C.A.L.S., P 29/18/1, 4, 9–10.

9 *Cart. Chester Abbey*, i, p. 117.

10 Ibid. i, p. 118.

11 *Cal. Papal Pets.* i. 82, 91, 134–5; *V.C.H. Ches.* iii. 138; 3 *Sheaf*, xxi, p. 52; xxx, p. 2; B.L. Harl. MS. 2063, f. 134; Burne, *Monks*, 91, 139.

12 3 *Sheaf*, xxxvi, p. 9.   13 Ibid. p. 54.

14 *List of Clergy, 1541–2*, 1.

15 Morris, *Chester*, 151, 153; 3 *Sheaf*, i, p. 32; P.R.O., SP 12/10, pp. 318–19.

16 York, Borthwick Inst., V.1578–9/CB.3, f. 18v.

17 3 *Sheaf*, v, pp. 9–10, 13–15; C.C.A.L.S., P 29/7/1, f. 12v.; P 29/7/2, p. 282.

18 Bridgeman, *Hist. Wigan*, ii. 297, 299.

19 1 *Sheaf*, i, pp. 47–8; 3 *Sheaf*, iv, pp. 75–6, 78–9; C.C.A.L.S., EDA 3/1, f. 220 and v.; P 29/7/2, p. 306.

unsatisfactory seating to the cathedral dignitaries and choir and had positioned the pulpit and the pew which he and the mayor shared in such a way that the mayor 'sat in the midst . . . and he [the bishop] was shouldered to the end'. In retaliation Bridgeman ordered the sermon to be preached not in St. Oswald's but in the cathedral choir, so incensing the corporation that they refused to attend services there and did not return until 1638.[1]

During the dispute St. Oswald's seems to have suffered further neglect. In 1633 the church was thought 'very indecent and unseemly', the fittings were in need of repair, and there had been no communion in the previous six months. Many parishioners attended other churches, and the vicar, a prebendary of the cathedral, neglected preaching, catechizing, and weekday prayers. Improvements were ordered to the paving and pews, the communion table was to be placed against the east wall, and altar rails were to be provided.[2]

During the Interregnum the ministers of St. Oswald's, then also known as Werburgh church, included the noted Presbyterian John Glendal (1642–*c.* 1648), and Henry Massey, who signed the Cheshire attestation in 1648. Immediately after the Restoration the Independent Thomas Harrison came there from Ireland.[3] He was ejected in 1662, and under his successor, another cathedral prebendary,[4] the lack of a font, surplice, royal arms, books, and other necessities was made good by 1664.[5] The dean and chapter appear to have maintained firm control of the church after 1662, and in the 1690s it was still repaired by them and said to be used by the parishioners only at their pleasure.[6] In 1708, however, they allowed the parishioners to erect a gallery at their own expense.[7]

By 1778 the church's inadequate accommodation forced many parishioners to worship in the cathedral choir or other city churches. The vicar was resident, and a curate was paid to officiate at Bruera. In St. Oswald's itself there was only a Sunday afternoon service, since parishioners were expected to attend morning service in the cathedral choir; prayers were read every Thursday. The sacrament was administered four times a year to between 100 and 150 people. The church's situation within the cathedral led the vicar to

complain that services were disturbed by people walking and conversing and by children playing in the nave and aisles.[8] In the late 18th and early 19th century the vicar, though resident, employed curates to serve both the church and Bruera chapel.[9] Communicants appear to have declined to *c.* 60 in 1804.[10] The single afternoon service still held in 1825 had been replaced by 1849 with matins and evensong, and in the 1850s an evening lecture was introduced.[11]

In 1868 the growing population of the parish led to the decision to build a chapel of ease, and land was obtained in Parkgate Road. The new chapel, dedicated to St. Thomas of Canterbury, was consecrated in 1872; services there included holy communion at least once a month on Sundays and on saints' days, as well as morning and evening prayer.[12] In 1880 the parishioners finally responded to the suggestion of the dean and chapter, first made in 1868, and agreed to surrender their rights in the cathedral and make St. Thomas's the parish church.[13] In the same year a new vicarage house next to St. Thomas's was begun.[14]

St. Thomas's opened as the parish church in 1881 with between 190 and 250 communicants. Services then included a weekly communion, held in the early morning or at midday. An experiment with a choral communion in 1889 did not meet with universal approval, and Sunday services remained unchanged for another twenty years.[15] More successful was the establishment in 1895 of the mission church of the Good Shepherd on South View Road in the western part of the parish. A curate was required for services there, and in the early 20th century the vicar generally had two curates.[16] In the early 1910s the congregation at the mission church usually numbered 50–80, ten or twenty of whom were communicants, but services were cut back in 1918 and discontinued in 1919. The building seems not to have been used regularly thereafter.[17]

H. E. Burder (vicar 1909–48) introduced Anglo-Catholic services at St. Thomas's, with a daily mass and a sung celebration on Sundays,[18] a tradition which continued under his successors.[19] From 1951 to 1967 the vicars of St. Oswald's had charge of Little St. John's, and in the mid 1960s the mission church of the Good Shepherd was finally closed.[20]

1 3 *Sheaf,* iv, pp. 85–6; Burne, *Chester Cath.* 104–5; *Cal. Chester City Cl. Mins. 1603–42,* pp. xxii–xxiii; Bridgeman, *Hist. Wigan,* ii. 295–305.

2 York, Borthwick Inst., V.1633/CB.2, ff. 436, 439v.–440; B.L. Harl. MS. 2103, f. 81; 1 *Sheaf,* i, pp. 47–8.

3 *Calamy Revised,* ed. A. G. Matthews, 224–5, 250–1; *D.N.B.*

4 Burne, *Chester Cath.* 131; *Walker Revised,* ed. A. G. Matthews, 98; C.C.A.L.S., ZML 3, no. 390.

5 C.C.A.L.S., EDC 5/1664/67.

6 Ibid. EDC 5/1695/4.

7 Ibid. P 29/7/4; EDA 2/4, pp. 114–15; 1 *Sheaf,* i, pp. 260–1.

8 C.C.A.L.S., EDV 7/1/8.

9 Ibid. EDV 7/2/6; EDV 7/6/125; EDV 7/7/118; DBE 30, f. 84.

10 Ibid. EDV 7/2/6; EDV 7/3/110.

11 Ibid. P 29/6/2; EDV 7/7/118.

12 Ibid. P 29/6/3; P 29/7/7; P 29/17/1.

13 Ibid. P 29/7/7.

14 Ibid. P 29/6/3.

15 Ibid. P 29/20/1–2.

16 Ibid. EDA 2/29, p. 393; P 29/7/7.

17 Ibid. P 29/3521/8; *P. & G. Dir. Chester* (1905/6), 34, 111; no entry in (1927/8), 53–6 or 171.

18 *Kelly's Dir. Ches.* (1914), 223, 232; *P. & G. Dir. Chester* (1935/6), 52.

19 C.C.A.L.S., P 29/20/7, 10.

20 *Chester Dioc. Cal.* (1951, 1965–7).

Buildings

Until the 14th century the church of St. Oswald was within the abbey, probably in the south nave aisle, for the maintenance of which the parishioners had special responsibilities.[1] About 1348 it was transferred to the new chapel of St. Nicholas within the abbey precinct.[2] That chapel was greatly extended in 1488, when a 'new church' of St. Oswald was added to its east end, largely at the expense of the abbey but with a significant contribution from the parishioners.[3]

In 1539 the parish returned to St. Werburgh's, presumably from the first being housed in the south transept, where it remained until 1881.[4] Its condition after the dissolution of the abbey was unsatisfactory,[5] and in 1624 the interior was refurbished.[6] Further repairs were undertaken *c.* 1703,[7] and more thoroughly in 1826 by the architect William Cole junior, whose fittings, with Gothic mouldings, included seats for the cathedral clergy, a bishop's throne, and a three-decker pulpit. In 1828 a new screen rising to roof level was added.[8] Those fittings were removed in 1876.[9]

The church of St. Thomas of Canterbury as built between 1869 and 1872 by George Gilbert Scott had a chancel with a south aisle and an aisled nave of three bays, all in an Early English style.[10] On becoming the parish church in 1881, it was enlarged to the designs of J. O. Scott with the addition of two bays to the nave, a north porch, and a tower which was never completed.[11] The red-brick vicarage of 1880 is by John Douglas.[12]

FIG. 89. *St. Oswald's church, doorway in cathedral south transept, 1876*

ST. PETER

A late tradition tells that St. Peter's was founded by King Alfred's daughter Æthelflæd and her husband Æthelred of Mercia, who transferred the dedication when they re-established as St. Werburgh's the minster formerly dedicated to St. Peter and St. Paul.[13] Soon after the Norman Conquest the church was given to Robert of Rhuddlan, who in 1086 unsuccessfully claimed that it stood on thegnland dependent on an extramural manor and was exempt from borough dues.[14]

The parish, always entirely intramural, had complex boundaries, possibly reflecting the holdings of an early burgess.[15] It was enlarged in the 1880s and 1960, and in

1972 was merged in the new parish of Chester, to which St. Peter's then served as a chapel of ease.[16] The church had no early burial rights and seems to have acquired a small churchyard only in the later Middle Ages.[17]

By 1081 Robert of Rhuddlan had granted the church to the Norman abbey of Saint-Evroul (Orne), a gift confirmed in the 1120s by Earl Ranulph I and King Henry I. Later in the 12th century the abbey transferred it to St. Werburgh's, whose position was consolidated when Simon fitz Osbern of Pulford (Ches.) and South Ormsby (Lincs.) and the rector, Alexander, also surrendered their interests.[18]

1 Above (Church Life).

2 Burne, *Monks*, 91; 3 *Sheaf*, xxxvi, p. 9.

3 3 *Sheaf*, iv, pp. 127–8; lv, pp. 32–3; B.L. Harl. MS. 2103, f. 25; Harl. MS. 2159, f. 112; Burne, *Monks*, 136; Morris, *Chester*, 134–5.

4 Burne, *Monks*, 139; *V.C.H. Ches.* iii. 138.

5 3 *Sheaf*, i, pp. 2, 32.

6 Ibid. iv, p. 110; C.C.A.L.S., P 29/7/1, f. 40.

7 Burne, *Chester Cath.* 164, 168–70; 1 *Sheaf*, i, pp. 197–8; *Diary of Henry Prescott*, i. 2.

8 C.C.A.L.S., EDP 76/6; Hemingway, *Hist. Chester*, ii. 66; H. Colvin, *Biographical Dictionary of Brit. Architects* (1978), 229.

9 Burne, *Chester Cath.* 258; C.C.A.L.S., P 29/7/7.

10 Pevsner, *Ches.* 171; C.C.A.L.S., P 29/17/1.

11 C.C.A.L.S., P 29/17/3–4.

12 E. Hubbard, *Work of John Douglas*, 250; Pevsner, *Ches.* 171.

13 H. Bradshaw, *Life of St. Werburge of Chester* (E.E.T.S. orig. ser. lxxxviii), 152.

14 *V.C.H. Ches.* i. 343 (no. 1e); *Domesday Surv. Ches.* 29–30, 85. 15 *J.C.A.S.* lxiv. 16–17.

16 Above, Local Government Boundaries: Parish Boundaries; *Lond. Gaz.* 30 June 1972, p. 7865.

17 Above, Collegiate Church of St. John; 3 *Sheaf*, xxxix, p. 111.

18 *Cart. Chester Abbey*, i, p. 83; ii, pp. 288–90.

Advowson, Income, and Property

St. Peter's was never appropriated, and until the 17th century the incumbent seems always to have been styled rector.[1] In 1627 there were appointments not only to the rectory but also to a vicarage.[2] After the Restoration incumbents were styled rector or vicar until 1701, when they became known as curates. The title of rector was reintroduced in 1837 and was retained until 1972.[3]

The advowson was kept by St. Werburgh's until the Dissolution, when it passed to the dean and chapter of Chester. By 1593 it was held by the Crown, which continued to present until 1624 and perhaps until 1627. After the Restoration the bishop of Chester became patron.[4]

From the 12th century St. Peter's paid an annual pension, never exceeding £3, to Chester abbey.[5] The benefice seems always to have been poor. In the 1530s it was valued at only £6 13s. 4d., and between 1628 and 1643 the parishioners paid their minister a yearly stipend of £26 13s. 4d.[6] During the Interregnum the benefice, which had no fixed income, was augmented with £150 a year from the revenues of the dean and chapter.[7] After that was taken away at the Restoration there was again no endowment,[8] and in the 1720s the income was only £12 18s. 4d., £10 of which came from surplice fees.[9] In 1760 and 1765 the living received grants from Queen Anne's Bounty,[10] and the income eventually rose to £120 in 1834.[11] Pew rents provided about half the total throughout the 19th century.[12]

A building known as the rectory house stood over the south door of the church by 1555. It was rebuilt in 1584, and demolished with the Pentice in 1803, though it had ceased to be occupied by the incumbent before the 1690s, when it was used to house the city records.[13] A new parsonage house was provided only after 1873.[14]

Church Life

In the 15th century the fraternity of St. George had a chapel in St. Peter's, probably in the south aisle, served by two or three chaplains. At its dissolution it possessed property in Chester worth *c.* £12 a year.[15]

Although in the late Middle Ages incumbents included two who were wealthy and apparently resident, Jordan of Marthall (1320–*c.* 1346) and Robert of Bredon (1350–77), St. Peter's seems generally to have been in the care of a parochial chaplain.[16] The church enjoyed close relations with the city authorities by the 13th century, when the Pentice was first built against its south wall.[17] The Assembly, which maintained the church clock from the 1460s or earlier,[18] established a trust fund for repairs in 1574,[19] and rebuilt the porch chamber in 1584.[20] By the early 17th century the city officers attended divine service alternately at St. Peter's and St. Oswald's, but a pew erected for them in St. Peter's in 1611 was pulled down on the orders of Bishop Lloyd, then in dispute with the corporation. A new pew was provided in 1612 and the mayor still worshipped there in 1627.[21]

In the 16th century St. Peter's appears to have been served by a curate paid by the rector. In 1541–2 the other clergy included two chaplains of St. George's fraternity and another paid by a city official.[22] The absentee rectors between the 1550s and the Civil War provided curates who by the 1590s were unlicensed and generally unsatisfactory.[23] In 1628 the parishioners engaged their own curate, John Glendal, to read the service and preach once every Sunday.[24] Glendal, a puritan, remained at St. Peter's until 1642 when he transferred to St. Oswald's. By 1648 he was again at St. Peter's, where he remained until ejected in 1662.[25]

The puritanism of St. Peter's was reinforced by its association with the city preachers, established in the reign of Elizabeth I to deliver sermons on Wednesdays

1   *Valor Eccl.* v. 207; C.C.A.L.S., ZMR 5, m. 4; ZMB 7, f. 16; ibid. EDV 1/15, f. 8; Ormerod, *Hist. Ches.* i. 326–7.

2   Gastrell, *Not. Cest.* i. 120; C.C.A.L.S., P 63/7/1, f. 6v.

3   C.C.A.L.S., EDV 2/7–9; *Cal. S.P. Dom.* 1682, 407; Jan.–June 1683, 11; F. Simpson, *Hist. of Church of St. Peter, Chester*, 6.

4   Gastrell, *Not. Cest.* i. 118–20; Ormerod, *Hist. Ches.* i. 326–7.

5   *Cart. Chester Abbey*, i, pp. 252–3.

6   *Valor Eccl.* v. 207; C.C.A.L.S., P 63/7/1, ff. 6v., 18, 108.

7   *Mins. of Cttee. for Relief of Plundered Ministers, and of Trustees for Maintenance of Ministers, 1643–54* (R.S.L.C. xxviii), 208, 216; C.C.A.L.S., ZAB 2, f. 78; ibid. P 63/7/1, f. 160; *Cal. S.P. Dom.* 1657–8, 241.

8   *Cal. S.P. Dom.* 1682, 407.

9   Gastrell, *Not. Cest.* i. 118.

10   C.C.A.L.S., EDV 7/1/10; C. Hodgson, *Queen Anne's Bounty* (2nd edn. 1845), p. ccl.

11   Simpson, *Hist. St. Peter's*, 6; Gastrell, *Not. Cest.* i. 118; Hodgson, *Queen Anne's Bounty*, p. ccl.

12   C.C.A.L.S., P 63/7/10, p. 175.

13   Ibid. EDV 7/2/8; ibid. ZAB 3, ff. 23v., 24v.; 3 *Sheaf,* xix, p. 93; above, Municipal Buildings: Pentice.

14   Simpson, *Hist. St. Peter's*, 12; C.C.A.L.S., P 63/7/10, p. 246.

15   *V.C.H. Ches.* v (1), Later Medieval Chester: Religion (Guilds, Confraternities, and Chantries).

16   e.g. C.C.A.L.S., ZMB 5, f. 104v.; Jones, *Ch. in Chester*, 14, 166–7; B.L. Add. Ch. 50141.

17   Above, Municipal Buildings: Pentice.

18   Jones, *Ch. in Chester*, 115; C.C.A.L.S., ZAB 1, f. 197v.; ZMB 28, ff. 71v., 123; Morris, *Chester*, 170.

19   C.C.A.L.S., ZCHB 3, f. 25 and v.; 4 *Sheaf,* vi, p. 29.

20   C.C.A.L.S., ZAB 1, f. 194v.

21   Ibid. P 63/7/1; *Cal. Chester City Cl. Mins. 1603–42*, pp. xxii, 52, 55; 3 *Sheaf,* xxiii, p. 72; xxvi, pp. 85–6; *V.C.H. Ches.* iii. 28.

22   *List of Clergy, 1541–2*, 1.

23   e.g. P.R.O., SP 12/10, p. 319; *J.C.A.S.* n.s. v. 411; C.C.A.L.S., EDV 1/14, f. 14v.; EDV 1/15, ff. 8–9v.; 3 *Sheaf,* i, pp. 68–9.

24   C.C.A.L.S., P 63/7/1, ff. 6v., 18.

25   Ibid. P 63/7/1; EDV 1/29, f. 2; EDB 61; *Calamy Revised*, ed. A. G. Matthews, 224–5; *V.C.H. Ches.* iii. 102.

and Fridays and partly paid by the corporation.[1] In the earlier 17th century they included such notable puritans as Nicholas Byfield (1608–15) and John Ley (1630–3 or later).[2] By the 1640s two preachers were appointed by the corporation to lecture in St. Peter's on Fridays and Sunday afternoons.[3]

St. Peter's was poorly provided with books and ornaments, and in 1553 its possessions were valued at 24s.[4] In 1605 it lacked even books of homilies and a new prayer book.[5] Improvements effected under Bishop Bridgeman included the repair of the pulpit in 1629, and the provision in 1639–40 of a new surplice, altar cloth, and liturgical books.[6] The church furniture, reordered at the rebuilding of 1637–40,[7] suffered in the bombardment of 1645.[8] The insalubrious churchyard, abutted by three alehouses, was paved only in 1657–8.[9]

A 'dish for baptizings' was in use by 1648 and the old font was destroyed in 1656,[10] the church retaining its puritan tradition until Glendal's ejection in 1662. With the coming of a new minister, William Thompson, in 1663 the church was furnished with a prayer book, altar rails, and surplice,[11] changes opposed by some parishioners, who were accused of disrupting a funeral service conducted in accordance with Anglican rites.[12] Thompson, a prebendary of Chester cathedral from 1675, remained rector of St. Peter's until his death in 1693.[13] A strong royalist and an active persecutor of Dissenters, he aroused much local hostility.[14] After 1683, when he received an additional living, he employed a curate at the church.[15]

St. Peter's retained its importance among the city churches in the later 17th century: it was the location of a monthly lecture for the reformation of manners established by Bishop Stratford and Dean Fogge in 1689,[16] and the corporation retained seats there, rebuilt in 1701. By the 1720s the newly refurbished church contained seating for all the city officers and prayers were said daily.[17] Communion was celebrated monthly and on the three great feasts, communicants numbering between 50 and 150. Residence among incumbents

varied. Some, such as Rigby Baldwin (1776–94) and John Halton (1815–36), lived in Chester and performed their duties in person; others, such as John Baldwin (1794–1815), resided on their other livings and employed curates.[18]

In 1817 a Sunday evening lecture was instituted, financed and run by a committee and popular enough by 1819 to require improvements to the accommodation in church. The lectures continued until 1852 when they were ended at the petition of the parishioners.[19] By 1803 payments were made to singers, and throughout the 19th century services appear to have had some musical accompaniment. In the 1820s and early 1830s the church had a paid organist and choir, but thereafter the organist alone was retained.[20]

By the earlier 19th century St. Peter's had developed a firmly protestant tradition, strongest perhaps under Charles Tayler (1836–46), appointed by the Evangelical Bishop Sumner and a prolific author with a strong bias against Roman Catholicism.[21] In the 1870s holy communion was celebrated only twice a month,[22] a pattern of worship which remained much the same until the 1920s.[23] In 1909 a worshipper protested at the performance of Stainer's *Crucifixion* in the church, and prompted the rector, Alfred Waller, publicly to declare his Low Church convictions.[24]

St. Peter's distinctive tradition helped to maintain congregations until after 1918 even as the population of the parish declined, by attracting worshippers from a wider area,[25] but from the 1920s financial problems led to a succession of brief incumbencies and the Low Church tradition was diluted. From 1959 to 1972 the benefice was held in plurality with that of St. Michael's with St. Olave's. In the 1990s, as part of the united parish of Chester, the church was in use as an ecumenical Christian centre and the base for the Anglican chaplaincy to Chester businesses.[26]

Building

The church of St. Peter, which is built of red sandstone, is almost square, with four aisles, the south-centre one

1 C.C.A.L.S., ZAB 1, ff. 246, 262v., 279, 300; *Cal. Chester City Cl. Mins. 1603–42*, pp. xxiii, 31 n.; W. Hinde, *Exemplary Life of Mr. John Bruen* (1641), 135; 3 *Sheaf*, viii, p. 5; I. E. Ewen, 'Short Hist. of St. Peter's Parish', *J.C.A.S.* [o.s.], iii. 383.

2 *D.N.B.* s.n. Ley; Hinde, *Life of Bruen*, 135; C.C.A.L.S., ZML 2, nos. 273–4; *V.C.H. Ches.* iii. 27; *Cal. Chester City Cl. Mins. 1603–42*, 160.

3 C.C.A.L.S., ZAB 2, ff. 60, 66, 67v., 84v., 124.

4 Morris, *Chester*, 151, 153.

5 C.C.A.L.S., EDV 1/14, f. 14v.; EDV 1/15, ff. 8–9v.; EDV 1/17, f. 40v.

6 Ibid. P 63/7/1, ff. 95v., 99; *T.L.C.A.S.* liii. 104, 111.

7 C.C.A.L.S., P 63/7/1, f. 96v.

8 Morris, *Siege of Chester*, 204.

9 C.C.A.L.S., EDV 1/14, f. 14v.; 3 *Sheaf*, xxxix, pp. 111–15.

10 C.C.A.L.S., P 63/7/1, ff. 133, 135v.

11 Ibid. ff. 164v., 167v.; EDV 1/34; York, Borthwick Inst., V.1662–3/CB.2, f. 1; *T.L.C.A.S.* liii. 104.

12 C.C.A.L.S., EDC 5/1663/26.

13 Burne, *Chester Cath.* 142–3.

14 *V.C.H. Ches.* v (1), Early Modern Chester: Religion, 1662–1762.

15 C.C.A.L.S., EDV 2/7–10; P 63/7/1, f. 204v.

16 *V.C.H. Ches.* iii. 46; *J.C.A.S.* [o.s.], iii. 375.

17 C.C.A.L.S., EDC 5/1668/18; EDC 5/1668/22; ibid. ZAB 3, ff. 94, 115; 3 *Sheaf*, xxxvi, p. 63; xlviii, p. 23.

18 C.C.A.L.S., EDV 7/1/10; EDV 7/2/8; EDV 7/3/111; EDV 7/4/187.

19 Ibid. P 63/7/8; P 63/7/10, pp. 26–8; Simpson, *Hist. St. Peter's*, 59–61.

20 C.C.A.L.S., P 63/7/8.

21 *D.N.B.*; Simpson, *Hist. St. Peter's*, 78.

22 *P. & G. Dir. Chester* (1878/9), 24.

23 Ibid. (1921/2), 50.

24 C.C.A.L.S., P 63/7/10, p. 420.

25 Ibid. pp. 385–6, 497.

26 Ibid. P 63/7/10, *passim*; *Chester Dioc. Year Bk. 1996/7*, pp. 42, 46; *1999/2000*, pp. 44, 47.

forming a nave of two bays and ending in a west tower; the unusual plan developed from the exigencies of the site, which allowed expansion only to the north. The church is built over part of the remains of the Roman headquarters building, from which some stones may survive in the western footings, and presumably for that reason has a south entrance at Row rather than street level.[1] From the 13th to the 19th century it was abutted to the south by various structures, including shops at ground level and the Pentice on the first storey.[2] The earliest surviving parts of the building are the 14th-century tower and the arcades, which like the rest of the building have been much reconstructed. In 1415 £10 was given to the fabric from the sale of lands bequeathed by Robert of Bredon's heir,[3] and in 1488–90 the steeple was repaired.[4] In the 1530s the church was almost doubled in size by the addition of the two northern aisles on land given *c.* 1528 by Fulk Dutton (mayor 1537–8). Dutton also gave £23 and the materials of the house demolished to make way for the extension, and paid for a large window containing the arms of himself and his wife.[5] The work, to which further bequests were made in 1535–6, was probably completed in 1539.[6]

In the later 16th century repairs were made by the city authorities, and in 1579–80 over 50 ft. of the spire was rebuilt.[7] Between 1637 and 1640 further major rebuilding took place. The east end and the south side were reconstructed, the aisles were flagged, and work was done on the roof and battlements. It was then too that galleries, the first in Chester, were introduced; by 1651 there was a gallery under the clock loft, a 'long gallery', and two others.[8]

In 1669 the spire was again rebuilt, at the parishioners' expense.[9] With the aid of a brief, further repairs were made to the south side and east end between 1713 and 1717, when new fittings were also installed.[10] The spire was taken down in 1780 after being struck by

FIG. 90. *St. Peter's from south, before 1669*

lightning,[11] and in 1803 the south side of the church was rebuilt after the removal of the Pentice.[12]

A north gallery inserted in 1769 was enlarged during restoration in 1848–9, when a south gallery was added at private expense.[13] Plans by the vestry to demolish the church were rejected by the corporation in 1879,[14] and in 1886 a thoroughgoing restoration was effected, during which new tracery was inserted in the windows of the south aisle, the west gallery was removed, and new fittings were provided.[15] Further restoration work was carried out in 1909 and 1957.[16]

MEDIEVAL CHAPELS

LITTLE ST. JOHN

The hospital of St. John without the Northgate, founded in the 1190s, had both a church and a chapel, where masses were said daily for the hospital's benefactors and services were conducted for the inmates and visitors. The church was perhaps a free-standing building, the chapel a room within the residential part of the hospital where services could be held for the infirm. Although the proper establish-

---

1 *J.C.A.S.* xxxviii. 2, 9–15.
2 Above, Municipal Buildings: Pentice.
3 B.L. Add. Ch. 50212.
4 3 *Sheaf*, viii, p. 79; xxix, p. 73; *King's Vale Royal*, [i], 76.
5 C.C.A.L.S., EDC 5/1616/1; below, Lists of Mayors and Sheriffs.
6 3 *Sheaf*, xviii, pp. 87, 99; xxi, p. 109; *T.L.C.A.S.* lvii. 73, 77, 99.
7 Morris, *Chester*, 170; 3 *Sheaf*, xxx, p. 30; C.C.A.L.S., ZAB 1, f. 194v.; *T.L.C.A.S.* lvii. 102.
8 C.C.A.L.S., P 63/7/1; Gastrell, *Not. Cest.* i. 120.

9 C.C.A.L.S., P 63/7/1.
10 Ibid. ZAB 3, f. 212; ZQSF 91; 3 *Sheaf*, xxxi, p. 65; xlviii, p. 23.
11 *J.C.A.S.* [o.s.], iii. 375; *T.L.C.A.S.* lvii. 114; 3 *Sheaf*, xxxi, p. 65.
12 C.C.A.L.S., ZAB 5, ff. 102v.–103; *J.C.A.S.* [o.s.], iii. 376.
13 C.C.A.L.S., EDA 2/7, ff. 83–4; P 63/7/10, pp. 209–10, 244–6, 250–1; *Chester Dir.* (1840), 81.
14 C.C.A.L.S., P 63/7/10, pp. 5–6.
15 Ibid. EDA 2/28, pp. 301–3; EDP 78/3.
16 Ibid. EDA 2/29, p. 830; EDP 78/3.

ment was three chaplains, by the 1520s there was evidently only one. The hospital survived the Dissolution and in the later 16th and earlier 17th century its masters continued to appoint a chaplain, salaried at £5 a year, to say daily prayers in the chapel for the almspeople and others,[1] including debtors imprisoned in the nearby city gaol.[2]

The chapel was destroyed with the hospital's other buildings during the siege of Chester in 1644 but evidently rebuilt while Col. Roger Whitley was governor of the hospital between 1660 and 1697.[3] The corporation of Chester took over the wardenship in 1703,[4] and promptly refurnished the interior of the chapel to include seating for the mayor and aldermen and stands for the civic regalia, appointing as chaplain the minister of St. Peter's.[5] Although the chapel was taken down and rebuilt at corporation expense as the south wing of the Blue Coat building in 1715–17,[6] its administrative arrangements were unaltered and in 1717 the Assembly specifically ordered that divine service was to be held in the new chapel as it had been in the old.[7]

The living came to be regarded as a perpetual curacy serving the tiny extra-parochial district of the former hospital precinct,[8] whose inhabitants comprised the almswomen of the hospital, the master and boys of the Blue Coat school, and until 1808 prisoners in the Northgate gaol. The corporation retained the patronage until compelled to give it up by the Municipal Corporations Act of 1835.[9] The living did not fall vacant again until 1864, when Bishop Graham, exercising the patronage for a turn, presented his son and namesake John. The next presentation, in 1873, was by the trustees of the St. John's Hospital charity, and the next after that, in 1881, by two private individuals who had acquired a turn. A Charity Commission Scheme of 1892 vested the advowson in the Chester Municipal Charities Trustees.[10]

The Assembly paid its appointee a salary which it increased from £6 13s. 4d. to £10 a year in 1717,[11] to £30 in 1820,[12] and perhaps to £50 by 1835.[13] Queen Anne's Bounty augmented it between 1802 and 1821 with capital sums totalling £1,800 and producing £90 a year,[14] and there were also pew rents. In 1825 the latter were said to amount to £50 a year, suggesting that under William Fish (perpetual curate 1803–28) the chapel was a fashionable place of worship,[15] and even at the reduced figure implied in 1835 the total income of £130 a year was larger than that of five or six of the city's parish churches.[16] Pew rents were abolished by an Order of Chancery, probably in 1852, after which all sittings not reserved for the almswomen and schoolboys were free to the poor.[17] The income from the living nevertheless grew steadily to £289 in the later 19th century.[18]

There was competition for what was virtually a sinecure even in the 18th century, when the income was distinctly modest.[19] In 1828 the position was 'closely contested' between the assistant appointed by Fish and a son of the city's recorder, the former proving successful.[20] In 1778 the services held by an incumbent who had been in post for the previous 20 years were confined to prayers on Wednesdays and Fridays, communion twice a year, and a grand service and sermon each year on the Sunday before a new mayor was elected. There was no regular Sunday service, and no baptisms, marriages, or burials.[21] In the later 19th and earlier 20th century regular Sunday services were held.[22] The clergy holding the living in the 19th and earlier 20th centuries also acted as chaplains at the new gaol or the Blue Coat or King's schools, or, in the case of John Graham, as diocesan registrar.[23] From 1951 the living was held in plurality with that of St. Oswald's, and the two benefices were united in 1967.[24] Services were discontinued in 1969.[25]

The building of 1715–17 is described elsewhere.[26]

---

1 *V.C.H. Ches.* iii. 180–2.

2 C.C.A.L.S., ZAB 1, f. 71.

3 *V.C.H. Ches.* iii. 182; below, Sites and Remains of Medieval Religious Houses: Hospital of St. John.

4 Above, Charities for the Poor: Municipal Charities (Almshouses: St. John's Hospital).

5 C.C.A.L.S., ZAB 3, ff. 115, 179v.

6 Below, Sites and Remains of Medieval Religious Houses: Hospital of St. John.

7 C.C.A.L.S., ZAB 3, f. 236.

8 e.g. S. Lewis, *Topographical Dictionary of Eng.* (1831 edn.), i. 401; *Bagshaw's Dir. Ches.* (1850), 63.

9 C.C.A.L.S., ZAB 3, ff. 185, 221; ZAB 4, ff. 30, 118v., 342v.; ZAB 5, pp. 5, 8, 173–4, 186, 194–5, 201; *Rep. Com. Mun. Corp.* p. 2631; Lewis, *Topographical Dictionary* (1848 edn.), i. 580.

10 C.C.A.L.S., EDP 71/1; *Alum. Cantab. 1752–1900*, iii. 109.

11 C.C.A.L.S., ZAB 3, f. 241; cf. ZAB 5, pp. 173–4.

12 Ibid. ZAB 5, pp. 385–6; C. Hodgson, *Queen Anne's Bounty* (2nd edn. 1845), p. cxcvii.

13 *Rep. Com. Mun. Corp.* p. 2631; but cf. *Chester City Cl. Abstract of Accts. 1854/5* (£30).

14 Hodgson, *Queen Anne's Bounty*, p. ccl.

15 C.C.A.L.S., EDP 71/1.

16 *Rep. Com. Mun. Corp.* p. 2631; above, Medieval Parish Churches.

17 J. Romney, *Chester and its Environs Illustrated* (Chester, [1853]), [45].

18 *Clergy List* (1842), 42 bis; (1859), 48 bis; (1866), 51 bis; (1881), 55 bis.

19 e.g. C.C.A.L.S., ZAB 4, f. 30.

20 Ibid. EDP 71/1; *Rep. Com. Mun. Corp.* p. 2631; for identification of the latter as Thos. Tyrwhitt: *Alum. Oxon. 1715–1886*, iv. 1457; Foster, *Baronetage* (1882), 622–3.

21 C.C.A.L.S., EDV 7/1/3.

22 Details in *P. & G. Dir. Chester* (1870), 21; (1905/6), 34; (1929/30), 56.

23 *Clergy List* (1842), 41; (1866), 138; (1881), 144; *Alum. Cantab. 1752–1900*, i. 28 (E. P. Alexander); *Crockford* (1935), 1293 (T. C. W. C. Teape-Fugard).

24 Above, Medieval Parish Churches: St. Oswald.

25 C.C.A.L.S., P 103 (TS. list).

26 Below, Sites and Remains of Medieval Religious Houses: Hospital of St. John.

ST. ANNE

The fraternity of St. Anne built a separate chapel within the precinct of St. John's church, probably when the guild was refounded in 1393. It stood until the Civil War siege.[1]

ST. CHAD

St. Chad's existed by *c.* 1250.[2] It lay in the area in the north-west of the city known as the Crofts and its status is uncertain but may once have been parochial.[3] By 1318 St. John's had appropriated it.[4] The church was mentioned in the late 14th century and *c.* 1500, but had probably disappeared by the 1530s.[5] Certainly no curate was associated with it in the 1540s.[6] By the early 17th century the exact site of the church had been forgotten.[7]

ST. JAMES (HANDBRIDGE)

Soon before 1358 John Spicer built a hermitage for himself within a walled enclosure at the south end of the Dee Bridge in Handbridge, between the river and the quarry east of the bridge.[8] In 1367 he was licensed to have an oratory there.[9] Spicer's establishment was presumably the hermitage and chapel of St. James in Handbridge whose occupants were a recurring source of anxiety to the authorities in the 1450s.[10] St. James's chapel yard survived in 1560, when it was termed a 'vacant place',[11] suggesting that the buildings had already been demolished.

ST. JAMES (IN ST. JOHN'S PRECINCT)

A chapel dedicated to St. James and long associated with an anchorite stood in the precinct of St. John's by the later 12th century. Disused for ecclesiastical purposes by 1589, it was probably demolished during the siege of Chester.[12]

ST. MARY (HANDBRIDGE)

A building in Kettle's Croft, Handbridge, west of the Dee Bridge and ruinous by the late 16th century, is supposed in antiquarian tradition to have been a chapel dedicated to St. Mary and belonging to the nuns of Chester.[13] No reference to such a chapel before the Reformation has been found.

ST. MARY (IN ST. JOHN'S PRECINCT)

A chapel of St. Mary, also called the White chapel, within the precinct of St. John's was in use as a grammar school in 1353. It was perhaps the same building as the 'basilica' or 'minster' of St. Mary recorded between 1086 and *c.* 1200. Although not recorded under its dedication after 1368 it may have been identical with the Calvercroft chapel in St. John's, also dedicated to St. Mary and in existence by the early 16th century. That chapel, which probably stood in the churchyard, survived the dissolution of the college of St. John's and was presumably destroyed in the 1640s.[14]

ST. NICHOLAS (IN THE ABBEY)

A chapel dedicated to St. Nicholas was built in the south-west corner of the abbey precinct in or shortly before 1348. It was perhaps intended from the start to serve as the parish church for St. Oswald's, which removed to it from the abbey church almost immediately. After being abandoned as the parish church *c.* 1539 it served a variety of uses, none of them ecclesiastical, and remained standing, very much altered, in 2000.[15]

ST. NICHOLAS (IN THE CROFTS)

A chapel dedicated to St. Nicholas stood in the Crofts, somewhere between Watergate Street and Black Friars, by the 1220s. It was acquired by the Dominican friars on their arrival in Chester *c.* 1237 and was perhaps put to use as their first church.[16]

ST. THOMAS THE APOSTLE

The chapel stood within the abbey precinct at the north-east corner of the great court (later Abbey Square) and after the Dissolution was incorporated into the Deanery (Fig. 91).[17]

ST. THOMAS THE MARTYR

A chapel dedicated to St. Thomas Becket stood by 1200 in the graveyard belonging to St. Werburgh's abbey outside the Northgate, in the fork of the later Parkgate and Liverpool roads.[18] Serving also as the meeting place for the abbot's manor court of St. Thomas,[19] it became

---

1 Above, Collegiate Church of St. John.

2 Ibid.; 3 *Sheaf*, xxxiii, p. 78.

3 J. McN. Dodgson, 'Place-Names and Street-Names at Chester', *J.C.A.S.* lv. 30–9.

4 Jones, *Ch. in Chester*, 7; *Blk. Prince's Reg.* iii. 74–5.

5 1 *Sheaf*, ii, pp. 116–17; 3 *Sheaf*, xii, p. 35; xxix, p. 64.

6 Not mentioned in *Valor Eccl.* or *List of Clergy, 1541–2.*

7 B.L. Harl. MS. 2125, f. 267v.

8 *36 D.K.R.* App. II, p. 439; for the quarry: *P.N. Ches.* v (1:i), 48; wrongly located by Morris, *Chester*, 168–9.

9 *Lich. Episcopal Reg. V: 2nd Reg. of Bp. Robert de Stretton, 1360–85* (Collns. Hist. Staffs. n.s. viii), p. 38.

10 Morris, *Chester*, 169; C.C.A.L.S., ZMB 4, f. 72; ZSB 1, f. 122; B.L. Harl. MS. 2057, f. 114v.; Ormerod, *Hist. Ches.* i. 354.

11 3 *Sheaf*, xi, p. 22; xxv, p. 81; xxxvi, p. 68.

12 Above, Collegiate Church of St. John.

13 B.L. Harl. MS. 7568, f. 211v.; Hemingway, *Hist. Chester*, i. 164; *P.N. Ches.* v (1:i), 53.

14 Above, Collegiate Church of St. John; 3 *Sheaf*, xiii, p. 52.

15 Above, Medieval Parish Churches: St. Oswald; cf. above, Municipal Buildings: Common Hall.

16 Below, Sites and Remains of Medieval Religious Houses: Dominican Friary.

17 Below, Cathedral and Close: Precinct from 1541.

18 3 *Sheaf*, xlv, pp. 43–7; *Cart. Chester Abbey*, i, p. 132; ii, p. 274.

19 Above, Law Courts: Middle Ages (Ecclesiastical Courts).

FIG. 91. *Former St. Thomas's chapel, as deanery, before 1788*

a private house called Green Hall after the Dissolution.[1] The building probably survived only until the demolition of the northern suburbs during the Civil War siege,[2] though in 1821 it was claimed that the former chapel was still in use as a barn.[3]

DEDICATION UNKNOWN

In the 13th century a chapel in or near Pierpoint Lane off the west side of Bridge Street belonged to the clerk Alexander Hone and later to the Amery family.[4]

MODERN PARISH CHURCHES

ALL SAINTS, HOOLE

A mission room was opened in Hoole in 1855, when it was still within the district of Christ Church.[5] After the building of a new church there in 1867 the area was served by a curate, maintained by congregational offerings, pew rents, and a small stipend from the incumbent of Christ Church.[6] The new church was consecrated in 1871, and a district comprising Hoole township was taken from Christ Church parish and assigned to it in 1872.[7] It became a fully independent parish served by a vicar in 1880.[8] The parish was extended east to the Chester bypass in 1989.[9]

The advowson was initially vested in a board of trustees composed of the incumbent of Christ Church, the 2nd marquess of Westminster, and local gentlemen,[10] but by 1900 had passed to the Simeon Trustees, with whom it remained in 2000.[11] The benefice's income came largely from endowments provided in 1872 and 1884.[12] A vicarage house south of the church was built in 1885–6.[13]

From the first All Saints was of a Low Church or Evangelical persuasion and the principal Sunday services were always morning and evening prayer.[14]

Building

The church of All Saints was built of stone in 1867 to designs by Samuel Dawkes,[15] and was enlarged with a south aisle and vestry in 1911–12 by J. Walley to designs by the late John Douglas.[16] As completed it consisted of a chancel with north organ chamber, aisled nave of five bays, south vestry, north porch, and south-west tower with spire. The detail of mouldings throughout is in the Decorated style.

CHRIST CHURCH, NEWTOWN

The church was opened in 1838, and in 1843 a district was assigned to it, covering the northern suburbs of Chester and formed from parts of the parishes of St. Oswald, St. John the Baptist, and Plemstall.[17] Reduced in size by the creation of a separate district for Hoole in 1872, it became an

1 e.g. B.L. Harl. MS. 1046, f. 172.

2 *V.C.H. Ches.* v (1), Topography, 900–1914: Early Modern and Georgian (Building Activity, 1550–1640; Effects of the Siege and Interregnum).

3 J. Broster, *A Walk Round the Walls and City of Chester* (1821 edn.), 85–6.

4 *Cart. Chester Abbey,* ii, pp. 467, 469.

5 C.C.A.L.S., EDP 153/4.   6 Ibid. P 161/8/9.

7 Ibid. P 161/5/6; *Lond. Gaz.* 13 Aug. 1872, pp. 3618–19.

8 C.C.A.L.S., P 161/9/1; S. C. Scott, *Hist. of St. John the Baptist Church and Parish,* 253; *Chester Dioc. Year Bk. 1996/7,* p. 44.

9 *Lond. Gaz.* 28 Jan. 1989, p. 564.

10 C.C.A.L.S., P 161/6/1.

11 Ibid. EDP 69/1; P 161/9–10; *Chester Dioc. Year Bk. 1999/2000,* p. 45.

12 C.C.A.L.S., P 161/6/2; P 161/8/9.

13 Ibid. EDP 153/5; P 161/6/4.

14 Ibid. P 161/15/1–41; *P. & G. Dir. Chester* (1878/9), 22.

15 C.C.A.L.S., P 161/5/1.

16 Ibid. EDP 153/2; P 161/5/10–11; E. Hubbard, *Work of John Douglas,* 203–4, 277.

17 C.C.A.L.S., EDA 2/19, p. 18; P 17/10/1; P 17/18/3; *Lond. Gaz.* 29 Sept. 1843, pp. 3174–6.

independent parish in 1879.[1] Thereafter the incumbents, originally styled perpetual curates, were known as vicars.[2] The benefice, whose patron was the bishop, was incorporated in the new parish of Chester in 1972, the church remaining in use.[3] The yearly value of the living rose from £150 in 1858 to £252 by 1874.[4] The Ecclesiastical Commissioners made grants towards providing a parsonage house in 1864 and 1881, and a house was built by 1887.[5]

Throughout the 19th century incumbents had the assistance of stipendiary curates.[6] In the 1870s Christ Church had between 25 and 40 communicants at the monthly eucharist and more at Easter.[7] By 1900 a weekly early celebration had been introduced at which communicants still numbered *c.* 20–40; Easter communicants, however, had risen steeply to over 400 and rose further to 640 in 1909.[8]

At about the same time the work of the church was extended into other parts of the populous and largely working-class parish. In 1895 the Revd. J. F. Howson bought a disused chapel in Back Brook Street from the pastor of one of the Welsh-speaking Congregationalist churches, Ezra Johnson, who had moved his flock to better premises the previous year. Around 1905 it was known as the mission church of the Atonement and provided a Sunday school and Sunday evensong, and *c.* 1930 evening services on three weekdays as well. Services were probably discontinued in 1934 or 1935, and the vicar let the building for other purposes from 1936. It was apparently demolished *c.* 1960.[9]

Howson also built the corrugated-iron St. Luke's mission church on land next to the vicarage house in Brook Lane, beginning services there in 1899. In 1905 the vicar or one of the two curates held morning service every Sunday and communion twice a month and on Thursdays in the summer. Services continued at St. Luke's until 1969, and the building was removed after 1971.[10]

At Christ Church itself a weekly, early morning, sung eucharist had been introduced by the 1930s, and under C. F. Leeper (vicar 1947–53) it replaced matins as the principal morning service.[11]

Building

As first built in 1838, to designs by Thomas Jones, Christ Church comprised chancel, transepts, and aisle-less nave.[12] In 2000 it consisted of a chancel with south chapel and north vestry, and an aisled nave with porch, the chancel and its chapel being of ashlar and the remainder of red brick with stone dressings. John Douglas was brought in as consultant in 1869, and the enlargement of the chancel dates to then or 1876. In 1893, to Douglas's revised designs in an Early Pointed style, the chancel was extended to the east, and between 1897 and 1900 he rebuilt the nave.[13] The porch was added in 1936.[14] The church contains a notable assemblage of Arts and Crafts fittings and glass, mostly by Douglas, Sir Charles Nicholson, and C. E. Kempe.[15]

HOLY ASCENSION, UPTON

In 1853 the rector of St. Mary's issued an appeal for funds to build a church in Upton to serve the large detached portion of his parish north of the city. The marquess of Westminster offered £1,000 as an endowment and £1,000 towards the building, and the church was consecrated as a chapel of ease to St. Mary's in 1854. The clergy were initially appointed by the rector of St. Mary's and held two Sunday services, administering communion monthly to 20 or 30 people in the 1860s. In 1882 Upton became an independent parish, with the patronage in the hands of the patron of St. Mary's, the duke of Westminster,[16] with whose descendants it remained in 2000.[17]

Building

The church of the Holy Ascension was built to designs by James Harrison based on the medieval work surviving and conjectured at Aldford. As originally built it consisted of a chancel with north vestry and organ chamber, nave with south porch, and tower with spire, all in the Decorated style of Aldford. A south transept and vestries were added in 1958 and a north transept in 1967, making the church cruciform.[18]

1 C.C.A.L.S., P 17/21/1–23; *Chester Dioc. Cal.*
2 *Chester Dioc. Cal.*; C.C.A.L.S., P 17/10/1.
3 *Lond. Gaz.* 30 June 1972, p. 7865.
4 *Bagshaw's Dir. Ches.* (1850), 65; *Morris's Dir. Ches.* (1874), 8.
5 C.C.A.L.S., P 17/8/1–4.
6 Ibid. EDP 69/1; P 161/8/9.
7 Ibid. P 17/4/1.
8 Ibid. P 17/4/2–3.
9 Ibid. P 17/12/20A–B; P 17/18/35, ff. 2–3; *P. & G. Dir. Chester* (1905/6), 34; (1927/8), 53; (1933/4), 48; not listed in (1935/6), 50; *Kelly's Dir. Chester* (1938), 6, and later edns. to (1958), 6; (1960), 6; (1962), 6.
10 C.C.A.L.S., P 17/6/10; P 17/8/7; P 17/10/2–4; P 17/19/1–4; P 17/20/1; P 17/3912/1; C.P.S., Brook La. (neg. AJAW 4/2).

11 C.C.A.L.S., P 17/4/4–7.
12 *White's Dir. Ches.* (1860), 89; E. Hubbard, *Work of John Douglas*, 131.
13 Hubbard, *Work of John Douglas*, 131, 200, 246–7, 262–3, 268–9, 271–2; C.C.A.L.S., EDP 69/2; P 17/6/1; P 17/6/3–5; P 17/6/14; *Chester Dioc. Gaz.* (1901), 110–11.
14 C.C.A.L.S., EDP 69/2; P 17/6/25B.
15 Ibid. EDP 69/2; P 17/6/6; P 17/6/14; *Chester Dioc. Gaz.* (1897), 118; Pevsner, *Ches.* 150; *Kelly's Dir. Ches.* (1906), 213; *Chester Dioc. Cal.* (1910), 149; (1911), 149.
16 C.C.A.L.S., P 176/4/1, items inserted at front; P 176/7/1.
17 *Chester Dioc. Year Bk. 1999/2000*, p. 47.
18 C.C.A.L.S., P 176/4/1, items inserted at front; P 176/5/1 (1965); P 176/5/14, 21; P. Howell, 'The Other "Harrison of Chester"', *J.C.A.S.* lxiii. 90.

HOLY TRINITY WITHOUT THE WALLS, BLACON

The replacement for the medieval parish church of Holy Trinity (above, pp. 133–6).

ST. MARK, SALTNEY

A chapelry known as Lache cum Saltney was formed in 1855 from the western part of St. Mary on the Hill parish within the liberties, the township of Marlston cum Lache (also previously in St. Mary's), and part of Saltney (previously in Hawarden parish, Flints.). It was extended eastward to Selkirk Road in 1923. The bishop of Chester was patron.[1] Services had been held in a barn at Corporation Farm, Saltneyside, since 1851, and in 1853 the marquess of Westminster gave a site for a church at Lache Eyes.[2] The church of the Holy Epiphany at Lache Eyes remained in use until 1893, when a new building, dedicated to St. Mark, opened in Hough Green.[3] Services were also held in a school at Mold Junction (in Saltney, Flints.) from 1891, and in 1911 a mission church dedicated to St. Matthew was opened near by in the hamlet of Saltney Ferry (Flints.). In the 1990s St. Mark's and St. Matthew's both remained in use and services were also held by the parish's team of incumbent and two curates at a 'family church' in Sandy Lane.[4]

Buildings

The parish church of St. Mark was designed by T. M. Lockwood in a 13th-century style. Of red Ruabon brick with a roof of Westmorland slate, it comprises a chancel with north vestry and south chapel, and a nave with north porch and south organ chamber.

The mission church of St. Matthew, Saltney Ferry, is of red Ruabon brick with a slate roof and consists of a chancel with south vestry, and a nave with western baptistery.

ST. MARY WITHOUT THE WALLS, HANDBRIDGE

The replacement for the medieval parish church of St. Mary on the Hill (above, pp. 142–6).

ST. MICHAEL, PLAS NEWTON

A church hall within the parish of All Saints, Hoole, opened in Devon Road, Newton, in 1965 and was used for evening services. It was rebuilt as a church with attached meeting rooms in 1982, when a parish was formed for it from all that part of All Saints north of the railway line, and a vicar was appointed. The patron, as at All Saints, was the Simeon Trustees. Services were Evangelical from the start and in 1996 the parish had a number of house-church groups. St. Michael's is a plain building of yellow brick, the church being simply a large rectangular room.[5]

ST. PAUL, BOUGHTON

The church was opened in 1830 as a chapel of ease to St. John's.[6] In 1846 a district was assigned to it, formed from Great Boughton township in St. Oswald's parish, the extra-parochial place of Spital Boughton, and a section of St. John's parish bounded by the canal, Steven Street, and the river.[7] The district became a parish in 1879, when its boundaries were extended at the expense of St. John's.[8] Its boundaries were altered in 1973, when territory was exchanged with Christleton and acquired from Bruera.[9] The vicar of St. John's remained patron until 1972, when the advowson was vested in the rector of the new united benefice of Chester.[10]

The curate's annual income, originally derived largely from pew rents, was *c.* £80 in 1831 but had risen to £150 by 1860.[11] The vicar continued to receive income from pew rents until 1915 or later.[12]

Congregations in 1851 averaged 330 on Sunday morning and 350 in the evening.[13] Incumbents were assisted by stipendiary curates throughout the 19th century and a mission church operated in Hoole Lane from 1887 to 1933 in a corrugated-iron and weather-boarded building still standing in 1996.[14] At St. Paul's an early celebration of holy communion every Sunday had been introduced by the 1870s, and by 1933 there was a weekly sung eucharist.[15] The sung celebration, which was made monthly in 1957, had again become the principal Sunday service by the 1970s.[16]

1 Ormerod, *Hist. Ches.* ii. 824; *Lond. Gaz.* 16 Oct. 1855, pp. 3796–7; 12 Oct. 1923, pp. 6854–6.

2 C.C.A.L.S., P 98/4/1; O.S. Map 6-inch, Ches. XLVI (1880 edn.).

3 C.C.A.L.S., P 98/4/2, 4.

4 Ibid. P 98/13/1; P 98/14/1–2; *Chester Dioc. Year Bk. 1996/7*, p. 45; *1999/2000*, p. 46.

5 *All Saints' Parish Church, Hoole and Newton, Chester: Centenary, 1871–1971*, 11 (copy at C.H.H.); *Chester Dioc. Year Bk. 1996/7*, p. 45; *1999/2000*, p. 47; inscriptions and leaflets at church; inf. from Mrs. Val Powell, who is thanked for opening the church.   6 C.C.A.L.S., P 51/26/1.

7 Ibid. P 51/26/2–4; *Lond. Gaz.* 10 July 1846, pp. 2532–3.

8 C.C.A.L.S., P 51/26/5–17; *Lond. Gaz.* 22 Aug. 1879, pp. 5123–4; S. C. Scott, *Hist. of St. John the Baptist Church and Parish*, 253.   9 C.C.A.L.S., P 162/10/6–8.

10 Scott, *Hist. St. John's Church*, 253; *Chester Dioc. Cal.*; *Lond. Gaz.* 30 June 1972, p. 7865.

11 *Rep. Com. Eccl. Revenues, 1828–31* [67], pp. 230–1, H.C. (1835), xxii; *White's Dir. Ches.* (1860), 89.

12 C.C.A.L.S., P 162/4/1–2.

13 P.R.O., HO 129/459/68.

14 C.C.A.L.S., EDP 77/1; P 162/7–8; *Chester Dioc. Cal.* (1888–9).

15 *P. & G. Dir. Chester* (1933/4), 50; (1935/6), 52.

16 C.C.A.L.S., P 162/10/3.

Building

The church of St. Paul, which is of brick and timber in John Douglas's distinctive local revival style, comprises an aisled nave terminating in a wide apse, a south-west baptistery, and an outer south aisle, added later.[1] The first church, which was built in 1830, was of stuccoed brick in an Italianate style with round-headed windows and a north-west campanile. The architect was William Cole the younger.[2] In 1876 the church was virtually rebuilt to the designs of John Douglas. The exterior was refaced, lancet and plate tracery windows were inserted, and an elaborate open timber roof topped by a spirelet was made. Inside there are timber arcades.[3] In 1900 a south aisle, designed by Douglas and Minshull, was added.[4] In the 1930s it was furnished as a side chapel.[5] The church contains notable glass by C. E. Kempe, Edward Frampton, and especially Morris and Co., all dating from between 1881 and 1925.[6]

ST. THOMAS, PARKGATE ROAD

The replacement for the medieval parish church of St. Oswald (above, pp. 149–53).

ROMAN CATHOLICISM

The clergy and nearly all lay people in Chester conformed with the Elizabethan religious settlement, and recusancy remained numerically weak and socially insignificant throughout Elizabeth's reign.[7] The handful of J.P.s and aldermen whose loyalty was suspected by the authorities in 1564 never became open recusants, and the only prominent citizens against whom proceedings were taken in the 1570s and later were a merchant, two lawyers, and several members of the Aldersey family. Of them only the lawyer Ralph Worsley proved obdurate. The searching enquiries made in 1592 revealed only forty actual or suspected recusants in the city. Recusancy was mainly confined to a few artisan families under the leadership of the Catholic gentry of west Cheshire, notably the Masseys of Waverton. The priests who served them probably lodged in gentry houses in the countryside. Ironically the main centre of Catholic activity in the city in the late 16th century was the castle, where recusants from elsewhere in Cheshire were gaoled in the 1580s and 1590s. The keepers of the castle gaol were lax and corrupt: some prisoners had liberty to walk about the city, priests were able to slip in to say mass, and one keeper's son became a convert.

Chester's importance in the history of recusancy was rather as a place frequented by Catholics travelling to Ireland. In 1594–5, for example, three groups of youths from other parts of the country were captured as they were trying to make their way abroad for a Catholic education, and presumably many others before and afterwards passed through the city without being apprehended. The town was also close to the strongly recusant districts of north-east Wales, which included the pilgrimage centre of Holywell (Flints.). There was, nevertheless, enough of a recusant community resident in Chester by the 1590s to provide safe houses for those *en route* for Ireland and to arrange for a prisoner who escaped from Northgate gaol to get clean away.

The features of Roman Catholicism in Chester established in the 16th century remained the norm until the early 19th.[8] It was the religion of a small, tightly knit group of families, mainly small tradespeople but including representatives of all classes except the governing élite, with wider leadership and refuges for priests provided by the Catholic country gentry. From 1622 the city was mainly served by Jesuit priests of the northern district. One active in 1654, Robert Grosvenor, was related to the Grosvenors of Eaton Hall, but the main gentry support came from the Fitzherberts of Swynnerton Hall (Staffs.), who had a house in Northgate ward. The number of Catholics, probably always under-recorded, rose only slowly. Sixteen were listed in the early 17th century; probably 15 in 1678; 104, including women and children, in 1705–6; and 130 individuals in perhaps 81 households in 1767.[9] The last figure accords well with the 138 sittings apparently provided at the chapel opened in 1799.[10] The continuing presence of even such small numbers was in part due to immigration; in 1767 perhaps a quarter of the Catholic families bore surnames of Irish, Scots, Welsh, or (in one case) French origin.[11]

1 The ritual positions are given; the church is in fact aligned north–south, with ritual east to the south.

2 C.C.A.L.S., EDP 77/4; *White's Dir. Ches.* (1860), 89; Scott, *Hist. St. John's Church*, 249; H. Colvin, *Biographical Dictionary of Brit. Architects* (1978), 229–30.

3 C.C.A.L.S., EDA 2/25, p. 762; EDP 77/2; *T.L.C.A.S.* lvii. 121.

4 C.C.A.L.S., EDA 2/29, pp. 905–7; EDP 77/2; *T.L.C.A.S.* lvii. 124.

5 C.C.A.L.S., EDP 77/2.

6 Ibid.; EDA 2/28, p. 305; EDA 2/29, p. 746; Pevsner, *Ches.* 173; A. Sewter, *Stained Glass of Morris and Co.*

7 This and next para. based on K. R. Wark, *Elizabethan Recusancy in Ches.* (Chetham Soc. 3rd ser. xix), esp. 2–3, 5–8, 14–20, 61–2, 70–3, 80–4, 88–92, 94–104, 106, 108–14, 124–7, 129, 138–73.

8 Para. based on M. W. Sturman, *Catholicism in Chester, 1875–1975* (Chester, [1975]), 9–25.

9 The last figure based on *Returns of Papists, 1767, Dioc. of Chester*, ed. E. S. Worrall (Catholic Rec. Soc. Occasional Publications, i), pp. 172–3.

10 The number in 1851: P.R.O., HO 129/459/55.

11 Sturman, *Catholicism in Chester*, 17–20; *Returns, 1767*, ed. Worrall, pp. 172–3; Sturman's analysis of immigration patterns from the 1767 returns (pp. 23–5) is unreliable.

Until the 1750s there was no permanently resident priest in Chester, masses being said either by a gentleman's chaplain, typically from Hooton Hall in Wirral or the Fitzherberts' house. From 1758, however, an almost continuous series of settled priests can be traced. Until 1838 they were normally, perhaps always, Lancastrians trained in the English seminary at Douai (Nord) or its successors, Crook Hall (in Brancepeth, co. Dur.) and Ushaw College (in Lanchester, co. Dur.). A permanent chapel was probably in use from the 1750s and by 1789 services were held in an upper room in Foregate Street. In 1799 the congregation built and registered a chapel near by on the west side of Queen Street. It was perhaps largely paid for by the Irish merchants who headed the list of those for whom perpetual masses were afterwards said.[1] They were very likely men who frequented Chester on business rather than permanent residents.

The Irish Catholic population of Chester grew rapidly in the 19th century, especially after the Irish famines of 1821 and the 1840s.[2] In 1826 the priest appealed for help for the many destitute Irish among his flock. In the 1830s many people born in counties Mayo, Roscommon, Galway, and Clare were settled in the city, and the Irish-born population reached over 1,000 by 1841, concentrated into a small area in and around Steven Street, between Boughton and the canal. There were also some Italian Catholic immigrants in the earlier 19th century, mainly shopkeepers. The average annual number of Catholic baptisms rose from 4 in the decade 1794–1803 to 20 in 1814–23, 48 in 1824–33, 63 in 1834–43, 86 in 1844–53, and 115 in 1854–63. Numbers attending mass in mid century were estimated at *c.* 700 at the bishop of Shrewsbury's first visitation in 1850, and 800 as the average Sunday attendance when the religious census was taken in 1851; the actual total attendance on Census Sunday in the latter year, however, was 570 adults and 100 children.[3] The growth in numbers later must have been due more to the natural increase of the settled population than to continuing immigration. There were an estimated 2,800 Catholics in Chester in 1889, 4,800 in 1929, 7,000 in 1951, and 10,000 in 1974.[4] As a proportion of the total population that represented a steady increase from probably under 8 per cent in the 1880s to about 12 per cent in the 1970s.[5]

The chapel in Queen Street was soon too small. Franciscan Capuchin friars from Pantasaph (in Whitford, Flints.) established a mission in Cuppin Street in 1858, saying mass first in a room and later in a temporary building, both located in Watergate Row South, before laying the foundation stone of a chapel in Grosvenor Street in 1862. The bankruptcy of the builder, an earth tremor, and a hurricane thwarted initial plans, but a temporary building, seating 500, was opened in 1864 and replaced in 1873–5 by the church of St. Francis. The friary behind the church in Cuppin Street was completed in 1876 and enlarged in the 20th century.[6]

Suburban churches were opened as the Catholic population moved away from the central area after the Second World War. In Upton masses were said in the village hall from 1939 and a church was opened in Plas Newton Lane in 1964. A parish for Blacon was established in 1956, and a church opened there in 1959. A church for south Chester was built by the Franciscans from the city-centre friary in 1960 on the Lache council estate.[7]

The earliest modern religious order established in Chester was the Faithful Companions of Jesus, who ran schools from their convent in Dee House, Little St. John Street, from 1854 to 1925, when they were replaced by the Ursulines, who left when the school closed in 1976.[8] The nursing order of the Little Sisters of the Assumption was established in Queen Street in 1911, building St. Augustine's convent and chapel in 1913 on land in Union Street given by Margaret Collins. They were succeeded there in 1957 by the Irish Sisters of Charity.[9] In 1976 there were also Sisters of Charity of Our Lady, Mother of Mercy, in Cliveden Road, Lache.[10] In 1995 the only order in the city apart from the Franciscans was a group of Benedictine nuns recently established in Curzon Park.[11]

The many Roman Catholic social organizations which flourished from the mid 19th century were based in the early 20th at no. 34 Queen Street, which closed in 1972 and was replaced in 1975 by a social centre in the former Bowling Green Hotel in Brook Street.[12]

Buildings

The old church of St. Werburgh, Queen Street, was a plain building in Classical style, of stuccoed brick with a Doric portico under a pediment, two panels with garlands decorating the upper wall, and tall round-arched windows in the side walls. An adjoining house became the presbytery and there was a burial ground to the rear. The chapel was converted into a school when

1 Sturman, *Catholicism in Chester*, 16, 25–31; description of chapel below.

2 Para. based, except where stated otherwise, on Sturman, *Catholicism in Chester*, 49–54, 61–2, 87.

3 P.R.O., HO 129/459/55.

4 *Shrewsbury Dioc. Year Bk.* (1974), 51–2.

5 Cf. above, Population.

6 O.N.S. (Birkdale), Worship Reg., nos. 8642, 9366, 16255; Sturman, *Catholicism in Chester*, 40, 47–8; description below.

7 Sturman, *Catholicism in Chester*, 91–3; O.N.S. (Birkdale), Worship Reg., nos. 67632, 68041, 71215; *Catholic Dir.* (1969), 427; (1976), 379.

8 Sturman, *Catholicism in Chester*, 66–7; *Ches. Observer*, 16 Feb. 1979; below, Education: 1944–74.

9 Sturman, *Catholicism in Chester*, 98; *Catholic Dir.* (1976), 380.   10 *Catholic Dir.* (1976), 379.

11 *Chester Chron.* 26 May 1995, p. 6.

12 Sturman, *Catholicism in Chester*, [109].

FIG. 92. *St. Werburgh's*

a replacement church was opened in 1875 and was demolished during the redevelopment of Queen Street in 1966.[1]

The new church of St. Werburgh was built between 1873 and 1875 to designs by Edmund Kirby of Liverpool, and extended in 1904 and 1914.[2] The site, fronting Grosvenor Park Road, required a reversed orientation. The church, built of pale yellow sandstone under a steeply pitched slate roof, has Early English details. It consists of an apsidal west sanctuary with a polygonal vestry adjoining it on the north and a western ambulatory, and a tall nave of six bays with

FIG. 93. *St. Columba's*

north and south aisles and a gabled east porch. All the windows are single lancets. There is a side altar flanking the high altar to the south, and an organ in the corresponding bay on the north. The pulpit was given by Patrick Collins in 1894.[3] The adjoining presbytery in Union Street is a red-brick house of two storeys with attics, enlivened by blue headers and prominent chimney stacks.

The church of St. Francis was designed by James O'Byrne of Liverpool in uncoursed sandstone with a slate roof.[4] It comprises a sanctuary flanked by shallow recesses for side altars, a wide aisleless nave of seven bays, and a small west porch. There are two further altars in the north wall, two confessionals in the south wall, and a west gallery. The west wall has two two-light windows with Decorated tracery but the nave windows are without tracery. The building debt was paid off through bequests from the Tatlock family in 1899.[5]

St. Theresa, Blacon Avenue, was designed by Reynolds and Scott in pale red pressed brick with stone dressings and flat roofs.[6] It consists of a sanctuary of one bay with a shallow polygonal apse, a tall nave, slightly raised over the western entrance, low north and south aisles, and a slender south-east tower. A west gallery over the lobby carries an organ. The attached presbytery stands to the north-east.

St. Clare, Downsfield Road, Lache, also by Reynolds and Scott,[7] is built in pale red and yellow pressed brick with tiled roofs. It comprises a sanctuary of two bays, a low north-east vestry, north and south transepts, a nave of four bays, and a slender south-west tower. The gabled

1 Sturman, *Catholicism in Chester*, 30–1; Pevsner, *Ches.* 153.
2 Sturman, *Catholicism in Chester*, 44; Pevsner, *Ches.* 153; *Dioc. of Shrewsbury Centenary Rec. 1851–1951*, 56.

3 Inscription on pulpit.
4 Pevsner, *Ches.* 151.
6 Pevsner, *Ches.* 171.

5 Inscription in porch.
7 Implied ibid.

end walls of the transepts and the west nave wall each have a small central hexagonal window circled by seven smaller ones, all filled with coloured glass. The nave and sanctuary windows are plain pointed arches with mullions. Inside there is a west organ gallery over the lobby, and confessionals are built into the north wall.

St. Columba, Plas Newton Lane, was designed in a non-traditional style by L. A. G. Prichard, Son, and Partners,[1] using a variety of walling materials and

copper roofs (Fig. 93). The ground plan is a symmetrical polygon, essentially half an octagon. A pyramidal spire rises over the altar. The internal space, apart from an enclosed lobby under an open organ loft, is semi-circular, arranged with low benches facing a semi-circular railed altar space against the east wall. The wall above the altar has 15 small triangular windows with red and blue glass. The lighting is suspended in clusters from a high wooden ceiling.

PROTESTANT NONCONFORMITY

EARLY PRESBYTERIANS AND INDEPENDENTS

The beginnings of Dissent in Chester can be traced back at least as far as William Prynne's visit of 1637, when, as a prisoner on his way to Caernarfon, he was entertained by several leading citizens, including Calvin Bruen, Peter Leigh, and members of the wealthy Mercers' company, a kindness for which the hosts suffered fines and imprisonment.[2] As early as 1641 Samuel Eaton preached Congregationalism in a sermon at St. John's, and after the fall of the city in 1646, as chaplain to the garrison, established the first Independent congregation in the city. He soon resigned and was succeeded by John Knowles, a brilliant preacher but a Socinian.[3] Knowles was later ejected and nothing more is known of the congregation, although Eaton certainly preached in Chester in the mid 1650s when at least two mayors, Edward Bradshaw and Peter Leigh, appear to have had Independent sympathies.[4] They and others of like outlook seem eventually to have gravitated towards Thomas Harrison, a former chaplain of Henry Cromwell in Ireland and minister of St. Oswald's 1660–2.[5]

Despite the presence of such an influential group of Independents, in Chester as in the rest of Cheshire Presbyterianism was from an early date the dominant form of non-Anglican Protestantism. In 1648 five of the city's ministers, Henry Massey of St. Oswald's, John Glendal of St. Peter's, Thomas Upton of Holy Trinity, William Peartree of St. Mary's, and Benjamin Ball of St. John's, signed the Cheshire *Attestation to the Testimony of Our Reverend Brethren of the Province of*

London, condemning Independency. Two, Upton and Glendal, retained influence in Chester until their ejection in 1660 and 1662 respectively,[6] while another Presbyterian, William Cook, curate of St. Michael's *c.* 1650–62, played a leading role in persuading the people of Chester to support Sir George Booth's rebellion in 1659 and was briefly imprisoned in London for his pains.[7]

From 1662 Chester had a number of Dissenting communities, focused upon ministers ejected from benefices within the city itself or elsewhere in the neighbourhood. William Cook, deprived of his living at St. Michael's despite his earlier efforts in the royalist cause, established a Presbyterian congregation of perhaps 50 or 60 people in the city, but soon came to the attention of Bishop Hall and in 1663 was imprisoned in the city gaol. After the passage of the Five Mile Act he withdrew to Puddington, seven miles away.[8] Peter Leigh, the ejected Presbyterian incumbent of St. John's, seems similarly to have remained in Chester until 1665.[9] The principal Independent conventicle, numbering as many as 100, met at the house of yet another local ejectee, Thomas Harrison, the former minister of St. Oswald's; he was still active in 1665 when Sir Geoffrey Shakerley, the governor of the castle, broke down the doors of his meeting and arrested over 30 worshippers, including Harrison himself, the former mayors Peter Leigh and Edward Bradshaw, Major James Jolly, and Mr. Gregg, the examiner of the palatinate exchequer. Described as 'of the first and worst stamp of sectaries', they were brought before the mayor and fined.[10] Shortly afterwards Harrison was imprisoned and securities were taken from Jolly.[11] In

1 Ibid. 172.

2 W. Urwick, *Hist. Sketches of Nonconformity in Ches.* 7–9, 13–15; M. J. Crossley Evans, 'Clergy of City of Chester, 1630–72', *J.C.A.S.* lxviii. 108–9, 119.

3 Urwick, *Sketches,* 15–20; *Life of Martindale Written by Himself* (Chetham Soc. [o.s.], iv), 74; *J.C.A.S.* lxviii. 111; *D.N.B.* s.n. Eaton.

4 F. Sanders, 'Quakers in Chester under the Protectorate', *J.C.A.S.* xiv. 39; for Bradshaw and Leigh: *Cal. S.P. Dom. 1664–5,* 461.

5 Urwick, *Sketches,* 19–21; *D.N.B.* s.n. Harrison; E. Calamy, *Nonconformist's Memorial,* ed. S. Palmer (1802), i. 330–1; *Calamy Revised,* ed. A. G. Matthews, 251.

6 F. J. Powicke, *Hist. of Ches. Congregational Union,* 2–3; Urwick, *Sketches,* pp. xxv–xxvi, 13; *Calamy Revised,* 224–6, 500; *V.C.H. Ches.* iii. 102–3.

7 Calamy, *Nonconformist's Memorial,* i. 326–30; *Calamy Revised,* 132–3; *J.C.A.S.* lxviii. 117–18; C.C.A.L.S., EDC 5/1663/73.

8 Urwick, *Sketches,* 21–2; H. D. Roberts, *Matthew Henry and his Chapel, 1662–1900,* 72–3; *J.C.A.S.* lxviii. 120; C.C.A.L.S., ZML 3, no. 390.

9 *J.C.A.S.* lxviii. 119, 121; cf. *Calamy Revised,* 320.

10 *Cal. S.P. Dom. 1664–5,* 461; Urwick, *Sketches,* pp. lxvi–lxvii; C.C.A.L.S., ZML 3, no. 390.

11 *Cal. S.P. Dom. 1664–5,* 550.

1665 Harrison introduced a young pupil, John Bailey, into Chester, but he too was imprisoned.[1] Harrison later withdrew from the city.[2]

Incoming ministers included John Wilson, a Presbyterian ejected from Backford in 1662, who took a house in Chester in which he held well attended meetings until he too was imprisoned.[3] Others were itinerant. William Colly, ordained priest in 1661, preached in and around Chester for several years, until in 1671 he was induced by Bishop Wilkins's 'soft interpretation of the terms of conformity' to accept a curacy at Churton Heath chapel.[4] John Gartside, a Presbyterian minister based primarily in Derbyshire and east Cheshire, also preached in the city 'very privately' between 1662 and 1672.[5]

In the earlier 1660s bishop and governor were active persecutors, and several leading adherents, in particular the pastors, suffered imprisonment under the Conventicle and Five Mile Acts.[6] The authorities believed that despite their efforts Chester remained the centre of a vigorous Dissenting community, and indeed members of that community were still a dominant force in such prominent local institutions as the Mercers' company.[7] In 1666 Shakerley alleged that the city was 'swarming with cardinal nonconformists', who had so penetrated the local magistracy that there was little hope of their being punished.[8] More relaxed attitudes came only with the advent of Bishop Wilkins in 1668 and the promulgation of the Declaration of Indulgence in 1672.[9] In accordance with the Declaration a number of meetings were licensed in the city, and by the end of the year there were complaints that the nonconformist congregations had grown so much that the city's parish churches were emptying.[10] Perhaps the most important and enduring of the Dissenting meeting rooms was that in White Friars, in the house of Anthony Henthorn, a sugar merchant, to which William Cook returned to preach in 1672. Cook, who was licensed to hold both Presbyterian and Independent meetings, continued to minister to his congregation until 1682. The application of another pastor, the Presbyterian William Wokey, to preach in Henthorn's house in 1672 was, however, denied.[11]

The city's other principal meeting in the 1670s was

in Northgate Street, where John Wilson, the former vicar of Backford, was licensed to preach to Presbyterian and Independent congregations in the house of Catherine Booth, daughter of George Booth, Lord Delamere. A popular pastor, who ministered to a large congregation thronging the hall, galleries, and part of the courtyard of Booth's house, Wilson died within a year or so of the Declaration.[12] His work was probably carried on by the Presbyterian William Jones, who like Wilson was licensed to preach in Booth's house in 1672.[13]

Other Presbyterian pastors licensed in 1672 included John Glendal, the minister ejected from St. Peter's in 1662, and Ralph Hall, ejected from Maer (Staffs.) in 1662 and granted permission to teach in Grange Lane (presumably Barn Lane) and also at Weaverham. A further Presbyterian meeting was permitted in the house of Hugh Harvey.[14] The Independents were less numerous. A licence was granted to Thomas Harrison, but he seems to have returned shortly afterwards to Dublin, where he died in 1682, and another meeting was permitted in the house of Henry Williamson.[15]

When the decade of toleration inaugurated by the Declaration of Indulgence ended in 1682 there were three main Dissenting congregations in Chester, those of Cook, Hall, and John Harvey, a former rector of Wallasey present in the city by 1680.[16] All three were broken up by the new persecution. Hall and Cook ceased to preach in 1682 and both died in 1684.[17] Harvey, however, preached privately and survived, assisted by visiting ministers.[18]

Late in 1686 the Presbyterian Matthew Henry paid his first visit to Chester, preaching at Henthorn's house in White Friars and at the houses of Harvey and Jolly. He made a good impression and was asked to come again. With the proclamation of the Declaration of Indulgence in 1687 Henry, who had just been ordained in London, came to Henthorn's house as preacher, at the request of Henthorn himself and Edward Greg, perhaps to be identified with the member of Harrison's congregation arrested in 1665. The assent of Harvey, the only surviving minister in Chester, had been obtained. Before Henry's arrival the congregation ceased to meet in Henthorn's hall and paid for the

---

1 Urwick, *Sketches*, 23–5; Calamy, *Nonconformist's Memorial*, i. 331–5.

2 *Calamy Revised*, 251.

3 Ibid.; Urwick, *Sketches*, 27; Roberts, *Matthew Henry*, 75 n.

4 *J.C.A.S.* lxviii. 121; *Calamy Revised*, 129.

5 Urwick, *Sketches*, 29; Roberts, *Matthew Henry*, 75 n.; *Calamy Revised*, 218.

6 e.g. C.C.A.L.S., EDC 5/1663/26, 73; EDC 5/1668/12; ibid. ZML 3, no. 390.

7 *J.C.A.S.* lxviii. 119–20.

8 *Cal. S.P. Dom.* 1666–7, 12; R. T. Jones, *Congregationalism in Eng.* 74.

9 *V.C.H. Ches.* iii. 43; G. L. Turner, *Original Rec. of Early Nonconformity*, iii. 104; *J.C.A.S.* lxviii. 121–2.

10 P.R.O., SP 29/319, no. 65, f. 74 and v., cited in D. Shorney,

Protestant Nonconformist and Roman Catholic Records: Guide to Sources in P.R.O. 17.

11 Turner, *Original Rec.* i. 228, 241, 286, 330–1, 354, 471, 485; iii. 651, 655.

12 Ibid. i. 369, 395, 457, 502, 515, 527, 581; Roberts, *Matthew Henry*, 75 n.; *Calamy Revised*, 536.

13 Turner, *Original Rec.* i. 581.

14 Ibid. i. 395, 502, 557; *Calamy Revised*, 224–5, 242.

15 Turner, *Original Rec.* i. 354, 553, 557; *Calamy Revised*, 251; cf. (in error) Urwick, *Sketches*, 19.

16 C.C.A.L.S., ZQSF 82; *Ches. Classis: Mins. 1691–1745*, ed. A. Gordon, 177; *Calamy Revised*, 251; H. Newcome, *Autobiography* (Chetham Soc. [o.s.], xxvii), 232.

17 Roberts, *Matthew Henry*, 75 n.

18 Ibid. 74.

conversion of a large adjoining stable into a permanent meeting house.[1] Initially services were held at church time in the morning, but were delayed in the afternoon until evensong was over. When Lawrence Fogge, one of the prebendaries of the cathedral, informed Greg that the separation was 'schismatical at any time' the practice was abandoned and both meetings were allowed to coincide with church services. Henry's new arrangements were also followed by Harvey at his house in Bridge Street, where meetings had hitherto been held only in the evening.[2]

A proposal from Henry to unite his congregation with Harvey's was refused, and he ministered to 45 hearers, chiefly former adherents of Cook and Hall. Thereafter the number of communicants rose rapidly, reaching 250 within three years and necessitating the enlargement of the meeting house in 1691.[3]

Henry and Harvey both joined the newly founded Cheshire classis in 1691. Their increasing co-operation was reflected in their joint participation in solemn monthly public fasts in the summers of the 1690s.[4] Owing to difficult relations with Henthorn's grandson, Henry's congregation moved in 1700 to a newly built chapel.[5] The first purpose-built chapel in Chester, it was built of brick, with three gables, two tiers of round-arched windows, and a central entrance. Inside there were two arcades of tall timber columns, with the pulpit placed between the windows on the north wall.[6] The chapel lay between Trinity Street and Crook Street, the land on the Trinity Street side being used later as a burial ground.[7] It was originally known as the Crook Street chapel, but by the 19th century the land between it and Crook Street had been built up, and it was generally referred to as the Trinity Street chapel.

By 1700 Harvey had died and been succeeded by his son Jonathan. The two congregations continued to co-operate. Harvey, however, was in poor health and soon after 1706 abandoned his meeting house in Bridge Street and resigned his ministry. His congregation decided to unite with Henry and in 1707 a gallery was added to the chapel in Trinity Street to accommodate them. By then there were 350 communicants and a normal congregation of 300.[8]

After rejecting many overtures from congregations elsewhere, Henry left Chester in 1712 to take up an appointment in Hackney (Mdx.), but died only two years later while visiting Cheshire and was buried in Holy Trinity church.[9] He was replaced at Trinity Street in 1713 by John Gardner, whose ministry lasted until 1765.[10]

FIG. 94. *Summer house behind Bollands Court, where Matthew Henry probably studied*

Chester remained a centre of predominantly Presbyterian Dissent for some time after Henry's departure. By 1720 Gardner was estimated to have 1,000 hearers, and his regular congregation included many gentlemen.[11] In the 1720s and 1730s the trustees of the Trinity Street chapel received large bequests in aid of Presbyterian ministers and divinity students.[12] From about 1750 Unitarian views gained a growing hold over the congregation. Gardner himself seems to have inclined towards unorthodoxy, and in 1751 he appointed a new assistant, John Chidlaw, of decidedly Unitarian opinions. Matters came to a head in 1765 when Gardner died and Chidlaw became sole minister. In 1768 there was an orthodox secession, mainly from the gallery where, perhaps, a differing religious tradition had been maintained since the arrival of John Harvey's followers in 1707.[13]

The new meeting started in a small room belonging to the Smiths' company on the south side of Common-hall Street, formerly the city corporation's common

1 Ibid. 75–9.
2 Ibid. 80; C.C.A.L.S., ZCR 151/86; ZQSF 85.
3 Roberts, *Matthew Henry*, 81–2.
4 Ibid. 88; *Ches. Classis Mins.* 6, 106, 122–3.
5 Roberts, *Matthew Henry*, 91.
6 R.C.H.M.E., *Nonconformist Chapels in N. Eng.* 6; Hemingway, *Hist. Chester*, ii. 152; *J.C.A.S.* xxii, facing p. 172.

7 J. Romney, *Chester and its Environs Illustrated*, [5].
8 Roberts, *Matthew Henry*, 90–3; C.C.A.L.S., ZQSF 90.
9 *D.N.B.*　　　　　　　10 Urwick, *Sketches*, 37–8.
11 Lond., Dr. Williams's Libr., MS. 38.4.
12 *31st Rep. Com. Char.* 411.
13 Urwick, *Sketches*, 37–8; *J.C.A.S.* xxii. 183–4. For the later hist. of the congregation, below, Other Churches: Unitarians.

hall.[1] In 1769 the congregation invited Dr. Jenkins, a Baptist minister from Wrexham (Denb.), to preach; he later affirmed that the group, which numbered *c.* 200, included only two or three from Chidlaw's congregation and that it was composed mainly of former Baptists and Methodists. Jenkins, who ministered to the congregation until early in 1770, professed himself anxious not to sponsor a permanent separation from Chidlaw, but interest was such that in 1770 the meeting moved across the street to larger premises. In 1772 the congregation was formally constituted an Independent church, and obtained a settled pastor, William Armitage.[2]

CONGREGATIONALISTS

William Armitage's appointment as pastor of the Commonhall Street Independent church in 1772 marked the beginnings of modern Congregationalism in Chester. In 1776, when it numbered *c.* 78 members, the congregation decided on new buildings in Queen Street. A brick chapel accommodating *c.* 900, a vestry, and a minister's house were built and services began on the new site in 1777.[3] In 1778 the incumbent of St. John's, whose parish included Queen Street, and his colleague at St. Mary's reported that the number of Independents was increasing;[4] by 1789, however, another vicar of St. John's alleged that the congregation was in decline and consisted of no more than ten or eleven families 'of the very lowest class'.[5] Armitage died in 1794 and until 1813 was succeeded by ministers whose generally short tenures were interspersed with prolonged vacancies.[6] The congregation, which in 1806 became one of the founding members of the Cheshire Congregational Union, seems, however, to have increased; in 1803 a Sunday School opened in Queen Street, and in 1812 a large and expensive gallery was erected in the chapel.[7] By 1814 there was also a preaching station at Great Boughton in Philip Oliver's old chapel,[8] which was still in use in 1840.[9]

Congregationalism briefly became fashionable in Chester between 1813 and 1818 with the ministry of John Reynolds, a former army officer and son of George III's physician, and for a while the congregation included leading families and officers from the garrison.[10] In 1838 the chapel was enlarged and adorned with a neo-Grecian façade of white stone with Doric columns *in antis*. The cost, with that of ancillary buildings, encumbered the church with debt for 20

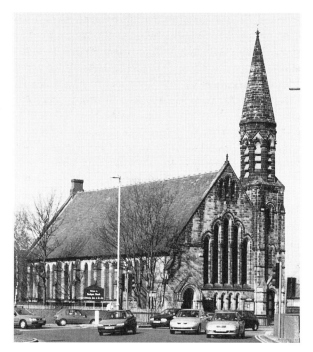

FIG. 95. *Congregational church, Upper Northgate Street*

years.[11] The Queen Street chapel was exceptionally successful under Richard Knill (1848–57) and survived the troubled pastorate of P. C. Barker (1865–9), who alienated many of the congregation before he eventually became an Anglican priest.[12] In 1851 the Congregationalists ranked third in numbers in Chester after the Anglicans and Wesleyans.[13] A Pleasant Sunday Afternoon Brotherhood was formed at Queen Street in 1892 and was at its height *c.* 1910, when it claimed an active membership of *c.* 700;[14] it continued until 1962.[15] The mother church at Queen Street remained the main focus of the movement in Chester until shifts in population from the city centre to the suburbs deprived it of its members. The church burned down in 1963, and in 1964 the congregation was dissolved.[16] The remains of the old building were largely demolished in 1978, except for the façade, retained as part of a Tesco supermarket, and a Doric screen from the lecture hall, resited at the northern end of a truncated Queen Street.[17]

In the mid 19th century Congregationalists proved adept at promoting new causes, and by 1851 there were four places of worship and *c.* 900 attenders at evening

---

1 C.C.A.L.S., EDA 2/6, f. 138; Urwick, *Sketches*, 39.

2 Urwick, *Sketches*, 39–42; Hemingway, *Hist. Chester*, ii. 165; Lond., Dr. Williams's Libr., MS. 38.7, ff. 207–8; C.C.A.L.S., ZCR 151/86.

3 Urwick, *Sketches*, 42–3; Hemingway, *Hist. Chester*, ii. 159–60; R.C.H.M.E., *Nonconformist Chapels in N. Eng.* 6.

4 C.C.A.L.S., EDV 7/1/2; EDV 7/1/4.

5 Ibid. EDV 7/2/2.   6 Urwick, *Sketches*, 43.

7 *V.C.H. Ches.* iii. 113; Powicke, *Congregational Union*, 26; C.C.A.L.S., ZCR 151/86, p. 51; ZCR 151/102.

8 E. Ll. Jones, *Great Boughton Congregational Church, Chester*

(copy at C.H.H.); Powicke, *Congregational Union*, 120.

9 *Parry's Dir. Chester* (1840), 82.

10 C.C.A.L.S., ZCR 151/86, pp. 51–3; Urwick, *Sketches*, 45.

11 C.C.A.L.S., ZCR 151/86, pp. 56–65; Urwick, *Sketches*, 46; R.C.H.M.E., *Nonconformist Chapels in N. Eng.* 6.

12 C.C.A.L.S., ZCR 151/86, pp. 59–60; ZCR 222/145.

13 *Census, 1851, Religious Worship*, p. cclv.

14 C.C.A.L.S., ZCR 572/27, esp. 10 Apr. 1911.

15 *Ches. Observer*, 6 Jan. 1962, p. 15; 12 Jan. 1963, p. 11.

16 C.C.A.L.S., ZCR 55/2/150; ZCR 151/20.

17 Harris, *Chester*, 162.

services.[1] The movement was first augmented by Mount Zion chapel in Commonhall Street, which in 1842 severed its links with the Calvinistic Methodists and adopted the principles of Congregationalism.[2] In 1875 Mount Zion moved to new premises in Upper North-gate Street, where it was apparently joined by a congregation which had met in the Music Hall in the 1850s and 1860s. The chapel, in the Early English style, of brick with a front and spire of Storeton Hill stone (Fig. 95), remained in Congregational hands until 1967.[3]

At Great Boughton, although there was no formal congregation, a Sunday school was carried on in Sandy Lane.[4] In 1863 Queen Street appointed a committee for the erection of a chapel. Land in Christleton Road was purchased in 1864 and in 1866 a chapel accommodating 150 adults was built to designs by T. M. Lockwood. In 1867 the chapel was constituted an independent church with a nucleus of 15 members. A new building of red brick in an Early English style, accommodating 450 worshippers, opened next to the 1866 building in 1873[5] and remained in use until 1976.[6]

At Handbridge a Sunday school established by Philip Oliver was continued under the auspices of Queen Street. A school room, purchased in 1863, closed in 1866 but reopened in 1868. In 1879 a Congregational church was formed in Oliver's old building in Greenway Street and in 1880 a new chapel of red brick with lancet windows was built on a new site in the main street of Handbridge.[7]

At Upton a handful of members of the Queen Street church, including one of the deacons, started open-air services in 1858 and built a chapel in 1860. It was replaced by a new church in 1900, enlarged in 1928 and 1965.[8]

In Hoole an iron mission room built in Walker Street in 1894 became a branch chapel of Queen Street in 1908[9] and a separate church c. 1937.[10]

In the 20th century further new congregations were established in the suburbs. An iron chapel opened in Whipcord Lane in 1909.[11] At Blacon, Free Church services held from 1943 in a garden hut at a private

house evolved into a Congregational church which had its own temporary premises on Saughall Road from 1949 and built a small chapel there in 1963.[12] In 1958 the church in Walker Street was replaced by a new and larger building in Hoole Road, of brick with a steeply pitched roof.[13] With the closure of Northgate church in 1967 many members joined an augmented church at Upton, where in 1969 work began on an extension to church and hall.[14] In 1964 the congregation of Queen Street was reconstituted as a new church in Green Lane, Vicars Cross. Besides those new buildings, earlier churches were still in use at Great Boughton, Handbridge, and Whipcord Lane in 1972, when the Congregational Church in England and Wales joined with the Presbyterian Church of England to become the United Reformed Church.[15] After the closure of the church at Christleton Road in 1976,[16] the U.R.C. joined with the Methodists in establishing the Caldy Valley Neighbourhood Church in 1983, which met at first mainly in Boughton Heath primary school before opening a new building in 1984, known locally as 'St. Sainsburys' from its location next to Sainsbury's supermarket on the Chester eastern bypass.[17]

There were also Welsh-speaking Congregationalists in Chester by 1850. They occupied a small brick chapel in Back Brook Street until 1860, when they bought the chapel in Pepper Street formerly used by the English Presbyterians. In 1870 they moved to a new building in Albion Park (later Albion Street), of brick with stone dressings in an eclectic Gothic style.[18] A second congregation formed in the 1870s in Frodsham Street had returned by 1884 to Back Brook Street, where it remained until 1894 when the Penri Memorial Chapel, of brick with a Decorated Gothic west window, was opened in Gorse Stacks. In 1898 the pastor, Ezra Johnson, sold the chapel to the Welsh Baptists, allegedly without the consent of the trustees, and the congregation evidently dispersed in acrimony.[19] The Albion Street chapel chose not to enter the United Reformed Church in 1972 and instead

1 *Census*, 1851, *Religious Worship*, p. cclv.
2 Urwick, *Sketches*, 48–9; C.C.A.L.S., EDA 13/1; below, this chapter: Later Presbyterians (Philip Oliver Connexion).
3 *Northgate Congregational Church, Chester, 1840–1940*; Powicke, *Congregational Union*, 124–5; C.C.A.L.S., ZCR 222/145; O.N.S. (Birkdale), Worship Reg., nos. 388, 22437.
4 Jones, *Great Boughton Congregational Church*.
5 *V.C.H. Ches.* iii. 113; Powicke, *Congregational Union*, 121; C.C.A.L.S., ZCR 158; ZCR 222/145.
6 *Ches. Observer*, 2 Jan. 1976, p. 25; 7 Jan. 1977, p. 5; C.H.H., RF 48, index cards.
7 C.C.A.L.S., ZCR 151/86, p. 68; ZCR 222/145; O.N.S. (Birkdale), Worship Reg., nos. 11102, 28188; Powicke, *Congregational Union*, 122–7.
8 *Upton Congregational Church, 1858–1970: A Short Hist.*; O.N.S. (Birkdale), Worship Reg., nos. 11104, 38229.
9 C.C.A.L.S., ZCR 225.
10 C.H.H., RF 48, index cards.
11 *Chester City Cl. Mins. 1908/9*, 425.

12 C.C.A.L.S., ZCR 151/18; ZCR 167; ZCR 575/2 (Sheila Parry, Hilda Pring, Mr. and Mrs. E. N. Kilver); *Ches. Observer*, 6 Jan. 1945, p. 3; inscription on bldg.
13 C.C.A.L.S., ZCR 225; O.N.S. (Birkdale), Worship Reg., nos. 62259, 66723.   14 *Upton Congregational Church*.
15 O.N.S. (Birkdale), Worship Reg., nos. 28188, 38229, 66723, 69109; *Kelly's Dir. Chester* (1972), 218, 360, 473; *Ches. Observer*, 5 Jan. 1973, p. 9.
16 *Ches. Observer*, 2 Jan. 1976, p. 25; 7 Jan. 1977, p. 5; C.H.H., RF 48, index cards.
17 Below, this chapter: Methodists (Methodism after 1932); local inf.
18 O.N.S. (Birkdale), Worship Reg., nos. 14733, 19788; *Bagshaw's Dir. Ches.* (1850), 66; *Slater's Dir. Ches.* (1855), 40; *White's Dir. Ches.* (1860), 91; *Morris's Dir. Ches.* (1864), 42.
19 *Chester Chron.* 5 Jan. 1884, p. 6; 6 Jan. 1894, p. 7; 5 Jan. 1895, p. 6; 24 Dec. 1898, p. 8; 14 Jan. 1899, p. 5; O.N.S. (Birkdale), Worship Reg., no. 34386; below, this chapter: Baptists.

joined the Union of Welsh Independents, but closed in 1985.[1]

LATER PRESBYTERIANS

Presbyterian Church of England

There was no orthodox English Presbyterian cause in Chester between 1768 and 1845, when a church belonging to the Presbyterian Church in England was founded by Major Anderson and Robert Barbour, the latter the driving force of the Presbyterians' Home Mission Committee. A chapel was rented in Pepper Street and by 1847 there were 19 communicants. The first minister was appointed in 1852 and numbers grew, partly because of Scottish migration to Chester to work on the railways and in other industries.[2] In 1857, with assistance from Barbour, a site was purchased in Newgate Street, and in 1860 a new church opened. Of brick with a stone front in the Decorated style, it was designed by the Liverpool architects J. M. and J. Hay in consultation with James Harrison,[3] and was extended by the same practice to include a lecture hall in 1884.[4] In the 1870s a missionary Sunday school was established in Commonhall Street. Thereafter the congregation remained relatively steady with 93 members on the communicants' roll in 1894[5] and c. 200 in 1960.[6] In 1972 it became St. Andrew's United Reformed Church,[7] and remained open in 2000.

Philip Oliver Connexion

Philip Oliver (1763–1800), a descendant of the Chester puritan John Bruen, was ordained by Bishop Porteous of Chester in 1787 and licensed to the chapelry of Bruera.[8] There he experienced an evangelical awakening, but shortly afterwards left Cheshire in poor health. When he sought to return, Bishop Cleaver, who had little love for evangelicals, did not offer him a living, and Oliver became a communicant member of the Queen Street Congregational chapel. In 1793 he began to conduct his own services on Sunday evenings at Boughton Lodge in Sandy Lane, where he converted outbuildings into a chapel, and soon afterwards forged links with the founder of Welsh Calvinistic Methodism, the Revd. Thomas Charles of Bala (Merion.), by whom he was persuaded to abandon the Anglican liturgy.[9]

Before Oliver died in 1800 he established other

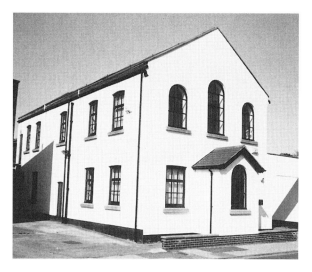

FIG. 96. *Windmill Lane chapel*

meetings at several places in the vicinity of the city, including Handbridge. His chapels formed a separate connexion under a scheme of government which achieved its final form in 1816. Supervision of them fell after Oliver's death to Thomas Charles, but because of the latter's responsibilities in Bala his duties were largely fulfilled by others, either ministers known personally to him or men trained in Lady Huntingdon's college at Cheshunt (Herts.). Her connexion was anxious to establish a new church in the city centre, and eventually Jonathan Wilcoxon, a trustee of Philip Oliver's Boughton chapel from 1800, seceded from it and rented the room in Commonhall Street vacated by the Baptists in 1806. Some members of the Boughton congregation followed him, and a church was formed in 1808, over which Wilcoxon presided until his death in 1837.[10] His followers afterwards built and moved to a small chapel in Windmill Lane (later Victoria Road), but had disbanded by 1867.[11] The Commonhall Street chapel itself remained connected with Oliver's churches and was rebuilt on the same site in 1839, but in 1842 abandoned Calvinistic Methodism in favour of Congregationalism.[12]

In 1813 the Oliver connexion moved from Boughton to the Octagon chapel at the Bars after the Methodists had vacated it. Thomas Charles died in 1814. Although in 1815 a permanent minister, James

1 *Ches. Observer*, 5 Jan. 1973, p. 9; *Chester Observer*, 25 Jan. 1985, p. 11; 1 Feb. 1985, p. 36; inf. from General Secretary's office, Union of Welsh Independents, Swansea.

2 C.C.A.L.S., ZCR 222/11; *Chester Guide* (1851), 113; J. H. Colligen, *Story of St. Andrew's, Newgate St., Chester*; O.N.S. (Birkdale), Worship Reg., no. 7946; K. M. Black, *The Threefold Cord: Sketch of Presbyterian Church in Eng.* 31–2, 43–4.

3 Colligen, *Story of St. Andrew's*; C.C.A.L.S., ZCR 222/36; O.N.S. (Birkdale), Worship Reg., no. 9463.

4 Colligen, *Story of St. Andrew's*; C.C.A.L.S., ZCR 222/68–73.

5 C.C.A.L.S., ZCR 222/104.

6 Ibid. ZCR 222/1–3.

7 O.N.S. (Birkdale), Worship Reg., no. 52807.

8 For this and following two paras. see G. Ll. Griffiths, 'Philip Oliver and his Connexion', *Cylchgrawn Cymdeithas Hanes Eglwys Methodistiaid Calfinaidd Cymru* (*Jnl. Hist. Soc. Presbyterian Church of Wales*), lvi. 68–77; lvii. 3–12; *Presbyterian Church of Wales, City Rd., Chester: Commemoration of Centenary* (1965) (copy at C.H.H.); J. Janion, *Some Acct. of Introduction of Methodism into Chester* (1833), 63–8.

9 *D.N.B.* s.n. Charles.

10 Hemingway, *Hist. Chester*, ii. 25; Aberystwyth, Nat. Libr. of Wales, MS. 12821.

11 C.C.A.L.S., ZCR 119/26, pp. 81–2, 84.

12 Urwick, *Sketches*, 47–9; above, this chapter: Congregationalists.

FIG. 97. *Presbyterian Church of Wales, City Road*

Bridgeman, was obtained from Lady Huntingdon's Connexion, the congregation at the Octagon was never part of that group and preserved its separate identity until 1854. Bridgeman and his assistant, John Williams, enjoyed a pastorate of *c.* 30 years, during which time the congregation varied from 'considerable' (1831) to 'not very numerous' (1843). In 1847 Bridgeman was succeeded by William Evans, a man trained in Thomas Charles's tradition, by then reconstituted as the Presbyterian Church of Wales. In 1854 the Philip Oliver Connexion, with chapels at Chester, Waverton, Tarvin, Delamere, Cotebrook, and Saughall, formally joined the Lancashire and Cheshire presbytery of that church.[1]

Presbyterian Church of Wales

The Octagon chapel was demolished in 1864 to make way for City Road and the congregation moved briefly to the Corn Exchange until a replacement had been erected near the original site. The new City Road chapel, designed by Michael Gummow of Wrexham, was of brick with a stuccoed Ionic portico *in antis*.

Accommodating *c.* 430 worshippers, it opened in 1865.[2]

Under William Evans's successor John Williams (1872–95) the church expanded. A schoolroom was built in 1880. A mission established by 1857 at Curzon Street, Saltney, moved to Saltney Ferry (Flints.) in 1886 and became a separate church in 1893.[3] The main congregation continued to occupy the premises in City Road in 2000, providing services of the Presbyterian Church of Wales in English.[4]

Welsh Calvinistic Methodist services in Welsh were being held in Trinity Street by 1804. The church moved to Mount Zion chapel on the north side of Common-hall Street in 1820,[5] and in 1854 was said to be the most numerous of the Welsh congregations in the city.[6] In 1865 the congregation purchased a site on the eastern side of St. John Street, where a church designed by W. and G. Audesley of Liverpool was erected in 1866. Of brick with an elaborate stone front in a 13th-century French Gothic style, it seated 700 people.[7] Welsh-language services of the Presbyterian Church of Wales were still held there in 2000.

1 O.N.S. (Birkdale), Worship Reg., no. 6272.
2 Ibid. no. 17236; *Cylchgrawn Cymdeithas,* lvii. 11–12; *Kelly's Dir. Ches.* (1892), 185.
3 *Presbyterian Church of Wales: Commem.*; *White's Dir. Ches.* (1860), 91; O.N.S. (Birkdale), Worship Reg., no. 7732; below, this chapter: Churches of Christ.
4 Inf. from Mrs. M. Newman, church secretary.

5 *Chester Guide* (1851), 112; *Parry's Dir. Chester* (1840), 82; *White's Dir. Ches.* (1860), 91; Hemingway, *Hist. Chester,* ii. 25, 165; O.N.S. (Birkdale), Worship Reg., no. 16053; P.R.O., RG 4/4417.
6 G. Borrow, *Wild Wales,* ed. D. Jones, 25.
7 *Stranger's Handbk.* (1891), 138; O.N.S. (Birkdale), Worship Reg., no. 18179.

BAPTISTS

A few Baptists from Chester attended a church in the parish of Grappenhall in the 1650s, and there were certainly Baptists active in the city in the 1660s.[1] In 1665 the presence of an 'Anabaptistical crew', reported by Sir Geoffrey Shakerley, governor of Chester castle, was confirmed by Bishop Hall.[2] In 1669 John Travers, a former captain in the parliamentary army, was arrested and imprisoned for holding an Anabaptist conventicle in Foregate Street. He was still active in 1670, but thereafter he seems to have gone to London.[3] In that year Shakerley recorded a further two Anabaptists imprisoned in the castle.[4]

Nevertheless, the cause was not strong in Chester and may have failed altogether. Allegations that the Baptists in the city abandoned separate meetings in order to join Matthew Henry's congregation[5] are refuted by the burial of one Hannah Amery of Chester at the Baptist mother church of Hill Cliffe, in Appleton, in 1709. Bishop Gastrell *c.* 1720 noted a meeting in St. Michael's parish. That congregation presumably included the Cestrian merchant Samuel Simpson, who in 1718 attended a Baptist ordination in Liverpool, and who was buried at Hill Cliffe in 1720.[6]

The continuing presence of Baptists in the city is shown by events at the Trinity Street Presbyterian church. The group which seceded in 1768 from what had become a Unitarian congregation attracted Baptists and indeed invited a Baptist minister to preach to them.[7] The Baptists among the seceders worshipped in a room in Foregate Street until 1777, when they moved to Commonhall Street, where successive pastors were Mr. Ecking, Dr. Jenkins of Wrexham, and Mr. Medley of Liverpool.[8] In the mid 1770s the Baptist minister and theologian John Fawcett (d. 1817) preached on at least two occasions.[9] The meeting was licensed,[10] and experienced a revival under pastor James Aston, who baptized 30 people in 1797.[11] In 1806 it moved to a chapel in Hamilton Place. The congregation, which was

Particular, did not join the Lancashire and Cheshire Association of Baptist Churches and did not prosper.[12] The chapel, which in 1851 had 250 sittings and a congregation of *c.* 100,[13] was closed in 1912 and demolished in 1913.[14]

By 1785 there was a second Baptist congregation, in St. Mary's parish, which sought a pastor from Archibald McLean, the leader of the Scotch Baptists in Edinburgh.[15] In 1800 they were meeting in Old Boarding School Yard at the back of Gamul House in Lower Bridge Street,[16] and in 1827 their pastor, the Revd. John Sim, bought materials from a former chapel in Bridge Street and built 'a little barn with Gothic windows' in Pepper Street to serve his small congregation. About 1845 that building was sold to the English Presbyterians, although the Scotch Baptists retained use of the vestry. The congregation, one of only 15 Scotch Baptist churches in England in 1851, still then numbered a dozen or so and was extinguished only in 1860 when the building in Pepper Street passed to the Welsh Congregationalists.[17]

In 1871 a new Baptist chapel was begun in the Pepper Street church just abandoned by the Welsh Congregationalists.[18] The number of sittings available to Baptists was thereby more than tripled, rising to 770.[19] The church joined the Lancashire and Cheshire Association in 1875, and in 1880 moved to new and much grander premises near Grosvenor Park. The new chapel, designed by John Douglas, was of brick with stone dressings in an eclectic Gothic style, the main body with grouped lancets and the street façade with tall Decorated windows and two low towers with high pitched roofs.[20]

An Ebenezer Strict Baptist mission, founded by members of the Hamilton Place congregation in 1877, had a membership of 50 by 1882, when it moved to a new brick-built chapel in Milton Street, Newtown.[21] It belonged to the Chester Evangelical Free Church Council from its foundation in 1897,[22] but later distanced itself from the local body, belonging instead by the 1970s to the Federation (later the

1 W. T. Whitley, *Baptists of NW. Eng.* 125; *V.C.H. Ches.* iii. 105.

2 *Cal. S.P. Dom.* 1664–5, 461; Urwick, *Sketches*, pp. xlv–xlvii; *V.C.H. Ches.* iii. 105.

3 *Cal. S.P. Dom.* 1668–9, 404; 1670, 248.

4 Ibid. 1670, 313.   5 Roberts, *Matthew Henry*, 121 n.

6 Whitley, *Baptists*, 64, 125, 155; Gastrell, *Not. Cest.* i. 108; J. Kenworthy, *Hist. Baptist Church at Hill Cliffe*, 33, 60–1, 63–4.

7 Above, this chapter: Early Presbyterians and Independents.

8 C.H.H., RF 48, MS. notes on Baptist chs.; Hemingway, *Hist. Chester*, ii. 165; Urwick, *Sketches*, 47; F. F. Bretherton, *Early Methodism in and around Chester*, 116–19.

9 Whitley, *Baptists*, 155; *D.N.B.* s.n. Fawcett.

10 C.C.A.L.S., EDV 7/3/112.

11 C.H.H., RF 48, MS. notes.

12 Whitley, *Baptists*, 155, 192, 331; Hemingway, *Hist. Chester*, ii. 165.

13 *Census*, 1851, *Religious Worship*, p. cclv.

14 Whitley, *Baptists*, 331; *Ches. Observer*, 6 Jan. 1912, p. 11; 4 Jan. 1913, p. 10.

15 D. M. Thompson, *Let Sects and Parties Fall: Short Hist. of Association of Chs. of Christ in G.B. and Irel.* 18; C.C.A.L.S., EDV 7/2/3; EDV 7/2/9.

16 C.H.H., RF 48, MS. notes; for the location of Old Boarding School Yard: J. Romney, *Chester and its Environs Illustrated*, [11].

17 Whitley, *Baptists*, 165, 259, 332; Hemingway, *Hist. Chester*, ii. 165; P.R.O., HO 129/459/67; *Census*, 1851, *Religious Worship*, p. lix; above, this chapter: Congregationalists.

18 C.H.H., RF 48, MS. notes.

19 *Nonconformist*, Dec. 1872; O.N.S. (Birkdale), Worship Reg., no. 21581.

20 *Kelly's Dir. Ches.* (1892), 185; O.N.S. (Birkdale), Worship Reg., no. 26197; E. Hubbard, *Work of John Douglas*, 249–50.

21 C.H.H., RF 48, MS. notes on Baptist chs. in Chester; *Kelly's Dir. Ches.* (1892), 185; O.N.S. (Birkdale), Worship Reg., no. 29761.

22 C.C.A.L.S., ZCR 572/1, p. 5.

THE CHURCHES AND OTHER RELIGIOUS BODIES · *Protestant Nonconformity*

Fellowship) of Independent Evangelical Churches.[1] A further mission, originally linked with Milton Street but from 1911 with Grosvenor Park, was opened in 1883 in Westminster Road, Hoole.[2]

In the 20th century the Baptists largely withdrew to the suburbs. The Milton Street chapel moved in 1970 to a new Ebenezer chapel near by in Francis Street when the whole area of Newtown was cleared of substandard terraced housing.[3] The Grosvenor Park chapel closed in 1974 and was reopened in 1977 by a Baptist congregation which, unlike its predecessor, did not affiliate to the Free Church Federal Council. It remained until 1980, when the members re-formed as Upton Baptist church, meeting at first in Upton Manor county primary school;[4] a new chapel, with low walls of brick and a barn-like pitched roof, was registered in 1989.[5] The mission at Westminster Road became an established Baptist church in 1952, with its own pastor from 1966.[6]

A Welsh Baptist congregation, in being by 1854,[7] met in the former Congregationalist chapel in Back Brook Street by 1864 but had moved out by 1878, when the chapel was in other hands. By 1884 the Welsh Baptists were meeting in Watergate Street, and moved from there in 1890 to Upper Northgate Street.[8] In 1898 they bought the Welsh Congregational chapel in Gorse Stacks and thereafter met as the Penri Memorial chapel, remaining open in 1995.[9]

QUAKERS

A meeting in Chester was recorded in 1653.[10] By then Quakers were established in sufficient numbers to alarm the authorities. Their sufferings between 1653 and 1657 under Mayors Edward Bradshaw, Richard Bird, William Wright, and especially Peter Leigh were detailed in a tract published in London in 1657.[11] Compiled by Anthony Hutchins, himself a sufferer, the pamphlet was augmented by a short contribution from George Fox, reproving the city's magistrates for their cruelties; Fox is known to have visited Chester in 1657.[12]

The earliest recorded persecutions were in 1653, when victims included the Quaker preacher Richard Hubberthorn (1628–62), arrested while on a visit to the city and imprisoned for three months.[13] Occasionally offenders were charged with attending a meeting, but more often they were arrested for abusing Presbyterian and Independent congregations or haranguing the public. In general, sentences were short, but they became more severe during the mayoralty of Peter Leigh (1656–7), when offenders were often confined for several hours in a cramped chamber known as Little Ease, in the grounds of the house of correction outside the Northgate. One unfortunate, Richard Sale, was imprisoned so often and with such brutality that he died of his injuries.[14]

Despite (or perhaps because of) such persecution, the Quakers remained a significant element among Dissenters in city and shire. At the Restoration 112 were imprisoned in the county gaol, and a further 10 were detained by the city authorities for refusing the oath of allegiance.[15] By 1665 Quakers were still to be found in at least four parishes within the city.[16] The castle governor and the bishop, Shakerley and Hall, though probably less brutal than their Commonwealth predecessors, proved vigorous persecutors. In 1665 *c.* 20 members of a meeting in Castle Lane were sent to the Northgate gaol,[17] and in 1669 the authorities attempted to suppress another meeting at the house of Richard Smith in St. John's Lane. Smith, a surgeon who in 1663 had been refused a licence and imprisoned, appeared before the justices with a number of associates, including two shoemakers, a tailor, and a labourer. All were fined.[18] Meetings, however, continued to be held twice every Sunday in the house, and in 1670 the society, whose members were then said to include a number of 'sequestrators and soldiers in the late rebellion', was once again subject to the attention of the authorities. Smith and *c.* 12 fellow worshippers appeared before the mayor and justices and were eventually fined sums ranging from £20 to 5*s.* for what was alleged in several instances to be their fifth

1 *Ches. Observer*, 7 Jan. 1972, p. 8; inf. from General Secretary's office, Fellowship of Independent Chs., Croydon.

2 Whitley, *Baptists*, 332; C.C.A.L.S., ZCR 662/39.

3 O.N.S. (Birkdale), Worship Reg., nos. 29761, 72388; C.H.H., RF 48, index cards; ibid. Y 1/1/516; *Ches. Observer*, 3 Jan. 1969, p. 9; 2 Jan. 1970, p. 8; 1 Jan. 1971, p. 7.

4 *Ches. Observer*, 8 Mar. 1974, p. 7; 5 Apr. 1974, p. 33; 7 Jan. 1977, p. 5; 6 Jan. 1978, p. 13; 5 Jan. 1979, p. 7; *Chester Observer*, 4 Jan. 1980, p. 10; 17 Dec. 1986, p. 11; O.N.S. (Birkdale), Worship Reg., no. 26197; below, this chapter: Other Evangelical Churches.

5 O.N.S. (Birkdale), Worship Reg., no. 78060.

6 C.C.A.L.S., ZCR 662/38–9.

7 G. Borrow, *Wild Wales*, ed. D. Jones, 25.

8 *Morris's Dir. Ches.* (1864), 43; *Slater's Dir. Ches.* (1880), 21; *Kelly's Dir. Ches.* (1896), 190; *Chester Chron.* 5 Jan. 1884, p. 6; 4 Jan. 1890, p. 6; 3 Jan. 1891, p. 2.

9 *Chester Chron.* 1 Jan. 1898, p. 3; 14 Jan. 1899, p. 6; inf. from Mr. S. R. Williams (church member); O.N.S. (Birkdale),

Worship Reg., no. 44972; above, this chapter: Congregationalists.

10 J. Besse, *Colln. of Sufferings of People called Quakers, 1650–89*, i. 99.

11 A. Hutchins, *Caines Bloudy Race Known by their Friends* (Lond. 1657), reprinted in *J.C.A.S.* xiv. 29–94, esp. 36–76. Cf. 4 *Sheaf*, v, pp. 9–28; Hemingway, *Hist. Chester*, ii. 168–70; Besse, *Sufferings of Quakers*, i. 99–102.

12 *Jnl. of George Fox*, ed. N. Penney, i. 285; *J.C.A.S.* xiv. 71–2.

13 *J.C.A.S.* xiv. 36–8; Besse, *Sufferings of Quakers*, i. 99; *D.N.B.* s.n. Hubberthorn.

14 *J.C.A.S.* xiv. 43–4, 50–5, 57–60, 62–7, 69; Besse, *Sufferings of Quakers*, i. 99–101; above, Law and Order: Municipal Prisons (House of Correction).

15 Besse, *Sufferings of Quakers*, i. 102.

16 C.C.A.L.S., EDV 1/34.

17 *Cal. S.P. Dom.* 1664–5, 226.

18 C.C.A.L.S., ZQSF 79 (pt. 2); Besse, *Sufferings of Quakers*, i. 103.

FIG. 98. *Quaker meeting house and burial ground, 1964*

offence.[1] The inability or reluctance of the city authorities to suppress the conventicle excited the indignation of Governor Shakerley, who lamented that the Conventicle Act was not being applied, and recommended the mayor and justices to exact the oath of allegiance and imprison those who refused. His advice was followed only in part and without enthusiasm, for the authorities discharged the Quakers despite their declared intention to continue their meetings.[2]

In the 1680s there were further persecutions, instigated in particular by Alderman William Harvey. In 1682 *c.* 28 worshippers, drawn from as far afield as Guilden Sutton, Hawarden, and Hope (Flints.), were again arrested and fined for attending the meeting in St. John's Lane. Two were committed to prison.[3] Small conventicles were broken up again in 1683 and 1684 by Harvey, but his attempts to secure the offenders' imprisonment met with only limited success; when they appeared at quarter sessions the jury found them not guilty and they were discharged. Harvey himself died in 1684 and thereafter there appears to have been little further persecution.[4] Those still in prison were released with the introduction of the new policy of toleration in 1686.[5]

In 1687 William Penn preached at Chester in the Quakers' meeting house to an audience which included James II.[6] A new meeting house was completed and registered for worship in 1703; among those contributing money was Joseph Maddock of Dublin, late of Chester, in his will of 1702.[7] It was a plain brick building with a burial ground in front, situated at the corner of Frodsham Street and Union Walk.[8] Meetings were also occasionally held elsewhere; in 1771, for example, the city magistrates authorized the use of a room at the timber yard in St. John Street, and in 1779, when the Friends held their octennial gathering at Chester, numbers were such that worship was held in a large temporary building in Linenhall field.[9] The capacity of the Frodsham Street meeting house was enlarged shortly before 1803 by inserting a loft.[10] By 1830, however, attendance at the weekly meeting had fallen to 15 or fewer, although it was swollen by members of other denominations when there was a visiting preacher.[11] Thereafter attendances remained modest, and in 1851 neither Sunday service drew more than 34.[12]

The second oldest place of Dissenting worship in the city, the meeting house in Frodsham Street was re-

1 C.C.A.L.S., ZMF 88; ZQSF 79 (pt. 3); *Cal. S.P. Dom. 1670*, 222; Besse, *Sufferings of Quakers*, i. 105.

2 *Cal. S.P. Dom. 1670*, 273.

3 C.C.A.L.S., ZMF 101.

4 Besse, *Sufferings of Quakers*, i. 110–11.

5 Ibid. i. 112.

6 T. Clarkson, *Memoirs of Public and Private Life of William Penn*, ed. W. E. Forster, 181; Hemingway, *Hist. Chester*, ii. 166.

7 C.C.A.L.S., ZQSF 90 (1703); *Quaker Rec., Dublin: Abstracts of Wills*, ed. P. B. Eustace and O. C. Goodbody, 65; D. M. Butler, *Quaker Meeting Houses of Britain*, i. 45.

8 Hemingway, *Hist. Chester*, ii. 166.

9 C.C.A.L.S., ZQSF 103; *Chester Chron.* 30 Apr. 1779.

10 Butler, *Quaker Meeting Houses*, i. 45.

11 Hemingway, *Hist. Chester*, ii. 166–70.

12 P.R.O., HO 129/459/57; *V.C.H. Ches.* iii. 108–9, 114.

modelled in the 19th century and repaired in 1960, but structural weaknesses in the building persuaded the Friends to sell it to a commercial developer for demolition in 1975, after which the society moved into new rooms, purpose-built over shops on the same site but entered from Union Walk rather than Frodsham Street, where they continued to meet in 2000.[1]

METHODISTS

Wesleyans

Chester was one of the earliest centres of Methodism in north-west England. There was a society in the city by 1747, when it was visited by the itinerant preacher John Bennet (1715–59), who reported to Wesley that the inhabitants received him gladly and were anxious for a visit from Wesley himself.[2] Bennet paid a second visit in 1748, but was barred from the city's churches.[3] As a result of his work Huntington Hall and a house in Love Lane were opened for preaching, and meetings were also held in the open air.[4] In 1752 the society moved to a barn at St. Martin's Ash, in which shortly afterwards Wesley held a well attended meeting on the occasion of his first visit to the city. His preaching aroused opposition and after his departure a local mob with the connivance of the mayor wrecked the barn.[5] In 1753 Wesley paid another visit to Chester and found the restored barn 'full of serious hearers'.[6]

In 1752 Wesley quarrelled with Bennet, who in 1749 had become assistant of a large circuit covering Cheshire, Lancashire, Nottinghamshire, Derbyshire, and parts of Yorkshire.[7] Although there were defections, the society at Chester remained loyal to Wesley and continued to receive frequent visits from him.[8]

In 1763 Chester became the focus of a circuit with four preachers serving the area between Warrington (Lancs.), Shrewsbury, and Wrexham. The congregation moved to a new chapel in 1765 in Boughton near what was later to become City Road,[9] its octagonal form reflecting Wesley's own preferences.[10] Wesley himself preached in the new chapel within two months of its opening.[11] The Octagon flourished in the 1760s and 1770s, its converts including Samuel Bradburn (1751–1816), who in 1792 was president of Conference, the Methodists' governing body nationally.[12]

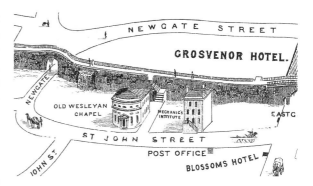

FIG. 99. *Wesleyan chapel, St. John Street, in 1867, looking west*

In 1776 an additional and more central place of worship was opened in Commonhall Street in premises vacated by the Congregationalists.[13] The new preaching room became the centre for the liberal faction within the society, and when in 1792 the congregation at the Octagon followed the decision of Conference to suspend the administration of the sacraments and to avoid holding services at times which conflicted with Anglican church hours, those at Commonhall Street adopted a policy more hostile to the Church of England and shortly seceded to help form the Methodist New Connexion.[14]

Although Wesleyan membership in Chester dropped after the secession, it revived in the early 19th century and by 1810 stood at 180.[15] In 1806 during a period of revivalist enthusiasm new building works, including a school, were undertaken at the Octagon, and opposition to holding services during church hours and to the administration of the sacraments was abandoned.[16] Larger premises were soon needed and in 1811 a 'capacious' chapel was opened in St. John Street. Designed by Thomas Harrison, assisted by Benjamin Gommer of Ruabon (Denb.), it was of brick with a semi-circular street front and entrances at both ends. The new buildings, which also included a school and preacher's house,[17] evidently attracted new worshippers, and in 1822 membership stood at 468, the largest recorded there in the 19th century.[18] By 1831, however, numbers had fallen

1 Lond., Friends' House, General Quarterly Meeting Rec. (Ches.) (inf. from H. G. Arnold); C.H.H., RF 48, index cards; Butler, *Quaker Meeting Houses*, i. 46.

2 F. F. Bretherton, *Early Methodism in and around Chester*, 26–7; E. A. Rose, 'Methodism in Ches. to 1800', *T.L.C.A.S.* lxxviii. 24–5.

3 *T.L.C.A.S.* lxxviii. 25.

4 Bretherton, *Early Methodism in Chester*, 28–9.

5 Ibid. 30–4; J. Wesley, *Jnl.* ed. N. Curnock, iv. 34–7.

6 Bretherton, *Early Methodism in Chester*, 35, 40–1; Wesley, *Jnl.* iv. 56.

7 Bretherton, *Early Methodism in Chester*, 28; *T.L.C.A.S.* lxxviii. 26.

8 e.g. Wesley, *Jnl.* iv. 184, 203, 311, 373, 446–7, 492, 522; v. 85–6, 109, 140–1, 162, 305–6, 329, 361, 403, 451; vi. 15, 101,

143, 174, 228, 271, 311, 402–3, 492; vii. 65, 98, 154, 257, 299, 375, 519; viii. 57.

9 Bretherton, *Early Methodism in Chester*, 54–5, 59–61.

10 *T.L.C.A.S.* lxxviii. 28; *Encyclopaedia of World Methodism*, i. 126–8.

11 Bretherton, *Early Methodism in Chester*, 59–60.

12 *D.N.B.*

13 Bretherton, *Early Methodism in Chester*, 115–19.

14 Below, this section: Methodist New Connexion.

15 Bretherton, *Early Methodism in Chester*, 274.

16 Ibid. 185–7.

17 Ibid. 243–58; J. Janion, *Some Acct. of Introduction of Methodism into Chester* (1833), 28; Hemingway, *Hist. Chester*, ii. 165; R.C.H.M.E., *Nonconformist Chapels in N. Eng.* 6–7.

18 Bretherton, *Early Methodism in Chester*, 274.

to 289 after a dispute led many of the congregation to secede to the New Connexion.[1]

The Chester circuit, which still stretched from Bunbury to Ellesmere Port in 1845, was reduced to a more manageable area round the city in 1868.[2] Its expansion within Chester was relatively slow. A small sandstone chapel in late 13th-century Gothic style was built at Hough Green to serve Saltney in 1856.[3] By 1868 there was a mission in Black Diamond Street, Newtown,[4] which closed when a new chapel, stone-built in a Gothic style with a tower and spire, was opened in City Road in 1873.[5] In Garden Lane a mission room was open by 1881,[6] and a small red-brick chapel was built in 1888 and extended in 1911.[7] In Bishopsfield (Hoole) there was a society by 1876 which closed in 1884, reopened in 1888, closed again in 1895, and was not re-established.[8]

Welsh-speaking Wesleyans had a meeting room at the south end of Northgate Street by 1804.[9] Until 1822 they belonged to the Chester circuit but then transferred to the Holywell Welsh circuit; in 1828 they moved to a small chapel in Hamilton Place.[10] It was sold to the corporation in 1884 and demolished to make way for an extension to the public market, the congregation moving to a new chapel in Queen Street, brick-built in a neo-Romanesque style.[11]

The total Wesleyan attendance on Census Sunday 1851 was the highest among the nonconformist denominations,[12] and adult membership of the English-speaking churches remained over 500 in the late 19th century.[13] The church in St. John Street was remodelled in 1906, when Harrison's western apse was replaced by a street front of red brick with stone dressings in a debased north European Gothic.[14] A chancel was added in 1926.[15]

Methodist New Connexion

In 1792 the more liberally inclined Methodists at the Commonhall Street chapel disagreed with the Wesleyan Conference's new policies of suspending the administration of the sacraments and avoiding conflict with the times of Anglican church services. In 1793 they formed a separate society and in 1794,

following expulsion from their premises by the proprietor, they took the highly unusual and decisive step of establishing an independent Methodist chapel at a new site in Trinity Lane. By 1796 they had formally broken with Conference. In 1797 the new society became the head of one of the seven original circuits of the Methodist New Connexion.[16] Its membership within the city, perhaps drawn mainly from a rather lower social stratum than the Wesleyans, numbered 48 by 1801, and in 1831 maintained a second preaching house in Handbridge, besides three Sunday schools.[17] Larger premises in the city centre were necessary, and in 1835 the congregation moved to a new chapel in Pepper Street, of brick with stone dressings and a stuccoed Corinthian portico *in antis*. It held 900 worshippers.[18]

The Pepper Street chapel remained the headquarters of a Chester circuit when the New Connexion joined with other Methodist groups to form the United Methodist Church in 1907, but it was closed in 1920 and the congregation moved to a modest hall in Egerton Street.[19]

Primitive Methodists

In the early 19th century the Primitive Methodists began to recruit in Chester. Their earliest preacher was Joshua Reynolds, a native of Saughall, but the real beginnings of the movement date from the missions of John Wedgwood in 1819 and Thomas Brownsword in 1821. The new society initially met in houses in Steven Street and King Street, but in 1823 a chapel was built in Steam Mill Street. It became the head of a circuit in 1826. Despite being in a discouragingly violent neighbourhood, the chapel, a plain brick building of five bays, remained the home of the congregation for nearly 40 years. Its construction burdened the society with debt and the early years were clearly precarious, although by 1832 the circuit reported 390 members.[20]

In 1861 the congregation decided to leave Steam Mill Street and in 1863 a new chapel and school, of brick with Gothic details, opened on the south side of George Street. From its earliest days the building was

1 Bretherton, *Early Methodism in Chester*, 274; Hemingway, *Hist. Chester*, ii. 162.

2 C.C.A.L.S., ZCR 55/33/1–3, 5.

3 Ibid. ZCR 55/21, sched. 1891.

4 Ibid. ZCR 55/33/2–3; *P. & G. Dir. Chester* (1871), 22.

5 *Kelly's Dir. Ches.* (1892), 185; O.N.S. (Birkdale), Worship Reg., no. 21460; C.C.A.L.S., ZCR 55/21, sched. 1891.

6 C.C.A.L.S., ZCR 55/34.   7 Ibid. ZCR 55/115.

8 Ibid. ZCR 55/33/6, 8, 10–11, 24–5, 28, 46–7; cf. ZCR 55/21, sched. 1891.

9 Ibid. EDV 7/3/110, q. 3.

10 Bretherton, *Early Methodism in Chester*, 294–5; Hemingway, *Hist. Chester*, ii. 163; *Stranger's Companion in Chester* (1821), 9.

11 O.N.S. (Birkdale), Worship Reg., nos. 5255, 27849; C.C.A.L.S., ZCR 119/26, p. 100; ZCR 286; *Chester Chron.* 5 Jan. 1884, p. 6; 3 Jan. 1885, p. 2.

12 *Census, 1851, Religious Worship*, p. cclv.

13 C.C.A.L.S., ZCR 55/33/8, 40.

14 Ibid. ZCR 55(3)/104, 113 (from TS. cal.); R.C.H.M.E., *Nonconformist Chapels in N. Eng.* 6–7.

15 C.C.A.L.S., ZCR 55(3)/92.

16 Bretherton, *Early Methodism in Chester*, 155–61; *Proc. Wesley Hist. Soc.* xxxvi. 8–9; Hemingway, *Hist. Chester*, ii. 163.

17 Bretherton, *Early Methodism in Chester*, 175; Hemingway, *Hist. Chester*, ii. 164; *Hist. of Methodist Church in G.B.* ed. R. Davies and G. Rupp, i. 309.

18 Bretherton, *Early Methodism in Chester*, 174; *Bagshaw's Dir. Ches.* (1850), 66.

19 C.C.A.L.S., ZCR 276 (TS. cal.); *Kelly's Dir. Ches.* (1923), 234, 242, 249.

20 *Centenary Souvenir of Introduction of Primitive Methodism into Chester and District, 1819–1919*; O.N.S. (Birkdale), Worship Reg., no. 801; *Chester Chron.* 9 Apr. 1887.

FIG. 100. *Primitive Methodist chapel (built 1888), George Street*

too small,[1] and in 1864 after a camp meeting in Chester a second society was founded. The congregation worshipped initially in a rented room in Pepper Street, then in Cuppin Street, but within three years had purchased Mount Zion chapel in Commonhall Street.[2] In 1874 the Chester circuit was divided between First and Second circuits, headed by George Street and Commonhall Street.[3]

Further expansion took place in the 1880s. In 1885 a new site was purchased in George Street, opposite the existing premises. A new chapel, designed by T. M. Lockwood in a Gothic style, of brick with stone dressings, with a squat tower and spire, opened there in 1888 and became the headquarters of the First circuit; the former chapel became a temperance hall and was in commercial use in 1995.[4] A chapel for Boughton built in Tarvin Road in 1884 became the head of a Third Chester circuit divided from the First circuit in 1889.[5]

The three circuits covered a wide rural area around the city, the First (George Street) to the north, the Second (Commonhall Street) south, and the Third (Boughton) east, co-operating in a Chester Primitive Methodist Council set up in 1895.[6] All three were still growing in strength *c.* 1900: the First circuit opened a mission room for Hoole in Faulkner Street in 1902,

which removed to a new chapel in Hamilton Street in 1903, designed by Henry Harper of Nottingham, of brick with stone dressings in a free Gothic style;[7] the Second circuit removed its headquarters from Commonhall Street to a new and larger chapel, of brick with stone dressings, with a tower and spire, in Hunter Street, called the City Temple, in 1899;[8] and the mother church of the Third circuit in Tarvin Road was enlarged in 1893.[9]

Independent Methodists

The United Free Gospel church, a small Methodist grouping, had a chapel in Back Brook Street (probably the former Welsh Baptist chapel) with its own minister in 1878, but had evidently left Chester by 1892.[10]

Methodism after 1932

With the union of the Wesleyans, the United Methodists, and the Primitive Methodists in 1932, the city was left with too many chapels. The process of reduction began with the closure of the small United Methodist church in Egerton Street in 1932 and the conversion of the City Road chapel into a central hall in 1934.[11] For the moment the four circuits, three formerly Primitive Methodist and one Wesleyan (renamed Chester St. John's circuit), remained separate, but in 1958 the St. John's and Hunter Street circuits were combined as Grosvenor Park circuit, and in 1963 they joined the others to form a united Chester circuit.[12] The former Wesleyan chapel in Saltney, renamed Hough Green in 1933 to distinguish it from the Primitive Methodist chapel in Saltney High Street (Flints.), had closed after uniting with the latter society in 1961.[13] Other closures followed the creation of the united circuit: Hunter Street in 1967 and George Street in 1970, both congregations moving to the St. John Street church, renamed Wesley in 1966 and remodelled 1968–70; and the City Road central hall in 1982, when a new society was formed in Great Boughton, which opened the Caldy Valley Neighbourhood Church, adjoining the Chester eastern bypass, jointly with the United Reformed Church in 1984.[14] Hunter Street, George Street, and City Road were demolished after closure.

1 *Centenary Souvenir*, 26–8; C.C.A.L.S., ZCR 55/2, 33, 130–2; ZCR 78/1–38; ZCR 94/1–37; O.N.S. (Birkdale), Worship Reg., no. 15774.

2 *Centenary Souvenir*, 15; *P. & G. Dir. Chester* (1871), 22; O.N.S. (Birkdale), Worship Reg., no. 23711; above, this chapter: Later Presbyterians (Presbyterian Church of Wales).

3 *Centenary Souvenir*, 15; C.C.A.L.S., ZCR 55/130/11–12, 35.

4 *Centenary Souvenir*, 28; C.C.A.L.S., ZCR 111/22–5; ZCR 745/23; O.N.S. (Birkdale), Worship Reg., no. 30733; *Chester Chron.* 9 Apr. 1887.

5 *Centenary Souvenir*, 17; *Kelly's Dir. Ches.* (1892), 185; O.N.S. (Birkdale), Worship Reg., no. 28364; C.C.A.L.S., ZCR 55/130/35; ZCR 55/156–65; ZCR 94/38.

6 C.C.A.L.S., ZCR 55/130/35; ZCR 55/130/40, p. 7.

7 Ibid. ZCR 55/2; ZCR 238 (TS. cal.); ZTRH 82, p. 348; O.N.S. (Birkdale), Worship Reg., no. 48513.

8 *Kelly's Dir. Ches.* (1902), 204, 211; *Centenary Souvenir*, 15–16; O.N.S. (Birkdale), Worship Reg., no. 36986; C.C.A.L.S., ZCR 55/2; ZCR 270/7–11; C.H.H., Y 1/1/510; *Methodist Church, Hunter St., Chester: Jubilee Celebrations, 1899–1949* (copy at C.H.H.).

9 Inscription on bldg.; *Kelly's Dir. Ches.* (1896), 190.

10 *Kelly's Dir. Ches.* (1878), 109; (1892), 192; *P. & G. Dir. Chester* (1878/9), 25; *Hist. Methodist Church in G.B.* ii. 323–6; cf. above, this chapter: Baptists.

11 C.C.A.L.S., ZCR 276 (TS. cal.).

12 Ibid. ZCR 55/33, esp. circuit plans for 1933, 1959, 1963.

13 Inscription on Saltney High St. bldg.; O.N.S. (Birkdale), Worship Reg., no. 18067.

14 C.C.A.L.S., ZCR 55/33, esp. circuit plans for quarters starting Nov. 1966, Aug. 1967; ZCR 234/13/13–14, 63–4, 70; O.N.S. (Birkdale), Worship Reg., no. 76623.

The Welsh church in Queen Street, which remained outside the Chester circuit, closed in 1977 and later passed to a Pentecostalist congregation.[1] In 2000 Methodist churches survived at St. John Street, Garden Lane, Hamilton Street, Tarvin Road, Caldy Valley, and Saltney (Flints.). The combined adult membership had fallen from 1,100 in 1966 to 800 in 1991.[2]

CHURCHES OF CHRIST

Chester had an important part in the early history of the Churches of Christ, an avowedly unsectarian evangelical movement stressing Scripture and the baptism of adult believers but shunning the emotional revivalism characteristic of many 19th-century evangelicals. Many early adherents in Britain were former Scotch Baptists, and the presence of a chapel of that sect in the earlier 19th century helped launch the movement in Chester and indeed nationally. An early leader in London was William Jones, who had been baptized at the Scotch Baptist church in Chester in 1786; in the 1830s his writings became known through the Chester Baptists to John Davies, lay preacher of a chapel at Mollington just outside the city boundary. Davies founded a new church in Chester possibly as early as 1836, the date later believed to mark the origin of a 'Baptist' congregation in the city. Davies also chaired the first general meeting of like-minded congregations at Edinburgh in 1842, which formalized the Churches of Christ as a separate denomination. The second general meeting, in 1847, was at Chester.[3]

Davies's congregation was perhaps the allegedly unsectarian group of fewer than 40 which in 1851 met in an upper room in Queen Street[4] and later used the meeting house, seating 90, which stood near by in 1872.[5] It dwindled after Davies's death in 1865. By the late 1870s it was in a much reduced state, and a missionary effort by the American arm of the movement in 1878 singled it out for special attention. The mission was a success, but the Americans differed enough in matters of church practice from the British churches to cause a split, the Chester church being expelled by the Association of Churches of Christ in 1883. The breach was healed only in 1917.[6]

The division did not hinder the progress of the church in Chester. By 1882 it had moved into a new building at the corner of Upper Northgate Street and Delamere Street,[7] and a second church was opened at Saltney in 1886 in the former Presbyterian Church of Wales mission chapel in Curzon Street.[8] They joined the newly founded Chester Evangelical Free Church Council in 1898 and 1899 respectively.[9] The Upper Northgate Street church was rebuilt in 1937 as a plain brick building with stepped round-headed lancets,[10] and the Saltney church moved to the former Methodist chapel in Hough Green in 1961.[11]

The Northgate Street church closed in 1981 after the Association of Churches of Christ had the previous year dissolved itself in order to allow individual congregations to join the United Reformed Church,[12] and the building was put to commercial use thereafter. The Saltney church, however, was among the minority which declined to join the U.R.C. and instead joined the newly formed Fellowship of Churches of Christ. It continued in 1995 as an independent evangelical church.[13]

UNDENOMINATIONAL MISSIONS
Chester City Mission

The mission was founded in 1845 on the model of the London City Mission by laymen from several denominations. Paid full-time missionaries and voluntary assistants held evangelistic cottage meetings, organized thrift clubs for the poor, and undertook charity work, notably in Handbridge and Boughton. In the 1850s and again briefly from 1870 four missionaries were employed, but the number was usually two and never more than three after 1872. The headquarters were at first in a barn off Upper Northgate Street, from 1853 in a room over a shop in Crook Street, and later in a mission hall built by Miss M. A. Walker next to the premises in Crook Street in 1881. Besides its cottage meetings, the mission held an annual Race-Week Gospel Campaign during Chester races, which were believed by Chester evangelicals to be a particular occasion for sin. In 1854 the organization opened a mission to canal boatmen, which was later hived off and operated as the Boatmen's Bethel. It came back under the wing of the mission in 1920, from 1924 most services were held in Crook Street, and after 1929 there was only one paid missionary. In 1959, when Crook Street was being redeveloped, the mission

---

1 *Ches. Observer*, 7 Jan. 1977, p. 5; 6 Jan. 1978, p. 13; O.N.S. (Birkdale), Worship Reg., no. 27849; below, this chapter: Pentecostal Churches.

2 C.C.A.L.S., ZCR 55/33; ZCR 234/13/15, 56, 93, 101; TS. list of ZCR 55 for inf. on churches open in 2000.

3 D. M. Thompson, *Let Sects and Parties Fall*, 7–10, 18–35, 40–3; C.H.H., RF 48, MS. notes on Baptist chs., where the 'third Baptist' church was actually the Church of Christ: *Chester Chron.* 5 Jan. 1884, p. 6; cf. above, this chapter: Baptists.

4 P.R.O., HO 129/459/58.

5 O.S. Map 1/500, Chester XXXVIII.11.17 (1875 edn.).

6 Thompson, *Let Sects and Parties Fall*, 57, 84–5, 109–11.

7 O.N.S. (Birkdale), Worship Reg., no. 26466; O.S. Map 1/2,500, Ches. XXXVIII.11 (1875, 1899 edns.).

8 Notice at church, Mar. 1995; O.N.S. (Birkdale), Worship Reg., no. 37499; cf. above, this chapter: Later Presbyterians (Presbyterian Church of Wales).

9 C.C.A.L.S., ZCR 572/1, pp. 38, 83.   10 Date on bldg.

11 O.N.S. (Birkdale), Worship Reg., no. 68413; C.C.A.L.S., ZCR 55/118–26 (TS. cal.); cf. above, this chapter: Methodists (Methodism after 1932).

12 Thompson, *Let Sects and Parties Fall*, 195–7; *Chester Observer*, 2 Jan. 1981, p. 10; 25 Dec. 1981.

13 Notice at church, Mar. 1995.

FIG. 101. *Sunday school children, City Mission Hall, 1958*

moved to the former ragged school in Princess Street, which was given to it by the city council. Thereafter the mission still undertook charitable work but from 1989 could not afford a full-time superintendent and its premises lay under the threat of the redevelopment of Princess Street. It secured instead the part-time services of the experienced former head of the Liverpool City Mission and the promise of a site in Hunter Street.[1]

Other Missions

In Hoole the marquess of Westminster in 1856 built an unsectarian mission church and Sunday school in Peploe Street (later Westminster Road); unsectarian services were still held there in 1901 but they probably ceased shortly afterwards.[2]

Other undenominational services were held at the Lecture Hall in Lower Bridge Street (presumably Oddfellows Hall), registered for worship in 1887;[3] and the Egerton Mission Hall in Egerton Street, built between 1906 and 1910, which was still open under that name in 1914,[4] but later passed into denominational use, first Methodist, then Spiritualist, and finally Christadelphian.[5] A mission to the deaf and dumb held services on alternate Sundays at no. 39 Northgate Street in 1910 and 1914.[6]

BRETHREN

Brethren of uncertain affiliation registered a meeting room at no. 6 Bollands Court, White Friars, in 1860.

They moved later to a room at the rear of Forest House off Love Street, registered in 1900, and then to a room in Westminster Road, Hoole, registered in 1938. The last room may have been long disused when it was struck from the register in 1964.[7]

Another group met at premises in Queen Street in 1871 but had disappeared by 1878.[8]

A third was by 1910 holding two services each Sunday at a mission room on the south side of Delamere Street, possibly in succession to one of the two gospel halls recorded in Frodsham Street between 1896 and 1906. The Delamere Street room was registered in 1927 and continued in use until *c.* 1940.[9]

Christian Brethren from Birkenhead began cottage meetings in Chester *c.* 1915; the congregation which formed was given a wooden building in Station Approach and opened it for services as the Brownhill Gospel Hall in 1918. In 1964 the church, which then had *c.* 35 members, built a new meeting place on the corner of Kingsway and Grasmere Road in Newton, called Kingsway chapel, whose membership had grown to *c.* 200 by 1995.[10] Brownhill Gospel Hall was used after 1964 by another group of Brethren, who ceased to meet some time after 1974.[11]

Yet another group was meeting over a café at no. 34 Lower Bridge Street by 1962 and continued until 1974 or later.[12]

Exclusive Brethren registered a meeting room in West Street, Hoole, in 1964, moving to Newton Lane near by in 1973; they apparently did not survive in 1995. In 1970 there was a secession from West Street by the more moderate members, and a small group set up its own meeting room in Spital Walk, Boughton, from where it moved in 1986 to establish a gospel hall in converted premises in Crewe Street, Newtown, where members still met for worship in 2000.[13]

SALVATION ARMY

The Salvation Army opened its campaign in Chester in the winter of 1881–2, holding services in the Linenhall and at the Pavilion roller-skating rink near the General railway station.[14] In March 1882 the local group ignored orders and marched through the Irish Catholic district around Steven Street, provoking a riot.[15] The Army opened a barracks in Commonhall Street in

1 'Citizen', *'Redeeming the Time': Hist. of Chester City Mission* [1945]; K. E. Boswell, *Brief Hist. of Chester City Mission, 1845–1995* (copies of both at C.H.H.).

2 C.C.A.L.S., ZCR 225; *Ches. Observer*, 5 Jan. 1901, p. 3; A. M. Kennett, *Chester Schools: Guide to Archives*, 9, 81, 83.

3 O.N.S. (Birkdale), Worship Reg., no. 30510.

4 *Kelly's Dir. Ches.* (1906); (1910), 226; (1914), 232.

5 Above, this chapter: Methodists (Methodist New Connexion); below, Other Churches: Spiritualists, Christadelphians.

6 *Kelly's Dir. Ches.* (1910), 226; (1914), 232.

7 O.N.S. (Birkdale), Worship Reg., nos. 9365, 37731, 57967.

8 *P. & G. Dir. Chester* (1871), 23; (1878/9), 25.

9 *Kelly's Dir. Ches.* (1896), 197, 206; (1902), 212; (1906), 221; (1910), 226, 233; later edns. to (1939), 83; *Kelly's Dir.*

Chester (1940), p. A41; (1941), p. A41; O.N.S. (Birkdale), Worship Reg., no. 50744.

10 Inf. from Mr. L. J. Scudamore, Hoole (church member); O.N.S. (Birkdale), Worship Reg., nos. 60749, 69586; cf. *Ches. Observer*, 1 Oct. 1960, p. 11; 17 Jan. 1964, p. 19.

11 Inf. from Mr. Scudamore; *Kelly's Dir. Chester* (1966), p. A9, and later edns. to (1974), 477.

12 *Kelly's Dir. Chester* (1962), p. A9, and later edns. to (1974), 477; C.P.S., Lower Bridge St. (neg. W 5/4).

13 O.N.S. (Birkdale), Worship Reg., nos. 69513, 73572, 74305, 77087; inf. from church member, Crewe St. Gospel Hall.

14 O.N.S. (Birkdale), Worship Reg., nos. 25904, 26027.

15 G. Watkinson, 'The Boughton Riots, 1882' (undated TS. at C.H.H.).

1889,[1] but in 1896 was temporarily based at the Union Hall in Foregate Street. It returned to Commonhall Street in 1899.[2] In 1908 or 1909 the Army moved to the Temperance Hall in George Street (a former Primitive Methodist chapel),[3] and from there successively to wooden huts on the south side of Castle Street in 1950,[4] a prefabricated hut at Northgate roundabout in 1973, and a newly built utilitarian headquarters in St. Anne Street, Newtown, in 1976,[5] still in use in 1995.

PENTECOSTAL CHURCHES

The Elim Foursquare Gospel Alliance registered the old village hall in Saughall Road, Blacon, for worship in 1960,[6] and remained there until 1967.[7] The Elim Alliance re-established itself in Blacon after a mission from Birkenhead in 1990: a minister was appointed in 1991, and in 1995 the Blacon Community Church was meeting in the West Cheshire College building in Blacon Avenue.[8]

The Emmanuel Assembly, affiliated to the Assemblies of God movement, was worshipping at no. 12 Bridge Street Row under its own pastor by 1952 and remained there until *c.* 1980, when it closed and the rump joined Chester Pentecostal Church. The latter had been founded in the mid 1970s also under the auspices of the Assemblies of God. Meeting at first in the minister's house, then briefly at the Penri Memorial

Baptist chapel, Gorse Stacks,[9] it took over the former Salvation Army building at Northgate roundabout in 1977, and moved from there to the former Welsh Methodist chapel in Queen Street as the Queen Street Christian Centre in 1986.[10] In the mid 1990s it was reckoned one of the four most successful non-Anglican evangelical churches in Chester, alongside Kingsway chapel (Christian Brethren), Hoole Baptist church, and Northgate church (Evangelical).[11]

OTHER EVANGELICAL CHURCHES

A dozen or so members of Hoole Baptist church separated in 1976, meeting at first as the Church of the Way in the arts centre in Northgate Street. They bought the former Congregational church in Upper Northgate Street and moved in as the Northgate church in 1978. In 1995 the church had *c.* 120 adult members and was connected with the Covenant Ministries International organization.[12]

An evangelical congregation bought the Matthew Henry chapel in Blacon from the Unitarians in 1987 and registered it under the name of the Matthew Henry Evangelical church in 1989.[13] It survived in 1995.

A congregation called the Zion Tabernacle moved into the former Baptist chapel in Grosvenor Park Road in 1980 and remained there in 2000, when it styled itself Protestant Evangelical.[14]

OTHER CHURCHES

The churches in this chapter are arranged in chronological order of their appearance in Chester.

HUGUENOTS[15]

Many Protestant refugees from France and the Rhenish Palatinate passed through Chester in the late 17th and the early 18th century *en route* for Ireland,[16] notably a party of over 3,000 Palatines who arrived in the city during a three-week period in 1709 and were assisted by the Presbyterian minister Matthew

Henry.[17] Others were in transit in 1713–14.[18] Some must have stayed, at least for a few years, since there was a French church at Chester in the 1710s. Jacques Denis was its minister in 1713,[19] but left for Ireland to serve the French church at Waterford in 1716.[20] His successor at Chester was M. Cortail, who was granted a royal pension in 1717 for the duration of his tenure.[21] The congregation was evidently conformist and its ministers presumably held services in one of the city churches.

1 O.N.S. (Birkdale), Worship Reg., no. 31940.
2 Ibid. no. 37198; *Kelly's Dir. Ches.* (1896), 197; (1906), 227.
3 O.N.S. (Birkdale), Worship Reg., no. 43683; above, this chapter: Methodists (Primitive Methodists).
4 O.N.S. (Birkdale), Worship Reg., no. 62688; C.P.S., Castle St. (neg. MET 1/28).
5 O.N.S. (Birkdale), Worship Reg., no. 74133; *Ches. Observer*, 5 Jan. 1973, p. 9; 4 Jan. 1974, p. 5; 2 Jan. 1976, p. 25; 7 Jan. 1977, p. 5.
6 O.N.S. (Birkdale), Worship Reg., no. 67957.
7 *Ches. Observer*, 6 Jan. 1962, p. 15; 6 Jan. 1967, p. 22; 5 Jan. 1968, p. 25.
8 Inf. from the Revd. G. Dalton, minister.
9 *Kelly's Dir. Chester* (1952), p. A32, and later edns. to (1974), 477; inf. from the Revd. M. Dixon, minister of Queen St. Christian Centre.
10 *Ches. Observer*, 7 Jan. 1977, p. 5; 6 Jan. 1978, p. 13; *Chester Observer*, 3 Sept. 1986, p. 25; 17 Dec. 1986, p. 11; O.N.S. (Birkdale), Worship Reg., nos. 75132, 77069; C.H.H., Y

1/1/589.
11 Local inf.
12 *Ches. Observer*, 2 Jan. 1976, p. 25; 7 Jan. 1977, p. 5; 6 Jan. 1978, p. 13; 5 Jan. 1979, p. 7; O.N.S. (Birkdale), Worship Reg., no. 75121; inf. from church office.
13 O.N.S. (Birkdale), Worship Reg., no. 77912; below, Other Churches: Unitarians.
14 O.N.S. (Birkdale), Worship Reg., no. 75656; above, this chapter: Baptists.
15 Thanks are offered to Messrs. R. Gwynn and P. Rambaut and Mrs. C. Hickey for their help with this section.
16 e.g. *Proc. Huguenot Soc. of Lond.* xv. 62; xxi. 412.
17 Ibid. xviii. 126; 3 *Sheaf*, x, p. 56.
18 *Proc. Huguenot Soc. of Lond.* viii. 124; *Diary of Henry Prescott*, ii. 397.
19 *Proc. Huguenot Soc. of Lond.* viii. 124.
20 Ibid. vi. 426; xi. 395; cf. i. 327; G. L. Lee, *Huguenot Settlements in Irel.* 94, 96.
21 *Proc. Huguenot Soc. of Lond.* i. 326–7.

UNITARIANS

Unitarian beliefs took hold in Trinity Street, at Matthew Henry's chapel (originally Presbyterian) in the mid 18th century and the remaining Trinitarians seceded in 1768 to a new Congregational church.[1] By 1778 the number of Unitarians had greatly declined,[2] and in 1822 the congregation, though 'highly respectable', was still small.[3] Maintenance of the minister, chapel, and Sunday school was assisted by charities established in 1640 and 1797.[4] The congregation remained small in the mid 19th century,[5] when the morning service on Census Sunday 1851 was attended by 102 adults and children.[6]

The Unitarians, as in other towns, were socially select, drawn from leading families in business and the professions, including the Frosts, the Moulsons (tobacco manufacturers), the Woods (of the anchor works at Saltney), the Brasseys (ironmongers), and the Johnsons (of the Hydraulic Engineering Co.).[7] Their wealth allowed for frequent improvements to the chapel, notably in 1862 when it was virtually rebuilt with a new front facing Trinity Street.[8] In 1902 the chemicals magnate and M.P. Sir John Brunner, Bt., a chapel trustee, paid for windows commemorating Matthew Henry and the prominent Unitarian James Martineau (d. 1900), and the galleries were rearranged in 1908.[9] The minister for much of the later 19th century, J. K. Montgomery (1860–96), was an influential figure in the city, notably in educational matters.[10] He introduced a congregational form of chapel government, an issue over which his predecessor had been forced to resign.[11]

In 1962 the chapel was closed for demolition during the redevelopment of the city centre, and the congregation worshipped at no. 16 Upper Northgate Street,[12] before building a new church to an uncompromising modernist design in the middle of a new housing estate at Blacon, but incorporating many of the fittings from Trinity Street, including the pulpit of 1700 and Brunner's windows. It opened in 1965 with the old name of Matthew Henry's chapel.[13] By the mid 1980s the dwindling congregation was unable to maintain the building, which it sold in 1989 to an evangelical church.[14] The Unitarians continued to meet fortnightly under the name of the Matthew Henry Fellowship, alternating between Stanley Palace and Waverton village hall, and in 1995 shared a minister with the Unitarian church at West Kirby and had *c.* 15 members.[15]

CHURCH OF JESUS CHRIST OF LATTER-DAY SAINTS

A Mormon evening service in Chester on Census Sunday 1851 drew 250 people, one of the largest gatherings anywhere in England in relation to the city's size. Morning and afternoon services were attended by 30 members.[16] The branch probably faded away through emigration to Utah. Services were again being held in 1908, over a shop in Northgate Street, with baptisms at the corporation baths,[17] but again they did not last. A third missionary effort resulted in the establishment of a church *c.* 1961. It met initially in the Newgate Street assembly rooms, from *c.* 1964 at Stanley Palace, and in 1965 built a church in Clifton Drive, Blacon. Before 1965 baptisms were held in the corporation baths, and later in the church at Rhyl (Flints.). The Chester branch was large enough by *c.* 1967 to have its own bishop, and in 1995 had *c.* 350 members and an average attendance of *c.* 110.[18]

CATHOLIC APOSTOLIC CHURCH

Members of the Catholic Apostolic church worshipped in a room over the post office in St. John Street before opening a church seating 250 in 1868 at the corner of Lorne Street and Church Street, off Garden Lane. The church, designed in an Early English style by O. Ayliffe of Manchester, was built of red brick with bands of blue brick and stone and had mostly lancet windows with a traceried west window and a west porch (Fig. 102, p. 182). The congregation had its own priest,[19] who held daily services in 1871.[20] The church was

1 W. Urwick, *Hist. Sketches of Nonconformity in Ches.* 37–8; H. D. Roberts, *Matthew Henry and his Chapel, 1662–1900*, 142–89; above, Protestant Nonconformity: Early Presbyterians and Independents. 2 *V.C.H. Ches.* iii. 109.

3 *Trans. Unitarian Hist. Soc.* v. 191.

4 *31st Rep. Com. Char.* 411–16.

5 *Bagshaw's Dir. Ches.* (1850), 65.

6 *Census*, 1851, *Religious Worship*, p. cclv.

7 *J.C.A.S.* xxii. 192–4.

8 *Gresty and Burghall's Chester Guide* [1867], 107.

9 *J.C.A.S.* xxii. 184–7; R.C.H.M.E., *Nonconformist Chapels in N. Eng.* 6.

10 *V.C.H. Ches.* iii. 117; *J.C.A.S.* xxii. 190–1; below, Education: 1870–1902.

11 *J.C.A.S.* xxii. 188–91.

12 O.N.S. (Birkdale), Worship Reg., no. 68905; *Ches. Observer*, 6 Jan. 1962, p. 15; 12 Jan. 1963, p. 11.

13 Inscription on bldg.; *Ches. Observer*, 1 Jan. 1965, p. 19; 14 Jan. 1966, p. 23; O.N.S. (Birkdale), Worship Reg., no. 69946;

R.C.H.M.E., *Nonconformist Chapels in N. Eng.* 6; G. and J. Hague, *Unitarian Heritage*, 106.

14 *The Inquirer*, 27 Feb. 1988, p. 5; 13 May 1995, p. 9; Char. Com., file 243388 A/1, Revd. J. Roberts to Char. Com., 2 Nov. 1989; above, Protestant Nonconformity: Other Evangelical Churches.

15 Inf. from Mrs. Carter, church treasurer.

16 P.R.O., HO 129/459/60; *Census*, 1851, *Religious Worship*, pp. cclii–cclxxii.

17 *Chester City Cl. Mins. 1907/8*, 452, 479–80, 618, 684.

18 O.N.S. (Birkdale), Worship Reg., no. 73307; inf. from Mr. and Mrs. Graham (church members).

19 Chester City Cl., departmental records: corporation deeds, C 1235/2–5 (Mar. 2002 held by Democratic Services: Legal Services); *Gresty and Burghall's Chester Guide*, revised J. Hickin [1867], 110–11; *Morris's Dir. Ches.* (1874), 9; date of 1864 given in error in *Kelly's Dir. Ches.* (1896), 190; O.S. Map 1/2,500, Ches. XXXVIII.11 (1875 and later edns.).

20 *P. & G. Dir. Chester* (1871), 23.

FIG. 102. *Catholic Apostolic Church, 1964*

evidently still meeting in 1941[1] and probably dis-banded in 1946, when the registration was cancelled.[2] The building was sold in 1952 and demolished to make way for the inner ring-road in 1964.[3]

PROTESTANT EPISCOPAL CHURCH

The Revd. Dr. Tudor Rogers, editor of *The Protestant*, a magazine 'established to oppose ritualism and sacer-dotalism', was minister of a congregation in Chester calling itself Emmanuel Protestant Episcopal Church, an 'unattached Church of England', which registered the Music Hall for worship in 1883 and moved to Pepper Street in 1885 but evidently disbanded in 1887.[4]

SWEDENBORGIANS (NEW JERUSALEM CHURCH)

The New Church formed a congregation in Chester in 1900 after two years of occasional lectures. The church at first rented a room in the Temperance Hall in George Street, then an old chapel in Victoria Road from 1906 to 1927, when it opened a small brick church in Newton at the corner of Brook Lane and Dickson's Drive. The site was said at the time to be ideal for the church's members, implying that they were largely drawn from the newer suburbs to the north of the city. It had a resident minister from 1936 (sometimes shared with Wallasey) and remained at Dickson's Drive in 2000.[5]

FIG. 103. *Christadelphian meeting room, Egerton Street, 1964*

SPIRITUALISTS

The First Spiritualist Church registered the former Salvation Army barracks in Commonhall Street for services in 1908, putting up a new church in the same street in 1956.[6] It was still there in 2000.

A second group had a Spiritualist Temple in Brook Street by 1912, which was called a Christian Spiritualist church in the 1940s and was registered as a church and

1 *Kelly's Dir. Chester* (1941), p. A41.

2 O.N.S. (Birkdale), Worship Reg., no. 21227.

3 Chester City Cl., departmental records: corporation deeds, C 1235/11–13, 18; *Chester City Cl. Mins. 1963/4*, p. 1094.

4 O.N.S. (Birkdale), Worship Reg., no. 27122; *Chester Chron.* 5 Jan. 1884, p. 6; 3 Jan. 1885, p. 2; 2 Jan. 1886, p. 2; 1 Jan. 1887, p. 2; 7 Jan. 1888, p. 7; B.L. cat. of printed bks., s.vv. Periodical Publications: Lond.; there is no reference to the church in F.

Vaughan, *Hist. of Free Church of Eng. otherwise called Reformed Episcopal Church.*

5 O.N.S. (Birkdale), Worship Reg., nos. 42074, 50979; *Chester Soc. of the New Church Golden Jubilee, 1900–50* (copy kindly supplied by the minister, the Revd. N. Ryder, and deposited at C.H.H.).

6 O.N.S. (Birkdale), Worship Reg., nos. 43021, 66663; inscription on bldg.

healing sanctuary in 1982.[1] In 1995 it operated as the Spiritualist Psychic Centre and Healing Sanctuary in rooms over a shop.[2]

A third Spiritualist church in Egerton Street, presumably occupying the old mission hall, was recorded only between 1934 and 1941.[3]

FIRST CHURCH OF CHRIST, SCIENTIST

Christian Scientists were meeting in Chester by 1908 and began public services at no. 68 Watergate Street in 1909 or 1910. They formed a society in 1921 and a separate church in 1926. Meetings were held in Pepper Street 1925–36, at Forest House in Love Street 1936–40, and in rooms above the Falcon café in Lower Bridge Street 1940–7. The church bought the elementary school behind St. Olave's church in 1946, and began holding services there in 1947. Another church was recorded in Hough Green in the 1960s. There were reading rooms at premises in St. Werburgh Street in 1940, a house in White Friars later in the 1940s, no. 3 Newgate Street in the late 1950s and early 1960s, and the redeveloped Pepper Row from the mid 1960s until 1993, when they were moved to the church building in St. Olave Street.[4]

CHRISTADELPHIANS

A meeting room in the Masonic Hall at no. 2 Queen Street was in use from the mid 1920s[5] and moved to the old mission hall in Egerton Street in 1950 (Fig. 103),[6] which was rebuilt in 1985[7] and where the Chester Christadelphian Ecclesia still advertised weekly meetings in 2000.[8]

JEHOVAH'S WITNESSES

The Jehovah's Witnesses who congregated in Chester in the later 1930s were drawn from an area extending as far as Mold (Denb.) and Deeside (Flints.). They met successively at no. 68 Watergate Street (formerly used by Christian Scientists), Eastgate Street, where a Kingdom Hall was registered in 1941, and a room in no. 3 Lower Bridge Street. Separate churches were later formed in Mold and Deeside, and the Chester group was itself large enough eventually to form three congregations, each numbering *c.* 100 in 1995. Northgate and Blacon congregations met separately in the Kingdom Hall purpose-built in Melbourne Road, Blacon, in 1969, and the Saltney congregation in its own Kingdom Hall in Boundary Lane, opened in 1990.[9]

GREEK ORTHODOX

Orthodox services were begun in 1985 at the Anglican mission church of St. Barnabas, Sibell Street, by the Community of St. Barbara the Great Martyr. In 1987 they moved to the Anglican cemetery chapel at Overleigh, where in 1995 the liturgy was conducted in English and Greek three times a month for a congregation mainly composed of English converts but also including Greeks, Russians, and Romanians.[10] Similar services continued weekly in 2000.

NON-CHRISTIAN RELIGIONS

JEWS[11]

No Jews are recorded in Chester in the Middle Ages.

The first Jew known to have resided in Chester after the Resettlement was Abraham Mendes (d. *c.* 1730), of a London merchant family with interests in Amsterdam and Barbados. He lodged in Chester with a draper, Daniel Hayes, and included among his executors Sir Henry Bunbury, Bt.[12] By the 1750s Chester had a lodging house for Jewish pedlars, and there was at least one settled shopkeeper by 1820.[13] A congregation was formed later in the century and met at first in a private house. It rented a room in Union Hall, Foregate Street, in 1894 and opened a synagogue in Bollands Court, White Friars, in 1900. The registration was cancelled in 1963[14] when the synagogue was united with that at Hoylake, which itself closed in the 1980s, after which the nearest synagogue to Chester was in

1 *Ches. Observer*, 6 Jan. 1912, p. 11; 6 Jan. 1940, p. 9; O.N.S. (Birkdale), Worship Reg., no. 76126; *Kelly's Dir. Ches.* (1928), 82, and later edns. to (1939), 83; *Kelly's Dir. Chester* (1940), p. A41, and later edns. to (1974), 477.

2 Notices on door, Feb. 1995.

3 *Kelly's Dir. Ches.* (1934), 82; *Kelly's Dir. Chester* (1941), p. A41; *Ches. Observer*, 6 Jan. 1940, p. 9.

4 Inf. from church recs. kindly supplied by Mrs. K. Nicholls; *V.C.H. Ches.* iii. 120; O.N.S. (Birkdale), Worship Reg., nos. 52682, 66759; *Kelly's Dir. Ches.* (1914), 232; (1923), 242; (1928), 82; (1934), 82; (1939), 83; *Kelly's Dir. Chester* (1940), p. A41; (1941), p. A41; (1952), p. A32; later edns. to (1974), 477.

5 *Chester Observer*, 4 Jan. 1985, p. 3; *Kelly's Dir. Ches.* (1928), 82, 96; *Kelly's Dir. Chester* (1940), p. A41, and later edns.

6 O.N.S. (Birkdale), Worship Reg., no. 62727.

7 *Chester Observer*, 4 Jan. 1985, p. 3; 15 Feb. 1985, p. 8.

8 Notices at church, Feb. 1995.

9 *Kelly's Dir. Chester* (1940), p. A41; O.N.S. (Birkdale), Worship Reg., nos. 59906, 72182; *Ches. Observer*, 1 Jan. 1965, p. 19; inf. from Miss M. Woodcock, member of Blacon congregation.

10 Inf. from the Revd. Deacon Pancratios Sanders, Wallasey; *Chester Chron.* 21 Apr. 1995, p. 16; *Dir. of Orthodox Parishes and Clergy in Brit. Isles* (1994/5), 17.

11 Thanks are offered to Mr. M. Brown, Jewish Historical Society of England, who supplied several of the references for this section.

12 P.R.O., PROB 11/645, ff. 373v.–375.

13 B. Williams, *Making of Manchester Jewry, 1740–1875,* 5, 32.

14 *Jewish Chronicle,* 14 Sept. 1894; 24 Aug. 1900; O.N.S. (Birkdale), Worship Reg., nos. 34535, 47927.

Liverpool. The community in Chester recongregated in 1973, and in 1988 numbered 30 families meeting each month in one another's houses. Formal services were occasionally held in Chester by a travelling minister sent by the chief rabbi's office.[1]

BAHA'IS

A Baha'i community existed in the city in 1963.[2]

MOSLEMS

Chester's small Moslem community registered the Shah Jalal mosque at no. 45 Egerton Street in 1988;[3] the Chester Islamic Society was based in premises at West Lorne Street, off Garden Lane, in the later 1990s.

1 Inf. from Mr. G. Viner, chairman of the community (1988), and Dr. I. S. Daniels (2002). Mr. J. G. Wolfson, Liverpool, is thanked for providing contact with Dr. Daniels.

2 *Chester City Cl. Mins. 1962/3*, pp. 940, 1025.
3 O.N.S. (Birkdale), Worship Reg., no. 77518.

MAJOR BUILDINGS

CATHEDRAL AND CLOSE

The foundation which became the abbey of St. Werburgh and eventually the cathedral church of Christ and the Blessed Virgin originated in the 10th century as an Anglo-Saxon minster.[1] As later, it probably occupied a precinct which comprised the north-east corner of the walled area of the city. The minster, of which nothing survived in 2000, was refounded as a Benedictine monastery in 1092, and shortly afterwards, or possibly in the late 1080s before the formal refoundation, work began on a new church and claustral buildings.[2] A major reconstruction of the entire complex began in the earlier 13th century and continued periodically throughout the 14th. A further building phase started in the late 15th century was incomplete at the Dissolution in 1540.[3] In 1541 St. Werburgh's became the cathedral church of the newly constituted diocese of Chester and the whole precinct passed under the control of the new dean and chapter.[4] It remained extra-parochial but until the late 19th century contained one of the city's parish churches, St. Oswald's, which was housed within the abbey and cathedral church except for the period 1348–1539 when it occupied St. Nicholas's chapel within the precinct.[5]

By the early 17th century the presence of commercial premises in Abbey Court (later Abbey Square) made the precinct disagreeable to the cathedral dignitaries.[6] Great improvements were made under Bishop Bridgeman (1619–52), but the most important changes came in the mid 18th century, when the bishop's palace (formerly the abbot's lodging) was largely rebuilt, and much of Abbey Court and Abbey Street were laid out with Georgian terraces. Further changes were introduced after the bishops moved out of the close in 1865; the palace was replaced by buildings which until 1960 housed the King's school and in 1979 became a bank.[7] In 2000 the Georgian houses in Abbey Square were given over to offices, flats for clergy and students, and the diocesan retreat house. The former deanery at the north-east corner had been turned over to the bishop's use in 1920.[8] Abbey Street remained largely domestic, and included the deanery and canons' houses.

ABBEY CHURCH TO 1541

At the Dissolution the abbey church of St. Werburgh comprised Lady chapel with side chapels, choir with north and south aisles, central tower, north transept with east chapel, aisled south transept, aisled nave, south-west tower, and porch. The cloister and domestic buildings were to the north, and the parochial graveyard and chapel of St. Nicholas to the south. The whole complex was built of the friable local red sandstone.

Nothing is known of the fabric of the Anglo-Saxon minster, except that it was beautified by Earl Leofric of Mercia (d. 1057) and his wife Godiva.[9] It is likely that it was a stone structure of some pretension. Work on its replacement, perhaps never completed, began with the refoundation as a Benedictine abbey and continued well into the 12th century. All that survives above ground is the north transept, the north wall of the nave aisle, and the lower parts of the north-west tower. There is, however, archaeological evidence for the ground plan of the eastern limb, for a south transept smaller than its successor,[10] and for the south wall of the nave, following virtually the line of that which survives.[11]

The earliest surviving structure is the north transept, datable on stylistic grounds to the 1090s. The interior, plain and unenriched by sculpture, includes an eastern arch leading into a chapel, originally apsed, and an arcaded triforium opening on a passageway in the wall above. To the west the wall was plain except for three blocked openings at triforium level which probably originally served another passage. Traces of a similar opening at the east end of the north wall indicate that the passageway was originally continuous round the transept. A blocked doorway in the monks' night stair in the north-east corner of the transept perhaps opened on to a wooden gallery.[12] All the arches are plain and unmoulded and the capitals simple cushions. Outside in the east walk of the cloister there were two doorways with jambs of long and short work and a heavy monolithic lintel, later blocked but perhaps originally giving on to recesses;[13] inside, a third similar feature in

1 A. T. Thacker, 'Chester and Gloucester: Early Eccl. Organization in Two Mercian Burhs', *Northern Hist.* xviii. 203–4.

2 *V.C.H. Ches.* iii. 133–4; R. Gem, 'Romanesque Archit. in Chester *c.* 1075–1117', *Medieval Arch., Art, and Archit. at Chester*, ed. A. Thacker, 31–44.

3 *V.C.H. Ches.* iii. 143–4.

4 Ibid. iii. 188; A. T. Thacker, 'Reuse of Monastic Bldgs. at Chester, 1540–1640', *T.H.S.L.C.* cxlv. 21.

5 Above, Medieval Parish Churches: St. Oswald.

6 *T.H.S.L.C.* cxlv. 35–7.

7 *V.C.H. Ches.* iii. 69, 232.   8 Ibid. iii. 80.

9 John of Worcester, *Chronicle*, ed. R. R. Darlington and P. McGurk, ii. 582–3.

10 Foundations of east wall located at north-east pier of transept in 1996: pers. comm. M. Morris and S. Ward, Chester Archaeology.

11 Footings seen just inside existing wall at fifth bay from west in 1987.

12 Gem, 'Romanesque Archit.'

13 E. Barber, 'Cloisters of Chester Cath.' *J.C.A.S.* n.s. ix. 10–11.

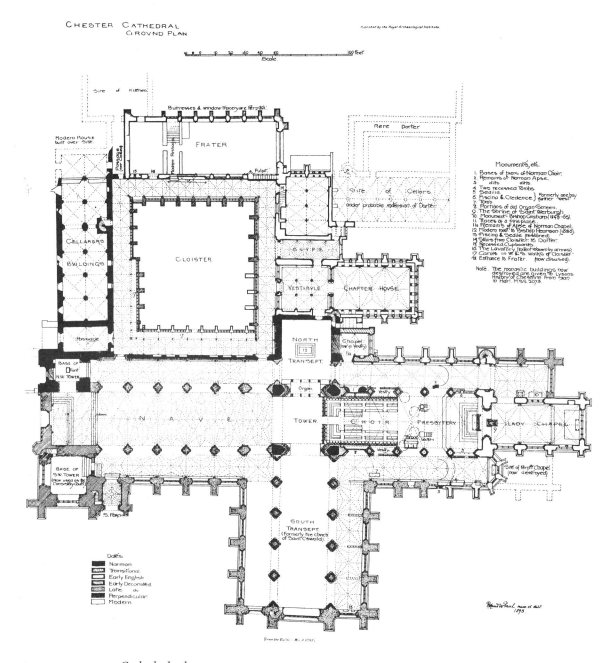

FIG. 104. *Cathedral, plan*

the north-east corner gave access to the night stairs and triforium passage.

Restoration work in the 19th century produced evidence of the ground plan of the Norman abbey's eastern limb. The foundations of large circular piers, 6 ft. 9 in. in diameter and believed to have formed the apsidal arcade of the church, were discovered by R. C. Hussey in the early 1840s. Hussey also claimed to have found on both sides of the choir the foundations of walling *c.* 6 ft. in width, which 'extended over the whole space between the bases of the pillars of the existing church'.[1] The findings suggested that the church combined two normally incompatible features: an ambulatory, usually associated with radiating eastern chapels, and a solid walled choir, generally combined with a triple eastern apse.[2] Later investigations during the restoration by Sir George Gilbert Scott (1868–76) modified that picture. Scott uncovered west of Hussey's finds the base of a circular pier and a reused circular scalloped capital, which he interpreted as the remains of a Norman choir arcade of two bays. Though he was unsuccessful in his efforts to find Hussey's apsidal arcade, Scott did discover evidence that both choir aisles ended in apses and were combined with an apsidal presbytery. The form of the main eastern chapel and ambulatory is, however, unknown (Fig. 105).[3]

1 *Arch. Jnl.* [1st ser.], v. 17–20.
2 e.g. A. W. Clapham, *Eng. Romanesque Archit.* ii.

3 *J.C.A.S.* [o.s.], iii. 164–5; *Arch. Jnl.* xciv. 308; Clapham, *Eng. Romanesque Archit.* ii. 34–5; Gem, 'Romanesque Archit.' 34–5, 42.

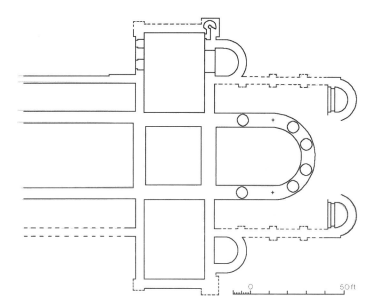

FIG. 105. *Reconstructed plan of eastern part of early Romanesque abbey church*

Little can be deduced about the elevation of the choir above the arcade. Presumably it rose to the same height as the surviving north transept and like it included a middle storey, either a modest gallery or a triforium passage.[1]

The Norman nave, which at ground level appears to have had virtually the same dimensions as its successor, was intended to terminate in a twin-towered west front. It was probably never completed, and in 2000 only the lower stages of the north-west tower survived. Outside, there is a deep recess with attached columns and a large pilaster with a sculptured capital. Inside, the details, though still comparatively plain, include keeled shafts and many-scalloped capitals, suggesting a date in the 1160s. Evidence of a clerestory wall-passage on the north side at the junction of the first and second bays suggests that the nave had a two-storeyed elevation comprising arcade and clerestory separated by blank walling at the level of the aisle roofs. Traces of an Early English arcade in the north-west bay at approximately the level of the Romanesque clerestory indicate that it was never finished or that it was remodelled soon after completion.[2]

The sources of the design of the Romanesque church remain unknown. The large circular piers of the choir resembled those in the collegiate church of St. John in Chester.[3] Another local parallel may have been Shrewsbury abbey, founded in 1083.[4] A more significant parallel is perhaps the eastern arm of the Romanesque

cathedral at Winchester, which also combined an ambulatory with three eastern chapels.[5]

There was further building in the late 12th and early 13th century. An Earl Ranulph, probably Ranulph III (1181–1232), took lands and revenues pertaining to the fabric into his protection, and ordered his officials to ensure payment to the directors of the work.[6] Grants to the fabric, mostly by Earls Hugh I (d. 1101) and Ranulph II (1129–53), were listed by Abbot Robert II (1175–84), who made further additions; the grants were confirmed by Abbot Hugh Grylle (1208–26), Earl Ranulph III, and Bishop Hugh of Coventry,[7] who instructed the archdeacon of Chester and his officials to enforce payment.[8] Grylle himself was afterwards remembered as a builder, and there is evidence that much work was done in his time.[9] In particular, he may have been responsible for the Early English clerestory arcade, traces of which remain in the north-west corner of the nave,[10] and for the early 13th-century changes to the east chapel of the north transept, which was given a square end and a ribbed vault. More extensive, though now lost, was the work done at the east end: numerous architectural fragments retrieved from the site attest to the scale of the undertaking, which probably involved wholesale rebuilding, including square-ended choir aisles.[11]

In the mid 13th century the community embarked on an ambitious reconstruction. It began with the Lady

1 Gem, 'Romanesque Archit.' 36. 2 Ibid. 36–7, 42.

3 Above, Collegiate Church of St. John.

4 *Cart. of Shrewsbury Abbey*, ed. U. Rees, i, pp. x–xii.

5 R. Gem, 'Romanesque Cath. of Winchester: Patron and Design in 11th Cent.' *Medieval Art and Archit. at Winchester Cath.* [ed. T. A. Heslop and V. A. Sekules], 4–5; Gem, 'Romanesque Archit.'

6 *Cart. Chester Abbey*, i, pp. xxviii, 72; *Charters of A.-N. Earls*, pp. 234–5 (no. 233).

7 Probably Hugh de Nonant (1188–98).

8 *Cart. Chester Abbey*, i, p. 72; ii, pp. 281–2, 286.

9 Morris, *Chester*, 118; Burne, *Monks*, 24; below, this chapter: Monastic Buildings to 1541; B.L. Add. MS. 11334, p. 31.

10 J. M. Maddison, 'Choir of Chester Cath.' *J.C.A.S.* lxvi. 34–5; cf. above, Collegiate Church of St. John.

11 *J.C.A.S.* [o.s.], iii. 167; V. Jansen, 'Attested but Opaque: the Early Gothic East End of St. Werburgh's', *Med. Arch., Art, and Archit. at Chester*, ed. Thacker, 57–65.

FIG. 106. *Cathedral, Lady chapel, one bay*

chapel, a building of three bays with lancet windows and a vault with ridge rib and tiercerons, perhaps inserted in the 1280s.[1] Between 1250 and 1280 the work was extended to include the reconstruction of the entire eastern limb of the church, a process which lasted until *c.* 1340 and involved at least six master masons.[2] The rebuilt choir was of six bays, with aisles ending in polygonal apses and a Chartres-like elevation comprising richly moulded arcade, trefoil-arched triforium, and tall clerestory. The new designs first appeared to the base level of the clerestory in the 1270s, and in their completed form by the early 14th century; they are of high quality and have been compared with work proceeding at Westminster, Acton Burnell (Salop.), and elsewhere under the influence of the royal court.[3]

Variations in the mouldings suggest that the first phase consisted of the arch into the Lady chapel, the polygonal chapels, the eastern responds of the choir arcade, and part of the first arch on the north side. The aisle apses were three-sided and rib-vaulted. They were destroyed in the late 15th or early 16th century, when the aisles were extended eastwards, but that on the south, reconstructed by Scott in the 19th century, retains a piscina with geometrical tracery. Of that on the north there survive the remains of a window recess much more elaborate than its neighbours in the Lady chapel, another piscina with geometrical tracery, and a doorway to an exterior spiral staircase. The work is characterized by complex mouldings of arch, capital, and base similar to those produced at Lichfield cathedral probably in the 1260s, and very closely related to part of the south chancel aisle of St. Mary's, Stafford, which may well have been by the same mason.[4] A second phase, similar to the first, but less distinguished, and dating probably from the 1270s, saw the completion of the first and second piers on the north side of the choir and the wall of the north choir aisle. At much the same time, a fully fledged Decorated style appeared in the first two bays on the other side of the choir. The master responsible for that, and perhaps other designers, carried the work as far as the first two bays of the triforium on the north side and part of the first bay of the triforium on the south, and also built the first two bays of the wall of the south choir aisle. Then, it seems, work stopped. The remaining four bays of the choir comprise a single design which shows clear indications of an early 14th-century date, notably in the use of the sunk chamfer. It has been argued that the long hiatus was engendered by the king's building works in Wales and at Vale Royal abbey, both initiated in 1277. Certainly the king borrowed 100 men from the abbot of Chester in that year for the building of Flint castle, and drew further on the community's resources in 1282, but, even so, as late as 1285 orders were issued to support the monks 'in the great work of building the church'.[5]

To preserve visual unity the early 14th-century master retained the arch mouldings of the north choir arcade and the hollow chamfers of the south, though amended the somewhat odd design of the north triforium. His principal innovation was to use the sunk chamfer, not only in the jambs of the clerestory windows but also in the piers of the arcade. The sunk chamfer first appeared at Caernarfon castle, and its employment at Chester could be evidence of the hand of Richard the engineer, who had worked in Wales with Master James of St. George and to whom the abbot of Chester pledged substantial sums in 1310 and 1312–13.[6]

Work was clearly still going on in 1315, when Abbot Thomas Birchills was required to surrender moneys received for the fabric of the church.[7] Building was presumably well advanced by 1323, when Birchills was buried amid his work, between the pillars on the south

1 *J.C.A.S.* lxvi. 33.

2 For what follows: ibid. 31–46; J. M. Maddison, 'Decorated Archit. in NW. Midlands' (Manchester Univ. Ph.D. thesis, 1978), 74–90.   3 J. Bony, *Eng. Decorated Style*, 14, 76.

4 Cf. *V.C.H. Staffs.* vi. 243; xiv. 51.

5 *Cart. Chester Abbey*, i, pp. 88–9, 212; Ormerod, *Hist. Ches.* i. 252; *J.C.A.S.* lxvi. 39–40; Morris, *Chester*, 122.

6 *J.C.A.S.* lxvi. 41–3.   7 Burne, *Monks*, 67.

side of the choir, set apart from earlier abbots.[1] By the 1330s the choir, including the clerestory, had been finished;[2] the abbot and monks recorded then that they had recently rebuilt the choir *de novo* at great expense, and needed fresh funds to reconstruct the body of the church and the bell tower, which were threatened with ruin.[3] The crossing and the last two bays of the south choir aisle seem also to have been under construction at that time; they bear a close resemblance to work at St. Mary's, Stafford, Audley (Staffs.), and Shifnal (Salop.), probably supervised by the same master mason between 1327 and 1337.[4] Only the vaults remained unfinished. The high vault was never built, while those over the aisles were added later, probably in the 15th century, and do not conform to the original scheme: except in the earliest bay of the north aisle the ribs of the springers have a more complex profile than those of the vaults. The vaults over the north side are simpler and probably earlier than those on the south: they have a ridge rib and an additional transverse rib in the middle of each bay, whereas in the south aisle vault the transverse ribs are replaced by two tiercerons, except in the most easterly bays (Fig. 107).[5]

The additional revenues secured by the abbey's appropriation of the rectory of Chipping Campden (Glos.) in 1340 perhaps encouraged an expansion of building operations. Then, if not earlier, the monastic choir was closed by a stone pulpitum, remains of which survived in 2000 reset as screen walls in the choir aisles.[6] Further modifications seem to have been made to the choir itself, including the elaborate sedilia with four canopied seats (much restored by Scott), and the gabled aumbries opposite, both features associated with the high altar.[7] Other closely related work of the period included the shrine of St. Werburg and the lower parts of the enlarged south transept and the nave.[8] Outside, the aisles have Decorated mouldings over window openings which were filled with appropriate tracery in the 19th century.[9] Inside, the work is characterized by continuous wave mouldings, filleted shafts, and capitals adorned with foliage and fleurons, an architectural vocabulary employed experimentally in varying combinations. The scheme for the south transept, which has east and west arcades with complex piers and arch mouldings, was repeated in the last five bays of the nave. The most easterly bay of the nave, however, is separated from the rest by a short stretch of solid wall and has a different scheme, characterized by continuous wave mouldings of a kind which derive

FIG. 107. *Cathedral, south choir aisle*

ultimately from work at Caernarfon castle.[10] It was presumably built a little earlier and in conjunction with the crossing; despite the considerable differences in design between the transept and the first bay of the nave they both belong to the mid 14th century, and there is no reason to believe that they were greatly separated in date.

The date of the nave arcades is uncertain. A local tradition, originating in the 17th century, attributes the south arcade to the 14th century and the north to Abbot Simon Ripley (1485–93), mainly on the strength of the monogram formed from his initials on the western respond and the single 'R' on the capital of the third column from the west.[11] The two arcades, both of which appear to have been built anew from the foundations,[12] are, however, almost indistinguishable in character, with identical piers and filleted shafts, and very similar coursing. Moreover, the responds of both are associated with identical unfinished vaulting shafts at the second bay from the east where the new scheme began. The pattern of the north arcade must therefore have been established at the same time as the south,

1 Ibid. 77; *J.C.A.S.* lxvi. 43; C.C.A.L.S., DCC 4, f. 59.

2 *J.C.A.S.* [o.s.], iii. 177; Maddison, 'Dec. Archit.' 210.

3 B.L. Harl. MS. 2148, f. 1v.; *V.C.H. Ches.* iii. 140 n.; cf. *Cal. Papal Reg.* iii. 166–7.

4 *J.C.A.S.* lxvi. 44–5.

5 Ibid. [o.s.], iii. 176; B. Willis, *Surv. of Cathedrals*, i. 321; plan of 1815 in J. and H. S. Storer, *Hist. and Antiquities of Cath. Church of Chester*.

6 B.L. Harl. MS. 2073, ff. 80–2; C.C.A.L.S., EDD 4/23, pp. 8–9; EDD 3913/3/10, p. 23.

7 Maddison, 'Dec. Archit.' 228, 265; cf. S. C. Scott, *Hist. of St. John the Baptist Church and Parish*, 35.

8 *J.C.A.S.* lxvi. 46; J. M. Maddison, 'St. Werburgh's Shrine', *Friends of Chester Cath. Ann. Rep.* (1984), 11–17; below, this section (Shrine).

9 *J.C.A.S.* [o.s.], iii. 179.

10 Maddison, 'Dec. Archit.' 91–7.

11 e.g. J. H. Parker, *Medieval Archit. of Chester* (1858), 24–5; F. L. M. Bennett, *Chester Cath.* 22, 53; Burne, *Monks*, 135.

12 Excavations in 1996: pers. comm. M. Morris and S. Ward.

and it is very difficult to detect any break in the work. Against such evidence must be set the fact that the arch mouldings, bases, and capitals of the north arcade look later than those of the south, and appear 15th-century. The foundations of the two arcades also differ: those on the north cut through an earlier sleeper wall, possibly of Norman date, whereas the southern piers rise from an ashlar plinth which rests on the earlier work.[1] The problem is further complicated by the fact that foliage very like that on the capitals of the north arcade is to be found in the south transept and on the aisle capitals of the easternmost and earliest of the complex piers of the south arcade. It has been suggested, therefore, that the two arcades date from successive building campaigns in the 15th century by a mason copying the design of the south transept.[2] If so, they represent a remarkable example of architectural historicism.

Building was undoubtedly undertaken during the abbacy of Richard Sainsbury (before 1352 to 1362).[3] Carpenters, masons, and other labourers were working continuously on the church in 1354,[4] but work seems to have lapsed by 1363, when Sainsbury's successor, Thomas Newport, complained of the urgent need for repairs and obtained a licence to employ six masons, a quarryman, and four stone-workers.[5] There is no other record of building in the 14th century, but the first bay of the nave, which differs from the rest at clerestory as well as arcade level, has late 14th-century window tracery and a unique vaulting scheme, which like its successor to the west was never completed. It is likely too that the double row of panelling which adorns the soffits of the east and west arches of the crossing was added in the late 14th century. It had the effect of doubling the thickness of the arches so that they could take a central tower, a feature presumably not intended in the 1330s.[6] The work was probably associated with the insertion of the wooden choir stalls in the 1380s. Strongly influenced by those at Lincoln, they originally comprised 48 canopied seats with misereres adorned with vivid carvings and fronted by a single row of desks; the high plinths of the crossing were presumably intended for their accommodation, evidence that the choir then extended one bay further west than at the Dissolution.[7]

The building campaign proceeded to such effect that

by 1413 Abbot Henry Sutton could be interred in the nave by the south pillar nearest the choir.[8] It probably also included work on the south transept, where the clerestory, although later renewed, was probably originally similar to that in the first bay of the nave.[9] The vaulting of the transept aisles was also begun, in the south-east corner with the chapel of St. Nicholas, where diagonal, longitudinal, and transverse ribs and numerous bosses were installed.[10]

Although Ripley is reputed to have been a great builder, his activities within the church are largely unrecorded, except for a late tradition that he built the stone pulpitum in 1491 at his own expense, an allusion, perhaps, to its removal to the eastern arch of the crossing.[11] Other less enigmatic work of the late 15th or early 16th century included the eastern extension of the choir aisles to embrace the two westernmost bays of the Lady chapel. Only the northern chapel survives, but the southern one was identical, of two bays with Perpendicular window tracery and vaults of similar design to that in the south transept.[12] In the nave, the roof and clerestory were apparently going up in 1501.[13] Another important enterprise begun in the early 16th century included the south-west tower and porch and the west front. The foundations were laid under Ripley's successor, John Birkenshaw, in 1508.[14] Expenditure on the repair and alteration of the church is recorded in the early 16th century.[15]

Inside, the roof of the north transept dates from the time of Cardinal Wolsey (d. 1530), whose arms appear with Henry VIII's on the bosses.[16] The vaults intended for the nave, aisles, and all but one bay of the south transept were, however, never built.[17] The south-west tower also remained unfinished, though some makeshift arrangement, perhaps a wooden belfry, permitted the hanging of three bells. One inscribed with the name of Abbot Birkenshaw was sold in 1551 and was in Conwy church (Caern.) in 2000.[18]

Shrine

The focus of the abbey was the shrine of St. Werburg, probably constructed in the 1340s and originally located in the easternmost bay of the presbytery, behind the high altar. At that time the altar was sited at least one bay west of its position in 2000.[19] One of a

---

1 Excavations in 1996: pers. comm. M. Morris and S. Ward.

2 Maddison, 'Dec. Archit.' 96–7.

3 *Blk. Prince's Reg.* iii. 88, 105; cf. ibid. 266, 286.

4 Ibid. 148–9.

5 Ibid. 461.

6 *J.C.A.S.* lxvi. 45; cf. Nantwich: Maddison, 'Dec. Archit.' 273–98.

7 B. T. N. Bennett, *Choir Stalls of Chester Cath.*; C. Grössinger, 'Chester Cath. Misericords: Iconography and Sources', *Med. Arch., Art, and Archit. at Chester*, ed. Thacker, 98–106; below, this chapter: Cathedral Church from 1541.

8 C.C.A.L.S., DCC 4, f. 62.

9 *J.C.A.S.* [o.s.], iii. 178–9; Maddison, 'Dec. Archit.' 291–2.

10 *J.C.A.S.* [o.s.], iii. 178.

11 Burne, *Monks*, 140; below, this chapter: Cathedral Church from 1541.

12 G. W. O. Addleshaw, 'Archit., Sculptors, Designers, and Craftsmen, 1770–1970, in Chester Cath.' *Archit. Hist.* xiv. 96.

13 P.R.O., CHES 29/202, m. 6; 3 *Sheaf*, x, p. 94.

14 *King's Vale Royal*, [i], 79; [ii], 192.

15 B.L. Harl. MS. 1994, ff. 31v., 38; *V.C.H. Ches.* iii. 143.

16 Burne, *Monks*, 144.

17 *J.C.A.S.* [o.s.], iii. 176, 178, 180–1; cf. C. Wild, *Illustration of Archit. of Cath. Church of Chester*; Storer, *Hist. Cath. Church.*

18 Burne, *Monks*, 143; Morris, *Chester*, 152–3.

19 Maddison, 'Dec. Archit.' 228, 259; *Friends of Chester Cath. Ann. Rep.* (1984), 12. Cf. burial of Thos. Yardley (d. 1434) in choir north aisle next to shrine: C.C.A.L.S., DCC 4, f. 63.

group described as 'box-type',[1] it is best interpreted as representing a miniature two-storeyed chapel, the lower storey forming the base and the upper housing the reliquary containing the saint's remains. The whole was richly ornamented, the upper section especially so with its traceried buttresses adorned with tiny gilded statues of saints. The lower section, which had votive niches ornamented with little vaults and panelling, seems to have been left incomplete, perhaps abandoned after the Black Death.[2]

The saint's remains were removed during the Reformation, perhaps in consequence of Bishop Lee's visitation of 1536, and the shrine was dismembered. In the 1620s, when it was described as a 'fair stone in the middle of the church', it served as the burial place for Bishop Downham,[3] and in 1635 the base and part of the upper section were adapted to make a throne for the bishop.[4] Missing portions of the base of the upper section, discovered during Scott's restoration in 1873, were reunited with the portions incorporated in the throne, and the whole was reassembled in 1888 by Sir Arthur Blomfield in the western bay of the Lady chapel.[5]

Burials and Monuments

No identifiable monument survives from the Middle Ages.[6] The 12th-century abbots were buried in the cloister, first in the south-east angle and later in the east range in front of the chapter house doors;[7] the Romanesque niches in the walls of the south cloister have been supposed to house some of their tombs.[8] In the 13th century, with a single exception, the abbots were buried in the chapter house, where Simon Whitchurch (d. 1291) had an especially splendid monument with a canopy supported by six marble columns.[9] From 1323 the abbots were generally buried in the choir, a fashion begun by Thomas Birchills, whose memorial slab, adorned with a brass effigy, was located between the pillars of the south choir arcade. His tomb was thought to have been discovered in 1787 east of the bishop's throne.[10] A further slab, bearing the matrix of a brass effigy with mitre and crozier and surviving in the south-east corner of the sanctuary in 1755, was perhaps that of William Bebington (d. before 1352), the first mitred abbot, who was laid to rest beside Birchills.[11] One

of the two 14th-century tomb recesses in the south wall of the choir may be that of William Merston (d. 1387), said to have been buried outside the choir near the 'pyramid'. Other abbots were buried in the chapter house, the easternmost bay of the nave, and St. Erasmus's chapel.[12] To the west of the two canopied niches in the south choir aisle was another grave, opened in 1874 and supposed to have been the tomb of the monastic chronicler Ranulph Higden.[13]

Supposed Tomb of Emperor Henry

The tradition that a German Emperor Henry (IV or V) was buried in the abbey church goes back, remarkably, to the late 12th century.[14] In 1728 it was believed that his bones were housed in a lead coffin enclosed within a stone monument located beneath the 'pyramid' which rose from the south choir aisle.[15] Later, however, he was said to rest in the north choir aisle, in an alabaster altar tomb adorned with trefoil- and quatrefoil-headed niches apparently dating from the 15th century.[16]

MONASTIC BUILDINGS TO 1541

Under Earl Hugh I (d. 1101) and his countess, Ermentrude, the abbey acquired buildings 'fit for the habitation of monks'.[17] The cloister was located north of the church, presumably because space was circumscribed to the south by the town and graveyard (Fig. 108, p. 192). Evidence of early activity in the east range includes two doorways or recesses; the chapter house, located on that side, was presumably complete by the 1120s, when it received the body of Earl Hugh I.[18] The west range was also built in the 12th century. It originally comprised the abbot's lodging and a substantial undercroft, surviving in 2000, which was divided into two aisles by circular columns with scalloped capitals similar to those of the choir arcade piers (Fig. 109, p. 193). A late 12th- or early 13th-century addition was the vaulted passage between the undercroft and the church, giving access to the cloister.[19] Above was the abbot's chapel, a three-bay structure which obscured the north window of the north-west tower.[20] The inside arch of the main refectory doorway may be Norman too, indicating that the north cloister range was also built in the 12th century.

1 *Jnl. Brit. Arch. Assoc.* cxxix. 15–34.
2 Maddison, 'Dec. Archit.' 259–60; *Friends of Chester Cath. Ann. Rep.* (1984), 17; Ormerod, *Hist. Ches.* i. 298–9; *J.C.A.S.* N.S. x. 77–81.   3 *King's Vale Royal*, [ii], 34.
4 Burne, *Chester Cath.* 116; *T.H.S.L.C.* cxlv. 41.
5 *J.C.A.S.* N.S. x. 82–3.
6 Unidentified late medieval sandstone altar tomb stood in south choir aisle in 1995.
7 C.C.A.L.S., DCC 4, ff. 51–2.
8 Ibid. ff. 50v.–54; EDD 3913/2/2 (18, 23, 25 Aug., 13 Sept. 1871); EDD 3913/2/3 (2 Feb. 1872); Willis, *Surv. of Caths.* i, facing p. 316.
9 C.C.A.L.S., DCC 4, ff. 55–9; cf. ibid. DCC 16/120, pp. 14–15; *King's Vale Royal*, [ii], 38.
10 C.C.A.L.S., DCC 4, f. 59; Ormerod, *Hist. Ches.* i. 252.

11 C.C.A.L.S., DCC 4, f. 60; B.L. Add. MS. 5836, f. 220.
12 C.C.A.L.S., DCC 4, ff. 60–3.
13 *J.C.A.S.* N.S. ix. 115–28.
14 Gerald of Wales, *Opera*, ed. J. S. Brewer (Rolls Ser.), i. 186; vi. 139–40; Ranulph Higden, *Polychronicon*, ed. C. Babington and J. R. Lumby (Rolls Ser.), vii. 466–8.
15 C.C.A.L.S., DCC 16/120, pp. 9–10; *King's Vale Royal*, [ii], facing p. 26; 3 *Sheaf*, li, pp. 35–6.
16 Ormerod, *Hist. Ches.* (1st edn.), i. 246; B.L. Harl. MS. 5836, f. 220.
17 *Cart. Chester Abbey*, i, pp. xxviii, 16.
18 Ibid. i, pp. xxviii, 47.
19 *J.C.A.S.* [o.s.], i. 65; [o.s.], iii. 166; N.S. xxxvii. 81–2; Pevsner, *Ches.* 145.
20 *J.C.A.S.* xxxvii. 82–3; Burne, *Monks*, 10.

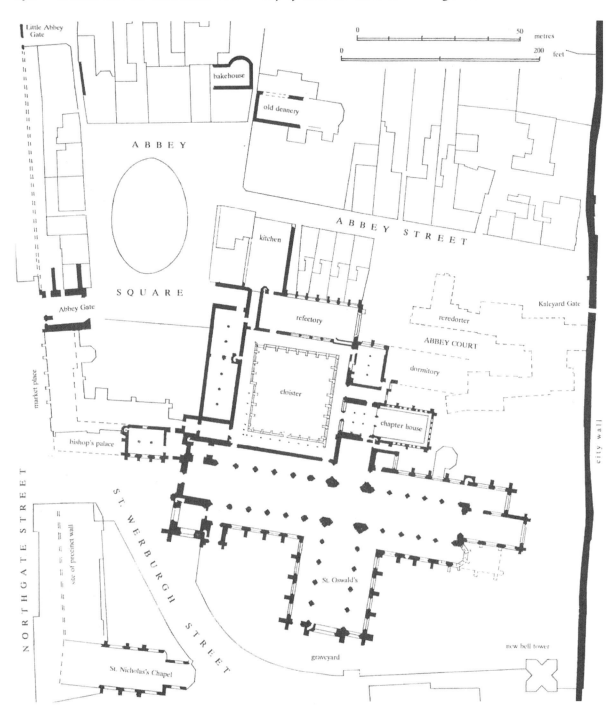

FIG. 108. *Abbey precinct in 2000. Surviving medieval fabric in black; probable buildings with dotted lines*

In the south walk of the cloister there are two groups of three tomb recesses with moulded arches and ornamented shafts, which probably date from the later 12th century; all slightly different, they were not bonded to the wall behind.[1] At the east end of the same walk is the elaborate late Norman doorway into the nave, adorned with three orders of columns with waterleaf capitals and water-holding bases.

During the 13th century many of the monastic buildings were rebuilt. Abbot Grylle (1208–26), for example, was authorized by Earl Ranulph III to extend his abbey's 'chantry' to the street and market place on land adjoining the churchyard gate.[2] One of the earliest of the new buildings was the chapter house vestibule, with simple rib vaults running uninterruptedly into eight-shafted piers, probably soon followed by the chapter house proper, which has lancets and a vault with a ridge rib and tiercerons. The chapter house may

1 e.g. C.C.A.L.S., DCC 4, ff. 51–2, 54; EDD 3913/2/2 (18, 23, 25 Aug., 13 Sept. 1871); EDD 3913/3/3 (2 Feb. 1872); above, this chapter: Abbey Church to 1541 (Burials and Monuments).

2 *Cart. Chester Abbey*, i, p. 251; ii, pp. 281–3, 286.

FIG. 109. *Abbot's lodging, undercroft*

well have been built by the workshop responsible for the chapel of St. Chad's Head and the south transept of Lichfield cathedral; in particular, the fluted columns attached to the walls and the arrangement of the wall-passages are strikingly similar.[1] To the north lay the parlour, the day stairs to the dormitory, and the slype, a group, perhaps dating from the 1230s or 1240s, characterized by doorways with three- and five-cusped heads and openings consisting of a quatrefoil inscribed in a circle.[2] The vault of the slype, which again has a ridge rib and tiercerons, is more elaborate and looks later than those in the chapter house. At much the same time work was being done in the north range of the cloister, including the lavatorium with three richly moulded arches, and the refectory. Work in the refectory can be divided into two phases. To the earlier belong the entrance from the cloister, the east end, which seems originally to have had a group of lancet windows, and the reading pulpit, reached by a stair in the thickness of the wall. The work, which included pointed trefoiled arches and quatrefoil openings, probably dates from the 1230s or 1240s.[3] The later phase included the windows of the main body of the building and those set high up at the east end of the south wall to light the pulpit, all of which appear to date from the earlier 14th century.

The west cloister range, which contained the abbot's hall and chapel, was untouched apart from some remodelling of the screens passage and great kitchen at the north end.

The outer precinct, and in particular its defences, also received attention during the 13th century. Its northern and eastern sides were enclosed by the city walls, through which in 1274–5 Edward I allowed the monks to make a postern gate to give access to the

FIG. 110. *Refectory pulpit*

monastic garden, the Kaleyards, situated just beyond. The Kaleyards themselves were fortified by a ditch probably in the 1260s, and later by a wall with a

1 Pers. comm. Dr. W. Rodwell.
2 Dates suggested by Mr. T. Tatton-Brown and Dr. W. Rodwell.

3 Bony, *Eng. Dec. Style*, 10; V. Jansen, 'Superposed Wall Passages and Triforium Elevation of St. Werburgh's, Chester', *Jnl. Soc. Archit. Historians*, xxxviii. 223–43.

FIG. 111. *Abbey Gate,*
looking into precinct

'great gate' which was replaced or supplemented by a smaller postern in 1322–3.[1]

On the western side of the precinct, the great gatehouse with its large segmental relieving arch containing two subordinate entrance arches recalls features of Edward I's Welsh castles, in particular the Queen's Gate at Caernarfon. Sunk chamfers on the arches and vaulting ribs suggest that it was contemporary with the early 14th-century phases of the choir.[2] At the same time, presumably, the precinct wall running northwards along Northgate Street was built. In 2000 substantial portions survived behind the houses fronting Abbey Square. The precinct north of the church, which contained all the claustral buildings, was thus enclosed from the early 14th century. Whether such defences extended south of the church, where the parochial graveyard was located, is unclear. By the 16th century a stone wall ran from the city walls along the line of the later St. Werburgh Street and turned north to join up with the great gatehouse.[3] That wall may have existed by the later 13th century, when a postern through it gave access to the precinct from a house by the abbey churchyard.[4] Almost certainly it was standing after the grant of a licence in 1377 to enclose and crenellate the abbey and church.[5]

Other work included the provision of a new water supply. At first the monks seem to have depended on wells within the precinct, but in 1278 they obtained a royal licence to make a conduit from a well in Newton, acquired in the 1240s, and pierce the city walls if necessary.[6] The supply was augmented in 1282 by the grant of a spring at Christleton, called Abbot's well, together with permission to lay pipes carrying the water to the monastery.[7] Cisterns connected by a conduit were built in the cloister garth and at the

spring, and licence to carry the pipe through the city wall was granted in 1283.[8]

In the mid 14th century a new chapel, dedicated to St. Nicholas, was built within the precinct south of the abbey church. In being by 1348, it soon housed the abbey's parishioners, probably when work was intended on the south aisle of the nave,[9] and was enlarged in 1488.[10]

New cloisters were built by Abbot Birkenshaw in the 1520s. A will of 1526 provided for the glazing of a new window there, and work was certainly being done on the north walk in the time of Abbot Marshall (1527 to 1529 or 1530), whose initials appear upon two bosses in the vault.[11] The tracery throughout, with its very late uncusped Perpendicular forms, resembles that in the nave clerestory. The new cloisters were of irregular shape. The south walk and the southern half of the west walk were enlarged by a row of nine columns framing glazed bays or recesses, which have been interpreted as carrels for monastic study (Fig. 112).[12] The work thus initiated was probably still continuing at the Dissolution. The ruthless way in which the cloister vaults cut into features of the surrounding buildings suggests that a larger reconstruction was intended to follow.[13]

At the Dissolution the precinct contained a considerable complex of buildings. Immediately north of the church the cloister included in the east range the chapter house and warming house with the dormitory over, in the north range the refectory and great monastic kitchen, and in the west range the cellarium and the abbot's halls. Adjoining the east range and running eastwards was a building with a vaulted undercroft, perhaps an extension of the dormitory. To the north of that, fed by the conduit which brought water into the reservoir within the cloister garth, lay a further

1 Burne, *Monks*, 62; Morris, *Chester*, 241–2; Hemingway, *Hist. Chester*, i. 345; below, City Walls and Gates: Gates, Posterns, and Towers (Kaleyard Gate and Walls).

2 *J.C.A.S.* lxvi. 41–3.

3 Morris, *Chester*, 135.

4 *Cart. Chester Abbey*, ii, pp. 339–40.

5 *Cal. Pat.* 1377–81, 56.

6 Ibid. 1272–8, 279; Burne, *Monks*, 38.

7 *Cart. Chester Abbey*, i, p. 225.

8 Morris, *Chester*, 121.

9 Burne, *Monks*, 91–2; *Cal. Papal Pets.* i. 82, 91, 134–5; above, Medieval Parish Churches: St. Oswald.

10 Burne, *Monks*, 136; *J.C.A.S.* [o.s.], i. 471–2; B.L. Harl. MS. 2103, f. 25.

11 B.L. Harl. MS. 2067, f. 37; 3 *Sheaf*, xx, p. 71; Burne, *Monks*, 154–6; *J.C.A.S.* n.s. ix. 12.

12 *J.C.A.S.* n.s. ix. 14–16.

13 Dr. J. P. Greene is thanked for this point.

FIG. 112. *Cloisters, south-west angle*

structure, probably the reredorter. Nothing of those buildings now remains, except for traces of the vaulting of the dormitory undercroft on the exterior of the warming house.[1] Near by, perhaps in another lost building, isolated and a little further north, was the infirmary.[2]

Immediately west of the cloister was the great court, the south side of which was formed by the abbot's lodgings, the west side by the abbey gateway and associated buildings including the monastic prison, a kiln, and drying floors, and the north side by other domestic structures, principally a brewhouse and a bakehouse.[3] At the north-east corner stood the chapel of St. Thomas the Apostle. The abbot's lodgings do not seem to have been especially grand. At first they included a great hall and chamber over the cellarium, as well as a chapel over the abbot's passage. Those rooms lay largely or entirely within the claustral west range and were approached by a porch from Abbey Court and a spiral staircase in the cloister. They were soon augmented by a range running westwards from the north-west tower of the abbey church to a tower on Northgate Street and containing at ground floor level a wine cellar in the tower, a beer cellar, a serving hall, a pantry, and a gateway leading from the 'gallery' in front of the abbot's garden into the churchyard. Above, on the first floor, were a second hall and chamber and a dining room. That extension probably dates from the time of Earl Ranulph III (1181–1232). A further range, running northwards along Northgate Street to the

abbey gateway, contained the abbot's kitchen, the porter's lodge, and other rooms.[4] Of all that there survive only the blocked remains of the gateway next to the pantry, and the 'beer cellar', an aisled vaulted chamber in the main range immediately west of the church.

The whole precinct was contained within an enclosure, comprising to the north and east the city walls and to the west a monastic wall pierced by the main gatehouse (Abbey Gate) and a lesser gateway (Little Abbey Gate) to the north composed of a single four-centred arch. A stone wall also surrounded the graveyard. Curiously, there is no record of a processional entrance from Northgate Street to the main door of the abbey church. Next to the south-west tower of the abbot's lodging, however, there was a gate or 'stile', from which a path presumably led to the great door and the gateway in the south range of the lodging, and which perhaps marked the formal entrance to church and graveyard for the citizens.[5]

CATHEDRAL CHURCH FROM 1541[6]

The interment of the former abbot (who also served as first dean of the cathedral) before the high altar within the choir in 1541 suggests that the Dissolution occasioned little immediate disturbance to the interior of the church.[7] The main change was presumably the dismantling of the shrine or at least the reliquary of St. Werburg.[8] More drastic alterations to the fabric began in 1550 with the removal of the stone altars,[9]

1 Cf. Ormerod, *Hist. Ches.* i. 255; B.L. Harl. MS. 2073, ff. 80–2.
2 Cf. B.L. Harl. MS. 2073, ff. 80–2.   3 Ibid.
4 Ibid.; *J.C.A.S.* xxxvii. 69–106; 3 *Sheaf*, xxv, pp. 53–4; *Lancs. and Ches. Wills and Inventories*, ed. G. J. Piccope, iii (Chetham Soc. [o.s.], liv), 1–8; *Cart. Chester Abbey*, i, p. 251.
5 *Cart. Chester Abbey*, i, p. 251; B.L. Harl. MS. 2073, ff. 80–2.
6 *T.H.S.L.C.* cxlv. 21–43.

7 *Lancs. and Ches. Wills and Inventories*, ed. G. J. Piccope, i (Chetham Soc. [o.s.], xxxiii), 125–30.
8 Cf. above, Collegiate Church of St. John; this chapter: Abbey Church to 1541 (Shrine); C. F. Battiscombe, *Relics of St. Cuthbert*, 86 n.
9 Morris, *Chester*, 152; C.C.A.L.S., EDD 3913/1/1, pp. 213–14; Burne, *Chester Cath.* 21.

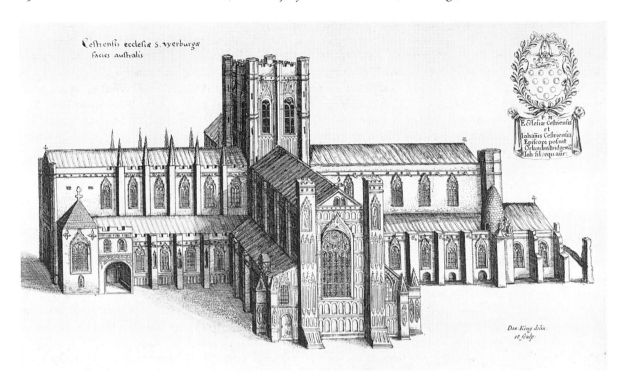

FIG. 113. *Cathedral from south, 1656*

and by 1553 the church had been stripped of almost all its ornaments.[1] The religious settlements of Mary and Elizabeth saw further changes, including the introduction in 1561 of a table of the Commandments.[2] The chapter was in financial difficulty after 1553, and by the 1570s the cathedral was in great decay, largely it seems because of the removal of its glass to the prebendaries' own benefices elsewhere.[3] Despite expenditure on the windows of St. Oswald's (that is, the south transept) in 1573, in 1578 the cathedral remained in want of lead, glass, and slate.[4] Improvement began only after 1580, when a commission headed by Lords Burleigh and Leicester recommended that the chapter's remaining rents be raised to provide for extra expenditure on the repair of the church.[5] By 1583 the chapter had set aside over £200, of which £100 had already been spent. In particular, eight new windows had been provided for the choir.[6] Even so, the cathedral was considered little better than a good parish church, its floor 'unpaved like a barn'.[7]

Although the nave was flagged in 1600,[8] and modest sums were spent in the early 17th century,[9] no major

work was undertaken until the 1630s. By 1631 the windows, especially in the choir, were so dilapidated that stones had fallen from them into the church. Work initiated by the chapter was furthered by Bishop Bridgeman, who between 1635 and 1637 refurbished the choir in the best Laudian manner. He caused the stalls to be painted and gilded, installed a new pulpit, galleries, and an episcopal throne incorporating parts of St. Werburg's shrine, glazed the east window with scenes from the life of Christ, and reordered the sanctuary, raising the steps to the communion table and blocking the eastern arch.[10]

St. Oswald's was also reordered in the 1630s and separated from the crossing by a new partition.[11] Other improvements included the whitewashing of the whole cathedral, the installation of a new font and pulpit at the west end of the nave, and the rehousing in 1635 of the consistory court in the south-west tower.[12] At the east end of the Lady chapel, which had formerly held the consistory court and retained its medieval east window with scenes from the life of the Virgin,[13] Bridgeman raised the great stone altar of the monastic

1 Morris, *Chester*, 151; cf. B.L. Harl. MS. 2103, ff. 68–9; Burne, *Chester Cath.* 108.   2 Burne, *Chester Cath.* 24–6.

3 Hist. MSS. Com. 58, *Marquess of Bath*, ii, p. 19; C.C.A.L.S., EDD 3913/1/2.

4 York, Borthwick Inst., V.1578; Burne, *Chester Cath.* 55–8.

5 Burne, *Chester Cath.* 84.

6 F. R. Raines, *Rectors of Manchester and Wardens of Collegiate Church*, i (Chetham Soc. N.S. v), 79.

7 Burne, *Chester Cath.* 80–1; B.L. Harl. MS. 2071, f. 147.

8 C.C.A.L.S., EDD 3913/1/3, pp. 356–63; Burne, *Chester*

Cath. 72.

9 C.C.A.L.S., EDD 3913/1/3, pp. 356–83; EDD 3913/1/4, pp. 19–26, 65–74, 101–8.

10 Ibid. EDA 3/1, f. 131; Burne, *Chester Cath.* 116; E. Barber, 'Chester Cath.: Jacobean Work', *J.C.A.S.* N.S. xii. 7–11.

11 Burne, *Chester Cath.* 106–7, 116–17; above, Medieval Parish Churches: St. Oswald.

12 G. T. O. Bridgeman, *Hist. of Church and Manor of Wigan*, ii (Chetham Soc. N.S. xvi), 447; Burne, *Chester Cath.* 105, 116–17.

13 *King's Vale Royal*, [ii], 33.

church, buried in the 1550s, a deed effected without the approval of a full chapter and successfully challenged by the puritan sub-dean, John Ley. Curiously, in yielding to the stone's removal, the bishop claimed that he 'had no thought of an altar' but intended only a 'repository' or table for preachers.[1]

Bridgeman's improvements did not long survive. In 1646 parliamentary troops defaced the choir, knocked the heads off the figures on the shrine fragments built into the bishop's throne, and broke the painted glass.[2] Seating was removed to refurbish St. John's elsewhere in the city, and contemporaries, perhaps with some exaggeration, talked of the ruin of the cathedral church.[3] The fabric itself was evidently maintained, since when the church was restored as a cathedral in the early 1660s the main expenditure needed was on plate and internal fittings rather than the building itself.[4] No work was done on the church until 1677, when the chapter borrowed £100 for the roof.[5] Fresh damage inflicted during a riot in 1682 included the destruction of Bridgeman's font and painted glass.[6] In 1701, when the dean and chapter sought a brief to raise £7,000, the cathedral's 'ruinous' state was attributed to its poor building stone and to harm done during the Civil Wars. It is doubtful whether the brief raised large sums. Although in 1708 the choir roof was allegedly 'newly planked' from money so collected, further repairs were needed and the chapter borrowed £300 for work on the Lady chapel.[7] Further improvements in the 1720s, including whitewashing the interior and placing the arms of the bishops, earls, and barons of Chester over the entrance to the choir, were paid for by a local inhabitant.[8] About then Nicholas Hawksmoor was apparently consulted about the repair or embellishment of the cathedral; he produced a ground plan of the church and bishop's palace and a sketch for rebuilding an aisle in his later classical manner.[9]

In the 1740s Bishop Peploe added north and south galleries to the choir, which in 1749 was declared to have been 'handsomely adorned and beautified, and the seats made uniform and decent'.[10] The flooring of the choir with marble, and further work on the nave, the south transept roof, and other buildings forced the chapter to borrow £500.[11] Thereafter, apart from flagging the nave in 1777,[12] little seems to have been done until the early 19th century, when the cathedral's 'mouldering outer form' attracted general censure,[13] and the chapter itself admitted that the church had fallen into decay through long neglect.[14]

In 1819 Thomas Harrison was commissioned to carry out major repairs. The work, funded by contributions from the diocese and a large gift from the dean and chapter of York, included repairs to the central tower, a new plaster ceiling for the choir, the replacement of the north window of the north transept, and, most importantly, rebuilding the front of the south transept, St. Oswald's.[15] In the 1820s there followed the internal refurbishment of St. Oswald's,[16] and work on the south choir aisle, including the addition of an octagonal turret to act as a buttress.[17]

A further major restoration took place between 1843 and 1848. The chapter launched an appeal which raised *c*. £4,000 to reorder and beautify the choir. As a first step the pulpitum was moved from the east to the west arch of the crossing, and shortly afterwards the Birmingham architect R. C. Hussey, aided by his mason George Haswell,[18] opened up the blocked eastern arch of the sanctuary, and installed new Decorated tracery in the east window and a quatrefoil balustrade in the clerestory. He replaced the existing roof with a groined vault of wood and stucco, moved the choir stalls westwards to the newly positioned pulpitum, and removed the galleries. Bridgeman's throne and pulpit were replaced by new stone structures, backed by stone screens with doors opening into the aisles. A new openwork screen, designed by James Harrison, was placed behind the high altar, and stained glass by William Wailes was inserted in the choir aisles.[19]

Hussey remained sole cathedral architect until

1 Burne, *Chester Cath.* 117–19; J. Ley, *Letter Against Erection of an Altar, 29 June 1635* (1641).

2 B.L. Add. MS. 5836, f. 219; J. C. Bridge, 'Organists of Chester Cath.' *J.C.A.S.* xix. 86.

3 Above, Collegiate Church of St. John; Morris, *Siege of Chester*, 205; *King's Vale Royal*, [iii], 46.

4 Burne, *Chester Cath.* 135; *Mins. of Cttee. for Relief of Plundered Ministers, and of Trustees for Maintenance of Ministers, 1643–54*, ed. W. A. Shaw (R.S.L.C. xxviii), 194, 208–9; *1650–60* (R.S.L.C. xxxiv), 103–4, 209, 287–8, 297–8; *V.C.H. Ches.* iii. 37.

5 C.C.A.L.S., EDD 3919/3/3, p. 18; Burne, *Chester Cath.* 150.

6 Dugdale, *Mon.* ii. 383; for the riot: *V.C.H. Ches.* v (1), Early Modern Chester: City Government and Politics, 1662–1762 (City Politics).

7 Willis, *Surv. of Caths.* i. 321; 2 *Sheaf*, i, pp. 34, 41–2, 52–3, 76, 88; 3 *Sheaf*, xii, p. 2; C.C.A.L.S., EDD 3913/3/4, pp. 60–1.

8 C.C.A.L.S., DCC 16/120, p. 10.

9 Wilton House, MS. F 6/27. Thanks are due to Mr. R. B. Hewling for supplying a copy of the drawings.

10 C.C.A.L.S., EDD 3913/3/5, pp. 14–15; Burne, *Chester Cath.* 205–6.

11 C.C.A.L.S., EDD 3913/3/5, p. 25; Burne, *Chester Cath.* 203.

12 Burne, *Chester Cath.* 223.

13 V. M. Jansen, 'Archit. of 13th-Cent. Rebldg. at St. Werburgh's, Chester' (Univ. of California, Berkeley, Ph.D. dissertation, 1975), 29–30, quoting G. Batenham, *Visit to Cath. Church of Chester* (Chester, 1823), 20, 40. Cf. Ormerod, *Hist. Ches.* i. 252–3.   14 C.C.A.L.S., EDD 3913/3/6, p. 17.

15 Ibid. pp. 19–23; Burne, *Chester Cath.* 243–6; Jansen, 'Rebldg. at St. Werburgh's', 31–2.

16 Burne, *Chester Cath.* 248–9; above, Medieval Parish Churches: St. Oswald.

17 V. M. Jansen, 'George Gilbert Scott and Restoration at Chester Cath. 1819–76', *Med. Arch., Art, and Archit. at Chester*, ed. Thacker, 81–107..

18 Jansen, 'Rebldg. at St. Werburgh's', 39, 340–50.

19 Ibid. 35–8; Addleshaw, 'Archit. 1770–1970 in Chester Cath.' *Archit. Hist.* xiv. 86–8, 101; Jansen, 'Scott and Restoration'; C.C.A.L.S., EDD 3913/3/6, pp. 23, 26–8.

c. 1855, when he was joined by George Gilbert Scott. By then the chapter had determined on a comprehensive refurbishment of the Lady chapel, into which Scott and Hussey introduced lancet windows in 13th-century style, allegedly on good evidence. The chapel was repainted, stained glass by Wailes was inserted, and mosaics were introduced behind the altar. The work was complete by the mid 1860s,[1] when, moved by the fear that the eastern limb was becoming unsafe, the chapter decided on a thorough restoration of the entire building. By 1868 sufficient funds had been obtained from the Ecclesiastical Commissioners, and until 1876 operations were in the hands of Scott, who had become sole cathedral architect, and James Frater, his clerk of works. The builders were the firms of Haswell and John Thompson and the carving throughout was by the firm of Farmer and Brindley.[2] The restoration was so drastic that it constituted virtually a rebuilding. The exterior, in 1868 so decayed that it resembled 'a mouldering sandstone cliff',[3] was refaced in red Runcorn sandstone. External features were remodelled to erase late medieval alterations: in particular, the gable, buttresses, and remaining Perpendicular windows of the Lady chapel and much window tracery elsewhere were reconstructed. Parapets were added to the Lady chapel, choir and choir aisles, central tower, south transept, south side of the nave, and south nave aisle. Pinnacles were placed at the east ends of the Lady chapel and choir, and turrets on the west end of the nave and the central tower, the last disproportionately large because they were intended to balance a spire that was never built.[4] The nave and south transept received flying buttresses and the south-west porch a fan vault, designed by George Gilbert Scott the younger. The most controversial change was the apsidal chapel with a high conical roof which terminated the east choir aisle, built as a memorial to the railway contractor Thomas Brassey.[5] Though Scott argued that there was good architectural evidence for it, the claim can scarcely have been justified.[6]

Inside, Scott introduced wooden ribbed high vaults over the nave, replaced those by Hussey in the choir, and inserted stone rib vaults in the nave aisles. The interior was cleansed of whitewash, mosaics designed by J. R. Clayton and made by A. Salviati were installed in the new apse terminating the south choir aisle, and the choir itself was greatly enriched; the new oak vault was decorated with paintings by J. R. Clayton, Hussey's

FIG. 114. *Cathedral, looking east from nave, 1876*

quatrefoil parapets in the clerestory were replaced, the choir stalls were remodelled and provided with extra rows of benches and desks, and a matching wooden throne replaced that of Hussey. An elaborate new pavement of tile and incised marble and a mosaic reredos were also installed, both designed by Clayton. The dean and chapter were especially concerned to obtain a clear view from the nave into the choir and Lady chapel,[7] and Scott therefore removed the screen behind the high altar and the stone pulpitum, the west face of which was divided and re-erected behind the reordered choir stalls. The stalls themselves terminated at a new open timber screen spanning the east arch of the crossing, and the back panels of the return stalls were removed. A similar desire for internal vistas also led to the removal of the timber screen which separated

1 Jansen, 'Rebldg. at St. Werburgh's', 42–6; Jansen, 'Scott and Restoration'; *Archit. Hist.* xiv. 88, 101; G. G. Scott, 'Archit. Hist. of Chester Cath.' *J.C.A.S.* [o.s.], iii. 170–1; C.C.A.L.S., EDD 4/23, pp. 2, 12.

2 Following acct. depends largely on C.C.A.L.S., EDD 4/16–17, 23; EDD 3913/2/1–5; EDD 3913/3/10; *J.C.A.S.* [o.s.], iii. 159–82; n.s. ix. 48–50, 55–8; *Builder* (1877), 210, 1006; J. S. Howson, *Handbk. to Chester Cath.* (Chester, 1882); *Archit. Hist.* xiv. 77, 80, 83, 95–8, 101; Jansen, 'Rebldg. at St. Werburgh's',

46–71; Jansen, 'Scott and Restoration'.

3 George G. Scott, *Personal and Professional Recollections*, ed. Giles G. Scott, 7, quoted by Jansen, 'Rebldg. at St. Werburgh's', 49.

4 *Archit. Hist.* xiv. 96.

5 C.C.A.L.S., EDD 4/23, p. 5.

6 *J.C.A.S.* [o.s.], iii. 173–5.

7 C.C.A.L.S., EDD 4/23, pp. 8–9; J. S. Howson, *Notes on Restoration of Chester Cath.* [*c.* 1873], pp. 17–18.

St. Oswald's church in the south transept from the rest of the building.

Other work in the choir included the replacement of Hussey's pulpit with a new wooden one, the installation of a new lectern in front of the high altar, and the introduction of 17th-century bronze candelabra into the sanctuary and 16th-century Spanish gates into the aisles. A great metal cross by F. A. Skidmore was suspended at the crossing,[1] and stained glass by Clayton and Bell, Wailes, and Heaton, Butler, and Bayne was introduced throughout the building.

Although Scott claimed to have been conservative, followed good evidence, and never wilfully displaced any stone 'retaining . . . its old surface',[2] undeniably the general impression created after 1876, especially by the exterior, was that of a Victorian building. Contemporaries were aware of that, and some at least were critical. In 1873, for example, a local artist commented in *Building News* that the church was a 'mockery', 'restored out of existence'.[3] Nevertheless, although Scott went beyond what was strictly necessary for preservation, introducing novel features and destroying medieval work in the process, he achieved much: above all, his conscientious structural work secured the building.[4]

Scott's work was continued in the 1880s by Sir Arthur Blomfield, who reinstated St. Werburg's shrine behind the high altar and restored the south transept after the removal of St. Oswald's church, installing a wooden high vault, a stone vault in the three northern bays of the east aisle, and a new Decorated south window with glass by Heaton, Butler, and Bayne to replace that of Harrison. Blomfield also renewed the stonework of the nave north wall, which was adorned with mosaic panels designed by Clayton and Bell, and created a baptistery by reopening the blocked internal arches of the northwest tower; the font installed there, which superseded that given in 1687 by Bishop Moreton of Kildare, was bought in Venice and, although then believed to be early Christian, was probably a fake made up from early panels.[5]

The remodelling of the interior of the south transept was completed as a memorial to the first duke of Westminster by C. J. Blomfield in 1900–2, when stone vaults were installed in the west aisle.[6] Between 1890 and 1904 stained glass by C. E. Kempe was introduced, and in 1906 Kempe refurbished the

chapel of St. Oswald. Giles Scott carried out further work on the exterior of the west aisle in 1908 and renovated the transeptal chapels of St. George and St. Nicholas in 1917 and 1921. In 1922 W. E. Tower refurbished that of St. Mary Magdalen.[7]

Thereafter little was done to the fabric. Inside, a rood replaced the chancel organ on Scott's screen in 1910.[8] The Lady chapel was redecorated between 1957 and 1962 by the cathedral architect, B. A. Miller,[9] and glass by W. T. Carter Shapland was inserted in the great west window in 1961.[10] Work executed for Dean Addleshaw in the 1960s by Miller's successor, George Pace, included the introduction of a painted ceiling into the crossing tower and new nave stalls incorporating panels from Bridgeman's choir pulpit.[11]

In 1973 a free-standing bell tower designed by Pace was built to the north-east of the cathedral; it comprised a concrete frame clothed in slate tiles rising from a base of red sandstone.[12]

Organs[13]

An organ in the abbey apparently survived the Dissolution. The early 17th-century instrument, which had a case with hinged shutters, was probably housed in a loft on the south side of the choir; it was gilded by Bishop Bridgeman in the mid 1630s. In the early 18th century a new organ, attributed to Bernard ('Father') Smith, was placed upon the pulpitum.[14] Rebuilt in 1825, it was replaced in 1844 by a new instrument, the second largest in England, located on the resited pulpitum. In 1875 that organ was itself superseded by an instrument built by a local firm and placed in a new case and loft designed by G. G. Scott on the north side of the crossing. A choir organ on the screen was removed in 1910, when the great organ was also rebuilt. The case was restored by George Pace in 1969.

Monuments

Although there were burials in the cathedral from 1541, the earliest surviving post-Dissolution monument, a tablet on a crossing pier, is to Thomas Green, a former mayor (d. 1602), and his two wives. Other early memorials include two 17th-century armorial boards painted by the Randle Holmes, in the south choir aisle in 2000, and a tablet above the west steps of the nave to two chancellors of the diocese, John and Thomas Wainwright (d. 1686 and 1720), designed by William

1 Pevsner, *Ches.* 205.

2 Jansen, 'Rebldg. at St. Werburgh's', 49.

3 Ibid. 48.　　　　　　　　　　4 Ibid. 48–63.

5 *Archit. Hist.* xiv. 77–8; *J.C.A.S.* n.s. ix. 103–6; xvi. 101–11; E. Barber, 'Baptistery of Cath.' *J.C.A.S.* n.s. x. 88–94; Burne, *Chester Cath.* 153, 158; G. W. O. Addleshaw, *Chester Cath.: Stained Glass, Windows, Mosaics, and Monuments* (Chester, 1965), 8.

6 *Archit. Hist.* xiv. 78; *J.C.A.S.* n.s. ix. 109–14.

7 *Archit. Hist.* xiv. 90, 98–9; F. L. M. Bennett, *Chester*

Cath. 62.

8 J. T. Belcher, *Organs of Chester Cath.* 4.

9 *Archit. Hist.* xiv. 91.

10 Ibid. 99.

11 Ibid. 93–4.

12 N. Pevsner, P. Metcalf, and others, *Cathedrals of Eng.: Midland, E., and N.* 62.

13 Para. based on Belcher, *Organs.*

14 Willis, *Surv. of Caths.* i. 321; Hemingway, *Hist. Chester,* ii. 41–2; C.C.A.L.S., EDD 16/120, p. 11.

FIG. 115. *Ruinous cloisters in early 19th century*

Kent with an inscription by George Berkeley. Another chancellor, Samuel Peploe (d. 1781), is commemorated by a tablet by Joseph Nollekens in the north transept. The most important 19th-century monuments are two tomb-chests: one in the north transept to Bishop Pearson (d. 1686), designed by A. W. Blomfield in 1864, the other in the south transept to the first duke of Westminster (d. 1899), designed by C. J. Blomfield with an effigy by F. W. Pomeroy in 1902. The cenotaph, also in the south transept, dates from 1933 and is by Giles Scott.

CLAUSTRAL BUILDINGS FROM 1541

The entire monastic complex, except for the former chapel of St. Nicholas, passed to the dean and chapter of the newly established cathedral in 1541.[1] The communal monastic buildings for which no use was found after the Dissolution suffered most, especially after the cathedral's impoverishment in 1553. The great kitchen, granted to the bishop in 1541, had disappeared by the 1620s.[2] The refectory only just survived. Used briefly by the grammar school in the 1570s, it needed repair in 1580, when it was recommended for conversion into a hall for chapter meetings. Eventually, in 1613, when it was returned (at least in part) to the grammar school, it was reroofed with slates and some internal partitions were inserted.[3]

On the east side of the cloister, the chapter house continued in use, together with a room over the vestibule on its west which later disappeared.[4] The

dormitory was intact in 1589, when the roof was repaired and locks were fitted to its doors. By 1631, when it contained a chamber inhabited perhaps by one of the conducts (the chaplains paid to read prayers in the cathedral), it had probably been subdivided.[5] The buildings to the east, designated 'priests' kitchens and cellars' in the 17th century, were probably used by the minor canons for common rooms and lodgings. In the 1570s and 1580s their dining hall was the former monastic misericord. After 1600, however, those buildings evidently fell into disuse.[6]

The cloister itself, reconstructed shortly before the Dissolution, was presumably in relatively good condition in the later 16th century. Apparently no work was done upon it until 1589–90, when some of the windows in the walks were roughly repaired with bricks.[7]

During the Interregnum the cloisters and chapter house were stripped of lead and glass and the dormitory was probably reduced to ruins.[8] Maintenance during the later 17th and 18th century was at best sporadic. The cloisters, for example, were clearly in decay in the 1680s and 1690s; though work was done in 1712, by the 1720s they were much neglected and the south walk was ruinous.[9] Apart from a new roof in 1751, no major work was undertaken in the 18th century,[10] and by the 1770s only three of the four walks remained.[11] The chapter house, long exposed to the elements, became 'a common receptacle for filth and rubbish' and was repaired only in 1723 at the

---

1 *V.C.H. Ches.* iii. 144, 188.

2 Below, this chapter: Precinct from 1541.

3 York, Borthwick Inst., V.1578–9, Thos. Purvis's responsion to interrogatory 9; Burne, *Chester Cath.* 12, 84; *V.C.H. Ches.* iii. 230.   4 B.L. Harl. MS. 2073, ff. 83–4.

5 C.C.A.L.S., EDD 3913/1/3, p. 43; EDV 6, petty canons' presentments, no. 19; Burne, *Chester Cath.* 64.

6 e.g. C.C.A.L.S., EDD 3913/1/3, pp. 7, 194.

7 Ibid. pp. 94–6; Burne, *Chester Cath.* 67.

8 C.C.A.L.S., DCC 16/120, p. 13.

9 Ibid. p. 11; ibid. EDD 3913/3/3, p. 70; EDD 3913/1/7; Willis, *Surv. of Caths.* i. 321; Burne, *Chester Cath.* 157.

10 e.g. C.C.A.L.S., EDD 3913/3/5, pp. 15–16; Burne, *Chester Cath.* 205.

11 T. Pennant, *Tours in Wales* (1810 edn.), i. 235; Burne, *Chester Cath.* 205.

initiative of the bishop and one of the prebendaries, when it received a new roof and windows and was converted into the cathedral library.[1] The ruinous dormitory disappeared entirely in the early 19th century.[2] By contrast, the refectory, which remained the home of the King's school, was repaired by the city corporation in 1657, and after 1660 was generally maintained by the chapter.[3]

Little was done to the claustral buildings until the mid 1850s, when R. C. Hussey rebuilt the entrance to the chapter house vestibule from the east cloister and the entrance into the chapter house itself.[4] His work was continued by G. G. Scott, who raised the gable, refaced the south side,[5] and installed a new east window by Heaton, Butler, and Bayne.[6] Blomfield restored the north side of the chapter house and added five grisaille side windows in 1882–3. He also rebuilt the roof to a steeper pitch in 1894 and renewed the west gable.[7]

In 1871–2 Scott reconstructed the south walk of the cloisters to match the surviving work.[8] Between 1911 and 1913 the late medieval vaulting, by then in a dangerous condition, was thoroughly restored by Giles Scott.[9] In the 1920s the cloisters were reglazed to designs by A. K. Nicholson and F. C. Eden.[10]

In 1913–14 Scott also started work on the refectory, vacated by the King's school in 1879, installing a new east window with Decorated tracery and restoring the windows on the south side to their original size.[11] In 1920 the east window was glazed to designs by J. W. Brown,[12] and in 1922 the whole building was thoroughly repaired.[13] In 1939 its restoration was completed with the installation of a steeply pitched hammerbeam roof by F. H. Crossley.[14]

On the west side of the cloister Giles Scott restored three rooms on the ruined upper floor and the newel staircase to them.[15] The Romanesque undercroft, much of which had long been a workshop, was restored in the early 1990s to house an exhibition on the church's history.[16]

The cloister gardens, laid out under Dean Bennett in

the 1920s,[17] received a sculpture by Stephen Broadbent in 1994.[18]

PRECINCT FROM 1541

There were few alterations to the precinct until *c.* 1550, when the dean and chapter were accused of pulling down certain buildings.[19] Thereafter the precinct was probably neglected by the largely absentee chapter, which in the 1570s rented out the prebendal houses.[20] In 1578 the precinct contained buildings lacking glass, slate, and lead, and the headmaster of the grammar school complained that the school building, then possibly housed in Abbey Court, was so poorly maintained that it endangered the lives of masters and pupils.[21] The churchyard too was neglected; defiled from the 1550s by animals and the filth repeatedly thrown into it, it was levelled and enclosed only in 1619, and still contained a dunghill in 1634.[22]

By 1583 the dean and at least three prebendaries were resident and work had been done on the grammar school.[23] In the early 17th century the outer court included the bishop's palace in the former abbot's lodgings, the deanery in the former chapel of St. Thomas,[24] and at least one prebendal house, perhaps on the site of the former bakehouse.[25] The condition of the court was nevertheless the cause of scandal and dispute, largely because of the 'noise, filth, and smoke' engendered by a brewhouse and bakehouse in the northern range, and the rowdiness associated with an alehouse in the abbey gate.[26]

Bishop Bridgeman, who in 1623 condemned the prebendaries' houses as 'base, little, noisome, and unfit for habitation',[27] initiated improvements. In 1626 on the site of the monastic kitchen he built four houses, each with a kitchen, hall, two chambers, two upper lofts, and cellars; reserved for the cathedral conducts, they were to be maintained by the dean and chapter.[28] The bishop also tried to ensure that the buildings on the north side of Abbey Court were reserved for the dean and chapter and other members of the church. His injunction was ignored, and in 1634

1 C.C.A.L.S., EDD 3913/3/4, p. 151; DCC 16/120, pp. 13–14; Willis, *Surv. of Caths.* i. 321–2.

2 Burne, *Chester Cath.* 235.   3 Ibid. 133, 139.

4 *Archit. Hist.* xiv. 88.   5 Ibid. 97.

6 Addleshaw, *Chester Cath. Glass,* 29.

7 Ibid. 30; *Archit. Hist.* xiv. 78.

8 *Archit. Hist.* xiv. 97.

9 Ibid. 98; *J.C.A.S.* xix. 223–5; xxi. 169–78.

10 *Archit. Hist.* xiv. 82, 92; Addleshaw, *Chester Cath. Glass,* 30–1; Bennett, *Chester Cath.* 99–100.

11 *Archit. Hist.* xiv. 98; *J.C.A.S.* xxi. 178–83.

12 *Archit. Hist.* xiv. 79, 95.

13 Bennett, *Chester Cath.* 109.

14 Ibid. 81; *Archit. Hist.* xiv. 81.

15 *Archit. Hist.* xiv. 98.

16 G. W. O. Addleshaw, *Pictorial Hist. of Chester Cath.* 22.

17 Ibid. 19, 24; Bennett, *Chester Cath.* 114.

18 S. Smalley, *Water of Life.*

19 *Acts of P.C.* 1552–4, 163, 218, 230; York, Borthwick Inst., V.1578–9, responsions to item 9 of interrogatories; Burne, *Chester Cath.* 24–6.

20 Hist. MSS. Com. 58, *Marquess of Bath,* ii, pp. 19–20.

21 Ibid.; P.R.O., SP 12/10, pp. 318–19; C.C.A.L.S., EDD 3913/1/2.

22 3 *Sheaf,* v, pp. 4–15; C.C.A.L.S., EDC 5/1634/96.

23 F. R. Raines, *Rectors of Manchester and Wardens of Collegiate Church,* i (Chetham Soc. n.s. v), 79.

24 Burne, *Chester Cath.* 226.

25 B.L. Harl. MS. 2073, ff. 80–2.

26 C.C.A.L.S., EDA 3/1, ff. 254v.–255v.; 1 *Sheaf,* iii, pp. 199–200, 204–5; Bridgeman, *Hist. Wigan,* ii. 399, 403–8; Burne, *Chester Cath.* 98–101; *Hist. of Retreat House, Chester,* 3–4.

27 Burne, *Chester Cath.* 101.

28 Ibid. 107–8; C.C.A.L.S., EDA 3/1, f. 226v.

FIG. 116. *House of 1761,*
north side of Abbey Square

the chapter renewed the brewhouse lease. In 1638, after the death of the tenant, Bridgeman sought help from Archbishop Laud. Although Chester was outside his metropolitan jurisdiction, Laud forbade the letting of any part of the court to a brewer or maltster, apparently to good effect.[1]

One reason for Bridgeman's demands for improvements was his increased residence in the palace at Chester from 1630.[2] In the 1630s he restored it, covering the 'tower' with lead, adding new rooms, reflooring and improving others, and reglazing the windows.[3] It was perhaps then that the episcopal chapel was refurbished with a new east window, screen, and, perhaps, plaster ceiling in the chancel.[4]

The Interregnum wrought great damage to the palace. Unoccupied after Bridgeman's flight in 1645, it was sold in 1650,[5] and the lead was stripped from the roof of the great hall and the adjoining 'Green Hall' or great chamber over the cellarium in the west range of the cloister.[6] In 1651 the city corporation negotiated unsuccessfully to buy the palace, and eventually it was used as a county gaol.[7] By 1660 the two halls were

ruinous, much had been demolished, and what remained was very dilapidated.[8]

Repair work began on the wrecked palace immediately after the Restoration. By 1663 the bishops had spent at least £900 and an estimated £700 was still needed.[9] Bishop Hall (1662–8) restored the battlements, and built a stair to the dining room and stone steps to the chapel. Work was also done on the chapel roof and the rooms above the chapel, and Hall's expenditure of £170 for plasterwork perhaps indicates that the chancel ceilings were his work rather than Bridgeman's.[10] Even so, in 1669, after over £2,000 had allegedly been spent, the halls above the west range of the cloister were still in ruins.[11] By then work had also been done on the prebendaries' houses, and the one standing at the north-east corner of Abbey Court had been leased out for rebuilding.[12]

There was also new building in the 1660s within the precinct, both on the site which developed into Abbey Green,[13] and in the lane later known as Abbey Street. At the eastern end of the latter Bishop Hall erected four houses for the petty canons.[14] Building continued

1 Bridgeman, *Hist. Wigan,* ii. 403–8; Burne, *Chester Cath.* 112–16.   2 Bridgeman, *Hist. Wigan,* ii. 332–4.

3 Ibid. ii. 446–9; C.C.A.L.S., EDA 3/1, f. 130v.

4 Burne, *Chester Cath.* 117.

5 Gastrell, *Not. Cest.* i. 11; *V.C.H. Ches.* iii. 36.

6 *J.C.A.S.* xxxvii. 302–7; Willis, *Surv. of Caths.* i. 321.

7 *J.C.A.S.* xxxvii. 302–3, 306.

8 Ibid. 302–11; B.L. Harl. MS. 1994, ff. 98–9; C.C.A.L.S., EDD 16/120.

9 *Cal. S.P. Dom.* 1660–1, 49; Bodl. MS. Tanner 144, ff. 13–15; *V.C.H. Ches.* iii. 37–8.

10 *J.C.A.S.* xxxvii. 310; cf. B.L. Add. MS. 5836, ff. 219–220v.

11 *J.C.A.S.* xxxvii. 307–11.

12 *Hist. of Retreat Ho.* 5.

13 C.C.A.L.S., EDD 3913/3/2, p. 20; EDD 3913/3/4, pp. 68, 104, 146; 3 *Sheaf,* xlv, pp. 14–15.

14 C.C.A.L.S., EDD 3913/3/2, pp. 93–4; Burne, *Chester Cath.* 148.

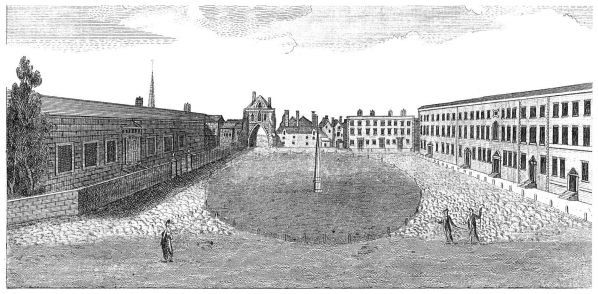

FIG. 117. *Abbey Square after 1761*

sporadically until the mid 18th century, especially in Abbey Court, which was known as 'the prebendaries' quadrangle' and formed the main residential area of the precinct. The former prebendal house at the north-east corner was reconstructed in 1675 and 1695, when the site was divided, and another next to Abbey Gate was rebuilt *c.* 1696.[1] In the 1720s the court was planted with lime walks.[2]

A major development of Abbey Court began with Bishop Keene's rebuilding of the palace. Work on the south range, west of the cathedral, started in 1754 under Robert (later Sir Robert) Taylor.[3] The new building, complete by 1757, was single-storeyed on the north side facing Abbey Court but two-storeyed to the south, where the ground level was lower. The north entrance front was rusticated and separated from the rest of Abbey Court by a ditch. It had a pillared central doorway approached by a flight of steps and flanked by three windows on either side. At both ends were two-storeyed ranges, that at the east being over an arched gateway opening into St. Werburgh's Lane.[4] The interior included two lofty and spacious rooms, a library, and a chapel. The whole cost £2,200, the equivalent of three years' income from the bishopric.[5]

Work on the palace stimulated activity around the other sides of Abbey Court. In 1753 Charles Boswell, a Chester brewer, took a lease of the northern half of the western side, where by 1760 he had built three houses.[6] In 1755 he acquired a further lease at the south end of

the precinct immediately west of St. Nicholas's chapel (by then the Wool Hall), on which he built a linen hall.[7]

On the north side of Abbey Court in 1754 the chapter leased to the chapter clerk and others 'certain old buildings' (presumably the former brewhouse and bakehouse) together with some adjoining land, sufficient for a terrace of four houses. Completed by 1761 and of brick with stone dressings (Fig. 116), the development was the grandest in the precinct and closely resembled the house which Bishop Peploe had built in the Groves *c.* 1741.[8] At the north-east corner of the court lay a house of the same date by a different architect, possibly Robert Taylor, built by one of the prebendaries on the site divided in 1695.[9] Another house was built on the east side in 1754.[10] In the court itself the lime walks were superseded by an oval of grass, in the centre of which was placed in 1761 a column removed from the Exchange in 1756 when the open ground floor was enclosed.[11]

The next area to be developed was the lane running from Abbey Court eastwards to the Kaleyards Gate, formerly known as Little Abbey Court and renamed Abbey Street in 1764.[12] The lessees there included three of the prebendaries and Charles Boswell. The new scheme involved the demolition of the two easternmost minor canons' houses, by then long let to tenants and ruinous, and the construction of three new houses.[13] Shortly afterwards there was development on a site leased to Alderman Thomas Boswell in 1768 and

1 C.C.A.L.S., EDD 3913/3/3, p. 112; EDD 3913/3/4, p. 10; EDD 3913/3/5, pp. 114–19; *Hist. of Retreat Ho.* 5–6.

2 Burne, *Chester Cath.* 188; C.C.A.L.S., DCC 16/20, pp. 11–12.

3 H. Colvin, *Biographical Dictionary of Brit. Architects* (1995 edn.), 965; C.C.A.L.S., EEB 99487, pp. 61–2.

4 C.C.A.L.S., DBE 50; EDD 3913/3/5, p. 35; B.L. Add. MS. 5836, ff. 219v.–220; *J.C.A.S.* xxxvii. 89–90; engraving in C. Hulbert, *Ches. Antiquities* (1838) (Fig. 117, above).

5 B.L. Add. MS. 5836, ff. 219v.–220.

6 C.C.A.L.S., EDD 3913/3/5, pp. 72–3; EDE, Box 3637 (draft

of lease); ibid. ZAB 4, ff. 156v., 233; Fig. 117.

7 C.C.A.L.S., EDD 3913/3/5, pp. 44–5, 87–8; B.L. Add. MS. 5836, f. 226; above, Fairs.

8 C.C.A.L.S., EDD 3913/3/5, pp. 36–8, 76–7; EDE, Box 3637 (drafts of leases).

9 Ibid. EDD 3913/3/5, pp. 46, 88; *Hist. of Retreat Ho.* 8–10.

10 Date on gutter; Bennett, *Chester Cath.* 117.

11 C.C.A.L.S., ZAB 4, f. 192; 3 *Sheaf,* xiii, p. 70.

12 C.C.A.L.S., EDD 3913/3/5, pp. 112–13.

13 Ibid. pp. 101–10, 112–13.

thereafter known as Abbey Green; a terrace of six houses was completed probably by *c.* 1775 and certainly before 1782.[1]

In the late 1780s the medieval chapel of St. Thomas in the north-east corner of Abbey Square, which had long served as the deanery, was taken down and replaced with a 'spacious mansion' by Dean Cotton.[2] The prebendal house by Abbey Gate was rebuilt in the early 1820s by the residing prebendary,[3] who shortly afterwards erected four more houses on a site on the north side of Abbey Street which had hitherto contained his coach house and stables.[4]

Between 1876 and 1881 the old infirmary buildings, then known as Little Abbey Court, were taken down and replaced by an open space.[5] By then the former palace, deserted by the bishop in 1865, had been demolished.[6] The chapel alone survived and was restored in the 1920s as the chapel of St. Anselm.[7] The precinct attained the form which in 2000 it largely retained with the construction of new buildings for the King's school on the site of the former palace. Designed by Sir Arthur Blomfield in a neo-Gothic style, the south wing was completed in 1877 and the west in 1879.[8] In 1920 the deanery was refurbished for the bishop's use.[9]

CASTLE

Founded by William I in 1070, the castle shortly afterwards came under the control of the earl of Chester and thereafter descended with the earldom.[10] It was temporarily in royal hands during the minorities of Earl Hugh II (1153–62) and Earl Ranulph III (1181–7), and passed permanently to the Crown with the earldom in 1237.[11] In 1254 it was granted to Henry III's son, the Lord Edward.[12] Acquired by Simon de Montfort after the battle of Lewes in 1264,[13] it was recovered by Edward in 1265[14] and remained with the Crown until 1322, when it was granted to Edward II's favourite, Hugh Despenser the younger.[15] With Despenser's fall in 1326 it reverted to the king, and thereafter it continued Crown property until the Interregnum.[16] Although the Crown resumed control at the Restoration, thereafter upkeep of the shire hall and other county buildings increasingly devolved upon quarter sessions, and from 1690 became their responsibility alone. The Crown, however, continued to maintain the military buildings and fortifications.[17] Those *ad hoc* arrangements were formalized under Acts of 1788 and 1807 which vested new county buildings occupying roughly the site of the former outer bailey in the *custos rotulorum* of Cheshire.[18] The dual

ownership thus established remained substantially unchanged in 2000.

ADMINISTRATIVE AND MILITARY FUNCTIONS

The castle was both the occasional residence of the Norman earls and their principal administrative centre, the base of such officials as the justice and chamberlain of Chester, their deputies and clerks.[19] Accounts were rendered at the exchequer there, and it was the location of the earl's chief court and prison.[20] Attached to it were certain lands. By the later 13th century, probably under an ancient arrangement, the castle demesne included 82 a. of land and 3 a. of meadow within the Earl's Eye, Handbridge, Brewer's Hall, Saltney, and Marlston cum Lache, all lying south of the Dee.[21]

After 1237 the castle remained the administrative centre of the palatinate, at first in the hands of royal keepers, later directly under the supervision of the Crown.[22] Daily administration was by a constable, first recorded *c.* 1216,[23] assisted by a staff generally including a keeper of the gaol, janitors of the upper and lower wards, serjeants, watchmen, chaplains, and clerks.[24]

An important base for royal operations against the

---

1 C.C.A.L.S., EDD 3913/3/5, pp. 134, 184; ibid. ZAB 4, f. 262v.; 3 *Sheaf*, xlviii, pp. 9–10.

2 Burne, *Chester Cath.* 226 n.

3 C.C.A.L.S., EDD 3913/3/6, pp. 29–30, 54.

4 Ibid. pp. 54, 58–9, 66, 77–81, 127–30; Burne, *Chester Cath.* 252–5.

5 C.C.A.L.S., EDD 3913/3/6, p. 408; EDD 3913/3/10, p. 210.

6 *V.C.H. Ches.* iii. 193.   7 Bennett, *Chester Cath.* 116–17.

8 *Archit. Hist.* xiv. 78; *V.C.H. Ches.* iii. 232.

9 *V.C.H. Ches.* iii. 80; *Hist. of Retreat Ho.* 18.

10 Orderic Vitalis, *Historia Ecclesiastica*, ed. M. Chibnall, ii. 236–7; B. Davison, 'Early Earthwork Castles: A New Model', *Château Gaillard Conference in Castle Studies*, iii. 37–46.

11 *Cal. Pat.* 1232–47, 184–5; *Ches. in Pipe R.* 27–8, 36–7; *V.C.H. Ches.* ii. 6.

12 *Cal. Pat.* 1247–58, 272; R. Studd, 'The Lord Edward's Lordship of Chester', *T.H.S.L.C.* cxxviii. 1–25.

13 *Cal. Chart. R.* 1257–1300, 54; *Cal. Pat.* 1258–66, 397, 416, 487.

14 *T.H.S.L.C.* cxxviii. 15–16; *Ann. Cest.* 94–5.

15 *Cal. Close*, 1313–18, 505; *Cal. Pat.* 1321–4, 194.

16 e.g. *Cal. Close*, 1327–30, 142, 288; *Cal. Pat.* 1327–30, 271; below, this chapter: Administrative and Military Functions.

17 C.C.A.L.S., QJB 13A (unfol.); QJB 14A, ff. 68v., 92v., 141, 178, 226; QJB 15A (unfol.); QJB 16A, ff. 3v., 15; QJB 20A (unfol.); *V.C.H. Ches.* ii. 71; below, this chapter: Buildings.

18 Chester Castle Rebuilding Act, 1788, 28 Geo. III, c. 82; Chester Castle Gaol Act, 1807, 47 Geo. III, Sess. 2, c. 6 (Local and Personal).

19 *V.C.H. Ches.* ii. 2–3; A. Thacker, 'Castle', *Chester 1900*, ed. A. M. Kennett, 13–16; D. Crouch, 'Administration of Norman Earldom', *J.C.A.S.* lxxi. 69–95.

20 *V.C.H. Ches.* ii. 3; cf. *Cal. Lib.* 1245–51, 76; below, this chapter: County Gaol.   21 *Cal. Chart. R.* 1257–1300, 282–3.

22 *Cal. Pat.* 1232–47, 184–5, 188–9, 240, 244.

23 B.L. Harl. MS. 2149, f. 172v.

24 *Ches. in Pipe R.* 36–8, 88; *Cal. Lib.* 1226–40, 348; 1245–51, 30; *Cal. Pat.* 1381–5, 265; C.C.A.L.S., ZMR 3, m. 1.

Welsh, the castle was visited by Henry III in 1241 before he overran north Wales, and again in 1245.[1] The Lord Edward also used it as a base during the Welsh wars of 1256–67.[2] Its significance is reflected in his forceful action to recover it from Montfort's officials in 1265, when it was besieged for over 10 weeks by an army led by James of Audley and Urien of St. Pierre, and eventually surrendered to Edward in person.[3] After Edward's accession in 1272, the castle attained its greatest importance during the conquest of Wales. The king stayed there while fruitlessly awaiting Llywelyn ap Gruffudd's response to his summons to do homage in 1275 and again in 1277,[4] and in 1276 it was the supply base of William de Beauchamp, earl of Warwick.[5] In the second and third campaigns of 1282–3 and 1294 it was again the king's headquarters and an important military base.[6]

Though the castle's military importance declined after 1300, in the early 14th century it was relatively well maintained. In Edward I's later years it seems to have been well supplied with arms and provisions, and was the base of a craftsman engaged in making weaponry (*attilliator*).[7] Edward II also repaired the castle and provided it with stores and armour, though elsewhere his castles suffered from neglect.[8] There was still a resident staff of 12 in 1313.[9] The king ordered the castle to be put into a state of defence in 1317,[10] and after his fall in 1327 custody was granted to Thomas of Warwick and orders were issued for its provisioning and repair.[11] In 1329 a new *attilliator* was appointed.[12] By then, however, the castle seems to have served primarily as an administrative centre.[13]

In the last years of Richard II's reign the castle again became a favoured royal base. In 1396 the office of master mason, which had lapsed in 1374, was reintroduced, and in 1397 the office of keeper of the king's artillery in Cheshire and Flintshire first appeared.[14]

Bolingbroke stayed there twice in 1399,[15] and in 1400 the castle, then occupied by the chamberlain of Chester, the county sheriff, and the constable, was unsuccessfully besieged during the Earls' Rising.[16] The rebellion temporarily enhanced the castle's military importance: early in 1400 it was garrisoned by 8 men-at-arms and 35 archers, and even in 1404 it was still protected by 8 archers. It also contained considerable stores of weapons and supplies.[17]

The Lancastrians replaced senior officials, including the constable, but left undisturbed such lesser men as the keeper of the artillery and the master carpenter.[18] The castle became primarily an administrative centre and a place of storage for the palatinate records,[19] and its military and strategic role again declined. Even so, the charter granted to the mayor and citizens of Chester in 1506 maintained its independence of the city.[20]

The castle became a base of the county justices introduced in 1536,[21] and in the later 16th century remained the seat of the principal palatine officials, including the vice-chamberlain; it also provided supplies and lodging for soldiers before they embarked for Ireland, especially during the revolt of 1579–81.[22] During the Civil War siege of Chester it was the royalist headquarters, with a garrison commanded from 1642 by a military governor. It escaped physical damage and in 1646 was surrendered with all its arms, ordnance, and ammunition intact, to become the headquarters of a parliamentary garrison under a new military governor.[23] During the Interregnum it remained a supply base for parliamentary troops in Ireland,[24] and the location of monthly courts held by the county sheriff in the shire hall.[25] In 1659 it was put into a state of defence during the rising of Sir George Booth, and shots were exchanged with the royalists who had entered the city.[26]

1 *Cal. Lib.* 1240–5, 70, 311; *Ches. in Pipe R.* 71, 76, 78–9, 81; *V.C.H. Ches.* v (1), Later Medieval Chester: City and Crown, 1237–1350.

2 *T.H.S.L.C.* cxxviii. 14–15; *V.C.H. Ches.* v (1), Later Medieval Chester: City and Crown, 1237–1350.

3 *T.H.S.L.C.* cxxviii. 15–16; *Ann. Cest.* 94–5.

4 *Ches. in Pipe R.* 113, 117, 120, 124–5; F. M. Powicke, *13th Cent.* 407–8, 410–11; *V.C.H. Ches.* v (1), Later Medieval Chester: City and Crown, 1237–1350.

5 J. E. Morris, *Welsh Wars of Edw. I,* 115, 118–20; *V.C.H. Ches.* v (1), Later Medieval Chester: City and Crown, 1237–1350.

6 M. Prestwich, *War, Politics, and Finance under Edw. I,* 30, 119–20, 157; Morris, *Welsh Wars,* 158–60, 244–5, 254; P.R.O., E 101/351/6; *Ches. in Pipe R.* 149; *Cal. Fine R.* 1232–1307, 189; *Cal. Chart. R.* 1256–1300, 268.

7 *Ches. in Pipe R.* 172, 208; *Ches. Chamb. Accts.* 10–11.

8 *Cal. Close,* 1313–18, 294; *Cal. Pat.* 1307–13, 427; M. Prestwich, 'Eng. Castles in Reign of Edw. II', *Jnl. Med. Hist.* viii. 159–78; below, this chapter: Buildings.

9 *Ches. Chamb. Accts.* 81.

10 *Cal. Close,* 1313–18, 505.

11 Ibid. 1323–7, 450; 1327–30, 288; *Cal. Pat.* 1327–30, 271; *Cal. Fine R.* 1327–37, 100.

12 *Cal. Pat.* 1327–30, 411.

13 Below, this chapter: Buildings.

14 *Hist. of King's Works,* ed. H. M. Colvin, i. 469; ii. 1056; Ormerod, *Hist. Ches.* i. 223.

15 Adam of Usk, *Chronicon,* ed. E. M. Thompson, 27–8, 176–9; *V.C.H. Ches.* v (1), Later Medieval Chester: City and Crown, 1350–1550.

16 P. McNiven, 'Ches. Rising of 1400', *Bull. John Rylands Libr.* lii. 387–9.

17 P.R.O., SC 6/774/13–15.

18 Ormerod, *Hist. Ches.* i. 223–4; 36 *D.K.R.* App. II, pp. 99–100, 137; *King's Works,* ii. 1056; 3 *Sheaf,* xxviii, p. 71; P.R.O., SC 6/774/13.

19 37 *D.K.R.* App. II, p. 359; *Cal. Pat.* 1441–6, 1.

20 Morris, *Chester,* 528, 535–6.

21 *V.C.H. Ches.* ii. 34, 45–7, 49.

22 *Cal. S.P. Dom.* 1547–80, 630, 633, 636, 669, 673; 1581–90, 30; J. Beck, *Tudor Ches.* 19.

23 J. S. Morrill, *Ches. 1630–60,* 128–38; *Memorials of Civil War in Ches. and Adjacent Cties. by Thos. Malbon* (R.S.L.C. xix), 199; *Cal. S.P. Dom.* 1645–7, 526, 529, 563.

24 *Cal. S.P. Dom.* 1652–3, 303, 474, 478; 1655, 256; 1656, 186.

25 Ibid. 1654, 132.

26 Ibid. 1659–60, 84, 87–8, 139, 141; 3 *Sheaf,* lvi, pp. 1–6.

The Cromwellian governor, Robert Venables, was removed in 1660.[1] Thereafter there seems to have been no garrison until 1662, when Sir Theophilus Gilbey was granted a warrant to enlist, arm, and keep under array c. 60 foot soldiers. The castle, whose strategic importance on the route to north Wales and Ireland continued to be recognized, was then felt to be in need of defence against sedition aroused by dispossessed nonconformist ministers. Late in 1662 Sir Evan Lloyd was appointed governor and shortly afterwards Gilbey asked for provisions, weaponry, and soldiers;[2] a garrison was then thought necessary to safeguard against the great numbers of Presbyterians in and around Cheshire.[3] After the 1660s, however, royal interest seems to have waned, though Chester remained one of the army's principal strongholds, under the command of a governor and much visited by dignitaries travelling to and from Ireland.[4]

In 1680 the governor, Sir Geoffrey Shakerley, was ordered to disband the foot company garrisoning the castle, and by 1681 there remained only three gunners.[5] At the time of the duke of Monmouth's visit in 1682 its undefended state caused the government alarm. New commissions to act as governor were issued to Shakerley and then to his son Peter, and a new garrison was installed.[6]

The castle retained its large garrison in James II's reign with men quartered in public houses and private dwellings;[7] a Roman Catholic chaplain was appointed, and in 1687 the king worshipped there.[8] Just before the fall of James, it housed eight companies of soldiers from Ireland,[9] together with arms and ammunition, maintained by a newly appointed 'furbisher' and supplied to troops travelling through Chester.[10]

Peter Shakerley was replaced as governor in 1689 by Sir John Morgan, Bt. Alarmed about the security of the numerous Irish prisoners because of Roman Catholic infiltration of the soldiery, he requested two new companies of 100 men, and by 1690 was involved in transporting troops to Ireland to repress Jacobites there.[11] Under his successor, however, the castle seems to have been less heavily manned, and in 1694

a company of c. 90 invalids was drawn from Chelsea hospital to form the garrison.[12] In 1696 the castle became one of five provincial centres to receive a mint for the recoinage. Staffed by a deputy comptroller (the astronomer Edmund Halley), a warden, master, assayer, and five other officials, it followed the processes used in London, issuing half-crowns, shillings, and sixpences, but functioned only until 1698.[13]

In the 18th century the castle's military significance declined. In the reign of George I military stores and ordnance, dating perhaps from the Civil War, were removed to the Tower of London. By 1728, though still commanded by a governor with two companies of invalid soldiers, the castle was described as 'destitute of arms almost for common defence'.[14] In 1745 an attack by the Jacobites was feared and attempts were made to remedy the situation, but in the event the castle saw no action.[15] The two companies of invalids remained until 1801, when they were disbanded,[16] but the castle was still notionally a garrison until 1843, commanded by a high-ranking governor and lieutenant-governor.[17] The rebuildings of the early 19th century had included barracks for 120 men and an armoury capable of storing 30,000 stand of arms.[18]

By the 1860s the castle was garrisoned by a company from a regiment stationed in Manchester and there was no barrack master. It was thus relatively unguarded, and in 1867 the Liverpool Fenians planned an attack. The plot was discovered and the garrison of 65 soldiers and 27 militiamen was reinforced by three additional companies from Manchester, local Volunteers, and, eventually, several hundred men from London and Aldershot (Hants). Although over 1,300 suspects were believed to have gathered in the city, and arms and ammunition were discovered in the suburbs, no attack took place.[19]

In 1873 the castle became the depot for the 22nd (Cheshire) Regiment.[20] The former exchequer court, housed in a block designed as barracks until its abolition in 1836, was transferred to the War Department in 1892.[21] Part of the block was made into the regimental museum in 1972.[22] In 2000 the castle remained the

1 *Some Accts. of Gen. Robert Venables* (Chetham Soc. [o.s.], lxxxiii), 6; *D.N.B.*

2 *Cal. S.P. Dom.* 1661–2, 49, 423, 435–6, 442, 452, 492, 498, 565, 570.

3 3 *Sheaf*, xviii, pp. 76–7.

4 J. Childs, *The Army, Jas. II, and the Glorious Revolution*, 9; *Cal. S.P. Dom.* 1672, 425, 471; 1675–6, 521.

5 *Cal. S.P. Dom.* 1679–80, 364; 1680–1, 143, 147, 153.

6 Ibid. 1682, 342–3, 354–5, 364, 458, 537.

7 Childs, *Army*, 24, 89.

8 Ibid. 24, 131; *Diary of Thos. Cartwright* (Camd. Soc. [1st ser.], xxii), 74–5.

9 Ibid. 345; 3 *Sheaf*, xliv, p. 6.

10 *Cal. S.P. Dom.* 1687–9, 76; cf. ibid. 295, 310, 314, 324.

11 Ibid. 1689–90, 104, 110, 114, 124, 139, 161, 560; Hist. MSS. Com. 20, *11th Rep. V, Dartmouth*, i, p. 252; 1 *Sheaf*, ii, p. 405; Bodl. MS. Rawl. A. 306, pp. 71, 107, 133.

12 *Cal. S.P. Dom.* 1693, 31; 1694–5, 312.

13 Ibid. 1696–7, 241, 537; W. Geddes, 'Chester Mint', *T.H.S.L.C.* cvii. 12–17; P. Ellis and others, *Excavations at Chester: Chester Castle: The 17th-Cent. Armoury and Mint, Excavation and Bldg. Recording in Inner Ward*, 17–18.

14 C.C.A.L.S., EDD 16/120, p. 53; 3 *Sheaf*, xlviii, p. 43.

15 1 *Sheaf*, i, pp. 108–9; below, this chapter: Buildings.

16 *Army List*, passim to (1801), 368; (1802), 381, clarified by (1803), 261.

17 Ibid. passim to (1843), 446; (1844), 447.

18 S. Lewis, *Topographical Dictionary of Eng.* (1848 edn.), i. 579; below, this chapter: Buildings.

19 *J.C.A.S.* xxvi. 111–15; 4 *Sheaf*, ii, pp. 45–6; *Army List* (1860), 465; (1866), 441; *V.C.H. Ches.* v (1), Late Georgian and Victorian Chester: Politics, 1835–1914 (Fenian Plot).

20 *Army List* (1873), 264; (1874), 264; J. B. M. Frederick, *Lineage Bk. of Brit. Land Forces, 1660–1978* (1984 edn.), i. 76.

21 *J.C.A.S.* xxvi. 117–18.

22 Below, Museums: Other Museums.

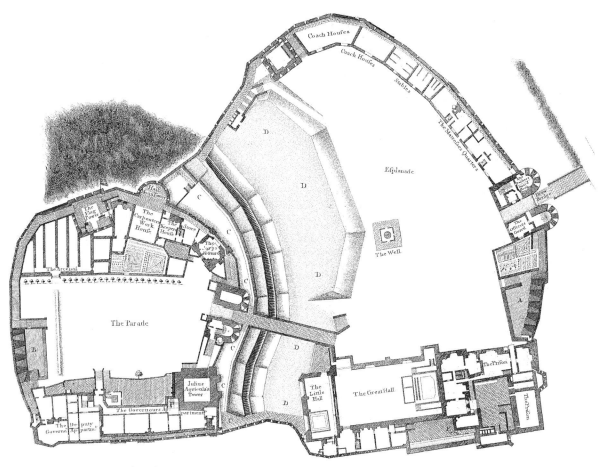

FIG. 118. *Castle, plan in 1745*

home of the regiment and of the Crown courts, for which a new building was provided in 1993. A new magistrates' court, designed by the county architect, was opened in Grosvenor Street in 1992.[1]

BUILDINGS

The complex no longer looks like a castle: the medieval remains are fragmentary and the site is dominated by buildings erected in the late 18th and the early 19th century. From the late 11th century there survives only the castle mound, part of a motte and bailey whose outer ward was probably co-extensive with the later inner ward. The earliest buildings, presumably of wood, were from the 12th century replaced in stone. There was building while the castle was in royal hands, and particularly heavy expenditure in 1159–60, when £102 was spent on works and fortifications and £20 on the castle bridge. There is, however, no reason to suppose that such activity was confined to periods of

royal guardianship; it is especially likely that there was building under Earl Ranulph III, who also established a new castle at Beeston in the 1220s.[2] The new defences, which incorporated an earlier keep and enclosed what became the inner ward, almost certainly consisted of a stone wall with square towers characterized by flat corner buttresses.[3] Two of the towers survived in 2000: the Flag Tower on the site of the early keep, and the Agricola Tower, built *c.* 1210 as the gatehouse and chapel.[4] Either may have been the 'keep' approached by a bridge mentioned in 1238.[5] The chapel in the Agricola Tower, the capitals and vaulting of which are closely related to those in the east chapel in the north transept of Chester abbey, was adorned with paintings soon after its completion. Not long afterwards, perhaps in the early years of Henry III's reign, they were replaced by a second decorative scheme, of very high quality and focused upon the Virgin.[6]

1 Inf. from Mr. J. Pepler, C.C.A.L.S.

2 *Ches. in Pipe R.* 2–3; *King's Works*, ii. 607; P. Hough, 'Excavations at Beeston Castle', *J.C.A.S.* lxi. 2.

3 Extant on Agricola Tower in 1995; cf. C.C.A.L.S., QAB 2/1/43; QAB 2/1/85; Ellis, *17th-Cent. Armoury and Mint*, 3–6, 33 (for Flag Tower).

4 The vault of its lower room is bonded into the outer walls and appears contemporary with the original building phase,

contrary to Pevsner, *Ches.* 158.

5 *Ches. in Pipe R.* 45; cf. ibid. 210; *Ches. Chamb. Accts.* 79; *Blk. Prince's Reg.* iii. 32; cf. Beeston, where perhaps the main gatehouse was called a keep: *Ches. Chamb. Accts.* 43; *J.C.A.S.* lxi. 5.

6 S. Cather, D. Park, and R. Pender, 'Henry III's Wall Paintings at Chester Cast.' *Medieval Arch., Art, and Archit. at Chester*, ed. A. Thacker, 170–89.

FIG. 119. *Chester castle from outer ward, 1777: great hall* (left), *inner ward* (background), *well house* (right)

Before the mid 13th century the castle was greatly enlarged by the addition north-west of the inner ward of a spacious outer bailey fortified by wooden palisading;[1] both enclosures seem to have contained halls from an early date.[2] From the early 12th century there was also a garden in the castle ditch, later reputed to contain Earl Ranulph III's 'resting-tree'.[3]

Royal ownership conferred a new importance on the castle, reflected in improvements to the fabric. In 1241 Henry III's first visit occasioned the construction of an 'oriel' before the doorway of the king's chapel,[4] and in 1245 the king's apartments were repaired, the paintings in the queen's chamber were renewed, and a bridge was made from the castle into the orchard to enable the king and queen to take exercise.[5] More significant was a series of major works in the later 1240s and early 1250s, which marked the beginning of the removal of the principal apartments to the outer bailey. Between 1246 and 1248 a chamber over a cellar was erected at the considerable cost of nearly £220 and the wooden palisade of the outer bailey was replaced by a stone wall; in 1249 the hall in the outer bailey was demolished and a new one, which was to cost over £350, was begun.[6] Though the work was still unfinished in 1253,[7] probably by then much had been achieved; early to mid 13th-century features long survived in the south-west gable of the hall and inside the adjacent building, later known as the parliament chamber and originally perhaps a chapel.[8] Thereafter, the structure in the outer ward was designated the great hall and that in the inner ward the lesser hall.[9]

Under Edward I the royal accommodation was further improved and enlarged. Repairs were undertaken in 1275, and in 1276 the 'king's houses' in the outer bailey were renovated for the earl of Warwick and given a new chapel.[10] In 1283 Edward I's visit necessitated further repairs to the hall and royal apartments, and to towers and domestic buildings in both wards.[11] New domestic buildings were begun in 1284, and between then and 1291 over £1,400 was spent. The major works, under the supervision of a Master William, included repairs to the king's houses, new chambers for the king and queen, and a stable, all probably in the outer bailey north and east of the great hall.[12] Further work in 1292–3 included a new gatehouse to the outer ward which cost over £318 and eventually comprised twin drum towers, a vaulted passageway with two portcullises, and extensive accommodation, including a prison. The master of works was William of Marlow, presumably the mason engaged at the castle in 1284–91.[13] Either then or a little earlier, a new inner gatehouse was built west of the Agricola Tower, which was blocked and given a new staircase, presumably in preparation for the conversion of its chapel into a treasury in 1301.[14] The decorative scheme in the tower chapel was then covered with limewash, removed only in the 1990s.[15]

By 1294 the castle comprised an inner bailey with hall, chapel, and apartments, and an outer bailey with great hall, exchequer, and further apartments for the king and queen, including separate chapels.[16] The decoration of the chapels and living quarters continued into the 14th century. Ten ceiling corbels in the king's

---

1 *King's Works*, ii. 608; *Cal. Lib.* 1245–51, 134; *Royal and Other Hist. Letters Illustrative of Reign of Henry III* (Rolls Ser.), ii. 45.

2 P.R.O., E 101/487/5; *Ches. in Pipe R.* 94–5; *Cal. Lib.* 1245–51, 258; *Close R.* 1247–51, 434.

3 N. J. Alldridge, 'Aspects of Topography of Early Medieval Chester', *J.C.A.S.* lxiv. 27; C.C.A.L.S., ZCR 63/2/120.

4 *Cal. Lib.* 1240–5, 70; *Ches. in Pipe R.* 38, 45, 52, 54, 59, 71.

5 *Cal. Lib.* 1240–5, 311; *Ches. in Pipe R.* 76, 79, 81; *Close R.* 1242–7, 327–8.

6 *Ches. in Pipe R.* 88, 94–5, 98–9; *Cal. Lib.* 1245–51, 29, 73, 134, 170, 223, 258; *Close R.* 1247–51, 434; *Royal and Hist. Letters*, ii. 45; *King's Works*, ii. 608.

7 *Close R.* 1251–3, 459.

8 C.C.A.L.S., QAB 2/1/122; Lysons, *Ches.* 455; *Gent. Mag.* lix (1), at p. 493; *V.C.H. Ches.* ii, plate facing p. 48.

9 e.g. P.R.O., E 101/487/5; *Ches. in Pipe R.* 123; *Cal. Lib.* 1245–51, 258.

10 *Ches. in Pipe R.* 113, 117, 120, 123–5; *Cal. Close, 1272–9*, 141; *Cal. Pat. 1272–81*, 169.   11 *Ches. in Pipe R.* 149.

12 Ibid. 157–8; *King's Works*, ii. 610.

13 *Ches. in Pipe R.* 166; *King's Works*, ii. 611; P.R.O., E 101/486/7.

14 *Ches. Chamb. Accts.* 8; *King's Works*, ii. 610.

15 *Medieval Arch., Art, and Archit. at Chester*, ed. A. Thacker, 170–89.

16 B.L. Harl. MS. 2073, f. 101; *Ches. in Pipe R.* 71, 123, 157–8, 209; *Ches. Chamb. Accts.* 8, 24, 124; P.R.O., E 101/485/25.

great chamber were coloured *c.* 1299, and shortly afterwards William of Northampton adorned the 'lesser chapel near the great hall' with a depiction of the murder of Thomas Becket. By then, too, glass windows had been installed in the 'greater' and 'lesser' chapels.[1]

All such work was under the control of Richard the engineer, perhaps as early as the 1270s and certainly by 1300. A royal architect much involved in the construction of the Welsh castles and a local man of substance, he retained the post of engineer until his death in 1315. After 1325 the office was discontinued and work was in the hands of master carpenters and masons, assisted by a small permanent staff.[2]

The castle's principal officials resided in the inner ward, where in 1328 the justice of Chester's deputy had his hall, chamber, and a new kitchen, and where Damory's Tower contained the former chamber of the justice himself. The constable also then had his lodgings in the inner ward.[3] The main administrative buildings, the shire hall and exchequer, were for long in the outer bailey, but in 1310 the shire hall was removed to a new position just outside the main gate.[4] A new exchequer was built within the castle in 1355, but in 1401 it too was moved outside to a building adjoining the shire hall.[5]

Although large sums were spent on repairs in the early years of Edward II's reign, especially to the outer gatehouse,[6] after 1329 the fabric suffered long periods of neglect, punctuated by occasional, often inadequate, refurbishments. In 1337, when over 100 yd. of wall had to be rebuilt, repairs were needed to the constable's hall and other buildings in the inner ward, and to the bridges leading to the two gatehouses.[7] By 1347 the Gonkes Tower, Chapel Tower, and Damory's Tower, the great chapel, the great chamber at the east end of the hall, the earl's smaller chamber and its chapel, and the great hall itself were all in disrepair.[8] Large sums were spent on the inner ward in the mid 1350s,[9] and further repairs were ordered by Richard II in the 1390s.[10] In Henry VI's reign expenditure on maintenance was generous, averaging £25 a year.[11] Work continued under the control of a master mason and master carpenter, of whom the latter at least had a

house within the castle. Under the Yorkists, however, the office of master mason lapsed.[12]

Henry VII, who appointed a master mason in 1495, continued to spend *c.* £25 a year on maintenance, higher than average for such buildings but still inadequate.[13] In 1511 repairs costing over £272 were made to the great hall, the gatehouses, and the shire hall outside the gate.[14] The Half Moon Tower in the inner ward may also have been built then.[15] By the 1530s, however, the great hall was in ruins, and between 1577 and 1582 it was almost completely rebuilt at a cost of £650 to house the shire court.[16] At the same time the 'parliament chamber', immediately south of the great hall, was reconditioned to accommodate the exchequer court.[17] No other repairs were made, and by the early 17th century the whole castle, including the prison, was in very poor condition.[18] Despite the expenditure of 500 marks in 1613, a survey undertaken in 1624 for the county justices, on whom the cost of maintenance increasingly devolved, found much of the castle in a bad state. The shire hall was very ruinous, the bridge into the castle so dangerous as to be unusable, and the castle chapel 'much more ruinous than heretofore'; other dilapidated buildings included the judges' and constable's lodgings, the protonotary's office, and the gatehouse prison. Although the royal earl's representatives felt that costs should be borne by the county authorities, they themselves reluctantly paid for repairs in 1627–8, including a new bridge.[19] The results were probably not entirely satisfactory: though earlier described as 'habitable', in 1636 the castle was condemned as 'old and ruinous'.[20]

Although the castle suffered no damage during the Civil War siege,[21] after the Restoration the fabric was far out of repair. Early in 1661 much of the outer gatehouse fell down, and the county surveyor, John Shaw, estimated the cost of restoring it and other buildings as at least £860.[22] Shaw began repairs, but work was delayed by his failure to obtain adequate authorization. In 1662, after a further survey, the cost of repairs was put at £5,000. In the event, between 1660 and 1664 only just over £546 was spent on repairs to the grand jury's chamber, the constable's lodgings, and

1 *Ches. in Pipe R.* 177, 179, 209–10, 219.
2 Ibid. 211; *King's Works,* i. 393, 468–9; ii. 1056; *Ches. Chamb. Accts.* 7–8.
3 P.R.O., E 101/487/11; *Ches. Chamb. Accts.* 122, 142.
4 *King's Works,* ii. 611; *Cal. Ches. Ct. R.* p. xviii n.
5 *Blk. Prince's Reg.* iii. 209; *Ches. Chamb. Accts.* 230; *King's Works,* ii. 612; P.R.O., SC 6/774/13.
6 *Cal. Close,* 1307–13, 187; 1313–18, 294; *Ches. Chamb. Accts.* 79–80.
7 *King's Works,* ii. 611; P.R.O., SC 12/22/96.
8 *Ches. Chamb. Accts.* 121, 124, 127; cf. ibid. 235, 241; *Blk. Prince's Reg.* iii. 465.
9 *Ches. Chamb. Accts.* 214, 230; *Blk. Prince's Reg.* iii. 209.
10 *Cal. Pat.* 1391–6, 433; 36 *D.K.R.* App. II, p. 216.
11 *King's Works,* ii. 609–10; cf. iii. 238.
12 Ibid. iii. 170, 238; P.R.O., SC 6/778/3.

13 *King's Works,* iii. 238; 37 *D.K.R.* App. II, p. 143.
14 *King's Works,* iii. 238; P.R.O., SC 6/Hen. VIII/340, m. 7.
15 Cf. blocked 16th-cent. doorway at rear of mint bldg.: Ellis, *17th-Cent. Armoury and Mint,* 7–9.
16 Cf. battlements and large bay windows of west front: Lysons, *Ches.* 455.
17 *King's Works,* iii. 238–9; *Cal. S.P. Dom.* 1547–80, 670; 1581–90, 30; B.L. Harl. MS. 7568, f. 131; P.R.O., E 101/489/21–5.
18 *King's Works,* iii. 239; *Cal. S.P. Dom.* 1603–10, 315, 363.
19 *King's Works,* iii. 240; B.L. Harl. MS. 2002, ff. 7–8; Harl. MS. 2091, ff. 311–19.
20 2 *Sheaf,* i, p. 80; Hist. MSS. Com. 78, *Hastings,* iv, pp. 340–1.
21 Above, this chapter: Administrative and Military Functions.
22 3 *Sheaf,* lv, pp. 64–5; *Cal. S.P. Dom.* 1661–2, 49; *King's Works,* iii. 241, gives date for collapse of outer gatehouse as 1660.

the protonotary's office. Shaw himself was paid only with reluctance in 1663.[1]

In 1666 fears of a rising of disaffected parliamentarians stimulated further action. The king ordered that the proceeds of the local mize, a county-wide tax, be paid to the governor, but seems to have overestimated the money available and work on the fabric proceeded very slowly.[2] In 1687 the castle received a new armoury in the west range of the inner ward, and an armourer's workshop, the Frobisher's Shop, behind the Half Moon Tower.[3] New fortifications, including a gun platform, were built in 1689, and further work was carried out on the armoury and barracks in 1691.[4] The county buildings, however, remained ruinous, the roof of the exchequer court and much of the protonotary's office having collapsed. They were repaired in 1685 and 1690, when £420 paid to the master masons Thomas and Peter Whitley proved to be the Crown's final expenditure upon them.[5]

The mint of 1696 was housed in the new extension to the Half Moon Tower.[6] Its installation involved the construction of mint ovens and chimneys and other alterations to the Frobisher's Shop, and after its closure in 1698 an estimate was ordered for the cost of restoring the shop to its former condition.[7] In 1699 the London mint paid £2,000 to the governor for the use of buildings within the castle.[8]

In 1745, with the rebellion of the Young Pretender, the lord lieutenant, George, earl of Cholmondeley, was zealous in putting Chester in a state of defence. He repaired the castle's decayed fortifications and added raised batteries in the inner and outer wards and a platform with a parapet south-east of the great hall. The military architect Alexander de Lavaux was engaged to draw up a plan to strengthen the fortifications, but his scheme, which consisted of four bastions joined by outworks flanking the ancient defences, was never carried out.[9]

Thereafter the castle was so neglected that in the 1760s a large portion of the curtain wall of the inner ward behind the armoury fell down. The breach was probably repaired in the 1770s, and further work was done in 1786, when Lord Cholmondeley's battery was reconstructed or refaced. Then or later the front of the curtain wall was cut back and the Flag Tower stripped of its external buttresses.[10]

When in 1785 quarter sessions ordered the rebuilding of the county gaol, a competition was held and won by Thomas Harrison, whose plans also involved the demolition and replacement of many buildings in the outer bailey, including the exchequer, grand jury room, protonotary's office, and eventually the shire hall.[11] In 1788 an Act of Parliament was obtained authorizing the scheme and setting up commissioners drawn from local gentry, clergy, and J.P.s to supervise its execution.[12] Harrison's early designs comprised a single block with a recessed portico and wings housing the shire hall, a room to serve both as grand jury room and exchequer, and other offices;[13] behind was the prison.[14] The main buildings, in the neo-classical style of which the architect was a master, were faced with Manley stone, while Runcorn stone and local red sandstone were used inside and in the foundations.[15] Harrison began in 1788 by demolishing the exchequer and the constable's house, and then moved on to build the prison and the southern parts of the main block.[16] As work proceeded he and the commissioners grew more ambitious. In 1789 a passage with a new gateway was opened into the upper ward, and the consent of the Board of Ordnance was obtained for the removal of the outer gatehouse, to be replaced by a new arch and guard rooms.[17] By 1791 the exchequer and grand jury room, the protonotary's office, and the prisoners' wards had all been finished, and the commissioners were anxious to proceed with the new shire hall. Harrison, however, submitted his plans only in 1792.[18] He continued to revise the scheme as late as 1793, some time after the demolition of the old shire hall; the portico seems to have caused him especial trouble, and went through several phases before achieving the imposing final design, with its double row of giant Doric columns.[19] Further difficulties arose from the discovery in 1794 that William Bell, the superintendent of works since 1788, had

1 *King's Works*, iii. 241; *Cal. Treas. Bks.* 1660–7, 479, 536; *V.C.H. Ches.* ii. 71.

2 1 *Sheaf*, i, pp. 163–4.

3 *Cal. S.P. Dom.* 1687–9, 76; 3 *Sheaf*, xiii, p. 67; Ellis, *17th-Cent. Armoury and Mint*, 15, 33–5; P.R.O., SP 44/126, p. 421; SP 44/164, p. 317.

4 *Cal. Treas. Bks.* 1689–92, 1301; 1700–1, 319.

5 Ibid. 1681–5, 1484; 1689–92, 168, 611; *Cal. Treas. Papers*, 1556/7–1696, 113; *King's Works*, iii. 241.

6 Ellis, *17th-Cent. Armoury and Mint*, 36–7; B.L. Harl. MS. 2099, f. 165v.

7 Ellis, *17th-Cent. Armoury and Mint*, 18, 36; 3 *Sheaf*, xiii, p. 67.

8 Ellis, *17th-Cent. Armoury and Mint*, 18, quoting P.R.O., MINT 1/6, p. 62; 3 *Sheaf*, xiii, p. 67.

9 1 *Sheaf*, i, p. 108; C.C.A.L.S., DCH X/9A/8, 17, 22, 36, 39.

10 Pers. comm. P. Hough, archaeologist for Eng. Heritage.

11 C.C.A.L.S., QAB 1/1/1, pp. 14, 21; QAB 2/1/2–3, 9; J. M.

Crook, 'Archit. of Thos. Harrison, II', *Country Life*, 22 Apr. 1971, pp. 946–7; M. A. R. Ockrim, 'Thos. Harrison and Rebldg. of Chester Castle: Hist. and Reassessment', *J.C.A.S.* lxvi. 57–75; *V.C.H. Ches.* v (1), Topography, 900–1914: Early Modern and Georgian (Public, Commercial, and Industrial Buildings, 1760–1840).

12 Chester Castle Rebuilding Act, 1788, 28 Geo. III, c. 82.

13 C.C.A.L.S., QAB 1/1/2, pp. 107–8; QAB 2/1/8, 42; drawing in Weaver Hall Mus., Ches.

14 Hemingway, *Hist. Chester*, ii. 184; *J.C.A.S.* lxvi. 69–72.

15 C.C.A.L.S., QAB 1/1/2, pp. 21, 54, 72–3, 99, 191; QAB 2/1/42; drawings in Weaver Hall Mus.; Hemingway, *Hist. Chester*, ii. 177–84.

16 C.C.A.L.S., QAB 1/1/2, pp. 27, 59–60, 69.

17 Ibid. pp. 43, 48–9, 53–4, 56, 102; QAB 2/1/43.

18 Ibid. QAB 1/1/2, pp. 107–8, 110, 123, 129.

19 Ibid. p. 140; QAB 2/1/1, 3, 8, 16–18, 35–6, 38, 42; watercolour in Grosvenor Mus., Chester.

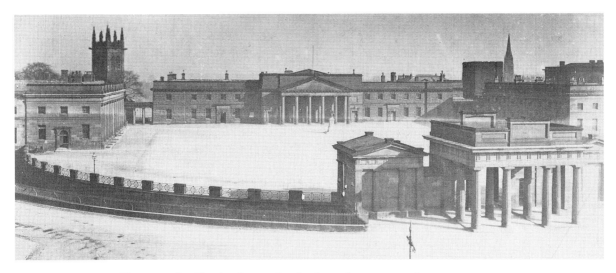

FIG. 120. *Chester castle: Harrison's completed scheme for outer ward*

wasted stone and embezzled funds and materials. Bell was dismissed, and Harrison, who seems to have been responsible for his exposure, replaced him as surveyor.[1] Examination of the work supervised by Bell revealed that the pillars in the prison chapel would not support the planned superstructure and there were additional delays while the foundations were relaid.[2] A new contractor, William Cole the elder, was appointed in 1797. By then the shire hall was substantially complete, except for the roof, finished in 1799: a 'magnificent hall of justice', it comprised a large semi-circular, semi-domed court room ringed with an Ionic colonnade. The main block seems to have been completed shortly after, for in 1800 the finishing touches were put to the portico and prison chapel.[3] In the form finally executed it had a façade of 19 bays, with a projecting portico of ashlar and rusticated wings on either side.

From 1795 the commissioners had been anxious to buy adjoining land to permit the enlargement of the castle yard and provide a suitable setting for the new buildings, and in 1803 they purchased all the buildings in Gloverstone.[4] Plans to enlarge the castle yard and build a new armoury, uniform with the main block, received the consent of the Board of Ordnance in 1804; the new building, which necessitated the demolition of the inner gatehouse, the Square Tower, and part of the curtain wall of the inner ward, was paid for partly by the Crown and partly by the county, which was responsible for the end walls and the front of nine bays with its attached Ionic half-columns.[5] A corresponding block, housing the barracks, military cells, and

exchequer court, was begun in 1806 north of the outer ward, on the site of the old cells and barracks, after similar arrangements to share the cost had been agreed between the county and the Barrack Master General.[6] Such major departures from the original plan required a new Act of Parliament, obtained in 1807.[7]

In 1810, though the barrack block was probably still incomplete, the final phase of the rebuilding began. A ditch faced with a stone wall was constructed round the castle yard and a new entrance was planned. Harrison's original scheme for a Doric gateway was altered in 1811 and made more elaborate in 1813, when four columns were added to the west side of the entrance. The completed 'propylaeum' comprised two pedimented lodges with east-facing porticoes and a central entrance block with columns projecting to the west,[8] the first use of the primitive Doric order in England.[9]

Harrison was perhaps also responsible for alterations to the inner bailey, including rebuilding the front wall of the armoury and refacing and refenestrating the old mint building and the Half Moon Tower.[10] His pupil, William Cole the younger, continued to work at the castle, and designed the military hospital, a plain brick building erected in 1826 in Castle Street.[11]

Further changes, begun in 1831, involved the demolition of the officers' barracks and judges' lodgings in the south-east range of the inner ward, to make way for a new armoury, and the conversion of the old armoury, Harrison's southern wing, into accommodation for officers and judges. The new works cost a little under £7,000, of which £1,000 was provided by the

1 C.C.A.L.S., QAB 1/1/2, pp. 21–2, 130, 196–203, 211, 214–19, 224; QAB 1/8.

2 Ibid. QAB 1/1/2, pp. 221, 242–3.

3 Ibid. pp. 345, 351; QAB 1/1/3, pp. 1–2; Hemingway, *Hist. Chester,* ii. 181.

4 C.C.A.L.S., QAB 1/1/3, pp. 54, 56, 249, 252, 254.

5 Ibid. pp. 77, 80–1.

6 Ibid. pp. 91–3, 99–100, 114–15.

7 Chester Castle Gaol Act, 1807, 47 Geo. III, Sess. 2, c. 6 (Local and Personal).

8 C.C.A.L.S., QAB 1/1/3 (unfol.).

9 *J.C.A.S.* lxvi. 72, citing M. Kappatos-Pavlakis, 'A Study of Greek Revival Archit. in Eng. before 1800' (Manchester Univ. Ph.D. thesis, 1974), 87.

10 Pers. comm. P. Hough.

11 C.C.A.L.S., QAB 2/6/1–3, 12–20.

FIG. 121. *County gaol from east* (left centre)

county. Among those who were then paid substantial sums was the Chester architect James Harrison, and it is possible therefore that he was responsible for the design of the new armoury, a plain rectangular free-standing building faced in local stone.[1] With the completion of the work in 1836 all that remained of the ancient castle was the Agricola Tower and the much altered Half Moon and Flag Towers.

There were important alterations to the south-west corner of Harrison's main block in the lower ward in the late 19th century. In 1875–7 a new *nisi prius* (civil) court was built, to designs by T. M. Lockwood, and in 1891 the protonotary's office was converted into a council chamber for the new county council.[2] The interior of the shire hall was rearranged c. 1881 and in 1895–6.[3] Harrison's barrack block was restored in 1922.[4]

After 1892 the site of the prison became a drill ground for the local Volunteer artillery. It was eventually occupied by a new county hall built between 1939 and 1957.[5] A new militia barracks for the permanent staff of the 1st Regiment of the Royal Cheshire Militia was built by the county authorities outside the castle precinct in Nuns' Gardens to designs by T. M. Penson in 1858–9. In an extravagant 13th-century castellated style with many towers and turrets and a gateway with a portcullis, it was sold to the War Department in 1874 and after 1882 housed married non-commissioned officers of the regimental depot. The building was repurchased by the county council in 1963 and demolished in 1964.[6]

COUNTY GAOL

The castle was used as a gaol by 1241, when Welsh hostages were confined there.[7] Under Edward I prisoners included local notables,[8] hostages taken from Prince Llywelyn in 1277,[9] and Llywelyn's brother Dafydd with five of his squires in 1283.[10] In 1294–5, when the gaol probably occupied the rebuilt outer gatehouse, it again received many Welsh hostages,[11] a few of whom were detained until c. 1300 and the last until the 1330s.[12] Besides the Welsh there were also six Scots, taken at Dunbar in 1296, and in 1301–2 still at the castle, which by then contained four prisons.[13] The castle was again briefly filled with hostages taken from the citizens at the time of Edward II's murder[14] and from the Welsh during Glyn Dŵr's revolt.[15]

By the 16th century the county gaol was situated in the outer gatehouse and the adjoining former exchequer.[16] It became a detention centre for recusants in the 1580s and 1590s, its importance enhanced by its position on the Irish route.[17] In 1648 it was refurbished and restored to use after the discovery of a royalist plot to recover castle and city.[18] The castle was again full of prisoners after the royalist defeat at the battle of Worcester in 1651, and was later the scene of the trial of notables.[19] It still contained prisoners, including a number of Scotsmen, in 1653.[20] The numbers detained rose again after the repression of Booth's rebellion in 1659.[21]

By 1681 the prison was in great decay. Although the Crown met the heavy costs of renovation, thereafter its

1 Hemingway, *Hist. Chester*, ii. 183; F. Simpson, 'Chester Castle, 907–1925', *J.C.A.S.* xxvi. 75–6; P.R.O., MPH 508 (1–3); WO 55/1886.

2 C.C.A.L.S., SF/Chester Castle; *J.C.A.S.* xxvi. 115, 118.

3 C.C.A.L.S., QAB 2/6/58–9; *J.C.A.S.* xxvi. 118.

4 *J.C.A.S.* xxvi. 120–8.

5 Ibid. 117–18; C.C.A.L.S., QAB 6/20; SF/Chester Castle; Pevsner, *Ches.* 158; inf. from files in custody of principal librarian, Ches. Co. Cl. Inf. and Record Services.

6 C.C.A.L.S., QAM 3; QJB 4/34, p. 25; QJB 4/35, p. 240; *Gresty and Burghall's Chester Guide* [1867], 75; C.P.S., Castle Esplanade; inf. from files in custody of principal librarian, Ches. Co. Cl. Inf. and Record Services.

7 *Ches. in Pipe R.* 78–9; cf. *Cal. Ches. Ct. R.* p. 18.

8 *Cal. Pat.* 1258–66, 49; cf. *Cal. Ches. Ct. R.* p. 158.

9 *Ches. in Pipe R.* 123–4.

10 Ibid. 149.

11 Ibid. 164; *Cal. Close*, 1288–96, 425; above, this chapter: Buildings.

12 *Ches. in Pipe R.* 164, 176, 181; *Ches. Chamb. Accts.* 79, 86, 113.

13 *Ches. in Pipe R.* 165, 173, 176, 181, 210; *Ches. Chamb. Accts.* 11; *Cal. Close*, 1288–96, 482.

14 *Cal. Close*, 1327–8, 142, 169, 187; *V.C.H. Ches.* v (1), Later Medieval Chester: City and Crown, 1237–1350.

15 *36 D.K.R.* App. II, p. 304.

16 *3 Sheaf*, lv, pp. 64–5; C.C.A.L.S., QJF 88/4/27.

17 Above, Roman Catholicism.

18 *Memorials of Civil War*, 214–16; *Cal. S.P. Dom.* 1648–9, 183.

19 *Cal. S.P. Dom.* 1651–2, 454, 457, 473; *3 Sheaf*, i, pp. 47–8.

20 *Cal. S.P. Dom.* 1652–3, 92, 168.

21 Ibid. 1659–60, 139, 141; *3 Sheaf*, lvi, pp. 1–6.

maintenance was left to the county authorities, who by the 1690s were raising levies for further repairs.[1] In 1715, after the government's victory at Preston, *c.* 500 Jacobite prisoners were brought to the castle. Because of a quarrel between the governor and Chester corporation they were held there until 1717 in crowded conditions, and disease spread from them to the soldiers.[2]

By the 1770s the prison in the north-east corner of the castle was clearly unsatisfactory; cramped and airless, it was compared by the reformer John Howard to the Black Hole of Calcutta,[3] and in 1784 it was presented at the assizes as out of repair and insufficient.[4] In 1785 the Cheshire quarter sessions ordered its rebuilding.[5] Thomas Harrison's new

prison, opened in 1793, was designed according to the enlightened principles advocated by Howard. Although planned before the publication of Jeremy Bentham's *Panopticon*, it was 'panoptic' in the sense that, as in Bentham's scheme, the gaoler's house overlooked the felons' yards.[6]

The prison, which had been found inadequate by the visiting justices in 1865, was transferred from county control to the Crown in 1877 and closed to civil prisoners in 1884, though there continued to be a small military prison in the castle until 1893. The gaol buildings were purchased by the county council in 1894 and demolished in 1900–2,[7] the site being used later for a new county hall.

CITY WALLS AND GATES

ROMAN DEFENCES[8]

When first built in the 70s and 80s, the legionary fortress was defended by an earth rampart topped by a wooden palisade and provided with wooden gates and towers spaced at regular intervals. The double turf-revetted rampart appears to have been constructed in a modular fashion on a base *c.* 6 m. wide and to a height of *c.* 3 m. Its core was composed of earth dug from the defensive ditches alongside, the whole structure being set on a log corduroy base and held together by layers of branches and brushwood. The wooden towers, set at intervals of *c.* 50 m., were *c.* 4.5 m. square and probably *c.* 7.5 m. high. The four main gates, undoubtedly also of timber, were probably similar to those at Inchtuthil on the river Tay.

The advent of the Twentieth Legion at the end of the 1st century saw the beginnings of a general reconstruction in stone. The work bears close similarities in design to the roughly contemporary walls at Gloucester and perhaps Inchtuthil, both also associated with the Twentieth. The rebuilding was abandoned, incomplete, in the early 2nd century and eventually finished over a hundred years later. Despite the hiatus, the walls were completed largely in accordance with the original intentions.

The stone curtain wall was not free-standing but rather a revetment of the earlier earthen rampart. A single face of masonry, it was built in a modular

fashion: the wall walk, for example, was set *c.* 4.9 m. above the base, and was augmented by interval towers approximately twice that in height. The new wall, which was clearly designed to impress, was built of *opus quadratum* set on a chamfered plinth and base course and surmounted by a remarkable and as yet unparalleled decorative cornice. Above the cornice there was a course of rounded rebated blocks in which was set the breastwork, topped with capstones, some of which were ornamented.

The north gate seems to have been a relatively simple single arch, while the east, south, and west gates were more elaborate with twin portals. The east gate, forming the main entrance, was especially impressive; perhaps of three storeys, it was built of *opus quadratum* adorned with elaborate cornices. Parts of it survived, embedded in the fabric of its medieval successor, until the 18th century.[9]

The stone defences were probably not extensively remodelled in Roman times and seem never to have acquired the projecting bastions typical of fortress walls of the late 3rd and 4th century. Maintenance continued to the end of the 4th century.

Throughout the Middle Ages the north and east walls appear to have been maintained wherever they survived in reasonable condition. In 2000 a particularly fine stretch survived to the level of the cornice in the north wall east of the Northgate. Even where the medieval fabric was completely replaced in the 18th

1 *King's Works*, iii. 241; *Cal. Treas. Bks.* 1681–5, 179, 196, 248; C.C.A.L.S., QJB 13A, sess. 12 Apr. 33 Chas. II; QJB 14A, f. 193; QJB 15A (unfol.).

2 J. H. E. Bennett, 'Ches. and the Fifteen', *J.C.A.S.* xxi. 30–46; 3 *Sheaf*, xxxvii, pp. 21, 60–1, 77, 82; lvi, p. 14.

3 J. Howard, *State of Prisons* (1780 edn.), 400–3; T. Pennant, *Tours in Wales* (1784 edn.), 206.

4 C.C.A.L.S., QAB 1/1/1, pp. 1, 8, 10.

5 *J.C.A.S.* lxvi. 58; above, this chapter: Buildings.

6 C.C.A.L.S., QAB 1/1/2, p. 181; QAB 2/1/62; Hemingway, *Hist. Chester*, ii. 184; *J.C.A.S.* lxvi. 58–60, 69–72.

7 C.C.A.L.S., QAB 6/120; SF/Chester Castle; Pevsner, *Ches.*

158; *J.C.A.S.* xxvi. 117–18; inf. from files in custody of principal librarian, Ches. Co. Cl. Inf. and Record Services.

8 This acct. is based on a draft by T. J. Strickland and relies heavily on C. LeQuesne, *Excavations at Chester: Roman and Later Defences, Pt. 1: Investigations 1978–90*. For other reports see T. J. Strickland, 'Defences of Roman Chester: Discoveries on N. Wall', *J.C.A.S.* lxv. 25–36; 'Defences of Roman Chester: Discoveries on E. Wall', *J.C.A.S.* lxvi. 5–11; 'Recent Research at Chester Legionary Fortress', *Archit. in Roman Britain*, ed. P. Johnson and I. Haynes; *V.C.H. Ches.* i. 120–3.

9 Below, this chapter: Gates, Posterns, and Towers (Eastgate).

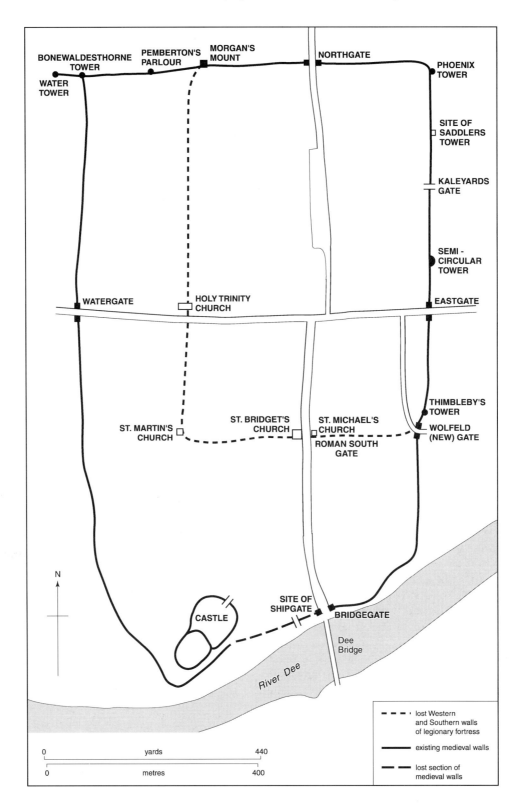

FIG. 122. *City walls and gates, plan*

and 19th centuries, the Roman foundations survived and Roman masonry was on occasion reused. In general the medieval walls diverged from the line of the Roman ones only where the latter had collapsed outwards and could not be retained as the base of a new superstructure.

Like the east gate, the north gate may well have survived largely intact within its medieval successor, disappearing only in the early 19th century. The interval towers were apparently less well designed; although at least one, that at Abbey Green, was still largely intact in the early 10th century, none appears to have survived above ground after A.D. 1000.

MEDIEVAL AND LATER WALLS

The extent to which the Roman defences were reused when Æthelflæd refortified Chester in 907 remains uncertain. One possibility is that she adopted the north and east walls, extending them to the river and creating thereby an **L**-shaped landward defence,[1] but there are also indications that the entire Roman *enceinte* was used.[2] Substantial sections of the north wall and portions of the east and west walls were repaired in early medieval times, in part with carved and inscribed Roman memorial stones.[3] Nevertheless, the likely length of the Anglo-Saxon defences, *c.* 1,700 yd., accords better with the **L**-shape than with the full legionary *enceinte*, and even if the Roman walls were refurbished it remains possible that the manned defences comprised only the northern and eastern sides of the fortress, extended to the river perhaps by earth walls.[4]

Whatever their form, the walls were probably complete by Edward the Elder's time (899–924), and were perhaps commemorated on a coin type apparently minted at Chester early in his reign, the reverse of which shows a tower.[5] They were kept in repair by the men of Cheshire at the rate of one man for every hide of the shire's assessment, an arrangement in force in 1066.[6]

The intrusion of the castle in the late 11th century probably involved the final abandonment of the south and west walls of the legionary fortress and the con-

struction of an enlarged *enceinte*. Shipgate, in the southern riverside wall, seems to have been built by the 1120s,[7] and the line of the western defences may have been moved further west about then to form the full medieval circuit, still standing almost in its entirety in 2000.[8] The considerable building activity which took place in 1160–2 perhaps marked the completion of the defences.[9] By Earl Ranulph III's time (1181–1232) all four principal gates had been constructed,[10] and in the 1190s the parish church of St. Mary on the Hill and the nunnery, both located near the castle and outside the line of the Roman fortress, were said to stand inside the walls.[11]

As elsewhere, upkeep was largely financed by murages, occasional duties on merchandise entering and leaving the city, levied by the city authorities under royal grant.[12] The first recorded murage occurred in 1249 and was for five years, the money being collected by two officials called murengers.[13] Further murages were granted in 1290, 1297, and 1299, for three, five, and seven years respectively.[14] Royal permission was also needed to breach the defences: in 1246, for example, Henry III allowed the Franciscans to penetrate the walls to bring in building materials.[15]

In 1264 the defences were strengthened by the construction of the town ditch on the north and east, an action which involved the destruction of property outside the Northgate and the taking of land near the Eastgate.[16] It was perhaps then that the drum tower and the Saddlers' Tower were built, at points on the east wall where the Roman wall had collapsed or been robbed, and on a line slightly behind the Roman defences.[17]

The principal gates were in the charge of hereditary serjeants or keepers, who by the late 13th century had responsibility for organizing watches on the walls and collecting tolls.[18]

In 1321 a murage was granted for two years, and in 1322 the citizens contracted with John of Helpston, a royal mason, for a new riverside tower in the north-west of the city (Fig. 123, p. 216).[19] Further murages were granted in 1329, 1352, 1355, 1358, and 1363, with work continuing under royal master masons and

1 *V.C.H. Ches.* i. 250–2.

2 LeQuesne, *Roman Defences.*

3 Ibid.; *J.C.A.S.* N.S. i. 177–83; ii. 1–10, 40–66; vii. 5–7.

4 Pers. comm. T. J. Strickland; cf. *V.C.H. Ches.* i. 250; P. H. Sawyer, *From Roman Britain to Norman Eng.* 228–9; *Med. Arch.* xiii. 84–92; *J.C.A.S.* lxiv. 10–11.

5 C. E. Blunt *et al., Coinage in 10th-cent. Eng.* 35–8, plate 4; J. D. Bu'lock, *Pre-Conquest Ches.* 58–60.

6 *Med. Arch.* xiii. 84–92; *Antiq. Jnl.* li. 70–85; *V.C.H. Ches.* i. 343 (no. 1d).

7 *Cart. Chester Abbey,* i, p. 49 (where *portam Clippe* is presumably a miscopying of *portam Shippe*); *Antiq. Jnl.* xxxiii. 24.

8 3 *Sheaf,* xliv, pp. 56–7, 61–2; xlv, p. 12; *J.C.A.S.* lxiv. 25–31.

9 *Ches. in Pipe R.* 4; *King's Works,* ii. 607.

10 Lucian, *De Laude Cestrie,* 7–8, 45–7, 49.

11 Ibid. 63; 3 *Sheaf,* xliv, p. 56.

12 K. P. Wilson, 'The Port of Chester in the Later Middle Ages'

(Liverpool Univ. Ph.D. thesis, 1965), 70–3.

13 *Cal. Pat.* 1247–58, 49.

14 Ibid. 1281–2, 344; 1292–1301, 310, 482; B.L. Harl. MS. 2162, ff. 394, 405v.

15 *Cal. Close,* 1242–7, 408; cf. *Cart. Chester Abbey,* i, p. 226; *V.C.H. Ches.* iii. 172.

16 *Ann. Cest.* 87–9; Morris, *Chester,* 17–18, 120, 256–8, 569; *Cal. Ches. Ct. R.* pp. 153–6, 158, 162, 188; *Cal. Inq. Misc.* i, pp. 127–8; B.L. Harl. MS. 7568, f. 178; 3 *Sheaf,* xxi, p. 44; xxxiii, pp. 98, 110, 112, 114; J. Brownbill, *Cal. of Deeds and Papers of Moore Fam.* (R.S.L.C. lxvii), p. 46 (no. 993).

17 LeQuesne, *Roman Defences.*

18 Morris, *Chester,* 554–9; *Cal. Ches. Ct. R.* pp. 181–4; C.C.A.L.S., ZCHB 2, f. 99v.

19 D. F. Renn, 'Water Tower at Chester', *J.C.A.S.* xlv. 57–60; Morris, *Chester,* 244; C.C.A.L.S., ZCX 6; B.L. Harl. MS. 7568, f. 196.

FIG. 123. *New Tower* (left), *spur wall,*
and Bonewaldesthorne Tower in later
18th century

in 1339 under the temporary supervision of a royal controller of murage.[1]

In 1387 Richard II authorized the city to use the murage to rebuild the Dee Bridge, and perhaps because of that by 1395 the walls were claimed to be in great disrepair.[2] Succeeding murages in 1395 and 1397 were devoted to their restoration, and no further money was diverted to the bridge until 1407.[3] It was evident that the defences could still assume a military importance during the Ricardian rising in 1400, when the rebels seized the keys to the gates, and again in 1408–9, when attempts were made to enforce the watch on the walls.[4]

Although in the earlier 15th century royal officials continued to supervise repairs,[5] care of the fortifications became increasingly a local affair. In 1409 Prince Henry as earl of Chester allowed the mayor and commonalty to take murages for the repair of the walls, gates, and bridge,[6] and thereafter they were frequently imposed.[7] After 1466 the murengers, who by then had a regular income from customs levied on goods entering and leaving the city, served for two years rather than one, one retiring each year.[8] In 1506 murages became a permanent custom under the administration of two annually elected officials.[9]

Such developments did not, however, bring much improvement in the upkeep of the walls. In 1410, 1452, and c. 1531 men were indicted for breaking them down

and carrying off stones.[10] By then the full circuit included some eight or nine watch towers, the four principal gates, and at least six posterns. The whole was embattled. Outside, to the north and east, lay the town ditch, and inside, except in the abbey precinct and between Eastgate and Newgate, a roadway to provide access.[11] In the later 16th or early 17th century the ditch was filled in.[12]

By the mid 16th century with the decline of Chester's trade the murengers' income had become inadequate. Some of the principal towers were rented and maintained as meeting places by the city's craft guilds, but the walls themselves were in poor condition.[13] In 1538–9 the city authorities agreed to pay a mason, Thomas Wosewall, 40s. a year and provide materials and two labourers to keep the entire circuit in repair.[14] Extensive renovations were undertaken in 1555–6, and in 1562 the contract was renewed,[15] but the results were not satisfactory: in 1569 a portion of the wall between the New Tower and the Watergate fell down, and in 1589 the entire defences were described as ruinous. In 1590 Wosewall surrendered his patent because he was unable to keep the walls in repair.[16] The murengers were increasingly reliant on special levies: in 1589 they were granted an assessment of £100 and in 1599 the profits from one year's toll on corn.[17] Even so, in 1600 the walls still endangered those walking on them, and a further assessment of £100 was ordered.[18] A 'great breach' between the New Tower and Watergate required £80 in 1608 and 100 marks in 1620.[19] Further assessments for repairs were levied in 1621, 1625, and 1629, but there appears to have been some resistance to their collection, and yields probably continued low, for the walls were still called ruinous in 1641.[20]

With the growing prospect of a civil war, measures were taken to improve the city's defences.[21] In September 1640 the corporation ordered repairs to the Eastgate, Newgate, and Bridgegate, and in 1641 it allocated all customs duties on wine imports (prisage) to the renovation of the walls. An additional assessment of 100 marks was granted in 1642.[22] In 1643, with the growing likelihood of a siege, new outer

1 *Cal. Pat.* 1327–30, 455, 559; 1330–4, 62; 36 *D.K.R.* App. II, p. 233; *Blk. Prince's Reg.* iii. 35, 88–90, 116, 292, 311, 425–6, 457, 489; Morris, *Chester*, 562–4.

2 36 *D.K.R.* App. II, pp. 94, 97; Morris, *Chester*, 264, 503–4.

3 36 *D.K.R.* App. II, pp. 97–8, 103; C.C.A.L.S., ZCH 21; ZCH 25; Morris, *Chester*, 509–10.

4 C.C.A.L.S., ZAF 1, f. 2; ZCHB 2, f. 67; Morris, *Chester*, 40, 47, 261–2; *Bull. John Rylands Libr.* lii. 386–92.

5 e.g. *Cal. Pat.* 1422–9, 158.

6 Morris, *Chester*, 510; C.C.A.L.S., ZCH 26.

7 Wilson, 'Port of Chester', 71; C.C.A.L.S., ZMB 2, f. 94; ZMB 3, f. 3; ZMB 4, f. 6v.; ZMB 5, f. 176; ZSB 2, f. 3; ZSB 3, f. 102v.; ZSB 4, f. 20v.

8 Morris, *Chester*, 566–8; Wilson, 'Port of Chester', 72; C.C.A.L.S., ZAB 1, f. 63; ZMUB 1; ZMUR 1.

9 Morris, *Chester*, 527.

10 Ibid. 55, 243.

11 G. Braun and F. Hohenberg, *Civitates Orbis Terrarum*, iii

(1588), no. 3; Morris, *Chester*, 569; Hemingway, *Hist. Chester*, i. 343.

12 B.L. Harl. MS. 7568, f. 178.

13 3 *Sheaf*, iii, p. 95; C.C.A.L.S., ZAB 1, ff. 219–20, 257.

14 B.L. Harl. MS. 7568, f. 196.

15 Morris, *Chester*, 210, 243–4; B.L. Harl. MS. 2046, f. 40.

16 3 *Sheaf*, iii, p. 95; Morris, *Chester*, 244; C.C.A.L.S., ZAB 1, f. 219; B.L. Harl. MS. 2046, f. 40.

17 C.C.A.L.S., ZAB 1, f. 257.

18 Ibid. f. 264; ZMB 28, f. 75v.; *Cal. Chester City Cl. Mins. 1603–41*, 17, 24, 41, 60, 80–1; 3 *Sheaf*, ix, pp. 17, 61.

19 3 *Sheaf*, ix, pp. 43, 71.

20 *Cal. Chester City Cl. Mins. 1603–42*, pp. xxxv, 108–9, 134, 154, 159, 162, 207.

21 For a full acct. see S. Ward, *Excavations at Chester: Civil War Siegeworks, 1642–6.*

22 *Cal. Chester City Cl. Mins. 1603–42*, 207, 211; Morris, *Siege of Chester*, 17, 19.

fortifications were built. They initially followed a line from the north wall near the Goblin Tower northwards to a point between Parkgate and Liverpool roads, and thence east to Flookersbrook Hall; from there they ran south and then east to Boughton, terminating at the river. The new works comprised trenches, mud walls, mounts, and pitfalls. Newgate and the New Tower were walled up, and the former ditch outside the Eastgate was perhaps re-excavated. In 1644 the line of the defences was brought back nearer the city to a turnpike at Cow Lane (later Frodsham Street), abandoning the enclosure of Flookersbrook; escarpments were deepened and widened, parapets raised, and new mounts thrown up around Cow Lane.[1] Finally, in February 1645 the fortifications assumed the form they had until the end of the siege: the outworks were brought back from the Cow Lane turnpike to Cow Lane Gate, and Morgan's Mount was constructed on the northern city wall near the Goblin Tower.[2]

The medieval defences suffered from the parliamentary bombardment during the siege. Two important breaches were made, a large one near the Newgate and a smaller one between the Goblin and New Towers, both in places where the fabric had already crumbled and been strengthened by earthen ramparts.[3] Modest disbursements were made in the later 1640s and 1650s to patch up the great breach near the Newgate and further breaches on either side of the Northgate. Major work costing over £120 was done near the Watergate between 1659 and 1661, and in the 1660s and early 1670s spending on repairs continued to be fairly heavy.[4] Yet the condition of the walls remained precarious. Although the antiquary Ralph Thoresby could describe them as in excellent condition in 1682, another opinion in 1686 was that they were 'far out of repair'.[5] In 1690 the corporation granted £160 for renovations, but there were still breaches in 1694. By 1700 the murage duties were in arrears.[6]

Nevertheless, the walls seem already to have become a popular promenade, perambulated for example by Thoresby in 1682,[7] and in 1707–8 the Assembly undertook major repairs with the object of restoring the entire circuit to use. The cost of £1,000 went towards repairing 'divers large breaches' and levelling and flagging the wall walk.[8] Thereafter the walls became one of the walks favoured by Henry Prescott, deputy registrar of Chester diocese, and his friends.[9] Access to the fashionable pleasure grounds in the Groves was made easier in 1720, when the corporation built Recorder's Steps, east of Bridgegate.[10] After all the improvements, the walls, though no longer of military use, were described in 1728 as 'of great delight and benefit' to the citizens.[11]

In the 18th century the walls were perambulated by such distinguished visitors as John Wesley and Samuel Johnson, though the walkway was not continuous as it was still interrupted by some of the towers over the main gates.[12] The reconstruction begun in 1707 continued piecemeal, and seems generally to have involved the total replacement of medieval fabric but the retention, where it existed, of Roman.[13] Work included the construction of the present unfortified parapet, the rebuilding between 1767 and 1810 of all the main medieval gates with wider arches, better for vehicles below and pedestrians above,[14] and attempts to render the wall walks more convenient by means of features such as the Wishing Steps, built in 1785 to ease the steep ascent east of Recorder's Steps (Fig. 124, p. 218).[15] Further work was done in 1828–9, when a collapsed portion between Abbey Street and the Phoenix Tower was rebuilt and Grosvenor Road was driven through the defences west of the castle;[16] shortly after, in 1830, part of the southern wall west of Bridgegate was moved further south to run along the new riverside embankment, a project involving the insertion of an archway to permit access to the extended enclosure of the castle.[17] In 1831 the walls were said to have been altered recently 'not so much for strength as for ornament'; the walks had been levelled, the battlements lowered, and the towers refurbished.[18]

The office of murenger was abolished in 1835, when its duties were vested in the corporation's finance committee.[19] The tolls at Eastgate, Northgate, and Watergate, most if not all of which were in the corporation's hands by 1662, were abolished in 1836.[20] Those at Bridgegate, acquired in the 17th century, had already been granted to the Dee Bridge Commissioners in 1824.[21]

Further work was done on the walls and towers in the late 19th century. In particular, at least 120 yd. of

1 Morris, *Siege of Chester*, 36, 58–9, 216–17, 220–1; Ward, *Excavations: Civil War Siegeworks*, 7–8; B.L. Harl. MS. 2135, f. 40.
2 Morris, *Siege of Chester*, 74, 222.
3 4 *Sheaf*, vi, pp. 1–25, esp. 9, 12–16.
4 C.C.A.L.S., ZCAM 3.
5 1 *Sheaf*, i, p. 99; C.C.A.L.S., ZAB 2, ff. 189v.–196v.; ZAB 3, f. 5 and v.
6 C.C.A.L.S., ZAB 3, ff. 24v., 45v., 77v., 145v.
7 1 *Sheaf*, i, p. 99; cf. 3 *Sheaf*, x, pp. 51–2.
8 3 *Sheaf*, xx, pp. 46–7; C.C.A.L.S., ZAB 3, ff. 145v.–146, 156–7; inscription on Pemberton's Parlour.
9 e.g. *Diary of Henry Prescott*, i. 214, 280, 297; ii. 355, 360–2, 364, 369, 568.
10 C.C.A.L.S., ZAB 3, f. 258v.; inscription by the steps has

erroneous date of 1700.
11 3 *Sheaf*, xlviii, p. 17.
12 1 *Sheaf*, iii, p. 115; 3 *Sheaf*, xi, p. 9; xvii, p. 14.
13 LeQuesne, *Roman Defences*.
14 Below, this chapter: Gates, Posterns, and Towers (Eastgate, Northgate, Watergate, Bridgegate).
15 F. Simpson, *Walls of Chester*, 67. No source for this date has been found.   16 1 *Sheaf*, ii, p. 119.
17 Hemingway, *Hist. Chester*, i. 366; *J.C.A.S.* lxviii. 80–3; C.C.A.L.S., ZAB 6, pp. 36–7, 39–40.
18 Hemingway, *Hist. Chester*, i. 343.
19 C.C.A.L.S., ZAB 6, p. 61.
20 Ibid. p. 85; ZAB 2, f. 138v.
21 Ibid. ZAB 5, p. 481; Ormerod, *Hist. Ches.* i. 357.

FIG. 124. *Wishing Steps, 1903*

FIG. 125. *Promenading the walls near King Charles's Tower, 1850s*

the north wall in Water Tower Street between the Northgate and Pemberton's Parlour were rebuilt or refaced in 1882–3, work which included a new gateway opposite Canning Street.[1] In 1887 and 1890–2 other stretches of the north wall west of the Phoenix Tower and west of the Northgate were reconstructed, and in both locations large numbers of inscribed and sculpted Roman memorial stones were found.[2] Attempts were made to strengthen the east wall north of the Kaleyards Gate in the 1930s,[3] and both that work and the earlier reconstruction in Water Tower Street were much renewed in the 1990s.[4] The city council remained responsible for maintenance work.

Alterations were made to the walls in 1846, when the Chester–Holyhead railway cut through the north-western corner; in 1900–1, when Castle Drive was laid out beside the river and the wall walk was re-routed; and in 1966, when the north walkway was carried over the new inner ring-road on a concrete footbridge, named St. Martin's Gate.[5] Despite such breaches and remodellings, the walls still in 2000 formed an almost unbroken pathway and a delight to visitors.

GATES, POSTERNS, AND TOWERS

The following description goes anti-clockwise from the Eastgate.

Eastgate

The earliest mention of the Eastgate is in the later 12th century.[6] It seems to have been enlarged in 1270, and a reference to it shortly afterwards as 'porta Cestriae' suggests that it was the principal gate of the city.[7] The keepers were responsible for the inspection of weights and measures, and were bound to find equipment for measuring salt.[8] The first known serjeant was Thomas of Ipgrave, whose widow Joan was granted the custody and tolls of the gate in 1275. Joan surrendered her rights in 1278 in return for a pension, and in 1286 the serjeanty was granted to Hervey of Bradford and his son Robert.[9] The Bradford family held it until 1376, when it was sold to William Trussell, from whose heirs it passed by marriage to the earls of Oxford.[10] About 1630 it was sold to Sir Randle Crewe.[11] In 1662 the Crewe family leased the tolls to the city, reserving for themselves the nomination of the serjeant. Thereafter the city appointed a keeper who remained responsible for inspecting the city's weights but who by 1666 had ceased to receive the profits of the gate or to pay the rent due to the Crewes.[12]

1 C.C.A.L.S., ZCCB 55, pp. 261, 272, 356; ZCR 63/1/14/9; *J.C.A.S.* N.S. i. 177; vii. 5; Simpson, *Walls*, 6; LeQuesne, *Roman Defences*.

2 Simpson, *Walls*, 6; *J.C.A.S.* N.S. ii. 1–131; N.S. vii. 6–7.

3 Inf. from T. J. Strickland.

4 LeQuesne, *Roman Defences*.

5 Simpson, *Walls*, 57; inscription at St. Martin's Gate; above, Railways.   6 *Cart. Chester Abbey*, i, p. 95.

7 *Cal. Inq. Misc.* i, p. 550; *Ches. in Pipe R.* 129, 132.

8 Morris, *Chester*, 223, 555.

9 *Ches. in Pipe R.* 129, 132; *Cal. Pat.* 1272–8, 357; *Cal. Close*, 1302–7, 281; 1307–13, 37; *Cal. Fine R.* 1272–1307, 92; B.L. Harl. MS. 2074, f. 201v.

10 Morris, *Chester*, 222–3; 3 *Sheaf*, xxviii, p. 64.

11 *Cal. S.P. Dom.* 1629–31, 294, 308; *Cal. Chester City Cl. Mins.* 1603–42, pp. xix, xxv, 161, 163–4.

12 C.C.A.L.S., ZAB 2, ff. 57, 155; ibid. EDD 16/120, p. 49; Ormerod, *Hist. Ches.* i. 357.

FIG. 126. *Old Eastgate, before 1768*

FIG. 127. *Eastgate, 1930s*

In its final form, reached perhaps in the reign of Edward III, the medieval gate, which incorporated much of the Roman structure, was the 'strongest and most lofty in the city'.[1] The east elevation seems to have consisted of a fairly narrow Gothic archway flanked by two tall octagonal towers, with perhaps two smaller outer towers.[2] The inner western face was dominated by a large round arch which by the early 18th century was regarded as Roman.[3] It suffered early neglect, and by 1631 was ruinous, stones from it falling on adjacent houses.[4] Repaired in 1640, it was much battered in the siege, when perhaps it lost its two smaller towers.[5] Though it was repaired again in the 1670s, it seems quickly to have fallen into decay once more.[6]

In 1707 as part of the general renovations the ancient pedestrian passage on the wall walk over the Eastgate was reopened.[7] By the 1750s the gate itself was thought narrow and inconvenient, and in 1768 it was demolished and replaced at the expense of Richard, Lord Grosvenor, by a wider elliptical arch flanked by low pedestrian arches designed by an otherwise unidentified Mr. Hayden.[8] In 1898–9 ironwork and a clock, designed by John Douglas, were placed on the tower to commemorate Queen Victoria's Diamond Jubilee of 1897.[9]

Tower

An unnamed tower lay north of the Eastgate *c.* 1588.[10] Its foundations, excavated in 1928 and surviving in 2000, show that it was semi-circular and bonded into a length of medieval wall set back slightly from the line of

the Roman defences. It was probably built in the 13th century at a point where the Roman wall had collapsed.[11]

Kaleyards Gate and Walls

Chester abbey's kitchen garden, known as the Kaleyards, lay just outside the east wall of the city beyond the town ditch. The garden was surrounded by its own stone wall,[12] and from 1274–5 it was reached by a postern in the city wall.[13] The arrangement caused dissension between the abbey and the citizens, anxious about the security of the city. In 1322–3 it was agreed that St. Werburgh's should keep the postern closed in peacetime and make and maintain a drawbridge across the town ditch. The monks were also to replace the gate in their own wall with a smaller postern.[14]

The abbey was equally concerned to prevent trespass in its garden from the city walls, and in 1352 the abbot was indicted for obstructing the wall walk with a door.[15] In 1414, however, Henry V granted the abbey licence to close two small gates on the walls between Eastgate and Northgate, on condition that it allowed access to the murengers and those in charge of the

1 3 *Sheaf,* xlviii, p. 38; LeQuesne, *Roman Defences.*
2 The Assembly Bk. refers to 6 towers, 2 directly 'under' and 4 'over' the gate, but the meaning is unclear: C.C.A.L.S., ZAB 2, f. 104.
3 P. H. Alebon *et al.,* 'The Eastgate, Chester, 1972', *J.C.A.S.* lix. 37–49; LeQuesne, *Roman Defences.*
4 *J.C.A.S.* lix. 48; *Cal. Chester City Cl. Mins. 1603–42,* 167, 169.
5 *Cal. Chester City Cl. Mins. 1603–42,* 205; B.L. Harl. MS. 7568, f. 202v.

6 *J.C.A.S.* lix. 48; C.C.A.L.S., ZAB 2, ff. 170 and v., 173, 176.
7 C.C.A.L.S., ZAB 3, f. 152v.
8 Ibid. ZAB 4, ff. 158v., 203v., 253v., 255–7.
9 *Chester City Cl. Mins. 1897/8,* 570; *1898/9,* 356; Pevsner, *Ches.* 163.   10 Braun, *Civitates,* iii, no. 3.
11 LeQuesne, *Roman Defences.*
12 1 *Sheaf,* ii, p. 33; *P.N. Ches.* v (1:i), 25.
13 Morris, *Chester,* 241; 3 *Sheaf,* xv, p. 59.
14 1 *Sheaf,* ii, p. 33.
15 C.C.A.L.S., ZQCR 5.

FIG. 128. *Old Northgate, before 1808*

defences in time of war. The licence was renewed in 1451 and 1538.[1]

The small gateway under the city wall existing in 2000 and leading into the former Kaleyards was probably built in the later 17th century.[2]

Saddlers' Tower

A square watch tower, shown on a map of 1745, stood *c.* 50 m. north of the Kaleyards Gate at a site marked in

2000 by buttress-like structures representing the stubs of its north and south walls. Aligned with the medieval defences, which stood 1.5 m. inside the Roman ones, the tower was built at a point where the Roman walls had collapsed or been robbed.[3] It was occupied by the Saddlers' company in the mid 16th century,[4] and was still their meeting house in the later 17th.[5] In 1690 it was repaired and said to be 241 years old.[6] The tower was taken down to the level of the walls in 1779–80 and demolished in 1828.[7]

Phoenix (formerly Newton, later King Charles's) Tower

By the later 16th century the tower was leased jointly to two city companies, the Painters and Stationers and the Barbers and Chandlers, who themselves occupied the upper storey and sublet the lower to other guilds. In 1612, when the tower had lost the lead from its roof and was almost ruinous, the two companies began its restoration.[8] A phoenix, emblem of the Painters, appears above the lower door. During the siege the tower had a gun in each storey and as a result was badly damaged. It was returned in 1658 to the companies, who carried out extensive repairs and continued to maintain it until *c.* 1773, when they abandoned it as a meeting place.[9] Further repairs were done by the city in 1773, but it was again described as dilapidated in 1838.[10] With the rise of tourism from the 1840s the tower was promoted as an attraction because of a supposed association with Charles I, who had allegedly stood on the roof to watch while his army was defeated at Rowton Moor in September 1645. In the early 1850s

FIG. 129. *Northgate*

1 *37 D.K.R.* App. II, pp. 137–8; *L. & P. Hen. VIII,* xiii (1), p. 226.   2 3 *Sheaf,* xv, p. 60.

3 Pers. comm. T. J. Strickland; LeQuesne, *Roman Defences.*

4 Morris, *Chester,* 245.

5 C.C.A.L.S., ZCAM 3; B.L. Harl. MS. 7568, f. 202.

6 *J.C.A.S.* xxxix. 96.

7 *Chester Guide* [*c.* 1828], 29; Hemingway, *Hist. Chester,* i. 345.

8 Morris, *Chester,* 245; *J.C.A.S.* xviii. 129–33; xxxix. 96; *Cal. Chester City Cl. Mins. 1603–42,* 65.

9 B.L. Harl. MS. 7568, f. 201v.; *J.C.A.S.* xviii. 141–2.

10 C.C.A.L.S., ZAB 4, f. 305v.; ZAB 6, p. 272; ZCAM 8.

FIG. 130. *Morgan's Mount, 1903*

FIG. 131. *Pemberton's Parlour*

the lower room was occupied by a print-seller, and from the late 19th century the tower housed a small private museum. By then it was commonly known as King Charles's Tower.[1]

Northgate

Recorded from the later 12th century,[2] the gate was granted in the time of Earl John (1232–7) to Robert of Anjou, in whose family the serjeanty remained throughout the 13th century, together with the North-gate gaol.[3] In the early 14th century Robert's great-great-grandson granted his rights to John Blund of Chester.[4] After 1360 the office passed by marriage to the Dutton and Derby families and in 1491–2 it was held by three co-heiresses of the Derbys. In 1498–9 the mayor and citizens laid claim to the Northgate, and by 1541 it was in the custody of the city sheriffs, with whom it remained until its demolition.[5]

The medieval Northgate comprised a narrow passage and pedestrian postern flanked by square towers, together with the gaol buildings.[6] Ruinous in 1617, it continued to be regarded as unsatisfactory until its demolition in 1808, after which it was replaced by a neo-classical arch, designed by Thomas Harrison and completed in 1810.[7]

Morgan's Mount

A watch tower probably preceded the building standing in 2000, which contains no medieval features and consists of a small chamber on the walls and a platform above, evidently a solid structure. Severely damaged during the siege, when it was converted into a battery, it was thereafter repaired.[8] The Mount was 'improved' in 1825.[9] Beside it is an arch opened in the early 19th century to facilitate access to the canal.[10]

Pemberton's Parlour

In the reign of Henry VIII the medieval watch tower on the site was known as Dille's Tower.[11] Later it became known as Goblin Tower, and was said to have been held by the Weavers' company.[12] It was apparently reconstructed in the early 18th century, and thereafter was used by John Pemberton, a ropemaker, to keep

1 J. Romney, *Chester and its Environs Illustrated*, [44]; Morris, *Chester*, 121; below, Museums: Other Museums.

2 *Cart. Chester Abbey*, i, p. 239.

3 P.R.O., CHES 29/59, m. 7; *Cal. Ches. Ct. R.* pp. 181–4, 188–9, 203; above, Law and Order: Municipal Prisons (Northgate Gaol).

4 P.R.O., CHES 29/59, m. 7; Ormerod, *Hist. Ches.* ii. 538; 3 *Sheaf*, xxxvii, p. 34.

5 Morris, *Chester*, 232; B.L. Harl. MS. 7568, f. 200 and v.; C.C.A.L.S., ZSR 261.

6 Morris, *Chester*, 233–4; C.C.A.L.S., ZCR 63/2/133; above, Law and Order: Municipal Prisons (Northgate Gaol).

7 *Cal. Chester City Cl. Mins. 1603–42*, 86; C.C.A.L.S., ZAB 2, ff. 125v., 163v., 182v., 183v.–184; ZAB 3, f. 176v.; ZAB 5, pp. 254, 257, 283; ZAC 1, ff. 19, 21; Harrison's design for the Northgate is at Weaver Hall Mus., Ches.

8 B.L. Harl. MS. 7568, f. 199v.

9 C.C.A.L.S., ZAB 5, p. 497; cf. ZAB 4, f. 114.

10 Hemingway, *Hist. Chester*, i. 353.

11 Morris, *Chester*, 245.   12 3 *Sheaf*, liii, pp. 42–3.

watch over his men working below. It fell down in 1893, and in 1894 was entirely rebuilt.[1]

Bonewaldesthorne Tower

A watch tower existed on the site by 1322, when the New Tower was built near by.[2] An irregular pentagon, it provided access to the walk along the spur wall to the New Tower. A blocked arch in the north wall near the tower, recorded in the early 19th century, was probably the remains of a postern giving access to the medieval harbour.[3]

Water (New) Tower

The round tower, which John of Helpston contracted to build in 1322 for £100, is joined to the main defences by a massive spur wall over 30 m. long, under which is a water gate restored in 1730. Many of the details show parallels with Edwardian works in Wales, particularly Conwy where there was a similar water tower. The tower was intended to be 'in the water of Dee', but had been left high and dry within a century.[4] By the 17th century it had long been abandoned, and in 1631 the Bakers' company offered to rent and repair it with the help of the city authorities.[5] In 1639 it was renovated at the city's expense,[6] and in the 1640s embrasures in the spur wall were converted into gun ports.[7] Leased as a storehouse in 1671,[8] the tower continued to be employed for similar purposes for much of the succeeding century, but in 1728 was described as useless and neglected.[9] In 1825 the corporation decided to improve it, and in 1837 it was leased as a museum, a function it generally retained thereafter.[10] The name Water Tower came into use in the 17th century and displaced the original name of New Tower, despite the Assembly's attempt in 1732 to insist on using the correct name.[11]

Watergate

Although Watergate Street was so named by *c.* 1220, the earliest references to the gate itself, in the late 12th century and 1249, allude simply to the 'west gate'.[12] In 1249 the gate was said to have been held by the ancestors of Christine la Paumere, whose husband

had been deprived of it by Philip of Orby (justice of Chester *c.* 1208–29), when he found the gate open before the proper hour. Philip had taken the gate into the earl's hand, and in 1249 it remained the king's.[13]

About 1270 Adam, son of Bernard of Salisbury, citizen of Chester, held the serjeanty of the Watergate by hereditary right.[14] Thereafter it passed through several hands until eventually, after 1432, it came into the possession of the Stanley family, who sold it to the city *c.* 1778.[15]

Tolls taken at the gate included fish, in the 13th century shared with one of the friaries.[16] By the later 15th century, however, takings appear to have been negligible.[17] In 1432 the yearly value of the serjeanty was 4*s.*[18]

The medieval gate consisted of a single Gothic arch and a small postern for pedestrians; whether it ever had towers is uncertain, but in the later 17th century it was described as a plain gate with a walkway over it.[19] In 1712–13 it was enlarged and rebuilt by the murengers,[20] and in 1760 a foot passage was constructed.[21] The corporation ordered the tollhouse at the gate to be demolished in 1782 and in 1788 the gate itself was replaced by a single neo-classical arch designed by the architect Joseph Turner, a member of the Assembly since 1776.[22]

Nuns' Gardens Postern

In the later 17th century the postern was said to have been granted to the prioress of Chester to facilitate access to her croft in the Roodee.[23] As late as 1718 burials were recorded 'nigh the Nun Gate'.[24]

Castle Postern

In the later 17th century the postern was described as 'an ancient port made for the benefit of them as lived in the castle to go to the river'. It was located by the castle ditch near the south-west corner of the defences not far from the Shipgate.[25]

Lowse Tower

A watch tower of that name faced the Roodee in 1573.[26]

---

1 Inscription and arms on tower; Simpson, *Walls*, 30–1; *J.C.A.S.* N.S. v. 127, 338–9.

2 *J.C.A.S.* xlv. 57–8; *P.N. Ches.* v (1:i), 24.

3 *J.C.A.S.* lv. 38; Hemingway, *Hist. Chester*, i. 357.

4 *J.C.A.S.* xlv. 57–60.

5 *Cal. Chester City Cl. Mins. 1603–42*, 166; *J.C.A.S.* xxxix. 96.

6 *Cal. Chester City Cl. Mins. 1603–42*, 200.

7 S. Ward, 'Recent Work on Medieval City Wall', *J.C.A.S.* lxviii. 79–81.

8 C.C.A.L.S., ZAB 2, ff. 172v., 173v.

9 Ibid. ZAB 3, f. 34v.; ZAB 4, ff. 102, 112, 145; 3 *Sheaf*, xlviii, p. 41.

10 C.C.A.L.S., ZAB 4, f. 497; ZAB 6, pp. 3, 186, 245; 1 *Sheaf*, i, p. 3; 3 *Sheaf*, vi, p. 8; below, Museums: Water Tower Museum.

11 *P.N. Ches.* v (1:i), 29; C.C.A.L.S., ZAB 4, f. 47.

12 Lucian, *De Laude Cestrie*, 8, 50–3; *Cal. Inq. Misc.* i, pp. 22–3; P.R.O., C 145/3/16.

13 *Cal. Inq. Misc.* i, pp. 22–3.

14 3 *Sheaf*, xi, p. 28.

15 Ormerod, *Hist. Ches.* i. 358; Morris, *Chester*, 225 (where the date of the city's acquisition is given as 1788); 37 *D.K.R.* App. II, p. 376; 3 *Sheaf*, xiii, p. 11.

16 *Sel. R. Chester City Cts.* p. lvii; Morris, *Chester*, 557–8.

17 Morris, *Chester*, 225–8; C.C.A.L.S., ZCAM 1.

18 37 *D.K.R.* App. II, p. 376.

19 Morris, *Chester*, 226; B.L. Harl. MS. 7568, f. 199; 3 *Sheaf*, xix, p. 91.

20 C.C.A.L.S., ZAB 3, f. 204v.; ZCAM 6.

21 Ibid. ZAB 4, f. 186.

22 Ibid. ZAB 5, ff. 11–12, 21, 44.

23 B.L. Harl. MS. 7568, f. 127v.

24 1 *Sheaf*, iii, p. 116.

25 B.L. Harl. MS. 7568, f. 127v.

26 Morris, *Chester*, 245.

Shipgate

The gate probably existed by the 1120s, and certainly by the 1270s.[1] In the 17th century it was said to have been opposite a ferry pre-dating the Dee Bridge. By the 14th century, when tolls were levied there, the gate was in the care of the keeper of the Bridgegate, who was bound to find a man to open and shut it. Dues were still charged there in the reign of Henry VI, but by 1534–5 it had been made 'useless', and in the reign of Edward VI it was blocked.[2] The gate, which comprised a single arch with battlements, was still standing in the later 16th century, but in 1707 was referred to in terms which imply that it had recently been removed.[3] If so, it must have been replaced, for it was expressly said to have been taken down in 1828 and was later re-erected in the garden of a house in Abbey Square.[4] In 1893 it was presented to the Chester Archaeological Society, and in 1897 was moved again by the city corporation to the Groves, where it remained in 2000.[5]

Bridgegate

Although in the late 12th century it was referred to simply as the south gate,[6] land near the Bridgegate and possibly the serjeanty of the gate had been given before 1150 by Countess Maud of Chester to her servant Poyns, probably keeper of the castle gardens.[7] The serjeanty and the keepership of the gardens remained combined throughout the 13th century. In 1269 Richard Bagot granted the serjeanty to Philip the clerk,[8] and thereafter the office was held by Philip's heirs, the Raby family, half from the heirs of the Bagots and half from the heirs of the Hose family.[9]

By 1321 tolls were levied at the gate,[10] and in 1349–50 the gate was said to have been worth 20s., in return for which the holder was obliged to find a man to keep it, the Shipgate, and the Horsegate. On the death without heirs in 1384–5 of Philip of Raby's daughter Catherine, the serjeanty remained divided into two shares, one of which, together with the castle garden, later passed to the Troutbecks and in 1521–2 to the Talbots, earls of Shrewsbury.[11] Both shares were eventually acquired by the city in 1624 and 1666.[12]

FIG. 132. *Shipgate, before 1828*

The medieval Bridgegate, which comprised a Gothic arch flanked by two round towers, was much altered in 1600–1 by the addition of a tall square tower housing machinery for conveying river water to the city. It was known, after its builder, as John Tyrer's Water Tower, and was destroyed in the siege of Chester. A new octagonal tower was afterwards erected, perhaps on a different site immediately behind the gate, but was disused by the late 17th century and was demolished in 1782.[13] The gate itself was repaired in 1640, and in 1645 an assessment was levied for building a drawbridge.[14] In 1728 the structure could still be described as an 'ancient, strong, and spacious stone building'.[15]

Repairs and improvements were considered in the 1770s, but in 1781 the old gate was taken down to be replaced by a classical arch with a balustraded parapet designed by Joseph Turner (d. 1807).[16] Steps leading from the gate into Skinners Lane were built in 1831.[17]

1 An early 12th-cent. reference to 'Clippe' gate may be a copyist's error for 'Shippe' gate: *Cart. Chester Abbey*, i, p. 49; 3 *Sheaf*, xlvii, p. 6. For the later reference see 3 *Sheaf*, xxxiii, p. 90.

2 Morris, *Chester*, 229–30, 256, 557; B.L. Harl. MS. 7568, ff. 141, 199.

3 Morris, *Chester*, 256; 3 *Sheaf*, xlvi, p. 62; xlvii, p. 20; B.L. Harl. MS. 7568, f. 137; C.C.A.L.S., ZAB 3, f. 156 and v.

4 *J.C.A.S.* n.s. v. 333–4. Simpson gives the date as 1831: *Walls*, 59.

5 *J.C.A.S.* n.s. v. 333–4; Simpson, *Walls*, 59; cf. *Chester City Cl. Mins. 1896/7*, 476.

6 Lucian, *De Laude Cestrie*, 47, 53, 60; 3 *Sheaf*, l, p. 23; *Charters of A.-N. Earls*, pp. 243–5 (no. 244).

7 Ormerod, *Hist. Ches.* i. 356; ii. 546; *Charters of A.-N. Earls*, pp. 57–8 (no. 42).

8 B.L. Add. Ch. 75138.

9 *Cal. Ches. Ct. R.* pp. 163, 166; Morris, *Chester*, 228; Ormerod confused Robert, son of Philip, with Robert of Raby (d. 1349–50): *Hist. Ches.* ii. 546–7.

10 Morris, *Chester*, 557; B.L. Harl. MS. 2125, f. 189v.

11 Ormerod, *Hist. Ches.* ii. 546–8.

12 Ibid. i. 357.

13 Morris, *Chester*, 229–30; 1 *Sheaf*, i, pp. 310–11; 3 *Sheaf*, lviii, pp. 14–15; *Cal. Chester City Cl. Mins. 1603–42*, p. xxxvi; C.C.A.L.S., ZAB 1, ff. 262v.–263; ZAB 3, ff. 34v.–35; ZAB 4, f. 345.

14 *Cal. Chester City Cl. Mins. 1603–42*, 205; C.C.A.L.S., ZAB 2, f. 71v.

15 3 *Sheaf*, xlviii, p. 38.

16 Ibid. xxxvii, pp. 56–9, 61–2; H. Colvin, *Biographical Dictionary of Brit. Architects* (1995), 998; C.C.A.L.S., ZAB 4, ff. 296v., 304v., 342 and v. 17 C.C.A.L.S., ZAB 6, p. 39.

FIG. 133. *Newgate, 1903*

FIG. 134. *Newgate*

Capelgate (Horsegate)

The gate, a postern east of the Bridgegate in being by 1321, was in the custody of the Bridgegate's serjeant.[1] Its primary object seems to have been to allow horses to be watered on the river bank.[2] Apparently only a modest archway in the wall, the gate was still standing in 1708.[3] In 1745 it was blocked, as part of the defensive measures taken against the Young Pretender.[4]

Postern Tower

A round battlemented watch tower east of Capelgate existed by the 1580s and was still standing in 2000.[5]

Watch Tower

A watch tower standing at the top of what later became the Wishing Steps was converted into a 'large, square, solid mount' to form a gun battery in 1643. Later furnished with a stone seat and windows commanding the view over the river, it was reduced in height in 1826 and entirely removed in 1843.[6]

Newgate (Wolfgate, Wolfeld's Gate)

The early name, Wolfeld's Gate, derived from a personal name, and occurs first in the late 12th century.[7] The gate lay adjacent to the point where Fleshmongers Lane, an early thoroughfare, breached the southern legionary wall and may date from before 1066.[8] No tolls were payable in 1321, though in 1754 tolls were said to have been taken from time immemorial.[9] The gate was the property of the city corporation in the later Middle Ages, and in 1489–90 was leased to a glover.[10] In 1573, after the abduction of an alderman's daughter, the city authorities ordered that it be shut at night.[11]

The medieval gate, which seems to have been set in a square tower, was repaired in the 1550s, but was condemned in 1603 as too narrow. At the order of the Assembly it was enlarged, but in the following year it was found to be in poor repair, and in 1608 it was taken down and entirely rebuilt.[12] The new gate was given a new door in 1640 and further repaired in 1651.[13] In 1674 a house in the form of a tower was built on the north side to be 'a defence and security to the . . . gate if

1 Morris, *Chester*, 557; Ormerod, *Hist. Ches.* ii. 547.
2 B.L. Harl. MS. 7568, f. 198v.   3 3 *Sheaf*, xxi, p. 41.
4 C.C.A.L.S., ZAB 4, f. 115v.
5 Braun, *Civitates*, iii, no. 3; 3 *Sheaf*, xx, p. 18; B.L. Harl. MS. 7568, f. 127.
6 Morris, *Chester*, 247; 3 *Sheaf*, xxi, pp. 18–19, 50; Hemingway, *Hist. Chester*, i. 354; B.L. Harl. MS. 7568, f. 127; *Gresty and Burghall's Chester Guide* [1867], 41.
7 *P.N. Ches.* v (1:i), 26; *J.C.A.S.* lv. 50–2; 3 *Sheaf*, lvi, pp. 72, 94.

8 *V.C.H. Ches.* v (1), Topography, 900–1914: Early Medieval (Layout of the City); *J.C.A.S.* lxiv. 12–13, 15, 21.
9 Morris, *Chester*, 554–8; C.C.A.L.S., ZCL 1511.
10 3 *Sheaf*, xvi, p. 74; C.C.A.L.S., ZAB 1, ff. 33v.–35v.
11 Morris, *Chester*, 237–41.
12 Braun, *Civitates*, iii, no. 3; Morris, *Chester*, 237; 3 *Sheaf*, ix, p. 43; xv, p. 50; xxiii, p. 76; xxx, p. 68; xxxiii, pp. 85–6; *Cal. Chester City Cl. Mins. 1603–42*, 35, 39 n.
13 *Cal. Chester City Cl. Mins. 1603–42*, 205; C.C.A.L.S., ZAB 2, f. 96v.

FIG. 135. *The Bars, before 1767*

occasion should require',[1] and in 1768 the gate itself was again rebuilt by the murengers, presumably as a single round arch, the form which it retained in 2000, when it was generally referred to as Wolfgate.[2] In 1938, as part of a road-widening scheme, a new gateway with two towers, designed by Sir Walter and Michael Tapper, was built immediately to the south.[3]

Thimbleby's Tower

A medieval watch tower, known in 1555 as Wolf Tower, it had an octagonal stone vault, built probably *c.* 1300, at the level of the wall walk. Rented by the Gamull family from the corporation in the earlier 17th century, it was a 'ruinous old place' until 1643, when it was put into repair during the siege. It may then have sustained damage, since in 1651 the Gamulls were asked to pay for repairs. In the late 17th century it was described as 'of no great use', and in the 18th century it served as a laundry.[4] The tower was repaired in 1879.[5] In 1994 it was given a steeply pitched tiled roof.[6]

OUTLYING GATES AND DEFENCES

The Bars

The gate, which had been built by 1241, stood east of the city on Foregate Street near the later junction with

FIG. 136. *Further Bridgegate, before 1784* (foreground)

City Road.[7] By the 17th century it had become a hindrance to traffic, and in 1609 a postern for pedestrians was inserted on the north side. The whole structure was demolished in 1767.[8]

Further Bridgegate (Dee Bridge Tower)

In 1387 Richard II directed that the profits of the murage and the ferry across the Dee were to be applied to the rebuilding of the Dee Bridge.[9] The work was not finished until 1407, when Prince Henry ordered that the tower on the bridge, begun in Richard's time, was to be completed.[10] By the 1590s it had become dilapidated and was replaced by a gatehouse, itself demolished in 1784.[11]

Cow Lane Gate

The gate, a single tall archway spanning the street, was built in 1630 and taken down in 1773.[12]

THE ROWS

Since the Middle Ages the most distinctive element of the four main streets of Chester has been the Rows, a system of largely continuous first-floor galleries, raised above undercrofts and incorporating public walkways which run parallel with the street below and give access

to shops on the inner side, and a stallboard or open area for the display of goods on the outer. Although galleries with shops were a common feature of medieval urban buildings, the Chester Rows are remarkable for running through groups of adjoining buildings in

1 C.C.A.L.S., ZAB 2, f. 179; *J.C.A.S.* xxx. 87–8.
2 C.C.A.L.S., ZAB 4, f. 255v.
3 Pevsner, *Ches.* 165.
4 Morris, *Chester*, 245; 3 *Sheaf*, xxi, pp. 76–7; Morris, *Siege of Chester*, 214; *J.C.A.S.* xxx. 82–4; Ward, *Civil War Siegeworks*, 5; B.L. Harl. MS. 7568, f. 203v.
5 Simpson, *Walls*, 70.
6 Inscription on tower.

7 *P.N. Ches.* v (1:i), 79.
8 Morris, *Chester*, 243; 3 *Sheaf*, lx, pp. 38–9; *Cal. Chester City Cl. Mins. 1603–42*, 40; C.C.A.L.S., ZAB 4, f. 249v.
9 *36 D.K.R.* App. II, p. 94.
10 Morris, *Chester*, 509–10; C.C.A.L.S., ZCH 25.
11 3 *Sheaf*, xiii, p. 11. Morris refers to a tower at either end of the bridge: *Chester*, 231 n.
12 B.L. Harl. MS. 7568, f. 173v.; 3 *Sheaf*, xv, pp. 44–5, 55–6.

FIG. 137. *Watergate Row South in later 18th century*

multiple ownership. The feature, which has been the subject of comment since the mid 16th century, is clearly ancient.[1] Despite the loss of almost all the medieval structural evidence above the level of the undercrofts, there are indications that Row galleries occurred in several widely separated places within the four main streets from an early period. Unambiguous traces of a gallery running through adjoining plots survived in 2000 at nos. 28–34 Watergate Street, where it was spanned by arches set within the party walls between the two houses and with a simple profile which, though obscured by stucco, is consistent with the mid 13th-century date of other parts of the buildings (Fig. 138).[2] A similar arch spanning the Row at no. 32 Eastgate Street survived until the mid 19th century,[3] and in the 1990s there were also traces of early gallery openings in party walls at nos. 48 Bridge Street and 6 Lower Bridge Street, both at some distance from the Cross.[4]

ORIGIN AND EARLY DEVELOPMENT

The Rows are unlikely to have originated much before 1200. The only indication of an earlier date is a tradition, probably 14th-century, that property on the north side of Eastgate Street recorded in 1155 was known as Lorimers' Row.[5] At the west end on that side of the street, however, the Buttershops or Bakers' Row occupied a site which was apparently still open ground in the 12th century.[6] Otherwise, Rows

were first recorded in 1293 near the Cross at the centre of the city.[7] One of them, Ironmongers' Row, lay immediately north of St. Peter's church, and may have originated in four shops which abutted the church by the 1220s. Whether the term Row already had the specialized meaning of 'elevated walkway' in the 1290s is uncertain, and the earliest unambiguous instance of such a usage is in 1356.[8] Ironmongers' Row was nevertheless probably elevated above the street, since Northgate Street is known to have had undercrofts by the 1280s and commercial premises above them by the 1340s.[9]

Although first mentioned only in the mid 14th century, Fleshers' Row on the north side of Watergate Street abutting St. Peter's was probably in the form of a Row by the late 13th century. Buildings on the site, owned by the influential Doncaster family in the 1290s, included two adjacent properties comprising shops and rooms over undercrofts by the 1340s.[10] By 1398 the Row ran west as far as Goss Lane.[11]

Opposite St. Peter's on the north side of Eastgate Street the building or group of buildings known *c.* 1270 as the Buttershops contained a Row by 1369.[12] It was exceptional in being located within substantial structures more than one storey high, shops with rooms above them, as early as 1361.[13] The Row ran into and was sometimes confused with Bakers' Row immediately to the east. That Row, named from its proximity to the important bakehouse belonging to St. Giles's

1 B. E. Harris, 'Debate on Rows', *J.C.A.S.* lxvii. 7–16.

2 *J.C.A.S.* lxix. 142.

3 J. M. B. Pigot, *Hist. of Chester* (1816), title page; Ormerod, *Hist. Ches.* i. 356.

4 Pers. comm. R. Harris, Dept. of Arch., Univ. of Reading.

5 *Cal. Pat.* 1399–1401, 297–8; *J.C.A.S.* xiii. 94.

6 K. M. Matthews and others, *Excavations at Chester: 3–15 Eastgate St.* 15–16, 65.   7 P.R.O., CHES 25/1.

8 C.C.A.L.S., ZCHD 2/1; 3 *Sheaf*, xix, pp. 19–20.

9 P.R.O., CHES 25/1; C.C.A.L.S., DBA 35, no. 4; ibid. ZD/HT

2; B.L. Add. Ch. 49975, 49982; *J.C.A.S.* n.s. x. 17.

10 C.C.A.L.S., ZD/HT 13, 20, 40–4; ZMR 3, m. 12; ZMR 8, m. 6d.; ibid. DBA 35; B.L. Add. Ch. 50052; P.R.O., CHES 25/1; Morris, *Chester*, 294.

11 C.C.A.L.S., ZMR 64. Thanks are due to Dr. J. Laughton for this reference.

12 J. Brownbill, *Cal. of Deeds and Papers of Moore Fam.* (R.S.L.C. lxvii), p. 146; 3 *Sheaf*, xxxvi, pp. 33–4.

13 *Talbot Deeds, 1200–1682*, ed. E. E. Barker (R.S.L.C. ciii), no. 73; cf. B.L. Add. Ch. 50196, 75161; C.C.A.L.S., DVE 1/CII/8.

FIG. 138. *Watergate Row North in 1849, showing 13th-century arches*

hospital, existed by 1293.[1] By 1375 it was associated with undercrofts, and it seems likely that it was a Row by the 1290s.[2] Other early Rows of similar form included Cornmarket Row on the south side of Eastgate Street, and Corvisers' Row, probably within the structures on the west side of Bridge Street known in the 1270s as the Shoemakers' Selds.[3]

In the late 13th and early 14th century Rows thus existed in many places in the four main streets. For long it was believed that they had evolved gradually, though the factors which engendered the development proved difficult to isolate.[4] Later, it was argued that they were deliberately planned after the destructive fire of 1278.[5] A detailed programme of interdisciplinary research conducted between 1985 and 1992 suggested more convincingly that the Rows emerged gradually between *c.* 1200 and 1350 through the adaptation of a common form of urban domestic building, the split-level house with an undercroft, to the unusual circumstances present in the centre of Chester.[6] One important element, recognized long previously, was the peculiar topography of the city centre, where the accumulation of material from collapsed Roman buildings caused the ground level to rise quite steeply on either side of the main thoroughfares.[7] The difference in levels was such that the characteristic Row building had its first floor fronting the street on a level with the ground floor at the rear. Moreover, because of the height of the rear levels and the presence of bedrock immediately beneath the street surface, the

first storeys had to be set relatively high. For external access they thus required substantial stairways which projected inconveniently into the highway and darkened the narrow frontages which gave the undercrofts their sole source of light. The Row walkway provided a means of limiting the number of stairways from the street without restricting access to the first-floor premises.

Another prerequisite for the Rows, 'a reasonably continuous occupation of the street frontages', had undoubtedly long existed in Chester.[8] The crowding of buildings on to the street frontages resulted from the commercial desirability of a location on the four main thoroughfares. It was apparent both in the concentration of shops and in the frequency with which property changed hands in the 13th and earlier 14th century.[9] Such pressure led to a demand for the maximum commercial space along the street, and hence to the appearance of so many shops at first-floor level.

It may be that such factors alone account for the emergence of the Rows. Certainly, they are consistent with the variable character and wide date-range of surviving Row buildings and with their evidently gradual evolution to become the norm in the principal streets. Nevertheless, the appearance of walkways running through adjacent properties in different ownership was remarkable. While there is no hint of anything so radical as a requirement upon house owners in the four main streets to reconstruct their property so that a public thoroughfare could run through it at first-floor

1 P.R.O., CHES 25/1; C.C.A.L.S., ZD/HT 18, 20, 24; ZMR 30; B.L. Add. Ch. 50151; Brownbill, *Cal. Deeds and Papers of Moore Fam.* pp. 148, 151; *J.C.A.S.* n.s. ii. 166–8.

2 C.C.A.L.S., ZMR 48.

3 Below, this chapter: Physical Form (Selds), Medieval Extent.

4 e.g. Morris, *Chester*, 288–94; P. H. Lawson, in 'Rows of Chester: Two Interpretations', *J.C.A.S.* xlv. 25–31.

5 J. H. Smith, in *J.C.A.S.* xlv. 32–41.

6 *Rows of Chester*, ed. A. Brown. Much of what follows is a revised and shortened version of ibid. 14–32.

7 T. J. Strickland, 'Roman Heritage of Chester', *J.C.A.S.* lxvii. 17–36.

8 Ibid. 39; *V.C.H. Ches.* v (1), Topography, 900–1914: Early Medieval (Layout of the City).

9 *V.C.H. Ches.* v (1), Later Medieval Chester: Economy and Society, 1230–1350 (Trades and Industries, Leading Merchants and Citizens).

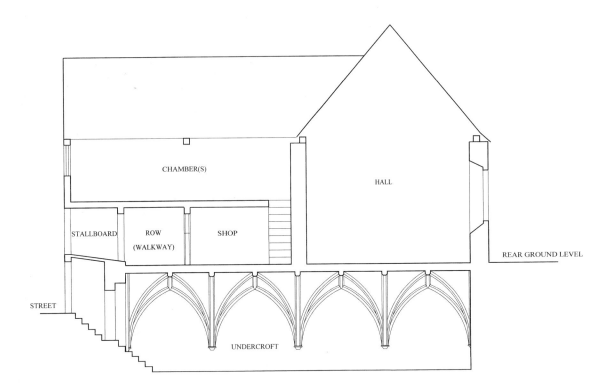

FIG. 139. *Elements of a typical house in the Rows*

level, it remains possible that a single early development somewhere in the city provided an influential model. The Rows seem always to have housed commercial premises and the earliest ones to be recorded were invariably linked with a single trade. That suggests that they may have owed something to the co-operation of members of the same craft, a process easier to secure in Chester than elsewhere because of the persistence there of a guild merchant covering all the trades and acting as a governing body for the whole city.[1] The selds, which contained a Row from an early date and were perhaps the area in which the stallboards were pioneered, were especially closely associated with the guild merchant, which met there until 1250.[2] Possibly the guild was responsible in the mid 13th century for laying out the first Row which became the pattern for others. Alternatively, the concentration of shops and early evidence of Rows around St. Peter's might suggest that the Rows originated in a comprehensive rebuilding on land associated with that church, perhaps the urban estate to which St. Peter's was originally attached.[3]

PHYSICAL FORM OF ROW BUILDINGS

Burgage Plots

One of the determinants of the form of Row buildings was the division of property along the main thoroughfares into long narrow plots in order to provide access to the street for as many owners as possible. In the early 13th century such holdings were occasionally described as 'burgages' (*burgagia*), but more often simply as 'land' (*terra*), 'plots' (*placeae*), 'messuages' (*messuagia*), or 'tenements' (*tenementa*).[4] As is implied by the use of such varied and unspecific terminology, the plots were in no way uniform. The few plot measurements recorded varied greatly, widths from as little as *c.* 5.5 m. to nearly 17 m., and lengths from *c.* 10 m. to over 48 m.[5]

Undercrofts and Frontages

The buildings erected on the plots were diverse in size but had a number of standard elements. Most striking are the undercrofts, many of which survived in 2000,

1 *V.C.H. Ches.* v (1), Later Medieval Chester: City Government and Politics, 1350–1550 (Decay of the Guild Merchant).

2 C.C.A.L.S., ZCR 469/542, f. 14v.; below, this chapter: Physical Form (Selds; 'Porches' and Stallboards); above, Municipal Buildings: Common Hall.

3 For further discussion see R. B. Harris, 'The Origins of the Chester Rows', *Medieval Arch., Art, and Archit. at Chester*, ed. A. Thacker, 132–51.

4 Aston charters: B.L. Add. Ch. 49968–50250, calendared in 3 *Sheaf,* xxviii–xxix; Shrewsbury (Talbot) deeds: B.L. Add. Ch. 72203–72329, 75107–75237, cal. 3 *Sheaf,* xxxiii; cartulary of St. Anne: B.L. Harl. MS. 2061, cal. 3 *Sheaf,* xxxvi; *Cart. Chester*

Abbey; Coucher Bk. or Chartulary of Whalley Abbey, ed. W. A. Hulton, ii (Chetham Soc. [o.s.], xi), pp. 339–84; Arley deeds: J.R.U.L.M.; Barnston deeds: C.C.A.L.S., DBA 35, cal. 3 *Sheaf,* xlii–xliii; Eaton charters: Grosvenor Estate Office, Eaton; Vernon deeds: C.C.A.L.S., DVE, cal. 3 *Sheaf,* lvi; Henry Taylor colln.: C.C.A.L.S., ZD/HT; Brownbill, *Cal. Deeds and Papers of Moore Fam.*; deeds relating to property which passed to Crown in 16th cent.: P.R.O., WALE 29; deeds enrolled in portmote ct.: C.C.A.L.S., ZMR. See also *Rows of Chester,* ed. Brown, 136–8.

5 e.g. B.L. Add. Ch. 50005, 50032, 50090–9, 72270; C.C.A.L.S., DVE 1/CI/41; *Rows of Chester,* ed. Brown, 1–32.

FIG. 140. *Undercroft at no. 12 Bridge Street, 1849*

which were almost invariably built at the front of plots and at right angles to the street, and were only partially below ground level.[1] Such structures were common in medieval English towns, doubtless because of the security which they afforded for the storage of valuable commodities, especially wine, and because they doubled the frontage available for commercial purposes. In the main streets of Chester they were exceptionally numerous, generally comprising single cells ceiled with heavy timbers, but also including grand stone-built examples, best represented in 2000 by the stone-vaulted and arcaded undercroft at no. 11 Watergate Street. They varied in size from 3.7 m. to 9 m. in width, and from 10 m. to 41 m. in length, and do not seem to have been the product of a single plan. Their existence provided an essential, though not of itself sufficient, precondition for the development of continuous first-floor walkways above them.

The undercrofts which can be traced to the 13th and 14th centuries were generally relatively wide. Above them, at Row level, were groups of small shops usually no more than 2 m. wide and 3 m. deep. A single merchant house might contain anything up to five such tiny lock-ups.[2] Such concentrations of shops above relatively high-set undercrofts made a common walkway at first-floor level especially desirable.

The nature of the medieval frontages to the undercrofts can be determined from a few known instances, at nos. 28 Eastgate Street, 6 Lower Bridge Street, and 11 and 25 Watergate Street. Each had a central doorway up to 1.5 m. wide with flanking windows. Access and illumination would otherwise have been difficult to

provide for: only one undercroft is known to have had a rear light-well, and only the Leche House (no. 17 Watergate Street) certainly had access by stairs to the rear of the undercroft.[3] The fact that the undercrofts were often divided into sections each requiring its own door and windows made especially heavy demands upon the frontage. At nos. 32–4 Watergate Street, for example, the surviving timber arcade, grooved to take wattle and daub partitions, implies a division into three longitudinal sections, each only 2.6 m. wide internally. If, as was probable, there were three upper-level shops, the benefits of a gallery approached by only a single flight of steps are clear. In 2000 such steps occurred on average at every third plot, a distribution which may well reflect medieval commercial groupings in the 13th and 14th centuries.

Domestic Accommodation

Behind the shops, at Row level and above, lay domestic accommodation reached by passages leading from doors opening on to the walkway.[4] Buildings took two main forms. In the simpler and much more common type the hall was placed at right angles to the Row, while in the grander houses, usually at corner sites, it ran parallel to the walkway across several undercrofts. The presence of the Row affected the layout of the houses, precluding the courtyard plan found in other towns. The Row's overriding importance in the planning is evident from the fact that the main entrance at the cross-passage of such houses was approached from the street only indirectly and inconveniently by steps at either end of the frontage.[5]

1 *J.C.A.S.* lxix. 115–45.

2 e.g. nos. 38–42 Watergate Street.

3 *The Past Uncovered: Quarterly Newsletter of Chester Arch.* (Spring 1998).

4 Except in the Selds: below, this chapter: Physical Form (Selds).

5 *V.C.H. Ches.* v (1), Topography, 900–1914: Later Medieval (Building Activity, 1230–1400).

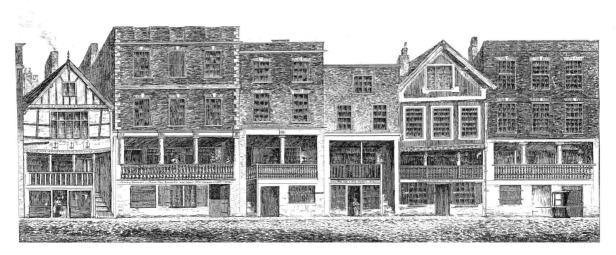

FIG. 141. *Access stairs and domestic accommodation in Watergate Row South, 1818*

Selds

The structures referred to in local sources as *seldae*, 'selds', have long been thought to have made an important contribution to the development of the Rows. In the past it has been suggested that they were long strips of property in front of the undercrofts, and that building over them was what enabled Row walkways to be developed at first-floor level.[1] That theory, however, is based on a misconception of the nature of selds. They are most plausibly viewed as 'private bazaars' into which were gathered stalls selling a particular form of merchandise, perhaps under privileged regulations.[2] The resemblance of Chester's selds to market halls is confirmed by a dispute in 1288–9 over the right of way through one of them.[3]

The selds were concentrated in Bridge Street, on the western side near Commonhall Lane.[4] They occupied the area in front of the common hall itself and extended northwards to the junction of Bridge Street with Watergate Street, where in the early 15th century lay the 'Stone Seld', probably that which in the 1270s adjoined Mayor John Arneway's seld in Bridge Street.[5] The whole quarter was known in the 13th and 14th centuries simply as 'the Selds'.[6]

In Chester a seld was sometimes an individual stall or booth but more usually a structure much bigger than a single shop. In the mid 13th century, for example, Mayor Arneway was granted half a seld measuring 10 ft. by 52 ft.[7] The tenement plots in Bridge Street immediately east of the common hall are very long and narrow. No. 32, for instance, is 40 m. long and less than 4 m. wide, dimensions similar to those of a seld recorded at Middlewich in 1334.[8]

Like those in London's Cheapside, the selds of Chester were elevated above undercrofts and probably fronted by shops.[9] They undoubtedly contained a Row. In 1356 the mayor and citizens granted a small piece of land in Bridge Street 'next to the new steps which lead towards Corvisers' Row at the end of the Fishboards, next to the pillory of Chester, in the corner towards the church of St. Peter'.[10] The 'Row' was thus an elevated walkway reached by steps and running along the west side of Bridge Street southwards from the junction with Watergate Street.[11] Although the steps were new in 1356, the Row was probably much older. In 1275 Robert le Barn, agent of Vale Royal abbey, leased to Alexander Hurrell, a former sheriff and later mayor of Chester, a group of 11 shops for the large sum of 40 marks.[12] The lease, originally for 12 years, was apparently soon terminated, since by 1278 Robert had granted the same properties in perpetuity to Vale Royal.[13] The shops were then called collectively the Shoemakers' Selds (*seldae sutorum*); they lay in Bridge Street between land belonging to St. John's hospital and that of Ralph of the pillory, probably the pillory

1 *J.C.A.S.* xlv. 26–7.

2 *V.C.H. Ches.* v (1), Later Medieval Chester: Economy and Society, 1230–1350 (Trades and Industries); D. Keene, *Winchester Studies*, ii. 137–8, 1091–2, 1098; idem, *Cheapside before the Great Fire*, 12–13. Cf. the great hall (*aula*) at Middlewich built as a seld for foreign merchants in 1334: *36 D.K.R.* App. II, p. 374; P.R.O., SC 6/783/15, m. 3; SC 6/783/16, m. 2d.; SC 6/783/17, m. 2; SC 6/784/5, m. 2. Thanks are due to Dr. J. Laughton for these references.　3 P.R.O., CHES 31/File 1A.

4 e.g. B.L. Add. Ch. 50058, 50117, 50152; C.C.A.L.S., ZD/HT 46; ZMR 5, m. 5; ZMR 30, m. 3; ZMR 35.

5 C.C.A.L.S., DVE 1/CII/21.

6 Ibid. ZCR 469/542; cf. ibid. ZMR 30, m. 3; ibid. DVE 1/CI/22; B.L. Add. Ch. 50152.

7 *Cart. Chester Abbey*, ii, p. 464.

8 Pers. comm. R. Harris; *36 D.K.R.* App. II, p. 374.

9 C.C.A.L.S., DVE 1/CII/21; D. Keene, 'Shops and Shopping in Medieval Lond.' *Medieval Art, Archit., and Arch. in Lond.* 38.

10 C.C.A.L.S., ZCHD 2/1. *P.N. Ches.* v (1:i), 21, wrongly places Corvisers' Row on the east side of Bridge St.

11 Morris, *Chester*, 295.

12 P.R.O., E 315/47/139.　　13 Ibid. E 326/3474.

FIG. 142. *Row walkway and stallboards, Bridge Street Row West, 1847*

which in the mid 14th century stood next to the steps leading to Corvisers' Row.[1] By 1334 Vale Royal owned 15 shops and a burgage in Chester, all apparently on a single site, and at least one of the shops was held by a corviser or shoemaker.[2] The connexion with Corvisers' Row is clear. It seems likely, therefore, that the Row existed in the 1270s when the Shoemakers' Selds were first recorded. Almost certainly it was linked with Saddlers' Row further south, which contained shops belonging to the Erneys family in 1342 and perhaps as early as 1293, and was evidently associated with their seld near the common hall.[3]

The selds declined and virtually disappeared after the earlier 14th century, although the structure on the corner of Bridge Street and Watergate Street continued to be known as the Stone Seld and later as the Staven Seld.[4]

'Porches' and Stallboards

In the earliest Row buildings the walkway was apparently flush with the frontage. Soon, however, the trading space within the galleries was extended by the addition of stallboards between the walkways and the street fronts, normally sloping gently up from the walkway side and used for the display of merchandise. Stallboards appear to have developed as the roofs of light lean-to timber shelters or 'porches' (*porcheria*) added at the front of the undercrofts.[5] Though such

structures nowhere survived in 2000, their existence may be inferred from the fact that in many cases the side walls below the stallboards were then predominantly of 18th- and 19th-century brickwork.[6] Stallboards supported by a stone porch in substantial townhouses such as nos. 38–42 Watergate Street were not apparently part of the original construction.

As early as 1293 indictments were made regarding the erection of obstructions to the public highway, including both steps and shelters. The 'porches' then erected by Hugh of Brickhill in front of four vacant houses in Bakers' Row in Eastgate Street represented an early example of encroachment large enough to support stallboards. Although the structures were initially condemned as injurious to the highway, commercial pressures were such that ultimately they were accepted by the authorities.[7]

Land annexed from the highway for porches was deemed to be still in public ownership. In 1508, for example, the Staven Seld at the corner of Bridge Street and Watergate Street was fronted by narrow strips of land which belonged separately to the mayor, sheriffs, and citizens of Chester.[8] In Bridge Street the strip was 2½ 'virgates' (2.3 m.)[9] wide and *c.* 18⅝ virgates (17 m.) long, dimensions which correspond with the length of the street frontage of the seld and the width of the pre-19th-century stallboard above. In Watergate Street, where the corresponding dimensions were 2 virgates

1 Ibid.; cf. *Ledger-Bk. of Vale Royal Abbey*, ed. J. Brownbill (R.S.L.C. lxviii), 131.

2 *Ledger-Bk. of Vale Royal*, 113.

3 C.C.A.L.S., DVE 1/CII/21; ibid. ZCHD 2/7; Morris, *Chester*, 250–1.

4 B.L. Add. Ch. 50152; P.R.O., CHES 25/1, m. 3; *Ches. Chamb. Accts.* 74; *P.N. Ches.* v (1:i), 23.

5 e.g. P.R.O., CHES 25/1.

6 e.g. nos. 19 and 37 Watergate St., 22 Northgate St., and 28 Eastgate St.

7 P.R.O., CHES 25/1.

8 C.C.A.L.S., ZCHD 2/7.

9 From the context *virgata* clearly meant a yard rather than a rod.

(1.8 m.) and 21½ virgates (19.7 m.), it may be significant that the medieval frontage lay 2.4 m. back from the modern line.[1]

The strips which fronted the Staven Seld had probably long been in civic hands. In 1356 the mayor and citizens owned a plot of land, 2 ells (2.3 m.) wide and 3 ells (3.4 m.) long, lying next to the steps leading to Corvisers' Row.[2] It thus appears that between the 1290s and the mid 14th century the local authorities abandoned their attempts to prohibit the extension of Row properties into the highway in the four main streets, but retained ownership of the land encroached on. Already in the late 13th century the encroachers included such leading citizens as Hugh of Brickhill. Perhaps Edward I's charter of 1300, in granting jurisdiction over Crown pleas to the mayor and bailiffs and licensing the citizens to build on vacant sites, removed any final constraint on the process, or at least allowed the civic community, as opposed to the king's representative, to charge rent for encroachments.[3]

The local use of the term *tabula* throws further light on the early development of stallboards. Though it could mean simply a trestle or stall, it was also applied in Chester to more permanent structures.[4] In 1355, for example, one holding included a tenement and two undercofts, a quarter share of a seld, a shop, and another undercroft and *tabula*,[5] the last evidently a fixture. In the mid 15th century one citizen paid the city 4*d.* a year rent for 'a certain piece of land under the *tabula*' of another.[6] It is unlikely that any use would have been found for a small piece of land under another man's stall. If, however, the *tabula* was a stallboard the rent may have been for the strip of ground below it at street level. In 1445 the same tenant was paying an identical rent for a piece of waste ground in Bridge Street flanked by undercrofts and between the house frontages and the highway. Very probably it was the same property.[7] Many of the *tabulae* were located in Bridge Street and several were expressly linked with selds.[8] Perhaps, therefore, the *tabulae* were at first newly developed structures in front of the selds for the display of cloth at Row level, possibly at fair time when commercial space was at a premium.[9]

Row Walkway

The ambiguous origins and legal status of stallboards and the land beneath them have parallels in the Row walkway itself. It began as private property and continued to be deemed an appurtenance of the property through which it passed. Nevertheless, it eventually attained the status of right of way under the control of the civic authorities. How and when that control was acquired is not clear. By the mid 14th century the Row in the Buttershops was regarded as a highway (*alta via*), and thus perhaps as public.[10] No civic regulations relating to the Rows survive before the early 17th century, when it was accepted that the owner needed the corporation's permission for any action which impeded access or caused obstruction to the Row walkway.[11] Possibly such regulation had been imposed in the earlier 16th century, when mayors such as Henry Gee were much concerned to define and codify civic custom and law.[12]

MEDIEVAL EXTENT AND APPEARANCE

There was relatively little building within the city centre in the later 14th and 15th century.[13] Where there was reconstruction, as at Leche House (no. 17 Watergate Street) in the late 15th century, or the Old King's Head (nos. 48–50 Lower Bridge Street) in the mid 16th, the new buildings continued to contain a Row.[14] Probably, therefore, there were few additions to the Rows system, which may be assumed to have reached its full extent by *c.* 1350. Almost certainly by then the following areas, identified by their modern street names, contained substantial lengths of gallery.

Eastgate Street North

The stretches of Row on the north side of Eastgate Street were known variously as Dark Lofts (or Row), Buttershop Row, Bakers' Row, and Cooks' Row.[15] Buttershop Row overlapped with Bakers' Row by the early 14th century, and galleries extended as far east as St. Werburgh Street by the 15th.[16] Hardly any medieval structures survived in 2000, though a stone arch spanning the walkway was recorded at no. 31 (just west of St. Werburgh Street) *c.* 1840.[17]

1 *J.C.A.S.* lxix. 124.

2 C.C.A.L.S., ZCHD 2/1; above, this chapter: Physical Form (Selds).   3 Morris, *Chester*, 490–3.

4 This analysis of the use of the term 'stallboard' in Chester was contributed by Dr. Laughton. For further details see *Rows of Chester*, ed. Brown, 137.

5 P.R.O., SC 6/784/5, m. 5; SC 6/784/7, m. 4; SC 6/784/11, m. 4; Eaton Hall, Ch. 321; cf. *Blk. Prince's Reg.* iii. 305.

6 B.L. Harl. MS. 2158, f. 194v.

7 C.C.A.L.S., ZCHD 2/3.

8 Ibid. ZMR 1, m. 1; ZMR 3, m. 2d.

9 Cf. removal of wall to extend Hugh the tailor's holding: B.L. Add. Ch. 49997, 50004.

10 C.C.A.L.S., ZCHC 11/3–5.

11 A. M. Kennett, 'Rows in City Recs.' *J.C.A.S.* lxvii. 50–1;

below, this chapter: Rebuilding and Enclosure.

12 *V.C.H. Ches.* v (1), Later Medieval Chester: City Government and Politics, 1350–1550 (Henry Gee and Reform of Civic Government).

13 *Rows of Chester*, ed. Brown, 63–75; pers. comm. Dr. Laughton; *V.C.H. Ches.* v (1), Topography, 900–1914: Later Medieval (Building Activity, 1400–1550).

14 *J.C.A.S.* lxix. 138–9; *Rows of Chester*, ed. Brown, 63–75.

15 Dark Lofts (1488): C.C.A.L.S., ZCHC 11/12; Buttershop Row: 3 *Sheaf,* xxxvi, p. 34; Bakers' Row: P.R.O., CHES 25/1; Cooks' Row (*c.* 1330): C.C.A.L.S., ZMR 30; ibid. DVE 1/CII/8; B.L. Add. Ch. 50196.

16 R. M. Montgomery, 'Some Early Deeds relating to Land on North Side of Eastgate Street', *J.C.A.S.* xxii. 117–41, esp. 131.

17 *J.C.A.S.* xlv. 15.

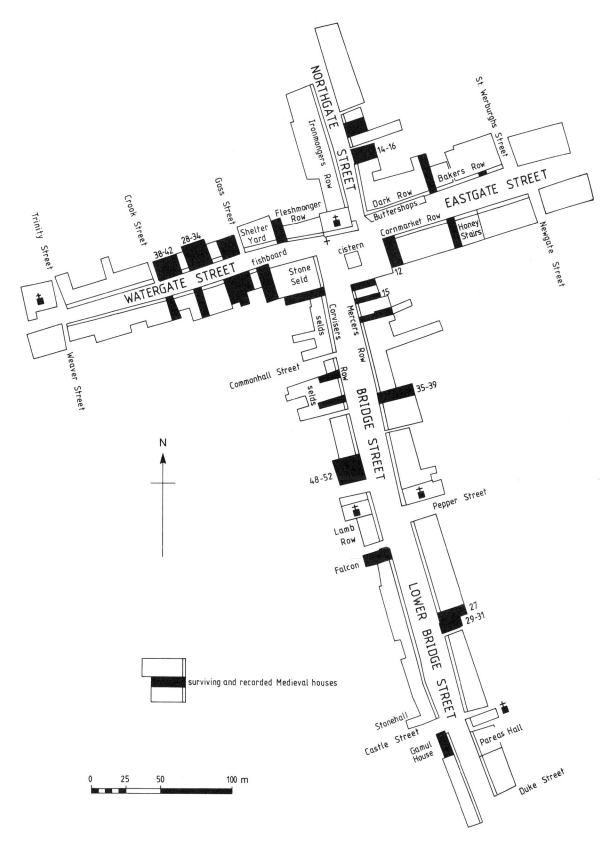

FIG. 143. *Probable extent of the Rows in the Middle Ages*

Eastgate Street South

Cornmarket Row was first mentioned in 1342,[1] and presumably ran through the complex of corn market, shops, kilns, and houses which existed by the 1270s.[2] A stone undercroft surviving in 2000 at no. 28, and two-centred chamfered arches shown in a 19th-century drawing as spanning the walkway at no. 32 were relics of the medieval Rows. Another stone-vaulted undercroft was recorded at no. 12 in 1855, but was later demolished.[3] The Row probably extended to Newgate Street; beyond that the walkway was presumably at street level, though in 1393 buildings with shops and undercrofts extended to the walls.[4]

Northgate Street West

Ironmongers' Row ran northwards from St. Peter's church to the market square by the late 13th century.[5]

Northgate Street East

Medieval undercrofts, surviving in 2000 only at no. 22, but formerly also at nos. 8 and 14–16, indicate that the Row extended northwards from the Buttershops to the market square.[6]

Watergate Street North

Fleshers' or Fleshmongers' Row ran westwards to Goss Street; beyond that the undercrofts and galleries at Booth Mansion (nos. 28–34) and at nos. 38–42 show that it continued at least to Crook Street, if not to Trinity Street. Medieval arches spanning the walkway at nos. 28–30 provide the earliest structural evidence of a gallery connecting adjacent holdings.[7]

Watergate Street South

The survival of a large number of medieval undercrofts, including three well built stone ones, suggests that the Row extended from the Cross at least to Weaver Street.[8]

Bridge Street West

Corvisers' or Shoemakers' Row ran south from the Cross through the Selds by the mid 14th century and probably by the 1270s.[9] Further south Saddlers' Row existed by *c.* 1300.[10] Undercrofts at nos. 12, 32, 36, and 48–52 suggest that the Rows ran along the full length of the street to Whitefriars.[11]

Bridge Street East

Medieval undercrofts at nos. 15 and 35–9 suggest that the Row extended south to Pepper Street. By the late 15th century it was called Mercers' Row.[12]

FIG. 144. *Terrace in front of St. Olave's, 1818*

Lower Bridge Street

South of the Two Churches (St. Bridget's on the west side of the street, facing St. Michael's on the east) there were certainly galleried buildings and perhaps Rows from an early date. In the 16th century Mercers' Row allegedly occupied the whole east side of Bridge Street from the Cross to Dee Bridge.[13] On the west side the Falcon (no. 6) still in 2000 contained a large medieval undercroft and early evidence of a gallery. In the early 19th century Lamb Row (nos. 2–4, since demolished) was also galleried.[14] Further south, where the street drops towards the river, there may have been a raised open walkway, such as that which still existed in 2000 at Gamul House (nos. 52–8), perhaps extending as far as Shipgate Street. On the east side medieval masonry has been noted at nos. 27 and 29–31. The Row probably ran to Duke Street, incorporating Richard the engineer's house. Some sections seem to have taken the form of a raised walkway with no oversailing buildings, such as the terrace which in 2000 survived in front of St. Olave's church (Fig. 144).[15]

Appearance

It is difficult to establish what the medieval Rows looked like. At Thun (Switzerland) there are first-floor walkways which are open and not oversailed by upper storeys, an arrangement similar to that which survived in 2000 on the west side of Lower Bridge Street and which may have disappeared from the eastern side only in the 19th century. In the city centre, however, in buildings such as nos. 28–30 Watergate Street, 48 Bridge Street, and 32 Eastgate

1 *P.N. Ches.* v (1:i), 22, citing C.C.A.L.S., DVE 1/CI/32.
2 P.R.O., E 315/47/139; WALE 29/272.
3 *J.C.A.S.* xlv. 12.
4 B.L. Add. Ch. 75179; cf. Add. Ch. 75154, 75202.
5 Above, this chapter: Origin and Early Development.
6 Ibid.; *J.C.A.S.* xlv. 15.   7 Above, this chapter: intro.
8 *J.C.A.S.* xlv. 19–23.

9 Above, this chapter: Physical Form (Selds).
10 Ibid.; *Ches. Chamb. Accts.* 74.
11 *J.C.A.S.* xlv. 2–6.
12 *P.N. Ches.* v (1:i), 21; Morris, *Chester*, 250.
13 *King's Vale Royal*, [i], 40. According to *P.N. Ches.* v (1:i), 21, Mercers' Row lay on the east side of Bridge St. only.
14 *J.C.A.S.* xlv. 6.   15 Ibid. 8–10.

Street, oversailing was clearly in place from the beginning, while similar arrangements were recorded in the 14th century in Ironmongers' Row in Northgate Street.[1]

Generally, it seems likely that the walkway was open at the front. In the earliest phases it probably overlooked the street, but by the later 13th century it was often separated from the street by an area for stalls or *tabulae*, a feature which originated in encroachment but was eventually an integral part of the structure.[2] In only one instance, the Dark Row, does the walkway seem to have been screened from the street by solid building, in the configuration preserved until the 1990s on the corner of Eastgate Street and Northgate Street. That it was unusual and made the Row notably ill-lit is indicated by the name.

REBUILDING AND ENCLOSURE, 1550–1850[3]

In the later 16th and early 17th century there was much rebuilding in the Rows, in particular of the superstructures above the undercrofts, the timber frames and elaborate frontages of which still survived in 2000 in considerable numbers. The new buildings continued to incorporate Row walkways, presumably because they remained commercially useful and because as earlier the upper storeys were in separate occupation from the undercrofts and therefore required independent access. Major projects included the rebuilding of the Buttershops and Dark Row in 1592,[4] and the new houses of Bishop Lloyd, Alderman John Aldersey, and the Mainwarings in Watergate Street.[5]

Although by then the Rows were under corporation control,[6] they continued in some sense to belong to the properties through which they passed, the owners of which were responsible for aspects of their maintenance, such as railings and stairways.[7] In the 1630s, for example, the corporation leased the Buttershops (or New Buildings) together with the Dark Row.[8]

The Rows remained an important and admired focus for trading. In the late 16th century William Smith praised the shops occupied by mercers, grocers, drapers, and haberdashers, to be found both at Row level and in the undercrofts; he was especially impressed by Mercers' Row which still apparently ran the full length of Bridge Street and Lower Bridge Street.[9] Elsewhere, however, undercrofts were used for storage, as workshops, and as taverns, and the best shops were at Row level.[10] By then, too, additional permanent retail structures were being created by the

FIG. 145. *Bishop Lloyd's House, Watergate Street*

enclosure of stallboards.[11] There was especial activity at fair time[12] and on market days; in the later 17th century, for example, the flax and linen market was often held in the Rows on Watergate Street or Bridge Street.[13]

Encroachment into the street in front of Row buildings continued to be licensed by the Assembly, whose income was increased by numerous small rents for the parlours, shops, and stairs thereby erected. Rent was also payable for extensions to upper storeys carried out over the street on posts. In the late 16th and early 17th century encroachments were especially numerous on the west side of Bridge Street.[14] By the mid 17th century they had a produced a notable rebuilding at nos. 22–6 (the Dutch Houses), timber-framed with two storeys above the Row adorned with twisted columns.

---

1 Above, this chapter: intro.; Origin and Early Development.
2 Above, this chapter: Physical Form ('Porches' and Stallboards).
3 Section based on *Rows of Chester*, ed. Brown, esp. 77–113.
4 C.C.A.L.S., ZAB 1, ff. 238, 240; Matthews and others, *Excavations at Chester: 3–15 Eastgate St.* 34.
5 3 *Sheaf*, xxxii, pp. 67–8; *J.C.A.S.* lxix. 140, 143.
6 *J.C.A.S.* lxvii. 50–3.

7 e.g. C.C.A.L.S., ZQSF 54, no. 39.
8 Ibid. ZCHD 3/14–16; *Cal. Chester City Cl. Mins. 1603–42*, 179.
9 *King's Vale Royal*, [i], 40.   10 Ibid. [ii], 19–20.
11 e.g. C.C.A.L.S., ZTAR 2/23.
12 e.g. ibid. ZAF 13/34.
13 Above, Markets: Wool, Flax, and Linen Markets.
14 e.g. C.C.A.L.S., ZAB 1, ff. 269, 337v., 338v.

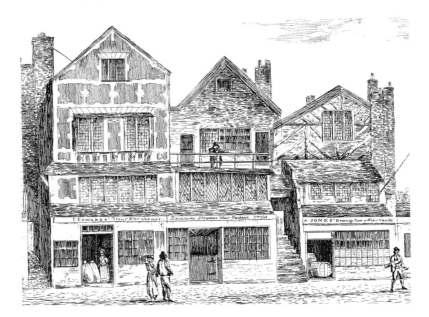

FIG. 146. *Enclosed Rows, Lower Bridge Street West, c. 1810*

Such developments radically changed the character of the Rows. The enclosure of stallboards darkened the Row itself and the rooms or shops which opened on to it, a development illustrated in 2000 by Tudor House (nos. 29–31 Lower Bridge Street). By the early 17th century there were already complaints that shops on stallboards were a nuisance which deprived legitimate Row traders of light, created shelter for 'lewd persons' at night, and were used as latrines.[1] Nevertheless, the process remained unchecked. By 1662 the Row walkways seem generally to have been flanked by shops on both sides,[2] and throughout the late 17th century there were frequent applications to build new shops and chambers in them.[3]

Stallboard enclosures perhaps encouraged a move away from the hall at Row level to the street chamber over the Row as the principal room in houses in the main streets. Especially fine examples survived in 2000 at Tudor House, no. 17 Eastgate Street, and Bishop Lloyd's House (no. 41 Watergate Street), the last with notable plasterwork.[4] There was also some development of a fourth or attic storey where rooms might be furnished with fireplaces and plaster ceilings.

The Rows' commercial function appears to have been greatly undermined between the mid 17th and the mid 18th century, a development marked by the enclosure of approximately a third of the walkways and their incorporation within private housing. Removal of the walkways was perhaps encouraged by their increasingly dark and noisome character and by extensive damage to Eastgate Street and Watergate Street through bombardment during the final stages of the siege in 1645.[5]

Enclosure was licensed by the Assembly and successful applicants had to pay a fine and an annual rent, charges later simplified into a single payment. The earliest known example occurred in 1643 when Sir Richard Grosvenor successfully petitioned to enclose a portion of the Row within his house at no. 6 Lower Bridge Street (in 2000 the Falcon Inn).[6] Nothing further was recorded until the 1660s, after which enclosure gathered momentum until the 1720s, petitioners often describing the Rows as useless, dangerous, or seldom used,[7] and occasionally as allowing disorder at night.[8] The greatest losses were in Lower Bridge Street, initially on the west side where a long section, running south from Grosvenor's house to Bridge House (nos. 18–24), had disappeared by 1687 (Fig. 146).[9] On the opposite side, enclosure began in 1700 at no. 51,[10] and between then and 1730 there were *c.* 20 further petitions for Bridge Street as a whole.[11]

In Watergate Street, too, enclosure began early, in the 1670s.[12] Although the Row was retained near the Cross even in such a major reconstruction as Booth Mansion (nos. 28–34),[13] further west there were many losses, with at least eight petitions to enclose between 1700 and 1745.[14] When in the mid 18th century the city began to oppose complete enclosure,[15] the Rows in Lower Bridge Street and in Watergate Street west of Crook Street on the north

1 C.C.A.L.S., ZAB 1, f. 342; ZAF 13/34; ZAF 14/22; cf. ibid. ZQSF 27, no. 131.

2 T. Fuller, *Worthies of Eng.* (1840 edn.), i. 290.

3 e.g. C.C.A.L.S., ZAB 2, ff. 180v., 192–4.

4 *J.C.A.S.* lxix. 140.

5 Morris, *Siege of Chester*, 204–5.

6 C.C.A.L.S., ZAB 2, f. 64.

7 e.g. ibid. ZAB 3, ff. 124v., 191, 208v.

8 Ibid. ZAB 4, f. 128.

9 e.g. ibid. ZAB 2, ff. 160 and v., 180v.

10 Ibid. ZAB 3, f. 75v.

11 Ibid. ff. 112, 113v., 124v., 160v., 185v., 192 and v., 198, 232, 241v.–242, 244, 247v., 258, 265; ZAB 4, ff. 3v., 12.

12 e.g. ibid. ZAB 2, f. 180v.

13 *J.C.A.S.* lxix. 142.

14 C.C.A.L.S., ZAB 3, ff. 97, 114, 150v., 192v., 208v., 209v.–210, 226; cf. ZAB 4, f. 76.

15 e.g. ibid. ZAB 4, ff. 66v., 95v.–96, 99v., 128, 130v., 138, 149.

FIG. 147. *Uniform frontages, Eastgate Street North, c. 1810*

side and Weaver Street on the south had almost entirely disappeared.

Although there were some early petitions for Northgate Street, few were implemented and the Row on the west side remained intact.[1] In Eastgate Street, the city's main commercial centre, the process began later and was generally resisted by the Assembly, although there were a few enclosures, usually for shops.[2]

Except in Lower Bridge Street, there were few complete rebuildings in the Rows in the later 17th and early 18th century. Much more common was the refronting of premises. The Assembly was often petitioned for permission to move forward the boundaries of properties on the main streets,[3] sometimes to fence front plots,[4] but mostly to enable them to push out the front walls of houses by a few feet,[5] to make them level and uniform with those adjoining.[6] On at least some occasions the reconstructed frontages were of brick with a first-floor colonnade to light the Row walkway.[7]

Permission to enclose declined from the mid 18th century and virtually disappeared after 1770. Although as a result no substantial new houses were built, in the late 18th and early 19th century renewal of frontages continued. Gradually the Row walkway came once again to be regarded as a desirable feature. Cast-iron columns were introduced, and by the early 19th century Row openings were heightened when the buildings

behind and above them were rebuilt. The stallboard structures, which darkened and obstructed the Rows and about which the Assembly had become concerned by the 1760s,[8] were largely removed in the early 19th century.[9] With the appointment of additional constables in 1815 and the introduction of gas lighting in 1818, the Rows were set to become once more respectable. In 1828, when William Brown built his grand store in Eastgate Street, the stone frontage in the Greek revival style incorporated a well lit Row walkway.[10] By then the Rows from the Royal Hotel on the south side of Eastgate Street to St. Michael's church on the east side of Bridge Street contained the best shops and formed a fashionable promenade.[11] Maintenance was further enhanced with the establishment of an improvement committee under the terms of the Chester Improvement Act of 1845. By 1847 the committee was requiring owners to repair the steps giving access from the street to the walkways.[12]

RECONSTRUCTION AND CONSERVATION, 1850–2000[13]

By the mid 19th century the Rows had become an antiquarian attraction and the Chester Archaeological Society was recommending that they be preserved and where necessary reconstructed with appropriate timber-framed buildings.[14] They were also highly

1 Cf. ibid. ZAB 2, f. 193v.

2 Ibid. ZAB 3, ff. 180, 237v., 285 and v.; ZAB 4, ff. 34, 36.

3 Ibid. ZAB 3–4, *passim.*

4 e.g. ibid. ZAB 3, ff. 143, 155, 239v., 242v., 252; ZAB 4, f. 134; cf. ZAB 4, f. 132v.

5 e.g. ibid. ZAB 4, ff. 181v., 183v., 204.

6 e.g. ibid. ZAB 3, ff. 121v., 124v., 150v., 172, 185, 242 and v., 252v., 255 and v.; ZAB 4, ff. 3v., 25, 40v., 75, 85v., 118v., 137v., 187v.

7 Ibid. ZAB 3, f. 149; cf. ibid. f. 256v.; frontage of no. 21

Watergate St.

8 C.C.A.L.S., ZAB 4, ff. 257 and v., 336.

9 Hemingway, *Hist. Chester*, i. 387.

10 *Browns and Chester*, ed. H. D. Willcock, 38.

11 Hanshall, *Hist. Ches.* 286; Hemingway, *Hist. Chester*, i. 387.

12 C.C.A.L.S., ZCCB 47, p. 689.

13 This section based on *Rows of Chester*, ed. Brown, 114–30.

14 Anon. 'Street Archit. of Chester', *J.C.A.S.* [o.s.], i. 463–4; cf. ibid. N.s. i. 33–4.

FIG. 148. *Vernacular revival buildings, Eastgate Street South: nos. 36–38 by T. M. Penson, 1857 (right) and nos. 40–44 by W. T. Lockwood, 1912 (left)*

prized for their picturesqueness by the increasing number of tourists whom Chester attracted.[1] Early examples of Row buildings in the revived vernacular style survived in 2000 at nos. 36–8 Eastgate Street and 40 and 51–3 Bridge Street, the first designed by T. M. Penson in 1857, the others by James Harrison in 1858.

Antiquarian interest was accompanied by a desire for conservation, first expressed over no. 9 Watergate Street (God's Providence House) in 1861.[2] Although that building was in fact completely rebuilt, something of the style of its former frontage was preserved. By then the stone-vaulted crypt at no. 28 Eastgate Street had been preserved and incorporated by Penson in an otherwise High Victorian Gothic building for Browns department store. Despite such developments the early fabric of the Rows continued to be eroded. A major loss was the stone-vaulted and aisled undercroft at no. 12 Bridge Street, demolished in 1861 despite a campaign by the Chester Archaeological Society for its preservation.[3] A further setback, again accomplished against public opposition, was the destruction of the Row at the east end of Eastgate Street North to make way in 1860 for the Chester Bank, a large stone building with a pediment and Corinthian columns.

Other relatively modest buildings of the 17th and 18th century were swept away during the full flowering of the vernacular revival led by the local architects John Douglas and T. M. Lockwood.[4] Such work was usually thorough in its replacement of all that had gone before. Notable achievements included Lockwood's work at

the Cross: the half-timbered no. 1 Bridge Street with its domed turret, built in 1888, and the brick and timber nos. 2–4 Bridge Street built opposite it in 1892.[5] Even more important was the reconstruction of Shoemakers' Row on the west side of Northgate Street, where a group of mainly 17th-century buildings had attracted low life and made the highway unduly narrow. The work was accomplished between 1897 and 1909, mostly to designs by Douglas, and although it did not incorporate an elevated walkway, the frontage preserved something of the character of the Rows, with a timber-framed arcade rising over low-set undercrofts or cellars.[6]

In 1909 W. T. and P. H. Lockwood, who had taken over their father's practice, rebelled against the prevailing half-timbered vernacular style and, under the patronage of the 2nd duke of Westminster, erected St. Michael's Row in Bridge Street, an incongruously bulky structure with a façade of white and gold Doulton tiles (Fig. 149). In 1911, however, in response to local protest, the duke, while professing his admiration for the building, personally paid for the façade to be replaced with the half-timbering deemed more appropriate. The tiles survived only on the ground floor and in the top-lit arcade of shops set behind and at right angles to the street frontage.[7]

The Lockwoods' experiment marked the end of a period of reconstruction within the Rows, when many new buildings were inserted, generally much larger than those which they replaced. Except in Shoemakers'

1 e.g. Henry James, *Transatlantic Sketches* (1875, repr. 1972), 12–13.

2 *J.C.A.S.* [o.s.], ii. 399, 405.

3 Ibid. 405, 410; n.s. xlv. 12.

4 *V.C.H. Ches.* v (1), Topography, 900–1914: Victorian and Edwardian (City Centre).

5 Harris, *Chester*, 49.

6 C.C.A.L.S., ZCCB 59, 11 Aug., 11 Nov. 1897; ZCCB 60, 14 June, 26 Sept. 1899; ZCCB 62, 13 July 1910; *Chester City Cl. Mins.* 1901/2, 184–5; E. Hubbard, *Work of John Douglas*, 272–3.

7 C.C.A.L.S., ZCCB 62, 2 June 1909; ZCCB 63, 15 Mar. 1911; *Chester Chron.* 17 Sept., 28 Oct. 1910.

FIG. 149. *St. Michael's Row as first built*

FIG. 150. *Nos. 55–61 Watergate Street*

Row they had all included a Row walkway, often made more convenient, with better lighting, more even floors, and improved steps from the street. The Rows system thus made a major contribution to the transformation of Eastgate Street, Bridge Street, and the southern end of Northgate Street into a modern shopping centre. Behind the improved frontages, however, the yards and rear buildings were until the 1930s crowded with much humbler workshops and residential buildings in insalubrious courts reached by narrow passageways from the Rows.[1]

Although the department stores in Eastgate Street continued to be enlarged between 1910 and the 1930s, no significant additions were made to the buildings within the Rows until the 1960s.[2]

In the early 1960s the insertion of the Grosvenor shopping precinct behind the Rows in Bridge Street East and Eastgate Street South greatly extended the retailing area to which the Rows gave access. In Water-

gate Street, until then relatively little altered, a medieval undercroft was lost to make way for Refuge House, and nos. 55–61 were replaced with a concrete brutalist building by Bradshaw, Rowse, and Harker of Liverpool (Fig. 150). Although that structure incorporated a Row, another new building of the period at nos. 42–8 Northgate Street did not.[3] A further replacement of Row buildings in modern materials took place at nos. 14–20 Watergate Street in 1970.

With the publication of the Insall Report in 1968, a number of dilapidated Row buildings including the Dutch Houses, Bishop Lloyd's House, and the Falcon were repaired. In 1988 a new building by Robin Clayton, of brick with a gabled façade, was erected at no. 12 Watergate Street, and in the early 1990s the Dark Row on the corner of Eastgate Street and Northgate Street was reconstructed by the Biggins Sargent Partnership, a development notable for its expansion of the Rows system.[4]

1 *V.C.H. Ches.* v (1), Topography, 900–1914: Victorian and Edwardian (Residential Development: The Courts); Twentieth-Century Chester: Housing and Suburban Development, 1918–39.

2 What follows based on *Rows of Chester*, ed. Brown, 131–4.
3 Cf. *Chester Chron.* 15 July 1964.
4 Matthews and others, *Excavations at Chester: 3–15 Eastgate St.* 69.

SITES AND REMAINS OF MEDIEVAL RELIGIOUS HOUSES

BENEDICTINE NUNNERY

Founded in the mid 12th century initially in Handbridge, the nunnery obtained its site in the Crofts north-west of the castle from Earl Ranulph II (d. 1153).[1] The stone-walled precinct formed an irregular quadrilateral extending north from the castle ditch to

Arderne Lane (later Black Friars), between Nuns Lane (Castle Esplanade) on the east and the city walls on the west.[2] The early conventual buildings were probably modest since the priory was never rich.[3] By the late Middle Ages they comprised the church of St. Mary in the centre of the precinct, the cloister to its south, a small inner court to the south-west, and a larger outer

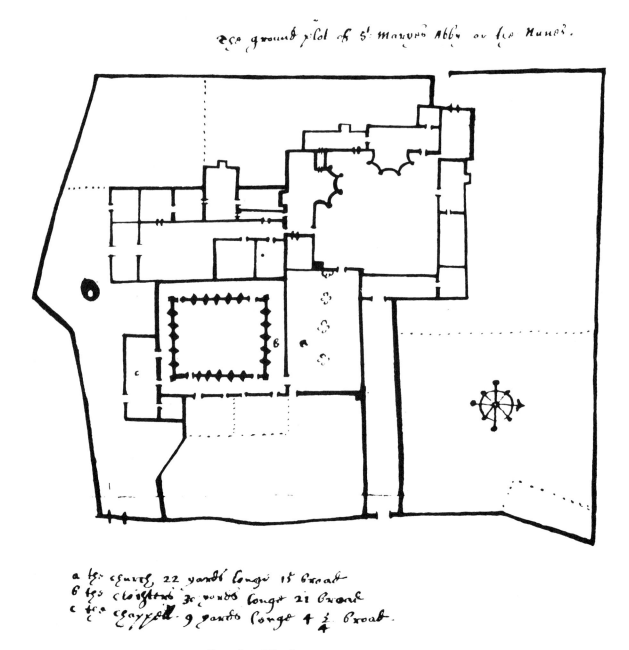

FIG. 151. *Nunnery, Randle Holme III's plan*

1 *Charters of A.-N. Earls*, pp. 110–12 (nos. 97–8).

2 B.L. Harl. MS. 7568, f. 140; S. W. Ward, *Excavations at Chester: Lesser Medieval Religious Houses, Sites Investigated 1964–*

83, 3, 10–11; *P.N. Ches.* v (1:i), 27, 37; Morris, *Chester*, 256.

3 W. F. Irvine, 'Notes on Hist. of St. Mary's Nunnery, Chester', *J.C.A.S.* xiii. 70; *V.C.H. Ches.* iii. 146–50.

FIG. 152. *Nunnery, remains, 1727*

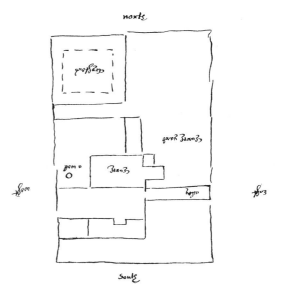

FIG. 153. *Franciscan friary, Randle Holme III's plan*

court to the north-west. Access was by a walled lane from a gate in Nuns Lane. South of the lane and east of the church was the graveyard.[1]

The buildings were predominantly late 13th- or early 14th-century in date,[2] but when the site was cleared in the early 19th century Romanesque and 15th-century architectural fragments were also found.[3] The church consisted of a chancel and a nave divided from a north aisle by an arcade of four piers dating from the 13th or 14th century, and was used for many burials.[4] In the early 15th century it contained at least 13 altars.[5] Outside, or perhaps over the western door, was the 'Jerusalem', from which anthems were sung during the Palm Sunday procession.[6]

The cloisters were being reconstructed in the 1520s.[7] On the south side they included a structure which probably served as the frater.[8] The smaller courtyard, which included the west cloister range, perhaps housed the prioress's lodgings, while the larger probably contained service buildings and guest accommodation.[9]

After the dissolution of the nunnery in 1540 the site was granted to Urian Brereton, whose descendants occasionally lived there.[10] The outer court seems to have been adapted for residential use by the addition of two large pentagonal bays, probably windows similar to those built at Little Moreton Hall in 1559.[11] The

mansion was pillaged by royalist soldiers in 1643 and never restored.[12] There was little on the site by the early 18th century, and it was transformed into a lawn in the early 19th.[13] An arch flanked by sections of wall adorned with niches was removed *c.* 1840 and eventually installed in Grosvenor Park, where it remained in 2000.[14]

The county police headquarters was opened on the site in 1967.[15]

FRANCISCAN FRIARY

Established in Chester in 1237 or 1238, the Grey Friars obtained royal approval in 1240 to build on a site in the Crofts extending north from Watergate Street roughly to Little Parsons and Dog Lanes (near the later Bedward Row) and west from Crofts Lane (later Linenhall Street and St. Martin's Way) to the city walls.[16] The rectangular precinct eventually occupied 7 a. and was surrounded by a wall which on the west ran inside the city walls.[17] Access was by a gatehouse at the south end of Crofts Lane.[18]

Henry III in 1245 allowed the community to take building stone from the castle ditch and to remove an

1 B.L. Harl. MS. 2073, f. 87; *Processional of Nuns of Chester*, ed. J. W. Legg (Henry Bradshaw Soc. xviii), 17; Ward, *Lesser Religious Houses*, 3, 9, 11–12; *P.N. Ches.* v (1:i), 37.

2 S. and N. Buck, *NW. View of Chester Castle* (1727); Ward, *Lesser Religious Houses*, 8, 12.

3 Ormerod, *Hist. Ches.* i. 347.

4 S. M. Rutland, 'St. Mary's Nunnery, Chester: Interim Report', *J.C.A.S.* lii. 26–32; Ward, *Lesser Religious Houses*, 4.

5 *Processional*, 7, 17; *J.C.A.S.* xiii. 86.

6 *Processional*, 5; Ward, *Lesser Religious Houses*, 13.

7 *Lancs. and Ches. Wills and Inventories*, ii (Chetham Soc. [o.s.], li), 7.

8 B.L. Harl. MS. 2073, f. 87; Ward, *Lesser Religious Houses*, 13.

9 Ward, *Lesser Religious Houses*, 11, 13.

10 *V.C.H. Ches.* iii. 149; *Medieval Arch., Art, and Archit. in Chester*, ed. A. Thacker, 154.

11 Ward, *Lesser Religious Houses*, 13.

12 B.L. Harl. MS. 2125, f. 134; Harl. MS. 1944, f. 98v.; Morris, *Siege of Chester*, 204.

13 Buck, *NW. View of Chester Castle*; Ormerod, *Hist. Ches.* i. 347, 359.

14 *V.C.H. Ches.* iii. 149–50; Ward, *Lesser Religious Houses*, 8.

15 Above, Law and Order: Policing.

16 *V.C.H. Ches.* iii. 171–2; J. H. E. Bennett, 'Grey Friars of Chester', *J.C.A.S.* xxiv. 11–16, 59–62; *P.N. Ches.* v (1:i), 36.

17 Ward, *Lesser Religious Houses*, 197–8; *J.C.A.S.* xxiv. 60–4; J. Speed, *Theatre of Empire of G.B.* (1611), plan of Chester; below, this chapter: Dominican Friary.

18 Morris, *Chester*, 256; *J.C.A.S.* xxiv. 61.

inconvenient lane.[1] The friars extended the precinct in order to enlarge their domestic buildings in 1332 and 1360.[2] By the late Middle Ages the church was *c.* 60 m. long, with north and south aisles, a transept, and a tower with a spire.[3] One burial is recorded within it, that of Robert Grosvenor in 1286.[4] Bequests were made for the repair of the church in the 1520s, when considerable work may have been done.[5] By 1528, however, the friars had clearly abandoned the nave, which was being used for the storage of sails and tools belonging to the city's merchants and sailors.[6]

The church lay on the south side of the precinct with the cloister to its north. A second courtyard north of the cloister may have included the infirmary, the east range of which abutted the friars' dormitory.[7] West of the church stood a house called the 'ostrye', a kitchen, and other chambers.[8] To the east were more chambers and the graveyard, and to the south a further range of buildings, perhaps the brewhouse and bakery.[9] Much of the rest of the precinct was occupied by orchards, pasture, and gardens, the western third forming a walled space later known as Grey Friars' croft or Yacht field.[10]

The friary was dissolved in 1538 and the site was sold first to Richard Hough in 1540 and again with the other friaries to John Cocks in 1544. Thereafter it passed to the Duttons, Warburtons, and finally in 1622 to the Stanleys of Alderley, who retained it until 1775. It is not clear whether it was ever occupied. By the time of the Civil War the buildings seem to have been ruinous, only the crossing tower certainly surviving.[11] In 1775 the site was again sold. The New Linenhall was built on the eastern half in 1778,[12] and in the 1780s Stanley Place, Stanley Street, and Watergate Flags were built on the remainder.[13]

DOMINICAN FRIARY

The Dominicans were settled in Chester by 1237 or 1238,[14] receiving a site in the Crofts of 5½ a., bounded by Watergate Street to the north, the later Nicholas Street to the east, Arderne Lane (later Black Friars) to the south, and the city walls to the west.[15] In its final form the precinct was divided by a substantial internal wall running east–west, presumably between the conventual buildings and the orchards and gardens.[16] The main entrance was by a gate in Nicholas Street giving on to an alley which crossed the precinct to a lesser western gate.[17]

A chapel dedicated to St. Nicholas apparently stood on the site in the 1220s, and was perhaps taken over as the friary church, which had the same dedication.[18] The church lay in the centre-west of the site with the main claustral range to the south. A further range of buildings lay to the north, perhaps an outer court entered from the alley.[19]

The conventual buildings may have been complete by 1276, when licence was obtained for a piped water supply.[20] The first church, a simple rectangle, was retained as the choir when in the late 13th or early 14th century a large nave with aisles, *c.* 30 m. long with seven bays, was added perhaps together with a transept and north-west tower.[21] Later a central tower was built over the crossing, the nave was shortened by one bay, and the north-west tower was removed. Those alterations were perhaps made in the mid 14th century, but floor tiles from the central tower are unlikely to pre-date 1400. In the later 15th century the crossing tower was removed and the choir widened, perhaps with the addition of an aisle. The nave was partially demolished in the early 16th century and foundations for a replacement were begun probably *c.* 1520. Work had apparently ceased before the Dissolution with the construction of a temporary retaining wall. Numerous interments took place in the nave and aisles throughout the Middle Ages. They included some children and a few women, but were mostly men, placed in the best positions at the eastern end of the nave aisles.[22]

In the mid 1520s Ralph Egerton left money for

1 *V.C.H. Ches.* iii. 171–2; *J.C.A.S.* xxiv. 16, 19–20; *Close R. 1237–42*, 171; *1242–7*, 339, 408; *Cal. Lib. 1240–5*, 68; *1245–51*, 6, 140.

2 *Cal. Pat. 1330–4*, 360; *Blk. Prince's Reg.* iii. 386; *J.C.A.S.* xxiv. 20–1.

3 *J.C.A.S.* xxiv. 33, 70–4.   4 Ibid. 72–3.

5 *Lancs. and Ches. Wills and Inventories*, i (Chetham Soc. [o.s.], xxxiii), 17; ii (Chetham Soc. [o.s.], li), 7.

6 *J.C.A.S.* xxiv. 29.

7 Ibid. 38, 59–70, 77–8; *V.C.H. Ches.* iii. 173; B.L. Harl. MS. 2073, f. 92/2; Ward, *Lesser Religious Houses*, 198–200.

8 *J.C.A.S.* xxiv. 37, 76–9.

9 Ibid. 38, 78; B.L. Harl. MS. 2073, f. 92/3; Ward, *Lesser Religious Houses*, 200–1.

10 *J.C.A.S.* xxiv. 62–5, 69–70; T. Pennant, *Tours in Wales* (1883 edn.), i. 236.

11 e.g. Speed, *Theatre of Empire of G.B.* plan of Chester; W. Hollar, *Ground Plot of Chester* (1585), printed in *King's Vale Royal*, [i], between pp. 36–7.

12 *J.C.A.S.* xxiv. 35–50, 63–5; Ward, *Lesser Religious Houses*,

197; above, Fairs.

13 *V.C.H. Ches.* v (1), Topography, 900–1914: Early Modern and Georgian (Residential Development, 1760–1840).

14 Ibid. iii. 174; J. H. E. Bennett, 'Black Friars of Chester', *J.C.A.S.* xxxix. 30–1; C. F. R. Palmer, 'Friars Preachers of Chester', *Reliquary*, xxiii. 97.

15 Ward, *Lesser Religious Houses*, 23, 63; *J.C.A.S.* xxxix. 32–3; *P.N. Ches.* v (1:i), 35.

16 Ward, *Lesser Religious Houses*, 63.

17 Ibid. 61; *J.C.A.S.* xxxix. 39; B.L. Harl. MS. 7568, f. 123.

18 3 *Sheaf*, xlvi, pp. 14–15, 22, 24–5; *P.N. Ches.* v (1:i), 35; *Cart. Chester Abbey*, i, p. 210; ii, pp. 301–2; J. Brownbill, *Cal. of Deeds and Papers of Moore Fam.* (R.S.L.C. lxvii), p. 146.

19 Ward, *Lesser Religious Houses*, 71–2.

20 Ibid. 60; *J.C.A.S.* xxxix. 44–5; *Cal. Pat. 1272–81*, 165; above, Public Utilities: Water.

21 Rest of para. based on Ward, *Lesser Religious Houses*, esp. 63–70.

22 Ward, *Lesser Religious Houses*, esp. 120–6; cf. *V.C.H. Ches.* iii. 176; *Reliquary*, xxiii. 99; C.C.A.L.S., ZMR 42.

FIG. 154. *Stanley Palace in 1867*

rebuilding the frater,[1] probably as part of an intended complete reconstruction of the cloisters. Only the southern and eastern ranges were standing at the Dissolution. The northern walk had perhaps been taken down with the nave. The western range, if it ever existed, must have been small, because of the position of the church, and the cellarer's range, guest houses, and service buildings usually to be found there were perhaps instead located in the unusually elongated eastern range or in an outer court.[2]

At the Dissolution the buildings included the 'old hall', the choir of the conventual church, the vestry, chapter house, two 'cloisters' (probably meaning two ranges of a single cloister), frater, dorter, several chambers, kitchen, buttery, and old buttery.[3] Three houses with gardens stood west of the church against the precinct wall.[4] Much of the rest of the precinct was occupied by a graveyard, probably for the brethren, east of the church, another graveyard for the laity to its south-west, and by orchards and gardens within the open area to the north.[5]

The friary was dissolved in 1538. In 1543 the main buildings were leased to Thomas Smith and Richard Sneyd, and in 1544 the entire site was sold to John Cocks.[6] In 1561 it passed to the Duttons and thereafter presumably to the Warburtons, reputed builders of the late 16th-century timber-framed house at the north-east corner of the precinct afterwards called Stanley Palace. The site later passed to the Stanleys of Alderley, who retained at least the eastern half until *c.* 1780.[7] By the early 17th century most of the friary buildings had been demolished, though the gate in Nicholas Street survived.[8] In 1745 the principal houses on the site were those of Mr. Smith in the south-west corner, and Sir Richard Brooke on the Watergate Street frontage west of Stanley Palace. Between lay extensive gardens reached by a lane perhaps on the line of the medieval alley.[9] Smith's house, later known as Grey Friars House, survived in 2000, a low two-storeyed building dating largely from the late 17th century but incorporating timber framing perhaps of the 16th.[10] Brooke's house was entirely replaced by Watergate House, built in 1820 by Thomas Harrison for Henry Potts.[11]

In the early 1780s the Stanleys and the architect

---

1 *T.H.S.L.C.* lxix. 110.

2 *J.C.A.S.* xxxix. 41, 53–4; Ward, *Lesser Religious Houses,* 70–3.

3 *V.C.H. Ches.* iii. 175; *J.C.A.S.* xxxix. 39–42, 93.

4 *J.C.A.S.* xxxix. 51, 53; Ward, *Lesser Religious Houses,* 63.

5 *J.C.A.S.* xxxix. 50–1, 53.

6 Ibid. 51–4; *V.C.H. Ches.* iii. 175.

7 *Reliquary,* xxiii. 103; Ormerod, *Hist. Ches.* i. 349; deeds in

custody of principal librarian, Ches. Co. Cl. Information and Record Services.

8 B.L. Harl. MS. 7568, f. 123; Ward, *Lesser Religious Houses,* 73.

9 Ward, *Lesser Religious Houses,* 72; Lavaux, *Plan of Chester; J.C.A.S.* xxxix. 35.   10 Ward, *Lesser Religious Houses,* 72.

11 H. Colvin, *Biographical Dictionary of Brit. Architects* (1978), 398; Hemingway, *Hist. Chester,* ii. 9–10.

Joseph Turner developed the eastern part of the site; a long Georgian terrace was erected on Nicholas Street, with a mews behind.[1] By the early 19th century Smith's Walk (later Grey Friars) had been laid out south of the earlier lane to provide access to the large house then belonging to Capt. Wrench.[2]

CARMELITE FRIARY

The Carmelites, first recorded in Chester in 1277,[3] were granted seven messuages by Hugh Payn 'in a suburb of Chester' in 1290 on which to build a convent and church.[4] It has usually been assumed that the land was in White Friars Lane, but 'suburb' is an unlikely description for that area, and the messuages were in St. John's parish and probably lay with the donor's lands in the eastern suburbs around the Bars.[5] Either the grant, which involved the friars in litigation, was not implemented or else the messuages were exchanged.

By the 1290s the community was established near White Friars Lane and Berward Lane (later Weaver Street), and in the time of Abbot Thomas Birchills (1291–1323) the precinct extended to Pierpoint Lane.[6] In 1350 the friars acquired and enclosed two lanes, one north of the friary, running towards Berwards Lane, and the other west, running from a barn towards White Friars Lane.[7] More land adjacent to the precinct was added in 1354.[8] The precinct eventually measured almost 80 m. from north to south and 120 m. from east to west, extending from White Friars Lane to Commonhall Lane, and from Berward or Alban Lane to the rear boundaries of houses on Bridge Street.[9]

There was much building activity in the mid 14th century,[10] and in 1495 the tower was rebuilt and adorned with a spire.[11] The conventual church of St. Mary lay at the eastern end of White Friars Lane.[12] At the Dissolution it included an entrance porch, a vestry, and a chancel furnished with five altars, three alabaster retables, and two organs, the greater over the doorway into the choir.[13] By the mid 14th century the church

was used for burials,[14] becoming especially popular in the early 16th century.[15]

The cloisters and conventual buildings presumably lay north of the church. At the Dissolution the dorter, reredorter, and prior's chamber probably occupied the east range, and the kitchen and frater the north range.[16] The graveyard perhaps lay east of the east range, and an outer court stood to the west with a gateway opening on to White Friars Lane.[17] There may also have been a gateway on Commonhall Lane.[18]

A barn once in the possession of the early 14th-century sheriff Gilbert Dunfoul had apparently been acquired by the friars before 1350.[19] It lay in the north-west corner of the precinct,[20] and parts of its walls and plan were preserved in the house called the Friary, which dates mainly from the late 17th and 18th century, with mostly 18th-century interiors and a south range rebuilt early in the 19th century. Within and adjoining the precinct there were other buildings, orchards, and gardens.[21] They included a house used by the Carpenters' guild for storing the props for their play.[22]

The friary was dissolved in 1538.[23] Its holdings passed in 1544 to Fulk Dutton, and a house, known as White Friars, was built on part of the site.[24] Thereafter the friary passed in 1583 to Edmund Gamull and in 1593 to Thomas Egerton, who in 1597 demolished the church to make way for a new building.[25] The site remained in the hands of Egerton's descendants until the later 18th century.[26] From the 1540s it appears to have been divided into two, an eastern portion comprising the church and conventual buildings within St. Bridget's parish, and a western portion including the barn perhaps in St. Martin's. Dutton's house, apparently distinct from the convent itself, was probably built on the latter, and Egerton's on the former.[27] The site was still divided between two tenants in the 1660s. The western portion, known as White Friars or the Friars, was tenanted in 1667 by Giles Vanbrugh, father of Sir John, and in 1679 by Anthony Henthorn, both sugar bakers.[28] By 1781 the Henthorns' former house, in Weaver Street, was known as the Sugar House,[29]

1 Deeds in custody of principal librarian, Ches. Co. Cl. Information and Record Services; Hemingway, *Hist. Chester*, ii. 11; *J.C.A.S.* xxxix. 35; J. Hunter and S. Weston, *Plan of Chester* (1789); J. Wood, *Map of Chester* (1833).

2 Hemingway, *Hist. Chester*, i. 363; ii. 11.

3 *V.C.H. Ches.* iii. 176.

4 P.R.O., C 143/13, no. 17; J. H. E. Bennett, 'White Friars of Chester', *J.C.A.S.* xxxi. 7–8.

5 *V.C.H. Ches.* v (1), Topography, 900–1914: Later Medieval (Extramural and Suburban Development).

6 C.C.A.L.S., DVE 1/CI/4; *Cart. Chester Abbey*, ii, p. 469.

7 P.R.O., CHES 3/2, no. 4; *J.C.A.S.* xxxi. 11–12; Ward, *Lesser Religious Houses*, 207.

8 *Blk. Prince's Reg.* iii. 177–8.

9 Ward, *Lesser Religious Houses*, 207.

10 *V.C.H. Ches.* iii. 176; *Blk. Prince's Reg.* iii. 122; *J.C.A.S.* xxxi. 13–14.

11 *J.C.A.S.* xxxi. 44; *V.C.H. Ches.* iii. 176, citing B.L. Harl. MS. 2125, f. 31v.; cf. Ward, *Lesser Religious Houses*, 209.

12 G. Braun and F. Hohenberg, *Civitates Orbis Terrarum*, iii (1588), no. 3; Hollar, *Ground Plot of Chester* (1585); W. Thompson Watkin, *Roman Ches.* 147–8; B.L. Harl. MS. 2125, f. 45.

13 *J.C.A.S.* xxxi. 27, 44–5.

14 e.g. ibid. 11, 16–24; B.L. Harl. MS. 2063, f. 62v.; 3 *Sheaf*, xvii, pp. 69–70, 105; *Lancs. and Ches. Wills*, ii. 7; Morris, *Chester*, 147.

15 e.g. *J.C.A.S.* xxxi. 20, 23.   16 Ibid. 43–7.

17 Ibid. 208–9.   18 Ibid. [o.s.], iii. 488.

19 Ibid. n.s. xxxi. 11; below, Lists of Mayors and Sheriffs.

20 *J.C.A.S.* xxxi. 32.   21 Ibid. 27–8.

22 Ibid. 28–9, 52 n.; *REED: Chester*, 31.

23 *V.C.H. Ches.* iii. 177; *J.C.A.S.* xxxi. 24–7.

24 *J.C.A.S.* xxxi. 27–33.

25 Ibid. 32–40, 44; B.L. Harl. MS. 2125, f. 45.

26 *J.C.A.S.* xxxi. 36–9.

27 P.R.O., CHES 2/259, m. 1.   28 *J.C.A.S.* xxxi. 36–8.

29 *Broster's Dir. Chester* (1781), 40, 92.

FIG. 155. *Hospital of St. John the Baptist (Blue Coat school), 1891*

presumably the same as the Friary, on the site of the medieval barn. Egerton's house was perhaps on or near the site of Bank House, which in the late 18th century included a courtyard facing Commonhall Lane.[1] By 1830 it had entirely disappeared,[2] and buildings had been erected along the eastern end of White Friars Lane, on either side of Bollands Court.[3]

HOSPITAL OF ST. GILES

The leper hospital of St. Giles was probably founded in the mid 12th century.[4] It lay in Boughton on the south side of Christleton Road at the easternmost limits of the liberties. Nothing is known of its medieval buildings, but since it was favoured by Henry III and by the early 14th century had extensive privileges and properties within the city, they may well have been substantial.[5] Although not dissolved in 1547, it was utterly destroyed in 1643 when the chapel, barn, and other buildings were razed by the city's royalist garrison lest they offer shelter to the parliamentary forces.[6] All that remained in 2000 was the graveyard, closed in 1854, the burial place of royalists killed in 1644 and of victims of the cholera epidemic of the 1830s, and used in the early 19th century by St. John's parish.[7]

HOSPITAL OF ST. JOHN THE BAPTIST

The hospital outside the Northgate obtained confirmation of its site from Earl Ranulph III in the 1190s,[8] and by *c.* 1200 had a church and a burial ground.[9] It

occupied a long narrow strip immediately outside the town walls and ditch, extending 120 m. west from Upper Northgate Street. In 1241 the brethren were permitted to erect a chapel apparently in addition to their existing church.[10] In 1341 the church, chapel, and other buildings had inadequate roofs and two large houses had collapsed for want of maintenance.[11] By 1396 the buildings included a single chapel, and a hall and barns with a chamber for the chief priest and administrator;[12] in 1414 there was also a garden.[13]

The hospital was not dissolved in 1547 and remained an extra-parochial place, within which the chapel, known as Little St. John's, exercised parochial functions until 1967.[14] In the early 17th century another building housed six poor widows, each with two rooms and a garden.[15] All the stone buildings, including the chapel and the precinct wall, were razed to the ground in 1644 by the city's garrison as a defensive measure.[16] Under the wardenship of Colonel Roger Whitley (1660–97) the hospital was reputedly rebuilt.[17] By 1703 the corporation had regained control and in 1715–17 the old chapel was taken down and new buildings erected. The main block, which housed the newly founded Blue Coat school, was paid for by private subscription. The corporation paid for the south wing housing the chapel, a rear courtyard containing almshouses, and the north wing containing the schoolmaster's house, which was added in 1730. When complete the building formed an open three-sided court facing Upper Northgate Street. The chapel,

1 *J.C.A.S.* xxxi. 44; B.L. Harl. MS. 2125, f. 45; J. Hunter and S. Weston, *Plan of Chester* (1789); T. Pennant, *Tours in Wales* (1883 edn.), i. 217.

2 Hemingway, *Hist. Chester*, ii. 148.

3 J. Hunter and S. Weston, *Plan of Chester* (1789); *P.N. Ches.* v (1:i), 10; Pennant, *Tours in Wales*, i. 235.

4 *Charters of A.-N. Earls*, pp. 202–3, 222–3, 236 (nos. 198, 222, 236).   5 *V.C.H. Ches.* iii. 178.

6 Ibid. 179; B.L. Harl. MS. 1944, ff. 98–9; Harl. MS. 2125, f. 135.

7 Inscription at graveyard; above, Public Utilities: Cemeteries.

8 *V.C.H. Ches.* iii. 180; R. Stewart-Brown, 'Hosp. of St. John

at Chester', *T.H.S.L.C.* lxxviii. 66–9; *Charters of A.-N. Earls*, pp. 221–2 (no. 221); P.R.O., CHES 29/52, m. 19; B.L. Harl. MS. 2159, f. 98v.

9 *Cart. Chester Abbey*, ii, pp. 299–300.

10 *Close R.* 1237–42, 329; *T.H.S.L.C.* lxxviii. 70–2.

11 P.R.O., CHES 29/52, m. 19; B.L. Harl. MS. 2159, f. 99v.; cf. *Blk. Prince's Reg.* iii. 98.

12 *Cal. Pat.* 1396–9, 286.   13 Ibid. 1413–16, 256.

14 Above, Local Government Boundaries: Parish Boundaries.

15 *V.C.H. Ches.* iii. 182; *T.H.S.L.C.* lxxviii. 79–81.

16 B.L. Harl. MS. 1944, ff. 98v.–99; Harl. MS. 2125, f. 148.

17 *V.C.H. Ches.* iii. 182; *T.H.S.L.C.* lxxviii. 82–3.

the 'ornaments' of which were partly paid for by Sir Robert Grosvenor, Bt., included room for the prisoners of the Northgate gaol and a gallery for the schoolboys. No early features survived inside the building in the 1990s.[1]

The Blue Coat school was closed in 1949,[2] and after a variety of uses the building was occupied in 2000 by the History department and other offices of Chester College.

1 *V.C.H. Ches.* iii. 182; *T.H.S.L.C.* lxxviii. 83–7; *31st Rep. Com. Char.* 345–6; C.C.A.L.S., ZAB 4, f. 29.
2 Below, Education: List of Schools.
3 *V.C.H. Ches.* iii. 184; J. H. E. Bennett, 'Hosp. and Chantry

HOSPITAL OF ST. URSULA

The hospital was founded under a licence granted in 1510 to the executors of Roger Smith (will proved 1508), with six almshouses and a chapel in the city's former common hall in Commonhall Lane. It may already have lapsed before its formal dissolution in 1547, when the chapel was sold. The almshouses continued until the 1870s.[3]

of St. Ursula the Virgin of Chester', *J.C.A.S.* xxxii. 98–126; above, Charities for the Poor: Municipal Charities (Almshouses: Sir Thomas Smith's).

LEISURE AND CULTURE

PLAYS, SPORTS, AND CUSTOMS BEFORE 1700

Chester's celebratory activities in the later Middle Ages and the Tudor period fell into three broad categories.[1] First, there were formal civic and guild occasions in which the mayor, aldermen, and guildsmen participated in their ceremonial robes, processing or standing in customary hierarchy. They included regular events such as the weekly attendance of mayor and aldermen at church or the election and accounting days of the craft guilds, and special occasions like the visit of a noble or royal personage. At the opposite end of the spectrum were the informal sports, recreations, and pastimes of the populace, often rowdy and even illicit, which at their most disorderly included frequenting brothels and drinking in alehouses. They might involve illegal games such as dice, cards, tables, bowls, and shovelboard indoors[2] and football outdoors.[3] The Midsummer bonfires built in 1546 and 1568 may represent the final futile attempts to sustain an old custom.[4] Cock fighting, and bull and bear baiting at the Cross,[5] were legal, though condemned by puritans as strongly as the illicit activities. Bowling greens were laid out in the 17th century.[6] Hawking and greyhound coursing went on in the area around Chester.[7] Additional entertainment might be had from a procession to execution, usually at the gibbet at Spital Boughton but occasionally by burning. Under the Tudors there were private archery butts in the city,[8] and public shoots were held on the Roodee, at which practice for children of six years and older was made compulsory in 1539–40.[9]

Between the two extremes was a range of customary activities which had the features and potential of the informal celebrations but were shaped to fulfil the civic functions of the more formal occasions: the Whitsun plays, the Christmas and Midsummer watches, the Sheriffs' breakfast, the Shrovetide homages, and the licensing of minstrels. Their origins are not all known, but in the Tudor period Cestrians accepted traditions linking them to important events in the city's history, constantly reinvented the exercises, purging them of unacceptable elements, and created new occasions, often a sporting and competitive character. They were valued in the early 17th century as evidence of the antiquity and continuity of the community of Chester, and as the means of furthering that sense of communal solidarity.[10]

Objections to indecorous and profane activities on religious and public order grounds increased from the later 16th century. In response, supporters sought new justifications, or modified or abandoned them. At the same time the range of civic celebration was extended through triumphs and shows sponsored by private citizens, and plays produced by touring professional companies or the boys of the King's school, making Chester familiar with large-scale visual spectacle, the developments of Elizabethan theatre, and classical drama. As a result, the identity of specifically local communal culture was undermined.

The Civil Wars and Interregnum increased the pressures, interrupting the city's celebratory cycle, but significantly the city sought to revive its celebrations after 1660. Chester seems to have clung to its customary practices more tenaciously than most other English cities, apparently needing to reassure itself in times of difficulty about a past which it imagined as more glorious and prosperous. The resurgence was artificial and brief: revived for sentimental reasons or as tourist spectacles to promote trade, the observances generally lacked their former social and economic functions, and most were discontinued during the later 17th or early 18th century.

THE CHESTER PLAYS

Corpus Christi Procession and Play

By the early 15th century and perhaps by 1399 Chester was clearly celebrating the feast of Corpus Christi (varying according to the date of Easter within the period 23 May to 24 June) with a procession escorting the consecrated Host through the streets.[11] The city companies or craft guilds were required to process and to provide a light, presumably a large shielded candle. In the 1470s the guilds processed in a set sequence, as on other civic occasions, from St. Mary's church to St. John's,[12] sites associated in earlier centuries with the earl of Chester and the bishop of Lichfield.[13]

The earliest reference to a play performed at Corpus

---

1 The data for this section derive from *REED: Chester*, and from research carried out by Elizabeth Baldwin and David Mills for *REED: Ches.* (forthcoming) and conducted with the support of the Leverhulme Trust and of the Humanities Research Board of the British Academy. 2 C.C.A.L.S., ZQRL 1–3.

3 e.g. Ormerod, *Hist. Ches.* i. 235.

4 C.C.A.L.S., EDD 3913/1/1, p. 68; EDD 3913/1/2, p. 61.

5 Below, this chapter: Sporting Customs (Civic Bull and Bear Baiting). 6 Below, Sport after 1700: Bowls.

7 e.g. C.C.A.L.S., ZQSE 11/29.

8 Ibid. ZCX 10. 9 Ibid. ZAB 1, f. 62 and v.

10 *REED: Chester*, pp. xxvii–xxxv; S. E. Hart and M. M. Knapp, 'The Aunchant and Famous Cittie': David Rogers and Chester Mystery Plays.

11 Cf. C.C.A.L.S., ZMB 1, ff. 55v.–56.

12 Ibid. ZMB 5, f. 216.

13 Above, Collegiate Church of St. John; Medieval Parish Churches: St. Mary.

Christi by the city's companies occurs in 1422,[1] when the Ironmongers' and Carpenters' guilds both sought assistance from the Fletchers and the Coopers in putting on their Corpus Christi pageant. The inquirers decided that the Fletchers were to continue to be responsible for the Flagellation, the Ironmongers for the Crucifixion, and the Carpenters for an unnamed pageant already assigned to them in what was called 'the original'. In 1429 members of the Weavers' company were assessed for contributions to the lights of Our Lady and Corpus Christi and to the Corpus Christi play each time the light was carried or the play performed.[2] Similar responsibilities lay with the Bakers *c.* 1463[3] and the Fletchers in 1468.[4] The problems and burdens which the play and procession presented for the companies were apparent in 1472, when the Saddlers complained of the reluctance of strangers to contribute to the costs incurred by the company in participating.[5]

The matter for which each guild was responsible was contained in an official document ('the original') and enforced by the city's administration. Nothing is known about the text, the method of production, or the place or places of performance. There was no specific mention of the Corpus Christi play after 1472, although in 1488 a claim was laid against the Cooks and Innkeepers' company for payment for performing the role of the demon in their play; as the claimant was a baker, not an innkeeper, performers were perhaps generally bought in from outside.[6]

By the early 16th century the civic Corpus Christi play had been replaced by a civic Whitsun play. The Corpus Christi procession and a play performed by the clergy, however, continued perhaps until Corpus Christi was cancelled as a feast of the English Church in 1548. The pre-Reformation banns announcing the Whitsun play indicated that it and the Corpus Christi procession had the authority of the city's governing body, the Assembly. The banns may have been composed to announce the change of date of the civic play from Corpus Christi to Whitsun and reassure the populace that the celebration would continue in its original form.[7]

Whitsun Play: History

A civic play at Whitsun, 11 days before Corpus Christi, was being performed by the guilds before 1521.[8] By then the guilds were clearly no longer obliged to contribute to a Corpus Christi play, and the pairing of responsibility for the Whitsun play and the Corpus

Christi light strongly suggests that the Whitsun play replaced that at Corpus Christi. In the mid 1520s the Cappers claimed that they had been given responsibility for their play, Balaam and Balaak, by Mayor Thomas Smith (who held office in 1504–5, 1511–12, 1515–16, and 1520–2). Their allegation that they had been promised financial help for the production from the Mercers' company implies that it was a recent responsibility undertaken only with such guarantees.[9]

A proclamation for the Whitsun play was drawn up by the town clerk, William Newhall, in 1531–2.[10] It contributed significantly to the myth of the play's origins,[11] and described it as 'a play and declaration and diverse stories of the Bible, beginning with the Creation and Fall of Lucifer and ending with the general judgement of the world'. It also set out the play's purpose as a mixture of religious edification and civic prosperity: 'not only for the augmentation and increase of the holy and catholic faith of our Saviour Jesus Christ and to exhort the minds of common people to good devotion and wholesome doctrine thereof but also for the commonwealth and prosperity of this city', a claim not, perhaps, without political significance in 1531–2. Its combination of spiritual and civic interests and sanctions against breakers of the peace, together with other details, suggests a possible origin in St. Werburgh's abbey, though responsibility for production clearly rested with the mayor. The proclamation referred to 'plays' in the plural and might suggest that an original single play had been divided into separate parts. It also contained indications that the traditions of performance had not been consistently maintained. A new beginning seems implied, combined with a desire to affirm solidarity with the past. Performance was said, vaguely, to be in Whitsun week, whereas the pre-Reformation banns announced that the play would be performed on Monday, Tuesday, and Wednesday of that week. As a three-day production, the play was evidently regarded as a trilogy rather than a single work. If those inferences are valid, then the shift from a one-day to a three-day production may have occurred between 1521 and 1531–2.

Whereas the Corpus Christi play was probably an annual event, the Whitsun play seems to have been less regular. It is unlikely that productions were maintained annually in the political and religious circumstances of the middle and later 16th century.

Both Newhall's proclamation and the post-Reformation banns for the Whitsun play defended it

1 Para. based on C.C.A.L.S., ZG 7/23.
2 Ibid. ZMR 85; *REED: Chester*, 7–8.
3 B.L. Harl. MS. 2054, f. 36v.
4 *REED: Chester*, 12.   5 P.R.O., CHES 2/144, f. 7.
6 C.C.A.L.S., ZSR 356, m. 1.
7 B.L. Harl. MS. 2150, ff. 86–88v.; R. M. Lumiansky and D. Mills, *Chester Mystery Cycle: Essays and Docs.* 272–310.

8 C.C.A.L.S., ZMB 12, f. 24v.
9 B.L. Harl. MS. 1996, f. 120; below, Lists of Mayors and Sheriffs.
10 Para. based on C.C.A.L.S., ZAF 1, f. 12 (emended version); B.L. Harl. MS. 2013, f. 1 (fair copy); ibid. Harl. MS. 2150, f. 86 (post-Reformation version, *c.* 1540).
11 Below, this section: Whitsun Play (Myths of Origin).

against expected opposition by an account of its alleged antiquity, its value to Church and town, and its alleged authorship and initiation.[1] In 1568 there was an 'original book', apparently the authorized version, in the custody of the mayor.[2] The text, however, had by 1572 been subject to revisions over a period of time, though the corrections had not always been adopted in performance.[3]

Performances were staged at recognized places in 1568 and on at least two previous occasions.[4] The penultimate performance took place in 1572 during the mayoralty of John Hankey. By then, opposition to it was mounting,[5] largely under the leadership of Christopher Goodman, a protestant reformer of national standing and a Cestrian by birth who had returned to the city in 1571. He lobbied the mayor, the president of the Council of the North, and the archbishop of York, apparently with the support of fellow preachers, and accused the bishop of Chester, William Downham, of supine acquiescence and the mayor's supporters of intimidation.[6] Accordingly, the archbishop sent an inhibition to prevent the production but it arrived too late and the plays were performed at Whitsun 1572.[7] Goodman reported the disobedience to the archbishop and complained of the treatment of those 'honest men' who, on conscientious grounds, had refused to pay their contribution towards the production and had been imprisoned.[8] The mayor was later called before the privy council to explain his responsibility in the decision.[9]

In 1575 the Assembly voted to hold that year's Whitsun play at Midsummer, and authorized the mayor, Sir John Savage, to amend the text after taking appropriate advice,[10] presumably bearing in mind Goodman's objections to its unscriptural and popish content. The move was probably caused by the threat of plague at Whitsun; when the threat receded preparations were evidently sufficiently advanced to hold a performance. Goodman protested privately to the mayor and publicly in a sermon.[11] The performance began on the afternoon of Sunday 26 June and ended on the evening of the following Wednesday.[12] The change of date transferred the play from the liturgical cycle to Chester's carnival period. Not all the plays were performed, some being thought superstitious,[13] and there was certainly dissent among the

citizenry,[14] partly because the play took place in only one part of Chester,[15] but also on puritan grounds.[16]

For ignoring a new inhibition of the archbishop of York, Sir John Savage was summoned before the privy council, but his assurance, supported by a certificate from his successor as mayor, that the decision to perform the play had been taken by the whole council appears to have satisfied the authorities.[17] Nevertheless, the claim that 'divers others of the citizens and players were troubled for the same matter' suggests that pressure was put upon all who were in any way connected with the production.[18] There is no evidence of further performances of the play, even though the Cappers, Pinners, Wiredrawers, and Linendrapers later claimed that they were ordered to receive the Bricklayers into their fellowship in 1589 to help carry the costs of the Whitsun plays.[19]

As in other cities, individual plays from the Whitsun cycle were occasionally performed before visiting dignitaries. In Chester the Assumption of Our Lady, the responsibility of the Worshipful Wives (perhaps a religious guild), was performed at the Cross for George Stanley, Lord Strange, in 1490,[20] and at the Abbey Gate for Prince Arthur in 1498, in the month of the feast of the Assumption (15 August).[21] In 1516 it was played with the Shepherds' play in St. John's churchyard, though the occasion is not known.[22] The play was part of the cycle before the Reformation but was dropped afterwards. The Shepherds' play was put on at the Cross by the mayor for Henry Stanley, earl of Derby, and his son Ferdinando, Lord Strange, during a private visit to Chester in 1577,[23] the last occasion before the 20th century that a play from the cycle was performed in the city.[24]

Whitsun Play: Myths of Origin

Official public pronouncements during the 16th century included statements about the authorship and origins of the plays. The constant claim before the Reformation was that they began in the mayoralty of John Arneway, who was later thought to have required a short rehearsal time and the provision of a carriage for each pageant. Until 1594, when errors in the official mayoral lists were revealed and the historical dates of his mayoralty established, Arneway was believed to have been Chester's first mayor. The proclamation of

1 B.L. Harl. MS. 2013; Harl. MS. 1944; Bodl. MS. 175; C.C.A.L.S., ZCX 3.   2 C.C.A.L.S., ZMB 19, f. 45v.
3 Denb. R.O., DD/PP/839, p. 121.
4 C.C.A.L.S., ZMB 19, f. 52.
5 B.L. Add. MS. 29777, no. 246.
6 Denb. R.O., DD/PP/839.
7 B.L. Harl. MS. 2133, f. 43.
8 Denb. R.O., DD/PP/839, p. 121.
9 C.C.A.L.S., ZCHB 3, f. 28; B.L. Harl. MS. 1046, f. 164v.
10 C.C.A.L.S., ZAF 3/25.
11 Denb. R.O., DD/PP/843.
12 C.C.A.L.S., ZCHB 3, f. 28v.
13 B.L. Harl. MS. 2133, f. 43v.

14 Ibid. Add. MS. 29777, no. 249.
15 Ibid. Harl. MS. 2125, f. 40v.
16 C.C.A.L.S., ZCR 60/83, f. 13.
17 B.L. Harl. MS. 1046, f. 164v.; Harl. MS. 2173, ff. 107v.–108; C.C.A.L.S., ZCHB 3, f. 28 and v.; ZAB 1, ff. 162v.–163.
18 B.L. Harl. MS. 1046, f. 164v.
19 C.C.A.L.S., ZAF 40c/35.
20 B.L. Harl. MS. 2125, f. 41; Add. MS. 29777, no. 163.
21 B.L. Harl. MS. 2057, f. 26v.; Harl. MS. 2125, f. 32; Add. MS. 11335, f. 23.
22 Ibid. Harl. MS. 2125, f. 33v.
23 C.C.A.L.S., ZCR 60/83, f. 13v.
24 Below, Revival of Mystery Plays.

1531–2 ascribed the text of the plays to a monk of St. Werburgh's, Henry Francis (fl. 1377–82),[1] but after the Reformation it was ascribed to Ranulph Higden (d. 1364), also a monk of St. Werburgh's and widely known as author of an influential universal history, the *Polychronicon*.[2] Higden's historical and Arneway's erroneous dates coincided, making it possible to claim that the cycle was composed and first produced *c.* 1327. The traditions were without historical foundation, though antiquarians of the late 16th and early 17th century attempted to reconcile them with more certain facts,[3] and their persistence has fostered the mistaken idea that Chester's plays were the earliest of the English cycles. They nevertheless hint at the possible political functions of the plays. The Arneway connexion linked their origins with the office of mayor, who certainly had complete authority over both the text and the allocation of the individual pageants.[4] Moreover, the transfer to Whitsun occurred in a period when other forms of civic ceremonial were being developed. Goodman attributed the initiative for the productions of the 1570s to the personal will of the mayors, and the privy council summoned Mayor Savage to answer the charge that he alone was responsible.[5]

The association with the abbey was less closely definable, but the proclamation asserted the play's Catholicism, and Goodman seems to have had that in mind in his objections. The post-Reformation banns responded to such criticism, defensively linking the play to two of the most famous Cestrians, the supposed first mayor and the abbey's greatest scholar. Higden presumably superseded the largely unknown Francis as a better known, more scholarly, and so more defensible author. The fact that he was a monk was addressed by representing him as a proto-protestant who, at considerable danger to himself, invented the play in order to bring the Scriptures to the people in their own tongue. The banns also emphasized the play's antiquity and stressed its archaic language and the lowly nature of both actors and audiences in the past: it was to be seen, in its original context, as a revolutionary work of which the city should be proud.[6] A similar view was held by David Rogers, who argued in 1609 (perhaps citing his father, Archdeacon Robert Rogers) that there was no longer need for such plays because the Bible had been translated into English.[7]

The claims made for the play's origins suggest a continuing civic function – the celebration of the mayoralty – and an occasional politicized religious function, varying according to the religious climate. Those diverse considerations may go some way towards explaining how the myths of origins developed and why the play was defiantly performed in the 1570s. The myths conferred upon Chester's cycle respectable scholarly credentials, implying a priority of text over production and linking the history of the play with that of the city. They reflected or created a pride in the cycle which seems unique to Chester among English towns with play-cycles and probably contributed to the survival of the written text.

Whitsun Play: Content, Text, and Performance

There are three kinds of evidence for the content of the Whitsun play. The first is lists of companies and their plays from the later 16th century; an earlier version may represent the order of guilds in the cycle, since it includes the Worshipful Wives and the title of their play, the only one to be named.[8] The second is the descriptions of the plays in the pre- and post-Reformation banns, and the third is the eight extant copies of part or all of the text, more than for any other English play-cycle.[9]

All the complete manuscripts of the cycle were copied long after the last production by men of scholarly pretensions and evident protestant orthodoxy. They derived from a common exemplar, presumably the city's book.[10] None seems to have been used in a production and all were probably prepared out of antiquarian interest. The manuscripts attest a cycle of 24 plays, of which the Flagellation and Crucifixion was divided into two separate plays in the four earliest manuscripts, recalling the dispute of 1422 about that section of the Corpus Christi play. The cycle has a stylistic uniformity and a thematic and structural coherence which support the view of single authorship or revision at some point in its development. Goodman's claim, however, that the text had been revised over a period of time can also to some extent be substantiated: copyists seem to have found many places in the manuscript where alterations had been made, sometimes not clearly, and had to choose between alternative versions ranging from individual words to a complete play.

The manner of production is known from David Rogers's description. On St. George's Day (23 April) a rider 'published the time and the matter of the plays in

1 Adlington Hall, deeds, bdles. 5.5, 16.2; B.L. Harl. MS. 2071, f. 23.
2 R. Higden, *Polychronicon* (Rolls Ser.).
3 e.g. B.L. Harl. MS. 2124, entry before f. 1.
4 Ibid. Harl. MS. 2150, f. 86.
5 C.C.A.L.S., ZCHB 3, f. 28.
6 *REED: Chester*, 240–7.
7 C.C.A.L.S., ZCX 3.
8 B.L. Harl. MS. 2104, f. 4.
9 Manchester Public Libr., MS. 822.11C2 (fragment of play 18, Resurrection; date uncertain); Nat. Libr. of Wales, Peniarth

MS. 399 (play 23, Antichrist; *c.* 1500); San Marino (California), Huntington Libr., MS. 2 (originally full cycle but now lacking play 1, Creation and Fall of Lucifer; 1591); B.L. Add. MS. 10395 (full cycle; 1592); C.C.A.L.S., ZG 7/5 (play 16, Flagellation; 1599); B.L. Harl. MS. 2013 (full cycle and post-Reformation banns; 1600); Bodl. MS. 175 (full cycle and part of post-Reformation banns; 1604); B.L. Harl. MS. 2124 (full cycle; 1607); *Chester Mystery Cycle*, ed. R. M. Lumiansky and D. Mills (E.E.T.S. suppl. ser. iii, ix).
10 'Texts of Chester Cycle', in Lumiansky and Mills, *Essays*, 3–86.

brief', accompanied by the stewards of the participating companies, and perhaps also by actors wearing play costume. On the performance dates, each pageant was performed first at the Abbey Gate in Northgate Street and then at the Cross. Rogers saw the route as symbolic of the partnership of Church and city; the clergy watched at the abbey and the mayor and his brethren at the Cross.[1] Each play moved 'then to Watergate Street, then to Bridge Street, through the lanes, and so to Eastgate Street'. The movement of the carriages was co-ordinated by reports taken from station to station. No single design for the carriages was possible: some plays (for example Noah's Flood) required a special vehicle. When the plays became a three-day production, carriage-sharing agreements were possible among companies playing on different days, like the earliest known, from 1532, involving the Vintners (Day 1, the Three Kings), the Masons and Goldsmiths (Day 2, Massacre of the Innocents), and the Dyers (Day 3, Antichrist).[2] Such agreements reduced the burden of storing, refurbishing, and dismantling what were clearly enormous and specially designed vehicles. The emphasis in the pre-Reformation banns was upon the spectacular carriages rather than the text.

The companies spent heavily in relation to the plays on food and drink, as well as on payments to actors and the renewal of props and costumes. Choristers from the cathedral and professional musicians were hired.[3] The cycle required over 200 actors for speaking parts, and if the 'putters' of the carriages and the back-up teams are included, it is clear that the celebration involved virtually the entire community.

CITY WATCHES AND MIDSUMMER SHOW

Chester's Christmas and Midsummer watches seem to have originated in practical arrangements for defence by the citizens, who were required to possess arms, produce them when required, and swear to defend the city. By the late 16th century the watches were largely ceremonial, traditions about their origins had developed, and they had become another means of manifesting civic hierarchy and promoting the established order.

Christmas Watch

The traditional origins of the Christmas muster of armour were set out in a speech written for the illiterate mayor Robert Brerewood, who learned it by rote and addressed the watch at Christmas 1584, and also by David Rogers *c.* 1620.[4] It was supposed to have been established after a Welsh raid on Chester at Christmas, when King William I gave lands to four men charged with defending the city. The responsibility remained

with those holding the lands. In the 16th century the watch was charged to safeguard the city against breaches of the peace, but in practice it was simply an occasion for civic banqueting. The participants, usually deputies for the landholders, were required to attend the mayor on the first night of Christmas and the sheriffs on the next two, in order to receive their commission to patrol the streets and protect the city from fire and criminal acts on those evenings. The mayor and sheriffs retired on each evening to banquet. The watch was not observed while the city charter was suspended, but its observance was resumed in 1672, only to fall victim to successive cancellations from 1678 and final abandonment in 1682.[5]

Midsummer Watch or Show

Chester's second watch was linked to the Midsummer fair, which until 1506 was under the jurisdiction of the abbot of St. Werburgh's. It developed into a great carnivalesque parade, more popular and enduring than the Corpus Christi and Whitsun plays. David Rogers claimed that the show was older than the play, but elsewhere its origins were attributed to the mayoralty of Richard Goodman in 1498–9, when Prince Arthur visited Chester and the north wing of the Pentice was rebuilt.[6] However, the first contemporary record of the show occurred only in an order of 1564 for the replacement of pageant figures which had evidently been destroyed,[7] implying that the show had been discontinued and was being revived in its traditional form.

Each guild was required to provide an armed escort, and its members attended the mayor in their gowns on St. John's Eve, where they were summoned by the crier to process in an established sequence from the Northgate round the other town gates, ending at the common hall. Repeated orders by the guilds reflected a reluctance of members to attend and to dress appropriately. In the later 16th century the show was primarily a carnivalesque celebration of the town and its hierarchy, Chester's equivalent of London's lord mayor's show, involving groups of armed men escorting the sheriffs, leavelookers, and mayor, together with the city's drummer and ensign, the waits, morris dancers, and men to keep the companies in their due order.[8] Each group had specially constructed figures: the mayor, his Mount; the sheriffs, the Elephant and Castle; and the leavelookers, the Unicorn, Antelope, Fleur-de-Lys, and Camel, with hobby-horses. Other features were four giants, and a dragon escorted by six 'naked boys'. In the 1660s preparations for the show took at least six weeks.[9]

---

1 Liverpool Univ., MS. 23.5.

2 C.C.A.L.S., ZAF 1, f. 11.

3 Below, this chapter: Music and Minstrelsy.

4 B.L. Harl. MS. 2150, f. 5v.; Harl. MS. 1948; C.C.A.L.S., DCC 19, on which rest of para. based.

5 C.C.A.L.S., ZAB 2, ff. 175v., 176v., 183, 187v., 189, 191, 195v., 196v.; ZML 3, no. 423.

6 e.g. ibid. ZCR 60/83, f. 8v.; above, Municipal Buildings: Pentice.

7 B.L. Harl. MS. 2150, f. 208.

8 Ibid. ff. 201–203v.

9 C.C.A.L.S., ZMF 87/46–7.

Rogers claimed that when the Whitsun plays were put on, the Midsummer show was not, and vice versa, but in fact the two celebrations interacted. The guilds might include in their Midsummer shows the more popular figures from their Whitsun pageants, including 'the devil, riding in feathers before the Butchers' (from their play, the Temptation of Christ) and 'a man in woman's apparel with a devil waiting on his horse, called Caps and Cans' (from the Cooks and Innkeepers' play, the Harrowing of Hell), as well as 'Christ in strings' (presumably from the Fletchers' play, the Flagellation).[1] The Cappers provided Balaam's talking ass from their play, Balaam and Balaak, evidently an elaborate structure since in 1610 they spent £4 1s. refurbishing it and making a new banner.[2] The Painters provided stilt-walkers described in 1577 as 'the two shepherds',[3] recalling their play of the Shepherds. By the 17th century, however, most companies were escorting a richly dressed boy on horseback. Nevertheless, the ready interchange between religious plays and carnival show invested the transfer of the 1575 performance of the plays from Whitsun to Midsummer with added significance.

The show encountered opposition during the later 16th century, both for its carnivalesque character and more particularly for the inclusion of quasi-Scriptural figures. In 1611, when Midsummer Day fell on a Sunday, the Assembly was concerned about profaning the sabbath and moved the show to the Saturday and the fair to the Monday, against opposition;[4] those arrangements were followed thereafter whenever Midsummer Eve fell on a Sunday. In 1600 the puritan mayor, Henry Hardware, had the giants broken up and banned the dragon, the naked boys, and the devil; instead, the show was led by an armed man with every company following a boy on horseback.[5] His successor, however, restored the figures and the company characters at popular request, to the disapproval of David Rogers in 1609. Nevertheless, their inclusion became increasingly unusual and in 1617, when Mayor Edward Button insisted that the Cooks and Innkeepers include their comic alewife and devils, it was to the disapproval of both clergy and people.[6] By 1622–3 Rogers felt that the reforms had gone sufficiently far to make the show a decorous activity bringing honour and profit (in all senses) to Chester.[7]

The show was discontinued during the Civil War, but in 1658 the mayor reported to the Assembly that the greater part of the companies desired its revival on commercial grounds.[8] The Assembly voted narrowly in favour of revival in 1659,[9] but the decision was perhaps not put into effect until 1661.[10] The requirement made in 1666, that all Assembly and company members attend the show, indicated continuing reluctance on the part of some citizens.[11]

In 1671 the show was moved to Tuesday in Whit week, on the grounds that it would attract many people 'by whom no little money may be expended'. Holding the show at fair time was said to be prejudicial to trade since, in order to take part, company members were compelled to shut their shops for lack of apprentices. The show was thus by then regarded as a tourist attraction held for commercial benefit.[12] In 1678 the Assembly finally decided to stop putting it on.[13] Proposals to revive it were voted down in 1680 and 1681,[14] by when it had apparently outlived even its commercial usefulness.

SPORTING CUSTOMS

Shrovetide Celebrations

In 1540, during the second mayoralty of Henry Gee, the Assembly approved an order reforming certain customary homages to the Drapers' company on Shrove Tuesday.[15] Three existing homages were covered. First, in the afternoon of Shrove Tuesday at the cross on the Roodee and in the presence of the mayor, the Shoemakers presented the Drapers and the Saddlers with a football, to be played from there to the common hall, an event conducted with much violence and injury. Secondly, at the same time and place, each master of the Saddlers, on horseback, presented the Drapers with a painted wooden ball on the point of a spear, decorated with flowers and arms. Thirdly, every man married in Chester during the previous year, or living in Chester but married elsewhere, offered the Drapers a ball of silk or velvet. The Drapers then provided bread and beer for the Saddlers, Shoemakers, and the mayor on Shrove Tuesday, leeks and salt on Ash Wednesday, and gave a banquet on the Thursday, all at the common hall. The customs were said to be long-standing, and perhaps dated from a time when the three companies separated from a united body.

Mayor Gee took the opportunity of Henry VIII's legislation promoting archery to change those customs. First, the Saddlers, instead of the football, were to give the Drapers six silver arrows, each worth 6d. or more, as the prize for a foot race to be run on the Roodee before the mayor. Secondly, instead of the wooden ball, the Saddlers were to give the Drapers a silver bell, valued at 3s. 4d. or more, as the prize for a horse race.

1 B.L. Harl. MS. 1948.
2 C.C.A.L.S., ZG 6/2, f. 28v.
3 Ibid. ZG 17/1, f. 66.
4 Ibid. ZAB 1, f. 312; B.L. Harl. MS. 2133, f. 47; cf. B.L. Harl. MS. 1948.
5 B.L. Harl. MS. 2125, f. 45v.
6 Toronto (Canada), Massey Coll., MS., f. 33v.
7 B.L. Harl. MS. 1948; C.C.A.L.S., ZQSE 9/69.

8 C.C.A.L.S., ZAB 2, f. 119.
9 Ibid. ZAF 37A/4.
10 Ibid. ZAB 2, f. 132; cf. ZAF 38A/5; ZAF 38B/5.
11 Ibid. ZAB 2, f. 155; cf. ZAF 39C/17.
12 Ibid. ZAB 2, f. 171 and v.
13 Ibid. f. 188.
14 Ibid. ff. 190v., 192.
15 This para. and next based on ibid. ZAB 1, ff. 64–5.

Thirdly, the married men's homage was commuted from a ball of silk to a silver arrow valued at 5*d*. or more, to be the prize in an archery competition with longbows. The feasting remained. The changes stemmed from a dual concern, to maintain public order and decorum under mayoral authority, and to rationalize a practice whose origins had been forgotten. Gee transformed a discrete series of homages into an organized sporting competition for the city while retaining the element of homage. In the early 17th century David Rogers commended the homage, but despite fines for non-compliance, there was evidently continuing laxity in its observance and in 1626 the mayor arbitrated over points of procedural difficulty.[1] The custom was reaffirmed in 1684, but dissent continued.[2] In 1691 the Drapers were fined for not keeping Shrovetide,[3] and when in 1698 the race was postponed to 22 March, the Drapers were particularly admonished to 'resume and perform their ancient ceremonies'.[4] Gee's reforms marked the origins of horse racing on the Roodee at Chester.[5]

Sheriffs' Breakfast

On the Monday of Easter week the sheriffs, mayor, and aldermen engaged in an archery contest on the Roodee. The practice is said to have begun in 1511.[6] After the contest, the participants processed to the common hall, the winners carrying arrows and the losers bows, to consume a breakfast of calves' heads and bacon, for which the winners contributed 2*d*. and the losers 4*d*. Two long tables were also set for what were variously described as 'loose' and 'straggling' people, making the occasion also one of public charity.[7]

The presence of the unofficial guests evidently made the occasion one of some rowdiness.[8] Perhaps for that reason, the breakfast was another of the customs reformed by Henry Hardware in 1600, though it was later restored.[9] A more determined attempt at reform was made in 1640, when the sheriffs provided a piece of plate for a horse race to be run on Easter Tuesday, and, by removing the long tables and excluding the unofficial guests, made the Easter Monday breakfast into a private dinner for the aldermen, gentlemen, and archers.[10] Some sheriffs and leavelookers evidently believed that the feast was observed at their discretion, but in 1674 the Assembly determined that it was not,

and levied retrospective fines for negligence.[11] Moreover, the substitution of a different sporting spectacle for the archery contest was resisted, since in 1681 a request to substitute an Easter Tuesday horse race was turned down.[12]

Civic Bull and Bear Baiting

Bulls and bears were baited in Chester as early as the late 12th century.[13] In later times each mayor's departure from office was marked by a bull bait at the Cross 'according to ancient custom',[14] the bull being provided by the companies of Butchers and Bakers. Bears were also baited there, as in 1611,[15] and elsewhere.[16] There was opposition to both sports, especially among puritans.[17] Mayor Henry Hardware had the bull ring taken up in 1600 and banned baits,[18] but baiting proved particularly resistant to suppression and survived in the city until 1803.[19]

MUSIC AND MINSTRELSY
City Waits

Chester employed a group of musicians, the city waits, by 1476.[20] In 1540 Mayor Henry Gee regularized their duties.[21] They were to play as accustomed in the mornings and evenings of Monday, Thursday, and Saturday, and additionally on Sunday and Tuesday mornings. The waits were entitled to a stipend, new cloaks every three years, and 10*s*. for playing upon 'any extraordinary rejoicing day', but complaints about non-payment and the lack of livery persisted into the 18th century, and from 1707 gowns were renewed only every five years.[22] The waits continued in existence until the 1770s or later.[23]

In 1591 the waits had hautboys, recorders, cornets, and violins,[24] and in 1614 a group which absconded left behind only a double curtal (a kind of bassoon) and a tenor cornet.[25] The waits could be hired, individually or collectively, as freelance performers for special occasions, such as the Whitsun play, the Midsummer show, guild election days or dinners, church gatherings, civic occasions like mayoral banquets, and private functions,[26] though sometimes the inducements of freelance playing conflicted with their obligations to the city.[27] Other musicians besides the waits laid claim to official recognition, and there were complaints in the early 17th century about 'apish

1 Ibid. ZAB 2, ff. 6v.–7v. 2 Ibid. ZAB 3, ff. 4v., 31v.
3 Ibid. f. 29v. 4 Ibid. f. 60.
5 Below, Chester Races.
6 B.L. Add. MS. 11335, f. 23.
7 Ibid. Add. MS. 29779, f. 49v.; Harl. MS. 2125, f. 133.
8 e.g. ibid. Harl. MS. 2125, f. 133.
9 Ibid. Harl. MS. 2133, f. 46.
10 Ibid. Harl. MS. 2125, ff. 64v., 133; below, Chester Races.
11 C.C.A.L.S., ZAB 2, ff. 177v., 185, 194.
12 Ibid. f. 194.
13 Lucian, *De Laude Cestrie*, 61.
14 B.L. Harl. MS. 2125, ff. 52v.–53.
15 Ibid. Harl. MS. 2158, f. 80.
16 C.C.A.L.S., EDV 1/14, f. 22v.; ibid. ZQSE 11/71.
17 Denb. R.O., DD/PP/844; C.C.A.L.S., ZAB 1, f. 243v.
18 B.L. Harl. MS. 2125, f. 45v.; Harl. MS. 2133, f. 46.
19 Below, Sport after 1700: Other Sports.
20 C.C.A.L.S., ZMB 6B, f. 44.
21 B.L. Harl. MS. 2150, f. 108.
22 C.C.A.L.S., ZAB 3, ff. 147, 149v.; ZAF 39A/22 (1666); ZAF 40C/23 (1672).
23 Ibid. ZAB 4, ff. 235v., 288, 305.
24 Ibid. ZMB 25, f. 45.
25 Ibid. ZMB 30, f. 22.
26 e.g. ibid. ZQSF 67, no. 6, 10 Aug. 1620.
27 e.g. ibid. ZQSE 9/2, f. 1v.

imitators' not only from the waits but from two private companies of musicians.[1]

Minstrels' Court

In 1477 the abbot of Chester, the mayor, and William Thomas were empowered to convene a court of minstrels at Midsummer, immediately after the Midsummer show.[2] Traditions recorded in the mid 17th century associated the court with a grant by Earl Ranulph III to his constable of authority over the 'cobblers, fiddlers, merry companions, whores, and such routish company' who had assisted him in a victory over the Welsh. The constable was supposed to have vested his power in the Dutton family, whose successors as owners of the manor of Dutton retained it in the 1640s. By then, the court had been elaborated into an annual event on Midsummer Day which began with a proclamation in Eastgate Street summoning musicians and minstrels to play before the lord of Dutton, who then rode to St. John's church, followed by the musicians playing. More music was played inside the church. A licensing court for minstrels was then held elsewhere, in later years at an inn. Courts were held by successive owners of Dutton until 1756.[3]

Other Musicians

Musical activity in the city was diverse. At one level were outsiders and itinerants, licensed in groups or solo and termed 'musitioners' or 'minstrels'. Many of them were pipers or fiddlers who played in inns or for private functions. A late but typical example was John Peacock, a piper resident with a Chester vintner in 1612.[4]

At the other extreme was George Kelly, member of a family of musicians and in 1607 the first musician enrolled as a freeman of the city. He was in the service of William Stanley, earl of Derby, apparently as the leader of the earl's musicians, but also had his own consort of musicians and taught dancing.[5] His group took over from the waits who absconded in 1614, with the understanding that they would provide their own instruments.[6] In 1615 he petitioned the Assembly to suppress incomers who had gained the favour of guilds and individuals and set up as teachers of music and dancing, an indication of increasing competition;[7] he also allied with other groups of musicians, including the waits, in petitioning the Cooks and Innkeepers, who were the main company patrons of musicians.

Among his earlier competitors had been his brother Robert, who served the Savage family with his own consort of musicians.[8]

There was also a tradition of amateur music-making in the city. Some of the wealthier families possessed virginals or viols, and by 1670 Chester had a specialist musical instrument maker.[9]

The Whitsun play contained a great deal of music, both sung and instrumental, and called for minstrels in certain pageants. The guilds also employed cathedral choristers and made use of various musical instruments, such as a portable organ or regal.[10] For the Midsummer show they hired musicians to accompany them. It is likely that the organizers drew upon all available resources: the waits and other official companies, licensed minstrels, and singing-men and choristers, according to availability and expense.[11]

PRIVATE PATRONAGE

Increasingly during the later 16th century and the 17th public celebrations became occasions of private patronage by prominent citizens, and professional touring companies began to visit the city. Those developments augmented the range of civic entertainment and changed the context within which the older celebrations were viewed. The new perception is evident in the defence of the Whitsun plays in the post-Reformation banns against criticisms more relevant to the conventions of later 16th-century drama, and in the elaboration of the minstrels' court in the following century. The decline of communal celebration was due in part to changes in religious and civic attitudes, in part to the spectacular and more spectatorial public entertainments which allowed more centralized control, and in part to the growth of private entertainments.

Entertainments in the private houses of the wealthy must always have been held. In 1568 Richard Dutton, the mayor, was said to have kept open house during Christmas, with a lord of misrule.[12] Mayors were expected to provide hospitality during their term of office, but Dutton's was unusual in its public lavishness. Mayor Thomas Bellin hosted a private performance of a Terence comedy in his house when the earl of Derby and Lord Strange visited the city in 1577,[13] and a masque was held at Lady Willoughby's house during the Christmas celebrations of 1582–3.[14] Christmas Day breakfasts and banquets, mummings,

---

1 C.C.A.L.S., ZG 13/46, unnumbered petition.

2 P.R.O., CHES 2/149, m. 11.

3 *REED: Chester*, 461–6; C.C.A.L.S., DLT/B3, ff. 143–144v.; Lysons, *Ches.* 523–7; Ormerod, *Hist. Ches.* i. 644, 651–4; 3 *Sheaf*, xi, p. 46; xl, pp. 121–2; *Notes & Queries* [1st ser.], ii. 21, 77; x. 244–5.

4 C.C.A.L.S., ZQSF 61, no. 47; cf. ZMB 20, f. 44v.; ZQSE 5/46; 3 *Sheaf*, lvii, pp. 51–2.

5 C.C.A.L.S., ZAF 10/53; ZAB 1, f. 302v.; ZG 13/46, unnum-

bered petition.

6 Ibid. ZMB 30, f. 22.   7 Ibid. ZAF 10/53.

8 B.L. Harl. MS. 2054, f. 101.

9 C.C.A.L.S., ZAF 40B/20.

10 B.L. Harl. MS. 2054, f. 18v.

11 R. Rastall, 'Music in the Cycle', in Lumiansky and Mills, *Essays*, 111–64.   12 B.L. Harl. MS. 2125, f. 39.

13 C.C.A.L.S., ZCR 60/83, f. 13v.

14 Ibid. ZQSF 34, no. 46.

and unlawful games were banned as a nuisance in 1555. The breakfasts, given by senior figures in the city, were a recent innovation, prohibited because they were held before the end of divine service and led to disorderly behaviour; but citizens were encouraged to provide hospitality on the other days of Christmas.[1]

Impromptu public entertainments included the stranger who performed a rope-dance at the Cross in 1606,[2] unspecified shows and pastimes staged by the mason John Brookes (d. 1614) on the steeples of Holy Trinity and St. Peter's, allegedly watched by thousands,[3] and the wager between William Hinckes and Jo Tizer in 1606–7, when Tizer failed to collect together 60 stones set in line before Hinckes completed a circuit of the city walls on horseback.[4]

Theatrical Companies

In 1529–30 an interlude, *King Robert of Sicily*, was performed at the Cross,[5] perhaps by a touring company. It is not clear if the performance of *King Ebrauk with all his Sons* in 1588–9 was a civic or a professional production.[6] The Queen's players performed for the dean and chapter several times between 1589 and 1592, and in 1606 William Stanley, earl of Derby, asked the mayor to allow the earl of Hertford's players to perform in the common hall.[7] Visits by noblemen's players were regarded as numerous in 1613.[8]

Interludes, minstrels, and tumblers were among the spectacles complained of by puritans in 1583,[9] while plays were banned within the city limits in 1596.[10] By 1615 plays put on at the common hall by permission of the city were frequent enough and their audiences sufficiently disorderly for the Assembly to ban all performances after 6 p.m.[11]

Triumphs and Shows

Triumphs were large, spectacular events in which the visual impact was more important than the text. On the Sunday after Midsummer 1564 the city sponsored a triumph devised by William Crofton, an officer of the palatinate, and Mr. Man, master of the King's school, of the history of Aeneas and Dido of Carthage, which was played on the Roodee and featured 'two forts raised and a ship on the water, with sundry horsemen'.[12] Triumphs on the Roodee were among the entertainments seen by Henry Stanley, earl of Derby, in 1577.[13] Local groups might also mount shows, in part to promote trade. In 1621 the citizens of Bridge Street put on a show for May Day, and those in Foregate Street another for St. James's Day (25 July), the latter drawing in many country people.[14]

The most elaborate show known was that sponsored by Robert Amery for the inauguration of the St. George's Day horse race in 1610. It consisted of a parade of characters: two giants, a horseman in the armour of St. George, Fame, Mercury, Chester, horsemen bearing the king's arms and regalia and a bell also dedicated to the king, others carrying the arms of the prince of Wales and a bell dedicated to him, the bearer of the St. George's cup, another St. George, Peace, Plenty, Envy, and Love.[15] The text of the show was published.[16] A further ambitious show was planned but not executed in 1621–2.[17]

The shows, with their mixture of folk and classical elements, reflected the growing fashion for allegorized spectacle set by national celebrations in London. Such events underlined the rise of individual philanthropy and professional entertainment at the expense of earlier, more communally focused celebrations.

CHESTER RACES

The race meeting on the Roodee, a 'perfect natural amphitheatre' framed by the river Dee and the city walls, is Chester's best known and longest established sporting event.[18] Regular races were first organized there in 1540 and have been held almost continuously ever since, interrupted only by civil war and puritanism in the 17th century,[19] and world war, strikes, and flooding in the 20th.[20] Continuity on the same racecourse justifies Chester's claim to be the oldest race meeting in the country.[21] With rare exceptions all the racing has been on the flat.

The original race, run on Shrove Tuesday for a silver bell given by the Saddlers' company, was devised by Mayor Henry Gee as an element in his reformed civic

1 Ibid. ZAB 1, f. 85.
2 Ibid. ZCR 60/83, f. 20; B.L. Add. MS. 29779, f. 34.
3 B.L. Harl. MS. 2177, f. 84.
4 C.C.A.L.S., ZCR 60/83, f. 20.
5 B.L. Harl. MS. 2133, f. 39; Add. MS. 29777, no. 204.
6 Ibid. Harl. MS. 2125, f. 43; C.C.A.L.S., ZCR 60/83, f. 15.
7 C.C.A.L.S., ZML 2, no. 184; E. K. Chambers, *Elizabethan Stage*, ii. 116–17.
8 C.C.A.L.S., ZCR 60/83, f. 24v.
9 Denb. R.O., DD/PP/844.
10 C.C.A.L.S., ZAB 1, f. 243.
11 Ibid. ZAB 1, f. 331v.; ZQSF 51, nos. 55, 57–8.
12 B.L. Harl. MS. 2125, f. 39.

13 Ibid. f. 41; C.C.A.L.S., ZCR 60/83.
14 B.L. Harl. MS. 2125, f. 53v.
15 Ibid. Harl. MS. 2150, f. 186 and v.
16 *Chester's Triumph in Honor of her Prince* (Chetham Soc. [o.s.], iii).　　　17 B.L. Harl. MS. 2057, f. 36.
18 R. M. Bevan, *The Roodee: 450 Years of Racing in Chester*, 14.
19 *V.C.H. Ches.* v (1), Early Modern Chester: Civil War and Interregnum (Economy and Society, 1646–60); cf. *V.C.H. Cambs.* v. 279.
20 Bevan, *Roodee*, 110, 113, 115, 121–2, 142, 148.
21 Cf. ibid. 15 with *V.C.H. City of York*, 159, 199; *V.C.H. Yorks.* ii. 507.

celebrations. It was evidently run only intermittently in the 17th century,[1] but was still taking place in 1705.[2] The lessee of the grazing on the Roodee for 1711–13 was required to allow the Shrovetide race to continue to take place,[3] though it had in fact recently been moved to another day.[4]

In 1610 a new race on St. George's Day (23 April) was inaugurated by Robert Amery, who gave two silver bells, returnable each year, as prizes. The winner and second also divided the stake money of 20*s*. a horse between them in the proportions 2:1. The city took control of the event in 1612.[5] In 1623 the mayor, John Brereton, increased the prize to a cup worth £8 and altered the course (from what form is not known) by moving the start north of the Water Tower and fixing the distance as five laps of the Roodee,[6] at least five miles in total. The starting stone, 4 yd. from the Water Tower, was still identifiable as a landmark in 1746 even though it was disused by then.[7]

A description of the races *c*. 1609 as 'for the public recreation of the whole city' may imply that they then remained primarily part of the annual round of civic ceremonial,[8] but in the 17th century the St. George's Day race became a 'county' event. As early as *c*. 1618 the mayor and Assembly were said to be accompanied at the race by 'such other lords, knights, ladies, gentlemen as please'.[9] In 1665 owners of horses taking part included the Cheshire gentlemen Edward Massey of Puddington and Sir Philip Egerton of Oulton Park.[10]

In 1640 a further race was started on Easter Tuesday. The prize, given by the city sheriffs, was a piece of silver plate worth £13 6*s*. 8*d*.[11] In 1706 the Shrovetide and St. George's Day races were moved to Easter Tuesday, but two years later all the racing was concentrated at a meeting on St. George's Day,[12] and the rules under which they were run were codified and confirmed. The principal race was the City Plate, supported by both the corporation and the guilds. Each owner could enter one horse carrying 10 stone. The race started at 2.30 and was apparently run round a right-handed circuit marked out by poles over three heats of three laps each (about three miles), with up to 30 minutes allowed for rubbing down the horses between heats. The prize went to the first horse to win two heats. Any which finished more than 120 yd. behind the winner of a heat did not run again. If three different horses won the heats they ran off in a fourth heat.[13] New 'chairs', presumably to mark the start and finish and perhaps the 120-yd. distance, were approved by the Assembly in 1714.[14]

The new rules marked the establishment of a fixed pattern of racing, and the St. George's Day meeting rapidly became a central event in Chester's social calendar. In the early 18th century 'a great concourse of people from all parts' attended,[15] owners included gentlemen from Cheshire, Liverpool, and Yorkshire, betting was important, and spectators were numerous and partisan.[16] The corporation long remained intimately involved. In 1694 it reaffirmed an old rule by ordering that horses entered for the races were to be stabled in the city for eight days beforehand (reduced to six days in 1708): the rule served to bring trade into Chester for a few extra days, and also made cheating more difficult because the horses were under supervision for longer.[17] The corporation was still closely involved in managing the races in 1777, ordering the weight carried by horses to be reduced to 9 stone, and setting the entrance fees for owners and the value of the prizes.[18]

The racecourse, extended towards the river in 1709,[19] assumed more or less its modern shape after the canalization of the Dee in the 1730s, when a new timber yard stretching from the Watergate to the river restricted racing to the area south of the Watergate.[20] The course, changed to a left-handed circuit, as it has remained, was marked by posts and had starting and distance chairs. The corporation viewed the races from a building near the Watergate called the Pentice on the Roodee, perhaps dating from 1607,[21] and others watched on foot or horseback, or from the city walls, which overlooked the finish.[22] In 1742 the Assembly required that individuals who wanted to erect booths, tents, or 'standings' against the walls had to seek its special permission first;[23] and in 1769–70 it built bigger starting and distance chairs, added a balcony to the Pentice,[24] and gave permission for Bennett Williams of Flint to build a small private grandstand against the

1 Above, Plays, Sports, and Customs before 1700: Sporting Customs (Shrovetide Celebrations); Ormerod, *Hist. Ches.* i. 380–1; C.C.A.L.S., ZAB 1, ff. 67–8.

2 *Diary of Henry Prescott*, i. 37.

3 C.C.A.L.S., ZAB 3, f. 184.   4 Below (this chapter).

5 Hemingway, *Hist. Chester*, i. 210–11, 212–13 n.; *Cal. Chester City Cl. Mins. 1603–42*, 44 n., 55; Hist. MSS. Com. 7, *8th Rep. I, Chester*, p. 366; C.C.A.L.S., ZAF 8/38; above, Plays, Sports, and Customs before 1700: Sporting Customs (Shrovetide Celebrations).

6 Hemingway, *Hist. Chester*, i. 211; B.L. Harl. MS. 2125, f. 126.

7 C.C.A.L.S., ZCHD 9/9, 29–30.

8 Above, Plays, Sports, and Customs before 1700: Sporting Customs (Shrovetide Celebrations).

9 *King's Vale Royal*, [ii], 16.

10 Bevan, *Roodee*, 19; Ormerod, *Hist. Ches.* ii. 222, 561.

11 Hemingway, *Hist. Chester*, i. 211 n.; C.C.A.L.S., ZAF 39C/7.

12 C.C.A.L.S., ZAB 3, f. 140v.; Ormerod, *Hist. Ches.* i. 384 n.

13 C.C.A.L.S., ZAB 3, ff. 158v.–159, 212.

14 Ibid. f. 215.   15 Hemingway, *Hist. Chester*, i. 361.

16 *Diary of Henry Prescott*, i. 4, 280; ii. 308, 355, 383–4, 437–8, 504–5, 570, 572, 630, 691.

17 C.C.A.L.S., ZAB 3, ff. 42v., 158v.–159; G. T. Burrows, *Ches. Sports and Sportsmen*, 38.

18 C.C.A.L.S., ZAB 4, f. 324 and v.

19 3 *Sheaf*, xxi, pp. 85–6.

20 *V.C.H. Ches.* v (1), Topography, 900–1914: Early Modern and Georgian (Building Activity, 1660–1760).

21 *J.C.A.S.* [o.s.], xii. 500.

22 S. and N. Buck, *SW. Prospect of Chester* (1728); Lavaux, *Plan of Chester*.

23 C.C.A.L.S., ZAB 4, f. 100v.

24 Ibid. ff. 201 and v., 266.

FIG. 156. *Chester races, 1753*

city wall.[1] In 1760 the Assembly had paid a carpenter, Richard Ledsham, for drawing plans for a grandstand but it is not clear that it was built.[2] In 1777 it decided to charge the owners of carriages 1 s. to bring them on the Roodee during the races.[3] By 1789 the course had been enlarged to make full use of the available ground and there were separate starting chairs for four-year-olds and older horses on the river side, the distance and finishing chairs remaining below the city walls.[4]

In the early 18th century the meeting lasted three days, each of which featured one race in heats. In each race the first horse to win two heats took the prize, a silver cup or plate given by subscribers. The three plates were worth much the same, especially after 1739, when parliament set a minimum value for prizes,[5] but the most sought after was the City Plate, by the 1710s provided each year through subscriptions from the corporation and guilds. The distance was increased from three to four laps in 1726. The race was run under different names (St. George's Plate, New Plate, Corporation Plate, and City Purse) until 1836,[6] when

the council realized that the Municipal Corporations Act of 1835 had made its own financial contribution illegal.[7] The second most highly regarded race in the 18th century was the Grosvenor Gold Cup, first offered by Sir Robert Grosvenor, Bt., in 1741;[8] the Grosvenors continued to provide prizes throughout the 18th and 19th centuries.[9]

Race week was moved to the first full week in May after the calendar reform in 1752, allegedly because the mayor, a draper, hoped to sell more summer dresses in warmer weather.[10] The programme of racing grew steadily in the later 18th century, a fourth day being added in 1751 and a fifth in 1758, with additional meetings held in 1739, 1744, 1754–5, and 1774–81,[11] testimony to Chester's popularity among racegoers. Owners *c.* 1730 included leading noblemen and gentlemen from the North-West, such as the Grosvenors, the earls of Derby, and the Williams-Wynns,[12] and sportsmen from a wider region which included Flintshire, Denbighshire, Shropshire, Staffordshire, Derbyshire, and Warwickshire. By the 1750s and 1760s, as the reputation of the meeting grew, owners were bringing their horses from Yorkshire, Northumberland, Herefordshire, and Gloucestershire, while in 1767 complaints were voiced that the meeting was dominated by 'Newmarket owners' (meaning the richest and most aristocratic owners who could afford to take part in racing at Newmarket, the country's most important racecourse) to the exclusion of northerners.[13]

The type of racing changed very little before the late 18th century: a race for four-year-olds over two-mile heats was added in 1751, but still in 1790 each day's racing consisted of a single race run in heats. Runners were not numerous: on average only four or five contested each race in the 1740s and 1750s.[14] The character of the meeting began to change only in the 1790s. Racing in heats was gradually abandoned in favour of races in their modern form, run in a single heat, though matches arranged privately between two owners were important for a time in the early 19th century. Already by 1800 there were as many ordinary races and matches as races in heats; by 1810 heats made up less than a third of the total; and by 1820 ordinary races were the norm. The change came about to accommodate the trend towards running younger horses over shorter distances, testing speed alone and not stamina. Chester had a race for three-year-olds

1 Ibid. ff. 264v.–265; ZCHD 9/58–9.

2 Ibid. ZTAV 2/44; *Rolls of Freemen of Chester*, ii (R.S.L.C. lv), 325.   3 C.C.A.L.S., ZAB 4, f. 326.

4 J. Hunter and S. Weston, *Plan of Chester* (1789).

5 Gaming Act, 13 Geo. II, c. 19, s. 2; cf. Gaming Act, 18 Geo. II, c. 34, s. 11.

6 C.C.A.L.S., ZAB 3, ff. 140v., 212; ZAF 50F, no. 26; ZG 6/3, s.a. 1705, 1713; ZTAB 2, f. 77; ZTAB 3, f. 30; ZTAB 6, ff. 8, 114v.; *J.C.A.S.* xviii. 156–7; xxi. 112; F. Simpson, *Chester Races: Their Early Hist.* (repr. from *Ches. Observer*, 25 Apr., 7 May 1925), 4–5; Bevan, *Roodee*, 37; *31st Rep. Com. Char.* 371.

7 5 & 6 Wm. IV, c. 76, s. 92; C.C.A.L.S., ZAB 6, pp. 72, 180;

Burrows, *Ches. Sports*, 49–50.

8 Bevan, *Roodee*, 24, giving the wrong forename: G.E.C. *Baronetage*, i. 191.

9 e.g. *Racing Cal. 1820*, 24–8; *1860*, 64–72; Bevan, *Roodee*, 29; C.C.A.L.S., ZCR 372/1; *Ches. Life*, May 1982, p. 58.

10 *J.C.A.S.* [o.s.], x/xi, p. 288.

11 *Hist. List Horse-Matches, 1729* and later edns. to *1770*; *Racing Cal. 1773* and later edns.

12 Ormerod, *Hist. Ches.* i. 382 n.

13 Bevan, *Roodee*, 27.

14 Ibid. 25; *Hist. List Horse-Matches, 1740* and later edns.; Ormerod, *Hist. Ches.* i. 382 n.

FIG. 157. *Chester races, between 1830 and 1840*

over two miles by 1800, and one for two-year-olds over four furlongs by 1820. In the latter year, of the other ten races four were over a mile, four over two miles, and only two over three miles. The switch to the modern pattern was complete by 1860, when the four-day meeting included twelve sprints of seven furlongs or less, nine races between a mile and two miles, and only two distance races.[1]

Several new races were introduced in the first third of the 19th century,[2] notably the Chester Tradesmen's Cup (later called the Chester Cup) in 1824. It was a handicap, something of a novelty and popular among gamblers. Its importance was established by 1836, when it was said that £1 million was wagered on its outcome. Its success also owed much to skilful handicapping by E. W. Topham, clerk of the course from the 1840s to his death in 1873.[3] During his time it attracted thirty or forty runners.[4] Once racing in heats had been abandoned there was less need for the meeting to last a full week, and it was reduced to four days in 1843 (though there was an additional October meeting 1843–57), and to three in 1878.[5]

The Assembly's disengagement from direct management of the races probably dates from around 1798, when it ordered the Pentice on the Roodee to be demolished and ceased attending in its official capacity.[6] In the early 19th century the races were instead managed by a committee which rented the Roodee from the corporation for a fortnight each year, the first week to allow for preparations.[7] In 1817, in response to the growing interest of polite society, a public subscription raised £2,500 to build a new grandstand. Among those involved in the grandstand committee

were Sir Watkin Williams-Wynn and the local newspaper proprietor John Fletcher. The city's innkeepers, who sold refreshments from tents and booths on the Roodee during the races, were opposed to it but failed to convince the corporation. The grandstand, designed by Thomas Harrison, was opened in 1819 on land leased by the corporation opposite the starting post. Entered from the city walls, it allowed the wealthiest racegoers to seclude themselves from the lower orders, and was enlarged in 1829.[8] A second subscription stand, the Dee Stand, was put up to its south by a separate company in 1840 and catered for the middle classes.[9] In the 1820s the social tone of the meeting was evidently high: a sympathetic observer wrote of the 'immense influx of affluent visitors' from Cheshire, Lancashire, Shropshire, and Wales during race week.[10]

Several factors might have curtailed racing during the 19th century. The switch to sprints put Chester at a disadvantage. The circuit was so tight that even five-furlong races could not be run on the straight, and owners of valuable young bloodstock were reluctant to enter them in races where they might be injured.[11] There was also growing opposition on moral grounds, especially from the city's nonconformists and evangelicals. In 1856 William Wilson inveighed against the races, which he asserted brought drunkenness, brawling, gambling, theft, prostitution, 'loathsome diseases', lunacy, suicide, and damnation to the city.[12] The attack was renewed in more measured tones in 1870–1 by the Anglican establishment, led by Dean Howson and Canon Kingsley,[13] and in 1898 by the Evangelical Free Church Council.[14]

The stridency of Wilson's attack in 1856 is evidence

1 *Racing Cal. 1780* and later edns. to *1860*.

2 Bevan, *Roodee*, 28.

3 Ibid. 33, 36–7, 43–5, 50, 56; J. Fairfax-Blakeborough, *Short Hist. Chester Races* (Chester Race Co. [1951]), 12.

4 Simpson, *Chester Races*, 8.

5 *Racing Cal. 1840* and later edns. to *1900*.

6 C.C.A.L.S., ZAB 5, p. 119; F. Simpson, *Walls of Chester*, 43.

7 e.g. C.C.A.L.S., ZCCB 30, 10 Jan. 1843.

8 Bevan, *Roodee*, 28–9; Hemingway, *Hist. Chester*, i. 362–3; H. Hughes, *Chronicle of Chester*, 94–5 and plate betw. pp. 66–7; [J. H. Hanshall], *Stranger in Chester* [1816], 47–8; C.C.A.L.S.,

ZAB 5, pp. 324, 367, 384, 404–5; ZCCB 38, pp. 309–14.

9 Bevan, *Roodee*, 40.

10 Ibid. 29, 33; Hemingway, *Hist. Chester*, i. 362.

11 C.C.A.L.S., ZCCB 38, pp. 330–2; cf. Bevan, *Roodee*, 104.

12 W. Wilson, *Chester Races* (Chester, 1856).

13 J. S. Howson, *Chester Races* (Chester, 1870); 'Chester Tradesman', *Chester Races: Do They Pay?* (2 pts. Chester, 1871); C. Kingsley, *Betting: Letter to Young Men of Chester* (Chester, 1871): copies of all four in Chester public libr. pamphlet colln.; Bevan, *Roodee*, 30–3.

14 C.C.A.L.S., ZCR 572/1, pp. 25–6.

that the race meeting had assumed a popular character on top of its long-standing appeal to the gentry. The railways were thought to have tripled attendance by 1850,[1] and as working-class leisure became more ample the crowds grew ever larger. Race week, especially Chester Cup day, was regarded in 1876 as 'a people's holiday' and 'one of the great sporting holidays of the North'. The size of crowds at open meetings before 1893 is difficult to estimate but they were clearly very large: the figure of 100,000 said to have attended on Cup Day in 1886 perhaps represents a wild guess, and a different observer writing in 1892 thought that the attendance was normally about 50,000.[2]

The third factor was unsatisfactory management. From 1840 there were three bodies with separate financial interests as lessees from the city: the Race Course Committee, the Grand Stand Committee, and the Dee Stand Committee. The stand proprietors were believed to make huge profits,[3] most of which they in fact ploughed back into the races as prize money.[4] At first the council remained at arm's length, taking a closer interest from the 1880s as pressure mounted to modernize both the meeting and the course. Its Roodee committee (later called the racecourse committee), set up in 1884, sought to fend off demands that the meeting be stopped altogether, and to make new arrangements after the grandstand leases expired.[5] In 1888 the issue was forced by the Race Course Co.'s declaration that it would not renew its lease when it expired in 1892. Negotiations among the parties directly interested, the Jockey Club, and the promoters of a new racecourse elsewhere made it clear that many wanted to turn Chester into a gate-money meeting, following the national trend among the surviving 'county' race meetings. The agreement that finally emerged owed much to Alderman H. T. Brown, chairman of the racecourse committee, who outflanked the anti-racing lobby by offering only a 14-year lease and one race meeting a year, not the 25 years and two meetings which the promoters wanted.[6] Opposition to racing lingered into the 1920s[7] but its force was broken by the tighter regulation of crowds made possible by the reorganization of 1893. The existing company re-formed itself as the Chester Race Co. in 1892, bought out the stand proprietors, and held the first 'closed' meeting, charging for admission, in 1893.

Admission charges at first reduced attendance to 20,000 on Cup Day 1893, but numbers soon rose again and from 1900 fully justified the description of 'gigantic throngs of humanity' clogging the streets of Chester and queueing for admission from the Roodee the full

FIG. 158. *Race-going crowds at the Cross and Eastgate Street, c. 1903*

length of Watergate Street to the Cross. New heights were reached after both world wars: 96,000 went racing on Cup Day 1920, 104,000 in 1946.[8] The races were still thought of as 'the great Cheshire holiday' in 1951,[9] but wider opportunities for leisure from the later 1950s quickly eroded the crowds. An evening meeting which drew 17,000 in 1974 was thought remarkable,[10] and the daily average in 1995 was *c.* 14,000.[11]

The crowds necessitated new facilities after 1893. At first there were only minor additions, such as a press box and telegraph office in 1894, and the company proposed merely to improve the existing stands, but the council's racecourse committee pressed for new stands meeting current standards and expectations. Thus was completed in 1900 the County Stand, a picturesque half-timbered building designed by Mangnall & Littlewoods of Manchester to accommodate 5,000 people under cover.[12] Its loss by fire in 1985 was much lamented, and in 1988 it was replaced by a new stand with improved facilities (Fig. 159, p. 260).[13]

More races were added to the programme after the

1 *Bagshaw's Dir. Ches.* (1850), 72.

2 Bevan, *Roodee*, 50–1, 58–9, 61–3, 89; *Chester in 1892, Illustrated* (publ. Robinson, Son, and Pike), 13; cf. 3 *Sheaf*, xviii, pp. 79–80.   3 e.g. Howson, *Chester Races*, 4.

4 e.g. C.C.A.L.S., ZCR 372/1.

5 Ibid. ZCCB 38, pp. 300–19.

6 Ibid. pp. 320–48; ZCCB 136, pp. 1–133; ZD/JWW 702.

7 Simpson, *Chester Races*, 12.

8 Bevan, *Roodee*, 87, 112, 122.

9 Fairfax-Blakeborough, *Short Hist. Chester Races*, 17.

10 Bevan, *Roodee*, 126, 130, 138, 144–5.

11 *Chester Chron.* 6 Oct. 1995, p. 29.

12 Bevan, *Roodee*, 84–5, 92, 96–7; C.C.A.L.S., ZCCB 136, pp. 79, 112–28.   13 Bevan, *Roodee*, 155–64.

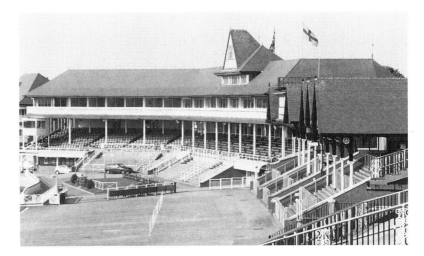

FIG. 159. *New grandstand, built 1988*

1893 reorganization, notably the Chester Vase in 1907,[1] but the Chester Cup retained its primacy, especially *c.* 1900,[2] and again in the 1930s, when it was regarded as a trial for the Derby.[3] Chester was slow to increase the number of days' racing in the 20th century, and in 1951 was one of only two flat courses with a single meeting each year.[4] Chester was awarded three extra days and an evening meeting in 1964; another evening meeting was added in 1987, a further two days in 1990, and a Sunday meeting before 1995, by when there were 11 days of racing between May and October each year.[5]

SPORT AFTER 1700

The sports played and watched in modern Chester have been influenced by the city's social character and by two natural assets, the Roodee and the river.[6] The Roodee was the setting not only for horse racing,[7] but also for bowls, and in the 19th and 20th centuries for amateur athletics, soccer, cricket, hockey, and polo. The stretch of the Dee above the weir enabled rowing and later canoeing to develop to a high standard, while skating was possible in the occasional winters when it froze over, as in 1822, 1895, 1917, and 1929.[8]

Among the sports long established in county towns bull baiting and cock fighting (the latter closely associated with Chester races) were in decline at Chester before they were banned in the earlier 19th century. From the 1840s the city's numerous middle classes gave an early impetus to amateur rowing and beagling. In the late 19th century and the Edwardian period the typically suburban games made a strong showing, especially golf, hockey, badminton, and lawn tennis.[9] The small size of the city's industrial working class did not prevent the growth of amateur soccer or working-class participation in swimming and rowing, and there was even pigeon racing,[10] but it did affect the

provision of commercial mass-spectator sport. Chester's professional football club was a weak latecomer; there was little professional boxing; and the greyhound track was built late in the pre-1939 boom. In the later 20th century aquatic sports and middle-class team games like hockey and lacrosse were relatively popular, but otherwise Chester's sports lost something of their distinctiveness, for instance with the appearance of newly fashionable minority sports like squash, basketball, and American football.

PUBLIC FACILITIES

The city council allowed the Roodee to be used for team games from the mid 19th century,[11] but did not have the power to let any part of it for permanent occupation. In 1900 it thus turned down a proposal from Chester Football Club and Chester Cycling Club for the council to build an enclosed football ground within a banked cycling track, to be rented to the two clubs.[12] The council opened swimming pools at the Union Street baths in 1901, and from 1911 it and Hoole urban district council provided public bowling greens and tennis courts.[13] From 1968 the Chester Area

1 Bevan, *Roodee*, 85, 98.

2 Fairfax-Blakeborough, *Short Hist. Chester Races*, 10, citing *Brit. Turf* (1901).   3 Bevan, *Roodee*, 118.

4 Fairfax-Blakeborough, *Short Hist. Chester Races*, 17.

5 Bevan, *Roodee*, 138–9, 157; *Racing Cal. 1960* and later edns. to *1988*; *Programme of Flat Meetings under Rules of Racing, 1989* and later edns.

6 Mr. K. Sykes, Frodsham, kindly provided a number of additional references for this chapter.

7 Above, Chester Races.

8 G. Huxley, *Lady Elizabeth and the Grosvenors*, 34; *Archives Photographs Series: Chester*, comp. M. Day and P. O'Brien (1996), 96–7.

9 J. Lowerson, *Sport and Eng. Middle Classes, passim.*

10 C.C.A.L.S., DDX 272.

11 Below, this chapter: Association Football, Cricket; *Chester City Cl. Mins. 1919/20*, 43–4.

12 *Chester City Cl. Mins. 1899/1900*, 420–2.

13 Below, this chapter: Bowls, Other Sports (Lawn Tennis, Swimming).

FIG. 160. *Northgate Arena*

Sports Advisory Council organized an annual sports week (later a fortnight) during which clubs held their own events. The event was run after 1986 by the Chester Sports and Leisure Association, to which individual clubs were affiliated.[1] After 1966 the River Dee Water Sports Association co-ordinated the interests of rowers, sailors, canoeists, anglers, and motorboat enthusiasts.[2]

The city council was concerned about playing fields by the 1920s.[3] In the 1970s it opened a floodlit all-weather pitch and a 9-hole golf course at Westminster Park,[4] public squash courts,[5] and the Northgate Arena leisure centre. The last, a striking building opened in 1977, included an 1,800-seat sports hall and practice rooms, but its pools did not meet the needs of serious swimmers.[6] The Arena was mainly used for practice and leisure activities: in 1994 the only competitive sports played there regularly were netball, squash, and professional basketball.[7] In 1991 the city council appointed a sports development officer for the first time.[8]

Chester's main sports ground in the late 20th century grew out of Cheshire County Officers' Sports Club, which began by 1936 on a large site off Newton Lane[9] and provided for soccer, hockey, cricket, tennis, and bowls. In 1975 the county council reopened Brookhirst Switchgear Ltd.'s former private playing fields in Upton as Cheshire County Council Sports Club, for the joint use of a nearby school, the County

Officers' Club (which moved from Newton Lane), and the public. It provided for a wide range of competitive sports and attracted existing hockey, soccer, athletics, fencing, and lacrosse clubs. By 1994 the county netball and badminton teams were also based there. Outdoor pitches for cricket, soccer, hockey, tennis, and netball were supplemented in 1993 by a floodlit all-weather artificial pitch.[10]

ASSOCIATION FOOTBALL

Soccer was played at Chester College and on the Roodee by 1867[11] and was well established in the city by the early 1880s, when several clubs used playing fields on the Roodee provided by the council.[12] Two of the clubs, Chester Rovers and King's School Old Boys, amalgamated in 1885 as Chester F.C. The club at first played in Hoole, moving to Whipcord Lane in 1904 and Sealand Road in 1906, when a limited company was formed. The first board of directors included a corn merchant, a baker, a butcher, an accountant, a stationer, a doctor, a clock maker, and an insurance manager,[13] but the largest shareholder was Alfred Mond of Brunner, Mond & Co., M.P. for Chester 1906–10.[14]

The club was a founder member in 1890 of the Football Combination, turned professional in 1902, and was admitted to the stronger Lancashire Combination in 1910, being promoted to the first division in 1911. After a hiatus during the First World War

1 *Chester Sports Week, 1968,* 3; *Chester Sports Fortnight, 1969,* esp. 3, 9, 27; and later edns. (copies in Chester public libr. pamphlet colln.); C.C.A.L.S., TS. list of ZCR 842.

2 W. J. C. Todd, *Royal Chester Rowing Club, 1939–88,* 63; River Dee Water Sports Association, 'Cal. of Major River Events, 1973' (TS. in Chester public libr. pamphlet colln.).

3 *Chester City Cl. Mins. 1923/4,* 296–7; *1937/8,* 71–5.

4 *Chester City Sports Week, 1970,* 28 (copy in Chester public libr. pamphlet colln.); below, this chapter: Golf.

5 Below, this chapter: Other Sports (Squash).

6 NW. Cl. for Sport and Recreation, *Dir. of New Facilities* (1977), 1; *Northgate Arena, Chester* (brochure for opening: copy in Chester public libr.); *Official Chester Guide Bk.* (1989 edn.), 52–3; local inf.

7 Inf. from Mr. J. Kelly, Northgate Arena.

8 Inf. from Ms. J. Peace, Sports Development Officer.

9 O.S. Map 1/2,500, Ches. XXXVIII.7 (1936 edn.).

10 Inf. from Mr. M. N. Fearon, manager.

11 J. L. Bradbury, *Chester Coll.* 136; *Gresty and Burghall's Chester Guide* [1867], 34.

12 Acct. of soccer based, except where stated otherwise, on 'Bevys', *Chester Football Club, 1885/6–1935/6: Reminiscences* (Chester, 1936); [Chester Football Club], *21 Years of Chester Football Club Ltd. 1931–52* (copy in C.C.A.L.S., ZCR 546/27); *Rothmans Football Yearbk.* 1992–3, 163; 1993–4, 159.

13 *Memorandum and Articles of Association of Chester Football Club Ltd.* p. 17 (copy in C.C.A.L.S., ZCR 242/1); *Kelly's Dir. Ches.* (1906) for directors' occupations; cf. Lowerson, *Sport and Eng. Middle Classes,* 226.

14 *D.N.B. 1922–30.*

Chester resigned from the Lancashire Combination in 1919 to help form the Cheshire County League, which it dominated throughout the 1920s. After a new grandstand was opened in 1920 matches against local rivals Connah's Quay attracted crowds of over 6,000.

From 1930 Harry Mansley as chairman and Charles Hewitt as the first full-time secretary and manager improved the ground and the club's finances and playing staff, and Chester were elected to the Football League (Division III North) in 1931. The club's most successful years followed, marked especially by a 5–0 win over Fulham in the F.A. Cup 3rd round of 1932 before a home gate of 14,000, a feat regarded by some as 'the greatest thing that had happened since the Romans evacuated the city'.[1]

Promotion from the bottom division (IV after 1958) eluded the club even in its heyday, and the years after 1946 saw poor results, falling attendances, a retrenchment to part-time professional players, and two re-elections to the League.[2] Chester won promotion to Division III in 1975 and a new stand was opened in 1979.[3] Its name was changed to Chester City in 1983. The club's finances, however, continued to deteriorate, and in 1990 it sold Sealand Road for development, shared Macclesfield's ground for two seasons, and returned to Chester in 1992 to the new 6,000-capacity Deva Stadium in Bumper's Lane. In the 1980s and earlier 1990s the team fluctuated between the bottom two divisions, but in the later 1990s the standard of playing and the club's finances both took a turn for the worse. The club was rescued from financial administration in 1999 by a new American owner with a controversial approach to management, team selection, and coaching, and was relegated to the Football Conference in 2000.[4]

Amateur soccer in Chester was represented by a Hospital Saturday Cup competition, organized intermittently from 1890,[5] and by the Chester and Runcorn Football Association and the Chester and District Football League, formed in 1893 and 1894 respectively. The latter included nearly 60 clubs in 1949.[6] In the 1990s the league had three divisions with 33 teams, and a Sunday league catered for 48 teams.[7] One of the strongest amateur clubs in the city was Chester Nomads F.C., formed in 1904, which settled at Boughton Hall in 1913 and was still playing there in the 1990s.[8] A women's team connected with Chester City was playing league soccer by 1994.[9]

ATHLETICS[10]

Foot races for prize money were staged in the 18th and early 19th century, commonly on the Roodee and often attracting large crowds.[11] Amateur athletics were first organized on a large scale during the 1860s boom in the form of the Chester Autumn Sports, held annually on the Roodee from 1863 and owing much initially to the support of W. Maysmor Williams, a prominent councillor. The event lapsed after 1893, was revived in 1925, and continued in 1993. Attendance in the 1930s and 1950s (when it was held on August Bank Holiday) occasionally topped 30,000, and the meeting was once regarded as one of the foremost in the North,[12] but the creation of proper athletics stadia in other towns had greatly reduced its importance by the 1990s. One of several 'athletic' clubs existing in the later 19th century (catering mainly for an interest in gymnastics), St. Oswald's, formed a group for runners ('harriers') in 1889.[13] Chester and District (later Chester and Ellesmere Port) Athletics Club, formed in 1967, at first used the track at Chester College,[14] moving to the County Sports Club at Upton in 1992.[15]

BOWLS

There was a bowling green in what became the Groves by 1630 and another on the Roodee in 1636.[16] A third at Bowling Green Bank at the east corner of the Gorse Stacks was new in 1700.[17] The Roodee green was restored to use after 1660,[18] and was still in use in 1800.[19] Those at the Gorse Stacks and in the Groves continued into the 20th century.[20] The Groves bowling green was used in 1910 by Chester Bowling Club.[21] That at the Gorse Stacks was attached to the Bowling Green House (later Hotel) by 1750.[22] In the 1860s and

---

1 Quotation from *21 Years*, 15.

2 Cf. 'Playing Rec. of Chester A.F.C. 1931–59', comp. J. H. Cunnington (C.C.A.L.S., ZCR 546/25).

3 *Chester City F.C.: Forward to the 80's* (copy in C.C.A.L.S., ZCR 546/32).

4 *Independent*, 3 May 2001, p. 26.

5 e.g. *135th Ann. Rep. of Chester General Infirmary*, 31; *138th Ann. Rep.* 42–3; *142nd Ann. Rep.* 39.

6 *Sportsmen's Evening at Town Hall, Chester, 21 Feb. 1949* (programme in C.C.A.L.S., ZCR 546/32).

7 *Chester Chron.* 9 Oct. 1992, p. 23.

8 A. Robinson, *Century at Boughton Hall: Hist. Chester Boughton Hall Cricket Club, 1873–1973* (priv. print. [1973]), 8; inf. from Mr. Robinson, Waverton.

9 *Chester Chron.* 5 May 1995, p. 28.

10 Several additional references for this and the following sections were kindly supplied by Mr. Sykes.

11 *Diary of Henry Prescott*, i. 159; Hemingway, *Hist. Chester*, ii. 253; 1 *Sheaf*, i, p. 165.

12 e.g. *Chester Autumn Sports and Carnival Programme* (1954) (copy at C.H.H.); ibid. (1950–5 and 1957) (copies in Chester public libr. pamphlet colln.); for Williams's role: *Gresty and Burghall's Chester Guide* [1867], 34.

13 *P. & G. Dir. Chester* (1871), 11; *Chester Chron.* 14 Sept. 1889.

14 e.g. *Chester City Sports Week, 1970*, 18.

15 Inf. from Mr. Fearon.

16 *Cal. Chester City Cl. Mins. 1603–42*, 164, 200, and map 1; *Chester: Contemporary Descriptions*, ed. D. M. Palliser (1980), 13; C.C.A.L.S., ZAF 11/24.

17 *P.N. Ches.* v (1:i), 65; 3 *Sheaf*, xx, p. 91; C.C.A.L.S., ZAB 3, f. 78.   18 C.C.A.L.S., ZAF 39A/13.

19 Ibid. ZAB 5, pp. 147–8.

20 e.g. ibid. ZAB 4, f. 4v.; Lavaux, *Plan of Chester*; J. Hunter and S. Weston, *Plan of Chester* (1789); Murray and Stuart, *Plan of Chester* (1791); *Brit. Atlas* (1805).

21 C.C.A.L.S., NVA 1/2, no. 3622.

22 3 *Sheaf*, xi, p. 69; C.C.A.L.S., ZCR 119/20.

1880s its members included city councillors, professional men, and successful tradesmen.[1] The green remained in use in the 1960s but was neglected when taken over and restored in 1975 by a Roman Catholic social club.[2] Other greens were attached to hotels or public houses. One at Flookersbrook in Hoole existed *c.* 1750,[3] and by 1818 the extensive grounds of the Albion Hotel in Lower Bridge Street included a green which continued in use until 1852 or later.[4] The Queen Hotel in City Road had a bowling green in 1889,[5] and the Egerton Arms in Bache (later the Bache Hotel) by 1923. The Deeside Bowling Club, established in 1868, had a green in Souters Lane,[6] and the Hoole and Newton Bowling Club played at Vicarage Road, Hoole, by 1910.[7] Apart from the Catholic club they all fell out of use during the mid and later 20th century.[8]

The first municipal greens were opened in 1911 by Chester city council near the Hermitage in the Groves and by Hoole urban district council at Alexandra Park,[9] and others followed at Buddicom Park in 1921,[10] Tower Fields in 1922,[11] and Cherry Grove in 1925 (moved to Stocks Lane 1974).[12] Buddicom Park closed during the Second World War.[13] The Hermitage green closed after 1966,[14] but a new green was provided in Upton (Wealstone Lane) and two at Westminster Park. In the 1990s Chester and District Bowls League included teams representing the five municipal greens, Bache, and the Catholic club, besides others from outside Chester.[15]

COCK FIGHTING

The place name Cockfight or Cockpit Hill at the north end of Frodsham Street was recorded from the late 16th century.[16] A circular thatched cockpit was built in 1619 by William Stanley, earl of Derby, near the walls south of Newgate.[17] By 1789 it had been replaced by an oval cockpit north of the same gate,[18] which in turn was succeeded by a brick building on the old site, put

up as a commercial speculation in 1825.[19] There were also cockpits in the yards of inns, including the White Talbot, Eastgate Street, in 1738,[20] the Elephant and Castle in the same street, which probably closed before 1796,[21] the Ship, Foregate Street, in 1776,[22] and the Feathers, described as new in 1815.[23] The inn cockpits presumably held matches all year round, but the high point of the cocking year was race week. By the 1730s matches took place on the mornings of race week and until *c.* 1760 were contested by individuals or between the gentlemen of Cheshire and Flintshire. From *c.* 1760 to 1800 gentlemen representing other counties in the North-West, north Wales, and the Midlands also participated. Private matches were again the rule from 1800 to 1834, but the last three race-week cock fights (1835, 1837, and 1839) were between Cheshire and Lancashire. From *c.* 1800 cock fighting by the gentry in connexion with race meetings was in decline, leaving Chester among the strongholds of a sport restricted to south Lancashire, Cheshire, and north Staffordshire.[24] The keeping of cockpits was made illegal in 1835 and cock fighting itself in 1849.[25]

Throwing at cocks was a traditional Shrove Tuesday sport which survived until the 1710s or later.[26]

CRICKET

Cricket was played on the Chester club's ground at Blacon Point by 1820,[27] on the Roodee by 1850,[28] and at Chester College before 1867.[29] The strongest club at first was Chester C.C., which went out of existence in 1898;[30] others included the Cestrian club by the 1840s and the Deva club by the 1860s, with annual subscriptions in the 1870s respectively of 1 guinea and 5*s.* reflecting a difference in social tone.[31]

Boughton Hall C.C. was formed in 1873 by John Thompson as an invitation eleven playing in the grounds of his house, Boughton Hall.[32] By the 1880s the club was financed by its members and had become

1 G. T. Burrows, *All About Bowls* (1948 edn.), 19; *White's Dir. Ches.* (1860), 101; *Chester Chron.* 31 July 1869, p. 8.

2 Inf. from Mr. J. S. Callister, Chester, who is thanked for advice on the history of bowls in Chester; above, Roman Catholicism.

3 3 *Sheaf,* xiv, p. 49; xx, p. 90.

4 *Georgian Chester*, ed. A. M. Kennett, 38; *Bagshaw's Dir. Ches.* (1850), 72; Burrows, *All About Bowls*, 13; J. Romney, *Chester and its Environs Illustrated*, [32].

5 O.S. Map 1/2,500, Ches. XXXVIII.11 (1875 and 1899 edns.); *Chester Chron.* 8 June 1889.

6 *P. & G. Dir. Chester* (1923/4), 24; (1933/4), 22.

7 C.C.A.L.S., NVA 1/7, no. 1311.

8 *P. & G. Dir. Chester* (1935/6), 22; inf. from Mr. R. G. Dawson, Chester and District Bowls League.

9 *Chester City Cl. Mins. 1910/11*, 472; C.C.A.L.S., ZTRH 84, pp. 319, 352–3, 401.   10 *Chester City Cl. Mins. 1920/1*, 471.

11 Ibid. *1921/2*, 473.

12 Ibid. *1923/4*, 60, 297, 553; *1925/6*, 408; *1974/5*, p. 268.

13 Ibid. *1942/3*, 197; *1944/5*, 397, 445–6; *1945/6*, 57.

14 C.P.S., Groves (neg. N 14/12).

15 Inf. from Mr. Dawson; *Chester Chron.* 21 Apr. 1995, p. 25.

16 *P.N. Ches.* v (1:i), 73.

17 Simpson, *Walls of Chester*, 67–8.

18 J. Hunter and S. Weston, *Plan of Chester* (1789).

19 Hemingway, *Hist. Chester*, i. 381–2.

20 1 *Sheaf,* i, p. 132.

21 *Chester Chron.* 23 Sept. 1796, p. 3.

22 Hughes, *Chronicle of Chester*, 127.

23 3 *Sheaf,* vi, pp. 40–2.

24 *Hist. List Horse-Matches, 1739* and later edns. to *1770*; *Racing Cal. 1779* and later edns. to *1841*.

25 Cruelty to Animals Act, 5 & 6 Wm. IV, c. 59, ss. 1, 3; Cruelty to Animals Act, 12 & 13 Vic. c. 92, ss. 1, 3.

26 *Diary of Henry Prescott*, i. 269; ii. 619–20, 677.

27 *Chester Chron.* 28 July 1820; cf. ibid. 10 July 1839.

28 *Bagshaw's Dir. Ches.* (1850), 72; 3 *Sheaf,* xviii, pp. 80, 84–5.

29 Bradbury, *Chester Coll.* 136.

30 A. Robinson, *Century at Boughton Hall: Hist. Chester Boughton Hall Cricket Club, 1873–1973* (priv. print. [1973]), 3, 6.

31 *Chester Chron.* 30 July 1847, 26 Nov. 1870; *P. & G. Dir. Chester* (1871), 11; (1878/9), 10.

32 Rest of cricket based on Robinson, *Century at Boughton Hall*; inf. from Mr. Robinson, Waverton.

the leading team in the city, dominating the short-lived Chester and District League (1894–c. 1900) and playing fixtures against teams in Cheshire and south Lancashire. Its early members were drawn from Chester's professional and commercial élite. In 1923 it joined the Liverpool Competition and made a consistently good showing in its unofficial rankings until 1939. The club became a limited company in 1925, bought its ground in 1945, and changed its name in 1955 to Chester Boughton Hall C.C. After 1945 the season was dominated by the Liverpool Competition (which evolved into a regular league) and from the 1960s there were also Sunday and evening matches in a variety of knock-out competitions. A second pitch was in use from 1974, allowing the club to field four teams in the 1990s. The club never employed a professional but in the 1990s had the services of a succession of junior players from the West Indies, several of whom graduated to Test cricket.

Cheshire first played at Boughton Hall in 1910 and held an annual minor counties match there between the wars and again from 1969. The county team often included Boughton Hall players.

City teams representing churches, offices, and commercial and industrial firms played in an annual knock-out competition at Boughton Hall from 1913. Crowds up to 1,000 before 1939 fell sharply in the 1950s and the competition was discontinued in 1966, though it had been resumed by 1994. Chester Women's Cricket Club played at Boughton Hall by 1994. In the 1970s the council provided pitches at Blacon, Hoole, and Westminster Park.[1]

GOLF

The first Chester Golf Club began playing in 1892 on an 18-hole course 6 miles from the city in Sealand (Flints.); it disbanded in 1940 when the land was taken for agriculture. Its namesake at Curzon Park began in 1901 as Bache Golf Club on a 6-hole course north of the county lunatic asylum in Bache, but moved the following year to a 9-hole course on the Bache Hall estate, then occupied by one of the club's founders, Major John MacGillicuddy. The club had over 200 members and employed a professional by 1906, and

had a ladies' section by 1909. A search for a new site began in 1910 when the owner of the Bache Hall estate proposed to sell the land to the asylum, and the last round was played there in 1912. In 1913 the club bought 108 a. at Brewer's Hall from Earl Howe, built a 9-hole course, removed its existing clubhouse from Bache Hall, and adopted the name Curzon Park Golf Club. The course was enlarged to 18 holes in 1920 and was modified several times thereafter. The club was called Chester (Curzon Park) Golf Club from 1923 and Chester Golf Club from 1964.[2]

Upton-by-Chester Golf Club was founded in 1934 by C. J. F. Owen on a 9-hole course, enlarged to 18 holes in 1937.[3] An 18-hole course opened at Blacon Point by T. B. Gorst was played only in 1937 and 1938; after it closed the land was used for an Army camp.[4] A 9-hole municipal course at Westminster Park was opened in 1976.[5]

ROWING

By the earlier 18th century fishermen and boatmen were racing professionally on the Dee,[6] and rowing for prizes continued into the earlier 19th century as a popular spectator sport. A regatta first organized in 1814 to celebrate the Peace of Paris became an annual event; prize money was offered in races for men, women, and boys, watched by crowds reckoned up to 10,000 strong.[7] Races for amateurs in 1832 still excluded only those actually employed on the river,[8] allowing other working men to take part, while the 1843 regatta included a race for 'mechanics or fishermen' besides one for gentlemen.[9]

From the 1840s, however, rowing became a principal focus of the cult of amateurism,[10] and in common with other rowing venues Chester soon had separate clubs for gentlemen amateurs and working men. Its distinctiveness was that the amateur club was especially early among provincial towns[11] and that it clung tenaciously to social exclusivity into the 1950s.[12] That club, formed in 1838 as Chester Victoria Rowing Club and renamed Royal Chester Rowing Club in 1840,[13] was the earliest gentlemen's boat club in the North.[14] It drew its patrons from landed society,[15] went in for elaborate banqueting,[16] and in 1843 even had its own chaplain,[17]

---

1 *Chester City Cl. Mins. 1974/5*, p. 831.

2 *Chester Golf Club Centenary, 1901–2001* (copy at C.H.H.); *Golfer's Handbk.* (1902 and later edns.); *Chester City Cl. Mins. 1905/6*, 639–40; for location of first club: P. Abercrombie, S. Kelly, and T. Fyfe, *Deeside Regional Planning Scheme*, map 1; *P. & G. Dir. Chester* (1919/20), 25; cf. *Chester Chron.* 20 Dec. 1890.

3 *Upton-by-Chester Golf Club: Official Handbk.* 6 (copy in Chester public libr.); *Chester City Sports Week, 1970*, 25.

4 *Golfer's Handbk.* (1937 and 1938 edns.); *Chester City Cl. Mins. 1937/8*, 75; C.C.A.L.S., ZDS 3/600; *Blacon Past and Present* (Blacon Hist. Group, 1990: copy at C.H.H.); *Blacon Community Nature Park* (1989) (leaflet at C.H.H.).

5 Inf. from Mr. J. P. Snead, Westminster Park.

6 N. Wigglesworth, *Social Hist. of Eng. Rowing*, 24; J. V. S.

Glass and J. M. Patrick, *Royal Chester Rowing Club, 1838–1938*, 47.

7 e.g. *Chester Chron.* 10 June 1814, p. 3; 17 June 1814, p. 2; 23 May 1817, p. 3; 2 June 1820, p. 2.

8 Glass and Patrick, *R.C.R.C. 1838–1938*, 9–10; Hemingway, *Hist. Chester*, i. 379 and n.

9 *Illustrated Lond. News*, 19 Aug. 1843, p. 122.

10 Lowerson, *Sport and Eng. Middle Classes*, 157–62.

11 Wigglesworth, *Social Hist. of Eng. Rowing*, 130, 201, 205–6.   12 Below, this section.

13 Glass and Patrick, *R.C.R.C. 1838–1938*, 10–12, 19.

14 Wigglesworth, *Social Hist. of Eng. Rowing*, 118.

15 Ibid. 122; Glass and Patrick, *R.C.R.C. 1838–1938*, 12.

16 Glass and Patrick, *R.C.R.C. 1838–1938*, 14–15, 23.

17 Ibid. 88.

but the rowing itself was also taken seriously, albeit at first by small numbers: 70 joined the club in 1838 but there were only *c.* 20 rowing members in 1841.[1] Crews competed on the Dee, widely in other northern regattas, and at Henley occasionally from 1855 and regularly after 1874.[2]

The club built a boat shed on the north bank of the Dee upstream from the Groves,[3] moving in 1877 to a new boathouse near by.[4] It bought the site in 1959.[5] The club's regatta was first held on coronation day in 1838; a committee separate from the club took it over in 1840, and it was revived in 1862, becoming a regular event thereafter.[6] The regatta course was fixed *c.* 1851 from Heronbridge downstream to the boathouse.[7] The Royals hired a professional trainer from the Thames in 1841[8] and another from the Tyne in 1854; while at Chester the latter, Mat Taylor, was influential in the development of shell racing boats and in training oarsmen in the new style of rowing which they required.[9] Standards of rowing fluctuated: there were several strong periods up to the 1890s, but not again until the 1930s.[10]

In 1876 the Royals were counted among only 10 rowing clubs catering exclusively for the 'upper class of amateur',[11] though the ethos was only then being finally refined: in 1872, for example, completely against the spirit of gentlemanly amateurism, there was heavy betting on the outcome of a race with the Mersey Rowing Club of Birkenhead.[12] In 1882, however, the Royals were a founder member of the Amateur Rowing Association, designed as and long remaining the guardian of a strict amateur code.[13] Chester was the only provincial club with a member on the A.R.A.'s management committee.[14]

The club remained exclusive until the mid 20th century. In the 1930s it was said to interpret A.R.A. rules 'to the letter'[15] and stood firmly against allowing ladies' rowing clubs to use its boats or premises.[16] It lifted an outright ban on manual workers and weekly wage earners in 1950 only in order to secure a grant towards a new eight from the Ministry of Education.[17]

In the 1950s new members were closely vetted by the committee[18] and the main annual social event was a white-tie ball.[19]

The tone of the club began to change in the 1960s. Boys from the King's school had begun to row for the Royals in the 1950s,[20] but in 1963 the club was still refusing to train oarsmen from scratch,[21] presumably as a means of excluding those thought socially undesirable. The demand for junior rowing and its importance in maintaining the club soon led to change, and a coaching scheme was put in place in 1968.[22] In 1975 the club admitted women and comprehensive-school boys as rowers.[23] In the 1980s the vitality and success of the club was largely dependent on student rowers from local schools and Chester Law College at Christleton.[24]

There were many other boat clubs in Chester besides the Royals. The Cestria club existed by the 1830s, had a boathouse behind Sandy Lane, and survived to the 1940s.[25] The Deva club competed for prize money in 1840,[26] and the True Blue Rowing Club was a rival of the Royals in the 1850s.[27] Small working-class rowing clubs based on a trade or a workplace flourished until the 1930s,[28] and there was an annual watermen's regatta in the 1920s.[29] The Grosvenor Boat Club was founded in 1869 for clerks and others who were barred from the Royals (Fig. 161, p. 266).[30] It had a boathouse in the Groves by 1892[31] and long remained the Royals' fierce rival,[32] surviving in 1994. The Athena club for junior women rowers was formed *c.* 1977.[33]

Competitive rowing events on a large scale were at first confined to the boat clubs' own regattas, of which the Royals' was the most prominent. From the mid 20th century other events of at least regional importance were devised: the North of England Head of the River for eights (1935), the Dee Autumn Fours (1948, organized by Grosvenor B.C.), and the Long Distance Sculls (1955, by the Royals). The Head and the Sculls were both rowed over 3¾ miles from Eccleston Ferry to the Royals' boathouse.[34] The new events kept Chester, if not always its own clubs, at the forefront of provincial rowing in the later 20th century.

1 Ibid. 12, 22. 2 Ibid. *passim*, esp. 28–31, 41.

3 Ibid. 13; Hughes, *Stranger's Handbk.* (1856), 121; O.S. Maps 1/2,500, Ches. XXXVIII.11 (1875 and later edns.).

4 Glass and Patrick, *R.C.R.C. 1838–1938*, 42.

5 W. J. C. Todd, *Royal Chester Rowing Club, 1939–88*, 46–7.

6 Glass and Patrick, *R.C.R.C. 1838–1938*, 11, 13, 18, 35–6.

7 Ibid. 19. 8 Ibid. 22.

9 Ibid. 26–9, 34.

10 Ibid. *passim*, esp. 70; Todd, *R.C.R.C. 1939–88*, *passim*.

11 Wigglesworth, *Social Hist. of Eng. Rowing*, 130.

12 Glass and Patrick, *R.C.R.C. 1838–1938*, 39.

13 Todd, *R.C.R.C. 1939–88*, 38, 131; cf. Lowerson, *Sport and Eng. Middle Classes*, 158–9.

14 Wigglesworth, *Social Hist. of Eng. Rowing*, 131.

15 Ibid. 135. 16 Ibid. 78.

17 Todd, *R.C.R.C. 1939–88*, 29. 18 Ibid. 39.

19 C.C.A.L.S., ZCR 419/3.

20 Todd, *R.C.R.C. 1939–88*, 42.

21 C.C.A.L.S., ZCR 419/4, cuttings of 21 Dec. 1961 and 4 May 1963.

22 Todd, *R.C.R.C. 1939–88*, 66.

23 Ibid. 78–80. 24 Ibid. 96–111, 120.

25 Ibid. 15; Wigglesworth, *Social Hist. of Eng. Rowing*, 64; *King's School Chester, Rowing Club Centenary, 1883–1983*, ed. A. G. Evans and others, 9, 17; *P. & G. Dir. Chester* (1919/20), 26, and later edns.; *Kelly's Dir. Chester* (1941), 292; not listed in *Brit. Rowing Almanack* (1950).

26 Wigglesworth, *Social Hist. of Eng. Rowing*, 122.

27 Glass and Patrick, *R.C.R.C. 1838–1938*, 25.

28 Wigglesworth, *Social Hist. of Eng. Rowing*, 157.

29 *Chester City Cl. Mins.* 1921/2, 608; 1922/3, 554; 1923/4, 630; 1924/5, 684; 1925/6, 705.

30 Wigglesworth, *Social Hist. of Eng. Rowing*, 160; *Chester Chron.* 31 July 1869, p. 8.

31 *Kelly's Dir. Ches.* (1892), 220.

32 C.C.A.L.S., ZCR 419/3–4.

33 *Chester Chron.* 5 May 1995, p. 30.

34 Glass and Patrick, *R.C.R.C. 1838–1938*, 74; Todd, *R.C.R.C. 1939–88*, 23, 26, 37, 39.

FIG. 161. *Grosvenor Boat Club members at their boat house*

OTHER SPORTS

American Football

Chester Romans American Football Club was formed in 1986 and from 1987 played in the national league, initially in Westminster Park but from 1994 at Wrexham.[1]

Badminton

A club representing Chester affiliated to the Badminton Association in 1911.[2] It remained a strong sport in the city: the Chester and District Badminton League was formed in 1948 with 12 teams, growing to 78 by 1974.[3]

Basketball

In 1993 the semi-professional men's team Cheshire Jets and its sister women's team Cheshire Cats moved from Ellesmere Port to the Northgate Arena and were renamed Chester Jets and Chester Cats.[4] The venue was highly regarded but the men's team was initially weak and poorly supported.[5]

Beagling

Beagling attracted a small but well-heeled following after the formation in 1854 of the Scratch Beagle Club, which had kennels in Brook Lane and social meetings at the Hop Pole Inn. The club was renamed the Chester Beagles in 1856 and Cheshire Beagles in 1890. It originally hunted over most of western Cheshire and

eastern Flintshire, though gradually abandoned its outlying meets. New kennels were built in Lache Lane in the 1880s, from where they were removed outside the city to Dodleston in 1957. New members and subscribers after 1918 were overwhelmingly from outside Chester.[6]

Boxing

Pugilists performed in the city in the early 19th century (Fig. 162), probably mainly at the Exchange.[7] Amateur boxers trained at a gym under St. Paul's church in Boughton in the later 19th century.[8] The Manchester fight promoter Harry Furness included the American Roller Rink among his venues *c.* 1940,[9] and there were contests at the Northgate Arena in the 1990s.[10]

Bull Baiting

A civic bull bait took place at the Cross as part of the annual mayor-making ceremonies in the early modern period. The corporation withdrew its sanction from the event in 1754 and ceased to attend in its official capacity, but failed in an attempt to suppress it in 1776. The *Chester Chronicle* came out against bull baiting in 1796, and in 1803 a clause in the Chester Improvement Act banned it within the city boundary. In October of that year, the first time that the ban was imposed, the police commissioners also printed and distributed a handbill warning against bull baiting, concentrating on Cow Lane (later Frodsham Street) and the flesh shambles, an indication that butchers

---

1 TS. 'Hist.' kindly supplied by Mr. L. Dillon, Whitegate, general secretary.

2 *Official Edn. of Laws of Badminton and Rules of Badminton Association* (1898 and later edns. to 1911/12); cf. Lowerson, *Sport and Eng. Middle Classes*, 109–10.

3 *Chester Sports Fortnight, 1969*, 19; *Chester City Sports Week, 1974*, 23 (copies in Chester public libr. pamphlet colln.).

4 Inf. from Mr. M. Burton, coach of Chester Jets.

5 *Chester Chron.* 21 Apr. 1995, p. 25; 21 July 1995, p. 30.

6 Anon. *Ches. Beagles, 1854–1954* (copy at C.H.H.); *Coun-*

try Life, 28 Mar. 1985, pp. 822–3; for Dixon and Walker: *Bagshaw's Dir. Ches.* (1850), 107; *White's Dir. Ches.* (1860), 134, 141.

7 e.g. Hemingway, *Hist. Chester*, i, facing p. 409; H. Hughes, *Chronicle of Chester*, 116–17; *Compilation of Papers Relating to Election for City Officers in 1809 and Parl. Representation of Chester* (1810, publ. J. Monk), p. vi.

8 3 *Sheaf*, xviii, p. 90; xix, p. 10.

9 D. Fleming, *Manchester Fighters*, 64.

10 e.g. *Chester Chron.* 21 Apr. 1995, p. 28.

FIG. 162. *Pugilism advertised at the Cross, c. 1820*

from Chester and the countryside remained prominent in its support. 'Bull Bait Monday', however, was revived at Boughton heath just outside the corporation limits in 1811, and evidently continued there until the sport was made illegal by national legislation in 1835. In 1822 a bull was baited on the foreshore of the river Dee below the high-water mark, also outside the mayor's jurisdiction.[1]

Canoeing

Chester Sailing and Canoeing Club was formed in 1957. The canoeing section produced several world-class competitors. Its main annual event in the city was the Chester weir slalom, held during Chester sports week from 1968. The national canoe marathon championship was held in Chester in 1992.[2]

Croquet

Hough Green Lawn Tennis Club also played croquet until *c.* 1920.[3] Chester Croquet Club was formed in 1977, playing at first on the former municipal bowling green at the Hermitage before moving to a purpose-made lawn in Westminster Park *c.* 1980.[4] Both were still in use in 2000.

Cycling

Cycle races were part of the Chester Autumn Sports on the Roodee in the later 1870s, when the city was also a popular venue for touring cyclists to visit. The Chester Cycling Club was established in 1888 at the Coach and Horses Hotel; its members toured the countryside and took part in an annual cycle parade to raise money for the Chester infirmary.[5]

Fencing

Fencing was taught as a social accomplishment in Chester until the 1850s.[6] It was re-established as a sport after the Second World War. A club formed in 1957 met for many years in the cathedral refectory,[7] moving later to Overleigh school and in 1993 to the County Sports Club in Upton.[8]

Fives

There was a fives court at the castle in the later 1850s.[9]

---

1 Above, Plays, Sports, and Customs before 1700: Sporting Customs (Civic Bull and Bear Baiting); Hemingway, *Hist. Chester*, i. 222–4; G. T. Burrows, *Ches. Sports and Sportsmen*, 11; Hughes, *Stranger's Handbk.* (1856), 50–1; *Browns and Chester: Portrait of a Shop, 1780–1946*, ed. H. D. Willcock, 67; C.C.A.L.S., ZTRI 3, f. 18; Cruelty to Animals Act, 5 & 6 Wm. IV, c. 59, ss. 1, 3.

2 *Chester Sports Week, 1968,* 19; *Chester City Sports Week, 1972,* 29 (copies in Chester public libr. pamphlet colln.); inf. from Ms. Peace.

3 *P. & G. Dir. Chester* (1919/20), 28; (1922/3), 28.

4 Inf. from Mr. R. Croston, Chester Croquet Club.

5 *Chester Chron.* 14 July 1877; 7 June 1879; 9 July 1888; 31 Aug. 1889.

6 *Bagshaw's Dir. Ches.* (1850), 116; cf. *White's Dir. Ches.* (1860), 133.

7 *Chester City Sports Week, 1970,* 27 (copy in Chester public libr. pamphlet colln.).   8 Inf. from Mr. Fearon.

9 C.C.A.L.S., QAB 6/49, datable by *Army List* (1861), 91, s.n. Elphinstone, Howard C.

Greyhound Racing

A track was opened in Sealand Road next to the football stadium in 1935[1] and closed after 1986.[2]

Hockey

Chester had a hockey club by 1895, and by 1900 a second club was based in Hoole. Both played on the Roodee, but the Chester women's team had faltered by 1912 and the men's followed suit *c.* 1920.[3] During the First World War staff at the Army Pay Office played mixed matches, leading in 1919 to the formation of Chester Casuals Hockey Club. About 1926 its men's teams disbanded and the women formed Chester Ladies Hockey Club, which moved to a new ground in Panton Road, Hoole, in 1930. Other clubs were the Chester and District Ladies from 1922 and a men's team representing Chester United Banks from 1925.[4] By 1964 the clubs which belonged to the county hockey associations were the County Officers (men and women), Chester and District (women), and Chester Ladies.[5] By 1992 there were two clubs catering for both sexes, Chester and County Officers.[6]

Hunting

In 1750 the Chester Hunt had as its kennels a building outside the Northgate which it rented from the corporation; the hunt master at that time was apparently Sir Richard Brooke, Bt., of Norton.[7]

Lacrosse

Chester Lacrosse Club had begun playing by 1975 at Boughton Hall cricket ground, moved to Cheshire County Council Sports Club at Upton in 1991, and in 1994 was the only club to have a team in both divisions of the Northern League.[8] An international match was played at Upton in 1995.[9]

Lawn Tennis

Chester Lawn Tennis Club was founded as Hough Green L.T.C. in 1890 in Wrexham Road, where it built a substantial wooden clubhouse. Its original three shale courts were later supplemented by tarmac and then by artificial grass courts, numbering seven in 1994.[10] Hoole L.T.C. began in 1896 in Vicarage Road and moved in 1904 to Hoole Road.[11] By 1908 other private clubs with their own courts included Glan Aber in Hough Green, Brookside in Sealand Road, and one in Liverpool Road. The last two did not survive. Other courts appeared between the wars in Newton and Upton.[12] In the 1930s ten clubs had their own courts[13] but the number later fell and in 1964 and 1993 only the Chester, Hoole, and Glan Aber clubs were affiliated to the county association.[14] Public courts were opened in Tower Fields in 1922,[15] and later in Hoole Alexandra Park and Wealstone Lane, Upton.[16]

Netball

Chester had a strong netball club in the 1990s.[17]

Polo

Chester County Polo Club was formed in 1874 and polo was still played regularly on the Roodee *c.* 1900.[18]

Quoits

Quoits was played by a club on a ground in Westminster Road, Hoole, in 1910.[19]

Rackets

There was a rackets court at the Brewer's Arms in Foregate Street in 1822;[20] another had been built by 1872 in the grounds of Arnold House school, Parkgate Road, but had gone by 1898.[21]

Real Tennis

A real tennis court on the south side of Foregate Street was probably in use between the 1680s and the 1710s but apparently fell into disuse before 1735.[22] The building, afterwards used as a theatre, survived in the 1860s.[23]

Rugby Union

A club existed from the late 1870s to 1884. The game was introduced to Chester College in 1889 and the

1 *Chester City Cl. Mins. 1935/6*, 495.

2 *Chester Observer*, 3 Jan. 1986, p. 27.

3 *Chester Chron.* 30 Mar. 1895; 31 Oct. 1896, p. 6; 3 Nov. 1900, p. 3; *Ches. Observer*, 11 Jan. 1902; *Chester City Cl. Mins. 1899/1900*, 481; *1900/1*, 218; *1902/3*, 917; *1906/7*, 506; *1922/3*, 615–16; *Gamages Hockey Annual and Club Guide* (1911/12 and later edns.).

4 *Chester Sports Fortnight, 1969*, 21; C.C.A.L.S., TS. list of ZCR 517; *Gamages Hockey Annual and Club Guide* (1922/3 and later edns.).   5 *Ches. Sports Guide, 1964*, 19, 21.

6 Inf. from Ms. Peace.   7 C.C.A.L.S., ZAB 4, f. 137.

8 Inf. from Mrs. M. Black, club secretary; inf. from Mr. A. Robinson, Waverton.

9 *Chester Chron.* 21 Apr. 1995, p. 28.

10 Subscription form, 1994, in possn. of V.C.H.; *P. & G. Dir. Chester* (1919/20), 28; (1922/3), 28.

11 Inf. from Mr. J. Cadman, citing club records.

12 O.S. Maps 1/2,500, Ches. XXXVIII.7, 10–11, 15 (1911 and

1936 edns.); C.C.A.L.S., NVA 1/6, nos. 10463, 10492.

13 *Chester City Cl. Mins. 1937/8*, 74–5.

14 *Ches. Sports Guide, 1964*, 29; *Lawn Tennis Association Handbk.* (1993), 157–8.

15 *Chester City Cl. Mins. 1921/2*, 473.

16 *Official Chester Guide Bk.* (1989 edn.), 53.

17 *Chester Chron.* 6 Oct. 1995, p. 30.

18 Ibid. 13 Sept. 1884, 26 May 1894; *Chester City Cl. Mins. 1906/7*, 506.   19 C.C.A.L.S., NVA 1/7, no. 1117.

20 Hemingway, *Hist. Chester*, ii. 276.

21 O.S. Maps 1/2,500, Ches. XXXVIII.11 (1875 and 1899 edns.); for the school: *P. & G. Dir. Chester* (1871), 92.

22 W. C. Braithwaite, *Second Period of Quakerism* (2nd edn., 1961), 138, 548, 708; *Georgian Chester*, ed. A. M. Kennett, 37; cf. J. M. Heathcote and others, *Tennis, Lawn Tennis, Rackets, Fives* (1890), 20.

23 *Gresty and Burghall's Chester Guide* [1867], 57; below, Places of Entertainment: Theatres and Music Halls.

FIG. 163. *Opening gala at Union Street baths, 1901*

college club affiliated to the Rugby Football Union, but none of the schools in Chester took it up and there was thus no firm basis for club rugby in the city. Chester R.U.F.C. was formed only in 1925, playing successively at Sealand Road, Blacon Point, and Bumper's Lane before moving to Boughton Hall alongside the cricket ground in 1932.[1] In 1959 it moved to its own new ground at Hare Lane off the Tarvin road,[2] outside the city, and after the creation of a divisional structure for the English game in the 1980s played at first in North-West Division One.

Squash

The first squash court in Chester was built at the castle by the Army and remained in use in 1994.[3] The 1970s boom led to increased provision of both private and public courts. The West Cheshire Squash Club opened in 1974 in Wrexham Road with six courts and became the base for the Cheshire county team.[4] Two private courts were built by the rugby club at Hare Lane before 1978, two public courts at the County Sports Club in

Newton in 1976, and four more at the Northgate Arena in 1977.[5]

Swimming

Nude male bathing in the Dee and the canal was regarded in 1822 as a nuisance which the mayor and J.P.s intended to eradicate.[6] In 1901 Chester Amateur Swimming Club was playing water polo in a roped-off section of the Dee near the Groves.[7] Swimming was popular in the Edwardian period and several workplace- and church-based clubs used the Union Street baths opened in 1901.[8] Chester Swimming Club had a successful water polo team in the 1920s.[9] The baths, managed after 1977 by Chester Swimming Association, continued in use for training in 1992, when Chester Swimming Club had over 500 members and was reckoned one of the strongest in the North-West.[10] Competitive events had to be staged outside the city, however, as neither the city baths nor the pool at the Northgate Arena met the standards required by the Amateur Swimming Association.[11]

PLACES OF ENTERTAINMENT

ASSEMBLY ROOMS

For most of the 18th century the most fashionable winter assemblies in Chester as well as the summer balls which were a feature of race week were held at the

Exchange.[12] Later in the century the Exchange came to cater mainly for tradespeople,[13] and after *c.* 1815 subscription assemblies for the gentry were invariably held instead at the Royal Hotel or the Albion Hotel.[14] By the mid 19th century the Exchange had virtually no

1 *Chester Chron.* 1 Nov. 1884; *Rugby Union in Lancs. and Ches.* ed. W. B. Croxford, 54–5; *Rugby Football Annual* (1913/14), 126; Bradbury, *Chester Coll.* 170.

2 Inf. from Mr. A. Robinson, Waverton.

3 Local inf. and personal observation.

4 Inf. from Mr. T. Sewell, West Ches. Squash Club.

5 NW. Cl. for Sport and Recreation, *Dir. of Facilities, 1978* (copy in Chester public libr.).

6 *Browns and Chester*, ed. H. D. Willcock, 68–9.

7 C.C.A.L.S., ZCCB 130, p. 243.

8 e.g. *Chester City Cl. Mins. 1901/2*, 78, 562; *1903/4*, 213,

621; *1905/6*, 302, 402, 605, 863, 974; *1906/7*, 55, 560, 719, 798; *1907/8*, 54, 361; above, Public Utilities: Baths and Wash-Houses.

9 *Chester Sports Fortnight, 1969*, 23 (copy in Chester public libr. pamphlet colln.); *P. & G. Dir. Chester* (1919/20), 27.

10 Inf. from Ms. Peace; *Chester Chron.* 22 Sept. 1995, p. 27.

11 *Chester Chron.* 21 June 2002, p. 28.

12 e.g. C.C.A.L.S., ZAB 3, ff. 263, 271; ZAB 4, f. 48.

13 *Georgian Chester*, ed. A. M. Kennett, 36.

14 E. M. Willshaw, 'Inns of Chester, 1775–1832' (Leic. Univ. M.A. thesis, 1979: copy at C.H.H.), 39.

FIG. 164. *Albion Hotel, Lower Bridge Street, 1856*

FIG. 165. *Theatre Royal entrance, Northgate Street, c. 1810*

social function.[1] Booth Mansion in Watergate Street housed a rival assembly room in the 1740s and 1750s, and new rooms were built by public subscription at the Talbot Inn, Eastgate Street, in 1777.[2]

The decisive abandonment of the Exchange for the most exclusive events came about because of politics.[3] Soon after the 1784 general election the Independents built the Royal Hotel behind the Talbot as their headquarters,[4] and the Grosvenors reacted in 1788 by buying the Talbot itself.[5] On the renewal of party conflict in 1807 the Independents held their assemblies and dinners at the Royal, leaving what was called the Grosvenor assembly at the Exchange.[6] Earl Grosvenor then bought the Royal Hotel in 1815,[7] to serve as his family's political and social headquarters in Chester,[8] forcing the Independents out. By 1830 political reconciliation had worked through to social life. In 1829, for example, a fancy-dress ball at the Royal during the autumn music festival 'commanded an immense company'.[9] Around that time the Royal had two assembly rooms, a newsroom, coffee room, and two billiard rooms.[10] About 1830 its main assembly room commonly attracted up to 300 gentry and was the usual venue for concerts.[11] The Talbot and the Royal merged under the ownership of the Grosvenors and when the two were rebuilt and extended as the Grosvenor Hotel in 1863–5 the new establishment incorporated the old assembly room.[12]

On their expulsion from the Royal Hotel, the Independents moved after 1815 to the Albion Hotel in Lower Bridge Street (Fig. 164),[13] converted from a private house to include a large assembly room. Its 2 a. of gardens stretched back to the city wall, and a newsroom and billiard room were accommodated in a house across the street. It became a fashionable place for ladies on summer afternoons,[14] but its trade was drawn away by the diversion of through traffic along Grosvenor Street after 1832, and after a lengthy decline it closed in 1867.[15]

THEATRES AND MUSIC HALLS

From the 17th century to the mid 19th the principal theatre in Chester was in the former St. Nicholas's chapel, commonly known as the Wool Hall.[16]

1 Hughes, *Stranger's Handbk.* (1856), 81.

2 *Georgian Chester*, ed. Kennett, 36; *Poole's Dir. Chester* [1791/2], 38; *V.C.H. Ches.* v (1), Early Modern Chester: Economy and Society, 1662–1762 (Chester as a County Resort).

3 Cf. *V.C.H. Ches.* v (1), Late Georgian and Victorian Chester: Politics, 1762–1835.

4 Hemingway, *Hist. Chester*, i. 414; J. Hunter and S. Weston, *Plan of Chester* (1789).

5 C.C.A.L.S., TS. cal. of Grosvenor MSS. at Eaton Hall, p. 164.

6 Hemingway, *Hist. Chester*, ii. 408–10, 413.

7 Ibid. i. 414.

8 Ibid. ii. 269, 280, 290, 419.

9 Ibid. ii. 295–6.

10 *Chester Chron.* 17 Sept. 1819, quoted in Willshaw, 'Inns', 12–13.

11 Hemingway, *Hist. Chester*, ii. 342–4.

12 Hughes, *Stranger's Handbk.* [1882], 53–5.

13 Willshaw, 'Inns', 54, quoting *Chester Chron.* 17 Mar. 1820.

14 *Georgian Chester*, ed. Kennett, 38–9; Hemingway, *Hist. Chester*, ii. 32, 269, 283; Hughes, *Stranger's Handbk.* (1856), 73–4.

15 Hughes, *Stranger's Handbk.* [1882], 93–4.

16 Above, Plays, Sports, and Customs before 1700: Private Patronage (Theatrical Companies).

Shakespeare's *Tempest* and a comedy were performed in 1692, by when there was a regular summer season.[1] *Richard III* was on the bill in 1727 and a comic opera, *The Maid of the Mill*, in 1769.[2] The 1751 season included a visiting company of rope-dancers and tumblers, who also staged a pantomime.[3] There were other venues in the mid 18th century. In 1752 the Exchange put on *Richard III*, vocal and instrumental music, and a 'tragi-comi-pastoral farcical operatical entertainment' called *The What D'ye Call It*.[4] The old real tennis court in Foregate Street was used by a different travelling company from London from before 1750 until 1768.[5]

The Wool Hall was refitted as the New Theatre in 1773. The proprietors ensured its continuance in the teeth of corporation hostility by obtaining a patent in 1777 licensing it as the Theatre Royal (Fig. 165).[6] Under that name it provided the main, perhaps the only, venue throughout the years that play-going was fashionable among county and civic society, opening each year to coincide with the peaks of Chester's season in the winter and during race week.[7] It was managed as part of a circuit which included Newcastle, Lancaster, Whitehaven, and Preston.[8] The programmes included Shakespeare, Garrick, Sheridan, and Otway, new comedies and farces, and pantomime, and all the leading actors of the day trod its boards between the 1780s and the 1820s, among them Edmund Keen, Sarah Siddons, and Grimaldi.[9] An extra tier of boxes was added in 1828.[10]

The lease of the Theatre Royal expired in 1853,[11] and it was refitted as the 1,400-seater Music Hall to designs by James Harrison, opening in 1855 to extravagant praise of its luxury and elegance.[12] Its managers, the Chester booksellers Messrs. Phillipson and Goulder, concentrated on musical performances – orchestral, choral, and brass-band[13] – to the apparent exclusion of theatre. It became a cinema in 1921.[14]

A large wooden building on the east side of City Road was used from *c.* 1866 for occasional plays and circuses. From 1869 it was called the Oxford Music Hall and in 1878 was refurbished as the Prince of Wales Theatre. It was let for short runs to popular entertainers, including circuses, waxworks, theatre companies, and 'Madame Beatrice's Frou Frou Com-

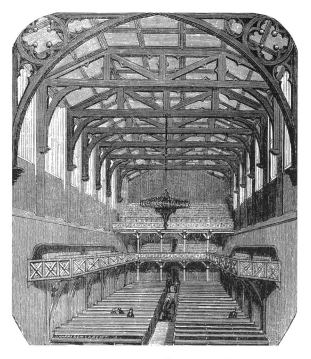

FIG. 166. *Music Hall, as refitted in 1855*

pany', all aiming for a lower niche in the market than the Music Hall. In 1882 it was replaced by an unremarkable brick building, the Royalty Theatre, which seated 2,000. Its owner from 1896, J. W. Carter,[15] floated it as a limited company that year, boasting of its monopoly of popular amusements in the city.[16] It occasionally offered high quality theatre,[17] but had opened with a pantomime and the usual fare in the early 20th century was music hall, variety, revues, melodramas, and farces.[18] By the 1960s amateur opera alternated with professional wrestling, and pantomimes with bingo and striptease.[19] In 1978 it began a brief incarnation as a skateboard rink[20] and in the 1990s housed a nightclub.

The Gateway Theatre was built as part of the 1960s Forum shopping centre jointly by the developer and the city council, and opened in 1968. Subsidized by public funds and commercial sponsorship, it put on a varied programme of theatre on a main stage and in a studio.[21]

Chester Theatre Club, founded in the 1940s, bought

1 *Georgian Chester*, ed. Kennett, 37; *Diary of Henry Prescott*, ii. 420.

2 Hemingway, *Hist. Chester*, ii. 246; 1 *Sheaf*, iii, pp. 205–6.

3 3 *Sheaf*, xv, p. 6.

4 2 *Sheaf*, i, pp. 84–5.

5 1 *Sheaf*, iii, pp. 221–2; 3 *Sheaf*, xi, pp. 36–7, 48; Ormerod, *Hist. Ches.* i. 367; *Adams's Weekly Courant*, 17 Nov. 1761, p. 3.

6 Hemingway, *Hist. Chester*, ii. 13–14; Chester Theatre Act, 17 Geo. III, c. 14 (printed in 3 *Sheaf*, xii, p. 57).

7 *Stranger's Companion in Chester* (1821), 35.

8 A. G. Betjemann, *Grand Theatre, Lancaster*, 2, 8, 11.

9 H. Hughes, *Chronicle of Chester*, 187–99; Hemingway, *Hist. Chester*, ii. 251, 253, 258, 260, 262.

10 Hemingway, *Hist. Chester*, ii. 14.

11 *J.C.A.S.* [o.s.], i. 251, 261.

12 Hughes, *Stranger's Handbk.* (1856), 82–4.

13 e.g. *Chester Chron.* 27 Apr. 1878, p. 7; 12 Apr. 1879, p. 1; *Kelly's Dir. Ches.* (1892), 186, 189.

14 Below, this chapter: Cinemas.

15 C.C.A.L.S., ZCR 119/24, pp. 196–8; *Kelly's Dir. Ches.* (1892), 186; Hughes, *Chronicle of Chester*, 202–3.

16 C.C.A.L.S., ZCR 119/24, p. 198A.

17 G. A. Audsley, *Stranger's Handbk.* [1899], 28.

18 Hughes, *Chronicle of Chester*, 203–4.

19 *Chester Chron.* 10 June 1966; *Ches. Observer*, 2 May 1959, p. 8. 20 Harris, *Chester*, 169–70.

21 *Chester Gateway Theatre, 1968–88* (copy at C.H.H.); Hughes, *Chronicle of Chester*, 205–8.

FIG. 167. *Odeon cinema*

the former Christ Church National school in 1962 and converted it into the Little Theatre, where it put on six amateur productions a year in the 1990s.[1]

CINEMAS[2]

William Freize-Green's claim to have shown the first ever successful moving pictures on 26 June 1890 at Chester town hall has been dismissed as either self-deluding or fraudulent.[3] In the 1900s showmen who visited Chester regularly exhibited films,[4] but the first permanent cinema was Will Hunter's Picturedrome, in the Corn Exchange, Eastgate Street, opened in 1909.[5] The Royalty Theatre, the Music Hall, and other venues also showed films.[6] The only purpose-built cinema before 1914 was the Glynn Picture Hall, opened in 1911 by a Shrewsbury company in a corrugated iron building seating 750 behind no. 110 Foregate Street. It was given a black-and-white vernacular front by the Chester architects Minshull and Muspratt.[7]

After 1918 there was much new investment in cinemas.[8] The Music Hall was refitted as an 820-seater in 1921.[9] Pat Collins, before the war a travelling film exhibitor, opened the 1,050-seat Cinema De Luxe at no. 95 Brook Street in 1921, behind a black-and-white frontage designed by W. Matthews Jones.[10] The

1 Leaflets and other inf. from theatre.

2 B. Hornsey, *Ninety Years of Cinema in Chester* (copy at C.H.H.); M. Perry, 'Electric Paradise: Chester's Cinema Era until 1937' (TS. [n.d.] in Chester public libr.).

3 Perry, 'Electric Paradise', 4–5; D. A. Ellis, 'Chester Cinemas Scrapbk.' (copy at C.H.H.).

4 Perry, 'Electric Paradise', 3, 5.

5 Ibid. 6; *Chester City Cl. Mins. 1909/10,* 136; *1910/11,* 638.

6 *Chester City Cl. Mins. 1909/10,* 136; *1910/11,* 75–6; *1911/12,* 432, 503, 655, 715; *1912/13,* 92; *1913/14,* 93; Hornsey,

Ninety Years, 3; C.C.A.L.S., ZCR 119/24, p. 175.

7 *Chester City Cl. Mins. 1910/11,* 206, 213–14, 276, 310, 547–8; Perry, 'Electric Paradise', 10; *Chester Chron.* 24 June 1911, p. 5.

8 e.g. *Chester City Cl. Mins. 1918/19,* 236, 320; *1919/20,* 305, 376; *1920/1,* 545; *1921/2,* 621, 686.

9 Hornsey, *Ninety Years,* 7; Perry, 'Electric Paradise', 9; *Chester City Cl. Mins. 1921/2,* 72.

10 *Chester City Cl. Mins. 1918/19,* 449–50; *1919/20,* 375–6; *1920/1,* 488; Perry, 'Electric Paradise', 15; C.C.A.L.S., ZCR 119/24, p. 176; *Ches. Observer,* 23 Apr. 1921, p. 10.

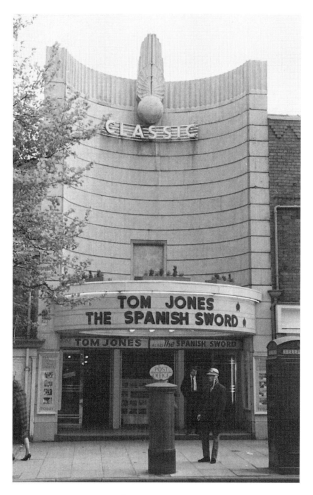

FIG. 168. *Classic cinema, 1964*

Park Cinema in St. Mark's Road, Saltney, was a 450-seater opened in 1923 by Messrs. Booth and Grierson.[1] The Picturedrome closed when its lease expired in 1924,[2] leaving four cinemas operating.

The early picture houses mostly had local owners, but the national cinema circuits moved into the city from the late 1920s, starting with the General Theatre Corporation, which in 1928–9 bought the Music Hall, the Glynn Picture Hall, and the Cinema De Luxe (renamed the Majestic in 1926).[3] The first of the 1930s 'supers' was the Gaumont Palace, a 2,000-seater auditorium with an opulent interior behind the black-and-white entrance front in Brook Street, opened in 1931;[4] next, in 1936, was the 1,750-seater Odeon, whose company architect toned down the circuit's usual modernism for a sensitive site in Northgate Street;[5] finally, in 1937, Associated British Cinemas Ltd. built the Regal, seating almost 2,000 in an equally restrained modernist style at the corner of Foregate Street and Love Street.[6] The Tatler News Theatre, erected at no. 56 Foregate Street in 1936, was one of the few provincial newsreel cinemas until it was taken over by the Classic chain *c.* 1957, renamed, and switched to feature films and pornography. It seated 530 and had a white-tiled neo-classical exterior.[7]

Only the Glynn succumbed to the increased competition, closing in 1931;[8] the building survived in 1994 but was badly neglected. Cinema closures began in earnest in the mid 1950s. The Majestic was converted, briefly, to a dance hall after it closed in 1956,[9] and only the front part survived as a shop. The Music Hall[10] and the Gaumont closed in 1961, the latter becoming briefly a ten-pin bowling alley, then a bingo hall,[11] which it remained in 1994. The Park closed in 1963,[12] the Classic closed in 1970 and was demolished in 1971,[13] and the Regal (renamed the A.B.C. in 1959)[14] became a twin-screen cinema in 1980, was sold and renamed the Cannon in 1987, and closed in 1990.[15] That left only the Odeon, remodelled to have three screens in 1976 and five in 1991,[16] and Metro-Goldwyn-Mayer's six-screen multiplex, opened as a replacement for the Cannon in 1990 at Greyhound Park, Sealand Road.[17]

CATHEDRAL MUSIC AND MUSIC FESTIVALS

The origins of Chester's music festivals lay in the musical tradition established at the cathedral after 1541.[18] The statutes of 1544 provided for six minor canons, six conducts or singing-men, eight choir boys,

1 *Chester City Cl. Mins. 1922/3*, 65, 631; *Chester Courant*, 23 May 1923; Hornsey, *Ninety Years*, 24; Perry, 'Electric Paradise', 16.

2 *Chester City Cl. Mins. 1923/4*, 241; Perry, 'Electric Paradise', 8; *Ches. Observer*, 22 Mar. 1924, p. 8.

3 Hornsey, *Ninety Years*, 7, 9, 11; *Chester City Cl. Mins. 1925/6*, 336; *1928/9*, 89.

4 *Chester City Cl. Mins. 1928/9*, 240; *1930/1*, 100–1, 357; Perry, 'Electric Paradise', 19–20; *Ches. Observer*, 7 Mar. 1931.

5 *Chester City Cl. Mins. 1934/5*, 683, 776; Perry, 'Electric Paradise', 25–6; C.C.A.L.S., ZCR 119/24, p. 176; *Chester Chron.* 10 Oct. 1936, p. 12.

6 *Chester City Cl. Mins. 1935/6*, 495; Perry, 'Electric Paradise', 20, 22–3; *Chester Chron.* 6 Nov. 1937, p. 14.

7 Hornsey, *Ninety Years*, 19; Perry, 'Electric Paradise', 33–5; Ellis, 'Scrapbk.'; *Chester Chron.* 5 Dec. 1936, p. 6; 15 Apr. 1961, p. 1; *Chester City Cl. Mins. 1933/4*, 905; *1934/5*, 55, 519.

8 Hornsey, *Ninety Years*, 9; *Chester City Cl. Mins. 1930/1*, 982.

9 Hornsey, *Ninety Years*, 13; *Chester City Cl. Mins. 1956/7*, p. 415; *Kelly's Dir. Chester* (1958), 19.

10 Hornsey, *Ninety Years*, 7, 9; *Chester Chron.* 29 Apr. 1961, p. 1.

11 Hornsey, *Ninety Years*, 15; *Chester City Cl. Mins. 1961/2*, p. 161; Perry, 'Electric Paradise', 19.

12 *Ches. Observer*, 2 May 1959, p. 18; Hornsey, *Ninety Years*, 24.   13 Hornsey, *Ninety Years*, 19; Ellis, 'Scrapbk.'.

14 *Chester City Cl. Mins. 1959/60*, p. 607; *1960/1*, p. 614.

15 Hornsey, *Ninety Years*, 21, 23; *Chester Observer*, 30 May 1980, p. 39.

16 *Ches. Observer*, 9 Apr. 1976, pp. 44–5; Hornsey, *Ninety Years*, 17, 19.   17 Hornsey, *Ninety Years*, 23.

18 This section draws heavily upon A. T. Thacker, *Chester Cath.: Its Music and Musicians* (Chester, [1981]). For other early musical activity: above, Plays, Sports, and Customs before 1700: Music and Minstrelsy.

and a choir master and organist.[1] A degree of continuity with the abbey is suggested by the fact that John Birchley, the monks' last organist, was re-employed by the new chapter.[2] By 1567 his office was sufficiently well regarded to attract Robert White, a distinguished composer of settings of the Latin liturgy, and later organist at Westminster Abbey. The cathedral was then the focus of considerable musical activity, and much involved in the musical side of the mystery plays.[3] White's successors, Robert Stevenson (1570–99) and Thomas Bateson (1599–1608), were also composers and maintained high musical standards at the cathedral.[4] By 1602 the lay clerks included Francis Pilkington, a composer of lute songs and madrigals, who became a minor canon in 1612 and precentor from 1617 until his death in 1638.[5] Between 1608 and 1646, however, the organists included only one figure of note, Randolph Jewett (1643–6), son of a former mayor, pupil of Orlando Gibbons, and composer of anthems.[6]

After the Restoration the cathedral's music was undistinguished. An attempt at improvement was made in 1727 when the chapter appointed Edmund Baker, a pupil of Thomas Arne and Chester's first professional organist since 1660, but the choir remained unsatisfactory and in 1741 Baker was unable to supply a conduct capable of singing at sight to help Handel rehearse *Messiah* while he waited at Chester to take ship for Dublin. Nevertheless, Baker was an accomplished musician and by the 1740s the city had become 'a very musical place'. By then John Prescott, a prebendary of the cathedral, held a weekly concert attended by 18–20 performers, gentlemen, and professors. Prescott, who was deprived of his stall in 1746, seems to have tried hard to promote an interest in music in Chester. He paid Baker to teach the harpsichord to singing boys and pupils of the cathedral school and in 1739 secured a free place there for the young Charles Burney.[7] Concerts were also occasionally performed at the Exchange, especially in aid of the infirmary from the late 1750s.[8]

Baker's successor, Edward Orme (1765–77), a man of some social position who became sheriff of Chester in 1773–4, organized the city's first music festival in 1772, at which three of Handel's oratorios, *Messiah*, *Samson*, and *Judas Maccabeus*, were performed in the cathedral nave. Further festivals took place in 1783, 1786, 1791, 1806, 1814, 1821, and 1829. Although Handel continued to dominate the programme, in 1806 Haydn's *Creation* was performed and in 1821 there were works by Mozart, Haydn, and Pergolesi. The festivals became

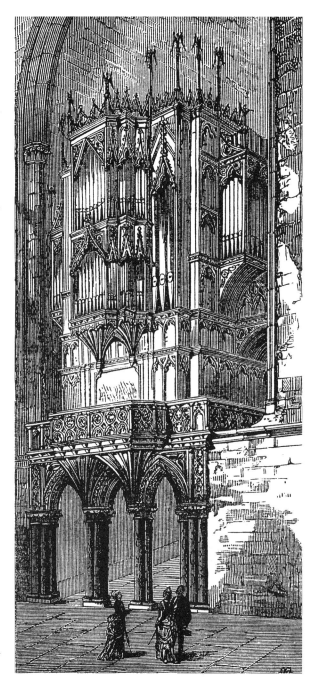

FIG. 169. *Cathedral organ of 1875*

increasingly grand, and by 1806 the four days of performances were a major social occasion attended by royalty and involving many of the principal musicians of the day. Their popularity, however, made the dean and chapter fearful of 'abuses and irreverence', and they refused permission for further festivals after 1829.[9]

1 C.C.A.L.S., EDD 2/55/2; *V.C.H. Ches.* iii. 188.

2 J. C. Bridge, 'Organists of Chester Cath.' *J.C.A.S.* xix. 65.

3 *New Grove Dictionary of Music and Musicians*, ed. S. Sadie, s.n. White; *D.N.B.*; *J.C.A.S.* xix. 67–70.

4 *New Grove*, s.nn. Bateson, Stevenson; *D.N.B.* s.n. Bateson; *J.C.A.S.* xix. 67–77.   5 *New Grove*, s.n. Pilkington; *D.N.B.*

6 *New Grove*, s.n. Jewett; *D.N.B.*; *J.C.A.S.* xix. 81–90.

7 *J.C.A.S.* xix. 103–9; C. Burney, *Sketch of Life of Handel*, 26; Burne, *Chester Cath.* 195, 200–1, 207–8; *New Grove*, s.n. Burney; *D.N.B.* s.n. Burney.

8 *Adams's Weekly Courant*, 2 May 1758, p. 2; 22 Aug. 1758, p. 3; 29 Apr. 1760, p. 3; 1 July 1760, p. 3.

9 C.C.A.L.S., ZCR 62/1–78; *J.C.A.S.* xix. 109–15; *New Grove*, s.n. Chester; A. T. Thacker, 'Handel and Chester', *Chester Summer Music Festival Souvenir Programme* (1985), 19; below, Lists of Mayors and Sheriffs.

Under Dean Anson (1839–67) the cathedral's musical standards were raised. A great new organ was introduced, the number of choristers was increased to the statutory eight, and a separate choir school was founded.[1] Further improvements took place under the precentor Hylton Stewart (1877–90) and organist J. C. Bridge (1877–1925) and in the 1880s large-scale choral works were occasionally performed and a triennial festival of parish choirs was established. Aided by another splendid organ installed in 1875, Bridge revived the music festival in 1885, with two days of concerts and choral evensong at the cathedral. Thereafter, festivals were held triennially. The performances, which included choral works by Handel, Haydn, Mendelssohn, Spohr, Verdi, and Berlioz, were generally held in the cathedral and invariably conducted by Bridge himself. The last took place in 1900.[2]

The cathedral continued its choral tradition throughout the 20th century, despite the closure of the choir school in 1977. In 1978 the music festival was again revived. By the early 1980s it had become a major annual event, lasting *c.* 10 days and involving soloists, ensembles, and orchestras of international distinction. By then it was held in several locations, of which the cathedral remained the principal.[3]

REVIVAL OF THE MYSTERY PLAYS

The 1818 edition by J. H. Markland, himself a Cestrian, of two plays from the Chester cycle represented the first modern edition of any English mystery plays. It was followed by improved editions of the full cycle, each in two volumes, published in 1843–7 and 1892–1916.[4]

A new interest in the performance of medieval plays was stimulated by William Poel's production of *Everyman* at the Charterhouse in London in 1901; it was paired with a production of Chester's *Sacrifice of Isaac*, the first performance of a Chester play in modern times.[5] One of Poel's company, Nugent Monck, formed his own company and staged versions of Chester's *Nativity*, *Shepherds*, and *Magi* plays in Bloomsbury Hall, London, in 1906. Monck wrote to the Chester Archaeological Society offering to produce the whole cycle in the traditional manner over three

FIG. 170. *Chester Historical Pageant, 1910: Midsummer Revels*

1 *J.C.A.S.* xix. 120–2; above, Cathedral and Close: Cathedral Church from 1541 (Organs).

2 *Grove's Dictionary of Music and Musicians*, ed. E. Blom (5th edn.), s.n. Bridge; C.C.A.L.S., ZCR 62/79–150; above, Cathedral and Close: Cathedral Church from 1541 (Organs).

3 *Chester Summer Music Festival Souvenir Programmes* (1983–92), esp. (1985), 10.

4 *Chester Mysteries*, ed. J. H. Markland (Roxburghe Club); *The Chester Plays*, ed. T. Wright (Shakespeare Soc.); *The Chester Plays*, ed. H. Deimling and Dr. Matthews (E.E.T.S. extra ser. lxii, cxv).

5 Para. based on D. Mills, 'Reviving the Chester Plays', *Medieval Eng. Theatre*, xiii. 39–51; idem, '"Reviving the Chester Plays": a Postscript', ibid. xv. 124–5; 'The Chester Mystery Plays: the Proposed Revival in Chester', *J.C.A.S.* xiv. 269–72.

FIG. 171. *Chester mystery plays in St. Werburgh Street, 1997*

days at Whitsun 1907. The proposal, which must be seen against the background of Chester's music festivals and the city's growing concern with its past, would have resulted in the first complete revival of any English play-cycle. The Society organized a public meeting chaired by the bishop to discuss it. Although the dean of Chester opposed the production, the cathedral organist, J. C. Bridge, supported it, and a number of Cestrians who had seen *Everyman* in London or on tour reported favourably on the production. Following the meeting, the three 'Nativity' plays were performed at the Music Hall in 1906 to test local reactions. An edition of the performance-text by Bridge was published to accompany the production.[1] The production was enthusiastically received, but the society then decided that the cost of staging the full cycle was too high and the scheme fell. Local interest, including that of Bridge, was diverted instead into the Chester Historical Pageant of 1910 (Fig. 170, p. 275).[2]

Objections to the alleged crudity of the plays' theology and drama, their lack of decorum, the danger of blasphemy, and the problems of understanding their language all surfaced again in the 1950s when the plays were revived as a full cycle. The first production took place in the cathedral refectory on 18 June 1951 to celebrate the Festival of Britain, the first time that the cycle as a whole had been performed since 1575.[3] The production mirrored the three-day original by being in three parts played on different days. Because of the enthusiasm of the amateur actors, public demand, and a desire to utilize the initial investment and impetus, the production was repeated the following year in a somewhat extended form. After that, performances in

various styles and using various texts were staged at roughly five-year intervals, becoming an established tourist attraction. To accommodate increasing audiences, the productions transferred from the refectory to Cathedral Green in 1967 and were thenceforth given in the open, except for the 1973 production, which was held in a circus tent. The early productions were marked by a reluctance to stage the more 'realistic' scenes, including the crucifixion, and by a dramaturgy wedded to a proscenium-arch stage. The transfer to Cathedral Green marked an extension of the scale of production, an increasingly full and authentic text, and a greater concern with communal involvement.

Those developments ran alongside academic investigations which generated a pioneer study in 1955 of the text in relation to the city's records, significantly advancing understanding of medieval drama.[4] A new scholarly edition appeared in 1974 and 1986,[5] and a major compendium of the city's drama records in 1979.[6] Interest in 'authentic performance' led to processional performances of the full cycle on the university campuses of Leeds and Toronto in 1983. Chester was fortunate in having the services of academics with an interest in practical drama (John Lawlor and Rosemary Sisson in 1967; Edward Burns and Robert Cheeseman in 1985 and 1992) and in the enthusiasm for drama in its schools, evidenced in the directorship of Peter Dornford-May in the 1970s and 1980s. Knowledge of Tudor production and ceremonial thus came to serve as the starting point and inspiration for adaptations which used the resources of modern theatre and sought to involve local people.

1 *Three Chester Whitsun Plays*, ed. J. C. Bridge; copies also issued bound with *J.C.A.S.* xiv.

2 *Chester Historical Pageant, 1910: Bk. of Music*, ed. J. C. Bridge; C.C.A.L.S., ZCR 62.

3 Rest of para. and next based on D. Mills, 'The 1951 and

1952 Revivals of the Chester Plays', *Medieval Eng. Theatre*, xv. 111–23; C.C.A.L.S., ZDPU 4–19.

4 F. M. Salter, *Mediaeval Drama in Chester*.

5 *Chester Mystery Cycle*, ed. R. M. Lumiansky and D. Mills (E.E.T.S. suppl. ser. iii, ix).   6 *REED: Chester*.

EDUCATION

BEFORE 1700

A grammar school is known to have existed at St. John's church in 1353, perhaps the same as that recorded in 1368.[1] There was also a school associated with the abbey, replaced in 1541 by a grammar school under the control of the dean and chapter of the cathedral.[2] The history of the new foundation, which provided for a master, an usher, 24 scholars, and eight choristers and was known as the King's school, is given elsewhere.[3]

The King's school remained a centre of classical instruction throughout the period, sending pupils to the universities, but it is highly probable that other privately run schools existed in Chester, of which no records have survived before *c.* 1700. In 1539 the Assembly ordered that all children over the age of six should be 'set to the school to learn their belief and other devotions, prayers, and learning, or else to such other good and virtuous . . . occupation whereby they . . . may obtain . . . an honest living'.[4] The phrase 'set to the school' might be a reference to the abbey school or to the existence of otherwise unrecorded petty schools in Chester. The Assembly was also linked with Robert Offley's charity, established in 1596, which provided an exhibition worth £5 at Brasenose College, Oxford, for the son of a Chester citizen, to be elected by the Assembly.[5] The surviving subscription books for schoolmasters and others in Chester diocese do not begin until 1669 and do not give the occupations of the subscribers.[6] Other than the master and usher of the King's school, there is little evidence for schoolmasters in Chester in the 17th century. The puritan John Glendal, curate of St. Peter's 1628–42, sent one of his pupils to Cambridge University,[7] and there was a private school in the period 1685–1705.[8] The educational functions performed by the well developed system of guilds were of considerable importance but were manifested in such matters as the rules governing apprenticeships rather than in formal schools.[9]

THE 18TH CENTURY

The 18th century was an age of benevolence and patronage in the development of education in Chester. As the commercial centre of a prosperous agricultural region and the seat of a bishopric situated close to the estates of a leading landowner (the Grosvenor family), Chester was well placed to be in the forefront of educational provision. The Society for Promoting Christian Knowledge had been founded in London in 1699 and only a year later a Blue Coat school on the model which it advocated was established by public subscription under the patronage of Nicholas Stratford, bishop of Chester, and Sir Richard Grosvenor, 4th Bt. A purpose-built school was erected in Upper Northgate Street in 1717 on a site donated by the corporation (Fig. 172, p. 278). One of the earliest schools of its type outside London, it concentrated on the teaching of the church catechism, reading, writing, and arithmetic, and provided boarding accommodation for 40 boys, who wore blue school uniform.[10] The cathedral authorities were also responsible for setting up a Blue Girls' school in 1720, where sewing, knitting, and spinning were added to the curriculum. The girls met at first in the boys' school building but later occupied a succession of other premises until a new school was built in Vicars Lane in 1872 by the 1st duke of Westminster. In 1783, largely through the initiative of Dr. John Haygarth, the pioneering physician of the Chester infirmary, the number of boarders at the boys' school was reduced to 25 and a day school was begun for 60 boys known as 'green caps'; their number was doubled to 120 in 1784.[11]

The social and economic character of the city also attracted middle-class nonconformists. Wesleyan Sunday schools were organized at the Octagon from 1781 and in St. John Street from 1782; a Congregationalist Sunday school met in Queen Street from 1803.[12] Dr. Haygarth was the prime mover in the establishment of a Society for the Promotion of Sunday and Working Schools for Girls in 1787. The enterprise was influenced by the growth of Sunday schools in Chester, but recognized the limitations of providing education on only one day in the week. It extended to girls attending on weekdays the type of vocational education already being provided for boarders at the Blue Girls' school.[13]

All the schools for poor children were supported by private patronage and were heavily religious in tone. The development of middle-class education took more

---

1 N. Orme, *Eng. Schools in Middle Ages*, 299, citing wrong p. in *Lich. Episcopal Reg. v: 2nd Reg. of Bp. Robert de Stretton, 1360–85* (Collns. Hist. Staffs. N.S. viii), p. 120; above, Collegiate Church of St. John.

2 Burne, *Chester Cath.* 9–10; A. F. Leach, *Schools of Medieval Eng.* 312.

3 *V.C.H. Ches.* iii. 230–2; v (1), Later Medieval Chester: Religion (The Dissolution).

4 C.C.A.L.S., ZAB 1, f. 62.

5 Ibid. ZCHC 9/1; *31st Rep. Com. Char.* 376–7; *Cal. Chester City Cl. Mins. 1603–42*, 155, 217; Johnson, 'Aspects', 206–7.

6 C.C.A.L.S., EDA 4/1–2.

7 [J. E. B. Mayor], *Admissions to St. John's Coll., Camb.* i, p. 45 (no. 18); above, Medieval Parish Churches: St. Peter.

8 D. Robson, *Some Aspects of Educ. in Ches. in 18th Cent.* (Chetham Soc. 3rd ser. xiii), 14.

9 *V.C.H. Ches.* iii. 197–9.

10 *Georgian Chester*, ed. A. M. Kennett, 29.

11 Ibid. 30.

12 J. C. Fowler, 'Development of Elementary Educ. in Chester, 1800–1902' (Liverpool Univ. M.A. thesis, 1968), 20–1, 28, 39.

13 Ibid. 15–17, 27; E. M. Sneyd-Kynnersley and M. E. Daws, *Story of Hunter St. School*, 5.

FIG. 172. *Blue Coat school entrance*

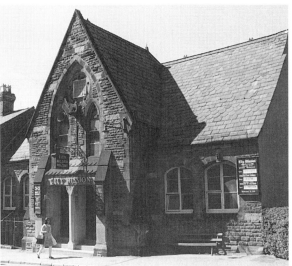

FIG. 173. *Bishop Graham Memorial Ragged School, used as Chester City Mission, 1966*

cognizance of secular subjects, and Chester in the 18th century became an important centre for private schools. The King's school retained its reputation as a classical school but by 1709 most of the 120 boys attending it were fee-payers; boarders were also mentioned later in the century.[1] In addition there were at least 44 private schools in existence during the 18th century, more after 1750 than before.[2] Over half were run by women, an indication of how middle-class girls received their education at a time when there was no public provision for them. In 1781 the *Chester Guide* listed 15 private school teachers: there were three women running boarding schools and 12 schoolmasters, including two dancing masters and a musician.[3] Private tutors also gave evening lectures on scientific and other subjects and contributed to the varied cultural life of the Georgian town.[4]

1800–70

Chester's rapid economic growth and the doubling in size of its population between 1801 and 1861 naturally had a considerable effect on the provision of education.

Private philanthropy remained the principal response but it was now organized on a more systematic basis, with the cathedral authorities playing a leading role. The Church of England founded the National Society for Promoting the Education of the Poor in 1811 and in the following year a National school for boys was established in Chester. In 1816 it was rehoused in a new building, on the corner of Upper Northgate Street and George Street, known as the Diocesan school.[5] The Sunday and working schools for girls were also reorganized in 1816 and became a National school for girls with the title of the Chester Consolidated Sunday and Working school. It met first in the basement of the Blue Coat school but moved to a new site between Princess Street and Hunter Street in 1854.[6] A third elementary school opened in Vicars Lane in 1813 and contained *c.* 300 boys and girls taught on the National system by a master and mistress appointed and paid by the marquess of Westminster.[7] It became known as the Grosvenor St. John's school.

In 1825, as the problem of educating very young children began to receive attention, the Chester Infant School Society was formed under the patronage of Charles Blomfield, bishop of Chester. Infants' schools were opened in the Kaleyards (1826), Russell Street (1827), Handbridge (1828), and later at St. Martin's-in-the-Fields (1860).[8]

The appointment of the liberal evangelical John Bird Sumner as bishop in 1828 gave further impetus to the provision of elementary education and to the training of elementary-school teachers. A diocesan board of education was set up in 1839 and its training college for schoolmasters, in Parkgate Road from 1842,[9]

1 *V.C.H. Ches.* iii. 231.
2 Robson, *Educ. in Ches.* 173–5.
3 *Broster's Dir. Chester* (1781); 3 *Sheaf,* x, pp. 98, 102.
4 Robson, *Educ. in Ches.* 176.
5 Fowler, 'Elementary Educ.' 46.

6 Ibid. 47; Sneyd-Kynnersley and Daws, *Hunter St. School,* 9.
7 *31st Rep. Com. Char.* 397; Fowler, 'Elementary Educ.' 48, 52.
8 Fowler, 'Elementary Educ.' 59.
9 Below, this chapter: Chester College.

FIG. 174. *Victoria Road British school*

opened a practising school for boys on the site in 1843 which became the male equivalent of the Consolidated girls' school, since both recruited their pupils from all the parishes in Chester.[1] For that reason the College boys' school and Consolidated girls' school came to be regarded as somewhat superior elementary schools.

Several parishes in the city set up their own National schools.[2] The Grosvenor family had already established a school in Vicars Lane for St. John's parish, and others were built by Christ Church in Cornwall Street in 1842 and by St. Mary's in 1846.[3] The new ecclesiastical district of St. Paul's, Boughton, held a day school from *c.* 1830, with a new building in 1857. Another National school was opened in Linenhall Street in Holy Trinity parish in 1869.[4]

The National schools charged small weekly fees, and a marked increase in the number of very poor children unable to pay led to the formation in 1851 of the Chester Ragged School Society, which recognized the need for free education for poor, orphaned, and neglected children. Ragged schools were established at Boughton (1852) and in St. Olave's parish (1852), with a third in Princess Street (1868) known as the Bishop Graham Memorial school (Fig. 173).[5] In 1863 the Boughton school was reorganized as an industrial school to which magistrates could send children who had committed minor offences.[6] Boughton, together with the workhouse school, which moved with the workhouse from the Roodee to Hoole Lane in 1878,[7] were the recipients of children who for social or other reasons could not be fitted into the contemporary educational system.

The non-Anglican churches also established their own schools in Chester during the period. A Wesleyan day school developed in 1839 from the Sunday school in St. John Street but the nonconformist British School Society did not establish a branch in Chester until 1867. A British school had opened in Christleton Road, Great Boughton, in the previous year and another opened in Victoria Road in 1867, with a new building in 1871.[8] Roman Catholic schools became eligible for government grants in 1847, and the St. Werburgh's schools were built in Queen Street in 1854. In the same year the Dee House convent opened a boarding school for Catholic girls, to which day pupils were later admitted.[9]

In the earlier 19th century, because of a decreasing demand for the classical languages, the King's school was in decline, in common with many other endowed grammar schools. By 1814 the classics were no longer being taught and, although Latin was later reintroduced, the school was classified by the Taunton Commissioners in 1867 as third-grade.[10] The mid 19th century was therefore the heyday of the private schools. In 1840 the *Chester Directory* noted 16 boarding and 26 day schools run by private individuals. Five of the boarding schools were for 'gentlemen' and eleven for 'ladies'.[11] In 1853 a private day school for boys, the Collegiate Institution, was set up by John Brindley in a house in Abbots Grange previously occupied by a girls' boarding school. Competition from other schools forced its closure *c.* 1857.[12]

The most valuable experiment in secondary education during the period was the science school which developed within the diocesan training college.[13] Several early training colleges ran schools for middle-class boys, whose fees were used to subsidize the largely working-class students training to be elementary-

1 Fowler, 'Elementary Educ.' 84–8.

2 All dates of opening and closure of schools from A. M. Kennett, *Chester Schools: Guide to Archives.*

3 Fowler, 'Elementary Educ.' 89–92.

4 Ibid. 135–7.

5 Ibid. 120–4.

6 Ibid. 125–6; D. H. Thomas, 'Chester Industrial School, 1863–1908', *Jnl. Educ. Administration and Hist.* xiii (2), 7–17.

7 *Archives and Records,* ed. Kennett, 80.

8 Fowler, 'Elementary Educ.' 128–9.

9 Ibid. 98–9; cf. above, Roman Catholicism.

10 *V.C.H. Ches.* iii. 231.

11 *Parry's Dir. Chester* (1840); cf. 3 *Sheaf,* x, pp. 4, 11–12; xi, p. 77.

12 *Bagshaw's Dir. Ches.* (1850), 108; *Whellan's Dir. Ches.* (1854), 1276; *Slater's Dir. Ches.* (1855), 29; *P. & G. Dir. Chester* (1871), 92; 3 *Sheaf,* xi, p. 53.

13 Para. based on J. L. Bradbury, *Chester Coll.* 133–8.

school masters, but only at Chester under the remarkable Arthur Rigg were science and technology given such prominence. In other circumstances, the science school might have developed into an independent public school similar to those at Liverpool (1843) or Rossall (1844), but it faded away following Rigg's retirement in 1869.

Scientific and technical subjects developed on a more permanent basis in response to a growing demand from older students, encouraged by a number of professional men in Chester, among whom Charles Kingsley, a canon at the cathedral, was the most notable example. A mechanics' institute was formed in 1810 and reorganized in 1835, moving to St. John Street in 1845, from which a public library developed in 1874.[1] A school of art was organized in association with it after 1853 and regular classes in science were also held after the founding of the Chester Society of Natural Science, Literature, and Art in 1871. Other branches of learning were stimulated by the Chester Architectural, Archaeological, and Historic Society, which was established in 1849.[2]

1870–1902

The majority of members of Chester city council opposed the formation of a school board under the 1870 Education Act, chiefly on grounds of expense, and claimed that Chester already had sufficient elementary schools provided by the voluntary bodies.[3] The Education Department in London adopted the rule of thumb that there should be sufficient elementary school places for a sixth of the population, but the calculation of school places in Chester was complicated by the uneven distribution of the schools and by the existence of a number of schools outside the city boundary (notably at Hoole and Saltney) which city children also attended. In 1872 it was agreed that there was a shortfall of 1,373 places. Virtually the whole deficiency was in places for girls and infants, reflecting the more generous provision already made for boys.[4]

The chief proponents of a school board were the nonconformists, led by the (Unitarian) Revd. J. K. Montgomery, secretary of the British Schools Association, who considered that non-denominational schools should be provided from the rates for 'the poorest class of children belonging to all denominations, and those unconnected with any'.[5] The council responded by setting up a school accommodation committee, which held its first meeting in 1873 under the chairmanship of the dean of Chester. It proposed that a voluntary rate of 6d. in the pound

should be raised to meet the £4,073 needed to supply the deficiency in school places, warning that otherwise a school board would have to be set up.[6]

Despite the warning, contributions to the voluntary rate were disappointing. The managers of several Anglican schools offered to extend their premises without calling on the rates, but money was still needed to accommodate more infants at the Victoria Road British school and in a proposed new British school to be held in a former chapel in Commonhall Street. By 1874 the voluntary rate had produced only £1,018, most of which was distributed to the British schools.[7] That to some extent satisfied nonconformist opinion, but the Commonhall Street school, which opened in 1875, was forced to close in 1876 through lack of funds.[8] No more was heard about a school board.

As the city's population rose, the number of pupils on the registers of the city's elementary schools increased, from 5,347 in 1877 to 6,988 in 1900.[9] The extra accommodation was provided wholly by voluntary effort. Infants' departments were opened by the Wesleyan school in 1871 and at the Boughton British school in 1880. The Roman Catholics expanded their schools at St. Werburgh's and in 1883 opened another in Cuppin Street in connexion with the new church of St. Francis. On the Anglican side, the duke of Westminster financed a new school at St. Mary's, Handbridge (1876), and rebuilt the St. John's school in Vicars Lane (1883). The new Grosvenor St. John's school was designed by E. R. Robson, architect to the London school board,[10] but was modified during construction. Other church schools were opened in the parishes of St. Oswald (1873), where the school was named after the new church of St. Thomas, and St. Peter (1874), while St. Michael's school (1879) took over from St. Olave's ragged school in Lower Bridge Street. An infants' school was opened in 1877 in the mission church of St. Barnabas, Sibell Street, and another off Sealand Road in 1883. By 1900 there were 20 elementary schools in the city, organized in 39 departments. In denominational terms, 11 per cent of the children were in Catholic schools, 19 per cent in nonconformist, and 70 per cent in Anglican.[11]

Although a school board had been avoided, the provisions of the Education Act of 1876 made it obligatory for the council to appoint a school attendance committee, which met at almost weekly intervals from 1877.[12] A school attendance officer was appointed, assisted by an 'out-door officer', a police constable in plain clothes. The implications of enfor-

1 B. Bracegirdle, 'Development of Further Educ. in City of Chester, 1834–1944' (TS. 1971, at C.H.H.), 133–43; below, Libraries.

2 Bracegirdle, 'Development', 150–63; *Chester Chron.* 9 Apr. 1853, p. 8; below, Learned Societies.

3 C.C.A.L.S., ZCB 2, 14 Dec. 1870, 8 Mar. 1871.

4 Ibid. ZCCB 113, list pasted inside cover.

5 Ibid. 7 Mar. 1873.

6 Ibid. 21, 30 July 1873.   7 Ibid. 27 Nov. 1874.

8 Ibid. 2 Aug. 1876.   9 Ibid. ZCCB 121–4 *passim.*

10 *Bldg. News,* 20 July 1883.

11 Calculated from *Chester City Cl. Mins. 1898/9*, table facing p. 602.

12 C.C.A.L.S., ZCCB 121, 23 Apr. 1877.

FIG. 175. *Technical school at Grosvenor Museum, c. 1906*

cing school attendance soon became clear. At the committee's behest, the collector of the improvement and lamp rates made a house-to-house survey and reported that 847 children aged between 5 and 13 were not attending any school.[1] Bylaws setting out the requirements of the Act were adopted and notices were sent to parents and employers outlining the new arrangements. Teachers were required to keep increasingly elaborate records, registrations of births were obtained on a regular basis, and a private medical practitioner was employed to certify absences through illness. In 1878 the committee sent out 2,513 notices to parents whose children were not attending school regularly, and many of the parents were called to interview by members of the committee. In 1878 the magistrates fined 112 parents and imprisoned five for the non-attendance of their children.[2] The number of fines rose to 460 in 1900 and each year some parents were imprisoned.[3] A small number of refractory boys were sent to the industrial school at Boughton or to the training ship *Clio* in the Menai Strait. Aided by such measures, school attendance rose from 75 per cent in 1878 to 82 per cent in 1900, matching the average for England and Wales as a whole. When the school attendance committee was replaced under the provisions of the 1902 Education Act, it was praised for its thoroughness, efficiency, and modest cost.[4]

The College school for boys and the Consolidated school for girls charged higher fees than the other elementary schools in the city and in 1885 became 'higher-grade' schools offering a somewhat more advanced curriculum.[5] The boys' school moved to a

new building on the college site in 1900, designed on the central-hall plan by the county architect, H. Beswick,[6] while the girls' school's building in Hunter Street was extended. The demand for secondary education was still largely being satisfied by private schools: in 1871 there were at least 40 private schools in Chester, 30 of them for girls. Several of the larger and longer established boys' schools in the 1870s occupied such notable buildings as the old Albion Hotel and Bridge House in Lower Bridge Street, 'Derby House' (Stanley Palace) in Watergate Street, and Forest House in Foregate Street, though Gamul House had closed as a boarding school in the 1860s.[7] However, the King's school was now being reformed, and acquired an impressive new building near the cathedral in 1879.[8] The Queen's school was established for middle-class girls in 1878 and moved to a new building in City Walls Road in 1883.[9]

Evening classes in art and science were held at the mechanics' institution in St. John Street, while the archaeological and natural history societies met in the Albion Rooms in Lower Bridge Street. Chiefly through the generosity of the duke of Westminster, all those activities were centralized in the Grosvenor Museum, completed in 1886 to the design of T. M. Lockwood. The classes were able to gain grants from the Science and Art Department at South Kensington.[10]

The city council adopted the Acts of 1889 and 1890 which permitted local authorities to raise a penny rate and to claim excise duties ('whisky money') in aid of technical education. In 1892 a technical day school for boys was established in the Grosvenor Museum and the

---

1 Ibid. 30 July 1877.   2 Ibid. 7 Oct. 1878.
3 Ibid. ZCCB 124, 8 Oct. 1900.
4 *Chester City Cl. Mins.* 1902/3, 769.
5 Sneyd-Kynnersley and Daws, *Hunter St. School,* 15.
6 *Perspectives of Chester Coll.: 150th Anniversary Essays, 1839–1989,* ed. G. J. White (copy at C.H.H.), 36–7.

7 *P. & G. Dir. Chester* (1871), 92; (1878/9), 90; *Gresty and Burghall's Chester Guide* [1867], 73.
8 *V.C.H. Ches.* iii. 231–2.
9 Ibid. 232–3.
10 Bracegirdle, 'Development', 158–63; Pevsner, *Ches.* 159; below, Museums: Grosvenor Museum.

council granted it £711 a year in return for representation on the school's governing body. The day-school fee of £10 a year proved to be too high to attract pupils and was later halved, while some scholarships for boys from the elementary schools were made available with the help of Robert Oldfield's charity.[1]

1903–18

Chester, a county borough, became a local education authority in 1902, and an education committee comprising 18 councillors and 9 co-opted members began work in 1903.[2] A. E. Lovell, previously on the staff of Chester College, was appointed director of education.[3] The abolition of fees in most of the elementary schools in 1907, and a declining birth rate, reflected in a drop in the average attendance in Chester's elementary schools from 6,243 in 1904 to 5,788 in 1913, largely solved the difficulties of securing school attendance, which rose to 90 per cent.[4]

The main problem facing the new authority was the unsatisfactory state of the voluntary school buildings, many of which were old and overcrowded. Government inspectors reported numerous deficiencies, confirmed by the city surveyor.[5] Although under the 1902 Act the authority was responsible for maintaining the voluntary schools, the external structure of the buildings remained the responsibility of the voluntary bodies. There was prolonged correspondence with the managers of the Wesleyan, British, and Catholic schools, and of the older Anglican schools, all of whom were short of funds. In the event, the Wesleyan school in St. John Street closed and was replaced by a new council school in Love Street in 1909. The Boughton British school was taken over by the authority in 1905 and replaced by a new council school in Cherry Grove Road in 1910. The Victoria Road British school was also taken over by the council in 1909 and later extended. The Roman Catholics were opposed to the non-denominational education given in the council schools: the managers further enlarged St. Werburgh's school, but in 1913 the Board of Education withdrew recognition from St. Francis's school because of the inadequate state of its building.[6] It carried on without government or rate aid and did not regain recognition until 1922.[7]

Some of the older Anglican schools were also forced to close. In 1908 Christ Church boys' school and the Diocesan boys' school were closed and the pupils transferred to a new council school in George Street.

The Bishop Graham Memorial school was taken over by the authority in 1909 and closed in 1915, while the infants in St. Barnabas's school and the Wesleyan school annexe in City Road were transferred to a new council infants' school which opened in Egerton Street in 1910.

The new council schools in Love Street and George Street were designed by H. Beswick, and those in Cherry Grove and Egerton Street by W. T. Lockwood in association with John Douglas.[8] The Love Street school was designed as a higher-grade school for boys and girls, matching the College and Hunter Street schools, which remained under Anglican control. Between 1903 and 1913 the authority spent £41,400 on new elementary school buildings, the Anglicans £6,800 on improvements, and the Catholics £5,000.[9] Annual expenditure on elementary education from the rates reached c. £12,000 before the outbreak of the First World War,[10] and the elementary school rate rose to 1s. 2d. in the pound. In 1911 Chester's elementary education rate was noted as 15th from the bottom in a list of 44 county boroughs,[11] a reflection of the continuing (though somewhat reduced) contribution of the voluntary bodies and, arguably, the better social conditions in Chester compared with the larger industrial towns; the authority did not, for example, consider it necessary to adopt the permissive Education (Provision of Meals) Act of 1906.[12]

Although from 1902 the King's and Queen's schools began to receive grants from the Board of Education, improvements were needed, especially in their provision for science teaching. Proposals that the local authority should make grants to them were opposed by the Ratepayers' Association, which considered that the parents whose children were benefiting from the schools should pay.[13] The Chester Evangelical Free Church Council, which disliked the Anglican connexions, particularly of the King's school, argued that rate aid should be limited to non-denominational schools.[14] Opposition also came from the private schools in the town,[15] which in 1905 were said to be providing as many secondary school places as the public schools. Among the numerous private establishments were Arnold House school in Parkgate Road, which had 90 boys, compared with 112 at the King's school, and a school in Upper Northgate Street which had 80 girls, compared with 170 at the Queen's school.[16] Arnold House had existed probably since c. 1871 but evidently closed in 1909.[17] The Dee House Convent school was

1 *Chester City Cl. Educ. Cttee. Mins. 1904/5*, 103–8.

2 *Chester City Cl. Mins. 1902/3*, 288, 379.

3 Ibid. 679; *Perspectives of Chester Coll.* ed. White, 64–6.

4 C.C.A.L.S., ZDE 1/3 (Director of Education's Reports to Education Committee), esp. *Rep. 1913*.

5 *Chester City Cl. Educ. Cttee. Mins. 1903/4*, 98.

6 C.C.A.L.S., ZDE 1/3, *Rep. 1913*, 27.

7 Ibid. *1922*, 3.

8 Ibid. *1907*, 7; *1908*, 6; E. Hubbard, *Work of John*

Douglas, 204.

9 C.C.A.L.S., ZDE 1/3, *Rep. 1913*, 28.

10 Ibid. 10.   11 Ibid. 53.   12 Ibid. *1908*, 19.

13 *Chester City Cl. Educ. Cttee. Mins. 1905/6*, 102.

14 Ibid. 145.   15 Ibid. *1904/5*, 221.

16 *Co-ordination of Schools*: memo. bound with ibid. *1905/6*.

17 *P. & G. Dir. Chester* (1871), 92; (1878/9), 90; *Kelly's Dir. Ches.* (1902), 226; (1906), 235; (1914), 246; *Crockford* (1907), 1124 (J. C. C. Pipon); (1926), 516 (A. H. Fish).

also gaining popularity, and took some non-Catholic girls.[1]

None of the schools met the needs of working-class parents, who wanted schools with more vocational courses and lower fees. They were provided for boys at the technical school in the Grosvenor Museum, while girls hoping to become pupil-teachers in the elementary schools attended classes which were transferred to rooms below the race stand on the Roodee in 1905.[2] Since many pupils at both institutions lived in the Cheshire education authority's area rather than the county borough, a joint scheme was agreed to build a new secondary school, which opened as the City and County school in Queen's Park in 1912.[3] Designed by W. T. Lockwood at a cost of £12,194, it provided accommodation for 120 boys and 150 girls in separate departments.[4]

When the boys moved out of the Grosvenor Museum, the evening classes for older students in technical and commercial subjects expanded. The administrative and financial complications arising from the fact that the museum also housed the school of art and local learned societies were finally resolved when the city council took over the museum building in 1915.[5]

1918–44

The Education Act of 1918 raised the minimum school leaving age to 14 and set out a programme of further advance in education, which fell victim to the economic crises of the ensuing years.[6] A. E. Lovell retired as director of education in 1923 and was succeeded by Richardson Peele, a young Oxford graduate who had read for the bar and was initially appointed as secretary to the education committee.[7]

Continuing inflation after the war raised costs without making much improvement in real terms. About half of the total expenditure on elementary education continued to be covered by government grants, but rate-borne expenditure also increased from £11,973 in 1913 to £30,378 in 1935, with the elementary school rate rising from 1s. 2d. to 3s. 6d. in the pound. Yet the number of children in average attendance in Chester's elementary schools declined from 5,788 to 5,399 over the same period. That was the result of a continued fall in the birth rate and of a larger proportion of children attending secondary schools. There was no new building and the number of elementary schools (five council and 13 voluntary) remained the same. In 1935 Catholic schools held 13 per cent of elementary school children in Chester, council schools 34 per cent, and Anglican schools 53 per cent.[8] Among the important advances made in elementary education during the period were the virtual elimination of non-certificated teachers, a reduction in the number of over-sized classes, and the further development of practical subjects for older children.

With the rapid rise in demand for secondary education between the wars, more free places were made available at the King's and Queen's schools, and in 1921 the Board of Education recognized Dee House Convent school as a secondary school.[9] All three schools received annual grants from both the city and county authorities, that from Chester rising from £718 in 1921 to £1,100 in 1935, when the rate for secondary education was 9d. in the pound.[10] The strength of parental demand, however, showed itself chiefly in relation to the City and County school. It had been designed for 270 pupils but by 1922 the number attending had risen to 497, and overflow classes were once again held in the Grosvenor Museum and at the racecourse.[11] In 1925 the school cloakrooms were converted into classrooms and the authority purchased an adjoining site upon which hutments were erected.[12] The number of children attending reached a peak of 580 in 1932.[13]

More than half of the pupils at the City and County school came from the county area, and the Cheshire authority paid capitation fees for them, but it was unwilling to share the cost of building another school in the city since it had its own plans for a new secondary school in Wirral.[14] In 1929 Richardson Peele, who had by then become director of education, wrote of the 'deplorably inadequate' accommodation at the school,[15] but the situation did not markedly improve until a new boys' school, delayed by the outbreak of the Second World War, opened in 1941. It was designed by Charles Greenwood, the city surveyor, in neo-Georgian style, and was called the City grammar school.[16] The 1912 building was then wholly occupied by the girls and was called the City high school.

The fees charged at the City and County school were considerably lower than those at the King's and Queen's schools and free places were also awarded annually on the results of an examination taken by 11-year-old children in the elementary schools. The number of free places awarded to city children remained fixed at *c.* 15 a year, while the number of fee-payers increased. Holders of free places constituted about half the total number of city pupils at the school in the 1920s, declining to a third in the 1930s when the pressure of numbers was at its height.[17]

1 W. M. Sturman, *Catholicism in Chester, 1875–1975* (Chester, [1975]), 67.

2 Kennett, *Chester Schools*, 29–30.

3 *Scheme with regard to Higher Educ.*: bound with *Chester City Cl. Educ. Cttee. Mins. 1905/6.*

4 C.C.A.L.S., ZDE 1/3, *Rep. 1912*, 21; *1913*, 42; Pevsner, *Ches.* 174–5.   5 C.C.A.L.S., ZDE 1/3, *Rep. 1915*, 20.

6 Ibid. ZDE 1/4, *Reps. 1921–35.*

7 Ibid. *1923*, 19.   8 Ibid. *1934/5*, list of schools.

9 Ibid. *1921*, 37.   10 Ibid. 37–8; *1934/5*, 21.

11 Ibid. *1922*, 19; *1923*, 16.   12 Ibid. *1925*, 27.

13 Ibid. *1932*, 17.   14 Ibid. *1924*, 25.

15 Ibid. *1929*, 6.   16 Pevsner, *Ches.* 175.

17 C.C.A.L.S., ZDE 1/3–4, *passim.*

The limited access to the grammar schools in Chester resulted in the further development of the three higher-grade elementary schools at the Love Street, College boys', and Hunter Street girls' schools, which became 'central' schools, recruiting their pupils on the results of the 11-plus examination.[1] Fees were abolished in 1919 and the number of pupils in attendance rose from 851 in 1922 to 971 in 1935, by which year half the senior pupils were above the statutory leaving age.[2] Though still classified as elementary schools, they had become embryonic secondary schools at which all the places were free. Children who were not selected for the grammar or central schools remained in the 'all-age' elementary schools. Elementary-school leavers could attend evening classes at the Grosvenor Museum or in Love Street school, though small fees were payable. There were on average *c.* 300 mainly part-time students in the school of art in each year during the period, with *c.* 400 in what was called the technical institute at the Grosvenor Museum, and *c.* 300 in the 'junior department' at Love Street.[3] In 1929 the director of education complained of the impossibility of expanding the work in the museum building and asked the committee to decide 'whether the present stagnation is to be permanent',[4] but improvements had to wait until after the Second World War.

In 1935 a new junior and infants' school was opened in Lache, in the first of the new housing estates planned for the outskirts of the city as the economic situation improved.[5] A notably innovative nursery school was also opened on the Lache estate in 1935 by a pioneering committee of women in connexion with the Nursery School Association. The principal benefactors were Mr. and Mrs. Alfred Haworth, who financed the building in memory of their daughter Hilary. It was run on a voluntary basis until the council took responsibility for it in 1940.[6]

With the establishment of more new housing estates in the previously agricultural districts of Newton and Blacon,[7] a new junior and infants' school was opened in Kingsway West at Newton in 1939 and a new junior school off Saughall Road, Blacon, in 1940, replacing a school which had been meeting in the village hall since 1930.[8] Largely as a result of the movement of population away from the centre of the city, three of the older Anglican schools closed: Holy Trinity in 1939, St. Michael's in 1941, and St. Peter's in 1942. The Blue Girls' school also closed in 1940 and the Blue Coat boys' school in 1949.

Private schools continued to be of some importance in Chester, though there were far fewer of them than before the First World War. Among the dozen or so were Walmoor College, a girls' boarding school established in Walmoor Hill, the house which the architect John Douglas had built for himself overlooking the river from Dee Banks, and its successor on the same premises after *c.* 1930, Hampton House, a boys' preparatory school earlier established at King's Buildings, King Street. In 1939 Hampton House advertised itself as preparing boys for public schools and the Royal Navy. It evidently closed during the Second World War.[9]

1944–74

Richardson Peele continued as director of education until 1960, when he was succeeded by his deputy, H. J. Hack, with the title of chief education officer.[10] On his retirement in 1966, L. E. Griffiths was appointed as his successor.[11]

The Second World War brought a halt to further development, but more significant was the Education Act of 1944, which had far more effect on education in Chester than the 1918 Act. Further changes were necessitated by the more rapid increase in the city's population from the 1930s and the incorporation of Hoole urban district into the city in 1954. That incorporation was followed by the reorganization of the church elementary schools in Hoole to form the Westminster Road Church of England junior school and the All Saints' Church of England infants' school; the elementary school built by the county council in Clare Avenue in 1912 became Hoole primary school in 1955. The former elementary schools in the rest of the city were also reorganized during the 1950s. As a result of the reorganization and the building of more new primary schools in Blacon and Newton, the number of children in Anglican schools was further reduced. In 1962, of the 6,093 children in primary schools in Chester, 64 per cent were in council schools, 20 per cent in Anglican, and 16 per cent in Roman Catholic.[12]

The King's, Queen's, and Dee House Convent schools became direct-grant grammar schools under the Education Act of 1944 and were largely financed by the Ministry of Education. About 40 free places each year were available to city children, but the main providers of free grammar-school education were the City grammar school for boys and the City high school for girls, which between them in 1962 accommodated

1 Sneyd-Kynnersley and Daws, *Hunter St. School*, 19.

2 C.C.A.L.S., ZDE 1/4, *Rep. 1922*, 2; *1935*, 3, 5.

3 Ibid. ZDE 1/3–4, *passim*.

4 Ibid. ZDE 1/4, *Rep. 1929*, 8.

5 *V.C.H. Ches.* v (1), Twentieth-Century Chester: Housing and Suburban Development, 1918–39.

6 Kennett, *Chester Schools*, 45.

7 *V.C.H. Ches.* v (1), Twentieth-Century Chester: Housing and Suburban Development, 1918–39.

8 *Blacon Past and Present* (Blacon Hist. Group, 1990: copy at

C.H.H.), 16–17.

9 e.g. *P. & G. Dir. Chester* (1923/4), 214; (1933/4), 270; (1935/6), 292–3; *Kelly's Dir. Ches.* (1928), 87; *Kelly's Dir. Chester* (1939), 250, 432A; (1941), 246; (1952), 36; *The Rare Old City of Chester: Chester Official Guide* [1929/30], 92; E. Hubbard, *Work of John Douglas*, 7–9, 188.

10 *Chester City Cl. Mins. 1959/60*, pp. 167, 648.

11 Ibid. *1966/7*, p. 276.

12 *Educ. in Chester* (issued by chief educ. officer, 1962); C.C.A.L.S., ZDE 2/23, list of schools, 18–20.

1,056 children or 28 per cent of the maintained secondary-school population.[1] Overall, about a third of Chester children over the age of 11 were receiving a free grammar-school education.

The secondary modern schools introduced in accordance with the 1944 Act were initially based on the central schools established before the war. In 1953, however, new schools were built on a large site which the authority had acquired on Old Wrexham Road. Overleigh secondary modern boys' school accommodated boys formerly in Love Street school, and St. Bede's Roman Catholic secondary modern school took boys and girls from the senior departments of St. Werburgh's school. In 1958 Hoole secondary modern school was built in Kingsway, Newton, for older children in Hoole and Newton, and in 1963 the College and Hunter Street schools were replaced by a new secondary modern school in Blacon Avenue called Bishops' school. Finally, in 1967 Charles Kingsley secondary modern school was opened in Blacon for the girls formerly at Love Street.[2]

The completion of the reorganization did not, however, satisfy public opinion in Chester. Although the 1944 Act had spoken of the need for 'parity of esteem' between secondary modern and grammar schools, the demand for grammar-school places continued unabated and overrode political and religious differences. In 1962 the education committee expressed its opposition to the introduction of non-selective comprehensive schools covering the whole range of ability, but allowed the General Certificate of Education examination to be taken in two of the secondary modern schools and permitted some late transfers to the grammar schools.[3] Nevertheless, parental opposition to the 11-plus selection examination increased still further and in 1963 the city council asked the education committee to devise 'a plan for an alternative method of selection for secondary education pending the ultimate introduction of comprehensive education'.[4]

When in 1965 the Department of Education and Science required all local education authorities to plan for comprehensive secondary education and for the proposed raising of the school leaving age to 16, wide-ranging discussions were held with parents and teachers in Chester and a number of possible schemes were considered.[5] The new chief education officer, L. E. Griffiths, favoured a three-tier system, chiefly to avoid the creation of very large schools, and in 1967 the authority agreed in principle that there should be 'a three-tier system of education on a co-educational basis with transfer at 8-plus and 12-plus and with

three high schools in the Hoole, Blacon and Queen's Park areas'.[6] Co-education for all secondary-school children was almost as radical a departure from traditional practice in Chester as acceptance of the comprehensive principle.

The new system was introduced in 1972, from which date most of the infants' schools became first schools, while most of the junior schools and two of the secondary modern schools became middle schools.[7] The secondary modern school at Hoole was enlarged to accommodate the full ability range and became Kingsway high school, the Charles Kingsley school became Blacon high school, and the City boys' and girls' grammar schools were united to form Queen's Park high school. In addition, a Roman Catholic high school was established in the building of the former Overleigh secondary modern school, in exchange for the St. Bede's school building, which became a local authority middle school. The Dee House Convent school was closed and its pupils transferred to the Catholic high school. The Anglicans objected to the designation of the Bishops' school as a middle school, and eventually, in 1984, it too became a high school, on a new site in Great Boughton.[8] The award of free places at the King's and Queen's schools came to an end in 1976, when direct grants were also withdrawn; they then became independent, largely fee-paying schools. The Queen's school remained in City Walls Road near the centre of Chester but the King's school had moved to a new building on Wrexham Road in 1960, where extensions were built with private funds and gifts from local businesses.[9]

Although the main focus of attention throughout the period was the development of primary and secondary education, courses for students who had left school continued to be held in the Grosvenor Museum and several other premises in Chester. In 1948 the authority decided to bring the courses together under one roof and purchased a large site in Eaton Road, Handbridge, for a proposed new college of further education. H. J. Long was appointed principal in the same year and the college was completed in instalments. The first phase opened in 1956 when classes in engineering and building were transferred, followed by science and general education (1957) and commercial subjects (1958). A library, refectory, assembly hall, and gymnasium were opened in 1958 and the school of art moved from the Grosvenor Museum to the new building in 1962. The completed college was officially opened in 1963.[10] H. J. Long retired in 1965 and considerable expansion took place during the principalship of A. J. Bristow between

1 C.C.A.L.S., ZDE 2/23, list of schools, 19.

2 Ibid. 9–10.   3 Ibid. 7.

4 L. E. Griffiths, *Proposals for Re-organisation of Schools* (1968), 1 (copy in C.C.A.L.S., ZDE 2/43).

5 Department of Educ. and Science, Circular 10/65.

6 Griffiths, *Proposals*, 4.

7 L. E. Griffiths, *Re-organization of Schools* (1971) (copy in C.C.A.L.S., ZDE 2/49).

8 Inf. from Canon J. G. White.

9 *V.C.H. Ches.* iii. 232, 234.

10 *100 Years of Further Educ. in Chester* (W. Ches. Coll., 1992).

FIG. 176. *Chester College, Parkgate Road: chapel* (left) *and College school* (right)

1966 and 1981. In 1972 there were 560 full-time and nearly 4,000 part-time students;[1] numbers were still rising when the county council took over the college in 1974.

1974–2000

In 1974 Chester ceased to be an independent local education authority, and the city's schools came under the control of the county council through a considerably enlarged education district with administrative headquarters in Ellesmere Port. Upton-by-Chester high school and six primary schools in Upton, Upton Heath, Vicars Cross, and Boughton Heath were added to the county borough's schools in the city's catchment area. The county council retained the comprehensive school system in Chester but during the 1980s reintroduced the more usual age range of 5–7 for infants' schools and 7–11 for junior schools. First and middle schools were phased out, and children over the age of 11 continued to be transferred to comprehensive high schools. In 2000 the total primary enrolment was 5,980 pupils, of whom 25 per cent were in Church of England and 11 per cent in Roman Catholic schools. There were 5,493 pupils in secondary schools, 18 per cent and 16 per cent respectively at the church-aided Bishops' Blue Coat Church of England school and the Catholic high school.[2]

Chester College of Further Education occupied a number of older buildings as its work continued to expand: Greenbank in Eaton Road (1983) for catering courses, the former Bishops' school in Blacon (1985) for art and crafts, and the Grange at Ellesmere Port (1985) for dance and drama. In 1986 the college was renamed West Cheshire College and in 1993, under the

provisions of the Further and Higher Education Act of 1992, was removed from local authority control to be financed by the Further Education Funding Council.[3] That was a clear indication of the growing intervention of central government in education as a whole and of the correspondingly reduced influence of local authorities.

A handful of private schools continued in existence at the end of the 20th century, including Abbey Gate school, begun as a kindergarten in Abbey Square *c.* 1934, which became a junior school after the Second World War, and later moved into the buildings of the former Victoria Road British school after its closure as a state-sector school in 1973.[4]

CHESTER COLLEGE

Chester College was founded as a diocesan training college for schoolmasters in 1839 and moved into purpose-built premises in Parkgate Road in 1842.[5] The architects were J. C. and G. Buckler and the building cost £10,000, most of which came from voluntary subscriptions.[6] A model or practising school, afterwards known as the College school, was at first held in the basement but moved to a separate wing *c.* 1844.[7] A chapel, designed by J. E. Gregan of Manchester, was added in 1847.

The first principal was the Revd. Arthur Rigg (1839–69), who had been educated in the Isle of Man and at Christ's College, Cambridge, where he graduated in mathematics in 1835. He was appointed at the remarkably young age of 27 and had charge of a small staff and three separate institutions within the same building. In addition to the training department for 50 young men intending to become elementary-school teachers, there

1 Chester Coll. of Further Educ., *Ann. Rep. 1972/3* (copy in C.C.A.L.S., ZDES 39/10).

2 Ches. Co. Cl. Education, *Primary Schools in Ches. 2000/2001*, 17–22.

3 Inf. from Mr. C. D. Rees, college principal 1981–93.

4 *P. & G. Dir. Chester* (1933/4), 106; (1935/6), 119; *Kelly's Dir. Chester* (1938), 227; (1952), 2; (1954), 255; (1973), 324;

(1974), 326.

5 This section is very largely based on Bradbury, *Chester Coll.*; the college magazine *Collegian* (1888–1987); and *Perspectives of Chester Coll.* ed. White.

6 Bradbury, *Chester Coll.* 75.

7 C.C.A.L.S., SC 1/42/7–8; *Perspectives of Chester Coll.* ed. White, 29–33.

was a day school for 110 local elementary-school boys, and a boarding school (called the commercial and later the science school) for 70 fee-paying boys.[1] Rigg was deeply interested in science and technology and his science school acquired a national reputation. Sir Henry Cole and Richard Redgrave of the Science and Art Department sent their sons to it and one of the science tutors was William Crookes, fellow and later president of the Royal Society.[2] The timetable provided that the students in the training department should spend two hours a day on 'industrial occupations', in which it appears that the boys of the science school also participated.[3] Out-buildings were used for such activities as metalworking, carpentry, stonecarving, and bookbinding.[4] A separate science laboratory was built in 1855.[5] The students themselves helped with the building of the chapel and made some of the stained-glass windows and interior furnishings; they also made scientific apparatus for sale to schools.[6] In the 1860s fears of the rising cost of education led to the introduction nationally of 'payment by results' and a severe drop in the demand for teachers throughout the country. In 1867, while there were 51 pupils in the science school, there were only five in the training department.[7] Rigg resigned in 1869 to pursue his scientific interests with the Royal Society of Arts in London.

Rigg was succeeded by the vice-principal, the Revd. J. M. Chritchley (1869–86). The Education Act of 1870 created a new demand for elementary-school teachers and the college governors decided to concentrate on teacher training, which they saw as the original purpose of the college. In 1873 there were 89 teacher-training students and only 19 boys in the science school.[8] By 1885 there were 110 students and the science school had closed.[9] The parts of the building occupied by the science school were taken over by the training department.

The next principal, the Revd. A. J. C. Allen (1886–90), quarrelled with the governing body and resigned. His successor, the Revd. J. D. Best (1890–1910), had been principal of the church training college at Derby. The number of students, all resident, continued to be *c.* 110 but student life became a little more varied.[10] A further broadening of horizons resulted from the use of practice schools in Liverpool and from the agreement made in 1908, as a condition of receiving a government grant, that up to half of the students could be non-Anglicans.[11] In 1900 a new model school was built and the old one became the students' dining room. A new lecture block was built in 1907.

The Revd. R. A. Thomas (1910–35), who succeeded Best, had been educated at the King's school in Chester and Trinity Hall, Cambridge. During the First World War the college was occupied by a public school evacuated from Kent, and Thomas became an Army chaplain. During the inter-war period the number of students averaged 150.[12] In 1928 land was purchased to enlarge the college site to 30 a. and in 1931 a new lecture block was built for more advanced work in science, art, and craft.[13] Most students took a two-year course, but in the 1920s the college was affiliated to Liverpool University, to which some students proceeded to take a degree; others took a three-year course in Chester which combined a teaching certificate with an external London degree.[14] In the early 1930s the falling birth rate and financial crises led to proposals from the Church of England Board of Finance that three of the strongest colleges (Chester, Lincoln, and Bristol) should be temporarily closed to enable the other church colleges to pay their way. The bishop of Chester, Geoffrey Fisher, led the opposition to the proposals, which were defeated in the Church Assembly in 1933.[15]

The Revd. H. S. Astbury (1935–53) succeeded Thomas. Two new hostels and a gymnasium were planned, but only the gymnasium was completed before the outbreak of the Second World War. The college was requisitioned by the Army, and Astbury, who had won an M.C. during the First World War, rejoined the chaplaincy service. The college reopened in September 1945. The Liverpool Institute of Education, set up to co-ordinate the work of the training colleges in the area, became the responsibility of Liverpool University in 1952.[16] Thereafter, university staff became involved in the setting and marking of college examinations.

Considerable development took place under the Revd. A. J. Price (1953–65), formerly principal of Goldsmiths' College, London. The rising birth rate after the war created an unprecedented demand for teachers. The number of students at the college rose from 150 to 550 and the teaching practice area for a time included Suffolk, Shropshire, and the Isle of Man.[17] New hostels planned before the war were completed in 1953 and 1954, an assembly hall was built in 1959, and a new dining hall in 1963. The former college school, which moved to Blacon in 1963, was taken over for college use and a second gymnasium and three more hostels opened in 1965. Of particular significance for the future was the admission of three female students (all married women) in 1961.[18]

1 Bradbury, *Chester Coll.* 80.

2 Ibid. 113, 135–6.   3 Ibid. 104, 115.

4 Ibid. 107; F. E. Foden, 'Arthur Rigg: Pioneer of Workshop Practice', *Vocational Aspect*, xxiii.

5 C.C.A.L.S., SC 1/42/1–6; *Perspectives of Chester Coll.* ed. White, 49 n.

6 Bradbury, *Chester Coll.* 120 n.

7 Ibid. 100.   8 Ibid. 144.

9 Ibid. 160.   10 Ibid. 180.

11 Ibid. 179.   12 Ibid. 185.

13 Ibid. 189, 206 n.; *Perspectives of Chester Coll.* ed. White, 19–28.

14 Bradbury, *Chester Coll.* 186, 196.

15 Ibid. 198–206.   16 Ibid. 216.

17 Ibid. 225, 236.   18 Ibid. 231.

Sir Bernard de Bunsen (1965–71) was the first lay principal of the college and had previously been the vice-chancellor of the University of East Africa. The number of students increased to 923 and a new tower block of lecture rooms opened in 1971. A four-year B.Ed. degree, validated by Liverpool University, was taken by a small number of matriculated students. The constitution of the college was democratized by the introduction of an academic council for the staff and a guild council for the students. A new social centre was opened in 1971.[1]

Sir Bernard de Bunsen was succeeded by Dr. Malcolm Seaborne (1971–87), a Cambridge graduate and formerly a senior lecturer at the University of Leicester School of Education. His aim was to phase out the non-matriculated entry and to develop a college in which all the students were reading for degrees.[2] In 1972 the number of students rose to 959, but in the following year the government announced a drastic reduction in teacher-training places which resulted in the closure or merger of many colleges. It became essential to diversify the college courses, and that was achieved with the help of Liverpool University, which agreed to validate courses leading to a B.A. in Combined Studies (General, 1975; Honours, 1983).[3] The university also agreed to validate a B.A. in Health and Community Studies (1980) and a B.Sc. (1985), to both of which Honours were later accorded. A postgraduate certificate in education, a range of specialist diplomas, and an M.Ed. degree were also introduced. By 1979 the student entry was fully matriculated, half of the students were women, and a third came from homes over 100 miles distant from the college.[4] In 1986 there were 559 undergraduates taking the B.A. or B.Sc. degree, 349 taking the B.Ed., and 58 mature students taking graduate or postgraduate courses; a further 266 students were taking degrees or diplomas part-time.[5] The main building work carried out was a new library (opened 1977), a new resource centre (1983), and a 'student village' of self-catering and self-financing flats (1987).

Dr. Seaborne retired in 1987 and was succeeded by the Revd. E. V. Binks,[6] previously principal of St. Katharine's College, Liverpool. The accelerating national demand for higher education led to a radical change in the methods of financing it. Colleges which took more students without increasing staff costs were permitted to extend their accommodation, and co-operation with local businesses and other agencies was actively encouraged. As a result of those policies, the numbers attending courses at the college increased rapidly and in 1992 there were 819 students taking the B.A., 666 the B.Ed., and 269 the B.Sc. full-time courses. The number of full-time postgraduate and in-service students had risen to 89 and the number of part-time students had also risen dramatically. Of particular importance was the participation of the college in 'Project 2000' for the education of nurses. In 1991 Chester College and the Chester and Wirral College of Nursing and Midwifery combined to provide education and training for 200 nurses a year preparing for a certificate in nursing studies validated by Liverpool University, and in 1992 student nurses from Crewe and Macclesfield joined with those in Chester and Wirral for a course leading to the award of a higher education diploma. The regional health authority financed a new headquarters building on the college site for nurse education (1991), while official funds and savings on staffing provided a library extension (1991) and a new building for art and technology (1992). A local industrialist helped to finance a new lecture hall complex (Molloy Hall, 1990). The profits derived from vacation conferences made possible the conversion of the principal's house in the old college building into a conference centre (1988). St. Thomas's vicarage was purchased for teaching rooms (1988), and new student flats were built alongside it (Douglas Court, 1992).[7] Further premises were brought into use in 1996, when the department of history was relocated to the former Blue Coat school, Northgate Street (leased from the Blue Coat Foundation). By the time Binks retired in 1998, students wearing gowns had become an annual event in Chester, the college having been responsible for the organization of degree ceremonies in the cathedral, on behalf of Liverpool University as the awarding body, since 1993.

The new principal, Professor T. J. Wheeler, led a bid for the college to be granted its own degree-awarding powers and oversaw continued expansion, including the opening of a new sports hall (1998) and the launch of a major new department of Business and Management (1999). By 1999–2000 there were c. 5,000 registered undergraduates (of whom about 1,000 were part-time) and 2,500 postgraduate students. Of the four schools of study into which the college was then arranged, 38 per cent of students were based in the school of Science and Health, 28 per cent in Arts and Humanities, 28 per cent in Nursing and Midwifery, and 6 per cent in Education,[8] a reflection of the shift of emphasis in the college's work which characterized the closing decades of the 20th century.

1 Bradbury, *Chester Coll.* 239–40.
2 *Collegian* (1973), 7.
3 Ibid. (1975), 5; (1983), 6.   4 Ibid. (1981), 36.
5 Ibid. (1987), 7; Liverpool Univ. Board of Coll. Studies, Minute 33, dated 12 May 1987.

6 Para. based on inf. kindly supplied by the Revd. E. V. Binks.
7 The rest of this account is by Prof. G. J. White, Chester College.
8 *Annual Rep.: Chester Coll. of Higher Education, 1999–2000*, 23.

LIST OF SCHOOLS OPENED BEFORE 1974[a]

	Name of School	Opened	Closed	Location
1	King's	1541		Cathedral precinct[b]
2	Blue Coat	1700	1949	Upper Northgate St.[c]
3	Blue Girls'	1720	1940	Blue Coat School?[d]
4	Consolidated Girls'[e]	1787	1963[f]	Hunter St.[g]
5	Diocesan	1812	1908[h]	Upper Northgate St.[i]
6	Grosvenor St. John's	1813	1964	Vicars La.[j]
7	Kaleyards Infants'	1826	1891	Frodsham St.
8	Russell Street Infants'	1827	1890	Russell St.
9	Handbridge Infants'	1828	1860[k]	Handbridge
10	Boughton St. Paul's	1830?	1973[l]	Boughton[m]
11	Wesleyan	1839	1909[n]	St. John St.[o]
12	Christ Church	1842	1855[p]	Cornwall St.
13	College	1843	1963[q]	Parkgate Rd.[r]
14	St. Mary's[s]	1846	1972	St. Mary's Hill
15	Lache cum Saltney	1851?[t]	1909	
16	Boughton Ragged[u]	1852	1908[v]	Boughton
17	St. Olave's Ragged	1852	1876[w]	St. Olave St.
18	Dee House Convent	1854	1972[x]	Little St. John St.
19	St. Werburgh's R.C.	1854		Queen St.[y]
20	Christ Church Girls' and Infants'	1855[z]	1960	Cornwall St.
21	Christ Church Boys'	1855[aa]	1908[bb]	Westminster Rd.[cc]
22	St. Martin's Infants'	1860[dd]	1862	Linenhall St.
23	Westminster Road Girls' and Infants'	1865	1955[ee]	Westminster Rd.
24	Boughton British (later Council)	1866	1910[ff]	Christleton Rd.
25	Victoria Road British (later Council)	1867	1973	Victoria Rd.[gg]
26	Bishop Graham Memorial Ragged	1868	1915	Princess St.
27	Holy Trinity	1869	1939	Linenhall St.
28	All Saints' C. of E. Boys'	1870	1955[hh]	School St.[ii]
29	Wesleyan Infants'	1871[jj]	1909[kk]	Pepper St.[ll]
30	St. Thomas's[mm]	1873		Walpole St.
31	St. Peter's Infants'	1874	1942	Hamilton Pl.[nn]
32	Commonhall Street British Infants'	1875	1876	Commonhall St.
33	Handbridge St. Mary's	1876	1984	Handbridge
34	St. Barnabas's Infants'	1877	1909[oo]	Sibell St.
35	Queen's	1878		City Walls Rd.[pp]

[a] The main list is confined to schools within the area of the former county borough of Chester. Based on A. M. Kennett, *Chester Schools: Guide to Archives*, and including schools not listed there which retained their records in 1993. Thanks are offered to the staff of the former Chester City Record Office and to head teachers for supplying information.

[b] 1876 to St. Werburgh St.; 1960 to Wrexham Rd.

[c] From 1717.

[d] 1810 to St. Martin's in the Fields; 1865 to Queen St.; 1872 to Vicars La.

[e] Founded as Sunday and Working schs.; reorganized and renamed 1816; usually known as Hunter Street from 1854.

[f] Replaced by no. 62.

[g] From 1854; previously at Blue Coat Sch. 1810, Vicars La. 1852.

[h] Replaced by no. 42. [i] From 1816.

[j] Rebuilt 1883. [k] Replaced by no. 22.

[l] Replaced by no. 75. [m] Rebuilt 1857.

[n] Replaced by no. 43.

[o] From 1842 (girls previously in St. John St., boys in Back Brook St.).

[p] Girls and infants remained in same bldg. (no. 20); boys moved out (no. 21).

[q] Replaced by no. 62. [r] Rebuilt 1900.

[s] Infants only 1866–1904 and from 1954.

[t] *Builder* (1851), 577. [u] Industrial sch. added 1863.

[v] Bldg. continued in use as no. 46.

[w] Bldg. continued in use as no. 36.

[x] Replaced by no. 72.

[y] 1953 seniors to no. 56; 1967 juniors to Love St. (reusing bldg. of no. 43); 1968 infants to Lightfoot St. (no. 68).

[z] Formerly part of no. 12 in same bldg.

[aa] Formerly part of no. 12. [bb] Replaced by no. 42.

[cc] 1870 to Black Diamond St.; old bldg. continued in use as no. 28.

[dd] Replacement for no. 9.

[ee] Bldg. continued in use as no. 57.

[ff] Replaced by no. 44. [gg] Rebuilt 1871.

[hh] Replaced by no. 57.

[ii] From 1887 (previously in Westminster Rd., bldg. formerly no. 21); old bldg. continued in use as no. 58.

[jj] Formerly part of no. 11.

[kk] Replaced by no. 45. [ll] 1899 to City Rd.

[mm] Renamed St. Thomas of Canterbury 1968.

[nn] Rebuilt 1888. [oo] Replaced by no. 45.

[pp] From 1883 (previously at Watergate Flags); preparatory dept. to Stanley Place 1932; juniors to Nedham House, Liverpool Rd., 1948.

LIST OF SCHOOLS OPENED BEFORE 1974 (*continued*)

	Name of School	Opened	Closed	Location
36	St. Michael's with St. Olave's	1879[qq]	1941	St. Olave St.
37	St. Francis's R.C.	1883	1972[rr]	Cuppin St.
38	Sealand Road C. of E. Infants'	1883	1921	South View Rd.
39	Technical Day	1892	1907[ss]	Grosvenor Museum
40	City and County Girls' (City High)[tt]	1905	1972[uu]	Queen's Park Rd.[vv]
41	City and County Boys' (City Grammar)[ww]	1907[xx]	1972[yy]	Queen's Park Rd.[zz]
42	George Street Council	1908[aaa]	1948	George St.
43	Love Street Council	1909[bbb]	1967[ccc]	Love St.
44	Cherry Grove Council	1910[ddd]		Cherry Grove Rd.
45	Egerton Street Council Infants'	1910[eee]	1992	Egerton St.
46	Boughton Reformatory	1911	1929	Boughton[fff]
47	Hoole Junior and Infants'	1912		Clare Ave.
48	Blacon Junior	1930		Warwick Rd.[ggg]
49	Lache Junior and Infants'	1935		Hawthorn Rd.
50	Hilary Haworth Nursery	1935		Sycamore Dr.
51	Newton Junior and Infants'	1939		Kingsway West
52	Boughton Nursery	1941	1973	Richmond Terrace, Hoole La.
53	Bowling Green Bank Nursery	1941	1953	off Brook St.
54	Blacon Infants'	1953[hhh]		Carlisle Rd.
55	Overleigh St. Mary's[iii]	1953[jjj]	1972	Old Wrexham Rd.
56	St. Bede's R.C. Secondary Modern	1953[kkk]	1972[lll]	Old Wrexham Rd.
57	Westminster C. of E. Junior	1955[mmm]	1972[nnn]	Westminster Rd.
58	All Saints' C. of E. Infants'	1955[ooo]		School St.[ppp]
59	Highfield Junior and Infants'	1955		Blacon Point Rd.
60	Hoole Secondary Modern[qqq]	1958		Kingsway (Kingsway High)
61	Woodfield Junior and Infants'	1959		Somerset Rd.
62	Bishops' High[rrr]	1963[sss]		Blacon Ave.[ttt]
63	St. Theresa's R.C. Infants'	1964		Blacon Point Rd.
64	Dee Point Infants' and Junior	1964		Blacon Point Rd.
65	Charles Kingsley Secondary Modern[uuu]	1967[vvv]		Melbourne Rd. (Blacon High)
66	J. H. Godwin Infants'	1968		Melbourne Rd.
67	Belgrave Infants'	1968		Five Ashes Rd.
68	St. Werburgh's R.C. Infants'	1968[www]		Lightfoot St.
69	Mount Carmel R.C. Junior	1969		Kipling Rd.
70	St. Clare's R.C. Primary	1972[xxx]		Hawthorn Rd.
71	St. James's C. of E. Junior	1972[yyy]		Hoole La.
72	Catholic High	1972[zzz]		Old Wrexham Rd.
73	Queen's Park High	1972[aaaa]		Queen's Park Rd.
74	St. Mary's Nursery	1972		St. Mary's Hill
75	Boughton St. Paul's Infants'	1973[bbbb]		Boughton
76	Victoria Infants'	1973		Cheyney Rd.

[qq] Reusing bldg. of no. 17.
[ss] Reorganized as no. 41.
[uu] Bldg. continued in use as no. 73.
[vv] From 1912 (previously at Roodee grandstand).
[ww] Renamed 1938.   [xx] Reorganization of no. 39.
[yy] Bldg. continued in use as no. 73.
[zz] From 1912 (previously at Grosvenor Museum).
[aaa] Replacement for nos. 5 and 21.
[bbb] Replacement for no. 11.
[ccc] Replaced no. 55 for boys (1953) and no. 65 for girls (1967); bldg. continued in use as no. 19.
[ddd] Replacement for no. 24.
[eee] Replacement for nos. 29 and 34.
[fff] Reusing bldg. of no. 16.
[ggg] From 1940 (previously in Blacon village hall).
[hhh] Formerly part of no. 48.
[iii] Secondary Modern 1953; Middle 1972; renamed 1984.

[rr] Replaced by no. 70.
[tt] Renamed 1938.
[jjj] Replaced no. 43 (boys only).
[kkk] Replaced no. 19 (seniors only).
[lll] Replaced by no. 72; bldg. continued in use as no. 55.
[mmm] Reusing bldg. of no. 23; replaced nos. 23 (girls only) and 28.
[nnn] Replaced by no. 71.   [ooo] Reusing bldg. of no. 28.
[ppp] 1981 to Clare Ave.   [qqq] Renamed 1972.
[rrr] Secondary Modern 1963; Middle 1972; renamed 1984.
[sss] Replacement for nos. 4 and 13.
[ttt] 1984 to Vaughan's La.   [uuu] Renamed 1972.
[vvv] Replacement for no. 43 (girls only).
[www] Replacement for infants' sch. at no. 19.
[xxx] Replacement for no. 37.
[yyy] Replacement for no. 57.
[zzz] Replacement for nos. 18 and 56.
[aaaa] Amalgamation of nos. 40 and 41.
[bbbb] Replacement for no. 10.

	Name of School	Location
77	Acresfield Primary	Acres La., Upton Heath
78	Boughton Heath Primary	Becketts La.
79	Mill View Primary	Wealstone La., Upton
80	Oldfield Primary	Green La., Vicars Cross
81	Upton-by-Chester High	St. James Ave.
82	Upton Heath C. of E. Primary	Upton La.
83	Upton Westlea Primary	Weston Grove, Upton

[a] Ches. Co. Cl. Education, *Primary Schools in Ches. 2000/2001*, 17–22.

LEARNED SOCIETIES

In the early 18th century Cestrians with scientific or antiquarian interests pursued them among small groups of friends like the circle of Henry Prescott, deputy registrar of Chester diocese.[1] Public lectures on practical science were being staged by 1750, and in the 1780s there was briefly a Free Conversation Society for cultivating 'moral and intellectual knowledge'.[2] A successor established in 1812, the Chester Literary and Philosophical Society, had among its two dozen members the chaplain of Little St. John's, the master of a commercial school, shopkeepers, clergymen, a physician, and the publisher of the *Chester Chronicle*, John Fletcher. It met to discuss papers and hear lectures, and bought scientific apparatus, but seems to have ceased after a year.[3] The Chester Cymmrodorion Society founded in 1822 had among its objects research into the history, customs, language, and literature of the Welsh, and held lectures and discussions at least in its early years but seems by the later 1830s to have become principally a dining club.[4]

The Chester Literary Improvement Society was apparently founded in 1847 by William Axon; probably the same body as the Literary and Scientific Society of 1849, its fate after 1855 is obscure.[5] A Chester Natural History Society lasted only from 1858 to 1859.[6]

The first of the two really successful learned societies, eventually known as the Chester Archaeological Society, was established in 1849 at a public meeting convened by the Revd. William Massie, rector of St. Mary's, which intended as much an architectural pressure group as a society for disinterested antiquarianism. The immediate inspiration seems to have been the 1849 meeting of the British Archaeological Associ-

ation in Chester. The local body's original name had the words 'Architectural, Archaeological, and Historic' in that order, and the first three of its five leading objects were the improvement of architectural taste and practice, the illustration and preservation of the remains of antiquity (probably mainly meaning old buildings), and the recommendation of plans for new and restored buildings. To those ends the committee was always to include four practising architects or builders. A fifth of the early members were clergymen, but there was also a serious attempt to attract ladies, 'young men . . . engaged in the shops and offices of the city', and 'the industrious and intelligent artisan' through six categories of membership. Almost as many women as clergymen joined in the early years, making the society relatively unusual. Meetings were at first held in the City Library, over the Commercial News Room in Northgate Street (Fig. 177, p. 292).[7] Part of the motivation for the society was an overt hostility to neo-classical architecture, as exemplified by the parish churches of St. Bridget (1829) and St. Paul (1830), and a corresponding adoration of Gothic in church architecture and 'medieval' timber-framing in domestic and commercial buildings, but opinion among members was not uniform,[8] and the society soon spread its interests into antiquarian matters broadly defined. For instance in 1852 it lobbied, unsuccessfully, for the retention locally of the palatinate records, as it did for their return in 1912–14.[9] Meetings certainly included architectural subjects but also ranged widely over archaeology and history.[10]

The society's impetus was faltering from the late 1850s and failed altogether in 1872: no minutes were kept, meetings became infrequent and informal, the

1 *Diary of Henry Prescott, passim.*

2 *Georgian Chester,* ed. A. M. Kennett, 39.

3 C.C.A.L.S., ZCR 163/1; members identified from ibid. ZAB 5, ff. 137, 201; *Pigot's Commercial Dir.* (1818/20), 99–108.

4 T. Edwards, *Chester Cambrian Societies, 1760–1906* (priv. print. 1906), 4–43.   5 C.C.A.L.S., ZCR 145/1–9.

6 J. D. Siddall, *Formation of Chester Soc. of Natural Science,*

Literature, and Art (1911), 6–7.

7 *J.C.A.S.* [o.s.], i, pp. i, iii, 1–4, 77; v, pp. vii–viii; A. G. Crosby, *Chester Arch. Soc. 1849–1999*, 5–15; *T.H.S.L.C.* cxlvii. 127–9.

8 *J.C.A.S.* [o.s.], i. 12, 31–43, 187; vi. 260–1; vii. 398–405.

9 Ibid. i. 326–9; n.s. xix. 233–4; xxi. 188–9.

10 Ibid. [o.s.], *passim.*

FIG. 177. *Commercial News Room and City Library*

Journal appeared irregularly and then not at all, and membership fell away, but the society was never formally wound up. It was relaunched as the Archaeological and Historic Society of the County and City of Chester and North Wales by Dean Howson in 1883 and was definitely afloat again from 1886, when a new constitution was adopted; the society's declared objects were now the publication of archaeological and historical information and the preservation of antiquities in the newly opened Grosvenor Museum. The *Journal* was restarted under the successive editorships of Thomas Hughes and J. P. Earwaker, and membership rose to 267 in 1888–9. The new museum played an important part in the revival, providing a location for meetings and storage for the society's library and collections, accumulated from the early years and hitherto kept in very poor conditions at the Albion Rooms in Lower Bridge Street.[1] The renewal of interest was also due in large measure to excitement over the discovery of extensive Roman remains in the city, and many members had an active involvement in local archaeology.[2] A regular winter lecture programme of six or seven meetings was established, excursions to places of historical interest were begun in 1894, and the *Journal* appeared regularly. Those core activities remained essentially the same in the 1990s.[3]

The revived society also renewed its role as an influential body of opinion in favour of conservation, but without the ecclesiological slant of the early years. It took a part, for example, in preserving Bishop Lloyd's House in 1898 and was especially active from the mid 1920s to the Second World War, when it helped to save St. Peter's church, the Blue Bell Inn, and the old Newgate. Although it resumed lobbying the city council in the 1950s, the formation of Chester Civic Trust in 1959 provided a new forum for such public campaigns.[4] Management of the Grosvenor Museum was transferred to the city council in 1915,[5] but the society was increasingly important as a collector of archival materials, especially the papers of such local antiquaries as J. P. Earwaker (1898), Canon Rupert Morris (1918), and Thomas Hughes (1925–6). Only with the appointment of the first city archivist in 1948 did the society willingly give up its role as a *de facto* local record office.[6] Archaeology returned to the forefront of the society's interests in the 1920s and remained there for the rest of the 20th century. Its centrality was signalled in the 1960s by the change of name to the Chester Archaeological Society. The society took a leading part in the excavation of the amphitheatre in the 1960s, but from the 1970s its role was restricted to providing volunteers for digs directed by professional archaeologists employed by the city council.[7]

The city's other long-lasting learned body, the Natural Science Society, was founded in 1871 under the direct inspiration of Charles Kingsley, who arrived in Chester as a canon of the cathedral in 1870 and gave a series of lectures on botany. The society took root and grew branches which by 1911 covered almost every aspect of natural science. Lectures on literature and art were dropped after the First World War. The society was a leading promoter of the Grosvenor Museum and of the School of Science, and had over 1,000 members in the early 20th century. Popular lectures and field trips, rather than active research, became the main emphasis from the 1920s. *Scientific Proceedings* were published 1874–1907 and 1947–51, and the society remained alive in 1995.[8]

1 *J.C.A.S.* n.s. i, esp. 99, 114–18, 130, 161–3, 228–32; Crosby, *Chester Arch. Soc.* 19–27, 49–52.
2 Crosby, *Chester Arch. Soc.* 53.
3 *J.C.A.S.* n.s. passim.
4 Crosby, *Chester Arch. Soc.* 37, 54–5, 63, 69–72, 88–90.

5 Below, Museums: Grosvenor Museum.
6 Crosby, *Chester Arch. Soc.* 58–60, 73–5.
7 Ibid. 36, 78–87, 92.
8 Siddall, *Formation*; H. Robinson, *Chester Soc. of Natural Science, Literature, and Art: First 100 Years* (1971).

LIBRARIES

Subscribers to an intended circulating library obtained permission to use a room in the Exchange in 1773,[1] but it is not certain that the venture was ever launched, and the earliest such library known to have operated had premises in Bridge Street in 1787.[2] In the early 19th century Chester boasted several small libraries, the most important of which was the City or Public library, owned by 120 proprietors, which began in premises in Whitefriars and moved to rooms over the Commercial News Room in St. Peter's churchyard in 1815. Members paid a high entrance fee and an annual subscription.[3] The others were circulating libraries run by or associated with booksellers,[4] one of which was the General Public library, opened in 1817 and connected with the newspaper proprietor John Fletcher.[5] Similar circulating libraries in the later 19th century included J. W. Huke's in Eastgate Buildings in the 1890s.[6]

Chester was a latecomer to the movement for working men's education. The Chester Mechanics' Institution was set up in 1835 in Goss Street.[7] The books and fixtures of the General library were bought with money advanced by William Wardell, and other donations brought the stock to 1,500 volumes, mostly non-fiction, by the end of 1835.[8] Evening classes were held for architectural, mechanical, and landscape drawing, music, foreign languages, elementary arithmetic, and literacy.[9]

In 1845 the Institution moved to rented premises in St. John Street, which it bought in 1856,[10] and in the following year it bought the stock of the City library.[11] From the late 1850s its educational activities began to fade; members preferred to read for amusement, and the library therefore bought more popular books.[12] Membership was never more than a few hundred, and the annual subscription of 10s. restricted it to the skilled working and lower middle classes.[13] The Institution was dogged by financial difficulties and survived only through philanthropic donations; in 1867 the management passed to trustees.[14]

At the suggestion of E. G. Salisbury, a former M.P. for Chester, the Mechanics' Institution was taken over by the city council in 1875 and converted into a free library under the Free Libraries Act of 1855.[15] Its opening was delayed by conveyancing problems and the need for repairs.[16] A periodicals reading room and the lending library were opened in 1877,[17] the latter largely restocked with novels, travel, history, and biography.[18] A reference room on the top floor was opened in 1883.[19] For the 1887 Jubilee T. M. Lockwood designed a new reading room in the garden behind the library and remodelled the front in a classical style with pilasters. The cost of the enlargement was met by

FIG. 178. *Public library, St. John Street, 1964*

1 C.C.A.L.S., ZAB 4, f. 297v.

2 *Broster's Dir. Ches.* (1787), 99.

3 C.C.A.L.S., ZCCB 114, p. 202; Hemingway, *Hist. Chester*, ii. 188, 190.

4 *Parry's Dir. Chester* (1840), 62–3.

5 Hemingway, *Hist. Chester*, ii. 191.

6 *Chester in 1892, Illustrated* (publ. Robinson, Son, and Pike), 40; cf. *Gresty's Illustrated Chester* [1864], advertisement at end.

7 C.C.A.L.S., ZCCB 114, pp. 202–3; *Parry's Dir. Chester* (1840), 26; K. Peate, 'Chester Mechanics' Institution, 1835–75' (Liverpool Univ. diss. for Diploma in Advanced Study of Adult Educ., 1984: copy at C.H.H.), 21.

8 Peate, 'Chester Mechanics' Inst.' 25, 32, 91–3.

9 Ibid. 32, 34, 39, 51, 55.

10 Ibid. 45, 50.

11 Ibid. 50; F. Simpson, *Chester Free Public Libr.* (priv. print. 1931), 6–7.

12 Peate, 'Chester Mechanics' Inst.' 49–50.

13 Ibid. 25, 78–84, 97; C.C.A.L.S., ZCCB 114, pp. 202–3.

14 Peate, 'Chester Mechanics' Inst.' 62–3.

15 C.C.A.L.S., ZCCB 37, pp. 431, 452–7, 467–8, 473–4; ZCCB 114, pp. 203–4.

16 Ibid. ZCCB 37, pp. 475–8, 487–8.

17 Ibid. ZCCB 114, pp. 8–9, 11, 13, 61, 63, 65, 81.

18 Ibid. ZCCB 37, pp. 526, 529, 535; ZCCB 114, pp. 40, 46–7, 84, 112–15, 157, 210, 492–3; ZCCB 115, p. 15.

19 Ibid. ZCCB 114, pp. 88, 163, 267–8, 386.

William Brown, of Chester's leading department store, who chaired the council's library committee from 1880 to 1900.[1] A separate reading room for ladies was opened in 1890.[2] In 1896 there was a short-lived and radical experiment to allow readers behind the librarian's counter to select their own books.[3]

The library also stored books owned by local societies and professional associations,[4] and let rooms to debating and learned societies for lectures and meetings.[5] When the School of Science and Art was established in the Grosvenor Museum the library bought books required by students, chiefly on architecture, building, civil and electrical engineering, and chemistry.[6] It also acted as a depository for course books needed for the Oxford University Extension scheme, launched in Chester in 1887.[7] The subjects favoured were mostly historical,[8] and their success inspired the library committee to hold its own evening lectures on similar lines in 1893 and joint lectures with the Oxford scheme in later years.[9]

The library opened a juvenile department in 1923,[10] and an extension in 1931, built with the help of the Carnegie Trust, which insisted on closing the separate ladies' reading room.[11] A branch opened at Blacon in 1937, and in 1954 the Hoole branch library, established in 1951 by the county council, was taken over by the city.[12] By then the St. John Street building was cramped, and from the 1950s the library committee sought larger premises, but a move was delayed until after the library service passed to the county council in 1974; it took over the former Westminster coach-building works in Northgate Street, latterly used as an arts centre, in 1984, creating a purpose-built library behind the distinctive front of the works building.[13] By then further branch libraries had been opened in Lache, Vicars Cross, and Upton.[14]

MUSEUMS

WATER TOWER MUSEUM

Within a year of its foundation in 1835 the Chester Mechanics' Institution resolved to establish a museum of working models, natural history, and antiquities. Benefactors gave objects for display and the city council offered a lease of Bonewaldesthorne Tower and the Water Tower on the city walls (often called the Upper and Lower Water Towers) at a nominal rent. An appeal raised £290 and the museum opened in 1838. Its hours were noon to 8 p.m. each day except Sunday.[15]

An admission fee of 6d. probably restricted entrance to well-off visitors, though a reduced rate of 3d. was later introduced for railway excursionists. A camera obscura, highly popular with visitors, was installed in 1840 and an observatory in 1848; in 1864 the Roman hypocaust and other remains recently discovered in Bridge Street were reassembled at the foot of the tower. The museum made a profit and was a source of great local pride,[16] but sophisticated visitors were conscious of its limitations: the American writer Henry James in 1872 called the towers 'receptacles for the dustiest and shabbiest of tawdry back-parlor curiosities'.[17]

The museum came into the ownership of the city council along with the rest of the Mechanics' Institution's assets in 1876.[18] The city recognized at an early stage that the Water Tower was unsuitable for a museum, but the council committee responsible had its hands full with arrangements for the new public library. The surviving exhibits were put into order and the museum opened each summer between the hours of 10 a.m. and 5 p.m.[19]

The Water Tower was closed in 1901–2 while the

1 C.C.A.L.S., ZCCB 114, pp. 576, 595; Simpson, *Chester Free Public Libr.* 13–14; Peate, 'Chester Mechanics' Inst.' facing p. 45; *Browns and Chester: Portrait of a Shop, 1780–1946*, ed. H. D. Willcock, 221.

2 C.C.A.L.S., ZCCB 115, pp. 96, 99.

3 T. Kelly, *Hist. of Public Libraries, 1845–1975*, 180; W. E. Doubleday, 'The Open Access Question from the Librarian's Point of View', *The Library*, N.S. i. 189; Mr. J. Tiernan, Liverpool, is thanked for providing the references.

4 Cf. C.C.A.L.S., ZCCB 114, pp. 221, 224; *Chester City Cl. Mins. 1937/8*, 752.

5 Cf. C.C.A.L.S., ZCCB 114, pp. 91, 94; *Chester City Cl. Mins. 1911/12*, 470–1.

6 C.C.A.L.S., ZCCB 114, pp. 583–4; ZCCB 115, pp. 12, 147–8, 215, 246.   7 Ibid. ZCCB 114, pp. 591–2.

8 Ibid. ZCCB 115, pp. 95, 152, 173; *Chester Chron.* 1 Mar., 3 May 1890; *Chester City Cl. Mins. 1898/9*, 411–12; *1900/1*, 416; *1901/2*, 62, 552; *1906/7*, 546, 708; *1907/8*, 238.

9 C.C.A.L.S., ZCCB 115, pp. 160, 183–5, 196, 202, 331–2, 337; *Chester City Cl. Mins. 1900/1*, 153.

10 Simpson, *Chester Free Public Libr.* 18.

11 *Chester City Cl. Mins. 1930/1*, 204–5; Simpson, *Chester Free Public Libr.* 28–9.

12 *Chester City Cl. Mins. 1936/7*, 781, 893; City of Chester, City Librarian's Rep. 1954/5; 1955/6, p. 6.

13 City of Chester, City Librarian's Rep. 1958/9, p. 298; 1963/4, p. 510; 1973/4, pp. 641, 745; M. Sugden and E. Frankl, *Chester*, 59.

14 *Ches. Tourism Dir.* [1984], 110–11.

15 K. Peate, 'Chester Mechanics' Institution, 1835–75' (Liverpool Univ. diss. for Diploma in Advanced Study of Adult Educ., 1984: copy at C.H.H.), 38–43; *Ann. Reps. of Chester Mechanics' Institution* (1837–64): copies in C.C.A.L.S., ZCR 542/3, 27–34; ibid. ZAB 6, pp. 181, 186.

16 *Ann. Reps. passim*, esp. *5th Ann. Rep.* (1840), 6–7; *13th Ann. Rep.* (1848), 5; *29th Ann. Rep.* (1864), 6; Hughes, *Stranger's Handbk.* (1856), 27–9; *Gresty and Burghall's Chester Guide* [1867], 30–1.

17 *Chester: Contemporary Descriptions*, ed. D. M. Palliser (1980), 32, quoting Henry James, *Transatlantic Sketches* (1875, repr. 1972), 12.

18 C.C.A.L.S., ZCCB 37, pp. 480–1.

19 Ibid. pp. 426–504, esp. 458, 490, 494–6, 500–2, 504; ibid. pp. 551–8, 599–601.

adjacent city wall was rebuilt; when it reopened in 1903 it attracted 12,000 visitors over the season, paying 1*d.* to get in.[1] In 1907 the exhibits included models of the Grosvenor Bridge, Overleigh Lodge, and the Northgate, and collections of militaria, prints, ethnography, and curiosities.[2] The Water Tower was closed to the public at the end of summer 1916. After taking advice from Professor Robert Newstead, the honorary curator of the Grosvenor Museum, the council decided in 1921 not to reopen it but to offer the collections to the Archaeological and Natural Science societies and sell whatever they did not want.[3]

Both towers were then let for non-museum use,[4] but by the early 1930s the city was aware of their tourist potential and in 1948 let them again on condition that the public be admitted.[5] In 1954 they were brought under the Grosvenor Museum, which reopened them in 1962 as an historical museum of medieval Chester, showing dioramas and local finds.[6] After refurbishment *c.* 1980 they were still open in 1995.[7]

GROSVENOR MUSEUM

The city council saw its acquisition of the Mechanics' Institution in 1876 as an opportunity to create a proper town museum, combining the existing collections of the Institution and the Natural Science and Archaeological societies with new galleries for sculpture and pictures. The existing Institution building in St. John Street was unsuitable for museum use and no alternative site immediately became available.[8] Meanwhile the societies, both of which had been collecting since their inception, and the Schools of Science and Art were all looking for permanent premises. An appeal for funds for a new building was launched in 1883 with the duke of Westminster as president and the dean of Chester as secretary. The duke gave a site in Grosvenor Street, which was enlarged by purchase, and £4,000 towards a total building cost estimated at £10,650. T. M. Lockwood designed an assymetrical museum in red brick with stone dressings in a free Renaissance style. When opened in 1886 it had the societies' natural history and archaeological displays and an art gallery on the ground floor, leaving the two upper floors for the (by then amalgamated) School of Science and Art. The building was managed by a committee on which the two societies together had equal representation with the school.[9] Both museum and school soon

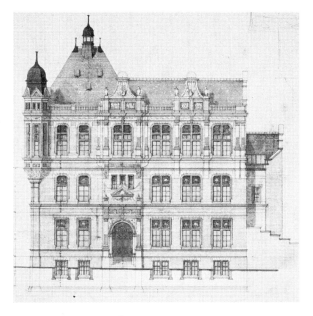

FIG. 179. *Grosvenor Museum,*
T. M. Lockwood's design, 1884

needed more space and a wing was added at the rear in 1895.[10]

From 1892 to 1912 the museum also housed a technical day school funded by the city council, and after the city became a local education authority under the 1902 Education Act it took responsibility for the building as a whole, including the museum.[11] The museum's voluntary management committee approached the council as early as 1904 with the proposal that the council take over its duties, and the council was keen to do so despite the objections of the Chester Traders' Association to supporting a museum from the rates, but the transfer was delayed until 1915.[12] Under the new arrangements the corporation leased parts of the building to the societies for meetings and displaying their collections.[13] Management of the building by the city council prolonged its use for further educational purposes, and the whole building (except for a lecture theatre used by the two societies) was turned over for museum use only when the School of Art left in 1962.[14]

In 1936 the council commissioned from the nationally renowned archaeologist Mortimer Wheeler a report on the city's future museum provision. It began to act on his recommendations in 1938 by

1 *Abstract of Accts. of Corp. of Chester, 1898/9,* 24–5; *1900/1,* 24–5; *1901/2,* 20–1; *1902/3,* 18–19; *1903/4,* 18–19; *Chester City Cl. Mins. 1901/2,* 124, 283–4, and other refs. from index s.vv. City Walls, Water Tower; *1902/3,* 59, 67, 441, 944.

2 C.C.A.L.S., ZCR 145/43; *Chester City Cl. Mins. 1906/7,* 545.

3 *Chester City Cl. Mins. 1915/16,* 279; *1916/17,* 133, 261; *1920/1,* 534–5; *1921/2,* 281.

4 e.g. ibid. *1922/3,* 343, 540; *1926/7,* 622, 787; *1932/3,* 510.

5 Ibid. *1931/2,* 129, 421; *1947/9,* pp. 280–1.

6 *Chester City Cl. Educ. Cttee. Mins. 1953/4,* 164; *1955/6,* 185; *1959/60,* 26; *Guide to Grosvenor Mus.* (1972), [37–40].

7 Harris, *Chester,* 95.

8 C.C.A.L.S., ZCCB 37, pp. 426, 436–8, 456–8.

9 J. D. Siddall, *Formation of Chester Soc. of Natural Science, Literature, and Art* (1911), 42–8; *J.C.A.S.* n.s. i. 117; C.C.A.L.S., ZDE 2/1.   10 *J.C.A.S.* n.s. v. 440–1.

11 Above, Education: 1870–1902, 1903–18.

12 *Chester City Cl. Mins. 1904/5,* 11–12, 770; *1907/8,* 223, 326–8, 790; *J.C.A.S.* xiii. 151, 154–5; xxii. 221; C.C.A.L.S., ZCR 119/24, p. 63; ZDE 1/3, *Rep. 1915,* 20; ZDE 2/7–8.

13 Grosvenor Mus., Hist. Files, Box 1: copy of 1915 agreement. Thanks are offered to Ms. K. Snowden for permission to consult the files.

14 Above, Education: 1944–74.

agreeing with the societies to take over direct management,[1] but further progress was delayed by the Second World War. The honorary curator, Professor Robert Newstead, who had served in one capacity or another since 1886, died in 1947, and his brother Alfred retired as part-time assistant curator in 1948,[2] when the city appointed as its first professional curator the Roman archaeologist Graham Webster. During his time (1948–55) existing collections were catalogued and redisplayed, assistant curators were appointed, and the creation of period rooms in a house in Castle Street behind the museum was begun.[3] The Grosvenor was thereafter in the hands of museum professionals and the augmentation of its collections, increase in its staff and activities (including archaeological and educational), and improvement of its displays were almost continuous.[4] The city council retained control at local government reorganization in 1974 despite being urged by the curator and the Archaeological Society to turn it over to the county council.[5]

The museum's most important collection, of national importance, was the Roman sepulchral monuments mainly discovered during repairs to the city walls between 1887 and 1892.[6] Other collections of local significance were Anglo-Saxon pennies acquired mostly in the 1950s, Chester-hallmarked silver, the topographical watercolours of Moses Griffith (1747–1819), and the 'consciously picturesque' and hugely popular watercolours of Victorian Chester by Louise Rayner (1829–1924).[7]

OTHER MUSEUMS

Chester's ever-growing appeal to tourists led to a proliferation of small museums in the 20th century. Already by 1900 the upper floor of King Charles's Tower on the city walls housed a small private museum,[8] though it underwent many vicissitudes. The city council let the tower in 1912 to Edward Davies, who showed a collection of artefacts connected with the history of Chester and was given an extended lease in 1917, despite being in arrears with the rent,

because Professor Newstead commended the value to the city of his local antiquarian knowledge.[9] Davies's collection remained on display[10] and was given to the city in 1955, after which King Charles's Tower was refitted by the Grosvenor Museum as an historical museum of the Civil War in Chester.[11]

Stanley Palace, bought by the Chester Archaeological Society for conversion to a museum in 1865 but sold back to the 15th earl of Derby in 1889, in the early 1920s housed 'a museum of 1,000 curios'.[12]

The Cheshire Regiment, which had a collection of old military equipment on display in the officers' mess at the castle by 1903, established a museum in the Agricola Tower there in 1923. In 1972 it moved to new rooms in the former barrack block as the Cheshire Military Museum, still under regimental control but augmented by the collections formed at Dale Barracks (at Moston, just north of Chester) and by the Cheshire Yeomanry at the Drill Hall in Albion Street. Artefacts belonging to other regiments were added c. 1978.[13]

After Holy Trinity church in Watergate Street was turned into a guildhall in 1963[14] a small museum was established in the former vestry to display documents and artefacts belonging to the city guilds.[15] Another redundant city-centre church, St. Michael's in Bridge Street, was converted by the city council in 1975 into the Chester Heritage Centre, publicized as Britain's first. Designed as a focal point for Chester's partication in European Architectural Heritage Year (1975), it contained displays about the city's historic buildings and their conservation.[16] The Grosvenor Museum later rearranged the displays to form an introduction to the history of the city and its buildings.[17]

The most substantial of the private-enterprise museums of the late 20th century was established in 1974 by Nickerson Investments Ltd., which turned the former Grosvenor St. John's school in Vicars Lane into the British Heritage Exhibition.[18] Its main feature was a full-size reconstruction of part of the Rows in Victorian times. In 1976 the Centre attracted 65,000 visitors, to the Grosvenor Museum's 119,000.[19] Nickerson sold

1 Grosvenor Mus., Hist. Files, Box 2: *Mus. Service for Chester* (1936); copies of agreements of 1938 and 1939.

2 Ibid. Box 1: TS. notes on Robert Newstead.

3 Ibid. Box 2: TS. notes by Webster on his career at Chester; *Chester City Cl. Educ. Cttee. Mins.* esp. *1947/9*, 110, 193, 263; *1949/50*, 103; *1950/1*, 150–2; *1953/4*, 39, 68, 111, 147.

4 *Chester City Cl. Educ. Cttee. Mins. passim.*

5 Crosby, *Chester Arch. Soc.* 88.

6 R. P. Wright and I. A. Richmond, *Cat. of Roman Inscribed and Sculptured Stones in Grosvenor Mus.* esp. 3–4.

7 Chester Arch. Service, *Newsletter* (1992, no. 2); *J.C.A.S.* xl. 68; Harris, *Chester*, 119; *Guide to Grosvenor Mus.* (1972), [29–36]; *Louise Rayner, 1829–1924* (Grosvenor Mus. 1978); quotation from Mr. P. Boughton, keeper of art, Grosvenor Mus., 1999.

8 *Ward Lock Guide to Chester* (1899/1900), 35; undated photograph in possn. of V.C.H.

9 *Chester City Cl. Mins.* 1903/4, 530; 1904/5, 188; 1908/9, 624; 1910/11, 628, 693; 1911/12, 215; 1913/14, 580; 1916/17, 61, 103.

10 C.C.A.L.S., ZCR 758.

11 *Cal. Chester City Cl. Educ. Cttee. Mins. 1953/4*, 164; *1954/5*, 210; *1955/6*, 185; *1956/7*, 29; *1957/8*, 203; *Guide to Grosvenor Mus.* (1972), [41–4].

12 A. G. Crosby, *Chester Arch. Soc. 1849–1999*, 15–16, 25; *The Rare Old City of Chester: Official Guide* [1923/4], 7.

13 *J.C.A.S.* n.s. x. 128; inf. for this para. supplied by Maj. T. Astle, assistant curator.

14 Above, Medieval Parish Churches: Holy Trinity.

15 'Cat. of Guild Mus.' (TS. 1971 and later edns.): copies in possn. of V.C.H.

16 C. M. Morris, 'St. Michael's Church: Brief for Heritage Centre' (TS. [1974] at C.H.H.); *Chester Heritage Centre* (undated leaflet in possn. of V.C.H.); above, Medieval Parish Churches: St. Michael.

17 *Chester Chron.* 18 July 1980.

18 Inf. for this para. from Mr. K. Wilson, owner.

19 Chester City Cl., *Greater Chester District Plan: Technical Rep. of Surv.* (1977), 99 (copy at C.H.H.).

the Centre in 1984 to a local businessman, who reopened it as the Chester Visitor Centre with craft shops inserted in the 'Victorian street'.

The other commercially run museums were Chester Toy Museum, opened in Lower Bridge Street in 1983;[1] the Dewa Roman Experience, opened in 1993 in a former motorcycle showroom in Pierpoint Lane off Bridge Street, which featured reconstructions of a Roman galley and streets and an archaeological excavation;[2] and On the Air, a museum of broadcasting opened in Bridge Street Row in 1994 as an extension of a business selling vintage gramophones.[3] Both the Toy Museum and On the Air, however, closed in the late 1990s.

NEWSPAPERS

Chester's first newspaper was the *Chester Weekly Journal*, begun by the printer William Cooke in 1721. It continued until 1733 and was superseded by Cooke's later ventures, the *Industrious Bee or Weekly Entertainer* (1733–4) and the *Chester Weekly Tatler* (1734). No copies of either of the last two are known.[4]

Cooke was evidently forced out of business by a rival title first published in 1732, *Adams's Weekly Courant*, which was established by another Chester printer, Roger Adams. After the deaths of Adams in 1741 and his widow Elizabeth in 1771 the business passed to their daughter Dorothy and her husband William Monk, formerly Adams's apprentice. Their son and grandsons retained control until 1832.[5] The paper included a short column of local news from 1758,[6] and changed its name to the *Chester Courant* in 1793.[7] John Dixon, owner from 1832, modernized the newspaper and reduced its price. Later difficulties led to its acquisition by the Cheshire and North Wales Newspaper Co. in 1891.[8] It was published mid-week.[9] The *Courant* was vigorously Tory in the later 1740s[10] and had a Conservative editorial line throughout the 19th century.[11] It ceased publication in 1984.[12]

The Whig *Chester Chronicle* was begun by the printer John Poole in 1775 and at first struggled to survive, changing its day of publication several times before settling on Friday in 1776. It was rescued in 1783 by John Fletcher (d. 1835), whose long life, business acumen, and growing political influence in Chester ensured its continuance.[13] It retained its Liberal affiliation after the Home Rule crisis,[14] and was still being published weekly in 2000, having shed its political ties in the 1950s and been acquired by Thomson Regional Newspapers in 1965.[15]

The *Courant* and the *Chronicle* both circulated widely throughout Cheshire and adjoining counties. In 1781, for example, they were distributed throughout the area as far as Denbigh, Shrewsbury, Stoke upon Trent, Macclesfield, Manchester, Wigan, and Ormskirk.[16] The earliest efforts to maintain a third newspaper failed in the face of their entrenched position. The *Chester Herald* (1810–13) did not long outlast the death of its founder Thomas Cutter in 1812.[17] The Whig *Chester Guardian*, despite influential support, was published only from 1817 to 1823. Joseph Hemingway, who edited the *Courant* and the *Chronicle* in turn, thought that Chester could not support a third paper.[18] His point was proved again by the *Chester Gazette*, which lasted from 1836 only to 1840.[19]

Conditions changed with the repeal of the stamp duty in 1855.[20] The *Cheshire Observer* was begun in 1854 by Henry Smith and Henry Mills. It started as politically neutral but evolved by the late 1850s into a popular Liberal paper, changing ownership several times.[21] After a short period when it was printed in Birkenhead (1861–3) it moved back to Chester and throve at the expense of the *Courant*. Both titles were taken over in 1891 by the Cheshire and North Wales Newspaper Co., a new venture whose Conservative backers included the duke of Westminster and the city's M.P., Robert Yerburgh.[22] The *Observer* was published on Friday and Saturday and the *Courant* on Wednesday, later Tuesday.[23] The group closed the *Courant*, whose circulation was falling sharply, in 1984,

1 Inf. from mus.
2 Inf. from mus.; brochure and leaflet in possn. of V.C.H.; *Chester Chron.* 9 Oct. 1992, p. 18.
3 Inf. from Mr. S. Harris, owner.
4 *Bk. Trade in Ches. to 1850: Directory*, ed. D. Nuttall, 73; D. Nuttall, *Hist. of Printing in Chester, 1688–1965*, 17–18; G. A. Cranfield, *Development of Provincial Newspaper, 1700–60*, 13–21; *J.C.A.S.* xxi. 25–9; 3 *Sheaf*, lvii, p. 71.
5 Nuttall, *Hist. Printing in Chester*, 18–26.
6 e.g. *Adams's Weekly Courant*, 22 Aug. 1758, p. 3.
7 Issues in C.C.A.L.S.; B.L. cat. of newspapers.
8 *Bk. Trade*, ed. Nuttall, 15; Nuttall, *Hist. Printing in Chester*, 46–8, 51–2; *Kelly's Dir. Ches.* (1892), 193.
9 C.C.A.L.S., list of newspapers held; *Kelly's Dir. Ches.* (1878 and later edns. to 1939); *Kelly's Dir. Chester* (1940 and later edns.).
10 Cranfield, *Development of Provincial Newspaper*, 51.
11 e.g. *Newspaper Press Dir.* (1857); *Kelly's Dir. Ches.* (1878), 110; (1892), 186.
12 *Benn's Press Dir.* (1982–5 edns.); B.L. cat. of newspapers.
13 Nuttall, *Hist. Printing in Chester*, 26–31, 49, 52–3.
14 e.g. *Kelly's Dir. Ches.* (1892), 186.
15 H. Hughes, *Chronicle of Chester*, 242, 246.
16 [P. Broster], *Chester Guide* (2nd edn., 1782), 66–8.
17 *Bk. Trade*, ed. Nuttall, 14, 74; Nuttall, *Hist. Printing in Chester*, 38; Hemingway, *Hist. Chester*, ii. 260; 3 *Sheaf*, xvii, p. 13.
18 *Bk. Trade*, ed. Nuttall, 18, 74; Nuttall, *Hist. Printing in Chester*, 38–9; Hemingway, *Hist. Chester*, ii. 264–5.
19 *Bk. Trade*, ed. Nuttall, 13, 75; R. Cowley, *NEWSPLAN: Report of NEWSPLAN Project in NW. Region*, no. 260.
20 Newspapers Act, 18 & 19 Vic. c. 27.
21 *Newspaper Press Dir.* (1857 and later edns.).
22 Nuttall, *Hist. Printing in Chester*, 47–53.
23 *Kelly's Dir. Ches.* (1878), 110, and later edns.

then passed into the ownership of the *Chronicle*, which ran the *Observer* as a mid-week paper before closing it in 1989 and instead starting *Cheshire Tonight*, an evening paper which lasted for only 18 months in 1989–90.[1]

R. M. Thomas started the *Chester Record* as a popular Liberal paper in 1857 and by 1864 was selling 1,200 copies a week in the city in vigorous competition with the *Observer*.[2] The *Cheshire News*, begun in 1866, was incorporated a year later into A. Mackie's *Chester Guardian*, founded in 1867 and politically unaligned. It was published as the *Chester News and Guardian* 1867–8, took over the *Record* in 1868, and appeared as the *Chester Guardian, Record, and News* 1868–9, the *Chester Guardian and Record* 1869–1946, and the *Chester Guardian* from 1946 to its demise in 1956. The *Chester Daily Guardian* appeared for 18 months in 1884–5.[3]

The *Farmers' Herald*, a monthly established in 1843 by W. H. Evans 'for the promotion of agricultural improvement and practical and scientific farming' and published in Chester, circulated among landowners and farmers well beyond the county, latterly as a magazine, until it closed in 1930.[4]

Several Welsh-language newspapers were published in Chester, the earliest *Y Geirgrawn* (*The Treasury of Words*) in 1796; the longest lasting was called successively *Goleuad Gwynedd* (*The Illuminator of Gwynedd*, 1818–19), *Goleuad Cymru* (*The Illuminator of Wales*, 1819–31), and *Y Drysorfa* (*The Treasury*, from 1847).[5]

The Chronicle group also published a free newspaper from 1970. Initially called the *Chester Mail*, it closed in 1985 but was replaced successively by the *Chester Express Mail* (1986–7), *Chester Mail* (1987–9), and *Chester Herald and Post* (from 1989). Other free papers were the *Chester and District Standard* (from 1986), *Chester Tonight* (1989–90), and the *Chester Evening Leader* (from 2000).[6]

OPEN SPACES AND PARKS

ROODEE

Chester's principal public open space is the Roodee, a flat, low-lying expanse south-west of the medieval walls. In the 20th century it covered 63 a., and the Little Roodee to the south-east, definitively severed from the Roodee when the embanked approach to Grosvenor Bridge was made in the late 1820s, covered 6 a.[7] In the Roman period the Roodee was part of the tidal salt-marsh at the head of the Dee estuary, the main river channel lying east of its present course under the line of the medieval walls.[8] Silting shifted the channel and gradually turned the marsh into meadowland but c. 1195 it was still covered by every tide.[9] A century later it may have been normally dry: by 1284–5 there was a way from the nunnery across crofts to the Eye (meaning the Little Roodee),[10] and in December 1288, a month when the river may well have been high, citizens were practising archery on the Roodee.[11] The name Roodee means 'the meadow with a cross' (rood eye),[12] and refers to a cross towards the south end which marked the boundary of Holy Trinity and St. Mary's parishes and of which the weathered pedestal and stump survived *in situ* in 2000.[13] Parish boundaries can hardly have been determined or the cross put up until the meadow was permanently dry, a period which can therefore probably be dated by the addition of the prefix 'rood' to the name of the meadow at some time between the 1280s and 1364.[14]

Presumably because it was land naturally reclaimed from the estuary the Roodee has always belonged to Chester corporation, and in 1401 it was declared tithe-free.[15] The mayor and citizens used it as security to raise a loan of £500 in 1697–8.[16] It was liable to regular winter flooding before an embankment alongside the Dee, called the Cop, was raised between 1706 and 1710 as part of the works to improve navigation on the river. The Roodee was still occasionally inundated in later centuries.[17]

By the 15th century the corporation was leasing the summer grazing (called the ley) on the Roodee, normally from early May to Michaelmas.[18] In the 1570s the rate was 10s. for a cow, with a total stint

1 *Benn's Press Dir.* (1982–5 edns.); *Benn's Media Dir.* (1989–90 edns.); B.L. cat. of newspapers.

2 *Newspaper Press Dir.* (1858 and later edns.).

3 Ibid. (1868 and later edns.); B.L. cat. of newspapers; Cowley, NEWSPLAN, nos. 261, 264–7.

4 *Newspaper Press Dir.* (1857 and later edns. to 1931); B.L. cat. of newspapers.   5 *Bk. Trade*, ed. Nuttall, 74.

6 Hughes, *Chronicle of Chester*, 244; B.L. cat. of newspapers; *Benn's Media* (1994 edn.), 122.

7 *J.C.A.S.* xlv. 52–3; *Chester City Cl. Mins. 1937/8*, 74.

8 *V.C.H. Ches.* i. 166, 178–9.

9 Lucian, *De Laude Cestrie*, 46; S. Ward, 'Course of River Dee at Chester', *Trade and Port of Chester*, ed. P. Carrington, 4–11.

10 *Cal. Pat.* 1399–1401, 301, dated by mayoralty of Robert the

mercer and sheriffdom of Hugh of Meols and Robert Erneys: below, Lists of Mayors and Sheriffs.

11 *Cal. Ches. Ct. R.* p. 156.

12 Cf. *P.N. Ches.* v (1:i), 63.

13 Ibid. 59; cf. Ormerod, *Hist. Ches.* i. 371.

14 *Blk. Prince's Reg.* iii. 466–7.

15 Ormerod, *Hist. Ches.* i. 371.

16 C.C.A.L.S., ZCHD 9/16; ZCR 371/3.

17 Ibid. ZAB 3, ff. 178, 182v.; *V.C.H. Ches.* v (1), Topography: Early Modern and Georgian (Building Activity 1660–1760); Ormerod, *Hist. Ches.* i. 371; Hemingway, *Hist. Chester*, i. 360 n.; ii. 246; above, Chester Races.

18 e.g. B.L. Harl. MS. 2158, ff. 205v., 208; C.C.A.L.S., ZAB 3, f. 63v.; Hemingway, *Hist. Chester*, i. 361.

FIG. 180. *The Roodee from west, 1950*

of 40 beasts,[1] but in later centuries horses were also grazed there and larger numbers of animals were permitted. The mayor and treasurers made the arrangements for the ley and were recompensed with an entitlement to 'horse grass', evidently the right to graze one horse for free. The rector of Holy Trinity parish also had horse grass, perhaps originally in lieu of tithes. A keeper of the Roodee, employed by the Assembly, was housed probably from 1607 in the rooms under the Pentice on the Roodee. Briefly from 1711 the Assembly leased the grazing as a whole to an innkeeper for a total of £350 over three years, but then restored the previous arrangements.[2] Payments for grazing were set in 1736 at 40s. for a horse and 30s. for a cow, and in 1759, when the rate had gone up by 5s. an animal, 54 horses and 44 cows were kept, bringing in almost £200. The number of horses kept on the Roodee later fell, so that by the 1820s there were up to 90 cows but never more than 10 horses.[3] In the 1840s the spring ley ran for a

fortnight in April and the summer ley from mid May to early October; lessees then paid £4 to graze a cow and £5 for a horse, the cattle being served by a bull provided by the corporation.[4] By 1904 only sheep were grazed there,[5] but during the drive for national self-sufficiency in the Second World War they numbered as many as 600.[6]

The Roodee originally extended north from the Watergate as far as the New Tower, but only as a narrow strip of land between the city walls and the river. North of the New Tower was land called the Saltgrass, never considered part of the Roodee proper. The first phase of work before 1710 to improve the Dee navigation entailed moving the course of the river between the Watergate and the New Tower 300 yd. to the west and building a new wharf. Samuel Taylor, who held corporation leases of both the northern end of the Roodee and the Saltgrass, built a new walled road from his existing warehouse outside the Watergate, which was now no longer on the river bank, to the new

1 Morris, *Chester*, 300–2.

2 C.C.A.L.S., ZAB 3, ff. 183v.–184, 185v., 193, 206v., 227; ZAB 4, ff. 19, 99v., 102v.–103; for the Pentice: above, Chester Races.

3 C.C.A.L.S., ZAB 4, f. 77; ZTAB 8, ff. 19–20v.; ZTAB 9,

ff. 21–2, 37–8; ZTAV 2/43, pt. 1.

4 Ibid. ZCCB 30, esp. 28 July 1843, 18 June 1844, 17 Nov. 1849.

5 *Chester City Cl. Mins. 1903/4*, 1051.

6 *Ches. Observer*, 15 July 1944.

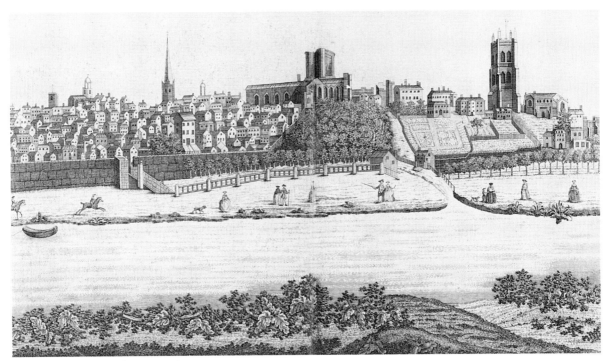

FIG. 181. *The Groves in 1760*

wharf. In 1708 he was given a permanent grant of the land over which the road was built but gave up everything to the south. Although flooding in 1720 destroyed the new wharf and probably Taylor's road, the renewal of navigation works in the 1730s allowed both to be restored and thus permanently closed off the Roodee on the north. Indeed thereafter the name Saltgrass was applied to what had formerly been the northern part of the Roodee, north of the Watergate and the wharf.[1] To the south-east the Little Roodee was already by 1765, and perhaps from 1710, walled off from the Roodee and leased separately, first to the Glovers' or the Skinners' guild as an extension of their working area on the river bank south-east of the castle, and later to private individuals.[2]

On the north-west side of the Roodee proper the permanent success of the navigation works of the 1730s made the land along the river bank south of the new wharf, outside the Cop, desirable for commercial purposes. A timber merchant briefly had part of it in 1742–3 and the workhouse was built there in 1759, but it was intensively occupied only from the early 19th century. The viaduct for the Chester–Holyhead railway

was built behind the riverside premises in the 1840s, narrowing the Roodee permanently on that side.[3]

The Roodee has been put to a great variety of uses besides grazing. It was the setting for civic pageantry in the later Middle Ages and afterwards,[4] for the races from their inception in 1540,[5] and for informal recreation of all kinds from archery in the 13th century to illegal rabbit coursing in the 20th.[6] In 1353, remarkably, it was the scene of a revival of the long outdated procedure of trial by battle, an occasion probably attended by the Black Prince and his household.[7] About 1600 it was used for archery, bowls, and walks by the Dee.[8] During the parliamentary siege of Chester in 1643–4 it was where the city's defenders were mustered.[9] One or more turns around the Roodee was the favourite walk of the church lawyer Henry Prescott in the early 18th century.[10] In 1823 there were ox-roasts for the birth of an heir to Robert Grosvenor, Viscount Belgrave, and for the coming of age of his political opponent Col. Roger Barnston's son.[11] In the 1850s the buttercups in full bloom were prized as 'a picturesque scene of superlative floral beauty'.[12] Later in the century thousands of militia

1 C.C.A.L.S., ZAB 3, ff. 97, 99 and v., 105v., 108v., 118v., 128v., 130, 148v., 157v.; ZCHD 9/22–3; Lavaux, *Plan of Chester*; above, Water Transport: River.

2 C.C.A.L.S., ZAB 3, f. 177v.; ZCHD 9/47, 66–7; Lavaux, *Plan of Chester*; J. Hunter and S. Weston, *Map of Chester* (1789).

3 C.C.A.L.S., ZAB 4, ff. 98–9, 101v.; ZCHD 9/74, 79–80, 83–4; above, Railways.

4 Above, Plays, Sports, and Customs before 1700: Sporting

Customs (Shrovetide Celebrations, Sheriffs' Breakfast).

5 Above, Chester Races.

6 *Cal. Ches. Ct. R.* p. 156; *Chester City Cl. Mins. 1902/3*, 245.

7 *Ches. Hist.* xii. 28.

8 Ormerod, *Hist. Ches.* i. 185.

9 Morris, *Siege of Chester*, 40, 64.

10 *Diary of Henry Prescott*, i, p. xi and *passim*.

11 Hemingway, *Hist. Chester*, ii. 279–80, 282–3.

12 J. Romney, *Chester and its Environs Illustrated*, [1].

FIG. 182. *The Groves, eastern end, 1856, with suspension bridge* (left)

Volunteers were reviewed, the 1858 Royal Agricultural Society show was staged,[1] and cattle which died in the 1866 plague were buried.[2] In the early 20th century the artillery Volunteers drilled,[3] local clubs played hockey, cricket, soccer, and polo,[4] balloons ascended,[5] racehorses were trained,[6] Lord George Sanger put on his circuses and Messrs. Barnum and Bailey their Wild West shows,[7] and parties of excursionists from trade unions, workplaces, and political and friendly societies in Liverpool and Birkenhead held sports days and rallies.[8] Meanwhile the Little Roodee was used for a pleasure fair during race week, pierrot shows over the summer, and also for touring circuses.[9] During the First World War the council had the Little Roodee seeded and was still letting it for grazing sheep in the winter of 1920–1, but in 1921 it was laid out as a parking ground for charabancs and other motor vehicles, complete with public lavatories. The race week fair and occasional circuses were still held there.[10] The Little Roodee remained a municipal car park in the later 20th century, when entertainments staged on the Roodee proper included sports meetings, circuses, and caravan rallies.[11]

THE GROVES

The riverside below St. John's church was also corporation property and used as a public walk by 1717.[12] In 1726 it was leased to Charles Croughton, who secured the river bank and planted an avenue of trees for the public benefit.[13] In 1745 the Dee Side walks extended from Souters Lane to a point east of St. John's.[14] By 1783 the promenade was called the Groves.[15] In 1881 the river bank from Souters Lane to the Dee Bridge was faced with rubble from the fallen tower of St. John's church, and the avenue was extended to the west, an improvement carried out at the expense of Charles Brown to commemorate his mayoralty.[16]

Boating excursions upstream from landing stages at the Groves, to visit the newly completed Gothic Eaton Hall, were an attraction by 1821.[17] In the mid 19th century the rise of tourist excursions to Chester turned the Groves into a popular resort. Pleasure boats could be hired on the river by the 1850s,[18] and in the later 19th century band concerts throughout the summer became a major attraction.[19] The concerts were at first arranged by a private committee, which built a

1 Hughes, *Stranger's Handbk.* (1856), 32–3; [1882], 32, 41.

2 C.C.A.L.S., ZCR 119/24, p. 144.

3 e.g. *Chester City Cl. Mins. 1902/3*, 601; *1903/4*, 683; *1904/5*, 286; *1905/6*, 525; *1906/7*, 297.

4 e.g. ibid. *1902/3*, 609; *1903/4*, 917; *1904/5*, 504, 879; *1906/7*, 506; cf. above, Sport after 1700: Association Football, Cricket, Other Sports (Hockey, Polo).

5 e.g. *Chester City Cl. Mins. 1905/6*, 704.

6 e.g. ibid. *1903/4*, 308; *1904/5*, 89.

7 e.g. ibid. *1902/3*, 346, 439; *1903/4*, 307.

8 e.g. ibid. *1906/7*, 578, 655, 734; *1907/8*, 80, 85, 297, 544, 610, 680, 755.

9 e.g. ibid. *1902/3*, 60, 67, 826; *1903/4*, 80, 92, 152; *1913/14*, 78; *1914/15*, 65–6, 571; *1918/19*, 137, 504–5.

10 Ibid. *1914/15*, 438; *1919/20*, 695; *1920/1*, 142, 200, 219, 303, 346, 474, 531, 618; *1922/3*, 52; *1923/4*, 626–7.

11 e.g. ibid. *1974/5*, p. 361.

12 C.C.A.L.S., ZAB 3, f. 236v.

13 Ibid. ZAB 4, ff. 4v., 6 and v., 41.

14 Lavaux, *Plan of Chester.*

15 *P.N. Ches.* v (1:i), 83.

16 *Browns and Chester*, ed. H. D. Willcock, 169–70; C.C.A.L.S., ZCB 3, f. 56ov.; ZCCB 55, pp. 1–2, 99–100, 103.

17 J. Broster, *A Walk Round the Walls and City of Chester* (1821 edn.), 48–9.

18 J. Romney, *Chester and its Environs Illustrated*, [54].

19 e.g. *Chester City Cl. Mins. 1901/2*, 612; *1909/10*, 631; *1910/11*, 738–9.

FIG. 183. *Grosvenor Park from south-east, 1867*

bandstand in 1913,[1] but were taken over by the city council in 1927,[2] when it also built kiosks for letting to traders.[3]

PUBLIC PARKS

The grounds at the foot of the Water Tower were laid out as an ornamental garden in 1859 by the Chester Mechanics' Institution, which had run a museum in the tower since 1838.[4] In 1863–4 Roman columns and a hypocaust excavated in Bridge Street were re-erected there,[5] creating what the novelist Henry James called 'one of those odd fragments of public garden, a crooked strip of ground called to social account . . . adorned with mossy fragments of Roman stonework'.[6] They were removed in 1949.[7] The city council extended the grounds in 1922, opening bowling greens and tennis courts.[8]

Grosvenor Park, 14½ a. north of the Groves, was presented to the city in 1867 by the 2nd marquess of Westminster with an endowment for its upkeep.[9] It was one of the first public parks in Britain outside the big industrial cities.[10] The park was designed by Edward Kemp and the black-and-white entrance

lodge by John Douglas;[11] a statue of the donor, by Thomas Thorneycroft, was put up in 1869 by public subscription.[12]

In Handbridge, 2¼ a. west of the Dee Bridge was laid out as a public park at the expense of the first duke of Westminster, who presented it to the city in 1892 with an endowment of £1,000 for its upkeep. At his insistence the long-established name of Kettle's Croft was abandoned in favour of the alternative name Edgar's Field, perpetuating the bogus antiquarian tradition that it contained the site of a palace of King Edgar.[13] It did include a Roman shrine to Minerva, long known to antiquaries,[14] which was restored in 1992.

Hoole urban district council opened a 6-a. park and recreation ground in 1904,[15] adding 3 a. fronting Hoole Road and renaming it Alexandra Park in 1911.[16]

In 1946 the 2nd duke of Westminster gave the city 46 a. between Hough Green and Lache Lane for a park to be called Westminster Park.[17] Two bowling greens were opened there in 1950[18] and plans were in hand from 1955 for playing fields,[19] but most of the land was let to a farmer while a scheme for an athletics track, cricket pitch, and grandstands was foiled by the duke's

1 *Chester City Cl. Mins. 1912/13*, 189–90, 483; *1923/4*, 365, 413.

2 Ibid. *1926/7*, 766; *1927/8*, 171.

3 Ibid. *1926/7*, 820; cf. *1912/13*, 427; *1921/2*, 369–70; *1922/3*, 426, 554.

4 *24th Ann. Report of Chester Mechanics' Institution* (1859), 9; cf. above, Museums: Water Tower Museum.

5 *29th Ann. Rep. Chester Mechanics' Inst.* (1864), 6; *V.C.H. Ches.* i. 145–7.

6 *Chester: Contemporary Descriptions*, ed. D. M. Palliser (1980), 32, quoting Henry James, *Transatlantic Sketches* (1875, repr. 1972), 11.   7 *Chester City Cl. Mins.* 1949/50, p. 246.

8 Above, Sport after 1700: Bowls, Other Sports (Lawn Tennis).

9 *Kelly's Dir. Ches.* (1878), 106; *Chester City Cl. Mins. 1937/8*, 74; Char. Com. file 509212.

10 H. Conway, *People's Parks: Design and Development of*

Victorian Parks in Britain, 74, 228–30.

11 Ibid. 114, 230; Hughes, *Stranger's Handbk.* [1882], 17; R. Desmond, *Dictionary of Brit. and Irish Botanists and Horticulturalists*, 395; E. Hubbard, *Work of John Douglas*, 46–8, 239.

12 *Chester Chron.* 3 July 1869; *Chester Courant*, 7 July 1869; R. Gunnis, *Dictionary of Brit. Sculptors, 1660–1851* (revised edn.), 393.

13 *Chester Chron.* 23 Apr. 1892, p. 2; *P.N. Ches.* v (1:i), 53; *Chester City Cl. Mins. 1937/8*, 74.

14 *V.C.H. Ches.* i. 183–4.

15 C.C.A.L.S., ZTRH 82, pp. 21, 60–2, 105–7, 120; ZTRH 109, p. 96; O.S. Maps 1/2,500, Ches. XXXVIII.7, 11 (1899 and 1911 edns.).

16 C.C.A.L.S., ZTRH 84, pp. 179, 265–6, 401, 408–9.

17 *Chester City Cl. Mins. 1943/4*, 93; *1944/5*, 288; *1945/6*, 132, 389.   18 Ibid. *1950/1*, pp. 77–8.

19 Ibid. *1955/6*, pp. 387, 617.

stipulation against large buildings and numerous spectators.[1] Only in 1972 did the council commit itself to building a golf course,[2] which was opened in 1973.[3]

The Roman remains at Water Tower gardens were moved in 1949 to a 'Roman Garden' laid out between the city wall and Souters Lane.[4]

THE MEADOWS

Agricultural land at the Meadows within the bend of the Dee upstream from the Groves was scheduled in 1926 to be acquired for public playing fields. In 1929 Mr. and Mrs. H. F. Brown gave the money to buy 64½ a. of low-lying ground, rather than the higher land intended.[5] It was used for football pitches and became a popular place for weekend recreation in the 1930s, but plans for an open-air swimming pool and a suspension bridge from Boughton foundered on lack on public money and the unsuitability of the site.[6]

HOUGH GREEN

Recorded from 1503 as waste ground belonging to the corporation,[7] Hough Green lay west of Handbridge in the southern part of the liberties and seems originally to have stretched from the Old Wrexham Road westwards for almost a mile. It thus covered the area on either side of the western part of the modern Overleigh Road as well as the road still called Hough Green. The name Hough indicated a hollow in higher ground, and the main road from Chester into north Wales crossed the eastern part of the green as a hollow way.[8] The green was bounded to the north by a steep slope down to the Dee, and north-west and south by farmland belonging respectively to the Brewer's Hall and Overleigh estates. Much of the corporation's interest centred on maintaining the road. It built a bridge across a watercourse on the green in 1598–9 and appointed overseers of highways for Handbridge and Hough Green in 1629.[9] By the late 17th century the road was paved and was referred to indifferently as the pavement and the causeway.[10] The Assembly was considering how to finance repaving it for carts as far as the city boundary at Saltney marsh from 1729, and in 1732 ordered that 20 roods (160 yd.) of paving be laid each year until the scheme was complete.[11] The road

passed into the control of a turnpike trust in 1756 and the toll gates were a prominent feature until the road was disturnpiked in 1883.[12]

Stone was probably quarried on the green from an early period, but the first specific reference to a quarry was in 1700. In the earlier 18th century the Assembly allowed various bodies to take stone: the churchwardens of St. Peter's, the undertakers of the navigation works in the Dee estuary, and the murengers (for repairs to the city walls), as well as some private individuals.[13] In 1720 it refused to allow an old quarry to be used for storing iron ore on its way to furnaces near Ruabon on the grounds that the city might still need to cut stone there.[14] A request for a 99-year lease on an existing quarry was turned down in 1763.[15] Most of the quarrying was evidently at the north-east corner of the green, occupied in 2000 by the rough ground called the Dingle and by the original part of Overleigh cemetery. Hough Green was also an importance source of brick earth, probably first put to heavy use when the rebuilding of the city after the Civil War siege began in the 1650s.[16] In 1670 the Assembly ordered that no bricks were to be made there without written permission and that those permitted should pay 6*d.* per thousand bricks made and level the ground afterwards.[17] Brick making continued on the green until the 1840s but was evidently intermittent, presumably subject to fluctuations in the building trade locally.[18]

There was a windmill on the green by the 1650s which stood until 1708 or later.[19] Other uses in the 18th century, intended or actual, included stacking the gorse used as firing by the city's bakers in the 1710s, limekilns on the river side at the east end of the green in 1755, and storage space for timber in the 1770s.[20]

Piecemeal inclosures of small plots for industrial purposes or housing were taking place from the 1650s, but the Assembly did not always agree to the petitions which it received. New buildings included a house and smithy in 1665, a small dwelling house 'many years' before 1678, a larger house owned successively by two aldermen, a stable, and buildings associated with a ropewalk after 1698.[21] The Cowper

1 Ibid. *1962/3*, p. 672; *1963/4*, p. 889; *1964/5*, p. 669.

2 Ibid. *1966/7*, p. 734; *1969/70*, pp. 514–15; *1971/2*, p. 657.

3 Above, Sport after 1700: Golf.

4 *Chester City Cl. Mins. 1942/3*, 41, 107, 152; *1949/50*, p. 246.

5 Ibid. *1923/4*, 296–7; *1925/6*, 702; *1928/9*, 75, 546, 685.

6 Ibid. *1928/9*, 625; *1929/30*, 378, 559, 840–1; *1931/2*, 536, 958; *1934/5*, 527–8, 915–16; *1937/8*, 457; *1945/6*, 206–7.

7 C.C.A.L.S., ZSB 5, f. 8.

8 *P.N. Ches.* v (1:i), 56.

9 C.C.A.L.S., ZAB 1, ff. 255, 258; ZAF 14/9.

10 Ibid. ZAB 2, f. 193; ZAB 3, f. 77.

11 Ibid. ZAB 4, ff. 18, 22v., 39v.

12 Above, Roads and Road Transport: Roads (Holyhead Road and North Wales).

13 C.C.A.L.S., ZAB 3, ff. 77, 129, 163, 210v., 212; ZAB 4, ff. 16v., 46. 14 Ibid. ZAB 3, ff. 254, 257.

15 Ibid. ZAB 4, f. 208.

16 *V.C.H. Ches.* v (1), Topography: Early Modern and Georgian (Effects of the Siege and Interregnum).

17 C.C.A.L.S., ZAB 2, f. 166.

18 Ibid. ff. 193–4; ZAB 3, f. 228; ZAB 4, f. 271; ZAB 5, pp. 154, 436; ZAB 6, pp. 12, 422–3; *V.C.H. Ches.* v (1), Late Georgian and Victorian Chester: City Government 1762–1835 (Finance).

19 C.C.A.L.S., ZAB 2, ff. 98v., 184; ZAB 3, f. 160v.; above, Mills and Fisheries: Other Mills.

20 C.C.A.L.S., ZAB 3, f. 209v.; ZAB 4, ff. 161, 306, 333.

21 Ibid. ZAB 2, ff. 98v., 107v., 153, 184 and v., 188v.; ZAB 3, ff. 63v., 149 and v., 160v., 162 and v., 170 and v., 172v., 196, 232, 242, 258, 262; ZAB 4, ff. 96v., 98, 176 and v., 179v.–180, 205v.–206; ZCHD 5/7, 10, 13–14, 16–18, 24; Lavaux, *Plan of Chester*; J. Hunter and S. Weston, *Plan of Chester* (1789).

family, owners of Overleigh Hall from *c.* 1660 and long prominent in civic affairs, encroached steadily on the south-east corner of the green. In 1700 the Revd. John Cowper had permission to inclose sufficient land to make a walled carriage drive from the highway to Overleigh Hall, and more land between the house and the road was taken into the grounds by his son, Alderman William Cowper, in the 1760s.[1]

In 1737 the Assembly resolved to inclose the green on the north side of the highway; work was apparently put in hand but rioters destroyed the new hedges and ditches, and the order to inclose was not renewed until 1751. The fences were again torn down, and were ordered to be rebuilt only in 1759.[2] A further part of the green, towards the Saltney end, was inclosed in 1800 for the benefit of the poor, and in the following year eight cottages were built on the north side of the road.[3] The corporation sold land on the south side in 1834 to the marquess of Westminster, who had recently bought the Overleigh estate and demolished Overleigh Hall, and in the following year decided to dispose of all the remaining common land.[4] It sold off building plots lining the north side of the highway from 1848,[5] after which Hough Green survived only as a road name for the stretch west of the new Grosvenor Bridge approach road and the Wrexham turnpike.

ZOO

Chester zoo was opened in 1931 on 9 a. at Oakfield, a house in Upton Heath, by George Mottershead, who had previously kept a small collection of animals at Shavington near Crewe.[6] The city council had refused planning permission but had been overruled by the government.[7] Mottershead formed the North of England Zoological Society to take over the zoo in 1934 and remained its director until his death in 1978. The zoo was firmly established as a visitor attraction by 1939 and expanded quickly and almost continuously between 1945 and the mid 1970s. Mottershead's successful breeding programmes and innovative ways of displaying animals (especially the large open-air enclosures divided from spectators only by wet or dry moats) exerted an international influence. The number of visitors grew to almost 500,000 a year in the early 1950s and a million a year between 1963 and 1973. His policies were continued by his successor as director, Michael Brambell. By 1994 the Society owned 400 a., of which 110 a. was used for the zoo, and had a permanent staff of 150, employing as many more during the summer. Visitor attractions (besides the animals) included extensive gardens, which were laid out from the early 1950s, waterbuses plying along a canal from 1957, and an overhead monorail from 1991.

1 C.C.A.L.S., ZAB 3, ff. 77 and v., 271v., 274v., 277; ZAB 4, ff. 32v., 79 and v., 87v., 246v.–247; ZCHD 5/20, 27, 30–1; Ormerod, *Hist. Ches.* i. 373–6.

2 C.C.A.L.S., ZAB 4, ff. 77, 79, 89v., 141v.; cf. Lavaux, *Plan of Chester.*   3 C.C.A.L.S., ZAB 5, p. 152; ZCHD 5/33.

4 Ibid. ZAB 6, pp. 53, 61; Ormerod, *Hist. Ches.* i. 374.

5 C.C.A.L.S., ZAB 6, pp. 766, 785, 813, 819, 830; ZCHD 5/35–61; *V.C.H. Ches.* v (1), Topography: Victorian and Edwardian (Residential Development: The Suburbs).

6 Acct. based on A. L. Howard, *Chester Zoo: First Half Cent.* [Chester, 1984]; inf. from zoo press office.

7 *Ches. Observer*, 7 Feb. 1931.

MAYORS AND SHERIFFS OF THE CITY OF CHESTER

THOUGH the names of Chester's mayors and sheriffs since 1506 are not in doubt, considerable confusion remains about the holders of both offices before that date, and especially in the 13th and 14th centuries. Moreover, no list has ever been published surveying the mayors and sheriffs as a whole. The following list is based on an extensive survey of the borough and palatinate records and of local deeds in Cheshire and Chester Archives and Local Studies (i.e. the formerly separate Chester City Record Office and Cheshire Record Office), the British Library, the Public Record Office, and the John Rylands University Library of Manchester. It is undoubtedly more accurate and more detailed than any other yet assembled.

The medieval and early modern mayors have been the focus of considerable interest since the late 19th century. In 1894 Canon Rupert Morris published a list which is still in many ways the most accessible and serviceable of those available. His findings for the period before 1350 were refined by W. Fergusson Irvine in lists published in the *Cheshire Sheaf* in the 1930s. Further very valuable work was done by Miss Annette Kennett, then City Archivist, and Dr. Brian Harris, first Editor of the Victoria History of Cheshire, between 1984 and 1986. The result has been a series of conflicting lists in great need of co-ordination and integration. One essential requirement for resolving the conflicts is a full consideration of the evidence, which is often derived from the analysis of deeds and other documents, themselves very difficult to date.

THE FIRST SHERIFFS

The office of sheriff of the city was first recorded in Chester in the 1120s, earlier than in any other English borough. In the 12th century the sheriff was appointed by the earl. The leading citizen of Chester, he presided over the city court (the portmote), maintained law and order, and accounted to the earl's chamberlains for the revenues of the city.

Winebald	occurs *c.* 1121×1129
Pain	occurs before 1178
William Gamberell	occurs 1190×1199
Richard Pierrepont	occurs *c.* 1210, *c.* 1220
Stephen Fresnell[1]	occurs before 1229, 1230s

THE EARLY MAYORS (TO 1300)

The office of mayor of Chester probably originated with Earl Ranulph III's grant of a guild merchant to the city in the 1190s. Although he was the head of the guild, the mayor ranked below the sheriffs. From the mid 13th century, however, the royal government increasingly treated him as the city's principal administrative officer. The first known mayor, William the clerk, attested a number of local deeds dating from the 1220s to the 1240s, but was identified in only three of them as mayor. Nevertheless, the fact that his name appeared either at the head of the witness lists or immediately after the sheriffs suggests that he was mayor throughout the period. The first precisely dated reference to the mayoralty was in 1244.

It is not known how the mayors were chosen in that early period. They did not change annually and some, such as Richard the clerk and John Arneway, held office uninterruptedly for many years. Towards the end of the century, however, there was a change. Though a man might be mayor several times, he does not appear to have held office consecutively for more than a few years.

Note: The mayoral year began on 29 September. It should not be assumed that mayors bearing the same name but with separated periods of office were necessarily the same person. In several instances, including Richard the clerk, Alexander Hurrell, and Hugh of Brickhill, two or more bearers of the name have been identified.

---

1 'Frednel, Freynel'. The last of the single officials nominated by the earl, he continued to serve alongside a colleague when the shrievalty was divided.

William the clerk	occurs before 1229, *c.* 1240
Walter of Coventry[1]	occurs 1241×1245
Walter de Livet[2]	occurs before 1245,
	1251×1255
Richard the clerk[3]	*c.* 1251–68
John Arneway	1268–78
Ranulph of Daresbury[4]	1278–1279/80
Alexander Hurrell	1279/80–1283
Robert the mercer	1283–5
Hugh of Meols	1285–1286–
Hugh of Brickhill[5]	1286×1289
Robert of Tarvin	–1289–90
Robert the mercer	1290–3
Hugh of Brickhill jun.	1293–7
Alexander Hurrell jun.	1297–1300

SHERIFFS, *c.* 1230–1300

At some point in the 1220s or 1230s the shrievalty was divided. The large number of different combinations of names suggests that although a man might be sheriff several times, there was some system of annual appointment or election. It is not clear whether specific duties or precedence were assigned to either of the sheriffs, or whether any significance attaches to the order in which they were named in the records (followed here).

Stephen Fresnell, Hamo Despenser	occur 1220s/
	1230s
William Saracen, Roger the clerk	occur 1230s
William Saracen, German Doubleday	occur 1230s
Adam the vintner,[6] Richard Bunce	1243–4
Robert son of Erneys, Adam the vintner	occur 1240s
Richard the clerk, Gilbert the marshal[7]	occur 1240s

Richard the clerk, John Ulkel[8]	occur
	1245×1251
Robert the mercer or le Prudemercer, Stephen Saracen[9]	1251–2
Stephen Saracen, Richard of Rhuddlan[10]	1252×1255
Richard the clerk, Stephen Saracen[11]	1251×1267
Stephen Saracen, Benedict of Rushton	1251×1267
John Grund[12]	1251×1267
Richard of Orby, Robert the mercer[13]	1251×1267
Richard the apothecary, Robert the mercer[14]	1251×1267
William of Hawarden, Roger Throstle	1251×1267
Oliver of Trafford, Robert of Tarvin	1251×1267
Richard Payn, Adam Godwyt	1251×1267
Stephen Saracen, John Ulkel	1256–7
Matthew of Daresbury, Stephen Saracen, Ralph Doubleday[15]	1257–8
Matthew of Daresbury, Ralph Doubleday	1259–60
Stephen Saracen, John Ulkel	1260–1
William of Hawarden, Oliver of Trafford	1265–6
William of Syston, Oliver of Stockton	1267–8
Alexander Hurrell, Laurence the vintner	1269–70
Hugh of Meols, Richard the spicer	1270–1
Alexander Hurrell, Richard the spicer	1271×1274
Matthew of Daresbury, William Cousin	1271×1275
Richard the apothecary, Robert the mercer	1276–7
Ranulph of Daresbury, Philip the clerk	1277–8
John of Berkhampstead, Matthew of Daresbury, Richard the spicer	1268×1278
Adam Godwyt, Richard the spicer	1268×1278
Richard the apothecary, Adam Godwyt	1268×1278
Hugh of Meols, Robert of Tarvin	1278–9
Robert of Hoole[16]	1280–1

1 Named as mayor in one deed, and attests another immediately after the sheriffs Richard the clerk and Gilbert Marshal.

2 Also de Lynet. Possibly to be identified with Walter of Coventry, he ceased to be mayor between 1251 and 1255. In Thomas Aldersey's mayoral list, compiled in the later 16th century and dependent upon lost records, he is said to have died in 1260.

3 According to guild records transcribed in the 16th century, he became mayor in 1250. In fact, Walter de Livet seems to have been mayor until 1251 or later. Richard cannot have become mayor much after 1251: the number of shrieval combinations known to have occurred during his mayoralty suggests a term of office of at least 16 years.

4 A 16th-century mayoral list drawing on records now lost assigns the year 1279–80 to Ranulph of Daresbury. There is, however, no known shrieval combination to assign to Daresbury's second year.

5 'Brichull, Birchull, Bircheles'. Hugh of Brickhill's mayoralty in the late 1280s is conjectural; his name occurs as mayor with sheriffs of that period in a number of undated deeds. Since those combinations of mayor and sheriffs cannot be assigned to the mayoralties of later bearers of the name in the 1290s and 1300s, they are likely to pre-date 1289. A Hugh of Brickhill, probably the sheriff and mayor of the 1280s, died in 1292.

6 Occurs as sole sheriff in a deed dating from no later than November 1246.

7 Probably sheriffs during the mayoralty of Walter of Coventry, who attested a deed immediately after them. Aldersey's list places them in that mayoralty.

8 Probably sheriffs during the mayoralty of Walter de Livet, who attested a deed immediately after them. They may have been sheriffs for the year 1250–1; in 1251 Walter de Livet, Richard the clerk, John Ulkel jun., and Robert the mercer were appointed viewers of the king's works in Chester.

9 They attested a deed the term of whose demise began Michaelmas 1251. This combination of sheriffs occurs under both Walter de Livet and Richard the clerk as mayor.

10 In the mayoralty of Richard the clerk.

11 They occur as sheriffs in a single undated deed. No mayor is named, but the grantee is Richard son of William the clerk, probably the mayor.

12 Occurs as sole sheriff in several undated deeds from the mayoralty of Richard the clerk.

13 Robert the mercer occurs alone as sheriff 1263×1265.

14 This combination is recorded only in Aldersey's list.

15 Matthew of Daresbury was succeeded as sheriff by Stephen Saracen between December 1257 and March 1258. The cause of his resignation is unknown; he became sheriff again in the following year.

16 Attested numerous undated deeds as sole sheriff during the mayoralty of Alexander Hurrell. Curiously, he also attested as sole sheriff under Hurrell's successor, Robert the mercer. Hoole was dead by 1284–5.

Robert of Tarvin,[1] Hugh of Meols	1281–2	
Robert of Hoole, Hugh of Meols[2]	1282–3	
Robert of Hoole	1283–4	
Hugh of Meols, Robert Erneys	1284–5	
Robert Erneys, Hugh of Brickhill	1285–6	
Robert Erneys, Hugh Payn[3]	1286×1289	
Hugh Payn, Andrew of Stanlow[4]	1286×1289	
Hugh Payn, Robert Harald[5]	1286×1289	
Robert Erneys, Nicholas Payn[6]	1289–90	
Alexander Hurrell jun.,[7] David the miller[8]	1290–1	
Robert Erneys, Alexander Hurrell jun.	1291–2	

Alexander Hurrell jun., Robert brother of Ithell	1292–3
Nicholas Payn, Roger Dunfoul	1293–4
Alexander Hurrell jun., Nicholas Payn	1294–5
Alexander Hurrell jun., Robert Ithell	1295–6
Roger Dunfoul, David the miller	1296–7
Robert Ithell, Andrew of Stanlow	1297–8
Roger Dunfoul, Robert Ithell	1298–9
Robert of Macclesfield alias Smallproud, Richard Candelan	1299–1300

MAYORS AND SHERIFFS, 1300–1506

Edward I's charter of 1300 confirmed the mayor's precedence over the sheriffs. The increasingly abundant records after that date show clearly that the sheriffs were chosen annually, though occasionally in the early 14th century the same pair held office for two consecutive years. The mayoralty, however, continued to be held for several years at a time until the earlier 15th century or later. By the 1340s, and probably as early as 1320, the mayoral and shrieval years ceased to run from Michaelmas to Michaelmas. Instead the new officials began their term of office on the Friday after the feast of St. Denis (9 October).

	Mayor	*Sheriffs*
1300–1	Hugh of Brickhill	Andrew of Stanlow, Robert Ithell
1301–2	William (III) of Doncaster[9] Hugh of Brickhill	Richard Candelan, Robert Ithell
1302–3	Alexander Hurrell	Richard Candelan, John of Tarvin
1303–4	Hugh of Brickhill	Roger Dunfoul, Robert of Macclesfield
1304–5	Hugh of Brickhill	Roger Dunfoul, Robert of Macclesfield or Smallproud
1305–6	Richard the engineer	Benedict of Stanton, John of Warwick
1306–7	Hugh of Brickhill	Richard Candelan, William son of Peter of Brickhill or the clerk or le Blake
1307–8	Hugh of Brickhill	William son of Peter of Brickhill, Henry Blackrod
1308–9	Hugh of Brickhill	William son of Peter of Brickhill, Robert of Macclesfield
1309–10	Benedict of Stanton	Richard of Wheatley, Henry Blackrod
1310–11	Hugh of Brickhill	Richard of Wheatley, Gilbert Dunfoul
1311–12	Hugh of Brickhill	John Blund, Richard of Wheatley
1312–13	Hugh of Brickhill	William son of Peter of Brickhill, Robert of Macclesfield
1313–14	Hugh of Brickhill	William (IV) of Doncaster, Richard Russell
1314–15	Benedict of Stanton	Gilbert Dunfoul, William of the Peak
1315–16	William (III) of Doncaster	Richard le Lewede, William Blund
1316–17	John Blund	William son of Peter of Brickhill, William of Milton[10]
1317–18	John Blund William (III) of Doncaster	Richard of Wheatley, Richard le Bruyn[11]
1318–19	William (III) of Doncaster	Gilbert Dunfoul, Robert of Strangeways
1319–20	William son of Peter of Brickhill	John of Daresbury, Roger Blund
1320–1	John of Brickhill	Richard of Wheatley, Richard Russell
1321–2	John of Brickhill William son of Peter of Brickhill[12]	Richard of Wheatley, Gilbert Dunfoul

1 Robert of Hoole was undoubtedly sheriff at the beginning of the mayoral year, in November 1281. Robert of Tarvin first occurs in December 1281. They may have been the same man.

2 In the mayoralty of Alexander Hurrell. This combination of mayor and sheriffs occurs only in Aldersey's list.

3 In the mayoralty of Hugh of Meols. Hugh Payn was certainly sheriff 1287–8.

4 In the mayoralty of Hugh of Brickhill. Andrew also occurs as Randal of Stanlow. This combination of mayor and sheriffs is undated, but cannot readily be assigned to the period after 1289.

5 In the mayoralty of Robert of Tarvin.

6 Occur in the mayoralties of Robert of Tarvin and Hugh of Brickhill.   7 Also called Alan Hurrell.

8 In the mayoralty of Robert the mercer, who is known to have been mayor in January 1291. The combination of mayor and sheriffs occurs in an undated deed, but cannot convincingly be assigned to any other year.

9 Only until some time between 2 and 10 November 1301.

10 'Mulneton'.

11 Possibly to be identified with Richard Russell.

12 Both John and William's names occur as mayor with these sheriffs, in undated deeds, probably to be assigned to this year.

	Mayor	Sheriffs
1322–3	William son of Peter of Brickhill	Richard le Bruyn, William of Basingwerk
1323–4	William son of Peter of Brickhill	Richard le Bruyn, William of Basingwerk
1324–5	Richard Russell	Richard of Wheatley,[1] William of Basingwerk
1325–6	Richard le Bruyn	Richard Erneys, Roger of Norley
1326–7	Richard le Bruyn[2]	Richard Erneys, Roger of Norley
1327–8	Richard Erneys	Richard of Wheatley, Thomas of Strangeways
1328–9	Richard Erneys	Warin Blund, Roger the harper
1329–30	Richard Erneys	Roger of Macclesfield, Madoc of Capenhurst
1330–1	William son of Peter of Brickhill	Henry Hurrell, Madoc of Capenhurst
1331–2	William son of Peter of Brickhill	William of Milton,[3] Roger of Blorton, Henry Wade
1332–3	Roger Blund	Madoc of Capenhurst, Roger of Norley
1333–4	Richard of Wheatley	Madoc of Capenhurst, John Bars
1334–5	John Blund	Henry Torrand, William of Kelsall
1335–6	Roger Blund	Robert of Ledsham, David Russell
1336–7	Roger Blund	David Russell, Roger of Capenhurst
1337–8	John Blund	Henry Hurrell, Madoc of Capenhurst
1338–9	Robert of Ledsham	John of Stoke, John of Hawarden
1339–40	John Blund	John of Hawarden, Edmund of Waterfall
1340–1	Richard of Capenhurst	Madoc of Capenhurst, Hugh of Rycroft
1341–2	Richard of Capenhurst	Madoc of Capenhurst, Thomas of Hegreve
1342–3	Richard of Capenhurst	Madoc of Capenhurst, Richard of Wainfleet
1343–4	John Blund	William (V) of Doncaster, Richard le Bruyn
1344–5	John Blund	William of Whitmore, Alan of Waley
1345–6	Richard of Capenhurst	Madoc of Capenhurst, Bartholomew of Northenden
1346–7	Richard of Capenhurst	John Bars, William of Hadley
1347–8	Henry Torrand	Hugh of Milton,[4] Richard of Ridley
1348–9	John Blund	Richard of Ditton, William of Capenhurst
1349–50	Bartholomew of Northenden[5] Richard le Bruyn	Alan of Waley, William of Derwaldshaw
1350–1	John Blund	Robert de Castell, John son of Adam White
1351–2	John Blund	Stephen Kelsall, William Huxley
1352–3	John Blund	Thomas Wise,[6] Adam of Hope
1353–4	Richard le Bruyn	William Bras,[7] Adam Ingram
1354–5	Richard le Bruyn	William Bras, Roger of Ledsham
1355–6	John Blund	John Dalby, Thomas Aldford
1356–7	John Blund	Benedict of Ridley, Hamo of Tuddesbury
1357–8	John Blund	John Colley,[8] Alexander Bellyetter
1358–9	John Blund	William of Beaumaris, Thomas of Appleton
1359–60	John Blund	John Colley, William of Meculfen
1360–1	Alan of Wheatley	John of Tranmere, Henry Walsh
1361–2	Alan of Wheatley	Henry Done,[9] Hugh Stretton
1362–3	Alan of Wheatley	William Burke,[10] Thomas Peacock
1363–4	Alan of Wheatley	Richard of Manley, Geoffrey of Flint
1364–5	Roger of Ledsham	David of Ewloe, John Cotton
1365–6	Roger of Ledsham	John Colley, William Brerecroft[11]
1366–7	John Dalby	Henry Stapey, Robert Fox
1367–8	John Dalby	John the chamberlain, William Hope
1368–9	Richard le Bruyn	Nicholas of Trafford, Richard of Hawarden
1369–70	Richard le Bruyn	John Armourer, William son of Ralph
1370–1	John Whitmore	John Armourer, Thomas Donne

1 Also occurs as Hugh of Wheatley.

2 On 14 July 1327 Richard le Bruyn, described as 'late mayor of Chester', was imprisoned in Chester castle for his adherence to the rebel earl of Mar.

   3 'Mulneton'. He was dead by June 1332.

   4 'Mulneton'.

5 Killed before December 1349 by Richard of Ditton, one of the sheriffs in the preceding year.

   6 'Wysse'.

   8 'Colle'.

   7 Also 'Braas, Braz'.

   9 'Doune'.

10 Possibly Burleigh.

11 Possibly Bancroft.

	Mayor	Sheriffs
1371–2	John Whitmore	Richard Dunfoul, Thomas del Frere[1]
1372–3	John Whitmore	Ralph Thorp, Robert Colley[2]
1373–4	John Whitmore	Richard of Birkenhead, Robert of Broughton
1374–5	Alexander Bellyetter	Robert the marshal, Hugh Dutton[3]
1375–6	Richard le Bruyn	Richard Bradburne, William Savage[4]
1376–7	Alexander Bellyetter	John Barber, John of Bebington
1377–8	Thomas of Bradford	Thomas of Appleton, John Armourer
1378–9	Thomas of Bradford	Henry le Bryn, Stephen de Cherlegh
	John the chamberlain[5]	
1379–80	John the chamberlain	Roger the potter, Ralph of Hatton
1380–1	John the chamberlain	John Hatton, Gilbert Bellyetter
1381–2	David of Ewloe	John Colley,[6] William of Barton
1382–3	David of Ewloe	Roger of Ditton, Richard the hewster
1383–4	David of Ewloe	Roger of Ditton, Robert Lancelyn
1384–5	John the chamberlain	Thomas Dodd, John of Preston
1385–6	John Armourer[7]	John Wych, Richard Strangeways
1386–7	John Armourer	John of Mossley, John Blackrod
1387–8	John Armourer	Henry Yate, John Hall
1388–9	John Armourer	Thomas Hurrell, John of Arrowe
1389–90	Robert the marshal	Ralph of Picton, John of Madeley
1390–1	John Armourer	Ralph of Hatton, John of Bebington
1391–2	Gilbert Trussell	Robert Daniel, Roger Potter
1392–3	Gilbert Trussell	Robert Lancelyn, John of Preston
1393–4	John Armourer	Richard the hewster, Thomas Piggott
1394–5	John Armourer	Hugh Dutton, Roger of Ditton
1395–6	John of Capenhurst	Roger of Ditton, William of Prestbury
1396–7	John of Capenhurst	John of Madeley, William Heath
1397–8	John of Capenhurst	John of Hawarden, Richard Strangeways
1398–9	John of Capenhurst	John of Hawarden, Richard Stalmin
1399–1400	John of Capenhurst	John of Hawarden, Richard of Bradley
1400–1	John of Bebington	Richard Stalmin, William Heath
1401–2	John of Bebington (died)[8]	John of Hawarden, Thomas of Acton (died), John of
	Robert the marshal	Arrowe (succ.)
1402–3	Roger Potter	Innocent of Chesterfield, William Kempe
1403–4	Ralph of Hatton	John Hall, John of Arrowe
1404–5	John of Preston	William Rochdale, Thomas Aleyn
1405–6	John Ewloe	Robert Chamberlain, John Hatton
1406–7	John Ewloe	John Hatton, Thomas Cottingham
1407–8	John Ewloe	John Walsh, Elias Trevor
1408–9	John Ewloe[9]	John Walsh, Hugh Moulton
1409–10	John Ewloe[10]	John Tarporley, Hugh Moulton
1410–11	Roger Potter	John Brown, Elias Trevor
1411–12	John Walsh	Richard Hatton, William Hope
1412–13	John Whitmore	John Hope, Hugh Moulton
1413–14	John Whitmore	John Hope, Richard Spicer
1414–15	John Whitmore	John Hope, John Overton

1 Possibly Thomas of Bradford. Both names occur in Aldersey's list as Dunfoul's co-sheriff during Whitmore's mayoralty.   2 'Coly, Colle'.

3 Aldersey's list is the authority for this combination of mayor and sheriffs. Aldersey knew of a record which identified Bellyetter as mayor in May 1375.

4 Aldersey notes the combination as recorded in October and December 1375. The list which he copied out also included Richard Dunfoul, mayor, Robert Colley and Hugh of Dutton, sheriffs, at about that date. As yet, however, no other record of

that combination has been identified.

5 John the chamberlain succeeded Thomas of Bradford 28 June 1379.   6 'Coly'.

7 Aldersey's list suggests that John the chamberlain was initially mayor in the year, but died and was replaced by John Armourer at early date.

8 Before August 1402.

9 Removed in August 1409 and replaced by John of Preston, as *locum tenens* of William Brereton, governor of the city.

10 Reinstated.

	Mayor	Sheriffs
1415–16	John Walsh	John Hatton, Robert Hope
1416–17	William Hawarden	John Hatton, Richard Spicer
1417–18	John Overton	Robert Hale, Thomas Cliff
1418–19	William Hawarden	Alexander Henbury, John Bradley
1419–20	John Hope	Robert Hale, Stephen Bellyetter
1420–1	John Hope	William Malpas, Nicholas Wervin
1421–2	John Hope	Richard Massey, William Malpas
1422–3	John Walsh	Robert Hewster, Nicholas Russell
1423–4	John Hatton	Hugh Woodcock, Richard Weston
1424–5	John Hope	Richard Massey, Adam Wotton
1425–6	John Hope	Richard Massey, William Stanmere
1426–7	John Hope	Roger Walsall, Thomas Wotton
1427–8	John Hope	Thomas Madeley, John Flint
1428–9	John Bradley	William Hulme, Thomas Bradford
1429–30	John Walsh	Edward Skinner, Hugh Green
1430–1	Robert Hope	John Freeman, Richard Hankey
1431–2	Richard Massey	John Pilkington, Richard Vickers
1432–3	Richard Massey	Thomas Walley, David White
1433–4	Thomas Wotton	William Rogerson, John Hickling
1434–5	Adam Wotton	Bartholomew Lyalton, Thomas Hamon
1435–6	John Walsh	John Cottingham, Robert Eaton
1436–7	William Stanmere	John Minor, John Layott
1437–8	Richard Massey	John Flint, John Wood
1438–9	Richard Weston	John Copeland, Thomas Clerk
1439–40	Nicholas Daniel	Robert Gill, Peter Savage
1440–1	John Pilkington	Henry Willaston, William Massey
1441–2	Hugh Woodcock	Thomas Lilley, Hugh Neal
1442–3	John Flint	Philip Rede or Hewster, Robert Walley
1443–4	Nicholas Daniel	John Loker, John Rothley
1444–5	Nicholas Daniel	John Loker, John Rothley
1445–6	Nicholas Daniel	Richard Barrow, William Overton or Barker
1446–7	Edward Skinner	Ralph Hunt, Richard Etchells
1447–8	Edward Skinner (died)	John Willym, Roger Ledsham
	William Rogerson	
1448–9	William Rogerson	John Yardley,[1] Robert Bruyn
1449–50	William Massey	John Southworth, Henry Herne[2]
1450–1	William Whitmore	Richard Hawarden, James Hurleton
1451–2	John Dutton	Richard Massey, Richard Rainford
1452–3	William Stanmere	Robert Rogerson, Thomas Gerard
1453–4	Nicholas Daniel	Ralph Marshall, John Trafford
1454–5	Nicholas Daniel	John Barrow, John Grosvenor
1455–6	John Cottingham	Thomas Kent, William Hawkin
1456–7	John Cottingham	John Runcorn, Richard Bower
1457–8	William Daniel	William Tricket, Richard Bulkeley
1458–9	William Daniel	Thomas Monkfield, Robert Acton
1459–60	John Southworth	William Lilley,[3] Nicholas Monkfield
1460–1	John Southworth	Roger Warmingham, Henry Day
1461–2	David Ferror	Thomas Cottingham, John Chamber
1462–3	Robert Bruyn	John Goldsmith, Hugh Frere (died), William Gough (succ.)
1463–4	Robert Rogerson	John Spencer, Alexander Stanney
1464–5	Roger Ledsham	Richard Green, William Runcorn
1465–6	Richard Rainford	James Norris, John Fenton
1466–7	William Lilley	William Rawson, William Thomason

1 'Erdeley'.   2 'Hyrne'.   3 'Lylle'.

	Mayor	Sheriffs
1467–8	John Southworth	Richard Sharp, William Sherman
1468–9	John Dedwood	Richard Gerard, Robert Nottervill
1469–70	Thomas Kent	John Smith, Henry Ball
1470–1	Thomas Cottingham	Thomas Fernes, William Richmond
1471–2	Robert Rogerson	Henry Port, Richard Harper
1472–3	John Spencer	John Evans, Nicholas Hopkin
1473–4	William Whitmore	John Barrow, William Sneyd
1474–5	John Southworth	Roger Hurleton, Robert Waley
1475–6	John Southworth	Richard Smith, Thomas Eccles
1476–7	Hugh Massey	Henry Warmingham, Roger Lightfoot
1477–8	John Southworth	George Bulkeley, Thomas Hurleton
1478–9	Robert Nottervill	Robert Elswick, John Monkfield
1479–80	William Snead	Robert Walker, Matthew Johnson
1480–1	John Southworth	Ralph Davenport, William Heywood or Cook
1481–2	Roger Hurleton	John Dedwood, Henry Frances
1482–3	Roger Hurleton	Roger Taylor or Wright, Roger Burgess
1483–4	John Dedwood	Peter Smith, John Runcorn
1484–5	Sir John Savage	John Norris, Hugh Hurleton
1485–6	Sir John Savage	Thomas Barrow, Richard Gardner
1486–7	Henry Port	Randal Sparrow, Richard Spencer
1487–8	Hugh Hurleton	Randal Sparrow, Nicholas Loker
1488–9	George Bulkeley	Thomas Bunbury, Robert Barrow
1489–90	Ralph Davenport	John Cliff, Thomas Monning
1490–1	John Barrow	Richard Wright, Richard Wirral
1491–2	Randal Sparrow	Edmund Farrington, Richard Hockenhull
1492–3	Roger Hurleton	Richard Goodman, Richard Barker
1493–4	Ralph Davenport	Ralph Manley, Richard Grosvenor
1494–5	George Bulkeley	Henry Balfront, John Waley
1495–6	Richard Wirral	Nicholas Newhouse, Randal Smith
1496–7	Thomas Barrow	Thomas Smith, Tudor ap Thomas
1497–8	Thomas Ferror	John Grimsditch, Randal Eaton
1498–9	Richard Goodman	Richard Fletcher, Thomas Thornton
1499–1500	John Cliff	Roger Smith, John Walley
1500–1	Thomas Ferror	James Manley, Richard Walton
1501–2	Ralph Davenport	William Rogerson, Richard Lowe
1502–3	Richard Wright	William Ball, Thomas Gill
1503–4	Richard Goodman	John Tatton, John Rathbone
1504–5	Thomas Smith sen.	Thomas Hawarden, William Sneyd jun.
1505–6	Thomas Thornton	Hamo Goodman, John Bradfield

MAYORS AND SHERIFFS, 1506–1835

The charter of 1506 confirmed the offices of mayor and two sheriffs, to be elected, as before, on the Friday after the feast of St. Denis.

	Mayor	Sheriffs
1506–7	Thomas Barrow	Robert Barrow, Hamo Johnson
1507–8	Richard Wirral	John Harper, Robert Golborne
1508–9	Thomas Hawarden	Edmund Smith, William Davidson
1509–10	Richard Wright	Thomas Croke, Richard Broster
1510–11	William Rogerson	Thomas Houghton, Henry Radford
1511–12	Sir Thomas Smith	Hugh Clerk, Charles Eaton
1512–13	Sir Piers Dutton	Thomas Middleton, David Middleton
1513–14	Sir Piers Dutton	John Birkendale, Robert Aldersey

	Mayor	Sheriffs
1514–15	Sir Piers Dutton	William Hurleton, John Loker[1]
	John Rathbone	William Goodman, Richard Grimsditch
1515–16	Sir Thomas Smith	Thomas Smith jun., Robert Wright
1516–17	William Sneyd	Hugh Aldersey, Randal Done
1517–18	William Davidson	William Offley, Nicholas Johnson
1518–19	Thomas Barrow	Piers Smith, Robert Middleton
1519–20	John Rathbone	John Griffith, Richard Anyon
1520–1	Sir Thomas Smith	Thomas Golborne, Christopher Warmingham
1521–2	Sir Thomas Smith	Ralph Rogerson, Thomas Bamvill
1522–3	William Davidson	Roger Barrow, John Woodward
1523–4	Edward Middleton	Roger Pike, Stephen Cross
1524–5	Robert Golborne	Richard Evans, John Dymock
1525–6	Robert Aldersey	John Walley, Henry Heyton
1526–7	Robert Barrow	Hugh Davenport, Fulk Dutton
1527–8	Sir Thomas Smith	Henry Gee, Thomas Hall
1528–9	Hugh Aldersey	Edward Davenport, Robert Barton
1529–30	Henry Radford	Thomas Rogerson, Ralph Goodman
1530–1	Sir Thomas Smith	Laurence Dutton, William Massey
1531–2	William Sneyd	Robert Brerewood, Thomas Barrow
1532–3	William Goodman	William Beswick, Richard Hunt
1533–4	Henry Gee	Randle Mainwaring, Hugh Hankey
1534–5	Ralph Rogerson	John Thornton, Thomas Martin
1535–6	Sir Thomas Smith	Robert Walley, Richard Wrench
1536–7	William Goodman	George Leech, George Lightfoot
1537–8	Fulk Dutton	William Glazier, Robert Whitehead
1538–9	David Middleton	Thomas Aldersey, Richard Dickon
1539–40	Henry Gee	William Aldersey, William Whiteley[2]
1540–1	Sir Laurence Smith	John Smith, Thomas Longley
1541–2	Hugh Aldersey	Richard Sneyd (died), Ralph Aldersey (succ.), Randle Bamvill
1542–3	William Beswick	Adam Goodman, Edmund Gee
1543–4	William Sneyd	Ralph Radford, John Rosengreve
1544–5	Robert Barton	William Leech, John Offley
1545–6	William Holcroft (died)	Richard Poole, Richard Grimsditch
	John Walley	
1546–7	Hugh Aldersey (died)	William Bride, Thomas Smith
	John Smith	
1547–8	Ralph Goodman	Richard Rathbone, Thomas Bavand
1548–9	Fulk Dutton	John Webster, Robert Johns
1549–50	Thomas Aldersey	Richard Massey, Morris Williams
1550–1	Edmund Gee (died)	Ralph Goodman, Piers Street
	William Goodman	
1551–2	William Glazier	Ralph Rogerson, Thomas Green
1552–3	Thomas Smith	Thomas Sanders or Steward, William Brownshank
1553–4	John Offley	Henry Hardware, William Ball
1554–5	Fulk Dutton	Robert Amery, John Cowper
1555–6	John Smith	Thomas Wetherall, John Rees[3]
1556–7	John Webster	John Hankey, Thomas Bellin
1557–8	William Bride	John Newall, Thomas Burges
1558–9	Sir Laurence Smith	John Yerworth, William Jewet
1559–60	Henry Hardware	Christopher Morrell, Simon Mountford
1560–1	William Aldersey	Robert Deerhurst, Richard Boydell
1561–2	John Cowper	Richard Dutton, Thomas Bellin
1562–3	Randle Bamvill	William Hamnet, John Harvey

1 All declared to have been improperly elected.   2 'Whitlegge'.   3 'Rysse, Res'.

	Mayor	Sheriffs
1563–4	Sir Laurence Smith	Hugh Rogerson, Gilbert Knowles
1564–5	Richard Poole	Henry Leech, Evan Denvevet
1565–6	Thomas Green	Edward Thompson, William Dodd
1566–7	Sir William Sneyd	William Bird, Robert Brerewood
1567–8	Richard Dutton	Edward Martin, Oliver Smith
1568–9	William Ball	Edward Hanmer, Roger Lee
1569–70	Sir John Savage	Richard Massey, Peter Litherland
1570–1	Sir Laurence Smith	John Middleton, William Styles
1571–2	John Hankey	Richard Bavand, William Wall
1572–3	Roger Lee	Richard Wright, Robert Gill
1573–4	Richard Dutton	William Massey, Paul Chantrell
1574–5	Sir John Savage	John Allen, William Goodman
1575–6	Henry Hardware	William Golborne, David Dymock
1576–7	John Harvey	Thomas Lyniall, John Barnes
1577–8	Thomas Bellin	Valentine Broughton, John Tilson
1578–9	William Jewet	David Mountford, Randulph Leech
1579–80	William Goodman (died)	Robert Brock, David Lloyd
1580–1	William Bird	Richard Bird, William Cotgreave
1581–2	Richard Bavand	Robert Wall, John Fitton
1582–3	William Styles	Thomas Cowper, Richard Rathbone
1583–4	Robert Brerewood	Thomas Fletcher, William Milton (died), Nicholas Massey (succ.)
1584–5	Valentine Broughton	William Aldersey sen., Henry Anion
1585–6	Edmund Gamull	Thomas Tetlow, Thomas Lynaker
1586–7	William Wall	Robert Amery, Richard Knee
1587–8	Robert Brerewood	Thomas Harbottle, John Williams
1588–9	Robert Brock (died) William Hamnet	Richard Spencer, William Mee
1589–90	William Cotgreave	Thurston Hollinshed, Godfrey Wynne
1590–1	William Massey	John Ratcliffe, Thomas Werden
1591–2	Thomas Lyniall	Randulph Allen, Richard Broster
1592–3	John Fitton	Peter Newall, John Taylor
1593–4	David Lloyd	John Littler, John Frances
1594–5	Fulk Aldersey	Henry Hamnet, William Knight
1595–6	William Aldersey sen.	Philip Phillips, William Leicester
1596–7	Thomas Smith	John Aldersey, Roland Barnes
1597–8	Sir John Savage (died) Thomas Fletcher	William Thropp, Robert Fletcher
1598–9	Richard Rathbone	John Brerewood, Lewis Roberts
1599–1600	Henry Hardware	John Owen, John Moyle
1600–1	Robert Brerewood (died) Richard Bavand	Richard Dutton, Edward Bennet (died), Thomas Wright (succ.)
1601–2	John Ratcliffe sen.	John Ratcliffe jun., Owen Harris
1602–3	Hugh Glazier	William Gamull, William Johnson
1603–4	John Aldersey	William Aldersey, William Manning
1604–5	Edward Dutton	Thomas Revington, Kenwick ap Evan
1605–6	John Littler	Robert Blease, Thomas Harvey
1606–7	Philip Phillips	Thomas Thropp, Richard Fletcher
1607–8	Sir John Savage	Robert Whitby, George Brooke
1608–9	William Gamull	Edward Kitchin, Robert Amery
1609–10	William Leicester	Charles Fitton, George Harper
1610–11	Thomas Harvey	Hugh Williamson, John Thropp
1611–12	John Ratcliffe	Nicholas Ince, Robert Fletcher
1612–13	Robert Whitby	Thomas Whitby, Peter Drinkwater
1613–14	William Aldersey jun.	Richard Bathoe, Thomas Percival

	Mayor	*Sheriffs*
1614–15	William Aldersey sen.	Richard Aldersey, Robert Bennett
1615–16	Thomas Thropp	Randle Holme (I), Thomas Weston
1616–17	Edward Button	Thomas Sutton (died), Thomas Bird (succ.), John Cook
1617–18	Charles Fitton	Fulk Salisbury, Gilbert Eaton
1618–19	Sir Randle Mainwaring	John Brereton, Robert Berry
1619–20	Hugh Williamson	Charles Walley, Thomas Ince
1620–1	William Gamull	Humphrey Lloyd, William Spark
1621–2	Robert Whitehead	William Allen, Richard Bridge
1622–3	Sir Thomas Smith	John Williams, Hugh Whickstead
1623–4	John Brereton	Christopher Blease, William Fisher
1624–5	Peter Drinkwater	Thomas Knowles, William Glegg
1625–6	Sir Randle Mainwaring	Robert Sproston, Robert Harvey
1626–7	Nicholas Ince	Richard Bennett, Thomas Humphreys
1627–8	Richard Dutton	William Edwards, Thomas Aldersey
1628–9	John Ratcliffe	Richard Leicester, John Leech
1629–30	Christopher Blease	John Aldersey, William Higginson (died), Robert Ince (succ.)
1630–1	Charles Walley	Thomas Thropp, Thomas Cowper
1631–2	William Allen (died) Thomas Bird	Richard Broster, William Jones
1632–3	William Spark	William Parnell, Robert Wright
1633–4	Randle Holme (I)	Randle Holme (II), Richard Bird
1634–5	Francis Gamull	William Ince, Thomas Eaton (died), Edward Evans (succ.)
1635–6	Thomas Knowles	Thomas Cross, Calvin Bruen
1636–7	William Edwards	Edward Bradshaw, Owen Hughes
1637–8	Thomas Thropp	Thomas Weston, William Wilcock
1638–9	Robert Sproston	Philip Sproston, William Drinkwater
1639–40	Robert Harvey	Richard Bradshaw, Ralph Hutton
1640–1	Thomas Aldersey	John Whittle, Edward Hulton
1641–2	Thomas Cowper	Thomas Mottershead, Hugh Leigh
1642–3	William Ince	William Crompton, John Johnson
1643–4	Randle Holme (II)	William Whittle, William Bennett
1644–5	Charles Walley	Humphrey Phillips, Ralph Davies (died), Randle Richardson (succ.)
1645–6	No election of city officers	
1646–7	William Edwards	Robert Sproston, unknown
1647–8	Robert Wright (died) Edward Bradshaw	William Wright, Richard Minshull
1648–9	Richard Bradshaw	Jonathan Ridge, Gerard Jones
1649–50	William Crompton	Thomas Parnell, Robert Capper
1650–1	Richard Leicester	John Anderson, Thomas Heath
1651–2	Owen Hughes (died) John Johnson	Thomas Harris, Hugh Mason
1652–3	William Bennett	William Wilson, Richard Townshend
1653–4	Edward Bradshaw	Daniel Greatbach, Charles Farrington
1654–5	Richard Bird	Arthur Walley, John Griffith
1655–6	William Wright	John Witter, John Pool
1656–7	Peter Leigh	Thomas Robinson, Ralph Burroughs
1657–8	Richard Minshull	William Street, William Bristowe
1658–9	Thomas Hand (died) Gerard Jones	William Heywood, Randal Oulton
1659–60	John Johnson	Thomas Wilcock, John Knowles
1660–1	Arthur Walley	Richard Taylor, Randal Bennett
1661–2	Thomas Thropp	Richard Harrison, John Hulton

	Mayor	Sheriffs
1662–3	Richard Broster	John Maddock, William King
1663–4	John Pool	Charles Leinsly, Edward Kingsey
1664–5	Richard Taylor	Robert Murray, Richard Key
1665–6	Randal Oulton	Gawen Hudson, Richard Annion
1666–7	William Street	Henry Lloyd, William Warrington
1667–8	Richard Harrison	William Harvey, Robert Caddick
1668–9	Charles Stanley, earl of Derby	Richard Wright, John Young
1669–70	Robert Murray	Thomas Simpson, Owen Ellis
1670–1	Thomas Wilcock	William Wilme, Thomas Billington
1671–2	William Wilson	Robert Townsend (died), William Wilson (succ.), Thomas Ashton
1672–3	Gawen Hudson	George Mainwaring, Benjamin Critchley
1673–4	Thomas Simpson	William Ince, Peter Edwards
1674–5	Richard Wright	Edward Oulton, Isaac Swift
1675–6	Henry Lloyd	Nathaniel Williamson, Thomas Wright
1676–7	John Young (died) John Maddock	Thomas Baker, Robert Shone
1677–8	William Ince	Thomas Hand, John Mottershead
1678–9	William Harvey	Hugh Starkey, Robert Fletcher
1679–80	William Wilme	Ralph Burrows, Francis Skellerne
1680–1	John Anderson	John Taylor, William Starkey
1681–2	George Mainwaring	William Allen, Henry Bennett
1682–3	Peter Edwards	Robert Hewitt, William Bennett
1683–4	William Street	John Wilme, Robert Murray
1684–5	Sir Thomas Grosvenor, Bt.	Richard Harrison, John Johnson
1685–6	William Wilson	Randal Turner, Richard Oulton
1686–7	Edward Oulton	Puleston Partington, Nathaniel Anderton
1687–8	Hugh Starkey	Edward Starkey, Jonathan Whitby
1688–9	William Street	Robert Murray, John Goulborn
1689–90	Francis Skellerne	Edward Partington, Randal Bathoe
1690–1	Nathaniel Williamson	John Warrington, Robert Dentith
1691–2	Henry Booth, earl of Warrington	Thomas Maddock, Michael Johnson
1692–3	Col. Roger Whitley	Joseph Maddock, John Burrows
1693–4	Col. Roger Whitley	Thomas Hand, John Kinaston
1694–5	Col. Roger Whitley	Arthur Bolland, Thomas Bolland
1695–6	Col. Roger Whitley	Timothy Dean, John Holland
1696–7	Peter Bennett	James Mainwaring, Owen Ellis
1697–8	William Allen	Peter Edwards, William Francis
1698–9	Henry Bennett	Thomas Parnell, Thomas Wright
1699–1700	William Bennett	Edward Puleston, John Bradshaw
1700–1	Richard Oulton (died) Hugh Starkey	Humphrey Page, Thomas Bowker
1701–2	Thomas Hand	William Allen, William Coker
1702–3	William George Richard Stanley, earl of Derby (died)[1] Michael Johnson	John Minshull, Thomas Partington
1703–4	Nathaniel Anderton	George Bennion, John Thomason
1704–5	Edward Partington	Daniel Peck, Thomas Houghton
1705–6	Edward Puleston	John Stringer, Randle Holme (IV)
1706–7	Puleston Partington	Thomas Davis, Francis Sayer
1707–8	Humphrey Page	Thomas Williams, Joseph Hodgson
1708–9	James Mainwaring	James Comberbach, Alexander Denton
1709–10	William Allen	Henry Bennett, Randal Bingley

1 Died 5 Nov. 1702: *Complete Peerage*, iv. 216.

	Mayor	Sheriffs
1710–11	Thomas Partington	Hugh Colley, Edward Burroughs
1711–12	John Minshull	Thomas Edwards, Thomas Wilson
1712–13	John Thomason	Robert Crosby, Lawrence Gother
1713–14	John Stringer	John Parker, Thomas Bolland
1714–15	Francis Sayer	John Parker, Peter Leadbeater
1715–16	Sir Richard Grosvenor, Bt.	William Hughes, Thomas Brooke
1716–17	Henry Bennett	John Pemberton, James Johnson
1717–18	Joseph Hodgson	Trafford Massie, George Johnson
1718–19	Alexander Denton	Thomas Williams, Peter Ellames
1719–20	Randal Bingley	William Johnson (died), Thomas Chalton (succ.), Thomas Bridge
1720–1	Thomas Edwards	Roger Massey, John Cotgreave
1721–2	Thomas Wilson	Nathaniel Wright, Thomas Hickock
1722–3	Lawrence Gother	John Marsden, Thomas Duke
1723–4	Robert Pigot	Peter Parry, Charles Bingley
1724–5	John Parker	Edward Twambrook, Samuel Jarvis
1725–6	Thomas Bolland	Edmund Parker, Arthur Mercer
1726–7	John Parker	James Burroughs, Thomas Davis
1727–8	James Comberbach	Thomas Maddock, Thomas Gother
1728–9	William Hughes	Joseph Parker, Randal Bingley
1729–30	Thomas Brooke	John Francis, Thomas Ravenscroft
1730–1	John Pemberton	Andrew Duke, George Fernall
1731–2	Trafford Massie	Henry Ridley, Edward Yeardsley
1732–3	George Johnson	Edward Nichols, William Edwards
1733–4	Peter Ellames	Charles Mytton, Robert Holland
1734–5	Roger Massey	Edward Griffith, Francis Bassano
1735–6	John Cotgreave	William Speed, Peter Potter
1736–7	Watkin Williams-Wynn	Thomas Bingley, John Hallwood
1737–8	Sir Robert Grosvenor, Bt.	Ralph Probert, Thomas Broster
1738–9	Nathaniel Wright	John Dicas, John Snow
1739–40	John Marsden	Henry Pemberton, William Vizer
1740–1	Thomas Duke	William Smith, Edmund Bolland
1741–2	Charles Bingley	Edward Partington, Benjamin Perryn
1742–3	Samuel Jarvis	Robert Cawley (died), William Cowper (succ.), John Page
1743–4	Thomas Davis	Benjamin Maddock, John Egerton
1744–5	Thomas Maddock	Peter Dewsbury, Richard Richardson
1745–6	Henry Ridley	George Griffiths, Thomas Massey
1746–7	Edward Yeardsley (died) Edward Nichols	Robert Maddock, Thomas Bridge
1747–8	William Edwards	Thomas Cotgreave, Edward Walley
1748–9	Edward Griffith	John Lawton, Peter Ellames
1749–50	Thomas Bingley	Charles Parry, Henry Hesketh
1750–1	John Hallwood	John Dicas, Holmes Burrows
1751–2	Ralph Probert	John Hickock, James Briscoe (died), John Bridge (succ.)
1752–3	Thomas Broster	Edward Burrows, Thomas Hart
1753–4	Edmund Bolland	Richard Ollerhead, Richard Ledsham
1754–5	Dr. William Cowper	Thomas Astle, John Kelsall
1755–6	John Page	Charles Boswell, Joseph Wilkinson
1756–7	Peter Dewsbury	John Johnson, George French
1757–8	Richard Richardson	Thomas Craven, Robert Lloyd
1758–9	Thomas Cotgreave	Thomas Randles, John Lawton
1759–60	Sir Richard Grosvenor, Bt.	Thomas Slaughter, Peter Morgan
1760–1	Thomas Grosvenor	Thomas Marsden, Samuel Dob
1761–2	Thomas Cholmondeley	Joseph Dyson, Joseph Crewe

	Mayor	Sheriffs
1762–3	Henry Hesketh	William Dicas, John Drake
1763–4	Holmes Burrows	Thomas Griffith, John Thomas
1764–5	Edward Burrows	James Broadhurst, Francis Walley
1765–6	Richard Ollerhead	Daniel Smith, John Hart
1766–7	Thomas Astle	Thomas Bowers, William Seller
1767–8	John Kelsall	Robert Williams, Gabriel Smith
1768–9	Charles Boswell	Joseph Snow, Pattison Ellames
1769–70	George French	Thomas Powell, Thomas Amery
1770–1	John Lawton	Henry Hegg, John Bennett
1771–2	Henry Vigars	John Dymock Griffith, Thomas Edwards
1772–3	Joseph Crewe	John Hallwood, Thomas Lea
1773–4	Sir Watkin Williams-Wynn, Bt.	Edward Orme, William Turner (died), Thomas Roberts (succ.)
1774–5	Joseph Dyson	Richard Ledsham, William Corles
1775–6	Thomas Griffith	Thomas Patton, John Chamberlaine
1776–7	James Broadhurst	John Monk, Peter Broster
1777–8	John Hart	John Wright, George Johnson
1778–9	William Seller	Thomas Richards, Charles Francis
1779–80	Gabriel Smith	William Birch, George Bingley
1780–1	Joseph Snow	William Harrison, Thomas Barnes
1781–2	Pattison Ellames	Rowland Jones, John Bramwell
1782–3	Thomas Patton	Joseph Turner, Samuel Bromfield
1783–4	Thomas Amery	Cotton Probert, Daniel Smith
1784–5	Henry Hegg	John Meacock, Richard Richardson
1785–6	John Bennett	John Larden, Thomas Jones
1786–7	Thomas Edwards	Charles Panton, Edmund Bushell
1787–8	John Hallwood	Nathaniel Dewsbury, William Edwards
1788–9	John Leigh	Andrew Davison, Thomas Bennion
1789–90	Robert Howell Vaughan	Robert Whittle, Joseph Wright (died), John Troughton (succ.)
1790–1	Thomas Powell	Thomas Rathbone, John Hassall
1791–2	Peter Broster	Roger Dutton, Thomas Jenkins
1792–3	John Wright	John Johnson, Peter Wilkinson
1793–4	Thomas Richards	William Seller, John Thomas
1794–5	George Bingley	Samuel Barnes, William Newell
1795–6	William Harrison	Thomas Evans, Robert Brittain
1796–7	Thomas Barnes	Francis Wood, John Bakewell
1797–8	Rowland Jones	Thomas Griffith, John Webster
1798–9	John Bramwell	Robert Bowers, Samuel Bennett
1799–1800	Daniel Smith	John Bedward, John Harrison
1800–1	John Meacock	John Johnson Cotgreave, Robert Williams
1801–2	John Larden	Joseph Bage, Thomas Francis
1802–3	Robert Hodgson	Henry Bowers, Thomas Bradford
1803–4	Edmund Bushell	John Tomlinson, Thomas Richards
1804–5	William Edwards	John Powell, John Williamson
1805–6	Thomas Bennion	Thomas Poole, John Swarbreck Rogers
1806–7	Thomas Rathbone	Timothy Whitby, James Bennett
1807–8	Robert, Earl Grosvenor	Joseph Johnson, John Stewart Hughes
1808–9	William Newell	Joseph Hornby, William Cortney
1809–10	Thomas Evans	William Massey, Joseph Grace
1810–11	Gen. Thomas Grosvenor	William Moss, Robert Morris
1811–12	Robert Bowers	George Harrison, James Snape
1812–13	Samuel Bennett	Josiah Thomas, Samuel N. Bennett
1813–14	Sir Watkin Williams-Wynn, Bt.	John Fletcher, George Hastings
1814–15	John Bedward	Thomas Dixon, Titus Chaloner

	Mayor	*Sheriffs*
1815–16	(Sir) John Cotgreave[1]	Richard Buckley, George Harrison
1816–17	Thomas Francis	Thomas Bagnall, William Gamon
1817–18	Henry Bowers	John Mellor, Thomas Whittell
1818–19	Thomas Bradford	Charles Dutton, John Dod
1819–20	John Williamson	George Wilding, William Sefton
1820–1	William Seller	Francis Massey, William Cross
1821–2	John Swarbreck Rogers	John Johnson, John Gardner
1822–3	William Massey	William Davenport, Edward Ducker
1823–4	Robert Morris	Jonathan Colley, George Walker
1824–5	George Harrison	John Harrison, Robert Shearing
1825–6	John Fletcher	Wilkinson Grace, William Bevin (died), Simeon Leet (succ.)
1826–7	John Larden[2] Thomas Francis	George Bridges Granville, Gabriel Roberts
1827–8	Henry Bowers	John Walker, Edward Titley
1828–9	Robert Morris	Thomas Bowers, George Allender
1829–30	William Moss	John Parry, Thomas Whittakers
1830–1	Titus Chaloner	Alexander Booth, Samuel Witter
1831–2	Richard Buckley (died) George Harrison	Richard Palin, Richard Phillpot
1832–3	John Fletcher	Joseph Janion, John Royle
1833–4	George Harrison	George Eaton, Joseph Ridgway
1834–5[3]	George Harrison	John Rogers, John Kearsley

MAYORS AND SHERIFFS, 1836–1974

From 1836 the mayor and a single sheriff were elected each year by the council as a whole.

	Mayor	*Sheriff*
1836	William Cross	Robert Whitley
1836–7	Thomas Dixon	John Palin
1837–8	Edward Samuel Walker[4]	John Williamson
1838–9	John Uniacke	Robert Miller
1839–40	John Uniacke	Thomas Griffith
1840–1	William Wardell	William John Seller
1841–2	William Brown	John Lowe
1842–3	William Henry Brown	Thomas Huxley
1843–4	Henry Kelsall	Samuel Gardner
1844–5	Charles Potts	Edward Tilston
1845–6	Edward Tilston	John Smith
1846–7	Richard Phillips Jones	John Rogers
1847–8	Richard Phillips Jones	John Trevor
1848–9	Sir Edward Samuel Walker	Robert Turner
1849–50	John Williams	Edward Russell Seller
1850–1	John Williams	Edward Johnson
1851–2	Philip Stapleton Humberston	Peter Eaton
1852–3	Henry Brown (died) Richard Phillips Jones	Thomas Quellyn Roberts
1853–4	John Smith	Samuel Peacock
1854–5	William Henry Brown	John Hicklin
1855–6	Edward Francis French	Samuel Seller

1 Knighted during his mayoral year, 5 July 1816: W. A. Shaw, *Knights of Eng.* ii. 317.   2 Ousted by *quo warranto*.   3 Under the Municipal Corporations Act of 1835 the mayor and sheriffs for 1834–5 remained in office until 31 December 1835.   4 Knighted in 1841: Shaw, *Knights of Eng.* ii. 343.

	Mayor	*Sheriff*
1856–7	Peter Eaton	John Jones
1857–8	Philip Stapleton Humberston	Joseph Baxter Musgrave
1858–9	Meadows Frost	William Johnson
1859–60	Meadows Frost	Robert Frost
1860–1	John Trevor	James Rowe
1861–2	John Trevor	Joseph Oakes
1862–3	John Williams	William Maysmor Williams
1863–4	Robert Frost	Robert Littler
1864–5	Robert Frost	Francis Butt
1865–6	William Maysmor Williams	Charles Dutton
1866–7	William Johnson	Thomas Bowers
1867–8	Joseph Oakes	Francis Arthur Dickson
1868–9	Thomas Gibbons Frost[1]	William Farish
1869–70	Francis Arthur Dickson	Robert Gregg
1870–1	Charles Dutton	Robert Roberts
1871–2	Robert Frost	James Gerrard
1872–3	Robert Gregg	Thomas Cartwright
1873–4	William Maysmor Williams	Thomas Hughes
1874–5	Thomas Quellyn Roberts	Charles Parry
1875–6	William Johnson	Charles Brown
1876–7	William Johnson	Charles Blelock
1877–8	William Farish	William Churton
1878–9	Leonard Gilbert	John Robertson
1879–80	Charles Blelock	James Salmon
1880–1	Charles Brown	Henry Richard Bowers
1881–2	Sir Thomas Gibbons Frost	John Cartwright
1882–3	Sir Thomas Gibbons Frost	John McHattie
1883–4	Charles Brown	Thomas Smith
1884–5	Charles Brown	Henry Brown
1885–6	George Dickson	George Dutton
1886–7	William Brown	Thomas Griffiths
1887–8	William Brown	John Smith
1888–9	George Dutton	Roger Jackson
1889–90	James Salmon	John Roberts
1890–1	Charles Brown	John Jones
1891–2	Charles Brown	Ernest Brassey
1892–3	Charles Brown	Henry Stolterfoth
1893–4	Leonard Gilbert	Alexander Hamilton
1894–5	William Churton	John Jones
1895–6	Benjamin Chaffers Roberts	John Goodie Holmes
1896–7	Benjamin Chaffers Roberts	John Foulkes Lowe
1897–8	John Goodie Holmes	James Huke
1898–9	Henry Stolterfoth	John Lightfoot
1899–1900	Robert Lamb	Henry Brown
1900–1	Henry Brown	Edgar Dutton
1901–2	James Frost	R. Cecil Davies
1902–3	John Roberts	Henry Dodd
1903–4	Robert Lamb	D. L. Hewitt
1904–5	Robert Lamb	A. Mann
1905–6	Robert Lamb	William Ferguson
1906–7	F. F. Brown (died)	R. H. Lanceley
	John Jones	
1907–8	John Jones	John Meadows Frost

1 Knighted 1869: *The Times*, 13 Nov. 1869, p. 7.

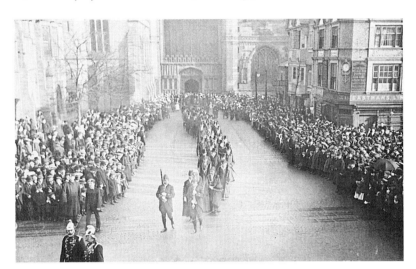

FIG. 184. *Mayor-making ceremony of 1904, procession leaving cathedral*

	Mayor	Sheriff
1908–9	R. Cecil Davies	Harry B. Dutton
1909–10	D. L. Hewitt	W. H. Denson
1910–11	D. L. Hewitt	H. F. Brown
1911–12	W. H. Denson	George Barlow
1912–13	Harry B. Dutton	J. Griffiths
1913–14	John Meadows Frost	John Dodd
1914–15	John Meadows Frost	W. H. Griffith
1915–16	John Meadows Frost	R. T. Wickham
1916–17	John Meadows Frost	John Owens
1917–18	(Sir) John Meadows Frost[1]	S. R. Arthur Wall
1918–19	Sir John Meadows Frost	John Williamson
1919–20	H. F. Brown	A. S. Dutton
1920–1	H. Sheriff Roberts	C. P. Cockrill
1921–2	W. H. Griffith	P. S. Brook
1922–3	S. R. Arthur Wall	W. Carr
1923–4	C. P. Cockrill	W. A. V. Churton
1924–5	D. L. Hewitt	T. S. Parry
1925–6	John Welsh	A. Hart Davies
1926–7	C. C. Taylor	Edwin Green
1927–8	Edwin Green	Stanley Gerrard
1928–9	W. A. V. Churton	John Morris
1929–30	John Morris	W. Matthews Jones
1930–1	John Morris	Robert Matthewson
1931–2	Stanley Gerrard	I. S. Fox
1932–3	I. S. Fox	J. H. Haselden
1933–4	Charles Sconce	F. D. Price
1934–5	J. H. Laybourne	W. H. Ebrey
1935–6	T. Davies Jones	W. H. Nightingale
1936–7	Robert Matthewson	P. H. Lawson
1937–8	George Barlow	Kate Clarke
1938–9	Phyllis Brown	J. M. Simon (died)
		Robert Frost
1939–40	Kate Clarke	Charles Jones
1940–1	W. Matthews Jones	E. W. Keyes
1941–2	W. Matthews Jones	Evan Owen
1942–3	W. Matthews Jones	Bert Reynolds

1 Knighted in 1918, some time after 3 June: *The Times*, 3 June 1918, p. 8b; *Who Was Who, 1929–40*.

	Mayor	*Sheriff*
1943–4	W. Matthews Jones	Stanley Dutton
1944–5	W. Matthews Jones	Edith Baty
1945–6	D. R. Owen	S. Jane Dunne
1947–9[1]	Robert Frost	Claude Crimes
1949–50	Bert Reynolds	W. R. Williams
1950–1	P. H. Lawson	H. C. Wickham
1951–2	E. W. Keyes	Charles Cullimore
1952–3	Charles Cullimore	Richard Davies
1953–4	Arthur Charmley	Charles Sconce
1954–5	J. Henry Reece	Leonard Edwards
1955–6	Thomas Price	Franklyn Hart Davies
1956–7	Franklyn Hart Davies	Revd. Eric Lawson
1957–8	Revd. Eric Lawson	T. F. Fazey
1958–9	Frank Wright	Beryl Nield
1959–60	H. W. Talbott	Mary Heaney
1960–1	John Groghan	J. T. Leese
1961–2	Beryl Nield	Florence Grogan
1962–3	T. F. Fazey	T. Sarl-Williams
1963–4	T. Sarl-Williams	Frederick Barker
1964–5	Mary Heaney	H. A. A. Howell
1965–6	H. A. A. Howell	John Arrowsmith
1966–7	Florence Grogan	Sylvia Harris
1967–8	Sylvia Harris	John Smith
1968–9	Frederick Barker	R. E. France-Hayhurst
1969–70	R. E. France-Hayhurst	J. M. V. Cottrell
1970–1	J. M. V. Cottrell	Cyril Gibson
1971–2	Leonard Edwards	C. N. Ribbeck
1972–3	C. N. Ribbeck	T. H. Tomlins
1973–4	John Smith	F. R. Cleeves

1 Under the Representation of the People Act, 1948, the term of office of mayor was changed to run from May to May, and the terms of the mayor and sheriff elected in 1947 were extended to May 1949.

CHESTER AND BEYOND

MANORS AND ESTATES IN AND NEAR THE CITY

Although Chester within the walls was regarded as the city proper, by 1066 it was grouped with nearby holdings to form a wider jurisdictional unit. The hundred of Chester included 'Redcliff' and the bishop's borough south-east of the walled city, Handbridge and Lee 'beyond the bridge' to the south, and Newton to the north-east.[1] All the holdings in the hundred, except Newton, were later included within the liberties, which emerged in the 12th and 13th centuries and had been defined with precision by the 14th.[2] This article focuses primarily on the manorial and estate structure of that area but also takes some account of the manors and estates immediately outside the liberties, holdings which were central to the local land market and whose owners and tenants often played an important role in civic life. In the 19th and 20th centuries many of those once-rural estates were built over to become part of suburban Chester, and wherever possible their disposal to builders and developers has been noted. Constraints of space, however, have made it impossible to cover their descents in full. More extensive treatment of estates outside the liberties is reserved for the detailed histories of the relevant townships in future volumes.

MANORS AND ESTATES WITHIN THE LIBERTIES

The rise of Chester as a town from the 10th century, and more particularly the emergence of a self-governing citizenry in the early 13th, restricted manorial development within the liberties, especially inside the walls. Although the king and earl had important financial rights in the late Anglo-Saxon town and maintained agents there, neither held a manor within the area of the later liberties.[3] Nor did the Anglo-Norman earls, whose castle, although some land was attached to it, never had manorial jurisdiction.[4] The two principal manors, those of the abbey and the nunnery, established in the late 11th and the 12th century, were largely extramural, the abbey's a compact holding to the north, the nunnery's smaller and more scattered to the south. Both had their own courts and associated privileges. Regarded with increasing suspicion by the citizens as the powers of the city courts grew, by the 16th century their business had been much reduced.[5]

The two principal manors, both of which retained their identity until the mid 19th century, were supplemented by other small manors and estates in the south of the liberties which were secular in origin and held mainly by local gentry. From the 18th century the Grosvenor family's accumulation of property intruded a new estate into what had been a largely stable structure, with substantial holdings both in the walled city and to the south and south-east.

ST. THOMAS'S MANOR

By the 12th century the most important manor within the liberties was that of the abbot of Chester. Although not expressly mentioned in the Domesday Survey or in the grants of the Anglo-Norman earls, its chief holdings in Chester were probably acquired at an early date. At its foundation in 1092, the abbey took over the 13 intramural houses of the Anglo-Saxon minster, while Earl Hugh I himself granted Northgate Street and his tenant Robert fitz Hugh two intramural tenements.[6] Earl Richard (1101–20) gave two more properties within the city and one outside the Northgate, and his tenants another three, two of them in the market.[7] Under Earl Ranulph I (1120–9) the abbey acquired a 'great shop' in the market place, together with a further six tenements, including two in front of the abbey church, one in Bridge Street, and one near the Shipgate.[8] Ranulph II (1129–53) gave two tenements before the abbey gates, and another outside the Eastgate was acquired in the time of Earl Hugh II (1153–81).[9] By the earlier 13th century the abbey also had intramural holdings in Parsons Lane (later Princess Street), Castle Lane, Cuppin Lane, and Fleshmongers Lane,

1 *V.C.H. Ches.* i. 326, 342–3 (no. 1), 344 (nos. 10–12, 14), 356 (nos. 181–3), 358 (nos. 210–12, 218).

2 Above, 9–10.

3 *V.C.H. Ches.* v (1), 24–5.

4 Below, this section, Castle Demesne.

5 Above, 25; Burne, *Chester Cath.* 251–2; *V.C.H. Ches.* iii. 146–7.

6 *Cart. Chester Abbey*, i, pp. 17–18, 37. Cf. ibid. i, pp. 237–42.

7 Ibid. i, pp. 40–1, 46.   8 Ibid. i, pp. 48–9.

9 Ibid. i, pp. 59, 95.

and also in the Crofts in the north-west corner of the city, the site of its principal barn. Thereafter the community continued to acquire land in the intramural area, and eventually had property scattered throughout the walled city but with a concentration in Northgate Street and Parsons Lane.[1] John Arneway's endowments for his chantry in 1278 constituted an especially important gift.[2] Under Abbot Simon Whitchurch (1265–91) in particular, the abbey also built up its holdings in the town fields outside the Northgate, which came to form the bulk of its property within the liberties, extending west to Portpool, north to Bache, and east to Flooker's brook. The extramural possessions were largely agricultural, the main house property being concentrated in Upper Northgate Street.[3]

After the Dissolution the manor of St. Thomas passed to the dean and chapter of Chester, who retained it until 1845. In 1663 the annual income of their estate, by then known as the Bailiwick of Chester and leased out, was £73.[4] The intramural holdings remained largely focused on Northgate Street and Parsons Lane, mainly on the west side of the market area opposite Abbey Gate, and in the Crofts. Scattered holdings were also retained in Watergate Street, Eastgate Street, Bridge Street, and Cuppin Lane. Outside the walls, the cathedral's main property lay mostly in the north and west of the liberties, concentrated between Liverpool Road and Parkgate Road, but stretching west to Finchett's Gutter and north to Bache and Flooker's brook. To the east, it continued to hold the Kaleyards immediately outside the walls, together with other property in Foregate Street and Boughton.[5]

The abbey's exemption from the urban courts and its special fair-time jurisdiction were also the subject of explicit grants, attributed to Earl Hugh I.[6] From the 13th century or earlier until the reduction of its business in 1509 the manor court was held at St. Thomas's chapel outside the Northgate.[7] No records survive. After the Dissolution the cathedral held manor courts within the precincts. By the 1670s there were two distinct bodies: St. Werburgh's court, held at fortnightly intervals, and St. Thomas's, which met irregularly and much less frequently.[8] The business of both seems to have been confined to petty presentments. By the late 18th century the dean's court, to which the manors of Great Boughton and Bridge Trafford paid suit and service, was held in Abbey Gate. In all, 83 tenants were required to attend, including (in Chester) 25 holding property in Northgate Street, five in Abbey Square, two in Parsons Lane, and one each in Watergate Street and Cuppin Lane.[9]

The cathedral's Bailiwick estate, which had been granted to Lyman Cotton on a 20-year lease in 1832, was ceded to the Ecclesiastical Commissioners in 1845. Reports by the commissioners' secretary, W. C. K. Murray, made then to assess the estate's potential, noted many changes since 1811.[10] In particular, there had been sales of land, the most significant, bringing in £9,000, to the Chester and Birkenhead and the Chester and Holyhead railway companies.[11] Murray put the annual value of the estate in 1845 at £3,048. He assessed the property under five headings: housing within or close to the city walls, with an annual value of £1,278; lands, chiefly small market gardens, at 'the skirts of the city' (£534); agricultural land in the north of the liberties around Liverpool Road and Parkgate Road (£574); other agricultural land, villas, and commercial buildings (£546); and tithe rent charges (£116 net). In addition the chapter retained 'considerable house property' in the city, mostly within the precinct and Northgate Street, the annual value of which had been estimated at £2,700 in 1811.

Murray considered that, with Chester's rising property market (in which, he noted, Earl Howe had already invested),[12] much of the extramural agricultural land was suitable for building, though the railways recently built across it had considerably weakened its value. His main recommendation was the immediate sale of 134 a. around Liverpool Road and Parkgate Road for development as villas. The commissioners heeded his advice, and over the next twenty years sold almost all the estate's extramural holdings, besides much of the property within the city acquired in 1845.[13]

In 1854 a second Order in Council transferred most of the dean and chapter's remaining holdings to the commissioners, including much of the precinct. By 1858, however, their re-endowment with a new permanent estate was under consideration, and in 1866, as part of that scheme, a further Order in Council returned to them property in Northgate Street and the precinct, including parts of Abbey Square and the Music Hall (the former chapel of St. Nicholas). Further transfers followed: in 1881 a house on the north side of Abbey Street to form a residence for the precentor, and in the 1890s much property in and around Abbey Square, Abbey Street, and Abbey Green. In particular, in 1899 the chapter purchased at a cost of £10,000 the abbey gateway and seven houses in Abbey Square,

1 *Cart. Chester Abbey*, i, pp. 166, 210, 242–5, 249, 253–6; ii, pp. 267–9, 343–8, 465, 468.
2 Ibid. ii, pp. 464–70.
3 Ibid. ii, pp. 267–8, 343, 346, 348–52; C.C.A.L.S., EDD 12/1.   4 Burne, *Chester Cath.* 260.
5 *L. & P. Hen. VIII*, xvi, pp. 535–6; C.C.A.L.S., EDD 12/1, 4; Lysons, *Magna Britannia: Ches.* 616.
6 *Cart. Chester Abbey*, i, pp. 14, 21, 23.
7 Above, 25, 27; Morris, *Chester*, 133–6.
8 C.C.A.L.S., EDD 11/1/1.
9 Burne, *Chester Cath.* 249–52.
10 Rest of section based on London, Church of England Record Centre, Ecclesiastical Commissioners' file 9544.
11 Cf. above, 91–2.
12 Cf. below, this section, Brewer's Hall.
13 *V.C.H. Ches.* v (1), 236.

together with stables, outhouses, and gardens to the north of the square, at the rear of Northgate Street, and north of Abbey Green.[1]

Thereafter the commissioners' main holdings in Chester were five houses in the late Georgian terrace of Abbey Green (the sixth having been transferred to the chapter in 1866). Those too were eventually sold, nos. 2 and 6 to local purchasers in 1923 and nos. 3–5 to the dean and chapter in 1925. Nos. 2 and 6 were bought by the dean and chapter in 1938 and 1947 respectively.[2] The cathedral retained its reduced estate within Chester at the time of writing.

OTHER HOLDINGS

In the 11th century there were seven or eight small rural estates immediately outside the walls, of which the bishop held one or possibly two in 1066.[3] Two belonged to Arni, a man of some substance who also possessed several manors near by in south Wirral and at Newton.[4] Two more were held by Leofwine and one each by Wulfnoth and by Gunnar, who was also probably lord of the nearby manor of Mollington Banastre.[5] Among their Norman successors, William fitz Niel the constable and Hugh fitz Osbern were important tenants of Earl Hugh for whom holdings near Chester would have been useful to ease their visits to the honorial capital.[6] Like other estates near the liberties, their importance waned as that function lost significance, and some of the holdings disappeared as separate entities.

St. John's College Estate. In 1086 the bishop had important financial rights and an agent in Chester. His small extramural estate at 'Redcliff', just outside the walls to the south-east of the city and assessed at two thirds of a hide, was assigned to the church of St. John in Domesday Book. It is uncertain whether 'Redcliff' included the bishop's borough, also referred to in the Survey and perhaps then free of geld. The status of the even smaller holding attached to St. Mary's minster, which lay near by and was assessed at 2 bovates, is similarly unclear, but it too seems to have been held by the bishop. All those estates, together with the minster's eight intramural houses, were probably eventually assigned to St. John's. The college's holdings were later augmented by chantry endowments and by property throughout the city given to the fraternity of St. Anne in the later 14th and 15th century. After its dissolution in 1547 or 1548

its property passed to the Crown and was sold, together with the fraternity's holdings and other obit lands. There was no mention then of any manorial rights.[7] The impropriate rectory was purchased in 1587 by Alexander Cotes of Chester and remained in the hands of his descendants until bought by Robert, 2nd Earl Grosvenor, in 1810.[8] The fraternity house in the churchyard was bought by Sir Hugh Cholmondeley shortly after the Dissolution and remained in his family until razed in the Civil War.[9]

'Redcliff': Secular Holding. Gunnar's small estate, assessed at a third of a hide, passed to Hugh de Mara before 1086. Granted by Hugh to St. Werburgh's abbey in the early 12th century, it has not been traced thereafter.[10]

Castle Demesne. The castle formed an extra-parochial precinct to which was annexed 85 a. of demesne, all in the south of the liberties or just outside them. In 1285 Edward I granted a large part of the holding, *c.* 29 a. in the Earl's Eye, to Randle of Merton.[11]

Handbridge. South of the river immediately beyond the bridge, at Handbridge, there were three small rural estates in late Anglo-Saxon times, assessed at 1 carucate each and perhaps of Hiberno-Norse origin. Arni's passed after the Conquest to William fitz Niel, Leofwine's to Hugh de Mara, and Wulfnoth's to Hugh fitz Osbern.[12] Their later history is uncertain, but they were perhaps among the lands in Handbridge which by the mid 12th century Earl Ranulph II and his tenants had granted to Chester nunnery. The earl also granted the prioress her own court and by the 14th century, when the nuns had consolidated their holdings in the south of the liberties, the estate was regarded as a manor.[13]

After the Dissolution the nunnery's holdings within the liberties, valued at £27 in 1535, were used to endow the new see of Chester.[14] In 1546, however, they were among the temporalities which the first bishop, John Bird, was forced to relinquish to the Crown.[15] Bird had apparently already leased the manor out,[16] and the Crown continued that policy, the early lessees, who held the manor courts, including the aldermanic families of Goodman and Gamull.[17] The manor remained at lease until the Interregnum,[18] when it was surveyed along with the rest of the late king's

1 London, Church of England Record Centre, Ecclesiastical Commissioners' file 9845.

2 Ibid. file 1515.   3 *V.C.H. Ches.* i. 344 (nos. 10–11).

4 Ibid. i. 320, 356 (nos. 181–3).

5 Ibid. i. 351 (no. 104), 358 (nos. 210–12, 218).

6 Ibid. i. 309–10, 313–14.

7 Ibid. i. 344 (nos. 10–12); ibid. v (1), 86; above, 129–30.

8 Lysons, *Magna Britannia: Ches.* 623–4; above, 138.

9 Above, 131; *V.C.H. Ches.* v (1), 223.

10 *Cart. Chester Abbey,* i, p. 19.

11 Above, 9, 204; below, this section, Earl's Eye.

12 *V.C.H. Ches.* i. 356 (no. 183), 358 (nos. 211, 218).

13 *Charters of A.-N. Earls,* nos. 97–8; *V.C.H. Ches.* ii. 147.

14 *Valor Eccl.* v. 206; *L. & P. Hen. VIII,* xvi, pp. 535–6.

15 *L. & P. Hen. VIII,* xxi (2), p. 295 (no. 574); P.R.O., C 54/445, m. 7; C 66/790, m. 29.

16 P.R.O., E 134/6 Chas. I/Mich. 43, which gives the date (erroneously) as Mar. 1536.

17 Ibid. E 210/10456; E 214/694; E 314/6 Chas. I/Mich. 43.

18 Ibid. E 134/14 & 15 Chas. I/Hil. 5.

possessions in 1650.[1] It was later granted as dower to Charles II's wife, Catherine of Braganza, and again put out to lease.[2] In 1762 it was granted to Richard, later 1st Earl Grosvenor (d. 1802), who, like his predecessors, continued to hold a regular court leet to which tenants in Handbridge and Claverton paid suit.[3] About 1815 Robert, 2nd Earl Grosvenor, failed to obtain a renewal of the lease, which was granted instead to his bitter political rival Sir John Grey Egerton.[4] In 1819 the Crown sold the manor to John Edwards of Chester, after whose death c. 1850 Thomas Higgins bought the manorial rights. By then the estate had been broken up: some land was sold separately in 1819 and more was bought by Richard Grosvenor, 2nd marquess of Westminster, in 1850.[5]

The survey of 1650 listed property in Chester itself, in the town fields of Handbridge and Claverton, and in Eccleston. By 1782 the manor's principal holdings were in Handbridge, largely on the north side of the main street, in Green Lane, and scattered through the town fields especially between Eaton Road and Wrexham Road. It also continued to include much property within the walls, on the east side of Nuns Lane (near the former precinct), in Watergate Street, Eastgate Street, Newgate Street, Bunce Lane, and Claverton Lane (later Duke Street), besides a few isolated tenements east of the city, in St. John Street, Foregate Street, and Boughton.[6] All that amounted to a sizeable estate, the annual income being reckoned at £480 in the late 18th century.[7] Until inclosure under an Act of 1805 much of the land in Handbridge remained an area of open-field arable farming, its tenants having rights of common pasture in Saltney marsh until 1781.[8]

Overleigh. Overleigh, one of the two small rural estates which comprised the Domesday territory of Lee, lay south-west of Handbridge, athwart the road to Wales. Leofwine's single virgate there had been granted by 1086 to Hugh de Mara.[9] Whether by descent or some other means, it evidently passed to the barons of Mold, for c. 1230 Robert of Mold granted it to the abbot and monks of Basingwerk (Flints.). In 1462 the convent leased it for 100 years to Elis ap Deio ap Gruffudd,

whose descendant, Matthew Ellis (d. 1574), a member of Henry VIII's bodyguard, bought it in 1545 from the Crown's grantees after the Dissolution. The timber-framed mansion and chapel of the Ellis family were destroyed in the siege of Chester, and after the Restoration a new brick house was built by Thomas Cowper (d. 1695), who had acquired the estate partly through descent and partly through purchase.[10] In the later 17th and 18th century Overleigh Hall remained the home of the Cowpers, a prominent Chester family, who included aldermen, a city recorder, and a celebrated local antiquarian. After improvements by the last, Dr. William Cowper (d. 1767),[11] the hall was inherited in 1811 by Charles Cholmondeley of Vale Royal and let to a tenant. Purchased in 1821 with an estate of 135 a. by Robert, 2nd Earl Grosvenor, the house was demolished in 1830 to make way for a new entrance to the Eaton estate.[12]

Netherleigh. Occupying an area directly south of Handbridge beside the river and on the road to Eccleston, Arni's estate, assessed at 1 virgate, had been granted by 1086 to William fitz Niel.[13] The latter's eventual successor, John de Lacy, granted it to Adam of Dutton, from whom it passed c. 1270 to the Orby family of Gawsworth and thence in the early 14th century to the Fittons. Later, perhaps c. 1604, part of the estate was acquired by the Stanleys of Alderley, by whom it was sold in 1735 to the Chester alderman John Cotgreave. Thereafter the Cotgreave family built a modest seat, Netherleigh House, on the west side of Eaton Road. A late Georgian two-storeyed brick building of c. 1813 with two shallow bows to the front and a three-storeyed mid 19th-century addition to the rear, it was purchased by the 1st duke of Westminster in 1878.[14]

The ancient mansion of Netherleigh Hall on its moated site passed with another part of the estate to the Browne family of Upton, who resided there in the 17th and 18th centuries until they sold it to John Bennett of Chester in 1774. The hall, which had been fortified by Sir William Brereton in 1645 for use as his headquarters during the siege of Chester, was eventually let to tenants, and in the early 19th century was

---

1 Ibid. E 317/Ches./13A, 13B; *Account of Manors held by Lease from Crown, reported by Commissioners to inquire in Royal Forests, Woods, and Land Revenues* (1787), App. 3.

2 *Cal. Treas. Bks.* 1714, 376.

3 C.C.A.L.S., TS. schedule of deeds and documents relating to the Grosvenors' Chester Estate (hereafter cited as Eaton Hall, Chester Estate Deeds), Box U, no. 2; C.C.A.L.S., ZTCC 77, 80; P.R.O., LR 3/14/1; Lysons, *Magna Britannia: Ches.* 628; Ormerod, *Hist. Ches.* ii. 821.

4 Thus Ormerod, *Hist. Ches.* i. 373, but there is no record of the lease in P.R.O., LR 1/167.

5 Eaton Hall, Chester Estate Deeds, Box T, no. 18; P.R.O., LR 1/168; Ormerod, *Hist. Ches.* i. 373.   6 P.R.O., MR 1/282.

7 *Account of Manors held by Lease from Crown*, p. 6.

8 P. J. W. Higson, 'Pointers towards the Structure of Agriculture in Handbridge and Claverton prior to Parl. Enclosure', *T.H.S.L.C.* cxlii. 55–86.

9 *V.C.H. Ches.* i. 358 (no. 210).

10 *26 D.K.R.* App. 34; Morris, *Siege of Chester*, 204; Lysons, *Magna Britannia: Ches.* 628–9; Ormerod, *Hist. Ches.* i. 336, 374–5; above, 303–4.

11 C.C.A.L.S., DCC 16/59.

12 Eaton Hall, Chester Estate Deeds, Box F2, no. 1.

13 *V.C.H. Ches.* i. 356 (no. 182).

14 P. J. W. Higson, 'Landlord Control and Motivation in the Parl. Enclosure of St. Mary's-on-the-Hill Parish, Chester', *T.H.S.L.C.* cxxxvii. 95, 111; Hemingway, *Hist. Chester*, ii. 230–1; Eaton Hall, Chester Estate Deeds, Box X, no. 4.

occupied by a farmer.[1] It afterwards disappeared and at the time of writing its site was unknown.[2]

Brewer's Hall. The estate, which lay west of the city on the river cliff overlooking the Roodee, was held by the Bradford family, serjeants of the Eastgate from the 1280s. It passed to the Trussell family of Warmingham in the 14th century and from them *c.* 1500 to the Veres, earls of Oxford. After its sale by Edward de Vere, 17th earl, in 1580, it passed successively to Hugh Beeston, Sir Thomas Egerton, and the Wright family, whose descendant sold it in the mid 18th century to William Hanmer of Iscoyd (Flints.). Hanmer's daughter Esther married Assheton Curzon, later 1st Viscount Curzon, whose grandson and heir R. W. P. Curzon-Howe, 1st Earl Howe, developed the estate, then disparaged as 'a cold bleak hill', in the 1840s.[3] The ancient mansion was demolished during the siege of Chester and was afterwards replaced by a farmhouse.[4]

Earl's Eye. The large tract of meadow known as the Earl's Eye, lying in a bend of the river east of the city, opposite Boughton and extending as far south as Claverton, seems to have been part of the castle demesne in the 12th and 13th centuries. In 1285 *c.* 29 a. of land and pasture there were granted by Edward I to Randle of Merton as part of an exchange. The holding remained in the hands of the Mertons and their heirs, the Gleggs of Gayton, until the 19th century.[5] Its western end was developed as the exclusive suburb of Queen's Park from the 1850s.[6]

Another holding in the meadows was acquired in 1568 by Gilbert Gerrard, probably from Sir Thomas Venables, and granted to William Gerrard, recorder of Chester, in 1569.[7] In 1588 the latter's heir, another Gilbert Gerrard, sold *c.* 30 a. of closes and pasture within the Earl's Eye to George Beverley of Chester for £400.[8] The origins and later history of the estate are unclear.

Ecclesiastical Precincts. Several small estates were formed from the city's main ecclesiastical precincts after the Dissolution. Sold by the Crown, they were developed by a variety of proprietors in the 17th and 18th centuries. The nunnery's conventual buildings were granted in 1541 to the Breretons, who established a mansion, Nuns Hall, which remained a seat of the family until it was destroyed in the siege of Chester.[9] Thereafter much of the site remained unoccupied

except for a house at its east end built for the Holme family, heralds and antiquarians, in the mid 17th century.[10]

The three friaries were all sold by the Crown within a few years of the Dissolution. Fulk Dutton bought the Carmelite site and built a mansion in the western part of the precinct.[11] The property later passed to Sir Thomas Egerton who built a second house east of Dutton's and whose descendants retained the estate until the late 18th century. Development along White Friars and within the precinct took place from the early 18th to the early 19th century.[12] To the west, both the Dominican and Franciscan sites were acquired by a branch of the Warburtons, an important Cheshire gentry family, by the late 16th century, and inherited by the Stanleys of Alderley in the earlier 17th. The late 16th-century timber-framed mansion later known as Stanley Palace was built in the north-east corner of the Dominican precinct, reputedly by Sir Peter Warburton, and two other gentry houses on the west part of the site by the 1740s. Much of the remainder together with the Franciscan precinct was developed by the Stanleys in the 1770s and 1780s.[13]

Grosvenor Estate. By far the most important later estate within the liberties belonged to the Grosvenors of Eaton. The family, which had long had a close association with the city through its hereditary serjeanty of the Dee, began acquiring land in Chester by the early 17th century, when Richard Grosvenor (d. 1619) held three messuages.[14] Investment on a grander scale began in the 18th century as the Grosvenors started to play a greater part in civic life. In the 1720s the family bought the Sun Inn in Northgate Street together with land in Eastgate Street, and in 1788 they made the important purchase of the Talbot Inn in Eastgate Street.[15] The main acquisitions, however, were between 1810 and 1821, under Robert, 2nd Earl Grosvenor (later 1st marquess of Westminster). Although he bought property all over Chester, his most significant purchases were in the relatively undeveloped block of land covering the remains of the Roman baths and lying east of Bridge Street, south of Eastgate Street, and around Newgate Street. There, in 1818, he bought the Royal Hotel, which lay on the south side of Eastgate Street next to the Talbot, with which establishment it was merged.[16] Another significant area of acquisition was south-east of the walled city in Love Lane and around

1 Ormerod, *Hist. Ches.* i. 373; Hemingway, *Hist. Chester*, ii. 230–1.

2 Pers. comm. Simon Ward, Chester Archaeology.

3 London, Church of England Record Centre, Ecclesiastical Commissioners' file 9544.

4 Above, 218; Lysons, *Magna Britannia: Ches.* 628; Ormerod, *Hist. Ches.* i. 373; iii. 229–30; *V.C.H. Ches.* v (1), 223.

5 Ormerod, *Hist. Ches.* i. 373; ii. 176, 179–80, 517–18.

6 *V.C.H. Ches.* v (1), 237.

7 P.R.O., CHES 11/59, 62.

8 Ibid. CHES 11/62.

9 Morris, *Siege of Chester*, 204.

10 Lysons, *Magna Britannia: Ches.* 576; above, 241.

11 Lysons, *Magna Britannia: Ches.* 576–7.

12 *V.C.H. Ches.* v (1), 224, 228; above, 244–5.

13 Above, 242–4.

14 Above, 84; Ormerod, *Hist. Ches.* ii. 836. Cf. Eaton Hall, Chester Estate Deeds, Box Y, no. 1.

15 Eaton Hall, Chester Estate Deeds, Box Y, nos. 2, 5.

16 Ibid. Box B2, no. 2.

St. John's church, the impropriate rectory of which Grosvenor bought in 1810.[1] The 2nd marquess, Richard Grosvenor, consolidated his father's acquisitions, especially in the 1860s, when he rebuilt the hotel in Eastgate Street as the Grosvenor Hotel[2] and bought the Feathers Hotel on the east side of Bridge Street together with holdings near by in Feathers Lane.[3] Thereafter there were fewer purchases, although the marquess continued to buy land and property around St. John's, in the Groves, and in Love Lane.[4]

Outside the walls but still within the liberties, the Grosvenors were building up their estates in Handbridge throughout the same period. From 1762 until 1815 they were lessees of the Crown's manor of Handbridge.[5] Purchases of cottages and land in the town fields of Handbridge were made continuously throughout the 18th and 19th centuries, although curiously the family did not acquire the manor of Handbridge when the Crown eventually sold it in 1819.[6] Between the early 18th century and the mid 19th the Grosvenors also bought most of the rural township of Claverton, immediately outside the liberties but part of Handbridge manor, an acquisition completed by the 1st duke of Westminster before 1882.[7]

From the mid 18th century the Grosvenors' impact upon the city was considerable. In the intramural area their most significant investment was in the large block of land bounded by Eastgate Street, Bridge Street, Pepper Street, and the walls. There, in addition to the Grosvenor Hotel, the family established St. Michael's Row in 1910, and, most conspicuously of all, developed a large shopping precinct between 1962 and 1964.[8]

Outside the walls, the 1st duke cleared squalid courtyard housing from his land in Handbridge and built the new church of St. Mary without the Walls in the 1880s. In the late 1940s the Grosvenor estate was responsible for a modest group of 40 houses in Brown's Lane.[9] In general, however, the family did not promote development in the southern and south-eastern reaches of the liberties. Much of the area south of suburban Handbridge, especially beyond Netherleigh and on the western side of Eaton Road, remained rural and heavily wooded after the 2nd earl's inclosure of a large part of the town fields to create a grand drive to Eaton Hall, the Chester Approach, under an Act of 1805.[10] Elsewhere the family used their land to establish public parks.[11]

MANORS AND ESTATES ADJOINING THE LIBERTIES

The liberties were mostly fringed by rather small estates, none of which was highly developed as a manorial centre. In the Middle Ages several were held by the abbey, and hence had no resident lord, while others belonged to prominent but largely non-resident gentry families. In the 13th and 14th centuries some members of the emerging civic élite took advantage of those circumstances to establish rural estates just beyond the liberties, especially in Claverton and Newton.

Although after the Dissolution the abbey's holdings were initially used to endow the new cathedral, the chapter soon lost control of them to fee farmers and they were progressively sold off, sometimes to long-established undertenants. By the late 16th century the city was thus encircled by a group of small country houses, some of which were in the hands of mayoral and aldermanic families. Although several houses were ruined in the 1640s during the siege of Chester and some estates never recovered, others continued in existence until the earlier 20th century, often still in the hands of the civic élite. After 1918, however, none

of the houses was occupied by the manorial lord and only a few by their owners. Most were let to tenants by 1939, and after 1945 those which remained standing were steadily enveloped in newly established housing estates.

The local gentry established on the margins of Chester were already by the mid 18th century being eclipsed as the dominant landowning influence on the city. The rise of the Grosvenors ensured that their seat at Eaton, three miles south of the Cross, became the main focus of aristocratic social and political power, a position it largely retained throughout the 19th and 20th centuries.

The arrangement of manors and estates in this section works clockwise from the north.[12]

BACHE

Immediately north of the liberties, on the far side of Bache brook, opposite the abbot's mills, lay the small manor and township of Bache. The abbey acquired the manor from Lettice of Malpas in the time of Earl

1 Ibid. Boxes Y, no. 8; Z, nos. 1–7; A2, nos. 1–3; B2, nos. 1–8; C2, nos. 1–2; above, 138.

2 See esp. Eaton Hall, Chester Estate Deeds, Boxes C2, no. 13; D2, nos. 1–2, 4, 6.

3 Ibid. Boxes C2, nos. 12, 14; D2, no. 3.

4 Ibid. Boxes C2, no. 10; D2, no. 5; E2, nos. 1–2.

5 P.R.O., E 367/5190, 7242; Lysons, *Magna Britannia: Ches.* 628.

6 Eaton Hall, Chester Estate Deeds, Boxes U, V, W, X; above,

this section, Handbridge.

7 Ormerod, *Hist. Ches.* ii. 821–2; Lysons, *Magna Britannia: Ches.* 627.

8 *V.C.H. Ches.* v (1), 232, 259.

9 Ibid. v (1), 235, 263.

10 Eaton Hall, Chester Estate Deeds, Box 3, no. 11; *T.H.S.L.C.* cxxxvii. 93–116; cxlii. 56–7.

11 Above, 302–3.

12 For maps see above, 2 (fig. 2), 13 (fig. 4).

Ranulph I (1120–9).[1] In the later 13th and the 14th century prominent citizens, including David the miller and members of the Doncaster family, had estates there, and by the 1430s the Chauntrells had established themselves as the principal landholders under the abbot. At the Dissolution the manor passed to the dean and chapter but in the 1550s was lost to fee farmers, under whom it continued to be held by the Chauntrells until 1606. It was then sold to the Whitby family, mayors and recorders of Chester, with whose descendants it remained until *c.* 1770. Thereafter the estate passed through various hands[2] until it was bought by the adjoining Cheshire county lunatic asylum shortly before 1914.[3] Bache Hall, the seat of the Chauntrells and the Whitbys, was destroyed in the siege of Chester, but was rebuilt afterwards and remained a gentry residence until *c.* 1910.[4]

UPTON BY CHESTER

Also north of the liberties, enveloping Bache, lay the substantial manor of Upton. In 958 King Edgar granted it to St. Werburgh's minster, but thereafter it was evidently lost.[5] Assessed at 4½ hides in 1066, it was held by Earl Edwin and at the Conquest passed to Earl Hugh.[6] Earl Ranulph I (1120–9) granted it to Chester abbey,[7] which retained it until the Dissolution and held a court there to which many of its other manors also paid suit. In the 14th century several prominent Chester families established out-of-town estates in Upton, including the Doncasters, Daresburys, and Hurrells. The manor passed to the dean and chapter at the Dissolution but was lost to fee farmers in the early 1550s. In the late 16th, 17th, and 18th centuries they included the Brocks, holders of the manor and resident at the hall, and the Brownes. In 1734 the manorial estate passed by marriage to the Egerton family of Oulton and remained in the hands of the Grey Egertons and their trustees in 1939.[8] Upton Hall was held by the Ithells, well-to-do tenant farmers, in the later 19th century and until the 1930s.[9]

NEWTON BY CHESTER

The township, which was included in the Domesday hundred of Chester, lay next to Upton and north-east of the liberties. By 1086 the Englishman Arni's estate of 1 hide had passed, together with his holdings within the liberty, to William fitz Niel,[10] who later gave it to the abbey of St. Werburgh to become part of the manor of Upton.[11] Fitz Niel's grant also included the services of Hugh fitz Odard, ancestor of the Duttons, who long held lands in Newton.[12] At the Dissolution the manor passed to the dean and chapter, but was among those holdings alienated in the 1550s,[13] and by the 1580s it was held by the Hurleston family of Picton, from whom it passed by marriage to John Needham, later 10th Viscount Kilmorey, in 1738.[14] Much of the township remained in the hands of the Needhams until the mid 1930s.[15] Thereafter their land was sold off, the Newton Hall housing estate being built over it 1957–60.[16] Newton Hall, residence of the Hurlestons and later let to tenants or sold, stands in Plas Newton Lane. Built *c.* 1700, it is two-storeyed, of brick with stone dressings.[17]

Leading Cestrian families held land in the fields of Newton and built up estates there. In the earlier 13th century the township gave its name to a family which had extensive holdings under the abbot and was perhaps descended from the Duttons.[18] A little later the Erneys family acquired land in Newton, receiving grants from Geoffrey of Dutton and the Newton family among others.[19] In the later 13th and early 14th century the mayoral family of Brickhill also acquired a considerable estate in the township.[20] Lands there later escheated to the city corporation, and by the later 17th century the city was making inclosures in the town fields of Newton.[21]

HOOLE

The township of Hoole also lay north-east of the city. Together with Mickle Trafford a component of the FitzAlan earls of Arundel's manor of Dunham on the Hill, it descended with the latter through the Trout-becks, who purchased it in the early 15th century, and thence by marriage *c.* 1510 to Sir John Talbot, ancestor of the Talbot earls of Shrewsbury. The earls held Hoole Lodge, then considered to be the ancient manor house, in the early 19th century, and were lords of the manor until the 1930s, although they had ceased to be significant landowners by the 1920s.[22]

1 *Cart. Chester Abbey,* i, pp. 51–2, 58. Cf. ibid. ii, pp. 274–5, 352.

2 Ormerod, *Hist. Ches.* ii. 773–6; Lysons, *Magna Britannia: Ches.* 616–17; *V.C.H. Ches.* v (1), 49, 54, 100.

3 *Kelly's Dir. Ches.* (1910), 56; (1914), 57; C.C.A.L.S., ZCR 856; above, 264.

4 Ormerod, *Hist. Ches.* ii. 776; Lysons, *Magna Britannia: Ches.* 616–17; Morris, *Siege of Chester,* 204; *Kelly's Dir. Ches.* (1857), 15; (1910), 56.

5 *Cart. Chester Abbey,* i, pp. 8–13; *V.C.H. Ches.* iii. 132.

6 *V.C.H. Ches.* i. 348 (no. 69).

7 *Charters of A.-N. Earls,* no. 13.

8 Ormerod, *Hist. Ches.* ii. 819–20; *V.C.H. Ches.* v (1), 54; C.C.A.L.S., ZCR 15/9; *Kelly's Dir. Ches.* (1934), 440; (1939), 444.

9 *Kelly's Dir. Ches.* (1857), 249; (1892), 494; (1934), 441; (1939), 446.   10 *V.C.H. Ches.* i. 356 (no. 181).

11 *Cart. Chester Abbey,* i, p. 40.

12 Ormerod, *Hist. Ches.* ii. 772; *J.C.A.S.* N.S. x. 49.

13 Ormerod, *Hist. Ches.* ii. 773.

14 C.C.A.L.S., ZCR 15/9; *Complete Peerage,* vii. 262.

15 Ormerod, *Hist. Ches.* ii. 773; *Kelly's Dir. Ches.* (1934), 300; (1939), 306.

16 *V.C.H. Ches.* v (1), 262.

17 Ormerod, *Hist. Ches.* ii. 773; Lysons, *Magna Britannia: Ches.* 618; *Kelly's Dir. Ches.* (1939), 306.

18 *Cart. Chester Abbey,* ii, pp. 356–8.

19 *J.C.A.S.* N.S. x. 43–7, 49.

20 Ormerod, *Hist. Ches.* ii. 772; *V.C.H. Ches.* v (1), 54–5.

21 C.C.A.L.S., ZAB 3, f. 32; ZCR 466/116, 119, 122–4; ZCHD 7/15.

22 Ormerod, *Hist. Ches.* ii. 36–42, 812–13; *Kelly's Dir. Ches.* (1906), 357; (1923), 386; (1928), 209; (1934), 202.

In the 13th and 14th centuries the Hoole or Holes family, which included a city sheriff in the 1280s, were mesne lords of the manor and probably resident, though by the late 14th century they had a mansion instead near Chester castle. They are not heard of after the mid 15th century.[1] By the 1450s the Bunbury family of Stanney resided at Hoole Hall, but the house was destroyed in the siege of Chester and the Bunburys sold their Hoole estate in 1757. The purchasers, the Baldwins, established a new hall. Built of brick, with five bays and two storeys, in the late 18th century, it was considerably extended in the 19th. Having passed by purchase through several hands, including members of the Potts family in the late 19th and early 20th century, Hoole Hall was derelict c. 1980, but by 1988 had been converted into a luxury hotel.[2]

From the earlier 18th century the Needham family, Viscounts and later earls of Kilmorey, also held property in Hoole.[3]

FLOOKERSBROOK

The estate of Flookersbrook, immediately east of the eponymous stream, lay partly in Newton and partly in Hoole. The estate, held by the Massey family of Kelsall, existed before 1450, and later passed to the Bruens of Tarvin and then the Sneyds, before being bought after 1538 by Sir Laurence Smith of Hough (d. 1582). Flookersbrook Hall, still held by the Smiths but then at lease, was destroyed in the siege of Chester and the estate was later sold to the Anderson family before being broken up in the 18th century.[4]

GREAT BOUGHTON

East of the liberties lay Great Boughton, probably part of the estate of Huntington given to St. Werburgh's minster by King Edgar in 958, and certainly held by the church in 1066.[5] Having passed from the abbey to the dean and chapter and thereafter to fee farmers, the estate was purchased by a younger branch of the Davenports, who already resided there, and was still retained by their descendants, the Currie family, in 1939.[6] The old hall, destroyed in the siege of Chester, was replaced in the 1650s, although the family had ceased to live there in the later 19th century. Boughton Hall, which became a centre for amateur sporting

activity in the early 20th century, was sold to its tenant in 1931.[7]

HUNTINGTON

Granted to St. Werburgh's minster by King Edgar in 958,[8] Huntington, which lay south of Great Boughton, was regarded from the foundation of Chester abbey as part of the Saighton fee. Passing successively to the dean and chapter and the fee farmers, it was held by a variety of largely non-resident owners, the capital messuage being simply a farmhouse. In 1772 it passed to the Brock family, by whom it was sold to the 2nd marquess of Westminster in the mid 19th century.[9]

The Cowper family of Chester also had an estate in Huntington from the 17th to the 19th century.[10]

CLAVERTON

In 1066 Claverton, which lay immediately south of the liberties, was clearly of some importance. Held by Osmær and assessed at 2 hides, like several other manors near Chester its appurtenances included burgesses (eight within the walls, four in Handbridge) and it also had a salthouse at Northwich. By 1086 it had passed to one of Earl Hugh's leading tenants, Hugh fitz Osbern.[11] In the 13th century its importance seems to have waned and it was apparently regarded as an extension of the town fields in the southern part of the liberties.[12] There was no manor house and probably few if any inhabitants. In the 13th and 14th centuries the main estate was held by the Pulfords, but other prominent citizens of Chester, including Philip the clerk, members of the Dunfoul family, and John Brunham, chamberlain of Chester, had agricultural holdings there.[13]

The Pulfords' holdings passed c. 1366 by marriage to the Grosvenors. With the partition of the Grosvenor estates in the mid 1460s, they were acquired by Peter Dutton of Hatton. The estate remained with his family until the early 17th century when it passed by marriage to the Gerrards, who held it until the 18th century.[14] During the 18th and 19th centuries the whole township was acquired piecemeal by the Grosvenors.[15]

MARLSTON CUM LACHE

Situated west of Claverton, in 1066 the township of Marlston cum Lache comprised two manors, Lache

1 Ormerod, *Hist. Ches.* ii. 812; *J.C.A.S.* n.s. x. 27, 32, 38–9; *Cart. Chester Abbey*, ii, pp. 342–3; *V.C.H. Ches.* v (1), 212, 218; above, 306–7.
2 Ormerod, *Hist. Ches.* ii. 813; Morris, *Siege of Chester*, 204; *Kelly's Dir. Ches.* (1892), 289; (1906), 357; (1910), 365; P. de Figueiredo and J. Treuherz, *Ches. Country Houses*, 244.
3 C.C.A.L.S., ZCR 15/9; *Kelly's Dir. Ches.* (1923), 386; (1928), 209; (1934), 202; (1939), 207.
4 Ormerod, *Hist. Ches.* ii. 773; iii. 503; Lysons, *Magna Britannia: Ches.* 619; Morris, *Siege of Chester*, 204; *V.C.H. Ches.* v (1), 117.
5 *Cart. Chester Abbey*, i, pp. 8–13; *V.C.H. Ches.* i. 344 (no. 18).

6 Ormerod, *Hist. Ches.* ii. 771; *Kelly's Dir. Ches.* (1939), 55.
7 *Kelly's Dir. Ches.* (1857), 47; (1892), 162; (1934), 53; (1939), 78; above, 262–4, 268–9.
8 *Cart. Chester Abbey*, i, pp. 8–13.
9 Ormerod, *Hist. Ches.* ii. 770; Lysons, *Magna Britannia: Ches.* 617–18.
10 Ormerod, *Hist. Ches.* ii. 770.
11 *V.C.H. Ches.* i. 367 (no. 332).
12 *V.C.H. Ches.* v (1), 216.
13 Ormerod, *Hist. Ches.* ii. 821; *J.C.A.S.* n.s. x. 33, 41.
14 Ormerod, *Hist. Ches.* i. 653; ii. 821.
15 Above, this section, Grosvenor Estate.

held by St. Werburgh's minster, Marlston by Arni. Marlston had passed to William fitz Niel by 1086.[1] Earl Hugh and his successors confirmed the new abbey in possession of a portion of Lache, but part of the manor appears to have been retained by the earl and was later given by Ranulph II to Basingwerk abbey.[2] Later a single manor of Marlston cum Lache was held of the earl by the Blund family, one of whom became serjeant of the Northgate in the 14th century.[3] In the 1350s and 1360s the nuns of Chester built up an extensive estate in Lache, including the manor.[4]

At the Dissolution the nuns' holding was granted to the Brereton family. In 1654 Sir William Brereton granted the manorial rights to Thomas Minshull, having let the land on a long lease to Col. Roger Whitley, from whom it passed by the marriage of his daughter Elizabeth to Sir John Mainwaring of Peover. The latter's descendant Charles Mainwaring purchased the manorial rights in 1773 and the Mainwarings remained lords of the manor in 1939.

Lache Hall was sold separately to the Manley family, who retained it until the mid 18th century. It was then bought by John Snow, a Chester alderman, in whose family it remained until the early 20th century.[5] Although the township was developed from 1919, Lache Hall was still occupied as a farm in 1934.[6] It had gone by 1959 when the Lache Hall housing estate was established.[7]

The Bradford family, serjeants of the Eastgate, held a further estate in Lache from the 1270s together with their estate at Brewer's Hall within the liberties. It descended like Brewer's Hall to the Trussells in 1376.[8]

BLACON CUM CRABWALL

The manor of Blacon lay north-west of the liberties. Assessed at 2 hides and held by Thorth in 1066, it passed by 1086 to Ranulph de Mesnilwarin, ancestor of the Mainwarings.[9] Probably subinfeudated shortly afterwards, it was once again held directly by the family in the 13th century. The estate went by marriage to William Trussell, in whose family it remained until it passed by marriage to the Veres, earls of Oxford, *c.* 1500. The Veres sold it to the Crewe family whose descendants remained lords of the manor until the First World War. A manor house leased by the earl of Oxford was recorded by John Leland in the earlier 16th century and became the seat of Sir Randle Crewe in the earlier 17th. It was destroyed in the siege of Chester.[10]

The estate of Crabwall was granted by the Mainwarings to the Arneway family in the early 13th century. John Arneway, mayor of Chester 1268–78, granted it to the abbot of Chester as an endowment to maintain his chantries in the abbey church and St. Bridget's.[11] After the Dissolution the estate was given to a younger branch of the Gamull family of Buerton, who built a residence there in the early 17th century, demolished by *c.* 1800. The estate remained in the hands of the Gamulls' descendants until the 19th century, when it was sold to Philip Stapleton Humberston.[12] Its later history has not been traced. At the time of writing Crabwall Hall comprised a small brick house refronted in the early 19th century and much extended in 1987 to form a luxury hotel.[13]

---

1 *V.C.H. Ches.* i. 345 (no. 35), 366–7 (no. 330).
2 *Charters of A.-N. Earls*, pp. 4, 40, 52.
3 Ormerod, *Hist. Ches.* ii. 822; above, 221.
4 *V.C.H. Ches.* iii. 148–9.
5 Ormerod, *Hist. Ches.* ii. 823; Lysons, *Magna Britannia: Ches.* 629–30; C.C.A.L.S., ZD/BC; *Kelly's Dir. Ches.* (1939), 273.
6 *Kelly's Dir. Ches.* (1934), 269. Not mentioned (1939), 273.
7 *V.C.H. Ches.* v (1), 263.

8 Ormerod, *Hist. Ches.* ii. 823; above, this section, Brewer's Hall.
9 *V.C.H. Ches.* i. 362 (nos. 270–2).
10 Ormerod, *Hist. Ches.* ii. 575–7; Morris, *Siege of Chester*, 204; *Kelly's Dir. Ches.* (1914), 188; (1923), 198.
11 *Cart. Chester Abbey*, ii, pp. 461–4.
12 Ormerod, *Hist. Ches.* ii. 577.
13 De Figueiredo and Treuherz, *Ches. Country Houses*, 226.

INDEX TO PARTS 1 AND 2

THIS index replaces that of persons and places published in Part 1 (pp. 273–88). Pages 1–8 of Part 1 and Part 2 are identical; both have been indexed.

Page numbers in bold indicate main entries in the text.

Page numbers in italics indicate an illustration on that page or the naming of the feature in question on a map on that page. The plates in Part 1, also italicized in this index, do not have page numbers.

Persons. All persons occurring in the text are indexed, arranged under their surnames (if they had them) or forenames. Persons bearing the same name are distinguished wherever possible. Dates are included only to distinguish persons of the same or a similar name.

Places. All places occurring in the text are indexed. Unless in Cheshire, places in Great Britain are identified by their counties before 1974.

Streets. Streets in Chester and its suburbs appear as main entries under their modern names, with cross-references from any former names. Those not identified by township were within the city liberties before 1835.

Buildings. Major buildings appear under their own names as main entries. Most lesser buildings in Chester are listed under the streets on which they stood, with cross-references from the name of the building.

school attendance i. 162; ii. 280–1, 282

university i. 256; *see also* Chester College

writing masters i. 144

see also Blue Coat school; Blue Girls' school; Chester College; King's school; Queen's school; schools

Edward the Elder, king of Wessex and Mercia i. 18, 19, 24; ii. 125

Edward the Martyr, king of England i. 22

Edward the Confessor, king of England i. 24, 217

Edward I (the Lord Edward before 1272) ii. 324, 326
  activities elsewhere i. 35, 37
  Chester abbey ii. 188, 193
  Chester castle i. 35, 218; ii. 204, 205, 212
  city charter of 1300 i. 37, 43, 44; ii. 9, 232
  city sheriffs i. 38
  Dee Mills i. 35; ii. 106
  impact on Chester i. 45, 46, 217
  importance of Chester to i. 3, 4; ii. 3, 4
  military operations in Wales i. 34, 35, 37, 217; ii. 205, 208
  taxes raised from Chester i. 34, 35
  Vale Royal abbey ii. 188
  visits to Chester i. 34, 35, 37; ii. 204, 205, 208
  Welsh castles i. 35, 52; ii. 188, 194

Edward II (Edward of Caernarfon) i. 37, 38, 54; ii. 204, 205, 209, 212

Edward III i. 38

Edward VII, as prince of Wales i. 170

Edward, prince of Wales (Edward of Woodstock, the Black Prince):
  created earl of Chester i. 38
  effects on Cheshire forests i. 217
  relations with Chester i. 58–9, 86; ii. 9, 77, 106, 127, 128, 133
  visits to Chester i. 38, 55; ii. 300

Edward, prince of Wales, son of Henry VI i. 57

Edward, the Lord *see* Edward I

Edward of Caernarfon *see* Edward II

Edward of Woodstock *see* Edward, prince of Wales (the Black Prince)

Edwards:
  Francis ii. 144
  John ii. 325
  Leonard ii. 321
  Peter (fl. 1673–83) i. 132; ii. 315
  Peter (fl. 1697–8, another) ii. 315
  Thomas (fl. 1711–21) ii. 316
  Thomas (fl. 1771–87) ii. 317
  Thomas, architect i. 231

William, M.P. (fl. 1627–47) i. 105, 106, 115, 120, 121; ii. 314

William (fl. 1732–48) ii. 316

William (fl. 1787–1805) ii. 317

Edwards' Court (off Princess Street) i. 230

Edwin, earl of Mercia i. 23, 24, 25; ii. 328

eels, trade in i. 44, 69, 73; ii. 112

Egerton:
  C.B. i. 157
  Francis, 2nd duke of Bridgewater ii. 87
  John (fl. 1743–4) ii. 316
  John (later Sir John Grey Egerton, Bt.) (d. 1825) i. 157; ii. 325
  Sir Philip (d. 1698) ii. 256
  Sir Philip de Malpas Grey, Bt., M.P. (d. 1881) i. 159
  Ralph ii. 242
  Thomas (fl. 1593–7) ii. 244, 245
  Sir Thomas, Lord Keeper i. 100; ii. 326
  family i. 63, 156, 214, 224; ii. 22, 244, 328

Egerton Arms *see* Bache: Bache Hotel

Egerton House *see* Upper Northgate Street

Egerton Iron and Brass Foundry i. 233

Egerton Street i. 221
  chapel (former mission hall) ii. 176, 177, 179, *182*, 183
  housing i. 228, 236
  industry and industrial buildings i. 184, 188–9, 197, 198, 233
  mosque ii. 184
  school ii. 282, 290
  social status i. 200

Eglaf, earl of Mercia i. 23

electricity supply i. 163, 164, 165, 170, 188, 189, 244, 245, 257; ii. **42–3**
  hydroelectric power station i. 163, 242, 244; ii. 41, 43, 104

Elephant and Castle Inn *see* Eastgate Street

Elis ap Deio ap Gruffudd ii. 325

Elizabeth II i. 265

Elizabeth (of York), queen of Henry VII i. 58

Elizabeth Crescent i. 263

Ellames:
  Pattison ii. 317
  Peter (fl. 1718–34) ii. 316
  Peter (fl. 1748–9, another) ii. 316

Ellen daughter of Richard the fisherman ii. 111

Ellesmere (Salop.) ii. 74

Ellesmere Canal i. 173, 174, 227; ii. 88–90

Ellesmere Port i. 191, 255; ii. 32, 42, 57–8, 76, 176, 266, 286

canal links with Chester i. 174; ii. 88–90
industry i. 186, 189, 190, 191, 242, 255, 256, 266, 267
  employment of Chester residents i. 255, 256, 258, 262
  lack of rail links with Chester i. 191; ii. 82
  road links with Chester i. 191; ii. 82
  shoppers in Chester i. 177, 178, 191, 268
  see also Cheshire Oaks Outlet Village

Ellington, E.B. i. 184

Ellis:
  Matthew ii. 325
  Owen (fl. 1669–70) ii. 315
  Owen (fl. 1696–7, another) ii. 315
  Robert i. 115
  family ii. 325

Elswick, Robert ii. 311

Ely abbey (Cambs.) i. 31

embroiderers i. 106
  craft guild i. 106; ii. 65, 115, 116, 122, 123

emigration i. 185–6, 204–5; ii. 62, 181

engineer:
  Amaury the *see* Amaury
  Richard the *see* Richard

engineering industry i. 173, 180, 183, 184, 188–90, 194, 197, 198, 200, 201, 202, 203, 233, 242, 254, 255, 267; ii. 82, 181

engineers i. 268
  canal and waterway ii. 85, 87
  civil i. 180
  electrical i. 163; ii. 43
  gas ii. 41, 42
  water and sanitary i. 161; ii. 35–6, 37, 38, 39

Englefield (Flints.) i. 45, 54

entertainment *see* agricultural shows; alehouses; assembly rooms; balloon ascents; balls; baths and bathing; bellringing; bingo; boating; bonfires; Christmas festivities; cinemas; circuses; cocoa house; coffee houses; Corpus Christi plays; dancing; Easter festivities; feasting; fire eating; fireworks; historical pageants; hotels; inns; learned dog; Midsummer festivities; mumming; music; music halls; mystery plays; nightclub; parks and recreation grounds; pleasure fairs; processions; promenades; public houses; regattas; rope dancing; Shrovetide festivities; sport; striptease; taverns; theatres and plays; triumphs; waxworks; Whitsun plays; zoo

Nonant, Hugh de, bishop of Coventry
    and Lichfield ii. 187
nonconformists i. 112, 127, 128–9,
    132, 169, 202–4, 227, 234–5;
    ii. 135, 139, 147, **165–80**, 206,
    258
  burial grounds ii. 48
  and education ii. 277, 279, 280
  see also Baptists; Brethren; Churches
    of Christ; Congregationalists;
    Evangelicals; Independents;
    Methodists; Pentecostalists;
    Presbyterians; Quakers; Salvation
    Army; United Reformed Church
Norfolk, duke of *see* Mowbray
Norfolk i. 196; *see also* King's Lynn;
    Norwich
Norley, Roger of ii. 308
Norman, John son of i. 211
Normandy (France) i. 48
Normans Lane *see* Commonhall Street
Norris:
  James ii. 310
  John ii. 311
Norse *see* Norway and the Norse
North & South Wales Bank i. 197,
    232, 232
North of England Zoological Society
    ii. 304
North Wales Flannel Manufacturing
    Co. i. 195
North West Securities *see* Capital Bank
North Western Gas Board ii. 42
Northampton, William of ii. 209
Northampton i. 186; ii. 82
Northamptonshire *see* Kettering;
    Northampton
Northburgh:
  Nicholas, dean of St. John's ii. 131
  Roger, bishop of Coventry and
    Lichfield ii. 128
Northenden, Bartholomew of i. 58;
    ii. 106, 308
Northern Counties Housing
    Association i. 235
Northgate i. 36, 53, 59, 135, 248,
    plates 21 and 24; ii. 33, 220, **221**,
    251
  custody by city sheriffs i. 152; ii. 32,
    221
  fabric i. 115, 145, 149, 223, 225;
    ii. 33, 88, 221
  gaol *see* Northgate gaol
  model ii. 295
  serjeanty and serjeants i. 40, 48;
    ii. 33, 221, 330
  tollhouse i. 152
  tolls i. 45, 48, 152; ii. 217
Northgate Arena leisure centre i. 265,
    270; ii. 261, *261*, 266, 269
Northgate arts centre *see* Northgate
    Street

Northgate Brewery *see* Chester
    Northgate Brewery
Northgate gaol i, *plate 21*; ii. **32–3**,
    33, 59
  chapel (in St. John's hospital) ii. 32,
    33, 157, 246
  charities ii. 32
  escapes i. 157; ii. 162
  footbridge over canal ii. 33, 88
  gallows i. 40; ii. 32, 33
  management i. 40, 98, 135, 151;
    ii. 22, 32, 221
  prisoners i. 128, 135; ii. 32, 95–6,
    101, 157, 173
  staff ii. 32
Northgate Iron Works i. 188
Northgate station *see* Chester
    Northgate station
Northgate Street i. 36, 90, 95, 206,
    213, 214, 220, 225, 232, 248,
    258, *plate 55*; ii. 35, 39
  arts centre ii. 180
  Blue Bell Inn i. 248, 260; ii. 292
  Boll Yard i. 65
  brewery *see* Chester Northgate
    Brewery
  buildings i. 213, 217, 218, 219, 221,
    223, 225, 228; ii. *270*; *see also*
    names of buildings among these
    subentries
  canal bridge ii. 88
  cistern ii. 30, 37
  Coach and Horses Hotel ii. 267
  Commercial News Room (later City
    Club) i. 226; ii. 291, 292, 293
  courts i. 229, 235
  Dark Row *see* Eastgate Street
  disorder ii. 27, 101
  drainage ii. 39, 40
  engineering works i. 189
  entertainments ii. 251
  fairground i. 213; ii. 95
  fire stations i. 233; ii. 30, 31, 32
  Forum Centre i. 259, 264, 268, 270,
    272; ii. 19, 98, 271
  Ironmongers' Row i. 59, 217; ii. 226,
    233, 234, 235
  library i. 270; ii. 294
  Little Abbey Gate i. 213; ii. 99, 195
  market buildings i. 149, 222, 231,
    233, 259; ii. 37, 96–9, *96*, *97*, *98*
  Market Inn ii. 19
  Market Square (or Town Hall
    Square) i. 233, 254, 269; ii. 45,
    98
  markets ii. 95, 96, 97, 98, 99
  medieval trades i. 75, 78
  Odeon cinema i. 247, 272; ii. *272*,
    273
  offices i. 259, 260; ii. 19
  pedestrianization i. 269
  Pied Bull (or Bull) Inn ii. 32, 82

places of worship i. 128; ii. 166,
    176, 181
property owners i. 31, 49, 53, 217;
    ii. 322, 323, 324
Rows ii. 234, 237; *see also* Northgate
    Street: Ironmongers' Row
Saracen's Head Inn ii. 19
Shoemakers' Row i. 229, 231–2,
    235; ii. 238
shops i. 50, 65, 197, 232
social status i. 200, 201, 223
Sun Inn i. 143, 226; ii. 326
Town Hall Square *see* Northgate
    Street: Market Square
Westminster Coach and Motor Car
    Works (formerly J. A. Lawton &
    Co.) i. 197, 198, 270; ii. 294
White Lion Inn ii. 82
see also Abbey Gate; Exchange; St.
    Nicholas's chapel; Town Hall;
    Upper Northgate Street
Northgate Village i. 271
Northop (Flints.) i. 73; ii. 74
Northumberland ii. 257; *see also*
    Corbridge; Hadrian's Wall;
    Newcastle upon Tyne
Northumbria, earl of *see* Uhtred
Northwich i. 65, 190, 191, 268; ii. 127,
    326
  railway links with Chester i. 191;
    ii. 94
  road links with Chester ii. 73, 75,
    81, 82
Norton priory (later abbey) (Ches.)
    i. 58, 68; ii. 126, 146, 268
Norway and the Norse i. 17, 19–20,
    23; ii. 136, 324
  kings *see* Harald III Hardrada;
    Magnus II; Olaf II Haraldsson
Norwich (Norf.) i. 4, 91, 142, 219;
    ii. 4
Nottervill, Robert i. 69; ii. 311
Nottingham i. 195; ii. 103, 177
Nottinghamshire ii. 175
Nun Gate *see* Nun's Gardens Postern
nunnery i. 31–2, 81–2, 213, 220; ii. 59,
    111, 145, 158, 215, 222, **240–1**,
    322, 324, 330
  burials i. 82; ii. 241
  chantries i. 82, 87
  church ii. 240, 241
  dissolution i. 88
  image i. 85
  prioress i. 81–2, 88; ii. 222, 324
  site (post-dissolution) i. 88, 221,
    222, 223, 241; ii. 326
Nuns' Gardens *see* Castle Esplanade
Nuns' Gardens Postern (or Nun Gate)
    ii. 222
Nuns Hall ii. 326
Nuns Road (formerly Nuns Lane) *see*
    Castle Esplanade
nurseries, plant i. 187, 199, 201

CORRIGENDA TO
VOLUME V PART 1

p. ix, plate 59: *for* Lache *read* Handbridge

p. ix, plate 60: *for* Eaton Road *read* Handbridge

p. 26*b*, line 8: *for* ap *read* ab

p. 31*b* lines 2–3: there is no evidence that the translation feast was known at Abingdon before the 12th century

p. 42*b*, line 3 up: *for* twice *read* thrice

p. 43*a*, line 2: *for* three *read* five

p. 54*b*, last line: *for* three *read* five

p. 68*a*, line 14: *for* priory *read* abbey

p. 83*b*, line 4: *for* 1396 *read* 1398

p. 109*a*, line 5: *for* 1609 *read* 1610

p. 144*b*, line 9 up: *for* dukes *read* duke

p. 163*b*, line 7 up: *for* ofan *read* of an

p. 189: *note 1 should be numbered note 16 on p. 188; notes 2–14 should be numbered 1–13*

p. 202, note 10: *for* Plate 38 *read* Plate 37

p. 203*a*, line 16: *for* Taylor *read* Tayler

p. 241*b*, para. 2, line 10: *for* Royson *read* Rayson

p. 257*b*, line 10: *for* Saltney *read* Sealand

p. 265*b*, line 9 up: *for* portmoot *read* portmote

plate 16 caption: *for* Giles *read* George

plate 59 caption: *for* Lache *read* Handbridge

plate 60 caption: *for* Eaton Road *read* Handbridge

THE V.C.H. CHESHIRE APPEAL

The following individuals and organizations contributed generously to an appeal for funds which enabled this volume to be completed.

SUBSCRIBERS

Sir Richard Baker Wilbraham, Bt., Rode
A. G. Barbour, Esq., Bolesworth
H. M. Bibby, Esq., Llansannan, Denb.
Mr. and Mrs. F. R. Brace, Mollington
Gyles Brandreth, Esq., London
Mr. and Mrs. Stephen Brown, Huntington
† G. Burkinshaw, Exeter
Dr. and Mrs. A. J. P. Campbell, Tattenhall
Mr. and Mrs. T. D. Carnwath, Sandiway
D. H. B. Chesshyre, Esq., College of Arms, London
Mr. and Mrs. K. G. H. Cooke, Kelsall
Professor J. Davies, Liverpool
S. de Ferranti, Esq., Henbury
Mrs. D. Dunn, Manley
E. P. Foden, Esq., Sandbach
C. F. Foster, Esq., Arley
Mr. and Mrs. C. M. Frazer, Kew, Surr.
Sir William Gladstone, Bt., Hawarden, Flints.
Lyndon Harrison, Esq., M.E.P., Chester
M. Hassall, Esq., London
E. M. Hawes, Esq., Kingsley
Mr. and Mrs. E. J. W. Hess, Wheatley, Oxon.
Mr. and Mrs. J. P. Hess, Chorlton by Backford
Mrs. R. H. Hobhouse, Nercwys, Flints.
Dr. T. D. S. Holliday, Chester
P. T. Hughes, Esq., Churton
Mr. and Mrs. D. M. Kermode, Little Neston
Mr. and Mrs. V. A. Knight, Chester
Mr. and Mrs. F. A. Latham, Alpraham
Mrs. R. F. McConnell, C.B.E., D.L., Chester
Mrs. S. M. McRoberts, Romiley
Mr. and Mrs. J. B. Makinson, Chester

The Hon. Mary Morrison, D.C.V.O., Fonthill Bishop, Wilts.
Dr. D. Nuttall, Dodleston
Mr. and Mrs. D. Okell, Great Barrow
J. H. Peacock, Esq., Little Sutton
Mr. and Mrs. D. O. Pickering, Higher Kinnerton, Flints.
Dr. and Mrs. C. Pownall, Chester
H. S. Proudlove, Esq., Chester
Ms. E. A. Renshall, Leeds
† Canon M. H. Ridgway, Rhyd y Croesau, Oswestry, Salop.
J. K. Shanklin, Esq., Dodleston
Mr. and Mrs. D. H. L. Shone, Wimborne, Dors.
J. Treloar, Esq., Huntington
M. A. T. Trevor-Barnston, Esq., D.L., Crewe by Farndon
Mr. and Mrs. A. W. Waterworth, Kingsley
Mrs. P. A. Wendt, Upton by Chester
Anne, Duchess of Westminster, Eccleston
Mr. and Mrs. G. Wolf, Disley

Barclays Bank plc, Chester
Cheshire County Council Archaeology Service
Cheshire County Council Conservation Action
Chester Society of Natural Science, Literature, and Art
Delamere Local History Group
Department of History, University College Chester
Duchy of Lancaster Estate Office, Crewe
Frodsham and District Local History Group
The Louis Nicholas Residuary Charitable Trust
Shell Chemicals UK Ltd., Chester
Simon Engineering Charitable Trust
Vauxhall Motors Ltd., Ellesmere Port
Wilmslow Historical Society
C. P. Witter Ltd., Chester

CONTRIBUTORS

Canon E. M. Abbott, Claughton, Birkenhead
Professor and Mrs. C. T. Allmand, Liverpool
Mr. and Mrs. M. A. Anderson, Burton
J. H. Beckett, Malpas
Sir Derek and Lady Bibby, Willaston
† Col. H. L. Birch, Tattenhall
R. E. Birkett, Esq., Macclesfield
W. K. Blinkhorn, Esq., Whiston, Lancs.

J. Blundell, Esq., Congleton
P. H. W. Booth, Esq., Birkenhead
Col. William Bromley-Davenport, Capesthorne
Dr. J. D. Bu'lock, Marple
Mrs. J. W. Burn, Rhyl, Flints.
P. Carden, Esq., Westbury, Salop.
Lord Carlisle of Bucklow, Mobberley
Mrs. J. Cooper, Haslington